The
AMERICAN HERITAGE
History of

THE GREAT WEST

By the Editors of AMERICAN HERITAGE
The Magazine of History

Editor in Charge: ALVIN M. JOSEPHY, JR.

Author: DAVID LAVENDER

Pictorial Commentary: RALPH K. ANDRIST

Published by American Heritage Publishing Co., Inc., New York

Book Trade Distribution by Simon and Schuster, Inc.

AMERICAN HERITAGE
The Magazine of History

Publisher: James Parton
Editor in Chief: Joseph J. Thorndike
Senior Editor: Bruce Catton
Editor: Oliver Jensen
Editorial Director, Book Division: Richard M. Ketchum
Senior Art Director: Irwin Glusker

Staff for this Book

Editor: ALVIN M. JOSEPHY, JR.
Assistant Editors: Ralph K. Andrist, Jane C. Flounders,
            Nancy Lindemeyer, Alice D. Watson
Editorial Assistants: Beverley Hilowitz, Frederick K. Poole,
            Melissa Sutphen
Copy Editor: Barbara Ackerman
Art Director: Eleanor A. Dye
Original Maps: David Greenspan

*Cover: Jedediah Smith by Harvey Dunn; South Dakota State
University. Front Endsheet: Temples and Towers of the
Virgen by William H. Holmes, Powell Survey; Clarence
Dutton, Atlas . . . Grand Cañon District, 1882. Half title:
Pimas shooting at saguaros; J. R. Bartlett, Personal Narra-
tive, vol. II, 1854. Title Page: The Promised Land by William
S. Jewett; Collection of Waddell F. Smith, Pony Express
Gallery, San Rafael, Calif. Below: Photograph of actual
gunfight at Quartzite, Arizona, 1904; Collection of Roscoe
G. Willson, Phoenix. Back Endsheet: Colorado's San Juan
Range by William H. Holmes, Hayden Survey; Atlas, 1877.*

TABLE OF CONTENTS

	Foreword	6
Chapter 1	BEYOND THE FIRST MOUNTAINS 1763-1779	15
Chapter 2	WHOSE WEST? 1779-1795	31
Chapter 3	THE TRANS-MISSISSIPPI MYSTERY 1792-1807	57
Chapter 4	BARREN BEGINNINGS 1804-1813	81
Chapter 5	WAR AND DEPRESSION 1810-1821	99
Chapter 6	SEVEN-LEAGUE BOOTS 1821-1833	121
Chapter 7	THE SOUTHWESTERN BARRIERS 1825-1844	153
Chapter 8	THE GREAT SURGE 1832-1846	177
Chapter 9	NEW EMPIRES 1846-1848	225
Chapter 10	THE MISERIES OF RICHNESS 1848-1854	249
Chapter 11	THE GREAT PRIZE 1852-1861	281
Chapter 12	CLEARING THE WAY 1854-1870	313
Chapter 13	HIGH, WIDE, AND UGLY 1870-1890	345
Chapter 14	NEW VALUES 1890-1914	385
	Acknowledgments and Index	410

THE PEOPLE OF THE GREAT WEST
A FOREWORD AND A DEDICATION

The story of America's westward movement is at heart the story of the men and women of all races and different origins and beliefs who helped shape the character of a nation. They lived a stirring epic, the telling of which grows ever more fascinating as it grows more remote. It has become a romance, a drama of many conflicts: of man against the forces of a stupendous land; of man against wild beasts, nameless terrors, and loneliness; of man against man. The grim image of a human pierced in the back by an arrow shaft and parted from his scalp (in the case above, a Crow Indian slain by an enemy warrior) is as good a trademark as any of the West of yesterday, for it exemplifies the pain and violence that tormented both white and Indian. Amid such symbols of a vanished environment the dynamic civilization that spreads today from the Appalachians to Hawaii was built. On these introductory pages are the portraits of a few typifying the many who contributed to the building. Some of the people are today remembered; most of them were never known except to their families and friends. All faced challenge and struggle, which accounts perhaps in large measure for our enduring interest in them.

MOUNTAIN MAN

Jim Baker went west with Jim Bridger in 1838, was a trapper with Kit Carson, then a scout and a guide.

MORMON PIONEER

Lucy Smith trekked with her husband to Utah in 1851 after he had fought persecutors in the Midwest.

VIRGINIA MOVER

David Poe, born 1799, kept going west. In 1856, seeking a new home in Nebraska, he froze on the plains.

SMALLPOX SURVIVORS

These sad Mandans of 1872 had seen their tribe all but wiped out by the white man's scourge.

FORTY-NINERS

Gold rush fiddlers, they were as much a part of the California scene (and as homesick) as the miners they entertained.

CHEROKEE HALF-BREED

Jesse Chisholm's wagon route, which he used as a trader, became the country's most famous cattle trail.

BAD WOMAN

Belle Starr's trail was crimson. A horse thief and consort of outlaws in the Indian Territory, she was shot to death.

The Appalachian Mountains

"It was on the first of May, in the year 1769, that I resigned my domestic happiness for a time, and left my family and peaceable habitation on the Yadkin River, in North-Carolina, to wander through the wilderness of America, in quest of the country of Kentucke...."

Daniel Boone in John Filson's *The Discovery, Settlement and Present State of Kentucke*, 1784

CHAPTER ONE

BEYOND THE
FIRST MOUNTAINS

1763-1779

Richard Henderson, judge of a back-country court in Colonial North Carolina, possessed, to borrow his own words, "a rapturous idea of property." In this he was not unique. Many Americans of his time, among them Benjamin Franklin, Patrick Henry, and George Washington, were similarly invigorated. During the energetic decades preceding the Revolution (and for many years thereafter), speculation in wilderness land was considered an honorable way of growing rich. The dealer's main problem, aside from finding suitable areas of a money-making size, lay in outwitting his own Government.

Richard Henderson's scheme for acquiring vast properties was more dazzling than most; but before we can appreciate its full arrogance, we need to glance at the whole question of early land titles. Exactly who owned the empty lands of North America? Theoretical jurists advanced several arguments. In general the philosophers granted to the Indians rights of possession based on occupancy. Geographical discovery of these Indian lands, backed by appropriate ceremony, gave to the home nation of the discoverer—in most cases either England, France, or Spain—a sort of primary option to purchase the aboriginal titles through solemn treaty, as though each savage tribe were a sovereign nation whose ideas of real property matched those of the Europeans.

This "option," so to speak, vested in the king. It could be conveyed by royal charter to the Colonial governments. Colonial administrators then entered into purchase agreements with local bands of red men and passed the land they acquired on to private owners by such

means as seemed best suited to encourage the spread of settlement. At times, private individuals hurried the matter along by buying land directly from the Indians without waiting for the sanction of a formal treaty. In general, however, this was frowned upon.

During the early years of the first American frontier, no one realized how wide the continent really was. As a result, the charters issued to Massachusetts, Connecticut, Virginia, both Carolinas, and Georgia blandly granted to each of the Colonies named all the land from its Atlantic frontage west to the Pacific Ocean, subject to the extinguishing of the Indians' title.

So long as the French sat glowering in the Ohio and Mississippi valleys, these sea-to-sea pretensions were meaningless. Then, between 1755 and 1763, war and the Peace of Paris ousted the French from the continent and confirmed England's dominion as far west as the Mississippi. Beyond the Mississippi, Spain blocked any sea-to-sea hopes, but there was plenty of land between the Allegheny Mountains and the river. Joyfully the Colonies reasserted their old claims, which were modified by the Spanish reality. Virginia's was the most sweeping. Ignoring the charters of Connecticut and Massachusetts and the tenuous claims that New York held to the land of the Iroquois, she contended that she controlled not just the area directly west of her—today's West Virginia and Kentucky—but all of what is now Ohio, Indiana, Illinois, Michigan, and Wisconsin, and part of Minnesota as well.

Devising methods of putting these Western lands into the hands of people who would utilize them was a persistent frontier problem. Speculators offered themselves as one useful channel. Their pattern of operation was, in theory, simple. A group of men formed a company that obtained from the Colonial governors or from the king a reasonably sound title to a stretch of wilderness. Through the blandishments of printed advertisements and sales-men called agents, they lured restless frontiersmen to-ward the area, broke the holdings into small pieces, and sold the plots at a dazzling advance in price. The specula-tors, and even the actual settlers whose land rose in value, insisted vehemently that whatever increment they gained was well earned. The Western lands were worthless until inhabited. Did not those who opened the country deserve a reward for their foresight and risk?

Many were eager to take the risks. By the middle of the eighteenth century a voracious land hunger filled the frontier. Nowhere was it stronger than in southern Penn-sylvania, birthplace of Daniel Boone, who was soon to be intimately associated with speculator Richard Hender-son. Squire Boone, Daniel's father, was an impatient man. Blocked by the mountains from an easy shift farther west, he gathered up six of his eight children and several grandchildren and about 1750 drifted south with a growing trickle of other "movers" who were seeking the future in the great trough that parallels the eastern base of the Appalachian Mountains—the valley that in Virginia is called Shenandoah. Beyond the Virginia bor-der, in the Yadkin country of North Carolina, the Boones and their fellow migrants met the vanguard of another thrust of people working from South Carolina northward along the rivers that head in the Blue Ridge Mountains and even beyond.

These movers were a new race. They or their parents had been born for the most part in England or its pos-sessions—the hill pockets of Wales, the Highlands of Scotland, or the wild moors of northern Ireland. With them were a few Huguenots from France and many Germans from the Rhine Palatinate. All but an excep-tional few were Protestants, the Scotch-Irish in particular being deeply tinged with Calvinistic individualism.

The frontier changed some of their characteristics and intensified others. They were, as a group, semiliterate, proud, and cantankerous, as dogged in their insistence on their own way of life as pine roots cracking granite to grow. Perhaps their greatest resource was their capacity to endure. They outlasted recurrent plagues of smallpox and malaria, uncountable Indian raids, and a steady pro-gression of natural accidents. They were incredibly pro-lific. Squire Boone's family of eight children was small by frontier standards. James Robertson, an eventual neigh-bor of Boone's and the founder of Nashville, had eleven children. Twice-married John Sevier, the first governor of

Tennessee, fathered eighteen; his long-time enemy, John Tipton, also twice married, produced seventeen.

The entire assets of one of these huge families often amounted, in the beginning, to little more than an axe, a hunting knife, an auger, a rifle, a horse or two, a few cattle and pigs, a sack of seed corn and another of salt, perhaps a crosscut saw, and a loom. Those that moved first into a new region lived for months at a time on wild meat, Indian maize, and native fruits in season. Yet if they were poor at the beginning, they confidently ex-pected that soon they would be rich and respected. The touchstone was land.

In a way almost impossible to define to urban dwellers, a slice of ground suitable for farming had come to repre-sent not just dollars and cents but dignity. In part the feeling sprang from a belief that at last, in America, a poor man could help fulfill the Scriptural injunction to subdue and replenish the earth. In Europe a poor family seldom achieved that particular integrity. On the frontier he could do so, or thought he could. The obsession brought shiploads of yearners every week to Boston, New York, Philadelphia, Baltimore, Charles Town (as the South Carolina port was then spelled), and Savan-nah. It sent them streaming westward into the wilderness after their pioneering predecessors to raise still more children who wanted still more land.

Out of this insatiable desire came one of the paradoxes of the American frontier. Having found their land after incredible toil, many of the seekers almost at once be-came dissatisfied and sought for something else farther on. The restlessness, so bone deep it seemed like a new human instinct, lasted as long as there was empty land to fill, and still leaves its imprint on the American character.

On, on, on. Did these perpetual movers see themselves as opening the way to the spread of civilization? Or were they fleeing from civilization's pressures? Could they have said themselves what they wanted? Whatever the answer, this self-renewing quest for a piece of earth that somehow meant fulfillment was the foundation upon which the early land speculators built their schemes.

In order to obtain land that could be passed on at a profit to the movers, these speculators unabashedly ma-nipulated the Colonial administrators. The administra-tors in their turn finagled the desired acreage from the Indians through small, ugly battles—sometimes deliber-ately provoked—and subsequent harsh treaties. The practices were flagrant enough so that after the close of the so-called French and Indian War, the home Govern-ment in London sought to control them by means of the famous Proclamation of 1763. Published on October 7, this decree laid down stringent rules for the conduct of

GULF OF MEXICO

SCALE
0   50   100   150 Miles

1763-79

the fur trade, forbade the purchase of Indian lands by private citizens, and ordered that settlement must not pass the crest of the Alleghenies until such time as the Indians agreed to an adjustment of the border.

The proclamation was a temporary expedient, designed in part to placate the Indians, who had been aroused to furious resistance by Pontiac's rebellion. It was also a clear announcement that seekers for land west of the mountains henceforth must look to the Government in London, not to the individual Colonies, for their grants. The change, though vastly irritating to the Colonies that claimed the Western territories, brought no pause to the speculators. Abetted by Benjamin Franklin, certain "Suffering Traders," as they called themselves, asked the king for millions of acres in Illinois and present-day West Virginia to compensate them for losses sustained during the French and Indian War. A group of Army officers, dubbed the Military Associates, felt their sacrifices deserved similar consideration. Both groups, and others like them, went ahead and laid out enormous tracts on the map and then fruitlessly petitioned the ministry to grant them confirmation.

Still other companies and individuals, including George Washington, used land warrants as a means of thrusting into the forbidden Indian country. A land warrant did not convey title. It was simply a document that permitted the holder to locate a specified number of acres, survey them, and register the claim in the land office. These warrants were a favorite method of paying soldiers. During the French and Indian War, Virginia alone issued warrants for nearly three million acres beyond the mountains. Industrious speculators bought these rights from the holders for a song and then asked piously whether the king's Government was going to force the Colony, through the proclamation, to default on its sacred obligations.

A more effective way of beating the proclamation was to ignore it. In Pennsylvania and in the northern part of today's West Virginia, thousands of settlers crossed the Alleghenies and in defiance of the Government hewed out farms along the rivers that meet near Fort Pitt (today's Pittsburgh) to form the Ohio. One estimate states that between 1764 and 1774 the line of settlement pushed from the mountain crest toward the Ohio River at an average rate of seventeen miles per year.

Before any of these titles could become legal, the proclamation line had to be shifted farther west. A start was made in the South in October, 1768, when the Indian Superintendent for the Southern Department, John Stuart, hard pressed by avid speculators, arranged with the Cherokees the Treaty of Hard Labor. This agreement

Back-country speculator Richard Henderson

won for the whites some of the North Carolina back country (but none of present Tennessee, as we shall see) and much of what is now West Virginia. The cession was not enough, however, for the more voracious whites, who wanted to swallow eastern Kentucky as well.

As a roundabout start in that direction the dealers went to work on the formidable League of the Iroquois, who had assembled during that same fall (1768) at Fort Stanwix in the Mohawk Valley of New York to discuss other treaties. There the Government's commissioners, badgered as remorselessly as John Stuart had been and possibly even bribed, at length prevailed on the Six Nations to accept trade goods worth £10,460 in exchange for southwestern New York, western Pennsylvania, and the contiguous parts of West Virginia. To this massive surrender the Iroquois added, as "a gesture of good will," such title as they possessed to all of what is now Kentucky and Tennessee.

Based on old war victories over the Shawnees, the Iroquois claims south of the Ohio were not very strong. But the yielding was a precedent, and now the speculators turned their attention to the Cherokees, who also claimed hunting rights to Kentucky. In 1770 the Treaty of Lochaber rearranged the boundary of Virginia at Cherokee expense so as to include still more Western territory. That was not enough, either. When surveyor John Donelson went into the field in 1771 to mark out the line, he prevailed on the Cherokees, by means now unknown, to let him push the border still farther west, to the Kentucky River. It is probably not entirely a coincidence that gigantic land schemes accompanied these readjustments, notably the proposed colony of Vandalia. Extending with the shifting boundary lines from southwestern Pennsylvania through what is now West Virginia into eastern Kentucky, Vandalia embraced approximately twenty million acres. If the Revolution had not intervened, it and various other land-grant entities probably would have been transferred from government control to ownership by the speculators.

Most of the dealers in Western land were moneyed people from the Atlantic seaboard with influence enough to catch the ear of the Colonial governors or the English ministers in London. They sought to bend the law to their service, rather than to violate it. Richard Henderson was an exception. From the first he set out to break the law, pressing ahead with a mounting presumption quite out of keeping with his title of judge.

Henderson understood the frontier. He had been born on the fringe of settlement in North Carolina. While studying law during his youth, he had served as an easy-going deputy under his father, the county high sheriff. He responded to back-country likes and dislikes even in such things as oratory. "You are," he told one group in the soaring metaphor they admired, "fixing the palladium, or placing the first cornerstone of an edifice, the height and magnificence of whose superstructure is now in the womb of futurity." When he began dreaming of a truly glorious tract of Western land that he might develop, no matter what the proclamation said, he turned with the sureness of his frontier instincts to the man best fitted to help him find it, Daniel Boone.

Boone's home—that is, the cabin where his wife, Rebecca, and their children stayed when he was off on his rambles, one of which took him as far as Florida—was in the remote Yadkin Valley of northwestern North Carolina. He was one of that now-legendary breed, the Long Hunters, so called because of the duration of their stays in the transmontane wilderness.

The principal goal of the Long Hunters was deerskin. In those days of hard-to-get money the hide of a doe was worth fifty cents or more, depending on its size and quality. The skins of a buck brought a dollar and up—hence the term "buck" as slang for currency. A stout little band of hunters could bring back several hundred, sometimes even a thousand, skins in a season, a heady stimulus to the cash-starved economy of the frontier. As a result, the whites did not take kindly to the Indians' assertion that *they* owned the game that roamed the forests. Did a farmer pretend to possess each raccoon that crossed his back forty? A pox on such reasoning! A wild creature belonged to whoever laid hands on it.

Most hunters were also farmers. They owned livestock and planted corn that their wives and children tended while the father was away. As land hungry as everyone else, the hunters watched for good soil as they roamed. Sometimes they marked off a piece for themselves by cutting slashes into tree trunks with their tomahawks, and hoped to make the appropriation stick when settlement caught up with them. Generally they failed to hold the land: some speculator obtained a grant to the entire area and disallowed prior entries.

Fierce contentions arose from such clashes of interest. Squatters often planted themselves defiantly on what they wanted, said their toil was what really gave the land its value (often enough they were hoping to resell at a profit and move on), and insisted on pre-emption privileges— the right of paying later for what they already were occupying. The resultant quarrels racked both the Colonies and the Government of the United States for years . . . but those accounts come later.

A man who worked for a speculative group could make his selections in advance and still avoid being dispossessed. This possibly was in Daniel Boone's mind when he made his first arrangements with Richard Henderson. The two men probably met about 1764 in Salisbury, North Carolina, a county seat into whose court various Boones were often hailed for debt. Poverty, a frontier commonplace, in no way vitiated a man's dependability as a land scout. Sometime during the latter part of the decade Judge Henderson offered to grubstake Boone in return for Daniel's reports on whatever good farmland he chanced to see during his hunts.

Results were negligible at first. Then, during the winter of 1768–69, shortly after the Iroquois had "opened" Kentucky to the whites, John Finley drifted into the Yadkin Valley with tales that set Boone into motion.

Finley and Boone had become friends years before, in 1755, when serving as wagon drivers for General Edward Braddock's ill-fated Pennsylvania campaign. Since then Finley had fallen on hard times. When he appeared in the Yadkin he was an itinerant peddler, leading a lone horse packed with gimcracks to sell to the back-country housewives, most of whom were too destitute to buy much. But he was stored with the kind of hunter talk Boone liked to hear. He had been an Indian trader before and after the Braddock fiasco and had seen something of the Kentucky country while slipping down the Ohio River in his canoe and, briefly, as a captive of the Shawnee Indians. The land beyond the mountains was a paradise of game, he said. He'd like to see more of it.

Boone invited him to spend the winter. During the long evenings they discoursed now and then about the population pressures building up behind them, and about the dissatisfactions of the back-country people with the

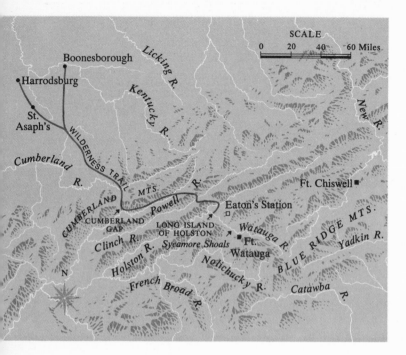

The Wilderness Trail to Kentucky is seen above, emerging from the maze of mountains and streams enfolding Cumberland Gap.

oppressive administration of Governor William Tryon, his venal courts and peculating sheriffs, and with the highhanded way the tidewater aristocracy passed legislation unfavorable to the Western settlements. Mostly, though, they wondered about the other side of the mountains, its fabulous herds of deer and buffalo. John Stuart, a brother-in-law of Daniel's, occasionally dropped by and added tales of what he had seen on his own epic adventure in 1766, when he had followed the Cumberland River to its junction with the Ohio.

By spring the three men had persuaded themselves to cross the hills for another look. They enlisted three more hunters and prevailed on Judge Henderson to furnish them with an outfit. The equipment they required for the trip was simple enough—horses, kettles, knives, and ample powder and lead for bullets.

They left on May 1, 1769, and worked west across the valleys formed by the headwater streams of the Tennessee River—down the Watauga to the Holston, through brushy gaps to the Clinch, across the Clinch's timbered ridges to Powell's Valley. There they found the Warrior's Trace, by which Cherokee war parties traveled north in search of enemy Shawnees, Wyandots, and Miamis as far away as the shores of Lake Erie. As Finley somehow had known it would, the Indian trace took the hunters up through the rocky, steep-sided Cumberland Gap, across the brawling headwaters of the Cumberland River, and on north to the rolling forests and open prairies that later

became known as the bluegrass country of Kentucky.

During the next two years the personnel of the little party kept changing. Some of the men returned to the settlements; replacements came out with fresh supplies. Boone himself stayed beyond the mountains, at times alone. His brother-in-law, John Stuart, vanished, probably killed by Indians. And when at last the group was homeward bound, Cherokees caught them, stripped them of every skin they had, and warned them to hunt no more in Kentucky, no matter what the Iroquois said.

If Boone's hunters carried back no hides that spring of 1771, at least they were freighted with wonders to relate. So delectable a land! Horses trampling through the wild strawberries in the gaps were stained with juice to their knees. Grapevines a foot thick spread lofty tendrils through the dense canopy of forest leaves; the way to pick grapes was to chop down the trees. And game! Pigeon roosts were a thousand acres in size. Wild turkeys were so fat that when they were shot and fell to the ground, their skins burst open. Deer, elk, and buffalo came in fantastic numbers to the "licks"—salt-impregnated earth surrounding saline springs. In places, their rough tongues had scraped a labyrinth of trenches into the ground deeper than the animals' own backs.

That sort of talk made the back-country settlers lift their heads. Pioneer farmers had to have salt for preserving meat and graining hides. The only way to obtain it far from the ocean was to find a salt spring and evaporate the water in large, flat-bottomed, shallow iron pans. In the land of Kentucky, the hunters said, everyone could be near such a salt spring.

Other tales were equally suggestive. If buffalo were ravenous for the thin green leaves of the cane that filled the valleys in dense mats as much as thirty feet tall, then cattle would like the feed just as well. If bears grew as round as tubs on the mast of beechnuts, acorns, and hickory nuts that carpeted the ground each golden autumn, then hogs would also thrive. The fact of those nuts was important to the settlers in still another way: soil where nut-growing trees flourished was reputed to be the best a farmer could find.

Pressures meanwhile were building up along the eastern toes of the mountains. For some years, settlers had been inching out of the Yadkin country into the brushy coves and fertile troughs formed by the headwater streams of the Tennessee. Bloody clashes with the government of North Carolina quickened the movement. In May, 1771, two months after Boone's return from Kentucky, armed bands of back-country farmers calling themselves Regulators gathered to protest certain actions of the governor and the legislature. The Colonial militia

This engraving of "An Attack of the Indians upon Dan'l. and Squire Boone & John Stewart" appeared in a History of Kentucky, *written by Humphrey Marshall in 1812. It helped spread the fame of America's first Western hero.*

defeated them at the Battle of the Alamance, whose casualties, counting those of both sides, came to eighteen dead and one hundred and twenty-two wounded. To escape retribution, streams of discontented farmers flowed across the first mountain ridges that lie along what is now the border between northwestern North Carolina and northeastern Tennessee. Most of them supposed they were locating in Virginia, where treaties with the Indians had made settlement legal. Surveys soon showed, however, that a large part of the section still belonged to the Cherokees.

Forbidden by the Proclamation of 1763 from buying the land, the settlers responded with an evasion. Acting as agents for the whites, James Robertson (who was simultaneously learning from his wife how to read and write) and Robert Bean leased, rather than bought, the area from the Cherokees. The group then formed the famous Watauga Association to govern the settlement and petitioned North Carolina for annexation in the hope the Colony could secure firm titles for them. (To jump briefly ahead: the lease was transformed into a purchase in 1775; annexation came the following year.)

Deterred perhaps by the troubled times, Judge Richard Henderson did not act immediately on the information Boone had brought him. But those same troubled times added to Daniel's desire to move on into Kentucky. Recruiting a few other families as companions, he set out in September, 1773, to open the transmontane West by himself, defying both his own Government, which had not yet opened western Kentucky to settlement, and the Cherokees, who two years earlier had ordered him to stay away from the region.

The Indians hit this new incursion just short of Cumberland Gap. Among those who died was Boone's eldest son. The survivors fell into a panic and stampeded back to the settlements. In disgust Daniel built a cabin at the foot of the mountains in Clinch Valley and sat down to wait for a second chance.

Northward, other adventurers, armed with land warrants as their justification, were pushing across the new boundary line of the Indian country and settling along the south bank of the Ohio. The squatting was illegal, the warrants notwithstanding, but the Colonial politicians were unwilling to try stopping them. Lord Dunmore, Governor of Virginia, reported to the Colonial Secretary in London, "They do not conceive that Government has any right to forbid their taking possession of a Vast tract of Country, either uninhabited, or which serves only as a Shelter to a few Scattered Tribes of Indians."

The Shawnees of Ohio, who each year hunted in Kentucky, took exception. They had ceded no territory. Let the whites stay out of their country.

In the hope of provoking a war that would silence them, a handful of settlers began fomenting incidents. Virginia indirectly encouraged the belligerence. She was quarreling with Pennsylvania over the western part of

21

their boundary line and early in 1774 sent John Connolly to Fort Pitt to seize control of the disputed area. Connolly was anti-Indian with a vengeance; he also claimed a large tract around modern Louisville. Knowing he could support them, the more rabid of the frontiersmen quickened their provocations. One instance will suffice: three traders invited several Indians, including a woman and her child, into their trading post fifty miles downstream from Pittsburgh, befuddled them with drink, and coolly slaughtered them all.

By spring war was inevitable. Before launching a general attack, the Virginia government warned the Watauga and Holston settlers to protect their southern flank by neutralizing the Cherokees, a mission successfully accomplished by James Robertson. Simultaneously, Daniel

Boone and another Long Hunter named Michael Stoner were sent into Kentucky to warn the scattered surveyors and settlers to seek retreat: trouble was coming.

Boone was amazed by what he found. Three years before, Kentucky had lain almost empty. Now land seekers swarmed through parts of the country. Near Dick's River, a tributary of the Kentucky, a party under James Harrod was actually laying out a town called Harrodsburg. Enviously, perhaps, Boone paused long enough to stake out a lot in the new settlement and build a semblance of a cabin. Then on he and Stoner went to alert the other camps. Sixty-one days and eight hundred miles after their departure, they were back east of the mountains. There Boone told Henderson, who had recently resigned his judgeship, that the whites were likely to win

The locations of various Indian nations in the interior of the Southeast are portrayed on this plan, copied from an 1825 Cherokee map. The original, on deerskin, was given by Cherokees to Governor Francis Nicholson of South Carolina. Charleston is seen at left.

22

their war and wring a cession from the Shawnees. If Henderson hoped to lay hands on that good land before the warrant holders gobbled it up, he had better move.

This time Henderson reacted swiftly. In August, 1774, while the war against the Shawnees was beginning in earnest (history remembers it as Lord Dunmore's War), he assembled several associates to discuss ways and means of thrusting into Kentucky ahead of other claimants. (Among his group was Jesse Benton, who a few years later would father Thomas Hart Benton, for decades the West's most vocal exponent in Congress.) They raised funds, formed what they eventually called the Transylvania Company, and in October sent Henderson and Nathaniel Hart to the Cherokee villages to sound out the Indians' willingness to relinquish whatever rights they possessed to a twenty-million-acre crescent of land between the Tennessee and Kentucky rivers. As a recent judge, Henderson surely knew he was inviting trouble. Under the Proclamation of 1763, private individuals could not buy land from the Indians, and settlements could not be planted west of the revised boundary line until all the Indians concerned had agreed. A mere unilateral, private deal with the Cherokees was clearly illegal. Furthermore, such an agreement would hardly sit well with the colonists who even then were battling the Shawnees for control of the same region.

On October 10, about the time Hart and Henderson were approaching the Cherokees, Lord Dunmore's soldiers defeated the Shawnees far to the north at Point Pleasant, near the confluence of the Great Kanawha and Ohio rivers. At the Treaty of Camp Charlotte, which followed the victory, the Indians promised to open Kentucky to settlement. Those were Shawnees, however—and Henderson meanwhile was dealing with Cherokees. They professed interest in his proposal and sent an emissary back to Fayetteville, North Carolina, to see what quality of goods the Transylvania Company would offer for their lands. No agreement had yet been signed. Nevertheless, Henderson's group was so sure of success that in December it began advertising for settlers.

This brought the project to the attention of the Colonial governors of Virginia and North Carolina. They reacted violently. By virtue of the recent victory over the Shawnees, Kentucky and Tennessee belonged to the citizens of their Colonies. Many veterans of several Indian fights held land warrants that could be satisfied by granting them acreage in the newly acquired area. Henderson's upstart company had shed no blood whatsoever and deserved no part of the spoils.

By official proclamation, Governor Josiah Martin of North Carolina warned that Henderson's fraudulent treaty with the Cherokees, if concluded, would not be recognized; Transylvania, he thundered inaccurately, was nothing more than a scheme for enabling debtors and other lawless persons to escape justice by fleeing across the mountains. On March 10, 1775, Governor Dunmore of Virginia followed Martin's proclamation with a public denunciation of the Transylvania Company's "unwarrantable and illegal Designs."

It was too late. The Transylvanians and the Cherokees had agreed to meet in March at Sycamore Shoals on the Watauga River for a final discussion of the sale. The whites let the Indians take a long look at the trade goods heaped to the roofs of the nearby cabins. Their mouths watered. A shortage of guns and ammunition had recently been the cause of their losing a fight with the Chickasaws, and here was more new armament than they had ever before seen in a single spot.

Gauging their eagerness even before they came to terms, Henderson on March 10 dispatched Daniel Boone at the head of twenty-eight axemen to cut a trail (not a wagon road yet) through Cumberland Gap to the Kentucky River. Four days later (March 14) the Transylvania Company sat down to talk terms with the Cherokees, overcame the objections of a dissident group led by Chief Dragging Canoe, and on March 17 completed the deal by formally exchanging the ten thousand pounds worth of trade goods for two thirds of modern Kentucky and a large slice of northern Tennessee.

Henderson's presumption in this freewheeling deal seems, from today's viewpoint, nothing short of astounding. But perhaps he sensed that times were sorely troubled and that none of the old English edicts might endure much longer. If so (and there is no way of proving this), he possessed remarkable prescience. For on April 19, 1775, while Boone's axemen were building cabins at the new town of Boonesborough beside the Kentucky River, and while Henderson himself was leading the first group of prospective settlers down the newly opened Wilderness Trail—on that fateful day a group of Massachusetts farmers, crouched behind stone walls on the road between Lexington and Concord, were cutting to pieces a column of British soldiers.

That spring, people sprouted in Kentucky as if by spontaneous generation. Families planning to buy from the Transylvania Company came down the Wilderness Trail at gratifyingly frequent intervals. Less amenable ones veered away to Benjamin Logan's station at St. Asaph's. Still more floated down the Ohio and clustered around the log town of Harrodsburg.

Henderson acted quickly to convince all of them that the Transylvania title was valid. On May 23, 1775, he assembled eighteen delegates from the different stations at a meeting under the elm trees at Boonesborough. A white lawyer paid by the Cherokees spaded up a square of turf and presented it to Henderson in symbolic yielding of sovereignty. Having made that point, Henderson next soothed the settlers' touchy individualism by letting the delegates believe they were drawing up their own laws for punishing crimes, establishing courts and militia, preserving game, and improving the breed of horses. The document looked democratic—"all power is in the people," it declared. Yet behind that facade the company retained certain arbitrary veto powers, the right to appoint the principal civil and military officials, the right to collect quitrents, and the privilege of reserving for its principal stockholders whatever choice land they wished.

For a time the maneuver sufficed, and the company's land salesmen did a roaring business. Henderson realized, however, that the settlers had a powerful string to their own bow: should they ever grow dissatisfied, they might appeal to the king or to the Colony of Virginia or to the new Continental Congress to cancel the company's title. He determined to act first. Returning to Oxford, North Carolina, he presented the problem to his partners.

There was only one solution. They dared not offer their settlements to Virginia as a *fait accompli* and appeal for recognition on that ground. Lord Dunmore had already branded the Cherokee treaty illegal; and even if the rebellious Virginians expelled Dunmore, as seemed probable, whatever government succeeded him was not likely to surrender at a breath its greatest resource, the trans-Allegheny farmlands. The king was an equally unlikely source, for Transylvania was a violation of the Royal Proclamation of 1763. This left only the Continental Congress. The proprietors hurried one of their number, James Hogg, to Philadelphia to offer Transylvania to the Confederation as a fourteenth state. Hogg was to be its delegate. Seating him would be tantamount to recognition by Congress of the company's title.

Aware of this and fearful of offending Virginia and North Carolina, whose support was desperately needed, Congress took no action. Meanwhile, the company tried to copper its bets, in case it lost the appeal, by cashing in quickly. It began charging more for its Kentucky lands, raised the quitrents, and boosted the cost of goods in the company stores. The proprietors swept into their own hands enticing lands near the Falls of the Ohio, where Louisville later was founded.

Resentment flared. Led by a redheaded, twenty-four-year-old surveyor named George Rogers Clark, the Kentucky settlers in June, 1776, called a protest meeting at Harrodsburg. After passing a resolution denouncing the company's greed, they elected Clark and lawyer John Gabriel Jones to journey through Cumberland Gap to Williamsburg with an appeal that Kentucky be made a county of Virginia and be given five hundred pounds of powder for fighting back the increasingly restive Indians. The creation of such a county would, of course, be a denial of the Transylvania Company's pretensions.

The two delegates, at times scarcely able to hobble because of "scald feet," an agonizing complaint brought on by too much walking in wet moccasins, reached Williamsburg after the Virginia assembly had adjourned. They learned, however, that sentiment was blowing their way. During the closing days of June, just before the signing of the Declaration of Independence, Virginia had uttered her own defiance of the king by nullifying the Proclamation of 1763 and asserting her ownership of the Western lands granted her by her original charter. To raise money, she adopted a system of selling this land without regard to the Transylvania claim. The following December, after listening to Clark and giving him his powder, she formally established Kentucky County.

Henderson fought bitterly, going himself to Williamsburg to challenge Virginia's action. Hogg appealed to Congress. Their intent was to save their economic hides, not to raise fresh questions of political philosophy. Raise them they nevertheless did. As a matter of fundamental law, who now controlled the Western lands? Was it the chartered Colonies or some suprasectional America, not yet fully glimpsed, but already struggling to rise above the jealousies of the individual states? If the Western settlements disliked the policies of their parent states, could they secede (as the original Colonies were seceding from England) and assert their own title? What rights, as against the rebellious Colonies, did the Indians have? What sort of power, exactly, would be legally able to extinguish those native rights?

Beset by the massive problems of prosecuting the war, the Continental Congress did not face the issues. Virginia's presumptions went temporarily unchallenged. That state did agree, however, to listen to the Transylania Company's suit for recompense. After all, Henderson's firm had spent ten thousand pounds buying the title from the Cherokee Indians, it had opened a usable trail across the mountains, and it had provided a semblance of order during the early days of settlement. In 1778 Virginia recognized the services by awarding the company two hundred thousand acres along the Green River near its junction with the Ohio. The balm was meager. The land lay scores of miles west of the nearest war-torn settlement, and many years must pass (twenty, as matters developed) before the proprietors could hope

This romantic view of Daniel Boone escorting pioneers through Cumberland Gap in 1775 was painted three quarters of a century later by George Caleb Bingham. It depicted the popular image of the opening of the trans-Appalachian West.

to realize a cent from their original investments and labor.

At the time, these academic abstractions about ownership seemed highly unrealistic. The Western Indians were on the upsurge, making bloody capital of the Revolution and seemingly on the verge of expelling the interlopers and reasserting their own title to the country.

The Cherokees made the first concerted move. In 1775 they had been well disposed toward the frontiersmen. At Sycamore Shoals they had sold not only their questionable rights to Kentucky but also the Watauga, Holston, Clinch, and Powell river areas south of Virginia, lands that until then the settlers had been leasing. A southern boundary to this cession was firmly agreed on, and another keg of rum was broached in friendship.

Almost immediately the whites violated the treaty, pushing down the Holston to its eastern tributary, the Nolichucky (a Cherokee word meaning "rapid" or "dashing"), and on toward the French Broad, almost within sight of the Cherokee villages themselves. At the same time, other settlers farther south in North and

South Carolina began crowding the tribe from the east.

To these provocations was added another motive. The image of Britain was bright in the minds of the American Indians, thanks to the compelling characteristics of several notable traders. This was true even north of the Ohio, where English-speaking wilderness merchants had replaced the French scarcely a dozen years before. It was doubly true in the South. There, energetic English packhorsemen thrusting westward from Charles Town and Savannah had proved as early as 1740 that they were more than a match for the indolent French of Mobile, New Orleans, and Natchez.

Of the scores of traders who settled contentedly among the Southern tribes, married Indian women, reared able half-blooded children, and extolled the king as the Great Father of them all, James Adair and Lachlan McGillivray were two of the most effective.

Adair, a native of Ireland, worked first among the Cherokees. At the behest of the South Carolina government he later opened trade routes among both the

By the time of the Revolution, the Cherokees—soon to be known as one of the Civilized Tribes—were no strangers to European ways. In 1730, these Cherokee headmen were pictured in white men's clothes during a visit to London.

Chickasaws and Choctaws. He was no illiterate woodsman. Fluent in Greek and Latin and a keen student of ancient history, he developed a theory that the American Indians were descendants of the Ten Lost Tribes of Israel. (A variant of the hypothesis later became incorporated into the doctrine of the Mormon Church.) To further his study he learned Hebrew and spent his declining years combing the Old Testament for Hebrew customs analogous to those he had observed among the Southern Indians. Retiring to London shortly before the Revolution, he published his findings (1775) in *The History of the American Indians*. Though Adair's anthropology is tedious, his descriptions of Indian life brought white readers their first solid account of the natives of the South. And to many of the Indians of that area, he brought through the years a glowing image of the English nation. Nothing they had seen among the American backwoodsmen could compare with it.

Of equal influence among the Creeks was Lachlan McGillivray, a Highland Scot to whom Adair dedicated his history. McGillivray settled about 1740 at the Creek

Indian town of Otciapofa, in the idyllic valley of the Coosa River, near today's Montgomery, Alabama. Hard by were the ruins of Fort Toulouse, a short-lived station of the French. Choicest relic of the French stay was Sehoy Marchand, daughter of a French army officer and a Creek "princess." At the time of McGillivray's appearance, Sehoy was married to an Englishman named Tait. Lachlan spirited her away. For her and their children he built a home near the Creek town of Little Tallassee, no porticoed mansion, to be sure, but a pleasant farm and trading post surrounded by an apple orchard, livestock pastures, and cotton fields tended by Negro slaves. Lachlan was particularly proud of his first-born, Alexander, whom he took to Charles Town to be educated by the boy's cousin, a Presbyterian minister.

When the Revolution erupted, the bulk of the traders stayed loyal to England. They were as opposed as the Indians were to an extension of settlement, for farming destroyed the fur-bearing animals on which their economy, as well as that of the savages, had come to rest. (A related essential: the traders paid for the pelts in merchandise; Long Hunters like Boone took the game as if it were theirs.) The traders believed that enforcement of the proclamation line, which the rebellious Colonies might repudiate, was the only hope of maintaining the integrity of the tribes until the Indians became civilized, a state that the Southern nations—the Cherokees, Chickasaws, Choctaws, and Creeks—were at last beginning to approach. They realized further, and made the Indians realize, that the Americans, oriented toward shipping and agriculture, lacked the industrial equipment to provide the manufactured goods on which the Indians depended. In short, so they argued persuasively, the Indians would be well advised to support the king.

The Colonies recognized this anti-American influence and fought it. They sent commissioners to the tribes and tried, with scant success, to win their neutrality. Georgia proscribed Lachlan McGillivray and confiscated a hundred thousand dollars worth of his property. Lachlan fled to Scotland. His son, sixteen-year-old Alexander, returned to his mother's people with an abiding hatred of every Georgian. Dozens of other traders also chose the wilderness and the Indians.

The Revolutionary frontier always blamed these traders for inciting the Indians to massacre. During the early days of the war the charge was not true, at least in the South. Although England wanted red warriors in readiness as auxiliary troops for fighting rebel soldiers, her strategists were reluctant to unleash the horror of raids on homes, women, and children.

The Cherokees, well armed by gifts of munitions from both sides, rejected the restraint. In Indian warfare female prisoners or female scalps were valid trophies: male children of the enemy made desirable captives to raise as replacements for men lost in battle. Furthermore, the frontier cabins, scars on their lands, were assailable representations of what they hated most. In their minds, passing by such places to wait for battle in open fields with better armed soldiers made little sense.

Fiery Dragging Canoe, who had resisted the sale at Sycamore Shoals, led the war talk in July, 1776. The Black Drink circulated through the bark-covered council houses. Made by boiling holly leaves in water and stirring the inky result to a froth, the decoction acted as a purgative, vomitive, and diuretic, purifying the drinker for debates in council, for the green corn celebration, and for war. In addition, its caffeine produced a nervous stimulation desirable for "medicine," the magic by which one sought to control the forces of destiny.

Among the Cherokees, certain female warriors called Ghigau, or Beloved Women, were privileged to prepare the Black Drink and participate in the councils that followed. One such Ghigau was half-breed Nancy Ward. Learning of projected attacks on the Holston and Watauga settlements and hoping to forestall bloodshed among her father's people, she secretly urged a trader named Isaac Thomas to alert the whites. Other accounts say that Henry Stuart, brother of John Stuart, British superintendent of Indian affairs for the Southern tribes, learned of the plot and hired Thomas. In any event, the settlers were warned in time.

They forted up in the nearest stockades—at Eaton's Station near the Long Island of the Holston and at Fort Watauga beside Sycamore Shoals. One hundred and seventy men marched out of Eaton's to meet the two hundred or so Cherokees that Dragging Canoe was leading toward them. The Indians fled from the short, fierce encounter, leaving thirteen dead and carrying with them an indeterminate number of wounded, including Dragging Canoe. Only four whites were hurt, none mortally.

The next dawn another band of Cherokees hit Fort Watauga, which was crowded with women and children and defended by only forty or fifty men. James Robertson was in command; blond, handsome, mercurial John Sevier, thirty-one years old, was his lieutenant. Kate Sherrill, tall, comely, and not yet twenty, had gone out at dawn with seven other women to nearby fields to milk a few cows. Indians ululated. The milkmaids scampered for shelter. The gates of the fort swung closed before Kate could reach them. John Sevier shot down her closest pursuer, leaned over the wall, caught her outstretched hand, and pulled her to safety. The sequel was inevitable. After Sevier's wife died early in 1780, he waited a few months and on August 14, married his Bonnie Kate, as he ever afterward called her.

After an intermittent siege, the Indians left Watauga. Stung by their failures, the Cherokees shifted targets. Joining the Creeks and several renegade Tories and led by trader Alexander Cameron, they ravaged the frontiers of both Carolinas and Georgia. Helped by Virginia militia, those Colonies struck back with equal savagery— South Carolina offered a bounty of seventy-five pounds for an Indian scalp, one hundred pounds for an Indian prisoner. By the winter of 1776 most of the thickly clustered towns of the Cherokees had been destroyed and the beaten tribe forced to sign peace treaties that yielded five million acres to the victors. Refusing to accept the terms, Dragging Canoe led a numerous band of intransigents called the Chickamaugans to shelter in the rough hill country near present Chattanooga and vowed to continue the fight from there.

For the time being, however, he had no strength to mount an offensive. The weakness saved Kentucky.

Shown above are the moves of George Rogers Clark and Henry Hamilton during the campaign in "the country of the Illinois."

Armed by Henry Hamilton, the British commander at Detroit, Shawnees and Delawares crossed the Ohio and attacked the Kentucky settlements with such effectiveness that by the opening of 1777 only Boonesborough, Harrodsburg, and St. Asaph's still held out. The one possibility of relief, George Rogers Clark decided, was to astonish the British by an attack on Detroit. To protect his flanks he would first have to seize the old French towns of Kaskaskia and Cahokia in Illinois and Vincennes on the Wabash. For this plan to have a chance of success, he would need help from Virginia.

Joining a party of retreating settlers who had had enough of Kentucky, he traveled, in October, 1777, back through Cumberland Gap to Williamsburg. There, with Jefferson's help, he prevailed on Governor Patrick Henry to give him twelve hundred pounds in depreciated currency for expenses, and authority to enlist three hundred and fifty men in the Fort Pitt area.

Military considerations took precedence in Henry's decision, but other points had their bearing. The states that owned no trans-Allegheny land to sell for financing their war contributions were looking askance at those that did. If the struggle was for the common good, should not the wilderness be a common resource? Furthermore, as the Western lands filled up with settlers, farms, and villages, they might greatly increase the owners' strength, to the detriment of those states that could not expand. The wilderness areas, the have-nots argued, should not become colonial appendages of the favored states but should be surrendered to the new nation as a whole.

The landed states resisted. Benjamin Harrison cried furiously in the Continental Congress that its members "shall not pare away the Colony of Virginia." Little Maryland retorted that she would not ratify the Articles of Confederation unless the land-holding states ceded their Western territories to Congress. The stand was not entirely altruistic. Speculators in Maryland and in other have-not states could not expect grants from Virginia and North Carolina, who would favor their own citizens. But they might win the ear of Congress if the nation held the land. Energetically those hopefuls tried to create sentiment in favor of the land cessions. They were, of course, met head on in their wiles by the legally wily speculators of the landed states, one of whom happened to be Governor Henry of Virginia.

If Virginia arms and Virginia money held the West against the British and Indians, then Virginia's claim to the area would be stronger when the showdown came. This as well as a desperate need for relief from the continuing Indian raids was in Clark's mind when he started back over the mountains by way of Pittsburgh.

Recruits would not join him to fight so far from home as Illinois. The total he mustered was one hundred and seventy-eight. To try to conquer the entire area between the Ohio, the Mississippi, and the Great Lakes with so minuscule a force seemed totally foolhardy. Yet his spies had brought him word that there were no British troops closer than Detroit, and that the French inhabitants of Kaskaskia and Cahokia were not likely to resist a surprise appearance of armed Americans. The chance seemed worth taking. Besides, something had to be done. Shawnee pressures were increasing. The Indians had even captured Daniel Boone and had exhibited him triumphantly in Detroit. Later Boone escaped and one week before Clark's departure for Illinois appeared at Boonesborough with a warning of fresh Indian attacks. The defenders needed that timely word. If the Kentucky forts fell, Clark would be helplessly isolated.

They held, and the story of Clark's triumphs in the Western country became an American legend. Moving his men with such secrecy that even the Indians did not know he was about, he captured Kaskaskia and subverted Cahokia and Vincennes without firing a shot. That same fall, 1778, Hamilton retook Vincennes after an epic march from Detroit, only to lose it again when Clark made a dramatic counterattack across the icy, flooded plains of the Wabash.

A swift follow-up would have plucked Detroit and the lake country for the Americans, but Clark was unable to

George Rogers Clark   *Henry Hamilton*

Seen above is the February 24, 1779, letter of George Rogers Clark to Henry Hamilton, written with determined hand and setting the American's terms for the surrender of Fort Vincennes.

muster adequate strength. Still, to Virginians his victories looked like powerful support for their argument about owning Kentucky and the Northwest. Ignoring increasingly strenuous demands for cession of the West to the nation, Virginia went ahead in 1779 and passed generous (and chaos-breeding) land laws designed to speed migration across the mountains.

Settlers responded eagerly. Although the Revolution continued badly in the East, the war beyond the mountains seemed over. Spain, entering the conflict as France's ally (not America's), captured the British posts at Natchez, Mobile, and Pensacola. John Bowman's Kentuckians burned the big Shawnee village of Chillicothe in Ohio; troops marching out of Pittsburgh spread havoc through the Seneca country; General Sullivan battered the rest of the hostile Iroquois. When Dragging Canoe's Chickamaugans ventured out of their mountain fastness, they were crushed by Evan Shelby.

All this while, Richard Henderson was scheming busily to salvage at least some land for the Transylvania Company. Virginia had denied his claims within her borders, but if he estimated geography correctly, part of the company's Cherokee purchase lay south of the Virginia line, in territory embraced by North Carolina's charter. Perhaps his native state would listen sympathetically to a project for establishing a settlement on the Cumberland. Perhaps Congress would be more amenable to his proposals for recognition once Virginia's pressures were gone. Perhaps cession of the trans-Allegheny territory to the United States would change the picture for everyone. Anyway, the waters were still troubled, and now that the Indian menace appeared over, Henderson was willing to fish in them once again.

Meeting with two famous Watauga leaders, John Donelson and James Robertson, he laid plans to send a strong expedition to the great bend of the Cumberland River, there to establish Nashborough—or Nashville, as it is called today—named for the Nash brothers of North Carolina: Abner, who was then governor, and Francis, a Revolutionary general killed at Germantown a year earlier. Henderson's plan was bold. But so was the one that had created Boonesborough. And both contained the same fundamental weakness: Richard Henderson never quite understood the forces he was trying to manipulate, sectionalism and nationalism. The struggle between them, swirling around his uncomprehending ears, had to be resolved before the United States could be more than a loose league of independent nations. During the two decades that followed, while Henderson was gradually shrunken to a cipher, the West would be continually agonized by the growing conflict.

Woodland of the Midwest

"The land we live on, our fathers received from God, and they transmitted it to us, for our children, and we cannot part with it.... Where is the land on which our children and their children after them are to lie down!"

Cornplanter, the Seneca leader, to President George Washington, 1790, prior to the making of a sacred treaty to last "as long as the grass shall grow." The United States broke the treaty in 1964.

CHAPTER TWO

WHOSE WEST?

1779-1795

In February, 1779, James Robertson, dour, stocky, and powerfully muscled, started with his brother, six other whites, and a Negro slave to locate a new colony for Henderson. After threading Cumberland Gap, they swung west from the traveled route and descended slowly through the enormous forest until they reached an elliptical, undulating valley, through which the Cumberland River curled. On the bluffs bordering the stream's south bank they found a big salt lick, French Lick, so called for a settlement of French hunters who had located there. Nearby was a natural ford. From this point, a well-traveled buffalo and Indian trail pointed to the southwest, toward Natchez.

Though Robertson was not sure he was south of the Virginia (now Kentucky) border, he decided this was a suitable place for the Nashborough colony. The party staked out several tomahawk claims, girdled trees to kill them, and planted corn. Leaving three of their number behind to guard the crop against animals and birds, they hurried east again, traveling with some Long Hunters who had happened by.

Somewhere Robertson managed to make connections with Henderson, who had meanwhile found employment as a member of the commission of North Carolina and Virginia surveyors running the boundary line between the Western holdings of the two states. Henderson approved Robertson's proposals for implementing the Nashborough migration, then grew so nervous about the settlement's location that he pushed ahead of the main boundary commission to run his own survey and satisfy himself that the site of the new colony really lay south of the line, in country beyond the reach of Virginia.

Although winter was at hand, Robertson prepared to lead a large group of men from the Holston, several of them driving livestock, back through Cumberland Gap and down the mountains to Nashborough. He felt, however, that the trail was too rough and the danger of Indians too great to justify adding to his party an unwieldy mass of women and children. Those appendages could travel more easily in bateaux and flatboats down the Tennessee River, where Indians ought not be a menace, for Dragging Canoe's Chickamaugans had just been whipped into peace. Robertson promised that messengers from Nashborough would leave written directions at Muscle Shoals (now under water upstream from Florence, Alabama) telling the flotilla members where to leave their boats so that they could continue to their new homes by land, for the planners thought the distance between the Cumberland and the Tennessee in that section to be less than it actually is.

Another thing the planners did not anticipate was one of the most severe winters in the history of Tennessee. Snow piled deep; weeks of low temperatures killed mile upon mile of canebrake; streams normally iceless were frozen so solid that Robertson's pioneers were able to trot across them on horseback. They did not reach the Nashborough claims until January 1, 1780.

It seemed pointless then to send messages to Muscle Shoals. The snowy woods were almost impassable. Besides, the flotilla of families, by that time supposedly having reached the rendezvous and finding no directions, probably had continued down the Tennessee to the Ohio, as had been agreed in case of a slip-up. From there they would ascend the Cumberland to Nashborough—a rough pull against the current, but at least they would know where to come. The essential service was to prepare food and shelter for them.

The corn had not fared well, and Robertson sent word of the shortage to Henderson. Early in March that indefatigable optimist left his surveying party and rode to Boonesborough to buy grain. What he saw must have brought pangs of envy. Freed of an immediate dread of Indians by Clark's and Bowman's military victories, settlers were flooding into what the North Carolinian had once hoped would be his own barony.

Most came by foot and horseback across the Wilderness Trail Boone had opened for the Transylvania Com-

This sketch of a flatboat, built on the Monongahela for use on Western waters, adorned Victor Collot's 1796 map of the Ohio.

pany. More daring souls were beginning to risk the Ohio in flatboats. These were ponderous craft, rectangular in shape, three or four feet deep, with a square cabin amidships. The sloping sides served as a pen for horses and oxen, which lived on hay stacked in one corner. Steering was provided by a pair of ponderous oars near the bow and, at the stern, by a giant sweep whose manipulation often demanded the full strength of two husky men.

Landing generally at Limestone (later named Maysville), the boat travelers scattered out to race for claims with the families crossing the mountains. On the chosen land they built rough log cabins just large enough, as a rule, to hold two beds, a rough table, a few split-bottom chairs and three-legged stools, corner shelves of crossed sticks for dishes, a spinning wheel, and a mud-daubed chimney rising from the flagstone hearth where meals

were cooked. When extra room was needed, a second cabin was added in line with the first but separated from it by a "dog-trot," or breezeway, both buildings sometimes shaded by one long gallery. New puncheon floors were polished by being sprinkled with corn siftings; friends were then invited to dance the oil into the wood—a bran, not a barn, dance.

These log cabins, stoutly chinked with long wooden wedges and clay, could resist nearly anything that the Indians brought against them except fire. Many a housewife, her husband absent or dead, successfully defended such a home with no help other than from her children. Mrs. John Merrill gained immortality of sorts by using an axe to split the heads of four Indians crawling through a hole they had hacked in her door, and burning a feather mattress to suffocate two more sliding down the chimney; when the choking pair tumbled into the fireplace, she used her axe on them, too.

At certain places the settlers built "stations" to which they could repair in case of heavy attack. A station consisted of several cabins surrounded by a tall stockade of pointed logs and guarded by blockhouses at opposite corners. Living crowded together inside one of the palisades could seem almost as bad to the settlers as facing Indians. One observer in 1780, the year Henderson went to Boonesborough for corn, described the spring of water inside Fort Harrod as fouled with ashes, sweepings, putrid flesh, dead dogs, and horse excrement, but utilized nevertheless for soaking deer hides and for washing clothes, as well as for drinking.

Until land had been laboriously cleared for rye, wheat, sorghum, tobacco, and peach and apple orchards, the staple crop was corn. Corn could be grown with no more cultivation than the use of a hoe on plots from which logs and dead, girdled trees had not yet been removed. It could be prepared in a variety of ways: roasted on the cob, leached with ashes into hominy, or pounded into johnnycake meal. Parched, it stored almost indefinitely.

Henderson bought quantities of this versatile grain and made arrangements for it to be taken by pirogue down the Ohio to the Cumberland and up that stream to Nashborough. After recruiting more settlers for the new colony from among Kentucky's malcontents, he returned to his surveying. Late in March he was astounded to receive the news that the little flotilla of Holston families bound for Nashborough was still struggling up the Cumberland. Hurrying off to the river, he met the immigrants on March 31 and from their captain, John Donelson, heard the story of their difficult trip.

Donelson was fifty-four years old. Once prosperous and three times a member of Colonial Virginia's House of Burgesses, he had lost his fortune in an ill-advised business venture. He had eleven children, the eldest already married. The youngest, Rachel, was thirteen. Tanned and nimble, she already showed signs of the striking beauty—"medium heighth, beautifully moulded form, full red lips"—that soon would disturb many men. When she was seventeen she married a Captain Lewis Robards. Five years later she ran away from Robards with a hard-drinking, high-living, intensely ambitious twenty-three-year-old lawyer named Andrew Jackson. But that is getting ahead of the story.

Donelson had left the Holston settlements on December 22, 1779, with forty men and one hundred and twenty women and children. They were crowded with their possessions into thirty flatboats, canoes, and dugouts. Ice stranded them. Not until late February were they able to inch southwest toward the high tablelands and bold cliffs of the Chickamauga country.

On March 6, Captain Hutchings' Negro slave froze to death. On the night of the seventh, the wife of Ephraim Peyton, a man who had gone to Nashborough by land with Robertson, was delivered of a child. The next day the Indians began a running attack. First they killed a young man whose canoe drifted in close to the north bank. Excited by that, they struck at a flatboat that was lagging in isolation behind the others because some of its twenty-eight passengers had just come down with smallpox. The savages captured or killed every person aboard the ill-fated craft. "Their cries," Donelson noted in his diary, "were distinctly heard."

Where Chattanooga now stands, the Tennessee River swung west and began a twenty-mile plunge through a deep canyon. The boatmen ran the rough water on March 8, Indians firing at them from both sides. On March 10, one of the boats crashed into a rock and hung there. Aboard were eight people: Mr. and Mrs. Jennings and their son, who was "almost grown," another young man, a Negro couple, Mrs. Peyton, and her baby, who was not yet three days old.

The Indians gathered, firing gleefully. Jennings yelled at the others to throw everything movable overboard in order to lighten the craft. Instead, his panicked son, the other young man, and the Negro male jumped into the river to try to swim away. The Negro drowned in the current. The Indians were able to seize the other two. Later they burned the young man at the stake but spared the Jennings boy and sold him to a trader.

Turned desperate by the desertion, Mrs. Jennings and Mrs. Peyton also leaped overboard, shoving at the craft while Jennings and the Negro woman pushed on the oars. The boat broke loose, and they scrambled aboard,

miraculously unhurt, although "their clothes," Donelson wrote, "were very much cut with bullets, especially Mrs. Jennings's." But the baby was dead, "killed upon the hurry and confusion consequent upon such a disaster."

The river looped down across what is now northern Alabama. On March 12, a Sunday, the party reached the upper end of Muscle Shoals, a thirty-seven-mile stretch of howling water. Nowhere could they find directions about how to reach Nashborough. After anxious consultation, they decided to follow their alternate plan: run the Shoals, continue down the Tennessee to the Ohio, find the Cumberland, and row up it—a total water trip from their starting point on the Holston, they estimated later, of nine hundred miles.

They shot the horrid stretch without accident in three hours—a fantastic twelve miles per hour for their ungainly craft. A week later they reached the Ohio. The prospect of fighting its current upstream so discouraged some of the party that they headed for other places—a few to Illinois, more to Natchez. Short of food, the rest toiled upstream. They met Henderson on the Cumberland on March 31. On April 24 they finally struggled into Nashborough. Scattering out in eight stations on both sides of the river, they set industriously to work building shelters and clearing land. Near his claim, John Donelson planted Tennessee's first cotton crop.

Henderson granted the Nashborough pioneers easier financial terms and a more liberal compact of self-government than he had offered the Kentucky settlers. Otherwise the pattern was the same—and came to the same end. North Carolina declared Henderson's title invalid and set aside most of the Nashborough area as a reserve of bounty lands for paying her soldiers. To recompense the Transylvania Company for opening the area, the state awarded it two hundred thousand acres in Powell's Valley. Added to the company's grant from Virginia, this brought the proprietors' possessions to four hundred thousand acres—no mean holding, yet a considerable diminution from the seventeen million acres they once had envisioned.

North Carolina's insistence on maintaining her charter rights as far west as the Mississippi ran counter to a growing sentiment in the rest of the nation: the Western territories should be common treasure. To set an example, New York in 1780 ceded to the Continental Congress her tenuous claim to the wilderness lands of the Iroquois. The next year Virginia's principal speculators (George Washington, Benjamin Harrison, George Mason, and Joseph Jones, the guardian of James Monroe) swallowed their private desires and let their state offer to the Confederation her claims north of the Ohio River, save for a military reserve along the Scioto River and a grant to George Rogers Clark across from Louisville. The offer carried strings, however: no prior speculative claims in the areas she relinquished were to be recognized.

Speculators interested in a dozen schemes immediately objected. Their influence was strong enough so that for the duration of the war they were able to block acceptance of the cession.

Although most of the shooting in the East ended in October, 1781, at Yorktown, the Indians and frontiersmen beyond the mountains continued striking at each other as ferociously as ever. In March, 1782, a gang of whites massacred ninety-six unresisting, Christianized Delaware Indian men, women, and children at their village of Gnadenhutten in eastern Ohio. The tribes retorted by butchering a column of soldiers under Colonel William Crawford. Crawford was captured and taken to a Delaware village, where he was slowly tortured—his ears sliced off, his body pierced by a burning stake, his head and body heaped with embers.

In August of the same year, Indians and Canadian rangers fell on Bryant's Station in Kentucky. Beaten back, they used their retreat to lure the Kentucky militia into an ambush where sixty men died. In retaliation, Clark led a vengeful force of a thousand Kentuckians up Ohio's Scioto River to burn to the ground the big village the Shawnees had rebuilt at Chillicothe. Only then did he receive word that the war was over and that he was forthwith relieved of his command.

Throughout this period (Yorktown to Chillicothe), the Continental Congress debated the land problem as though the Western territories without question would stay in American hands. Actually, there was real doubt that they would. From a European point of view, the American Revolution was only a part of a larger imperial struggle between France and Spain on one hand and England on the other.

France was far less interested in strengthening America than in placating Spain, to whom she had promised British-held Gibraltar. Unable to deliver that Mediterranean stronghold, she had suggested that Spain take instead the western tip of Kentucky, the western half of Tennessee, and all of present Mississippi and Alabama, thus gaining full control of the Mississippi River below the mouth of the Ohio. It was thought that England would agree to this massive transfer if she were allowed to keep the rich fur country west and north of the Ohio River, as far as the Mississippi. Spain, of course, already held the entire trans-Mississippi West.

On discovering France's abrogation of United States "rights," the American envoys repudiated their French obligations and dealt directly with the English. Negotiations were long, complex, and amazingly successful. In spite of furious objections by the Montreal fur traders, the northern boundary of the American West became a line through the Great Lakes and along the fur-trade canoe route from Lake Superior to Lake of the Woods. The country's western boundary became the Mississippi. (What to do about the awkward gap between Lake of the Woods and the source of the Mississippi became a matter for contention that lasted several years.) Spanish pretentions were also whittled away. Instead of receiving most of the Old Southwest as originally proposed, she had to be content with a strip of land below the 31st parallel; today the parallel forms the northern boundary of eastern Louisiana and of western Florida. The strip substantially strengthened Spain's position, however. It made the Gulf of Mexico a Spanish "lake" and put into Spain's hand the power of closing the lower Mississippi to American navigation whenever she chose.

The treaty was concluded on September 3, 1783. The West as far as the Mississippi at last belonged legally to someone in the United States. Now it was up to the nation to decide who the owners were.

Georgia and South Carolina, both hard pressed for funds and claiming an enormous block of wilderness between the 31st parallel and the southern boundary of the Tennessee country, refused to give up a square foot of their holdings. North Carolina wavered over what to do about Tennessee. Under various pressures she finally decided to cede—but as little as possible. As already noted, she had held out a large military reservation around Nashborough. Desperate for revenue (her legislators were being paid in corn), she next offered the entire remaining area for sale at prices as low as five cents an acre in hundred-acre plots—all without extinguishing the Indian title, which in effect threw the Chickasaws straight into the arms of Spain. Speculators went wild. In seven months they located, surveyed, and entered claims for a crazy patchwork of four million acres. If North Carolina's cession materialized, only the poorer sections would remain for the United States.

In the North, sentiment was strongly in favor of cession. Massachusetts and Connecticut promised to yield their rights as soon as Virginia ceded, though Connecticut did hold out a military reservation in northeastern Ohio, the famous Western Reserve, with the site of Cleveland-to-be in its heart. Brushing aside the objections of the speculators, Congress appointed committees to study the best ways of managing the territory when it came into the nation's hands. How was it to be governed? By what orderly method were titles to be transferred to individual

citizens? What was to be done about the Indian tribes?

Conservatives like George Washington advocated carefully controlled expansion. Land was to be obtained by treaty from the Indians in narrow north-south strips as needed; the Army was to patrol the borders and make sure Indian country was not invaded before each newly acquired strip was fully settled. Such a system, Washington believed, would check the provocations that led to Indian wars and would keep the West, in his words, from being usurped "by a parcel of banditti who will bid defiance to all authority while they are skimming and disposing the cream of the country."

Jefferson, who headed two Congressional land committees, doubted the ability of the Army to control the westward rush of migration and the wisdom of having it try. He did accept Washington's strip theory to the extent of ruling off the Old Northwest into tiers of states stacked north and south and blessing them with such resounding names as Cherronesus, Assenisipia, Metropotamia. He recognized the need for negotiating with the Indians to extinguish title, but he would let circumstances, not rigid lines on the map, determine the westward progression. Most importantly, he believed that the settlers should from the outset have a voice in their own affairs, and that as each territory attained a voting population of twenty thousand, it should enter the Confederation as a full-fledged, sovereign partner of the others, not as an inferior appendage.

While debating this Ordinance of 1784, as it was called, the original states gave notice that they opposed colonialism within the new nation. In other respects, however, the bill drew heavy censure. Its prohibitions against slavery were stricken out by the South, the West objected to rigid boundaries determined without regard to natural features, and the Eastern states feared that the great number of units proposed (up to sixteen) would result in their being dominated by the radical debtor classes beyond the mountains. Hammered thus from every side, the ordinance never went into effect. But it did plant usable seeds concerning governmental policies for the new territories—seeds that soon grew into the famous Northwest Ordinance of 1787.

One of Jefferson's land committees, searching for an orderly method of putting the public domain into private hands, faced two main problems: price and measurement. So far as price was concerned, the determining factor was a prevailing belief in Congress that land, should be sold to raise revenue, rather than passed out cheaply as an inducement to settling. Accordingly, the minimum price was set at a dollar an acre. Since land was to be offered first at public auction, optimists hoped that this minimum would often be exceeded. The minimum amount to be sold was set by the same committee at one square mile, or six hundred and forty acres, in the belief that this would allow individual farmers an opportunity to bid against speculative land companies. Matters did not develop as anticipated, however. A square mile of forestland was more than a single family could clear, and the price of six hundred and forty dollars proved to be more than most Western migrants could raise for a single payment. Ignoring both provisions, squatters moved defiantly onto the public lands during the next fifteen years. Meanwhile, agitation for more liberal laws intensified, especially in the matter of granting credit. At last, in 1800 (to move briefly ahead of our story), a man was allowed to buy as little as three hundred and twenty acres and to pay for it in four installments.

Obviously, the bounds of a piece of land had to be determined before it could be sold. How were these outlines to be determined—by the so-called Virginia system, established for Kentucky in 1779 and favored by the South, or by adaptations of New England's township method? The Congressional committee studying the matter quickly decided against the Southern system. It had proved chaotic. Under it, a Kentuckian had simply stepped off whatever he wanted, regardless of shape, guiding himself by natural landmarks—hollow oak trees, creek beds, and the like. Afterward, he had the plot surveyed and registered in the land office. Inevitably, furious quarrels arose about overlapping boundary lines and priority of selection. The inadequate staffs of surveyors and clerks in the land offices could not keep up with the flood of entries; yet until land was properly filed, infinite opportunities existed for honest mistakes and dishonest sleight of hand. Lawyers waxed; speculators throve; homeseekers were in turmoil. Confusion and technicalities were such that pioneers like Daniel Boone lost every acre they tried to claim. Disgusted and as restless as ever, Boone in 1799, aged sixty-five, moved on west of the Mississippi to the central part of Missouri and, in exchange for land that he could more surely call his own, took the step of becoming a Spanish citizen.

The Congressional committee studying the problem decided to end the chaos by surveying the Western lands in precise pattern before permitting occupancy. Drawing on various precedents, particularly the land system in vogue in New England, the group proposed as the basic unit of measurement a square, six miles to a side, called a township. Each township was to be divided into thirty-six pieces called sections, each a mile square. The north-south boundary lines of the townships were called "range lines," the east-west boundaries, "township lines."

Showing Fort Harmar in 1790, with the infant town of Marietta across the Muskingum River where it meets the Ohio (left), this lithograph, based on an early view by Joseph Gilman, was published in The American Pioneer *in 1842.*

Astronomical observations determined where measurements were to begin, and the mathematical precision of each step so enthralled Josiah Meigs, Commissioner of the General Land Office, that in 1819 he exclaimed, "So wise, beautiful, and perfect a system was never before adopted by any government or nation on earth." Individualistic Southerners who wanted to draw their lines so as to include only good soil and avoid taxes on poor sidehills or swamps were slow to agree. Eventually, however, the pattern prevailed and became the official surveying method of nearly every civilized nation in the world.

Immediately after the system was enacted on May 20, 1785, Thomas Hutchins, Geographer of the United States, began surveying the first seven range lines west of the Ohio River where it parallels, roughly, the Pennsylvania border. Supposedly, Indian claims to western New York, northwestern Pennsylvania, and eastern Ohio north of the river had been extinguished by the second Treaty of Fort Stanwix in 1784, and by another signed in January, 1785, at Fort McIntosh, two dozen miles down the Ohio from Pittsburgh. Elsewhere, Indian lands were deemed to be inviolate. To show its good intentions, the

Government ordered General Josiah Harmar to drive squatters out of all unceded Ohio lands and build Fort Harmar at the mouth of the Muskingum River to be sure to keep them out.

It was a futile gesture. The squatters slipped back as fast as they were removed and drew up manifestoes denouncing the Government's action. "All mankind," declared one, ". . . have an undoubted right to pass into any vacant country and there form their constitution, and the Confederation of the whole United States Congress is not impowered to forbid them."

The Indians were equally recalcitrant. As fast as a treaty was negotiated, it was denounced by the tribes (not always with complete accuracy) as having been signed by spurious chiefs, minority groups, or outside bands that had no right to the lands they alienated. Capitalizing on the seething unrest, Joseph Brant, an educated Mohawk leader who had been one of England's most ruthless allies during the war, went about urging an Indian confederation. If the united tribes struck hard while time remained, he argued, they might force the Americans to recognize the Ohio River as the boundary of an independent nation

An unknown British officer, dating his work July 25, 1794, painted this view of Detroit. The peaceful scene was deceptive; fought over many times in the past, the strategic post would see more conflict during the War of 1812.

of red men lying between the United States and Canada.

The fur traders of Montreal abetted the Indians. They had been outraged by the surrender of the fur country south and west of the Great Lakes, "a lavish unnecessary concession," that, they said, cost them an annual one hundred and fifty thousand pounds in pelts. An Indian nation between the lakes and the Ohio would let them retain this harvest and would also act as a buffer to protect Canada from the land-grabbing Americans.

Swayed by the arguments and half anticipating that the young United States Confederation might fall apart anyway, the English Government lent unofficial support to the red men's dream. It did this by declining to evacuate the border forts it occupied on American soil at Lake Champlain, Oswego, Niagara, Detroit, and Michilimackinac Island in the strait between Lakes Huron and Michigan, claiming in justification that American citizens were not paying debts owed to loyalists before the war.

From the shadow of these posts British traders continued to send, as they had since 1763, munitions and other manufactured goods to the restless Indians. When Brant in 1785 launched his plans for an Indian confederacy, these traders added unofficial but inflammatory suggestions about war on the feeble whites of the United States. Alarmed by the stiffening determination of the Indians, belligerent Kentuckians tried to terrify them by sending brutal raiding parties (also unofficial) across the Ohio. Although mutual jealousies among the tribes kept an effective union from forming in opposition, sporadic attacks by individual bands spread slaughter along the Pennsylvania border and across the river into Kentucky. This led to further white retaliation; but destructive thrusts into the heart of the Indian country only increased the Indians' fury. Settlement north of the Ohio River obviously was going to be precarious for an indefinite period of time.

In spite of this uncertain future, Hutchins' government surveyors made some progress toward laying out the first seven ranges beyond the Ohio. In one of the field parties, not by chance, was Benjamin Tupper, close friend of General Rufus Putnam of Massachusetts, who was a man keenly interested in the speculative possibilities of Western land. Tupper's main purpose on the survey was to acquire, for his and Putnam's use, information about profitable sites for a colony.

He returned singing paeans about the Muskingum Valley, which was protected from Indian attack by Fort Harmar, at the river's mouth. The upshot was the formation soon afterward of the Ohio Company for the purpose of buying up depreciated continental certificates—a form of paper money—and using them to purchase a huge block of land in the Ohio country.

Negotiations with Congress were entrusted to the Reverend Manasseh Cutler of Ipswich, Massachusetts, a buoyant, full-bodied man with an encyclopedic mind, a bottomless appetite for fine food and wine, and a picayune ministerial salary further shrunken by inflation. "Purchasing lands in a new country," he later wrote, "appeared to be ye only thing I could do to secure a living to myself and family."

He appeared before Congress in July, 1787. The legislators, engrossed in writing a new constitution for the United States and clinging to the principle of selling the public domain in small pieces, at first paid Cutler little attention. Just as he was ready to give up, he was approached by William Duer, Secretary of the Confederation's Board of Treasury. Duer said that several "principal men" of New York City wished to buy Western lands from the nation but could not because of their positions in government. These anonymous speculators included Duer himself, General Arthur St. Clair, who was the president of Congress, and several other congressmen: This group of influential men planned to incorporate their venture as the Scioto Company.

Duer's proposal to Cutler was unabashedly blunt. If Cutler and the Ohio Company would front for the Scioto Company in an appeal for five million acres, Duer and his associates would push through Congress legislation enabling the United States to overlook its own requirements about price, public auctions, and payment in full at time of sale. Western land sales were not producing the revenue anticipated: units were too large and the Indian menace too severe. Under the circumstances, Duer said, the prospect of selling many millions of acres in huge blocks would be tempting to the Government.

To whet Cutler's interest still further, Duer said his associates would lend the Ohio Company money enough for a down payment on one and a half million acres for itself. He also promised that Cutler and others in the Ohio Company would receive stock in the Scioto purchase. Cutler immediately accepted the offer.

The necessary legislation went through Congress with scarcely a ripple. This was not enough for Cutler, however. He felt that prospective settlers could not be lured westward without a guarantee of stable government. He proposed accordingly that Congress appoint a committee to revamp Jefferson's Ordinance of 1784, leaving out its objectionable features but incorporating its good points. He then invited himself to join the deliberations.

Within days the committee produced the famed Ordinance of 1787. Though turgid in language and shortsighted in some of its political philosophy—for example, on Indian problems and in an insistence on property qualifications for voting—the document was an important landmark in providing workable machinery by which the Western territories could develop, as their populations grew, toward full and independent statehood. Again,

colonialism within the United States had been rejected.

The Ohio Company used its privileges well. In April, 1788, a carefully chosen, well-equipped advance party began building at the mouth of the Muskingum, opposite Fort Harmar, a neatly planned community called Marietta. Even the conservative Washington approved, declaring, "No colony in America was ever settled under such favorable auspices."

Other colonies were less remarkable, notably the hard little towns of Columbia and Cincinnati, which were founded on a tract of land purchased from the Government late in 1787 by a New Jersey judge, John Cleves Symmes. Eventually Cincinnati and its neighbors struggled into prosperity, but the colony established by Duer's Scioto Company never did.

The Scioto group, with Cutler's help, had obtained its option on five million acres. To raise money for meet-

The whites' advance into the eastern part of the Northwest Territory is shown on this map of Ohio from the Revolution to 1795.

39

ing their payments, the Scioto speculators sent Joel Barlow, a Connecticut poet, to Paris to sell stock. Barlow fell into the hands of an English schemer ironically named William Playfair. Together they formed the Compagnie de Scioto and flooded France with hyperbole: the Ohio country was "the most salubrious, the most advantageous, the most fertile" ever seen. Five hundred American "cultivators," they said untruthfully, were already erecting houses and planting this "garden of the universe" in preparation for the coming of settlers fortunate enough to secure acreage.

The bombast fell on wistful ears. The Bastille had fallen; mob rule threatened France's established order. Jewelers, dancing masters, wigmakers, provincial noblemen, and indentured servants besieged the Compagnie offices with their money. During February and March,

Fournier's portrait of Joel Barlow

1790, five ships carrying more than five hundred hopeful men, women, and children plowed across the Atlantic toward what the passengers visualized as a Utopian heaven of gleaming white houses, to be named Gallipolis.

Playfair absconded. When the French landed at Alexandria, Virginia, they learned that the Scioto Company had not met its payments and therefore owned no land. Duer, the originator of the Scioto scheme, made amends of a sort. He helped secure lands for the bewildered newcomers opposite the mouth of the Great Kanawha, inside the Ohio Company tract. He arranged for John Burnham to recruit fifty men (four soon deserted) at twenty-six cents a day to clear a few acres and build barracks—several rows of drab log buildings divided into eighty rooms. There most of the shockingly unprepared immigrants settled down to rebuild their lives, many of them hanging on at Gallipolis even after the United States

Government offered them, free of charge, other lands in Ohio as a recompense for their shabby treatment.

South of the Ohio, the country was plagued by problems that were in many ways similar to those facing the North. Angry Indians were making common cause with a foreign power, in this case Spain.

Worried lest the explosive American frontiersmen sweep on across Texas toward the silver mines of northern Mexico, Spanish colonial administrators had devised three countermeasures. One attempted to domesticate the wolf, so to speak: American emigrants were given land if they became Spanish citizens. The second policy was to set up the Indians as a buffer, much as the English were doing in the North. The third was to weaken the United States by encouraging disaffection among independence-minded Westerners. Engineer of the three devices was canny Esteban Miró, Governor of Louisiana.

The Indians were ready to listen to Miró. North Carolina had already enraged the Chickasaws by opening Tennessee to settlement without consulting them. Georgia had been equally highhanded. In 1783 that state appropriated Creek lands north of present Augusta through a treaty with two minor chiefs. The next year she blandly granted still more Creek lands, these around Muscle Shoals, to a speculative company whose officers included such frontier leaders as John Sevier, William Blount, and John Donelson, leader of the river migration to Nashville. In 1785 she endeavored to seize the Natchez country, which Spain also claimed, by creating Bourbon County, with boundaries running west to the Mississippi.

The Indian chief Miró used in coalescing the resentment toward these American encroachments was young Alexander McGillivray, the quarter-breed son of the proscribed British trader Lachlan McGillivray. In some ways, Alexander seemed scarcely like a Creek. He avoided active participation in war and hunting. Though tall and lean, he had a frail physique further weakened by dissipation. He lived in white style at Little Tallassee, far better educated and more cultured than many of the frontiersmen who feared and despised him. With the additional skill of a consummate diplomat, he had made himself, during the uneasy times of the Revolution, absolute master of the thirty-four Creek towns.

When Miró began dickering with him, Alexander forced the Spaniards to withdraw trading privileges from Spanish traders and assign their licenses to the house McGillivray favored, the English firm of Panton, Leslie & Co. This guaranteed to the Creeks a surer supply of munitions and other necessary goods than the inefficient Spaniards could have furnished. It lined McGillivray's pockets. And it guaranteed a desolating time for the

40

Georgia settlements and for the Nashville community when the Creeks, Choctaws, Chickasaws, and, to a lesser extent, the Cherokees unleashed their attacks in 1784–85. The plans laid by speculators for a Muscle Shoals settlement never got off the ground.

So far, so good. The Westerners, meanwhile, were meeting Spanish expectations by growing more and more disgruntled with the East. Conservative mercantile interests along the seaboard were inclined to sneer at the transmountain people as radical malcontents who, although not contributing their share of taxes, demanded excessive amounts of national money for protection from the Indians and for internal improvements—roads, canals, and the like. Westerners believed, on the other hand, that the East exploited them, gobbling up the country's natural resources without granting adequate recognition to those who had suffered and died to gain the treasures for the nation.

In the years immediately following the Revolution, Western dissatisfaction was generally directed not so much at the Confederation as at the parent states of Virginia and North Carolina. Throughout most of a decade, Kentucky kept begging Congress to help her assert her independence. Virginia kept retorting that the young county beyond the mountains was not yet ready for self-government, a stand that in 1783 led Kentucky petitioners to a famous, if somewhat illogical, rejoinder: "... if our society is rude, much wisdom is not necessary to supply our wants, and a fool can put on his clothes better than a wise man can do it for him."

While the Kentucky pioneers pleaded, those in eastern Tennessee acted. In 1784 North Carolina finally decided, in a very close vote, to cede to the nation what remained of her Western lands, provided that Congress recognize all grants made before May of that year. (Further entries were not to be allowed after May.) Congress was given one year in which to accept the offer.

The act caused an uproar in the overhill counties—Washington, Sullivan, Greene—that embraced the growing Holston and Watauga settlements. The pioneers did not wish to be left dangling for a year, uncertain whether or not the Continental Congress would accept the cession with its provisos. Meanwhile, who would assume responsibility for the debts North Carolina owed the Cherokees for certain Western lands? North Carolina apparently would not, in the hope that eventually the nation would. Yet if the debts were not paid when due, the Indians would attack the Western settlements.

There were other disaffections. Pleading poverty, North Carolina had declined to grant the overhill counties superior courts or militia organizations of their own. Were they to be without orderly government while waiting for Congress to make up its mind about accepting the cession? Too, there was the matter of expansion. North Carolina had arbitrarily declared that after May, 1784, settlement should not pass the French Broad River, a restriction that severely cramped the ambitions of both "movers" and speculators. To cap all this, the tidewater aristocrats had characterized the Westerners, during the debate on cession, as "off-scourings of the earth, fugitives from justice," whom North Carolina should be happy to pass on to the Confederation.

Meeting in tumultuous convention in Jonesborough, the people of eastern Tennessee on August 23, 1784, declared themselves an independent state named Frankland —"land of the free." Soon they changed it to Franklin, hoping to entice assistance from Benjamin Franklin. (He

John Sevier by Charles Willson Peale

gave them little more than flowery phrases.) Their idea, so far as the hot protests embodied a coherent idea, was to set up what they wanted in the way of courts, militia, Indian boundaries, land laws, and the like, then seek admission to the national Confederation, not as a territory, but as a full-fledged state whose organization could not be modified. The Cumberland settlements farther west, it should be noted, were extended an invitation to join the Franklinites but turned it down.

The uproar gave the anticession party in North Carolina an excuse for demanding reconsideration of the act relinquishing Tennessee to the nation. On reconvening, the members of the legislature repealed the bill and passed various measures that they hoped would placate the rambunctious Westerners. The Franklinites spurned the gestures. Buoyed by their enthusiasm, they assembled again at Jonesborough in December, 1784, whooped through a constitution, and elected John Sevier governor.

Glib, handsome, bold, and opportunistic, Sevier was the hero of the mountaineers. During the Revolution, in October, 1780, he had helped lead a militia army of fifteen hundred backwoodsmen on a spectacular dash out of the brushy hills to crush an English force on King's Mountain. A little later he had swept the Cherokees out of the French Broad and had forced them to open that area to settlement. The fine, stout home he built for his Bonnie Kate stood beside the cascading Nolichucky. Because of that, his neighbors called him Nolichucky Jack —"dashing," "rapid." The name fitted.

North Carolina's governor fired off a series of manifestoes declaring Franklin to be illegal. Sevier answered with a paper bombardment of his own. Greenville, thirty-some miles southwest of Jonesborough, was selected as Franklin's capital. William Cocke, a onetime Boonesborough pioneer who had returned to Watauga, was elected the new state's representative to Congress, and rushed to Washington to obtain recognition. Sevier, meanwhile, marched once more against the Cherokees and wrested from them another block of territory reaching almost to the Little Tennessee River, a stream that flows out of the western end of what is today the Great Smoky Mountains National Park.

None of the moves succeeded. Congress not only refused to seat Cocke but also ignored Sevier's Indian dealings. Instead, it negotiated its own Treaty of Hopewell (November, 1785) with the Cherokees. Under this agreement, the Indians yielded the Nashville area to the whites but recovered most of the land Sevier had recently taken from them. Greenville, the Franklin capital, was left within the borders of Indian country, and settlers who had taken up claims on the strength of Sevier's victory were ordered to vacate.

Nolichucky Jack's prestige was slipping. To repair it, he sought an alliance with Georgia, which was hard pressed by McGillivray's Creeks. Georgia needed help: raiders were striking everywhere, killing even redoubtable John Donelson of the Cumberland flotilla. Tentatively she promised to recognize Franklin in return for fighting men. Then internal squabbles intervened, and Georgia dropped the proposed campaign. Sevier's situation grew desperate.

All this time, North Carolina had continued to assert her jurisdiction over the seceding counties by appointing justices of the peace and militia officers side by side with those named by Sevier. The leader of the North Carolina officials was John Tipton. In February, 1788, the month in which Massachusetts ratified the new Federal Constitution and Rufus Putnam's advance party of Ohio Com-

pany settlers started for Marietta, Tipton seized the courthouse at Jonesborough from the Franklin officials and made off with its records. He also laid hold of some of Sevier's Negroes and took them to his own "fortress-like" home, where he had them held allegedly as security for money Sevier owed North Carolina.

Sevier and two hundred followers besieged Tipton's home. A heavy snowstorm upset their strategy. Reinforcements slipped past Sevier's sentries, and on February 28 the strengthened Tipton men risked a charge. In the snow-shrouded battle they killed two Franklinites, wounded more, and routed the rest. Among their prisoners were two of Sevier's sons. Tipton wanted to hang the young men but was dissuaded by cooler heads.

Retreating to the lower settlements, Sevier distracted his unhappy followers with another set of brutal Indian raids. None of this helped Franklin's stark bankruptcy. Unable to pay Sevier's salary in cash, the legislature voted him one thousand deer skins and five hundred raccoon hides a year, commodities that were also declared acceptable in payment of taxes. Lesser officials received correspondingly lesser emoluments.

Into this troubled scene rode James White. Recently one of North Carolina's delegates to Congress, White had become a Spanish agent, assigned to furthering the third of Spain's would-be checks against American expansion to the southwest—keeping the West unhappy and the United States weak. In pursuit of this policy, Spain was resorting to various devices, some of them extraordinarily devious. To understand them, and also to understand what James White hoped to accomplish in Franklin, it is necessary to backtrack to June, 1784, when the Spaniards declared that the Mississippi River would be closed to American navigation.

Closure was a powerful economic lever. Produce from western Pennsylvania and Kentucky—tobacco, flour, salt pork, rye whisky—was too bulky to be transported to Eastern markets on horseback. Realizing this, George Washington in 1784 had studied means of building roads and canals for moving goods eastward across the mountains. The job was too big to be accomplished quickly, however. For years Western agricultural products could reach buyers in the West Indies or on the Atlantic seaboard only by traveling the rivers to New Orleans, there to be deposited in warehouses while waiting for ocean-going vessels. If Spain plugged this Mississippi River outlet, Westerners were certain to cry to their Government for help. If help was not forthcoming . . . well, who could tell what might happen?

Don Diego Gardoqui, appointed Spanish chargé d'affaires in New York, arrived in that city to negotiate.

What he said he wanted, on the strength of certain obscure post-Revolutionary agreements, was a boundary line far enough to the east so that the Mississippi River would be fully protected from the Americans—a boundary, specifically, that would give to Spain all of the present states of Mississippi and Alabama, and the western quarter of Georgia. Failing to obtain this, he might still handle the Mississippi question in such a way as to keep the West in ferment.

At first he was successful. Although the American Confederation's Secretary for Foreign Affairs, John Jay, resisted Gardoqui's boundary proposals, he yielded to commercial blandishments. Tentatively accepting trading privileges in Spanish ports—a boon to New England —Jay promised in return that the United States would not press its demands for navigational rights on the Mississippi for twenty-five years.

Furious at being thus abandoned by the East, hotheads in western Pennsylvania, Kentucky, and Tennessee fell into Spain's trap and began rumbling of their own declaration of independence and their own nation west of the Alleghenies. Loyalists rebuffed the idea, and in the welter of arguments that followed, opportunistic plotters saw a chance to make hay for themselves. Foremost among them was James Wilkinson.

Handsome, brave, hard-drinking, and everlastingly greedy, Wilkinson seems to have been a compulsive intriguer. Although he had fought skillfully during the Revolution, he had been stripped of his honors for joining the Conway Cabal, an abortive scheme to remove

Washington as commander of the American Army. In 1784 Wilkinson came to Kentucky. There his energetic espousal of separation from Virginia won him a considerable following. This strength, which he bolstered by working to undermine the influence of George Rogers Clark, he hoped to be able to sell at a high price to the Spanish administrators in Louisiana.

Luck played into his hands. In 1786 Clark led an ill-disciplined force of Kentucky volunteers across the Ohio and up the Wabash on a punitive campaign against the Indians. The base of the expedition, which desertions turned into a fiasco, was the old French settlement of Vincennes. While the troops were there, three traders, citizens of Spain, arrived from New Orleans without passports. Clark's officers confiscated their vessel and cargo. After returning to New Orleans, the trio instituted suit against Clark, who received no help from either Virginia or the United States on the ground that he had not been acting under official orders.

Wilkinson used the episode to justify a secret letter to Spanish officials. In his communication he angrily denounced Clark's action, suggested falsely that Clark intended to seize Natchez, and hinted that he possessed other data of value. On the strength of this, Spanish Governor Miró of Louisiana gave the conspirator permission to descend the river with several flatboats loaded with produce. The stroke made Wilkinson's prowess shine still brighter in the eyes of his envious neighbors.

In New Orleans the American swore secret allegiance to Spain and promised to foment rebellion in Kentucky.

Western Pennsylvania immediately after the Revolution was still a partial wilderness of Indians, small settlements, and forts. One of the latter, guarding Sinking Spring Valley, was Fort Robertdeau, pictured in the Columbian Magazine *about 1787 (above).*

In return he received a generous "loan" and a trading monopoly: of all Westerners, only James Wilkinson or men named by him could bring flour, tobacco, whisky, and the like down the river. Highly pleased, he sailed home by way of Philadelphia. Behind him, as contact man, he left a trusted agent, swarthy, handsome, eighteen-year-old Philip Nolan, whom Wilkinson had all but raised in his own household.

While Miró was intriguing with Wilkinson, Don Diego Gardoqui in New York was using James White to sound out Sevier in the disintegrating state of Franklin. Sevier outmatched the clumsy White. In return for swinging Franklin into Spain's orbit, he demanded munitions and money for his feeble state and help for himself in establishing a colony at Muscle Shoals. Excited over the prospects, White sailed by way of Havana to consult Miró.

The Louisiana governor was unimpressed. He doubted Sevier's ability to deliver what few assets Franklin offered, and he had no interest in alienating the Creeks by establishing an American colony on their land. Besides, he was jealous of Gardoqui and reluctant to listen to his envoy. Cavalierly he brushed White aside.

Sevier, meanwhile, was using the Spanish threat to his own advantage. Franklin had collapsed. In October, 1788, North Carolina lawmen arrested the governor and took him to Morgantown, North Carolina, for trial. The Morgantown sheriff, who had served under Sevier at King's Mountain, declined to jail him. While Sevier was lounging unguarded in a local tavern, his sons and a group of loyal followers galloped up. Away Sevier went. There was no pursuit. He whipped the Cherokees again and then dropped hints that he might join the Spanish, unless. . . . What bargaining ensued is unknown. Anyway, charges against him were dropped, and on February 17, 1789, he swore an oath of allegiance to North Carolina. Promptly thereafter he was seated in the state legislature as senator for the overhill counties.

Like Sevier, James Robertson of Nashville also used the Spanish threat to further his policies. The most immediate problem was the Indians. Believing that Miró could restrain the natives if he chose, and hoping also to develop markets in New Orleans for Tennessee tobacco and cotton, Robertson began hinting of an alliance. As evidence of his good faith he named Tennessee's western judicial district after the Spaniard, but misspelled it Mero. Having thus prevailed on Miró to listen, he then waved the Spanish bugaboo at jittery North Carolina.

Of the original thirteen states, only North Carolina and Rhode Island had not yet ratified the new Federal Constitution, although the revitalized Government, with George Washington as its President, had begun to func-

tion. Robertson and his Nashville associates hoped that Tennessee might fare better as a territory of the national Government than it had under North Carolina. Before a territorial administration could be established, however, North Carolina must ratify the Constitution and again cede her Western lands to the United States. To push her along this path, the Nashville leaders wrote influential Easterners that discontented Tennesseans were beginning to emigrate to Spanish territory. Unless there was federal jurisdiction to bring stability to the area, the entire Mero district might secede and join Spain, "in hopes," said Daniel Smith, one of Robertson's colleagues, "of getting their Calamities alleviated."

Again the effect of this conniving cannot be evaluated. In any event, on November 21, 1789, North Carolina ratified the Constitution and three months later finally ceded Tennessee to the United States, to be formally established as Southwest Territory. It became the state of Tennessee in 1796.

Only Georgia still refused to relinquish her Western land claims. Anxious to profit while she could, she sold, on December 21, 1789, a total of 25,400,000 acres to three speculative land companies. The price was $207,580. All three purchases lay far from the nearest Georgia settlement: two bordered the Mississippi; the third embraced Muscle Shoals. All were in regions claimed both by the Indians and, somewhat more nebulously, by Spain. The purchasers, Georgia said, would have to face the responsibility of dealing with those powers and with the new federal union as best they could.

The most aggressive of the three groups was the South Yazoo Company, which held, on paper, a broad swath of land across the entire middle part of the present state of Mississippi. The general agent of the company was Dr. James O'Fallon, an engaging Irish swashbuckler who had landed in North Carolina just before the Revolution.

As soon as his company completed its negotiations with Georgia, O'Fallon hurried to Kentucky to recruit colonists for a settlement at Walnut Hills (present Vicksburg), at the mouth of the Yazoo River, and to enlist the assistance of Wilkinson in persuading Governor Miró that he should tolerate the colony.

O'Fallon's promises to settlers were lavish. The first woman to land at Yazoo, he said, would receive five hundred acres. Another five hundred acres would go "to her who shall bring forth [in the colony] the first live child, bastard or legitimate." To Miró he wrote in a sterner vein, saying that he planned to arrive soon with "from three to five thousand well armed men without the incumberances of Females or Children." This formidable settlement, he told the Louisiana governor, would serve

The Spanish ships Sutil *and* Mexicana, *seeking a Northwest Passage, are seen in this view of Nootka harbor. The drawing was probably made by José Cardero, an artist on the* Mexicana, *which stopped at Nootka in May, 1792.*

Spain as a rampart to hold back aggressive Americans.

To Miró, several thousand armed men sounded more like danger than security. There was little prospect that such a force would materialize, however. Spain was no longer stirring the wrath of the frontier. Worn by the effort of guarding her New World territories from the tip of South America to Alaska and alarmed by revolutionary developments in France, the Government had decided to placate, rather than antagonize, the United States. Miró's superiors in Madrid told him to counsel the Indians toward restraint and to open the Mississippi to American navigators who paid certain specified duties. About the time O'Fallon was busily making his bombastic claims of armed legions, sixty flatboats sailed joyfully from Ohio River ports for New Orleans. Recruiting for Walnut Hills went badly. Although he was disgruntled by the shattering of his trade monopoly, Wilkinson secretly betrayed O'Fallon and wrote Miró saying that there was nothing to worry about.

Almost immediately, however, a fresh worry did spring alive, born of unexpected developments on the farthest fringe of the continent. Years before, in the late 1760's,

Spain had been aroused by the Russian advance from Siberia eastward along the Aleutian Peninsula toward Alaska. As a counter, the *visitador-generales* in Mexico ordered missions strung along the California littoral, culminating in Anza's founding of San Francisco in 1776. Concurrently, Spanish naval expeditions under Juan Pérez and Bruno Heceta pushed cautiously northward along the foggy coasts. In constant dread of Indians, they landed here and there to take possession of the unknown Pacific Northwest in the name of their king.

In 1778, not long after the scurvy-ridden Spanish mariners had retreated to Mexico, Captain James Cook of England led his two exploring ships, *Resolution* and *Discovery*, into deep, timber-girt Nootka Sound, on the western side of what later was named Vancouver Island. During Cook's stay at Nootka to cut new masts, his sailors traded buttons, metal dishes, and bits of iron to the Indians for lustrous sea otter pelts. In Canton they sold these furs at astronomical prices.

Learning of the episode, the handful of English traders in the Orient stampeded to Nootka to take over this alluring new commerce. When the Spanish learned of the

45

The imperial intrigues of the latter part of the eighteenth century are mirrored by this secret Spanish map, which shows the close watch being kept on the westward-advancing Americans by Spain's officials in New Orleans. The map portrays, with considerable accuracy, "the territory which is occupied by the new Establishments of Kentucky, Cumberland, and Franklin." Noted, among other significant features, are the Wilderness Trail and the settlements of "Boonsbourough" and "Harrodsbourough." The map, made about 1789, was found in the Spanish Historical Archives in Madrid.

intrusion, they objected. In the summer of 1789 a pair of warships commanded by Esteban José Martínez sailed into Nootka harbor, seized the vessels of a slippery British trader named John Meares, and took them to Mexico.

(The clash was watched with some fascination by two Yankees, Robert Gray and John Kendrick, who had been supplied by a Boston syndicate in a belated effort to cut into the trade. For some unexplained reason, Martínez did not bother them.)

Meares rushed to London to appeal to his Government for help. The political situation in Europe, muddied by the growing French Revolution, was such that the British ministry decided to make an issue of the seizure. Spain retorted belligerently, and by May, 1790, the issue had reached such proportions that Europe was on edge over the prospect of war between the two countries.

Word of the danger reached the United States while President Washington was at last coming to grips with the Western problem. At once he intensified his efforts to remove the sources of trans-Allegheny discontent, fearful that armed clashes between Spain and England in the Mississippi Valley might lead to new and more reckless opportunism by the frontier plotters. He had reason to worry. Ever since 1788, for instance, the Governor General of Canada, Lord Dorchester, acting often through loyalist John Connolly, had been hinting of armed support if a force of Kentuckians were to march against New Orleans and open the Mississippi by force.

As one step in wooing back the allegiance of the frontier, Virginia was prevailed upon to promise independence to Kentucky. (Statehood was not achieved until 1792, however.) Western leaders who had flirted with Spain were soothed with high offices. Speculator William Blount was named governor of Southwest Territory. John Sevier and James Robertson became brigadier generals in the territorial militia. Wilkinson was made a lieutenant colonel in the United States Army; two years later he was elevated to a generalship.

The Nootka explosion, threatening a new imperial clash, reacted even on the Southern Indians. Should an English fleet blockade the Spanish Florida coast, essential supplies might be impossible to get. Alexander McGillivray, whose interest in Spain had never been more than expedient, decided to listen to the commissioners Washington had sent to treat with him. He journeyed to New York, was wined and dined, flattered, and given a general's commission in the American Army at a salary of twelve hundred dollars a year. Thus beguiled, he surrendered Creek lands in central Georgia to the whites but recovered those claimed by the Yazoo companies. The date was August 7, 1790, the same day on which

Blount was named governor of Southwest Territory.

(Two days later Robert Gray sailed his ship *Columbia* into Boston, the first American captain to circumnavigate the globe in an American vessel. He gave his excited countrymen a firsthand report about the sea otter war on the other side of the continent. Then, after a rest of seven weeks, he sailed back to Nootka for more pelts. During that second adventure he made a profound geographical discovery that had eluded the navigators of both Spain and England. In May, 1792, he found the great river of the West and named it the Columbia, after his ship. This meant that now the United States also had a claim to that far-off Pacific coast.)

The Nootka excitement lent new energy to James O'Fallon. Hoping for British support, he told Miró that if his colonists were not given permission to settle at Walnut Hills in peace, they would take the area by force. At this point Wilkinson openly cut away from the foolish partner he had been betraying in secret. Undaunted, O'Fallon turned to George Rogers Clark and asked him to take command of the colonists' army. Debt-ridden, alcoholic, and bitterly resentful of the Government for rejecting the drafts he had signed to supply his Revolutionary campaigns, Clark agreed. To hold Clark in line, O'Fallon, aged forty-one, married the disgruntled soldier's fifteen-year-old sister.

Washington responded to the plot with a proclamation denouncing the Yazoo project. Even in the angry West, the President's prestige was so enormous that his mere word was enough to dissuade would-be participants. Another blow came in the fall. England's fierce sword rattling frightened Spain into signing the Nootka Convention, which in effect ended Spanish pretensions along the Northwest Coast. This meant that O'Fallon would receive no help from Canada in the event of a clash with Miró. His men melted away, and the scheme died.

Other conspirators continued chasing shadows. Wilkinson talked the Spanish into paying him an annual pension in return for troublemaking in Kentucky. In the South, his handsome henchman, Philip Nolan, obtained passports to travel west as far as San Antonio, Texas. His business was capturing wild horses, some of which he sold to flatboatmen who had landed at New Orleans and needed mounts for returning north over the dangerous Natchez Trace. As he passed back and forth, he diverted himself by seducing the wife of his friend Antonio Leal, a trader at the frontier post of Nacogdoches. He also made detailed maps of the Texas countryside. No one knew quite why. The Spanish were suspicious, in spite of Nolan's connection with Wilkinson. Finally they revoked his passports. When he went defiantly back with a rugged band of freebooters, a group of Spanish soldiers in 1801 ran him down and killed him.

Despite occasional gestures at conciliation, fear of Americans remained perennial in Louisiana. On succeeding Miró as governor, Héctor Carondelet tried to reinstitute the threadbare plan of an Indian buffer state in the South. He bribed McGillivray by paying him more than the Americans did, but the tribes had begun fighting each other and no longer listened so compliantly to the old Spanish songs. Though Carondelet could still create froths of trouble by tampering with navigation on the river, the Spanish danger was dwindling.

North of the Ohio, the Indian threat remained undiminished. The tribes were well armed, relatively united, and confident that the English garrisons at their backs would support them. The Americans did nothing to awe them. When General Harmar marched a grumbling force of ill-equipped regulars and militia north from Fort Washington in Cincinnati, the Indians let it blunder into an ambush, inflicted almost two hundred casualties, and routed the rest. The following year an elaborate second attempt under gouty old Arthur St. Clair, Governor of the Northwest Territory, was shattered even more disastrously. Near the head of the Wabash the savages fell on his sleeping camp, slaughtered six hundred and thirty men, and wounded two hundred and eighty-three more —a far worse disaster than Custer's more publicized stand three quarters of a century later on the Little Bighorn, where some two hundred and fifty men died.

Dismayed, Washington called on Anthony Wayne, stern hero of Brandywine, Germantown, Stony Point, and Yorktown, to reform the Western army. Yet the President dared not risk still another defeat if negotiations, including major concessions to the Indians, would work instead. While Wayne was held to drilling his troops, first in Pennsylvania and later at Fort Washington, conciliators were sent to contact the tribes.

They fared badly. Missionaries assigned to spreading propaganda about the peaceful intentions of the United States were unable to pass the fringes of settlement. A pair of notable traders, one of them Connecticut-born Peter Pond, who had opened the Athabaska region of western Canada for the North West Company, were stopped by the British authorities at Niagara. Two officials were murdered in the wilderness. Commissioners traveling through Lake Erie to attend a huge Indian conclave on American soil at the mouth of the Maumee (present Toledo, Ohio) were shunted aside to Detroit by the arrogant British commander. There Indian spokesmen mocked them. The Americans had money to pay for land, had they? Then pay it to the settlers at Marietta and Cincinnati for their holdings and take the interlopers home. Henceforth the boundary was to be the Ohio River.

Brazenly the British erected a fort beside the Maumee River, on American ground. In the summer of 1794, Wayne was at last ordered to march. He moved cautiously, building forts as he went to protect his supply routes. The Indians barricaded themselves at Fallen Timbers, a chaos of downed trees beside the Maumee. Expecting an immediate charge, the Indians followed custom by fasting before the battle. Wayne sat tight for three days. After hundreds of starving Indians had drifted away to eat, he attacked the remnant and sent it reeling back toward the British fort.

The survivors found no help there. While Wayne had been preparing for his campaign, the international situation had been changing in ways the Indians could not understand. The French Revolution was engulfing Europe in war. Fearful that the United States might support its French allies, either actively or through restrictions on trade that Britain needed, the English Government ordered its Western commanders to cease supporting the Indians. The change was made concrete by slamming the gates of the Maumee fort in the faces of Indians clamoring for refuge. Utterly disheartened by the desertion, the Indians capitulated. The next year, at the Treaty of Greenville, they relinquished to the United States the southern two thirds of Ohio, part of Indiana, and sixteen enclaves where American trading posts and military installations could be built inside Indian country.

American diplomacy also took advantage of Europe's turmoil. In November, 1794, John Jay concluded a treaty under whose terms the English withdrew their garrisons from the border forts; but Jay infuriated Western fur men by letting Canadian traders carry on their commerce south of the border without restrictions, just as they always had. In the South, after Alexander McGillivray had died and Tennessee militia had inflicted a series of painful defeats on the discordant tribes, faltering Spain also decided to sit down at the council table with the young nation she once had thought to circumvent by cloak-and-dagger plots and economic pinchings. By the Treaty of San Lorenzo (1795) she promised to abandon two forts recently built on the American side of the Mississippi, relinquish her claims north of the 31st parallel, and open the river to American commerce.

Although Governor Carondelet was slow in carrying out the stipulations of his Government's treaty, the Western problem at last seemed on its way to solution—until abruptly the issues were raised again by the unexpected appearance of a new, dangerously aggressive power on the western banks of the Mississippi, Napoleonic France.

A NORTH VIEW of FORT FRANKLIN on French Creek.

THE WEST
OF THE NEW NATION

Spain conspired to split off the American West and used the Indians whenever possible as instruments of her policy. This cartouche symbolizing friendship between Spaniard and Indian embellished a directive by the Baron de Carondelet, Governor of Louisiana, in 1794, ordering the military of the province to respect Osage chief Kuchechire and his tribesmen.

The United States came into being after the Revolution with a vast hinterland of almost untouched wilderness beyond the Appalachians and an army of land-hungry citizens eager to move out and people it. The foundling Government was forced to deal with frontier problems almost as a first order of business: to work out a system of land distribution, to protect the settlements against enemies, white and red, to provide a plan for eventual transition to statehood.

The region was not without liabilities and encumbrances. England, quickly regretting her cession of so much territory, refused to give up important frontier posts in the Northwest. In the Southwest, Spain held the mouth of the Mississippi and with it the power to throttle Western growth. And there were the Indians—always the Indians. The Government forbade settlement on any Western lands until the Indians had ceded their rights, but few frontiersmen paid any attention to the rights of an Indian. Fort Franklin in western Pennsylvania (above, as painted in 1787 by Captain Jonathan Heart, in charge of construction) guarded the border against resentful Senecas; it was one of hundreds that would be built during more than a century when frontier and Indians would be virtually synonymous.

IMAGES OF THE WILD LANDS

A Beaver 26 inches long from the head to the tail

wild Beeves

A beeve catch'd by ÿ horns with ropes

A beeve attackd with Spears

A Savage springing upon a beeve

Savages drying their meat

The French Baron de Lahontan traveled widely in America and wrote a book about it in 1703, a combination of fiction about noble savages who discussed philosophy and of purported fact that today seems almost as fanciful. His drawing of a beaver, shown at left, from an English edition of his book, owes its face of a dyspeptic minor official to nothing worse than poor draftsmanship, but the vignettes of Indians hunting "wild beeves" (buffalo) appear to have been drawn from imagination and secondhand reports. Not only are his beeves unlike any buffalo that ever existed, but it is difficult to imagine Indians taking one of the huge beasts by lassoing its horns, much less by leaping onto its back and spearing it.

New Voyages to North America, YALE UNIVERSITY LIBRARY

'The land on the southside of Lake Erie, from Presque Isle, puts on a very fine appearance; the country level, the timber tall, and of the best sort, such as oak, hickerie and locust; and for game, both for plenty and variety, perhaps exceeded by no part of the world." Thus wrote Major Robert Rogers, renowned leader of Rogers' Rangers, as part of a glowing description of the wild lake-shore region, which he crossed in 1760. For many generations the world had learned about the West from such reports, made by explorers, Indian traders, travelers, and frontiersmen; as early as the seventeenth century, books about travels in the American West were best sellers in Europe and the Colonies. Many of the early accounts contained outrageous misinformation, but by the time of the post-Revolutionary surge of settlers, fact had been fairly well separated from fancy, and the main features of the trans-Appalachian empire as far as the Mississippi were known with reasonable accuracy.

Through the Interior Parts of North America in the Years 1766, 1767, & 1768, N.Y. PUBLIC LIBRARY

The Indian on the warpath symbolized for most Americans the worst terrors of the frontier and was a never-failing theme for artists and writers. The Iroquois warrior (above), about to scalp an unhappily conscious victim, is the work of J. Grasset de St. Sauveur in the late 1700's. St. Sauveur was known for his accuracy in depicting Indian dress, but for some very strange reason, he painted palm trees into a far northern landscape.

Minnesota's Falls of St. Anthony on the upper Mississippi were seen by Jonathan Carver in 1766; this picture is from his book on his three-year explorations. On the far side of the river is Spanish territory; after 1783 this far-northwestern cataract lay on almost the most distant of all the boundaries of the young nation.

Pulpit Rocks, a natural wonder of the frontier (in the Alleghenies near today's Altoona, Pennsylvania), were pictured in Philadelphia's Colum-bian Magazine in 1787. Illustrated articles about Western travels were to remain favorites for a century.

STATE HISTORICAL SOCIETY OF WISCONSIN

OPENING THE OHIO

During the first years after the Revolution, the Ohio country remained officially closed to settlement while the Government tried to plan for orderly movement into the new lands—and squatters ignored both laws and Indians to filter in and take up land. In two of its first acts, the Government made a far-seeing beginning to a frontier policy that thereafter was not always marked by wisdom: it provided in the Northwest Ordinance for the eventual transition of the West to statehood, and it instituted a system of land survey prior to settlement to prevent confused and overlapping claims. It was a system that would be carried all the way to the Pacific.

But these steps could mean nothing until the Indians had been taken care of. The tribesmen, increasingly goaded into retaliation by settlers' callous disregard of their rights, routed one army sent to punish them, half-annihilated another, but were defeated by General Wayne in 1794. The cost to twelve beaten tribes was tremendous; they were forced to give up lands in most of present Ohio and in a strip of Indiana.

The great survey of the Western lands was begun at the Ohio River with the laying out of seven ranges of townships, each township six miles square and divided into 36 mile-square sections. The township in the survey map above was one of the first laid out; like most on the easternmost ranges, it lacks some of its 36 sections because the Ohio River cuts into it.

FORDHAM UNIVERSITY COLLECTION, NEW YORK

The watercolor sketch at left of Pittsburgh in 1790 by landscape artist Lewis Brantz is the earliest known view of the city that was destined to serve for many decades as port of entry to the Ohio Valley.

The defeat of the Indians by General Anthony Wayne at Fallen Timbers was serious but not fatal to them. But the land cession he forced from them in the Treaty of Greenville was the blow from which they never recovered, for it was the first of many land grabs that ultimately pushed them into limbo. The map below, showing the westernmost part of the Greenville cession after it had been surveyed, notes the individual claims of newly arrived settlers. The blank space to the left was still Indian land at the time; to the right was more Greenville treaty land, which, however, did not concern the maker of this map.

Anthony Wayne by John Trumbull

LEFT AND ABOVE: NATIONAL ARCHIVES

53

A Shawnee warrior of the Ohio country

A SPY'S DRAWINGS OF THE FIRST WEST

Frenchman Victor Collot viewed the West with the specialized eyes of a military spy. In 1796, with France dreaming about recovering her American empire, the French minister in Philadelphia sent Collot to gather information about the Ohio and Mississippi rivers. Collot was ideal for the job: a professional soldier, capable cartographer and artist, fluent in English. With him went Joseph Warin, a young French officer who had served in the American Army, a skilled map maker too.

Their secret was badly kept, and orders were sent to the governor of Northwest Territory to find some pretext to seize the pair's papers. In the meantime, they went on their way, mapping rivers, towns, and fortifications in exquisite detail and making drawings of settlements and even of Indians. They were arrested at American Fort Massac on the Ohio but were later permitted to go on. Warin was attacked by two Indians who had followed them and died of his wounds on the lower Mississippi, and in New Orleans the Spanish governor seized and copied Collot's papers but later returned them. The map and drawings on this page are among those made by the pair on their strange trip.

Collot's map of the junction of

Marietta, Ohio, was eight years old when the two spies recorded its appearance.

The Falls of the Ohio in 1796 were lined

PARTIE DE LA LOUISIANE SUPERIEURE

PLAN DE St LOUIS
DES ILLINOIS

LE MISSISSIPI FLEUVE

...sissippi and Missouri rivers, with its careful plan of St. Louis and the small inset depictions of fortifications, indicates his chief interest.

the very beginnings of Louisville.

Collot's meticulous draftsmanship did not omit even the Spanish flag above Fort Natchez.

55

Old Faithful geyser, the Yellowstone

"The Bearer ... has charge of ... a Savage delineation on a Buffaloe Pelt, of the Missouri & its South Western Branches. ... This Rude Sketch ... exposes the location of several important Objects ... among other things a little incredible, a volcano ... on Yellow Stone River. ..."

Letter accompanying an Indian map of the unexplored Louisiana Purchase, from James Wilkinson, Governor of Louisiana Territory, to President Thomas Jefferson, St. Louis, October 22, 1805

CHAPTER THREE

THE TRANS-MISSISSIPPI MYSTERY

1792-1807

France had never been reconciled to the stripping away of her colonial empire in North America by the 1763 Treaty of Paris. Dreams of repossession intensified after the overthrow of the monarchy and the establishment of the French Republic in the summer of 1792. Girondists in Paris, abetted by such American expatriates as Thomas Paine, who was working on his explosive *Rights of Man*, and Joel Barlow of the Gallipolis fiasco, eagerly discussed plots to upset the entire Western Hemisphere.

One scheme had a Venezuelan adventurer, Francisco Miranda, kindling popular revolts against Spain throughout South America. The United States, by treaty still an ally of France, was either to launch, officially, supporting attacks on Florida and New Orleans and then sweep on to Mexico, or was to look the other way while unofficial American filibusterers did the work. If the most ardent schemers were able to manage events their own way, the young American nation as a whole would benefit very little. As the plotters envisioned matters, France not only would wrest for herself the trans-Mississippi regions from Spain and perhaps Canada from England but, capitalizing on frontier discontent, would help the Western pioneers set up an independent government, as Spain had tried to do. The United States would thus be choked off behind the Allegheny Mountains.

The man chosen to further the intrigues in the West was a mild-seeming scientist, André Michaux. Years before, Michaux had plunged into a study of botany in order to forget the death of his young wife. After preliminary work in the Pyrenees, he had gone to Persia, where he had botanized in the dangerous, scientifically unknown regions between the Tigris and Euphrates rivers. In 1785 the French Government sent him to the United States to find trees that might be cultivated in Europe, particularly for naval construction. Michaux established one nursery at Hackensack, New Jersey, and another just outside Charleston, South Carolina. His chief assistant was his motherless son, also named André.

Father and son botanized industriously in the southern Appalachians and in Florida, where they must have become aware of frontier discontent and of the plots involving Spain. In 1790 young André returned to France and became an ardent revolutionist. The father stayed in America, journeying in 1792 as far north as the regions around Hudson Bay. In passing through Montreal, where he sought information among the Canadian fur traders, he presumably learned of Alexander Mackenzie's project of crossing overland from Lake Athabaska, in the Canadian Northwest, to the Pacific. This in turn may have fired Michaux's ambitions—but first we need to look at Mackenzie's own overpowering desires.

Supplying the Athabaska fur posts by canoe from Montreal was so backbreaking and expensive an effort that Mackenzie's firm, the North West Company, hoped to find a more economical river route heading inland from the Pacific. Mackenzie made his first eager attempt in the summer of 1789, but the river he laboriously followed (it now bears his name) landed him on the shores, not of the Pacific, but of the Arctic Ocean. Determined to try again, he went to London during the winter of 1791–92 to learn how to make astronomical observations for lati-

Twelve years before Lewis and Clark, Alexander Mackenzie, via this route, made the first continental crossing above Mexico.

tude and longitude and to bone up on what little was known of the geography of the Northwest coast, principally as reported by England's great navigator, James Cook. In the spring of 1792 Mackenzie hurried back through Montreal and up the interminable rivers to Lake Athabaska so that he could launch his adventure to the Pacific coast the following spring.

(To cast ahead a little: he left a temporary post on the Peace River above Lake Athabaska on May 9, 1793, in a twenty-five-foot canoe crowded with six *voyageurs,* two Indians, a clerk named Alexander McKay, a dog, and a ton and a half of supplies. They struggled through the howling Peace River Canyon, crossed the Continental Divide over a portage eight hundred and seventeen paces long, and coursed down the Fraser River of today's British Columbia until its frantic gorge forced them to turn up a western tributary. After climbing more mountains and obtaining a canoe from Bella Coola Indians, they reached salt water on July 22, 1793. But the way was too arduous for commerce, and for the time being, the North West Company lost interest in exploration.)

When Mackenzie and, a bit later, Michaux went through Montreal in 1792, the town was still humming with talk of Nootka's meaning to the fur trade and of the

possibility of linking the beaver with the sea otter trade. The botanist was forty-six then, rather old for grueling exploration. (Mackenzie that year was either twenty-eight or twenty-nine.) Nevertheless, Michaux almost surely felt the excitement, and it may have been a strong factor in leading him toward plans for emulating Mackenzie's efforts farther south, using the Missouri River as a highway. Returning to the United States late in 1792, he appealed to the American Philosophical Society for financial aid. This brought him to the attention of the society's vice-president, Thomas Jefferson.

Jefferson, an ardent student of natural history, was also an advocate of Western exploration. Nine years before, on December 4, 1783, he had casually sounded out George Rogers Clark about leading an expedition overland to checkmate a rumored Pacific colony of British citizens. Although nothing came of either the proposal or the colony, Jefferson's interest remained active. Three years later, while United States minister to France, he listened sympathetically to the harebrained plan of John Ledyard of Connecticut, who had seen Nootka in 1778 as one of James Cook's marines. Ledyard proposed to tramp across Siberia to the Kamchatka Peninsula and catch a Russian ship to Alaska. Accompanied only by a dog or two, he would then walk across North America to the Atlantic. As Jefferson said, Ledyard was sanguine. (". . . Do not think," Ledyard wrote him once, "that mountains or oceans shall oppose my passage to glory. . . . I have pledged myself. . . my heart is on fire—ye stimulate, & I shall gain the victory.") Armed with passports Jefferson helped him obtain, the adventurer managed to push deep into Siberia before Russian officials, turning suspicious, ordered him to go back.

And at this point, after his trip to Canada, Michaux appeared in 1792, offering still another plan to cross the continent—doubly important now that Mackenzie was making the same effort for Great Britain. The American Philosophical Society blessed Michaux with its prestige and $128.25, of which Washington contributed $25, Jefferson and Alexander Hamilton, $12.50 each. His instructions were "to find the shortest & most convenient route of communication between the U.S. & the Pacific ocean," paying particular heed to the Missouri and a far-western river "called Oregon." The latter was completely mythical, its name plucked out of Indian talk fifteen years before at Michilimackinac by the famed Colonial ranger, Robert Rogers. The Columbia, to be sure, lay about where the Oregon was supposed to, but Jefferson had not yet heard of Gray's discovery of the Columbia.

Michaux could hardly have expected to launch even a small expedition for one hundred and twenty-eight dollars, but the matter was no longer pertinent—if, indeed, it ever was. Somehow, probably through his son, he had made contact with the French plotters mentioned at the beginning of this chapter. Their fiery plans at once metamorphosed his proposed journey of exploration into a handy disguise for Western intrigue.

The swiftly moving scheme soon involved George Rogers Clark. Early in 1793, that decaying warrior wrote a letter to a French official in New York City, offering his services for a proposed attack against Spanish Louisiana: "Out of Kentucky, Cumberland, the settlement on Holston, the Wabash and Illinois I can (by my name alone) raise 1500 brave men—and the French at St. Louis and throughout the rest of Louisiana, together with the American Spanish subjects at the Natchez will, I am sure of it (for they all know my name) flock to my standard."

His suggestion traveled into what seemed a favorable whirlwind of change. France declared war against England on February 1. On March 9 she also declared war against Spain. In between the two events, Edmond Charles Genêt, the new minister from the new French Republic, sailed for the United States to stir up as much trouble as possible against both enemies.

Landing in Charleston, South Carolina, Genêt commissioned American privateers to raid English shipping and sounded out American land speculators concerning raids on Spanish Florida. Although President Washington dampened the Frenchman's ardor by a neutrality proclamation of April 22, Genêt still hoped that Michaux and Clark would be able, in spite of the President, to launch the proposed Western attack on Louisiana.

Enthusiasm for Republican France was high in Kentucky, but mere enthusiasm, unsupported by hard cash, was not enough. Alexander Hamilton refused to give to Genêt any part of the debt that the United States owed France. As a result, Genêt could send no money to Clark, who discovered to his mortification that his name alone really was not sufficient to recruit and supply fifteen hundred men. The wilting project died completely when Washington, after publicly denouncing it, demanded Genêt's recall. Michaux, his ambitions wilting with it, traveled no closer to the Pacific than Kaskaskia, Illinois.

New confidence was filling the trans-Allegheny settlements. Anthony Wayne, as noted, humbled the Indians; treaties with England and Spain removed other pressures that had impeded the American settlers. Kentucky and Tennessee achieved statehood, and Ohio began agitating for similar status. These evidences of stability intensified the flow of people across the mountains. Cities germinated. Although Federal law prohibited private citizens from purchasing lands from Indians, Moses Cleaveland bought a tract by Lake Erie from them for meat, whisky, and five hundred pounds and launched the settlement that still bears his name, though it is spelled somewhat differently. Nathaniel Massie founded Chillicothe near the spot in Ohio where a Shawnee Indian village of the same name had stood only a few years earlier.

A mania for roads and ferries grew with the towns. Ebenezer Zane cut a curving trace from the east bank of the Ohio, opposite Wheeling, through Chillicothe to a terminus opposite Maysville, Kentucky. For most of its rough two-hundred-mile course, Zane's Trace was little more than a slit through the forest. The ferry over the Muskingum consisted of two canoes joined by a log; but the road and the crossing turned a wilderness river bottom into modern Zanesville.

Farther south, hearing that Kentucky had voted appropriations to turn the Wilderness Trail into a way suitable for wagons, Daniel Boone in 1796 applied for the job: "I think my Self intitled to the ofer of the Buisness as I first Marked out that Rode in March 1775 and Never rec'd anything for my trubel." The contract, however, went elsewhere—yet another reason contributing to Boone's decision to move to Spanish Missouri.

During two summer months in 1795, an estimated twenty-six thousand people tramped along the Old Walton Road, the main thoroughfare to the Cumberland settlements of north-central Tennessee. Tens of thousands more floated into the entire Ohio Valley on ungainly flatboats. The demand for land became so insatiable that the Government could not negotiate new treaties fast enough to suit the inpouring, and violations of Indian territory became daily causes of antagonism between the two races.

The Federal Government, to which the Constitution had assigned full control of Indian affairs, tried to deal honestly with the red men. It recognized their title to the land they occupied and held that the United States had acquired nothing more from England than a pre-emptive right to obtain that land by treaty. To the frontiersmen, this interpretation was an outrage. They insisted that they had fought England for possession as well as for freedom; the degraded savages were mere tenants at will, replaceable as soon as another race (meaning their own) appeared that was capable of making more efficient use of God's wilderness.

In spite of their protests, Congress passed a series of measures designed to protect the Indians in dealings with rapacious whites. As a guarantee of good behavior, traders had to buy licenses and post bonds, both of them to be forfeited in case of violations of the law. Individuals were not permitted, on paper, to sell alcohol to Indians inside Indian country or to purchase either land or horses from them. Squatters who entered unceded territory were to be evicted. None of the measures worked, however. Prosecutors of illicit traders, grogsellers, and squatters could seldom secure convictions from resentful back-country juries. Agents and military men who dared make arrests were often sued and found liable for trespass.

Other laws, meanwhile, tried to meet the problem more positively. Humanitarians believed that if the red men became civilized, they would not need so much land for supporting themselves and would be more willing to sell their surplus acreage to the whites. The contentions over land thus being ended, the Indians could gradually be absorbed into the frontier communities. This civilizing process was furthered by private missionaries and by government-appointed agents who lived among the tribes, reported on happenings in their areas, and by precept and actual instruction urged husbandry and agriculture on their charges.

Another political and humanitarian device, repeatedly urged on Congress by President Washington, was the government trading house. The Indians, he pointed out, were deeply attached to the traders who brought them the manufactured goods they needed. Unfortunately for the security of the United States, the most proficient traders in the North were those from Montreal. In the South the dominant firm was the Spanish-licensed, British-operated house of Panton, Leslie & Company. In Washington's mind, private United States traders were not an adequate answer to these canny, long-experienced foreigners. Motivated by greed, private individuals cheated the Indians, corrupted them with whisky, and urged them to maintain the hunting state on which trading profits depended. The President recommended combatting these undesirable persons through government-supported trading posts, called factories, which would drive private operators from the field by underselling them. Fair dealing by the government factors, meanwhile, would draw the Indians to commercial friendship with the United States and would also increase the natives' yearning for domestic goods. This in turn, it was hoped, would induce them to leave their enormous forests and settle down on small farms.

After some preliminary experimentation, Congress on April 18, 1796, passed "an act for establishing Trading Houses with the Indian tribes" and appropriated one hundred and fifty thousand dollars for stocking the establishments to compete with private enterprise. At the same time, the Government continued licensing private traders —a philosophically unsound ambivalence that was vehemently protested on the frontier. Partly because of the protests, the factories spread slowly. The first pair, aimed partly at countering Spanish influence, were located among the Creeks in Georgia and the Cherokees in Tennessee. Not until 1802 were others added near Mobile Bay and at Chickasaw Bluffs (present Memphis), Fort Wayne, Indiana, and Detroit.

The headlong rush of settlement outstripped all these foot-dragging measures, and soon visionaries were looking for more land across the Mississippi. As early as 1782 St. John de Crèvecœur, author of *Letters from an American Farmer*, had asked rhetorically about the West, "Who can tell how far it extends? Who can tell the millions of men whom it will feed and contain?" In 1789 the Reverend Jedidiah Morse, who wrote textbooks for children in order to support himself at the Yale Theological Seminary, declared in his *American Geography*, "The Mississippi was never designed as the western boundary of the American Empire." He did not necessarily mean the United States would ever actually cross the river; distances were considered too great to permit a single continent-wide union. But he did mean that settlers emigrating from the United States and linked to her by bonds of culture and kinship were not going to be halted by either Spain or the Indians.

If Spain had retained Louisiana, some sort of clash almost certainly would have developed. Such prominent Americans as Rufus King, minister to England, and Robert Livingston, minister to France, discussed seizing Louisiana by force. But Spain did not hold her vast province. Napoleon unexpectedly intervened.

Since 1796 Spain had been France's ally and accordingly listened when Napoleon demanded Louisiana. Spain no longer wanted the colony. For years it had cost her more than it had returned, and expenses were likely to soar as pressures from the United States mounted. Accordingly, at the secret Treaty of San Ildefonso, October 1, 1800, she returned Louisiana to France in exchange for territorial acquisitions in Tuscany and Napoleon's promise to retain the trans-Mississippi area as a buffer between the United States and Mexico.

Napoleon soon abandoned the war that obtaining Tuscany for his ally would have cost him and then brazenly demanded and received Louisiana from Spain without compensation. During these developments, the hapless Spaniards continued administering Louisiana as usual. In spite of their pretense, Jefferson's administration learned something was afoot. Meanwhile, French troops had begun moving into the West Indies, ostensibly to subdue a revolt in Santo Domingo. Jefferson took alarm, foreseeing correctly that Napoleon meant to strike at the lower Mississippi as a first step in re-establishing France's colonial holdings in North America. Rather than let this happen, Jefferson was prepared to form an alliance with England. Instructions to this effect were carried to Robert Livingston, the American minister in Paris, by Pierre S. Du Pont de Nemours, a Frenchman who was a refugee from the excesses of the Revolution.

Shortly thereafter a new wrench was given to affairs in the West by the Spanish intendant at New Orleans. For three years American flatboatmen had been coming down the Mississippi without political hindrance, often abusing their privileges with flagrant smuggling and offending the ruling elements in New Orleans with their raucous behavior. Abruptly, in October, 1802, acting on orders from Madrid, the intendant (still administering Louisiana) in effect closed the Mississippi to United States commerce by revoking the right of deposit—that is, the right to store goods in New Orleans warehouses until they could be loaded on ocean vessels.

The West, which by now knew that Louisiana belonged to France, incorrectly suspected that Napoleon had instigated the move. France, of course, was a far more dangerous threat to American well-being than Spain had been. Stung to alarm, the Mississippi and Ohio valleys reacted with a noisy truculence that, in Jefferson's words, "threatens to overbear our peace." Jefferson nevertheless granted the soundness of the frontier's stand: whatever foreign power holds the mouth of the Mississippi is "our natural and habitual enemy." He made certain warlike gestures of his own toward France and Spain, but meantime lent a sympathetic ear to a suggestion by Pierre Du Pont de Nemours that the problem might be solved if France proved willing to sell New Orleans to the United

In 1812 Manasseh Cutler's son, Jervis, published a journal purportedly kept by a French-Canadian trader, Charles LeRaye, who said Crows in 1802 had taken him to the Bighorn River, where no whites had yet been. The drawing above appeared in the journal.

States. Hopefully, while the turmoil over the closure of the river increased, he sent James Monroe to join Livingston in Paris with expanded orders containing a concrete offer: the United States would pay up to ten million dollars for the city and the Floridas.

So far Jefferson had said nothing official about the bulk of Louisiana Territory; yet the entire trans-Mississippi area was on his mind. His political thinking, reflecting the agrarian society that had molded him, embraced both the romantic concept of the noble farmer and the more hardheaded belief that the dynamic quality of the United States rested on sturdy "cultivators" to whom ample amounts of independence-bringing land were always available. "The small landowners are the most precious portion of the State," he said once. (Ironically, large plantations, responding vigorously to Eli Whitney's cotton gin and manned by slave labor, were even then beginning to expand more rapidly in the South than the small freeholds that he admired were spreading in the North.) Thus, on the one hand, Jefferson could argue for humane treatment of the Indians, and on the other, he could support the rapacity of such Western politicians as William Henry Harrison of Indiana, who during Jefferson's administration bamboozled millions upon millions of acres from the increasingly stubborn tribes.

More millions lay beyond the Mississippi. It might be, as Jedidiah Morse suggested, that this almost inconceivable domain would some day furnish space for new nations that, while not part of the United States, would be intimately related to her by cultural ties. Or perhaps the area would serve better as a place into which the indigestible Indians of the East might eventually be moved. There they would be safely out of the way of the small landholders, who entertained an almost pathological hatred toward Indians and whose pace into the Ohio Valley had been accelerated by a law of 1800 allowing them to buy their farms from the Government on credit.

These were the long-range considerations confronting the United States. More immediately pressing were problems of foreign affairs. Nations that in Europe were deadly enemies of one another ringed the United States—Spain in Florida, Spain and France in Louisiana, England in Canada. At any moment (this was 1802), England might resume her long war with the other powers. If so, what might this mean to the United States?

Certain hints existed. Jefferson knew, and assumed that the members of Congress knew, Alexander Mackenzie's recently published account of his voyages to the Arctic and Pacific oceans. The last chapter of that book contained a detailed plan whereby Great Britain could set up bases at the mouth of the Columbia, drive off

American ships that were gradually dominating the sea otter commerce, and eventually control both the fur trade and the fisheries of the northern part of North America. Other arguments for his plan, Mackenzie went on, italicizing the key word, came from "many *political* reasons, which it is not necessary here to enumerate."

Those reasons were plain to Jefferson. If France held land between the Pacific and the Mississippi and if war between France and Great Britain were resumed, England almost surely would seize the area. The United States would then be fenced in tightly from Maine to New Orleans. And if so powerful a nation as England closed the Mississippi, the results would be far more damaging than when Spain had done it. Any such threat had to be challenged before it could become dangerous.

There were ways. The United States had a claim to the Columbia country through the discoveries of Robert Gray in 1792. This claim might be strengthened by an expedition crossing overland to the Columbia's head-waters and coursing the river's length ahead of the British. Once the United States was established both on the Mississippi and on the Northwest coast above Spanish California, then by all logic what would happen to the intervening country called Louisiana?

Before Jefferson could start to answer this or any other question implicit in his thinking about settling either small farmers or Indians in the West, he had to learn something about the unknown area. In an extraordinary bit of presumption—for France still owned, and Spain still administered, Louisiana Territory, and Monroe had not yet gone to Paris—Jefferson instructed his private secretary, Meriwether Lewis, fresh from Army service in Ohio, to study botany and navigation and prepare to lead an exploring party across foreign soil to the Pacific.

Funds for the expedition had to be authorized by Congress. Jefferson made his appeal in a secret message of January 18, 1803. He backed into the request in curious fashion. First he talked about Indian policy. More land had to be acquired from the natives between the Ohio and Walnut Hills (today's Vicksburg) so that the United States could oppose a solid line of territory on the east bank of the Mississippi against France on the west bank —in other words, he wished to leave no wedge of Indian country for the French to infiltrate The Indians, however, already had alienated so much land that they were opposed to giving up more. They must therefore be taught agriculture; then, Jefferson predicted, they would be willing to sell the forests they no longer needed. He said nothing in this message about transporting them west.

Unfortunately, the training program was opposed by private traders who constantly endeavored, Jefferson said, "to excite in the Indian mind suspicions, fears, & irritations toward us." These disruptive men must be driven from the field by an extension of government trading houses. No lasting hardship would be involved, for the displaced traders could turn to richer opportunities on the Missouri River, whose upper reaches currently were pouring pelts into the coffers of England.

Having thus barely touched on some of the West's keenest concerns—the new French ownership of Louisiana, the Indian problem, and the furs English traders were snatching from American hands—the President at last came to his main point, the proposal of an expedition by ten or twelve men to learn what Louisiana was like. He said he particularly wanted to know whether trade might be developed across the continent (that is, with the Orient, which he did not have to say in so many words) by means of the waterways of the Missouri and Columbia rivers. Another commercial point: the Missouri was farther south and presumably freer of ice than the Saskatchewan, the river by which the Montreal fur men reached their distant posts; if connecting tributaries were found, then it might be possible to lure pelts out of Canada to the open water of the Missouri and on into the United States. Beyond commerce, there was the matter of knowledge for its own sake. The expedition, the President told Congress, would of course study the natural history of the Western country. This scientific aspect of the project would persuade France, Spain, and Britain to issue passports to the explorers—or so Jefferson suggested, although less than two months earlier the Spanish minister had frowned on the idea.

As is evident from this summary, Jefferson did not mention some of the implications outlined earlier. How much these unmentionables ruled his thinking (even secretly, one did not cast covetous eyes on foreign territory; besides, New England was opposed to unlimited agrarian expansion and would resist hints of territorial ambitions) and how deeply Congress read between the lines of his message is impossible to say. Yet it is hard to believe that all the members supposed, in view of the uneasy foreign situation, that the expedition was designed merely to study another country's geography. Some of his listeners must have recognized at least the value of having a few trained men and full reports on hand in case the European whirlpool sent eddies across the Western wilderness. In any event, the lawmakers voted Jefferson the twenty-five hundred dollars he requested.

Almost at once, the rush of events tumbled into his lap a greater piece of luck than he could possibly have anticipated. Yellow fever and guerrilla warfare had so decimated the French forces in Santo Domingo that military

Meriwether Lewis   *William Clark*

campaigns based on the West Indies were no longer possible. Abruptly Napoleon lost interest in attacking England in the Western Hemisphere. Yet wherever he attacked, Britain might retaliate by occupying the Mississippi from north and south and appropriating Louisiana. To prevent this and to raise money for other wars, Napoleon broke his promise to Spain not to transfer the American West to another power and offered the entire, vaguely delineated area to the astonished envoys of the United States. After boundaries finally were settled, the area took in a little more than nine hundred and nine thousand square miles—forty-three thousand miles *larger* than the entire area of the United States at the time of purchase. The price, after certain French claims and interest on purchase bonds had been added, eventually reached $23,213,567.73, or about four cents an acre.

Thanks to Jefferson's preparations, Meriwether Lewis was already in motion. He had spent the winter learning a few rudiments of scientific observation and ordering supplies—instruments, medicines, ammunition, Indian trade goods, a rapid-fire air gun, a twenty-two-oar keelboat to be built in Pittsburgh, a canoe with a collapsible iron frame for use in shallow streams (it proved impractical), and so on. In June he offered joint command to an officer four years older than he with whom he had served under Wayne in the Ohio country, William Clark, red-headed younger brother of George Rogers Clark.

Lewis was in Pittsburgh when he learned definitely that Louisiana belonged to the United States. Instantly the mission became a full-dress affair of national policy. In addition to investigating fur trade routes and finding, if possible, a usable transcontinental waterway, his party must now reach the Columbia without fail in order to nail down America's claim to a Pacific outlet, with all that this implied about commerce to the Orient. Politically, they must warn British fur traders on the upper Missouri to follow the regulations of the United States; and as a related matter, the Americans must convince the distant Indians that they owed allegiance to a new power

—one of which most of them had never heard. Lastly, as Albert Gallatin, Secretary of the Treasury, put the matter to Jefferson, the group should ascertain "whether from its extent & fertility that country is susceptible of a large population, in the same manner as the corresponding tract on the Ohio." Distant though the region was, who dared predict when the overflow of people might reach and fill it—or what this change in conditions would do to the Indians who might be moved there?

The explorers spent the winter of 1803–4 in camp on the Illinois shore of the Mississippi, opposite the mouth of the Missouri. Their party had grown from the ten or twelve men originally envisioned by Jefferson to about fifty, and just how the President obtained additional funds for equipping and paying them remains another of the story's unknown elements.

Most of the group were frontiersmen of heterogeneous background. Some were expert Kentucky woodsmen; some, like George Drouillard, were French-Canadian hunters and interpreters; some were craftsmen—a carpenter, a blacksmith, and the like. There were interpreters for talking to the Indians and a few French voyageurs for manning the boats. Professional soldiers, the majority of them chosen from frontier garrisons on the basis of wilderness experience, formed the group's hard core. "Robust, helthy, hardy," the young men at times during the first winter and on the first leg of the trip needed heavy handling by their captains, who were also products of the forest wars and knew how to deal with unruly personnel. The insistence on discipline paid. When the group later ran into morale-sapping difficulties—near-starvation in the Idaho mountains and a dreary, rain-swept winter on the Oregon coast—there were no crises of spirit to complicate matters. Sergeant Charles Floyd, the only man lost during twenty-eight months and seven thousand miles of arduous travel, died near today's Sioux City, Iowa, of natural causes, probably appendicitis.

The group started up the Missouri on May 14, 1804. They traveled in two narrow, multioared wooden canoes called pirogues and in the Pittsburgh keelboat, fifty-five feet long and propelled, as occasion warranted, by its twenty-two oars, by setting poles thrust against the bottom, by towrope, or, at blessed intervals when the wind sat right, by a square sail. In addition to the men, the boats were sorely crowded by twenty-one bales of presents for the Indians—beads, looking glasses, ribbons, medals, and the like—plus tools, powder, lead, and such supplementary provisions as meal, pork, flour, and salt.

They did no exploring the first summer. During the mid-1790's the Spanish had put into motion a series of expeditions designed to reach the Pacific. None had passed the villages of the Mandan Indians in the central part of today's North Dakota, but the British-born leaders of those abortive Spanish efforts, James Mackay and John Evans, had thoroughly sketched the lower sixteen hundred miles of the river. Lewis and Clark had copies of their maps. The Americans were familiar also with maps drawn in London by Aaron Arrowsmith, incorporating bits of useful data about the upper Missouri as learned or guessed at by surveyors of the Hudson's Bay and North West fur companies. From Vancouver's charts they knew something of the course of the lower Columbia, including the names of such prominent landmarks in the distant Cascade Range as Mt. Hood. But of the land that lay between the Mandan villages and the Cascades, they knew nothing.

They had no idea of the elevation and, particularly, the breadth of the Rockies, which upset their calculations by turning out to be a series of parallel ranges, rather than a single wall. They did not anticipate the great distance between the Rockies and the Pacific. Until they learned better during a long, worrisome loop through what is now the southwestern part of Montana, they fully expected to cross the continent entirely by water, save perhaps for a half day's portage over a "height of land," as low divides between watersheds were called. After all, they had already heard how Alexander Mackenzie in 1793 had negotiated the Continental Divide on a portage only eight hundred and seventeen steps long, and in 1804 who could have guessed that Canada's great explorer had luckily stumbled onto the only riverways in North America by which such a feat was possible?

Although Lewis and Clark's expedition did not explore on the lower Missouri, they labored prodigiously. The river was swift, turbid, dangerous. Surging currents collapsed the sandy banks. The opaque water hid snags and sawyers—the latter pointed, crippling tree stubs sink-

Lewis and Clark's expedition, above, the first official U.S. penetration of the Rockies, presented the West, in the words of Bernard DeVoto, "as something with which the mind could deal."

ing and rising on the eddies. Mats of driftwood protruding from the banks produced forbidding boils. Sudden squalls provided unwelcome excitement; mosquitoes, a permanent torment.

The captains held meetings with whatever Indians could be persuaded to attend: Council Bluffs, near present Omaha, received its name from such a gathering. At these conclaves Lewis and Clark passed out gifts, told the warriors that the United States was now in charge, and enlisted chiefs to go East with an interpreter to meet the Great Father (the President) and be awed by the might he commanded. The only showdown between Indians and white men came near modern Pierre, South Dakota, where Teton Sioux tried to turn the expedition back lest it carry goods and arms to their enemies up-

stream. Coolly the whites bluffed through without a fight.

Early in November, after halting for the winter, they built log quarters in a cottonwood grove a little below the five villages of the Mandan and Hidatsa (whom they called Minnetaree) Indians—five clusters of sunken, round, warm, odorous, earth-covered huts. The cold days passed busily. The men hunted, built boats, chopped mountains of firewood; diversion was furnished by Sioux raids on the Mandan horseherds and by venereal-tainted Mandan girls—"a sett of handsome tempting women," Clark noted. The captains wrote up their notes and prepared maps and natural history specimens to send downstream to Jefferson. As they had been doing all the way up the river, they explained American commercial regulations to the river traders, including several Britons who arrived overland from the north and offered to go along with the Americans to the Pacific, a gesture crisply declined.

Clinging of necessity close to the mighty river, the explorers could not give more than perfunctory heed to Gallatin's injunction that they study the potentials of the land for settlement. Such maps of the plains country as existed classed the area as a desolate waste. The dearth of trees, save near water, always astonished men from the forested East. Yet Meriwether Lewis saw what he wanted to see. In the spring of 1805, just before advancing farther west, he declared in a long letter to his mother that the prairies were not "barren, steril, and sandy. . . ." The lack of timber came from fires set by the Indians (a mistaken theory, of course), and actually the Missouri "waters one of the fairest portions of the globe, nor do I believe that there is in the universe a similar extent of country, equally fertile. . . ." Not until the arrival of dryland wheat boomers three quarters of a century later would anyone else make a similar remark about the arid western half of the Dakotas.

Throughout the winter the explorers avidly sought information from the Indians about the way ahead. Most of it was relayed through two voyageurs who lived in the villages, René Jessaume and Toussaint Charbonneau. From these talks the captains gathered a workable idea about the river as far as the mountains, but beyond that point everything was uncertain. They did learn, however, that they would need horses for the crossing, and that these might be obtained from a tribe called the Shoshonis. This gave sudden importance to a sixteen-year-old Shoshoni girl named Sacajawea, who had been captured from her people some years earlier by the Minnetarees, and who recently had become the wife of old Charbonneau. In order to obtain her services, Lewis and Clark enrolled Charbonneau as interpreter and agreed to let Sacajawea bring along her infant, born that winter with more difficulty than generally accompanied Indian deliveries. On Jessaume's advice, Lewis aided her labor by sending the young mother powdered rattlesnake rattles, which she was to mix in water and drink.

Early in April, shortly after the breakup of the ice, the voyageurs from St. Louis and a detachment of soldiers started downstream in the keelboat. The remaining twenty-nine Americans, including Clark's amiable slave York, plus Charbonneau and his family, moved upstream in the pirogues and in six canoes hollowed during the winter from cottonwood logs.

Cheerful in the face of dreadful toil on the towropes, the explorers crept west to the rapids bracketing thunderous Great Falls. They circled these by an eighteen-mile portage, dragging the canoes up the bluffs and over the cactus-studded prairie on solid truck wheels sliced from a cottonwood trunk. (By that time, the heavier pirogues and a few supplies for the return trip had been left behind in caches.) The persistent southward trend that had developed in the river worried them. With horses they might have cut due west toward the mountains, but they had no horses. Strangely, they had not sighted an Indian, although wondering natives were watching them.

At last Sacajawea reassured them by recognizing landmarks. They reached the beaver-teeming Three Forks area and turned up the Missouri's western branch, which they named the Jefferson. This in turn also forked three ways. They clung with their canoes to the brawling central branch, the Beaverhead, sparkling in a deep, barren valley—dense willows along the stream, sagebrush on the slopes, a ruffle of trees on the rounded mountaintops. The stream, clogged with boulders, gravel bars, and beaver dams, was all but impassable for the men, dragging ahead on lacerated, ulcerating feet. But without horses they had no choice.

As desperation grew, Lewis and three men went ahead to try to find the Shoshonis. The first Indian they saw fled. Hiking on through country still largely treeless, they crossed the Continental Divide on August 12 at Lemhi Pass, 7,373 feet above sea level west of today's Armstead, Montana. On the western slope Lewis with supreme cajolery persuaded a group of suspicious Shoshonis to visit the main party. By incredible coincidence, the band's chief turned out to be Sacajawea's brother. Through him they bought the horses that staved off failure.

Now they turned north, so that their back trail described a giant arc with its base to the south. Horses slipped and slid in an early snowstorm as they worked down into lovely Bitterroot Valley. Near today's Missoula, Montana, they at last veered west again over the dangerous Lolo Trail, which Nez Perce Indians used

James Wilkinson   Zebulon Pike

when traveling east to hunt buffalo on the plains. They were famished and, Clark wrote, as "wet and as cold in every part as I ever was in my life."

At a Nez Perce village on the Clearwater fork of the Snake River they left their horses, hollowed out five canoes, and took to water again. On October 16, in a brown, bare, sun-smitten valley lined by vast buttes of lava, they reached the glittering Columbia. They whirled down its great, rapid-torn gorge through the Cascade Mountains and on November 7 sighted the broad estuary. Moving a few miles inland among the enormous trees on the south shore, within sound of Pacific breakers, they raised crude log cabins, surrounded the buildings with a stout palisade, and settled down for the rainy winter.

Far behind them, in St. Louis, General James Wilkinson, the perennial schemer, was midway through another busy adventure. As Anthony Wayne's successor in command of the Western army, Wilkinson in the fall of 1803 attended the ceremonies at New Orleans that symbolically transferred Louisiana first from Spain to France, then from France to the United States. He brightened the festivities by serving, at United States expense, upwards of six hundred gallons of choice wine, two hundred and fifty-eight bottles of ale, forty or so gallons of hard liquor, and eleven thousand three hundred and sixty cigars. On the side he sold to the Spanish, for twelve thousand dollars, information that proved worthless. The windfall was not enough for Wilkinson. In Washington the following spring he held secret meetings with Vice-President Aaron Burr. Burr helped him obtain, in addition to his military command, the governorship of Upper Louisiana (eventually renamed Missouri Territory), at an annual salary of two thousand dollars.

A few months prior to Wilkinson's appointment as governor, Burr had killed Alexander Hamilton in a duel, and the downslip of his political career accelerated. He launched feverish schemes to reassert his fortunes. No one has ever learned what the plans really involved, probably because Burr let expediency take command. At times he considered inveigling money from England to use for recruiting troops in the disgruntled West and tearing Texas and Mexico from Spain, setting himself up as emperor of the new entity. When the wind blew right, he apparently thought of attaching the trans-Allegheny South to his banners. As his desperation increased, he may have hoped to involve the United States in a war with Spain so that he could clutch at whatever pieces shook loose during the explosion.

In furtherance of his schemes, he toured Kentucky in May and June, 1805, then dropped down the Mississippi to visit New Orleans. En route, at Fort Massac, near today's Paducah, he conferred at length with Wilkinson. Almost immediately thereafter, Wilkinson ordered Lieutenant Zebulon Montgomery Pike, a devoted twenty-six-year-old follower of the general's (and an Army acquaintance of Meriwether Lewis), to explore the upper Mississippi. Neither this expedition nor Pike's second trip to the southern Rockies was authorized by President Jefferson or by the War Department, although both trips were approved after they had been launched. To what extent they were related to the Burr-Wilkinson intrigues, if at all, can only be surmised.

Zebulon Pike, slim, blue-eyed, ruddy, with an odd habit of tilting his head to one side, was more than a little pompous, but highly ambitious and efficient. Within weeks he had selected twenty competent soldiers and had prepared a seventy-foot keelboat. The explorers left Bellefontaine, a new Army post a little north of St. Louis, on August 9, 1805. (By that time, Lewis and Clark had passed Three Forks and were toiling toward the Lemhi Pass.) Without particular incident, Pike's group rowed and sailed among the river's maze of islands to the lead mines operated by Julien Dubuque, near today's Dubuque, Iowa. Pike investigated the mines (conspirators might need lead for bullets), then continued to the old French town of Prairie du Chien, which was nestled under striking bluffs a little above the mouth of the Wisconsin. There he picked out a site for a United States military installation (it was never used), counseled the British-favoring Indians about their new obligations to the United States, and warned the town's unimpressed English and French traders to heed American regulations. He also got rid of his ponderous keelboat, exchanging it for two faster-moving barges.

On September 23, at an impressive meeting with Sioux Indians on an island at the junction of the Mississippi

Pike's first trip, above, took him to Leech Lake, which he thought the Mississippi's main source, but he missed Lake Itasca, to the west, later established as the river's true source.

and Minnesota rivers (southern suburbs of Minneapolis and St. Paul straddle the site today), Pike purchased a military reservation of one hundred thousand acres for his Government. To the continuing annoyance of the Indians, however, payment was not made, and the fort, Indian agency, and trading house that he had promised to build on the land were not started until 1819.

Nights grew bitter. Racing winter, Pike pushed his men so hard that Sergeant Henry Kennerman, "one of the stoutest men I ever knew, broke a blood-vessel and vomited nearly two quarts of blood." Near present Little Falls, Minnesota, fifteen hundred river miles from St. Louis, Pike stopped and had the men build a crude, square stockade. Half the party stayed there. On December 10 the other half, dragging their equipment on sleds, set out to walk to the headwaters of the Mississippi. It was a cold, brutal trip—toes and fingertips froze—and

An encounter with a grizzly bear was depicted in Sergeant Patrick Gass's ghostwritten account of the Lewis and Clark party.

could not have succeeded without the hospitality of the British fur trading posts that were situated at intervals along the Mississippi and its lakes.

These posts, located on American soil, illegally flew the British flag and dealt in goods on which the traders had paid no duty. Pike estimated that the British traders' activities resulted in America's losing twenty-six thousand dollars a year in revenue. He warned the foreigners to mend their ways. When one Union Jack was not lowered at his request, he went so far as to have his men drop it by shooting out the pin that fastened its halyard. In spite of such strong measures, the British trader involved, Hugh McGillis, and two of his voyageurs went with Pike and a single soldier to Cass Lake, which the American guessed (incorrectly) might be the upper source of the Mississippi. Pike turned back then. In the course of the return journey he made attempts at various times, without success, to persuade representatives of the Northern

tribes to visit the United States with him. On April 30, 1806, he rowed into the docks at St. Louis.

During Pike's absence, Burr had found a financial angel in the unlikely shape of Harman Blennerhassett, a rich Irishman who had married his own niece and had fled the scandal to an island in the Ohio River, fourteen miles below Marietta. There Blennerhassett had laid out formal flower gardens, planted a farm and orchard, and built a two-story mansion, painted white, its curving wings housing his offices and laboratory. While he conducted experiments in chemistry and electricity, his niece-wife, Margaret, held musicales or galloped about the estate in a red riding habit topped by a white hat jaunty with an ostrich plume.

Somehow Burr persuaded Blennerhassett to start building a fleet of barges capable of moving an army of thirteen hundred men. The purpose was something of a mystery. Whether the filibusterers hoped to seize New Orleans and form an independent nation under the protection of Spain, or to fight Spain, with Texas and Mexico as their prize, is uncertain. The latter seems the more likely.

Before roaring off westward, Burr needed to have some idea of where he was going. Wilkinson possessed charts of southeastern Texas that had been prepared by Philip Nolan a few years earlier. Burr had made a surreptitious copy of the map of western North America that Europe's greatest scientist, Alexander von Humboldt, had recently put together for the Spanish Government, a replica of which Humboldt left in Washington in 1804 on his return from Mexico City. (The map was not officially published until 1811.) Did the conspirators want still more information about Mexico's northern provinces—about the Spanish fortifications, for instance, and trails along which an army might march?

It seems so. It seems, too, that Spanish spies in St. Louis immediately learned that Wilkinson proposed to send a scouting trip across the plains, ostensibly to look for the headwaters of the Red River, which supposedly rose somewhere near Santa Fe. Conceivably Wilkinson himself sent the information to the Spaniards, in return for another payment.

The news struck tender Spanish nerves. The United States was arguing that the Louisiana Purchase extended to the Rio Grande. Spain retorted that the Red River, which runs through the western part of the present state of Louisiana and then along the southern border of Oklahoma, was the true boundary. She backed her contentions by checking, or preparing to check, in 1804 and 1806, two parties under William Dunbar and Thomas Freeman that Jefferson had ordered to explore the Red. And now here was talk of still another party crossing over the prairies to locate the headwaters of the river.

The word went down-river to Natchez, through southern Texas, to Government headquarters at Chihuahua, Mexico. In alarm the commandant sent orders north to Santa Fe. Find the Americans, turn them back! Lieutenant Don Facundo Malgares mounted five hundred militia and one hundred regular troops on white horses (the officers rode blacks), packed another 1,475 animals with supplies, and in mid-June sallied forth. For once the Spanish were too prompt. In June Pike, chosen to make the trip, was still in St. Louis, making ready.

Wilkinson's official orders—a few historians think there may have been other, secret instructions—told Pike to steer carefully clear of Spanish territory. Wilkinson, however, also granted permission to a young doctor named John H. Robinson to go along with the expedition. Robinson fully intended to penetrate as far into New Mexico as Santa Fe in search of a trader named Baptiste La Lande. This La Lande had gone earlier to New Mexico with goods belonging to a Kaskaskia merchant and had not returned. Chasing him down to collect may have been a legitimate errand—or it may have been a means whereby spies could work open a chink in Spain's jealously guarded frontier. Again, one can only guess at the true motivation.

Meantime, the border quarrel between the United States and Spain was growing increasingly tense. In the spring the War Department ordered Wilkinson, commander of the Western army, to Natchitoches on the Louisiana frontier, there to counter whatever aggressions Spain might make. If Burr wanted to provoke a war in aid of his schemes, here was the opportunity. Yet incredibly enough, Wilkinson disobeyed orders and did not start south until he was sure that Pike would get off in good shape on July 15, 1806. Then the general rushed forth to save his country.

Pike moved west with a party of twenty-two men in two barges. Their first goal was the Grand Osage village located on the present Missouri-Kansas border, to which the lieutenant was returning fifty-one Osage Indians to whom the Government had guaranteed safe conduct. The Osages walked the distance, which may have been an easier means of travel than rowing and poling the awkward boats up the shallow Osage River.

By July 15, meanwhile, the Lewis and Clark party was well started on its way home. In May they had picked up the horses they had left at the Nez Perce village on the Clearwater. Late in June, tortured by "the Musquetors our old companions," they wallowed through the snow of the Lolo Trail across present Idaho. After a brief rest in the Bitterroot Valley, the group split. Clark and the

bulk of the party turned south to pick up the boats and goods they had cached on the upper Beaverhead when they had bought horses from the Shoshonis. Nine men, led by Sergeant Ordway, would take these craft to the cache at Great Falls, while Clark and the rest of the men crossed Bozeman Pass and explored the Yellowstone River to its junction with the Missouri.

Lewis at the same time led nine men directly east over the Continental Divide at Montana's low (6,323 feet) Lewis and Clark Pass, thus drawing a chord across the roundabout southern arc the party had followed on its way west. At Great Falls, where ten thousand buffalo (Lewis's estimate) shook the air with their "tremendious roaring," another separation took place. Five men cleared out the caches while waiting for Ordway's canoe party. Lewis and the remaining three cut north on horseback across hot, woodless prairies to learn whether the

BOTH: N.Y. PUBLIC LIBRARY, RARE BOOK DIVISION

Another picture from Gass's book, the first published on the expedition (1807), shows the explorers parleying with Indians.

Marias River reached far enough toward the Saskatchewan to furnish a way by which furs could be practically transported into the United States.

It didn't. Disappointed, Lewis turned back. Almost at once his group encountered a small party of Blackfeet. Reds and whites camped together that night. Lewis foolishly told the Indians that he had been west of the mountains and had seen their enemy, the Tushepahs (Flatheads). He hoped the tribes would make peace, for soon traders from the United States would be following him up the river to bring goods to both groups.

The Blackfeet did not want the Tushepahs to get either guns or merchandise—unless Blackfeet carried such goods as they chose for a middleman's profit. At dawn they tried to kill the whites. Instead, the whites killed two of them and sent the rest fleeing. Fearing retaliation, Lewis and the others then rode one hundred and twenty miles back to the Missouri almost without pausing. Hav-

69

*Maps that Pike made were confiscated by the Spaniards. The one
at left, preserved by his captors, and with north at the top,
shows Pikes Peak (top, center) and the dotted-line route of
the explorers up the Arkansas from the region of present-day
Pueblo, Colorado (on the plains, right), to the Royal Gorge and
the river's headwaters, hemmed by mountains (left). At the
map's bottom is a sketch of the famous peak and its satellites.
Below is the entire route of Pike's controversial expedition.*

SCALE

0   50   100   150 Miles

ing survived the expedition's one fight with Indians, Lewis shortly thereafter was drilled through the buttocks by one of his own hunters, who mistook the captain's buckskin breeches for an elk's hide.

On August 12 the parties reunited below the mouth of the Yellowstone. They stopped at the Mandan villages long enough to persuade a minor chief, She-he-ke, to travel East with them to interview the President. Eager for home, they rowed swiftly down the river, pausing now and then to converse with traders who were ascending the stream. On September 10, a few miles above the site of the present-day city of St. Joseph, Missouri, they learned that General Wilkinson had moved south with his troops and that "Mr. Pike and young Mr. Wilkinson [the General's son] had Set out on an expedition up the Arkansaw river—or in that direction."

On September 23, 1806, the inhabitants of St. Louis lined the docks to give them a "harty welcom." Almost at once Lewis and Clark began work on preliminary reports for Jefferson, emphasizing—as John Jacob Astor of New York soon would learn—the possibility of employing caravans of cheap Indian horses for carrying furs from the Missouri to navigable waters of the Columbia. And the Columbia, as Astor knew, pointed directly toward the profitable fur markets of China.

That same September Wilkinson advanced with a show of belligerence to Natchitoches, Louisiana. The Spanish at Nacogdoches, Texas, a hundred miles west, rattled their swords right back at him. Both sides sent patrols toward the Sabine, the present boundary between Louisiana and Texas, but before an inflammatory incident occurred, Wilkinson received two unsettling messages. One led him to think that the Government was aware of his duplicity. The other, in cipher from Burr, made him wonder whether his partner could deliver the money, men, and munitions he had promised.

Adroitly Wilkinson turned coat again. Twelve days after receiving Burr's letter, he wrote dramatically to Jefferson, exposing the dreadful plot. A few days after that, he and the Spanish commander negotiated a truce that established a neutral area between the Arroyo Hondo (Natchitoches, roughly) and the Sabine, to endure until the governments of their two countries settled the boundary dispute by treaty. Blandly but fruitlessly, he then asked 121,000 pesos from Spain for his work in upsetting Burr's evil designs on Texas. Then he rushed back to New Orleans, declared martial law, arrested suspects, and in general made a noisy show of suppressing a dangerous revolt.

Farther north, Ohio militia seized the boats Blennerhassett was building at Marietta. When the would-be revolutionist fled to join Burr at the mouth of the Cumberland, vandals joyfully smashed everything movable in his island mansion.

On reaching Louisiana, Burr vigorously protested that he was interested only in a colonizing project. Orders were nevertheless issued for his arrest. Bidding adieu to a twenty-year-old Southern beauty whom legend says he had been wooing, he belatedly fled, in mid-February, 1807, up the Natchez Trace. A posse caught him in a somber grove of giant oaks and took him to Richmond, Virginia, for trial. Wilkinson testified against him, then himself was searchingly investigated. Both men were freed, but in public opinion, at least, both were guilty.

By February, 1807, Pike too was under arrest. He had spent the first month of his trip toiling up the Osage River to the main village of the Grand Osage Indians. After exchanging his barges for horses, he angled northwest across what is now Kansas. At a Pawnee village on the Republican River, he learned that a large force of Spanish soldiers mounted on white horses had been looking for him—an indefensible violation of United States territory. After persuading the Pawnees to exchange the Spanish flag Malgares had given them for the Stars and Stripes (and then returning the alien banner to the Indians!), Pike swung almost due south to the drab valley of the Arkansas, which was bordered by monotonous sand hills. Young Lieutenant Wilkinson and five soldiers left the main group there and descended the river to the Mississippi in a frail boat built of buffalo hides stretched across a frame of green cottonwood.

Pike rode on west. The increasing aridity of the central plains drew no such response from him as the northern ones had from Meriwether Lewis. In his opinion those sandy deserts, "incapable of cultivation," would forever limit the spread of the frontier. And yet he also estimated that the short, curly grass along the banks of the Arkansas supported enough buffalo "to feed all the savages in the United States territory one century." Such grass would support cattle as well, but in those days cattle range was not needed. Indian range was, and Pike's remarks gave material for thought to men who wanted to move every aborigine in the United States somewhere off beyond the Missouri.

On November 15 the explorers sighted a distant peak and raised "three cheers to the Mexican Mountains." Two weeks later they were nearing the point at which the Arkansas River emerges from its spectacular gorge. The peak they had first sighted rose grandly to the north. Though the weather was cold and the men were ill clad in light summer uniforms (Pike had supposed winters that far south of Minnesota would be warm), he, Dr. Robinson, and two privates set out to climb the mountain.

It was farther away than it looked in the clear air. They walked three days, lost themselves in the ravines, and by mistake climbed what later was named Cheyenne Mountain. In freezing temperatures, waist-deep in snow, they gaped at the summit, five thousand feet higher than they were, and decided that under the circumstances no one could have scaled the "Grand Peak." They did not name the mountain, but later trappers did, and in 1843–44 Frémont made the label official—Pikes Peak.

The next weeks were a horror. The men wandered almost aimlessly through the front range of the Rockies, behind what is now Canon City, Colorado. They were looking, Pike said, for the Red River; actually, it heads far to the southeast, in the Panhandle of Texas. They did see the beginnings of the South Platte and thought wildly that they detected the source of the Yellowstone, which in truth was hundreds of miles away in the north.

Their confused meanderings brought them back to the very part of the Arkansas from which they had started. A shortage of game would not let them stay there through the winter. Half-starved, they heaved their equipment onto their own backs and struck west. At intervals, five men collapsed with frozen feet and were left behind. Those still ambulatory floundered into the San Luis Valley and so reached the upper Rio Grande, very definitely inside Spanish territory. Looking for timber with which to build, Pike led the shivering remnants of his party five miles up an east-flowing tributary of the river, the Conejos, just north of today's Colorado–New Mexico border. In a grove of cottonwoods he erected a stout palisade twelve feet high, surrounded by both a moat and an overhang of sharpened stakes.

Volunteers went back to help the men left in the mountains. (Eventually all emerged.) In an amazing maneuver never explained, Dr. Robinson started south, afoot and absolutely alone, in winter weather, to see whether he could find Santa Fe. He did. One hundred Spanish soldiers immediately marched north to capture the Americans, which may have been what Pike wanted, either because his situation was desperate, or because it was a way to get inside the town and spy for Wilkinson.

On February 26, 1807, the New Mexican troops appeared outside the Conejos stockade. Pike voiced astonishment on being told he was on not the Red but the Rio Grande. Obligingly he hauled down the American flag and went with his captors to Santa Fe, a city of five thousand inhabitants who lived in low, cramped adobe houses scattered around a large central plaza. The bedraggled appearance of the newcomers led the wretched inhabitants to flock around with sympathetic clucks.

Were all Americans so ragged? At home did they live in houses, like civilized men, or in tepees, like Indians?

To his surprise, Pike found a few Americans already there—the trader La Lande, a Kentucky hunter named Pursley, or Purcell, and a survivor of Nolan's last filibuster into Texas. All were forbidden to leave the city, however, and if Pike managed to return home, he would be the first of his nationality to bring back an eyewitness account of the mysterious city of the conquistadors.

It was Spain's policy to let no information leak. The commandant confiscated Pike's papers and maps. But he feared that the United States might raise an issue over these troublesome soldiers, and so he decided to get rid of them by sending them to Chihuahua, Mexico, under charge of Lieutenant Malgares—at last Malgares had found his Americans.

The governor in Chihuahua decided that the safest move was to send the captives back through Texas to Natchitoches. He warned the escort to let Pike make no notes en route, but the lieutenant managed a few jottings while relieving himself in private. Some of these scraps of paper he hid in the barrels of the unloaded muskets his soldiers had been allowed to keep as a courtesy. The notes later refreshed his amazing memory as he prepared an account of his adventures for publication.

The party reached Natchitoches on July 1, 1807, and Pike immediately was suspected of complicity in Wilkinson's plotting. Pike never quite lived the charges down, in spite of his stubborn insistence that neither he nor his general, to whom he was devoted, was guilty of anything contrary to the good of their country.

The abject collapse of the Burr conspiracy showed, among other things, that separatism was no longer a factor in the West. The Louisiana Purchase not only had ended the Mississippi question but, more importantly, had lifted the eyes of the nation to the vast and challenging lands beyond the river. What was there? What did it mean to the United States as a whole?

Pike and Lewis and Clark had come back with useful accounts about the northern and southern fringes. But the heart remained a mystery. Congress had declined Jefferson's request for additional explorations up several of the Mississippi's and the Missouri's principal tributaries. Because the Government was absorbed by threats emanating from the Napoleonic Wars and by its own fluctuating embargo policies toward Great Britain, no more official expeditions into the new territory were likely for some time. Whatever was learned would come from private effort. That was unfortunate. What is privately learned is likely to remain private. Yet knowledge to be useful as a national resource needs wide dissemination.

*Alexander Mackenzie
by Thomas Lawrence*

Northwest Passage

One of the great will-o'-the-wisps of history was the Northwest Passage, a sea route by which ships could sail from ocean to ocean through North America. Early explorers on the Atlantic coast hopefully sought it in each new river and inlet, and the Hudson's Bay Company was required by its charter to search for the passage as it traded into new territory. On the lesser known Northwest Pacific coast, legends persisted of a mysterious Strait of Anian and of a mythical voyage of a probably mythical Spanish Admiral de Fonte, who was said to have found a northern channel that carried him through to the Atlantic. At last, in 1778, Britain's Captain James Cook, carefully exploring the Canadian and Alaskan coasts, proved there was no passage through the continent. However, the expedition did discover that the sea otter pelts it obtained from the Indians brought tremendous prices on the Chinese market, and soon British and American traders in increasing numbers were coming to the Northwest coast. One of them, Captain Robert Gray, in 1792 gave the United States a basis for its first West Coast claim when he discovered, and sailed some ten miles into, a large stream he named Columbia's River for his ship, the *Columbia Rediviva* (pictured above in a squall by George Davidson, who accompanied Gray). Abandoning the long-held dream of a Northwest Passage, Canadian fur trader Alexander Mackenzie in 1793 made the first crossing of the continent above Mexico, but his route from Montreal to the Pacific through a maze of waterways was too arduous for practical use. It remained for someone else to find a more feasible path across North America.

LANGSDORFF, *Voyages and Travels*, 1812

Russia's trading post at Sitka, viewed by George Langsdorff in 1805

NATIONAL MARITIME MUSEUM, GREENWICH, ENGLAND

Britain's Captain Cook on the Pacific coast in 1778, by John Webber

MUSEO NAVAL, MADRID

The Spanish mission at Carmel, California, in 1791, by José Cardero

CONTINENTAL STAKES

PUBLIC ARCHIVES OF CANADA

Nootka Indians like this man, painted by Webber, supplied traders with furs.

At the turn of the nineteenth century the United States was still a weak country sharing North America with giants. The problems of diplomacy had been difficult enough east of the Mississippi; the Louisiana Purchase and a growing interest in the Northwest coast soon involved the nation on a continental scale.

Still hoping to regain the Great Lakes and eastern Canada, France until 1803 retained an active interest in the Mississippi Valley. Russia, continuing the expansion that had colonized Siberia, established herself in Alaska and pushed on down the Pacific coast; in 1811 she would build a fort just north of San Francisco. Spain had responded to the threat by moving, in 1769, into hitherto empty California. And into this arena the British moved boldly by sending vessels to establish a claim to the region between California and Alaska—a land the Spanish insisted was theirs and almost caused a war over by seizing British vessels in Vancouver Island's Nootka Sound. In the midst of this contention among empires, America soon established claims of its own.

French spy Victor Collot (see pages 54–55) arrived in St. Louis in 1796, soon after the return of J. B. Truteau's Spanish expedition up the Missouri. Collot secured Truteau's map (made by Antoine Soulard) and, adding conjectural information from Truteau, prepared this pre-Lewis and Clark map of the West, reproduced here for the first time.

Northwest Indian arrow

Coastal Indian hat

Plains "battle axe"

A "pheasant" of the Rockies

The expedition's Missouri River keelboat

A bighorn sheep

Great canoe of coast Indians

Head flattening, lower Columbia

Plan of Fort Clatsop, where the expedition wintered near the Pacific

Indian weir for trapping salmon

Indian rock painting

An "evergreen shrub"

Columbia River salmon trout

The mountain quail (above) and horned toad (right) were among paintings by Charles Willson Peale done from specimens brought back by Lewis and Clark and meant for inclusion in the explorers' story of their trip. When costs rose, the book was published without pictures.

Lean, hardened, self-assured, Meriwether Lewis (left) was portrayed in frontiersman's garb by Charles Saint-Mémin during 1806, immediately after his return from the great trip west.

"BY LAND FROM THE U. STATES"

Before their epic journey to the Pacific began, President Jefferson emphasized to Lewis and Clark the paramount importance of gathering all possible information about the unknown Far West; among the many things they were to observe were Indian tribes, weather, river courses, fur trade possibilities, soil fertility, and plant and animal life. He also directed that every literate member of the expedition should keep a diary, and he thought that, for safety's sake, one diary should be kept on waterproof birch bark. So, as they traveled, the two leaders kept records as ample as the grueling exertions of the journey permitted (in quaintly unique spelling, in the case of the frontier-reared Clark), occasionally making little sketches (left) on their journal pages—very rough, for neither man was an artist. After their return, they made plans, at Jefferson's urging, to use their records in writing a joint account of their great adventure for the public, but in 1809 Lewis was murdered or took his own life while traveling to Washington on the Natchez Trace. Clark turned the project over to an editor; the work was finished in 1814, but much of the flavor of the original journals was gone.

Daniel Boone stayed ahead of the civilizers. He was in Missouri when Chester Harding made his life portrait of him.

Cleveland, founded in 1796, had 1,300 inhabitants by 1800, but Captain Allen Gaylord's sketch that year of Lake Erie and the mouth of the Cuyahoga River, now in the heart of the city, showed only one cabin.

ALL THE WAY TO SHAWNEETOWN

In the trans-Appalachian country the settlers were coming on. The Ohio River, leading from the Alleghenies westward, was ideally suited to carry a migrating people into wilderness regions where roads were almost nonexistent. And as the river was the great highway, the flatboat was the universal carrier, first of the settlers, and later of their produce on its way to down-river markets. Boats by the hundreds moved with the current, and the banks echoed a popular boatmen's song: "Hard upon the beech oar!—She moves too slow! All the way to Shawneetown, Long while ago." Timothy Flint, minister and Western writer, described many of the settlers' boats as "fitted up with chairs, beds, tables and stoves. It is no uncommon spectacle to see a large family, old and young, servants, cattle, hogs, horses, sheep, fowls, and animals of all kinds, bringing to recollection the cargo of the ancient ark, all embarked, and floating down on the same bottom." Even the advent of the steamboat did not end the stream of flatboats.

Cincinnati was founded by land speculators in 1788 on the Ohio opposite the mouth of the Licking River with the tricky name Losantiville—"L" for Licking, "os" for mouth, "anti" for opposite, "ville" for city. Happily, it was renamed the next year when it became the capital of the Northwest Territory. This painting was made in 1807 by C. Williams.

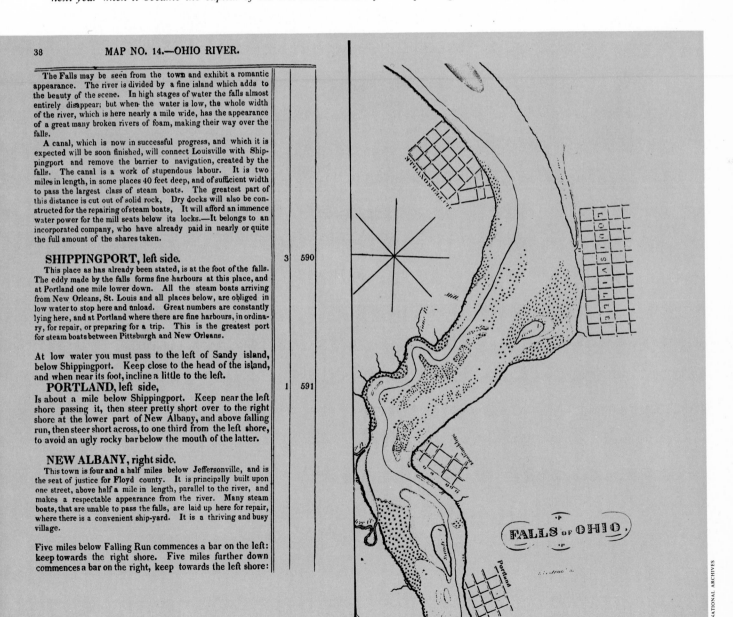

38   MAP NO. 14.—OHIO RIVER.

The Falls may be seen from the town and exhibit a romantic appearance. The river is divided by a fine island which adds to the beauty of the scene. In high stages of water the falls almost entirely disappear; but when the water is low, the whole width of the river, which is here nearly a mile wide, has the appearance of a great many broken rivers of foam, making their way over the falls.

A canal, which is now in successful progress, and which it is expected will be soon finished, will connect Louisville with Shippingport and remove the barrier to navigation, created by the falls. The canal is a work of stupendous labour. It is two miles in length, in some places 40 feet deep, and of sufficient width to pass the largest class of steam boats. The greatest part of this distance is cut out of solid rock. Dry docks will also be constructed for the repairing of steam boats. It will afford an immence water power for the mill seats below its locks.—It belongs to an incorporated company, who have already paid in nearly or quite the full amount of the shares taken.

SHIPPINGPORT, left side.
This place as has already been stated, is at the foot of the falls. The eddy made by the falls forms fine harbours at this place, and at Portland one mile lower down. All the steam boats arriving from New Orleans, St. Louis and all places below, are obliged in low water to stop here and unload. Great numbers are constantly lying here, and at Portland where there are fine harbours, in ordinary, for repair, or preparing for a trip. This is the greatest port for steam boats between Pittsburgh and New Orleans.

At low water you must pass to the left of Sandy island, below Shippingport. Keep close to the head of the island, and when near its foot, incline a little to the left.

PORTLAND, left side,
Is about a mile below Shippingport. Keep near the left shore passing it, then steer pretty short over to the right shore at the lower part of New Albany, and above falling run, then steer short across, to one third from the left shore, to avoid an ugly rocky bar below the mouth of the latter.

NEW ALBANY, right side.
This town is four and a half miles below Jeffersonville, and is the seat of justice for Floyd county. It is principally built upon one street, above half a mile in length, parallel to the river, and makes a respectable appearance from the river. Many steam boats, that are unable to pass the falls, are laid up here for repair, where there is a convenient ship-yard. It is a thriving and busy village.

Five miles below Falling Run commences a bar on the left: keep towards the right shore. Five miles further down commences a bar on the right, keep towards the left shore:

3	590
1	591

The Ohio and Mississippi rivers had innumerable navigation hazards, and a great comfort to inexperienced settlers in flatboats were chartbooks such as Samuel Cummings's Western Pilot *(above), which told how best to navigate every mile.*

River boats came in many varieties, but most common was the broadhorn flatboat (left), so called from its long steering sweeps on each side.

Hells Canyon of the Snake River, between Idaho and Oregon

"... we had just started out, when—What was my astonishment and distress!—I beheld Mr. Crooks and his party on the other side of the river.... Poor man!... he had gone three days' march further down; ... the mountains there are even higher and come closer to the river, which at that spot is compressed into a canal not more than sixty to a hundred feet wide between precipitous rocks; ... it was impossible for men in their condition to proceed, because, for six days, their only animal food had been one of their dogs.... It was necessary therefore ... to retrace my steps...."

Wilson Price Hunt, leading starving Astorians, Snake River canyon, December 6, 1811

CHAPTER FOUR

BARREN BEGINNINGS

1804-1813

On November 19, 1804, fur-trading Pierre Chouteau, Sr., of St. Louis, the newly appointed agent for the Indians of Louisiana Territory, reported to his superiors in the War Department that "an immense number of merchants coming from Michellimakina"—i.e., Britons—had stampeded up the Missouri to trade. Chouteau disapproved of the intruders. Indians, he said, were "easy to seduce," and these foreigners, who carried quantities of liquor with them as an extra inducement to further their bartering, might act in ways that would prove to be inimical to the interests of the United States.

Since Chouteau's time, lovely little Michilimackinac Island (today Mackinac) has become one of Michigan's most popular summer resorts. Commerce seems ill suited to its tiny size, three miles by two. But at the time of the Louisiana Purchase, Mackinac was the nerve center of the fur trade along the northern border, handling each year blankets, coarse cloth, trade guns, deer hides, and beaver and muskrat pelts worth, in terms of today's currency, many millions of dollars.

Geography gave the bluff-lined, forest-crowned islet its extraordinary dominance. Lying just east and slightly north of the narrow strait connecting Lakes Huron and Michigan, it commanded vital water routes leading to the western side of the lower Michigan Peninsula; to the St. Joseph River of Indiana, which in turn opened into the Wabash country; to Chicago and thence the Illinois River; to Green Bay and the strategic Fox-Wisconsin link with the Mississippi. A short swing east and north from Mackinac brought traffic to the St. Marys River, which

in turn led to Lake Superior, the myriad streams of northern Wisconsin, and the maze of lakes beyond Fond du Lac, near today's Duluth.

Fragile birchbark canoes and clumsy Mackinaw barges served this entire area. The barges, flat-bottomed and propelled by six or eight oars, looked like overgrown rowboats. Thirty feet long and equipped with masts on which sails could be raised, these sturdy craft served as the work horses of the trade.

Swifter and more manageable than barges where portages had to be made were the *canots du maître*. Built of strips of birch bark sewn with fibers of tree roots over a pliable frame of red cedar, the graceful, dancing craft were thirty-five to forty feet long and up to six feet wide. Although they weighed less than five hundred pounds, they could transport four to five tons of merchandise each, plus a crew of eight to ten singing voyageurs and a passenger or two. Their great drawback was their flimsiness. They had to be unloaded and taken from the water every night and frequently waterproofed with pine resin. Seldom did one survive more than a single season. A barge, on the other hand, lasted for years.

During the fall and winter, trade goods were assembled in Montreal. Calico and strouds (a kind of heavy cloth the Indians liked), knives, kettles, and awls, beads, muskets, and powder came from abroad. Traps, iron tomahawks, and silver brooches and earrings were fabricated in Montreal. Rum, whisky, high wine (an explosive, high-proof distillation), lyed corn, and salt pork for the men were imported from the West Indies and the United States. This merchandise was lashed into ninety-pound bales, a convenient weight for being carried across the portages on human backs. Shortly after the ice went out of the rivers in late April, the bales were carted to the head of Lachine Rapids, a few miles up the St. Lawrence from Montreal. There they were loaded into barges or canoes for the long trip to one of the West's two great rendezvous points, Mackinac Island or Fort William, the latter a baronial log complex on the northwest shore of Lake Superior, gateway to the beaver streams of Canada.

Barges were rowed and poled up the St. Lawrence to Lake Ontario, where sometimes their cargoes were transferred into undependable little schooners. But since both barges and men were valuable in the West, the straining crews often rowed on across Lake Ontario to Niagara. Wagons hauled boats and goods around the Falls to Lake Erie. The rowers then toiled past Detroit into Lake Huron or sought a difficult short cut by way of York (now Toronto) and the rivers between Lake Simcoe and Georgian Bay. A traverse of Huron's full length then brought them to Mackinac.

These lake routes were the cheapest way to go. Canoes took the faster, more expensive way up the foaming Ottawa and Mattawa rivers, crossed to Lake Nipissing, and swept down the French River to Georgian Bay. The trek was tormented by eighteen portages and an equal number of *décharges*, where the canoes were partially unloaded and towed through the white water. Mosquitoes stained the gasping men with blood: insects were one reason voyageurs wore their hair long. But with a good crew and good luck it was possible to make the nine-hundred-mile trip from Montreal to Mackinac in eleven or twelve days—grueling eighteen-hour stretches from dawn at three until dark at nine. Barges needed more than twice that many days to make their roundabout voyage through the lakes.

Traders coming with pelts from what is now Michigan, northern Indiana, Illinois, Wisconsin, and Minnesota met suppliers at the island rendezvous in June, July, and early August. Indians drifted in from all sides, until there were a thousand or more living in wigwams on the beach and padding with the whites through the little town that lay under the guns of the stone fort high on the hill. It was a roaring time. As Washington Irving summed it up in *Astoria*, "They feast, they fiddle, they drink, they sing, they dance, they frolic and fight."

Mackinac waxed because of the economic situation in Canada and along Canada's unsurveyed boundary with the United States and (until 1803) Spanish Louisiana—that broad sprawl of watery forest from Lake Superior, past the headwaters of the Mississippi, where Pike had found North West Company traders in 1805, to the Red River of the North, which today separates Minnesota and North Dakota. From that hazy line northward, two ruthless monopolies, the Hudson's Bay Company and the North West Company, were supreme. True, a group of rebel Nor'Westers calling themselves the XY Company did furiously challenge their former partners at the turn of the century, but it was a family quarrel.

Unable to break into this long sweep of northern territory, independent operators based on Michilimackinac Island turned south and southwest. To the disgust of the American frontier, Jay's Treaty (1794) legalized these forays within the borders of the United States as they then existed. The experienced British quickly made the most of the privilege. They brought the not-so-naive Indians better merchandise than the Americans could offer; indeed, most of the goods used by United States traders also had to be imported from England. The French-Canadian employees of the British—and many employers as well—married Indian women and so won the loyalty of the tribes, whereas American frontiersmen made themselves suspect by fighting the Indians for their land. By 1803 many of the Mackinac-based Britons were acting as arrogantly as if there had been no Revolution and the area around the upper Great Lakes still belonged to them.

At least their presence within the United States was legal. West of the Mississippi, in Spanish Louisiana, it was not. But the Great Lakes area was getting overrun. Even before Jay's Treaty, Mackinac traders had begun traveling through Prairie du Chien on the upper Mississippi and up the Des Moines and St. Peter's (Minnesota) rivers into territory claimed by Spain. By the end of the 1790's a few of their pack trains had even crossed the Missouri to seek Pawnees along the Platte, in present-day Nebraska. Other smugglers, led by a big, redheaded Scot named Robert Dickson, ventured regularly into eastern South Dakota to trade with the Sioux.

The traders of Spanish-governed St. Louis who tried to compete with these invaders were, in the main, naturalized Frenchmen or Englishmen. They imported first-class merchandise from Europe by way of Montreal, Michilimackinac, Green Bay, and the Fox-Wisconsin and Mississippi river systems. Spain's mercantile policies, however, crippled the advantages that the traders' bloodlines and goods should have brought them.

In general, the Spanish governor in St. Louis allowed only one trader per tribe of Indians and sold the license to the highest bidder. To recoup, the licensee charged the Indians exorbitantly and at the same time toadied to them in an effort to maintain their favor. The contemptuous Indians soon learned that they could get better prices from the unlicensed British. They swung so completely

Water routes of fur men, from the St. Lawrence to the Mississippi, the Missouri, and central Canada, are seen above.

into the foreign orbit that, Meriwether Lewis wrote somewhat ungrammatically to Jefferson in 1806, they "have been known in several instances to capture boats on the Missouri, in their descent to St. Louis, and compelled the crews to load themselves with heavy burdens of their best furs across the country to their towns, where they disposed of them to the British merchants."

A growing number of Britons competed for this illicit trade. East of the Mississippi the supply of high-class fur, notably beaver, was shrinking steadily as the expanding United States wrung more and more hunting land from the Eastern Indians. Meanwhile, the economic chaos created by Napoleon's wars was reducing fur prices while increasing shipping costs. Sobered by this dousing of financial cold water, the XY and North West companies in 1804 made peace and amalgamated their competing posts and supply caravans. The union threw many men out of work. Those who wished to stay in the business had to look for new locations south of the United States border. They did not like what they saw. The independents there were trying to make ends meet by slashing prices, pouring out whisky, and stealing each other's credits—that is, the furs due a trader in payment for goods delivered. This left the trans-Mississippi West as the sole remaining field offering a reasonable hope of success.

At that point the United States acquired Louisiana. In Canadian minds this legally opened to them the very

ground they wanted, for Jay's Treaty specified that Canadian merchants could do business within the United States simply by complying with American laws. The Montreal importers rushed orders to England for more trade goods, and in 1804 the wilderness merchants launched the stampede to the Missouri of which Indian agent Pierre Chouteau complained so bitterly.

Chouteau was not alone. United States Indian traders were unanimously enraged by this threatened engrossment of what they felt should have been their plum. Furthermore, they were deeply suspicious of the Britons. Tensions between the United States and England were building up again because of British interference with American ocean shipping. Was it safe to let potential enemies move unrestrained among Western Indians, whose prejudices they could manipulate at will by means of their long experience and superior merchandise?

After consulting with Chouteau and other officials, but acting entirely on his own responsibility, General James Wilkinson, the new American governor of Louisiana, decided to stop the British. Treaty rights? They had none. Louisiana Territory had not been a part of the United States at the time Jay's Treaty had been signed; therefore the privileges that the treaty accorded British traders in the East did not apply in the West.

On the strength of that reasoning, Wilkinson on August 26, 1805, issued a proclamation that declared,

83

"No person the Citizen or Subject of a foreign Power will be permitted to enter the Missouri River for the purpose of Indian trade." Only residents of the United States could import goods from abroad, and employees of the traders were ordered "to take & subscribe an oath of fidelity to the United States and of abjuration to all other Powers." As Wilkinson himself admitted by letter to Secretary of War Henry Dearborn, the sweeping edict was "somewhat extrajudicial," but he insisted that circumstances demanded it.

The ruling brought consternation to the British traders moving down the Mississippi with their loaded barges. The season was too late for them to shift to alternative trading grounds of any value. Unless subterfuges were found, their year's investments would be lost.

Some of them managed. James Aird, for instance, got his four boats through by invoking a clause in Jay's Treaty that said that all residents of the border posts (Mackinac, Detroit, etc.) at the time of the British evacuation in 1796 were, unless they declared otherwise, automatically regarded as United States citizens. Aird insisted he had made no such declaration, and Wilkinson had to let him through. Aird's clerks—one of them an eighteen-year-old Scot named Ramsay Crooks, destined to become a dominant figure of the American fur trade—thereupon swallowed whatever patriotic scruples they had, swore oaths of fidelity to the United States, and were allowed to continue.

Though a few people like Aird and Crooks did slip through the blockade, the harassment was acute enough to dismay the entire Mackinac community. The rush of Britons slowed down. Otherwise, they almost certainly would have pressed on into the Rockies and there have joined hands with the Nor'Westers who were working through Canada to the upper Columbia. What difference this might have made to the history of the West is hard to gauge. One can argue, however, that in this case, at least, Wilkinson's arrogance did his country some good.

Wilkinson raised a few other question marks for historians that summer. On September 8, 1805, two weeks after the proclamation, he wrote Secretary of War Dearborn that he was sending a small expedition to the Yellowstone River. (Only a month before this, he had started Pike up the Mississippi.) What was his purpose? Lewis and Clark were already in that country. And did Wilkinson's expedition actually materialize? It seems not. Clark, who coursed the Yellowstone on his way home in 1806, does not mention any such party, nor do those members of the expedition who traveled down the Missouri. Still, it is a huge country, and the explorers easily could have missed a small party. And by 1807, as we shall see, there

were more Americans in the northern Rockies than written history accounts for. How did they get there?

That same Wilkinson letter of September, 1805, adds small twists to the Burr conspiracy. Wilkinson was planning, he said, to send a certain Captain John McClallen of New York to Santa Fe with trade goods—a year before he actually sent Zebulon Pike off in that direction. A little after this, the governor ordered his troops to build a fort at the mouth of the Platte, on the grounds that the Spanish were exciting the Pawnees and Osages against the Americans and a bastion was necessary.

The Secretary of War canceled the fort and censured Wilkinson for assuming too much power—yet let him remain in command of the Army. No objection was raised to Captain McClallen's adventure. A year later he was still planning the trip. On September 17, 1806, he met Lewis and Clark, homeward bound, a little below the site of today's Kansas City and gave them a full rundown on his strategy. He said that first he would build a post near the mouth of the Platte, the site of Wilkinson's abortive fort. There he would win the friendship of the Pawnee, Oto, and Comanche Indians and prevail on them to escort him to the New Mexican capital. "Through the influence of a handsome present" (Clark's words), he would win permission from the Spanish governor to set up a store at a point near enough the border so that the New Mexicans could reach him for trade.

Curiously, Pike on that very day was no more than one hundred and seventy-five miles farther west, in central Kansas, bound toward New Mexico and carrying with him a letter from Wilkinson, dated August 6, that enjoined him to put a stop to exactly that sort of Santa Fe performance by another St. Louis trader who was far more influential than McClallen—Manuel Lisa, Spanish by heritage but automatically a citizen of the United States under the terms of the Louisiana Purchase. According to Wilkinson's letter, Lisa was planning to press close to Santa Fe after establishing trade relations with the Pawnee and Comanche Indians of the Western plains. He too would offer the governor presents, but if permission could not be obtained that way, then he would barter clandestinely from his border deposit. No good could come to the United States from such a project, Wilkinson told Pike, and therefore ". . . you must take all prudent and lawful means to blow it up."

In short, what was satisfactory for McClallen was not satisfactory for Lisa. Why? Was McClallen enrolled as a Wilkinson spy, whereas Lisa was not? Or were other jealousies at work? No one knows.

Another curious note: McClallen in 1806 told Meriwether Lewis (so Lewis wrote in his "Observations . . . on

. . . Louisiana") that the one thing he (McClallen) did not like about the Spanish plan was "the disadvantages it laboured under from the free admission of the British merchants" to the United States. He was ready to call off the adventure "unless these merchants were prohibited from entering the river." In short, he did not think Wilkinson's exclusion order of 1805 was effective and feared, as Meriwether Lewis also did, that the British might prove able, in spite of restrictions, to engross not just the trade of the Missouri but that of the entire West—a large-scale bogeyman indeed, and indicative of the resentful admiration the British traders commanded.

Or perhaps McClallen was just making excuses; anyway, he seems not to have continued with his Spanish plans. Neither did Lisa, either because of Wilkinson's objections or because of a keener interest in the Missouri. But two of Lisa's associates, Jacques Clamorgan and Louison Beaudoin, persisted and in the summer of 1807 crossed the plains to Santa Fe. The Spanish officials there proved as suspicious of them as they had been of Pike a few months earlier and, as they had done with Pike, hustled the traders to Chihuahua for questioning. Apparently not enough gain resulted for the pair to risk repeating the adventure. In any case, whatever they learned they apparently kept to themselves. Even on the frontier the affair created no stir; memory of it melted

ARCHIVES OF ST. JOHN'S CATHEDRAL, WINNIPEG

Fur trade loyalties caused many Indian migrations. Peguis (above, painted by Peter Rindisbacher), led his Chippewas from Lake Superior to the British at Lake Winnipeg.

away, and today scarcely a detail can be resurrected.

The early West abounds with tantalizing tales like that. For instance: on August 12, 1806, Lewis and Clark met, in what is now the extreme western part of North Dakota, two Illinois trappers named Forest Handcock and Joseph Dickson. Trappers, note. The traditional way of obtaining fur was to let the Indians do the work (after all, the natives claimed the game in their territory) and then to obtain the pelts by barter. Beaver in particular were best obtained with traps. The Western Indians, however, did not understand trapping and in 1806 had not yet developed a strong enough desire for manufactured luxuries so that they were willing to learn the arduous business. So, at the risk of incurring the wrath of the aborigines, the impatient whites had taken to the streams themselves. Lewis and Clark had found French trappers working the Missouri above the Mandan villages as early as the spring of 1805.

Handcock and Dickson were of this new breed. They had been away from civilization for two years. Indians had robbed them of the few furs they had taken and had wounded Dickson during a scuffle. Yet when they heard from Lewis and Clark's men that beaver abounded farther west, they determined to press on. One of the Lewis and Clark expedition's stoutest members, John Colter, caught the fever, obtained his release, and went with them. But no record exists of their adventures.

An even more intriguing expedition was one headed by a Charles Courtin, or Courter, or Corta. Courter (or Courtin—the name is spelled both ways, and more besides) was a French Canadian from Michilimackinac. He had gone to Missouri at least as early as 1805, perhaps as a clerk of James Aird, and therefore must have become a nominal citizen of the United States. When David Thompson ran across Courter's traces in Montana a few years later, he called him an American.

On July 9, 1806, according to the records of John Kinzie, a trader at Chicago, Courter, James Reed, and Ramsay Crooks (the latter two definitely clerks of Aird's) dragged their boats across the Chicago Portage into Lake Michigan. Reed and Crooks were on their way to Mackinac to buy goods for Aird to use on the Missouri during the ensuing winter. Courter, however, cut loose on his own. Gathering a group of men from somewhere, he spent the winter of 1806–7 among the Maha Indians in the northeastern corner of present Nebraska. (Query: Did two of Lewis and Clark's men hurry back up the river to join him after obtaining their discharges in St. Louis late in September, 1806? It may be so.)

The Mahas were overrun with traders that winter. Crooks was there, representing Aird. Also on hand, representing himself, was wiry little Robert McClellan (no kin to Wilkinson's John McClallen), who reputedly could jump over a covered wagon and who had served as a fabulous Indian scout under Anthony Wayne in Ohio.

As soon as the ice broke, Courter pushed on up the Missouri. The move excited Crooks and Robert Mc-Clellan, who determined to hurry to St. Louis, wind up their business, obtain financing, and follow him—but more of that later.

The North West Company was also thrusting westward. Their latest move had begun in 1800 or so, after Kutenai Indians had slipped timorously across the Continental Divide to Rocky Mountain House on the North Saskatchewan River to buy guns for fighting the Blackfeet. Because of the Blackfeet, it was a dangerous trip. The Kutenais promised many beaver if the company thereafter would assume the risk by bringing goods over the mountains to them. David Thompson, the Nor'-Westers' great map maker and astronomer, agreed and sent two half-breed *engagés* west with the Indians to establish relations. Later, Thompson and Duncan Mc-Gillivray both tried to find passes through the Rockies easy enough to be turned into commercial routes. Although one or the other of them may have reached the western slope of the divide late in 1801, the distance from Montreal was so great that further explorations were suspended. Later, after the consolidation with the XY Company had released new energies, the moves resumed. In 1805 grouchy Simon Fraser built posts high up the Peace River and from them reached, the next year, the somberly beautiful country he called New Caledonia, the northern part of today's British Columbia.

In 1806, also, David Thompson was ordered to reestablish contact with the Kutenais. As a first step his half-breed clerk, Jacques Finlay, called Jaco, left Rocky Mountain House in the fall to open a usable horseback trail. The following spring, moving circumspectly so that neither Blackfeet nor rivals from the Hudson's Bay Company would realize what he was up to, Thompson followed with a party that included his half-Cree wife and their three small children. The backbone of the group was red-bearded Finan McDonald, six feet four inches of restless energy. After waiting two weeks for snow to melt in what later was named Howse Pass, the Thompson party floundered down Jaco's wretched trail beside steep Blaeberry River, torrential with spring runoff.

They reached the Columbia toward the end of June. Following directions the Kutenai emissaries had given him earlier, Thompson turned the group upstream to the river's head. In mid-July, near what is now called Lake Windermere, they started to build a post. Indians soon

appeared with word that forty-two Americans, two of them veterans of the Lewis and Clark expedition, were putting up a rival fort at the junction of the two "most southern & considerable branches of the Columbia," which might have meant the confluence of the Bitterroot and the Clark Fork, the Salmon and the Snake, the Clearwater and the Snake, or even the Snake and the Columbia. In any event, the Americans were not far away, because the Indians had with them a letter dated July 10, 1807, Fort Lewis, Yellow River, Columbia.

This letter, signed by a Lieutenant James Roseman and a Captain Zachary Perch, was addressed to "Foreigners who may at present be carrying on a Traffic with the Indians within our Territories," and claimed its authority from "General Braithwaite," commander of the newly acquired land north and west of the Illinois. The writers said that information picked up in the Mandan villages had led them to suspect the British might try to usurp the Columbia. This was not to be allowed. The United States owned the Pacific Northwest, and trade could be conducted only under certain stringent regulations, which the letter outlined.

United States Army records for 1807 contain no such names as Braithwaite, Perch, Roseman, or Fort Lewis. Thompson, of course, had no way of knowing this. He accepted the letter as genuine and in his journal noted that the American establishment, Fort Lewis, might give a new turn to events. But he also realized that bravado in the wilderness was not likely to be conclusive in the national capitals. He filed the letter without answering it and went on with his building. The Indians drifted back to report to the Americans.

Uncomfortable weeks followed. The Britons had nothing to eat save salmon turned flabby from spawning and meat from a few wild horses. Truculent Piegans of the Blackfoot confederation dropped by from time to time, angry that Thompson dared trade with their transmontane enemies. At one point they besieged the fort. For three weeks the defenders nibbled dried food and got water by lowering kettles over a steep bank to the river.

Having survived that, Thompson was unimpressed on December 24 to receive via the Indians another letter from the Americans. This one, dated September 29 at Poltito Palton Lake, was signed by Lieutenant Jeremy Pinch. There was no Pinch in the U.S. Army, either.

The new letter chided Thompson for his "tacit disrespect" in ignoring the first notice and threatened force if he did not heed regulations. This time Thompson sent off a reply, suggesting mildly that explorations made on the lower Columbia by Lieutenant Broughton of Vancouver's expedition perhaps gave prior rights to Great

Manuel Lisa

Britain. And that was the last he heard of the matter.

Who were the Americans? Did they choose spurious names because they were pretending an official authority that they did not possess? Were they members of the party Wilkinson had said he was sending out in the fall of 1805? If so, they had authority, and there is no clear reason why they did not use Wilkinson's name, rather than inventing a General Braithwaite.

Were they of Courter's (Courtin's) party? It had left the Maha villages early enough in 1807 to have reached the head of the Missouri by July 10, the date of the first letter. No other party of record could have gone so far so early. What of the two Lewis and Clark men? Were they from the contingent that had been sent down from the Mandan villages in the spring of 1805? Or had they gone to Courter's Maha camp from St. Louis in the fall of 1806? Or were they another invention by "Pinch-Perch"?

How far west did these mysterious Americans go? The locations used in the headings of their letters seem to be phonetic renderings of the names of two Indian bands, kindred of the Nez Perces, whom Lewis and Clark had encountered on and near the Clearwater River of west-central Idaho. One band, known today as the Palouse, the explorers called the Pelloat Pallahs. Thompson himself knew the Salmon River of central Idaho as the Pallahtopallah. (Compare Pinch's Poltito Palton.) The other band, today's Wallawallas, were Lewis and Clark's Yelletpo. (Compare with Zachary Perch's Yellow Lake.) Finally, the Snake River, which absorbs both the Salmon and the Clearwater in western Idaho, was then called Lewis's River. And that suggests Perch's Fort Lewis.

All these names occur well west of the Continental Divide. Courter, at least, would have had difficulty

reaching them by July 10, 1807. The Western names may have been bluff, however, picked up perhaps from the two Lewis and Clark veterans and used grandly in an effort to make Thompson think Americans had traveled farther west than was actually the case. Having dispatched the first letter from, say, the upper Missouri, the Americans may then have followed it across the divide into Flathead country before writing the second. At least Thompson noted in his journal that a group of Flatheads, cut off by Piegans from coming to him, had swung about to trade with the newcomers. So by winter they were somewhere beyond the divide, the first private group of Americans to have reached so far.

Tantalizing though the mystery is, the significant point is not identity, but timing. Formal exploration had accomplished as much as it was going to for the next several years, and in 1807 private adventurers were setting out to fill the gaps, thrusting southward into New Mexico as well as north toward the Columbia. In hindsight it seems historic inevitability, rather than coincidence, that United States and British fur gatherers planted themselves on Columbia drainage during the same summer months. Though they did not meet, the challenge was prophetic. Even in 1807 Louisiana, though bigger than the original United States, did not stretch far enough either north or south to satisfy American expansionism. If the headlong pace continued, so would conflicts with two familiar enemies, Great Britain and Spain.

Parties that provided history with clearer records were also moving up the Missouri in 1807. The first to leave St. Louis was one led by Manuel Lisa. His troubles with Wilkinson, mentioned earlier in this chapter, may have prompted him to abandon his proposed venture to Santa Fe with Clamorgan and Beaudoin and turn instead to the muddy river. On this enterprise his partners were William Morrison and Pierre Menard, both of Kaskaskia, Illinois. The Kaskaskia pair did not travel with the party's two keelboats but hired as their representative George Drouillard of the Lewis and Clark expedition. Other veterans of the great crossing whom Lisa signed on in St. Louis were John Potts and Peter Wiser.

On the way upstream the trapper-traders bucked the usual gamut of troubles—snags, blockading mats of driftwood, lashing hail and thunderstorms, agonizing mosquitoes. Men too were troublesome. When one deserted, Lisa's short patience snapped, and he ordered Drouillard to bring the fellow back dead or alive. Drouillard took orders literally and shot the man. The next year he was put on trial in St. Louis for murder and acquitted: he had been acting under orders, and besides, it was felt that *engagés* must accept the extraordinary discipline needed for mastering the wild Missouri River.

At the mouth of the Platte the group met John Colter, returning alone from his winter of trapping with Handcock and Dickson. Why he had left them is unknown. But the mountains gripped him still. He signed on with Lisa and faced upstream again.

The Arikaras, who lived in northern South Dakota in three villages of oval mud huts, met Lisa with ugly threats. He bluffed, cajoled, passed out gifts. Perhaps he sold them guns and hinted that another party coming behind had plenty of trade goods. For whatever reason (the matter has been endlessly debated), the Indians let him go and settled down to wait for the next group.

That one was a double-barreled affair. Part of it consisted of soldiers commanded by Ensign Nathaniel Pryor, who had been a sergeant with Lewis and Clark. Promoted, Pryor was responsible in 1807 for returning to his home the Mandan chief She-he-ke, who had gone downstream with the expedition the year before to visit President Jefferson. Accompanying this Government party and likewise bound for the Mandans was a trading group led by Auguste Pierre Chouteau, the eldest son of Indian agent Pierre Chouteau.

When the parties' keelboats neared the Arikara towns, several hundred inhabitants, fortified by many Sioux, swarmed to the riverbank. Shooting across the bows, they forced the travelers to halt. Discovering She-he-ke, the attackers demanded that Pryor hand him over, on the ground that they were at war with the Mandans. Pryor refused and barricaded the chief in the low-roofed cabin of one of the keelboats. Councils deadlocked and more shooting erupted, this time in earnest.

Possibly Lisa's sly propaganda had stirred the attack. Additional incentive came from a rascally French trader who lived among the Rees (Arikaras) and who wanted to make trouble for these potential rivals. He added inflammatory words. The Indians were not hard to arouse; they were feeling their oats and did not want either She-he-ke or supplies to reach the enemy Mandans. During the fifteen-minute exchange they killed three whites, wounded nine, one mortally, and drove the others back. This blow to American prestige inflamed every tribe along the middle river.

As the whites retreated, they met Robert McClellan and Ramsay Crooks moving upstream on a large keelboat with a strong force of eighty voyageurs, traders, and trappers. Size was no substitute for resolution, however. French-Canadian boatmen in general had no stomach for fighting. Fearful of disaster if they challenged the aroused Indians with so limp a crew, McClellan and Crooks changed their plans and dropped back downstream to trade with the less aggressive Indians between the Maha towns and the mouth of the Platte.

Save for Courter's party somewhere up ahead, Lisa now had a clear field. Toiling industriously, he reached the Yellowstone and ascended it to the mouth of the Bighorn in south-central Montana. This was the land of the Crow Indians, safer neighbors, as he may have learned from John Colter, than the Blackfeet who roamed the upper Missouri. The tribe might prove lucrative customers indeed, for they had learned trapping from Nor'Westers who occasionally wandered into their country. François Larocque, for instance, had visited the section with a Crow escort during the summer of 1805.

Using timber hewn from a grove of trees between the winding Yellowstone and the Bighorn, Lisa's voyageurs began erecting a fort he named Remón, or Raymond, for his small son in St. Louis. Before its walls were up, he sent out several men to find Indians and bring them in to trade. Not all the emissaries proved reliable. In order to curry favor with the Crows, one ferocious mulatto named Edward Rose gave away the samples he carried and on his return pummeled Lisa sorely for daring to criticize him. Fired, Rose went back to live with the Indians.

Two other scouts, George Drouillard and John Colter, repaid their *bourgeois* (leader) in far better fashion. Drouillard made two trips southward into the Bighorn Basin, making rough maps of the country he traversed. He was looking for Spaniards as well as Indians: Lisa, a Spaniard by blood, was still interested in opening trade with Santa Fe, even from the Yellowstone, which indicates the geographical haziness of the times. Drouillard returned to Fort Raymond with Indians, reports of beaver, and indications that the Crows traded directly either with New Mexicans or with Spanish-oriented Indians, a point Lisa kept remembering.

Colter's trip was even more phenomenal. Possibly alone but more likely with Indian guides, he rode and walked through the dead of a Rocky Mountain winter more than five hundred miles across several rugged ranges, with only thirty pounds of supplies on his back. Conceivably he also encountered some of Charles Courter's men and obtained directions and powder from them. (Query: How on earth did Courter's group support itself in the Montana Rockies without fresh supplies for nearly three years, as it seems to have done?)

Colter's itinerary cannot be accurately reconstructed, although many people have tried on the basis of vague lines William Clark sketched on his master map of the West after talking to the wanderer more than two years later in St. Louis. A few historians conjecture that he may have reached South Pass, at the southern extremity of Wyoming's Wind River Mountains. Others have him crossing directly over the Wind River Range—an almost incredible feat in winter—then traversing Jackson Hole and climbing over Teton Pass into eastern Idaho. Though he skirted Yellowstone Park, he did not see its geysers; the section later known as Colter's Hell embraces the rumbling thermal springs and sulphurous gas vents near today's Cody, Wyoming.

The tales he and Drouillard told, added to the results of the winter trade at the fort and of the spring trapping on nearby streams, put Lisa's imagination astir. If capital could be found, why not enlist a hundred or more men and fan them everywhere through the virgin mountains?

Drouillard and a few boatmen went with their bourgeois as he hurried the winter's harvest of pelts to St. Louis. Most of the other trappers stayed in the mountains. Searching for still more Indian customers, Colter traveled west toward the Continental Divide and perhaps crossed it. According to Thomas James, who heard the story from him the following year, he found five hundred Flatheads and started with them toward Fort Raymond. They had reached the Gallatin River and were headed toward Bozeman Pass when they were hit hard by fifteen hundred Blackfeet. Wounded in the leg early in the fight, Colter crawled into the brush and kept firing as fast as he could pour powder into his hot musket and ram home the balls. The uproar of the battle attracted three hundred Crows. They helped drive the Blackfeet away. The defeated did not forget.

Though wounded, Colter made his way alone to the fort and sat quietly while his leg healed. By the time the fall trapping season arrived, he was ready to go again. With John Potts he returned to the headwaters of the Missouri, this time to the Jefferson, where three years before, Lewis and Clark had not seen a single Indian.

This year, 1808, several hundred Blackfeet caught the two trappers. Recalling Colter's earlier bloodletting and resentful of whites' stealing their beaver and arming their enemies, the Indians decided to make a vivid object lesson. They robbed the pair of traps and furs, killed Potts when he resisted, and fixed their inventiveness on the survivor. Stripping him naked, they told him to start running. Eager young warriors, well armed, set out in pursuit. One outdistanced the others. Unable to gain on him, Colter whirled abruptly and managed to kill the

This first map of the Bighorn River was drawn in 1808 by William Clark, from information provided by George Drouillard. North is at top, toward which the Bighorn flows past the twisting Little Bighorn (center) to the Yellowstone (upper left corner). At left center, the "Stinking Water" (today's Shoshone River) flows into the Bighorn east of present Cody, Wyoming.

Indian with the latter's own spear. Then on he pounded to a river pool covered with driftwood. Diving under it, he found a tiny air pocket and stayed hidden in the icy water until dark. Naked alternately to the cold nights and the burning days, subsisting on roots, his feet lacerated by cactus, he spent a week (some accounts say nine or ten days) hobbling to the fort by the Bighorn.

Two thousand miles away, in St. Louis, Lisa raised the capital he needed by forming the St. Louis Missouri Fur Company, more familiarly the Missouri Fur Company. Among his new partners (Morrison and Menard stayed) were old Pierre Chouteau; Andrew Henry, a stalwart lead miner who came from the Ste. Genevieve district of Missouri; Reuben Lewis, brother of Meriwether; and William Clark. The last-named pair brought Governmental connections that today probably would be suspect.

As a reward for the transcontinental crossing, Meriwether Lewis had been appointed governor of Upper Louisiana (Missouri) Territory. William Clark was made brigadier general of its militia and agent for the Western Indians. Reuben Lewis, a competent young man, was his subagent. In 1808, when Lisa came out of the mountains, Reuben was working with Clark on the building of Fort Osage in western Missouri.

The new company, Reuben Lewis and William Clark among its directors, promptly executed with Governor Meriwether Lewis a lucrative contract for equipping one hundred and twenty militiamen to take the Mandan She-he-ke home. In addition to a seven thousand dollar fee, the company won Governor Lewis's promise not to issue licenses for other traders to go above the Platte River before the Missouri Fur Company had started.

The trading-trapping part of the expedition was composed of almost two hundred American backwoodsmen, French voyageurs, and a few Shawnee and Delaware Indian hunters. The combined groups floundered up the river in two dozen or more barges and keelboats.

The size of the expedition cowed the hostile Sioux—some of whom were carrying British flags—and the Arikaras. After the Indians had promised to be good, the traders left outfits with them and labored on. The militia delivered She-he-ke to his people and returned home. The others advanced a dozen or so miles beyond the Mandan and Minnetaree towns and in September, 1809, halted to build what was intended as their main post, Fort Mandan. There they were joined by various trappers, including Colter, who had stayed in the mountains, and from them learned that the Blackfeet would war on any Americans who ventured into the Three Forks area.

The need for furs to pay bills was so great that in spite of the discouraging reports, Andrew Henry and Pierre

Menard led horseback and boat parties through the icy fall weather to Fort Raymond. There they waited out the worst months of winter. At the first sign of spring, 1810, Colter guided them across Bozeman Pass to the Three Forks country—almost too soon, for several of the men suffered from snow blindness.

They built a crude stockade about two miles from the confluence of the three rivers (the Jefferson, the Madison, and the Gallatin) and scattered out to trap. On April 12, within ten miles of the fort, Blackfeet killed five hunters and made off with horses, skins, and many traps. A little later the savages caught George Drouillard and two Shawnees up the Jefferson a way, killed them, chopped off Drouillard's head, and disemboweled him.

Midway between the two encounters, John Colter decided he had stretched his luck far enough. On April 21 or 22 he left the mountains forever. The discouraged partners who remained behind sent out letters by him. Pierre Menard wrote gloomily to Pierre Chouteau that unless peace could be made with the Blackfeet, "it is idle to think of maintaining an establishment at this point." Reuben Lewis, writing to his brother Meriwether, blamed a familiar enemy: "I am confident that the Blackfeet are urged on by the Brittish traders. . . ."

Actually, the Blackfeet (or, more properly, the Piegans) were as furious at the English for arming the Western Indians as they were at the Americans. While Manuel Lisa had been struggling to master the Yellowstone and the upper Missouri, David Thompson of the North West Company had been unraveling the geographic and commercial puzzles of the upper Columbia. Although burning to learn whether the lower river would furnish a usable supply route to the Pacific, he first had to protect his flanks against the Americans. In the spring and early summer of 1808 he examined what is now northern Idaho; and when he at last had to leave to take out his furs over Howse Pass, he ordered big Finan McDonald to stay behind and spend the next trade season (1808–9) in the vicinity of present Libby, northwestern Montana.

After his return the next summer, Thompson worked deeper into Idaho. About the time Lisa's men were building Fort Mandan on the Missouri, the Nor'Westers started a post called Kullyspell House near the point where the Clark Fork pours into Pend Oreille Lake in northern Idaho. From there Thompson moved southeast up the Clark Fork into Montana and built Saleesh House (near today's Thompson Falls) for trade with the Flatheads, a fine, cleanly tribe with perfectly normal skulls.

Charles Courter (or Courtin), the Canadian who had sworn allegiance to the United States in order to ascend the Missouri, was somewhere east of him, perhaps in the

While She-he-ke the Mandan was in Washington, he was portrayed by Saint-Mémin.

vicinity of modern Missoula. In February, 1810, Courter was out in the broad central valleys of the mountains with some Flatheads, trapping beaver and hunting buffalo, the latter a vital source of dried provisions. Blackfeet, indifferent to the white man's nationality but not to his association with the enemy tribe, killed him and one Indian and wounded several more. Thompson helped recover some of the dead man's furs from the Flatheads and distributed the property among Indians and whites as equitably as he could. Courter's party evidently disintegrated after that.

For the time being, that ended competition from Americans west of the Continental Divide. Thompson again went out with his furs, leaving Finan McDonald behind. Like Courter, McDonald ran afoul of Blackfeet while out hunting buffalo with a band of Flatheads. McDonald was clearly a Britisher—but Blackfeet leaped on him too. His Flatheads, however, were more potent than Courter's. Armed with guns Thompson had brought them, they fought the Blackfeet to a standstill—a moral victory. In a fury those implacable savages shifted north to the Saskatchewan, determined to halt Thompson on his return and prevent his taking firearms to the Western tribes. Of that episode, more shortly.

The Americans under Henry and Menard at Three Forks had not even a moral victory for consolation. Disheartened, some of them followed John Colter's example and left the country. The others, led by Andrew Henry, decided to move south beyond reach of the Blackfeet. A likely section had been found in 1808 or 1809 by Lisa's wandering men, particularly Jean Baptiste Champlain

and Peter Wiser. Five or six days' travel up the Madison and across an easy pass to a tributary stream of the Snake, these scouts reported, would bring the men to an "illigable" place for a fort.

Just before the whites started, they had another tangle with the Blackfeet. One American died in exchange for twenty-two Indians—a victory of sorts, but it came too late to alter Henry's plans. He moved his crew up the grassy valley of the Madison toward either Targhee or Raynolds Pass, gentle gaps in the Continental Divide immediately west of today's Yellowstone Park. Along the way, Crow Indians stole most of their horses. Turning themselves into beasts of burden, the grumbling men moved on among sunny meadows and dark stands of evergreens to a point on Henrys Fork of the Snake a mile or two below present St. Anthony, Idaho. There they built a cluster of cabins since known as Henry's Fort.

How much farther they and their predecessors pushed remains unknown. They certainly touched the headwaters of the Green. Recognizing it as the beginning of an entirely new drainage system, they called it the Spanish River and wondered whether it might lead them to Santa Fe. (It wouldn't. They were confusing it with the Rio Grande.) Their guesses about the Snake, whose lower end Wiser and Colter had seen with Lewis and Clark, were sounder. Although the river flows south after absorbing Henrys Fork, the men knew—probably through Indian talk—that it bent west and north again to join the Columbia in what today is southeastern Washington. But they did not travel far enough along it to see the horrible lava canyons it hews through southern Idaho. They jumped to the natural conclusion that since its headwaters were gentle, the rest of its course, like the Missouri's, would also be navigable. After interviewing Henry in October, 1811, a reporter from the *Louisiana Gazette* stated that the easy terrain of the passes and the placidity of the waterways would make "intercourse with settlements which may be formed on the Columbia, more easy than between those on the heads of the Ohio, and the Atlantic states." Long after other mountain men had learned better, this geographic oversimplification continued to muddy the oratory of expansionist congressmen.

The shift in bases benefited Henry very little. Even for the Rockies, the weather was severe. Game vanished, and for long periods of time the men subsisted mainly on roots. Spring added torrential rains to the heavy runoff of snow water, so that trapping along the flooded streams was arduous. Although Henry succeeded in making forty packs of furs, a good haul, he went back to Fort Mandan sick of the mountains—so sick that he made scant effort to hold his group together for another season of trapping.

Lake
Athabaska

Ft. Chipewyan ■

ROCKY MOUNTAINS

Finlay R.

Parsnip R.

CONTINENTAL DIVIDE

INDEFINITE BOUNDARY

Peace R.

Athabaska R.

N. *Saskatchewan R.*

BLACKFEET CONFEDERACY

ATHABASKA PASS

BLOOD

□ Rocky Mtn. House

HOWSE PASS

Columbia R.

Blaeberry R.

BLACKFEET

BRITISH

Fraser R.

Thompson R.

Kootanae House □
Lake Windermere

KUTENAI

S. *Saskatchewan R.*

COAST RANGES

Nootka Sd.

VANCOUVER I.

OREGON

COUNTRY

SELKIRK MTS.

THOMPSON 1807-8

PIEGAN

NATURAL BOUNDARY

Wood R.

Columbia R.

Clark Fork

Kootenai R.

PACIFIC

OCEAN

Astoria
(Ft. George) ■

Ft. Clatsop ■

Spokane
House □
*Pend Oreille
Lake*
Thompson Falls →

Kullyspell
House

*Flathead
Lake*

Saleesh
House □

← *Great Falls*

Missouri R.

PALOUSE

CASCADE RANGE

Willamette R.

Columbia R.

Clearwater R.

WALLAWALLA

CAYUSE

NEZ PERCE

FLATHEAD

ROCKY

Clearwater R.

COAST RANGES

HELLS CANYON

Salmon R.

Bitterroot R.

Jefferson R.

Three Forks

Gallatin R.

Madison R.

Missouri R.

BOZEMAN PASS

Yellowstone R.

Ft.
Raymon

CROW

Boise R.

Lewis's (Snake) R.

Henry's Ft. ■

Henrys Fork

TARGHEE
PASS

TETON RANGE

Clarks Fork

COLTER 1807-8
(Conjectural)

Bighorn R.

Tongue R.

Powder R.

Colter's
Hell

UNION
PASS

INDEFINITE BOUNDARY

TETON
PASS

WIND RIVER RANGE

Wind R.

SHOSHONI

ROCKY MOUNTAINS

Green R.

SOUTH PASS

SPANISH POSSESSIONS

*Great Salt
Lake*

ATSINA

Some headed on their own toward St. Louis. A few started for Santa Fe—a mystery. What was their purpose? Did they arrive? No surviving record says.

Because Blackfeet had deflected his trappers southward, Lisa did not come into conflict with the Nor'-Westers beyond the Rocky Mountains. That clash was reserved for a man with a broader imagination and far greater resources, John Jacob Astor of New York.

Astor, who bought many furs each year in Montreal, was aware of Canadian dreams of supplying their western posts by riverways that opened into the Pacific. He knew of the sea otter trade based on Nootka. His agents were old hands in Canton, a market that the Montrealers could not exploit because of a monopoly held by the London-based East India Company, but to which Astor's ships regularly took choice pelts, ginseng root, and silver specie in exchange for tea and silk. Finally, he resented paying high prices in Montreal for skins obtained by the Canadians on United States soil south of the Great Lakes.

The reports brought back by Lewis and Clark of the fur-rich Rockies precipitated these varied elements into a plan for taking over the entire United States pelt trade from Michilimackinac Island west to the Columbia. The Canadians anticipated him, however. Before Astor could move toward the Great Lakes, the Montreal supply firms that controlled the North West Company welded the principal independents south of the border into a partnership called the Michilimackinac Company, which was capitalized for eight hundred thousand dollars, a sizable figure in terms of today's purchasing power. The year was 1806, the same year that these same men directed David Thompson to expand North West Company trade by carrying it across the Rockies toward the Pacific. The North West Company, incidentally, was capitalized for one million dollars.

Astor at first treated this power with gingerly respect. Having obtained in 1808 a charter for his American Fur Company, he went to Montreal, mentioned his new plans, and pointed out that *his* ships could get into China, whereas the Montrealers' could not. He then offered the Canadians five hundred and fifty thousand dollars for the Michilimackinac Company, plus another fifty thousand for a free hand on the lower Columbia.

The Montrealers rebuffed him. Reluctantly, then, Astor decided to challenge them. Through Russian officials in the United States, he offered to use his ships and merchandising connections in London to supply the Alaska posts of the Russian American Fur Company.

The theatre of the far-western fur trade of the Americans and British in the decade after Lewis and Clark is seen at the left.

(One offshoot of this was an agreement whereby the Russians let the Columbia alone; moving farther south, they established Fort Ross, or Fort Russia, a little north of Spanish San Francisco in 1812.) Astor began plans to build a sea-supplied headquarters fort at the mouth of the Columbia and early in 1809 sounded out Wilson Price Hunt, a young merchant of St. Louis, about leading an expedition overland to the Western river.

The wild gyrations that the Napoleonic wars brought to United States politics played into his hands. As difficulties grew with Great Britain and France, Congress invoked a series of nonimportation and embargo decrees. When it became impossible for the Canadians to import goods to Michilimackinac, the Montrealers turned to Astor, hoping that if an American were associated with them, the restrictions might be relaxed.

As part of his price for helping them around the Great Lakes, Astor demanded that the North West Company buy one third of the Columbia adventure, which by then he was calling the Pacific Fur Company. His idea, of course, was to keep them from competing with him on the Columbia. The Montrealers agreed tentatively, but their wintering partners, as actual traders in the wilderness were called, proved reluctant. They wanted all of the upper Columbia, not a mere third. Finally the winterers decided that the only way to attain the monopoly and still retain Astor's friendship at Michilimackinac was to go ahead with the deal and then quietly hold the Pacific Fur Company to the lower Columbia. Accordingly, they rushed an express west to Rainy Lake to intercept David Thompson, on his way east to attend the annual rendezvous at Fort William. The express ordered Thompson to return to the Columbia, do what he could to win the Indians, and stake out as much of the river as possible for Great Britain—and for themselves.

While hurrying obediently westward, Thompson ran into Piegan Indians aching to revenge the mauling Finan McDonald's Flatheads had given them earlier in the year. Rather than fight them, Thompson risked the Canadian winter to veer northward through what is now Jasper National Park. In January, 1811, he and his terrified voyageurs dragged sleds across Athabaska Pass and dropped down Wood River, reaching the Columbia where it makes its hairpin bend around the Selkirks. Soft snow pinned him there for several weeks. Then, as the ice began to break, he forced a way southward up the river and across the portages to Saleesh House on the Clark Fork in western Montana.

Since the members of Astor's overland party might come that way, he left them a note scrawled on a piece of board and struck for the coast with eight men, journeying by way of a new post that Jaco Finlay and Finan McDonald had built during the winter near the site of present-day Spokane. Riding on to the Columbia, he built a canoe. On his way to the ocean, he paused frequently to talk about trade—English trade—with every band of Indians he could induce to come near him.

On July 9, 1811, where the Snake River poured into the Columbia, he set up a small wooden stake bearing a gigantic ambition: "Know hereby that this country is claimed by Great Britain as part of its territories and that the N.W. Company of Merchants from Canada . . . do hereby intend to erect a factory. . . ." That done, his chanting voyageurs paddled on down the sun-smitten water to learn whether the sea party of Americans had arrived yet at the river's mouth.

Far behind, in New York, the fluctuating policies of the United States Government had altered matters again. Trade restrictions against foreigners had been relaxed, and the Montreal merchants had backed out of the deal with Astor. Grimly he prepared to fight. Because experienced fur men were hard to find in the Eastern United States, he brazenly hired his partners and best clerks from among the Nor'Westers' own disgruntled employees. Save for a great bear of a man named Donald McKenzie, all these Canadians, plus a few green American clerks, sailed from New York in September, 1810, aboard the ship Tonquin. McKenzie, meanwhile, was to travel overland with a party led by Wilson Price Hunt, who in 1810 agreed to take charge of it.

Rough weather around the Horn and explosive quarrels with the Tonquin's martinet captain, Jonathan Thorn, marred the seven months' sea passage. Eight men drowned in attempting to find a way across the Columbia's tumultuous bar. After unloading a supply of merchandise at a fort site on the south shore of the inner bay, Thorn recrossed the deadly shoals and sailed north to trade with the coastal Indians. At Nootka the natives surprised him and massacred the entire crew. It was a costly victory. A wounded white man crawled to the ship's powder magazine and blew the vessel, himself, and a crowd of prancing Indians into bits.

The Canadians at the new post, named Fort Astoria, had not yet heard of the loss when David Thompson appeared. They greeted him warmly as a former associate and perhaps as a new partner; after all, he had letters saying the North West Company owned a third of the enterprise. But the tales Thompson told of the poverty of the upper country did not deter them, and they went ahead with their plans for David Stuart to ignore the claim stake at the mouth of the Snake and build a post farther inland. The spot Stuart chose turned out to be at

This historic photograph of surveyors crossing the Canadian Rockies between the Saskatchewan and the Columbia Basin was taken at Jasper's House, an old stopping place for Hudson's Bay Company "expresses" near the Continental Divide.

the mouth of the Okanogan, a highly profitable district.

Gloom spread after Thompson and David Stuart had started upriver. Word of the *Tonquin* disaster trickled down the coast and so excited the local Indians that they began to act as though they meant to attack. Meanwhile, where was the party that Wilson Price Hunt supposedly was leading overland? Had some accident befallen it, too?

The overland group got off to a slow start. Instead of going directly to his jumping-off place in St. Louis, Hunt traveled first to Montreal to hire experienced voyageurs. He recruited one boatload there and continued to Mackinac. On Mackinac he hired more men and also picked up Ramsay Crooks, whom he had enlisted earlier. Not until September 3, 1810, at about the time the *Tonquin* was preparing to sail from New York, did the overlanders at last reach St. Louis. There they made efforts to strengthen their crew of timid voyageurs by hiring enough expert riflemen to guarantee passage through the lands of the hostile Indians of the Missouri.

Presumably Hunt asked William Clark about routes. As cartographer of the first crossing, Clark had sketched every mile of the way. On his return he had worked the rough charts into a master map designed to illustrate a narrative of the trip that Meriwether Lewis had planned to write. Lewis had never found time to finish it. During his governorship of Missouri Territory, he had run into severe political and financial storms. (One of the latter was connected with the expedition to return the Mandan

chief She-he-ke to his home.) Seeking to straighten out his troubles, Lewis had started for Washington over the Natchez Trace in September, 1809. Along the way he was either murdered or committed suicide. It is not likely the truth will ever be determined.

At Jefferson's request, Clark assembled his dead friend's notes and made arrangements for Nicholas Biddle of Philadelphia to put the material into publishable shape. (Various contretemps delayed publication until 1814.) Meanwhile, Clark had added to his map the data he had secured in 1808 from George Drouillard and in 1810 from John Colter.

As a Government employee, Clark should have given Hunt access to this material. But as a partner of the Missouri Fur Company, he was suspicious of Astor's intentions. Did Hunt mean to drop off some of his trappers in country claimed by the Missouri Fur Company? Would Clark's firm and Astor's clash on the Snake, where Andrew Henry had taken his party just that summer? Was it wise to give such information to competitors?

In the end Clark may have proved cooperative. Lisa did not. By spreading innuendo and rumor, he tried to keep Hunt from acquiring the trained men he needed. Hunt outmaneuvered him, mostly through the help of Joseph Miller, an associate of Ramsay Crooks's whom Hunt had also lined up earlier for the crossing. The adventurers then rowed four hundred and fifty miles up the Missouri to a spot well removed from temptations to desert, and one where they could support themselves during the winter by their hunting. At this camp they picked up still another associate of Crooks's, his former partner, Robert McClellan.

Hunt's head start worried Lisa. He knew that Crooks and McClellan suspected him, perhaps wrongly, of having incited Sioux Indians to cut them off from the upper river in 1809. He feared that the Astorians might now repay him in kind. Besides, if the river Indians were hostile, the more guns the whites faced them with, the better. Lisa had only twenty hands, whereas the others had sixty. Driving those twenty prodigiously throughout the spring of 1811, he succeeded in overtaking the Astorians eleven hundred or so miles upstream from St. Louis. They did not make him welcome—at one point pistols were drawn but not fired—and in stiff unfriendliness the rivals rowed and towed their clumsy keelboats up opposite sides of the river to the Arikara villages just below the present North Dakota–South Dakota border.

Hunt, meanwhile, had met and hired first two and then three experienced hunters descending from the mountains. As Colter had done earlier, the five told him dire tales of Blackfeet. The three hired last added a solution. They had wintered with Andrew Henry on Henrys Fork of the Snake, and they told Hunt (as Henry himself a few months later told the *Louisiana Gazette*) that the Snake was navigable to the Columbia. Furthermore, the trio said, they could lead the party to the Snake by a route far enough south to avoid the Blackfeet. But to make the trip, the party would have to switch its baggage to horses.

Hunt's decision to leave the river turned Lisa almost friendly. He offered to speed the Astorians out of his country by selling them several horses he had at Fort Mandan, two hundred miles farther up the Missouri. Crooks and a small party fetched these back, while Hunt dickered for more animals with the Arikaras. All told, the horse buying consumed a month, and during the long days the Astorians unquestionably heard a great deal of shoptalk about the newest developments in the West.

One item concerned the Santa Fe trade, a recurrent interest of Lisa's. In August of the preceding year (1810) one of his best men, Jean Baptiste Champlain, had left Fort Mandan with a score of hunters to work southward along the eastern toes of the Rockies. Early in the spring of 1811 he returned for supplies. He brought exciting news with him. On the Arkansas River (probably in the vicinity of present-day Pueblo, Colorado), his party had opened trade with Arapaho Indians and from them had learned that Santa Fe was within reach. To Lisa he now proposed a three-way venture. He would return with his men to the South Platte River near the site of today's

Robert Stuart

Denver and there split his party. Some would trap in the Colorado Rockies; some would trade with the Arapahoes. And some would venture into New Mexico.

Lisa agreed. During the winter word had reached St. Louis that a revolt in northern Mexico—*el grito de Dolores* of Father Miguel Hidalgo—had spread triumphantly into Texas. If it had reached New Mexico as well, the rebels might welcome outside traders. Champlain's men would be the first on the scene, save perhaps for a small group of Missourians led by a man named McLanahan and guided by a Spaniard called Manuel Blanco. This party, almost unknown today, had left Missouri late in 1809 and had not been heard of since. In any event, it was not potent enough to be a threat, and the Spanish plum just might be Lisa's for the picking.

Actually, the Mexican revolt had been temporarily strangled, but the men on the Missouri did not know that. Anyway, the matter was of only academic interest to Hunt's Astorians. August was at hand, and the party's sixty-two men, one Indian woman, and two children (the family of interpreter Pierre Dorion) had far to go before winter. Loading their equipment on eighty-two pack horses, they plodded west and southwest through searing heat to Wyoming's Wind River. Game disappeared. From Snake Indians they picked up along the way, they learned that buffalo abounded on the other side of the mountains at the head of Green River, or, as Hunt called it in his journal, the Spanish River. They tugged their sore-backed horses over Union Pass to the Green. They then dried three tons of meat, limped on northwest, crossing over Teton Pass, and in an October snowstorm reached Andrew Henry's deserted cabins on Henrys Fork.

Navigable water! Heartily sick of their horses, the canoe-oriented voyageurs hollowed several pirogues out of cottonwood logs. Five men (including Joseph Miller) dropped out to trap, as three others had done earlier. The rest joyfully launched their little fleet, expecting to finish the journey with ease.

The appalling lava canyons of southern Idaho shattered the hope. One man drowned; several canoes were lost. Convinced at last that the Western rivers were not as amenable to water travel as those in the East, the party cached its baggage, broke into sections, and groped ahead on foot. Cold, hunger, deep snow, desertions, and more deaths racked them. The first small detachment reached Astoria in January, 1812. Hunt arrived with the main section on February 15. Crooks and John Day, left behind because of illness, did not appear until May.

By that time another supply ship had arrived from New York, and the Astorians were energetically preparing to open trade with the Russians and spread posts throughout the Columbia. The activity did not impress Crooks and McClellan. The loss of the *Tonquin* and competition from the North West Company would delay profits for a long time, and the Indians they had seen on the way west did not strike them as promising customers. They decided to surrender their shares in the company and return home, traveling with young Robert Stuart, who, assisted by three survivors of the westbound crossing, had been delegated to carry dispatches to Astor.

Nothing in particular happened until the group reached southern Idaho. There they encountered four of their detached trappers, including Miller, who had roamed far and wide before being stripped of everything they owned by Arapahoes. There, too, Stuart heard from an Indian of a short cut around the southern base of the Wind River Mountains, the famed South Pass of later emigrations. Augmented by Miller (the other trappers stayed behind), the party pressed toward the gap.

Horse-hungry Crow Indians frightened them northward toward Hunt's trail. The evasive action proved useless: the Crows followed and made off with every animal. Quarreling at times and once on the starved edge of cannibalism, the whites walked back across Teton Pass, then veered south again. On October 18, 1812, about twenty miles southeast of modern Pinedale, Wyoming, they encountered a village of destitute Snakes.

From these Indians Stuart's group acquired a single horse and several items of information that indicate how amazingly some kinds of news traveled from tribe to tribe. They heard of the movements of certain deserters from Hunt's westbound party who had pilfered its bag-gage caches. They learned that Lisa's man, Jean Baptiste Champlain, and a few of his hunters had been slain by Arapahoes on the Arkansas River.

Lisa also learned of Champlain's disaster at about the same time. He had hoped for better reports. Blackfeet, the accidental burning of twelve thousand dollars in supplies at a post among the Sioux, poor fur prices, the difficulty of obtaining goods from England because of the embargo, and mutual ill feeling among his partners had gradually sapped the company's strength. The Arikaras had brought in very few skins during the winter of 1811–12, and the once-friendly Minnetarees near Fort Mandan, inflamed by British whispers, had turned hostile. Trying desperately to recoup, Lisa had built a new post, Fort Manuel, twelve miles above the Arikara towns. From there, in September, 1812, he had dispatched Charles Sanguinet and two *engagés* southward to learn why no word had arrived from Champlain.

He had also instructed Sanguinet to open trade relations with New Mexico in case Champlain had failed. This last was important. As Lisa had learned in St. Louis, nine or ten Missourians led by Robert McKnight, James Baird, and Samuel Chambers were even then bound for Santa Fe. Lisa did not want them to establish themselves before he could counter the move.

Sanguinet never reached New Mexico. Somewhere in Wyoming, Indians told him more about Champlain's disaster than Stuart knew. The trader-trappers had fought with Indians. The leader and several men were dead. The survivors had cached their furs and scattered. Some were still in the mountains. Though Sanguinet did not know this, Ezekiel Williams, perhaps traveling alone, had started east for help. Others of the disintegrating party had headed toward Santa Fe. Like the New Mexico roamers from Andrew Henry's dissolving Snake River brigade, these last left no recoverable records.

Probably Sanguinet was wise when he decided not to follow. For after the McKnight-Baird-Chambers group reached the New Mexico capital, Spanish officials took them under arrest to Chihuahua and imprisoned them there for nine years.

Aware only that Champlain and some of his men were dead, Stuart's party led its lone horse eastward through the broad, bleak wastes of South Pass. After sitting out the winter in two different Wyoming bivouacs—Arapahoes frightened them from the first—the men resumed their long journey down the Platte in March, 1813. On nearing the Platte's confluence with the Missouri, they met traders who told them that another war with Great Britain had been turning the Mississippi Valley upside down for almost a year.

Eroded plains country, Platte River Basin, Nebraska

"In regard to this extensive section of country, I do not hesitate in giving the opinion, that it is almost wholly unfit for cultivation, and of course, uninhabitable by a people depending upon agriculture for their subsistence. . . . the scarcity of wood and water, almost uniformly prevalent, will prove an insuperable obstacle in the way of settling the country. . . . The whole of this region seems peculiarly adapted as a range for buffalos, wild goats, and other game. . . ."

Major Stephen H. Long, U.S. Topographical Engineers, *General Description of the Country Traversed by the Exploring Expedition,* 1819–20

CHAPTER FIVE

WAR AND DEPRESSION

1810-1821

Doubling the geographic area of the country through the Louisiana Purchase seemed to reduce in proportion the wits of some frontiersmen. Local stump orators forgot that they had recently been agitating for a separate republic west of the Allegheny Mountains and began crying instead for still greater expansion by the Stars and Stripes, an irresistible surge (in their minds) that would easily brush away the Spaniards from the South, the British from the North, and the Indians from wherever they were.

A seething economic discontent gave dangerous substance to the ranting. The very fertility of the Midwestern land was mocking the thousands of farmers it had lured from the East. The eager newcomers had produced such an abundance of grain and salted pork, of rice and cotton and hemp, that they could not sell it all. Even New Orleans, the gateway that once had promised so much, turned gray. Many an anxious farmer made the long, dangerous trip by flatboat only to catch yellow fever or some other tropical disease; others were robbed by land pirates during the ride back over the Natchez Trace. And for what? Prices in New Orleans were almost as low as in Cincinnati, in the main because of the annual glut from upriver, but also because of England's blockade of the principal receiving ports in Napoleonic Europe. Emotionally speaking, England was a more satisfying villain to blame than was overproduction.

The only answer that many ill-educated husbandmen had for the problem of dropping farm prices was to raise still more crops. Children of the "movers" who had poured across the Alleghenies during the last quarter of the eighteenth century acted in typical fashion during the first decades of the nineteenth. They cleared trees from a few acres (or had slaves do it in the South), exhausted the soil through a few years of careless farming, sold the holding, and looked for another place, shouting meanwhile at their Government for help in reaching new markets and opening new land. Since many political philosophers of the time believed that the country's strength rested on a base of sturdy small farmers, the Government was inclined to listen.

The Louisiana Purchase did not suit the demands for fresh land: most of it was too far away and too barren to be attractive. Farmers were still bound to the past and set in their ways, not yet ready to change their methods to adapt to the new conditions imposed by the new land that was available. After centuries of seeing crops spring riotously from the leaf-fertilized soil of forest clearings, pioneer agriculturists had grown convinced that deciduous trees were essential to good earth. They shied away from prairies, whose heavy sod was hard for their primitive plows to break. They wanted ready timber for their cabins and split rail fences. And finally, for the sake of future sales appeal, land clearers and speculators both wanted traditional types of soil.

If the Louisiana Purchase was ruled out, only three sources of land remained. One was the fertile wedge of the Ontario Peninsula between Lakes Huron and Erie, across from the ambitious ports of Buffalo, Erie, Ashtabula, and Cleveland. A second, particularly tempting to the cotton planters in the South, was Spain's long crescent around the northern circle of the Gulf—East and

West Florida, and Texas beyond the Sabine River.

Defenseless West Florida, indeed, proved irresistible. It bordered the Mississippi from the 31st parallel to the Gulf, save for the enclave of New Orleans, and thus was an affront to every American descending what he deemed to be his river. In September, 1810, a gang of highjackers —or patriots, depending on one's view—decided to remedy the matter. Arguing, without much justification, that the Louisiana Purchase extended east to the Perdido River (the western border of today's Florida), they seized the Spanish fort at Baton Rouge, killing one of its commanders. They then declared West Florida independent of Spain and petitioned the United States for annexation. President Madison promptly obliged them.

The acquisition was so easy that an ex-governor of Georgia, George Mathews, began, with Madison's tacit blessing, to create a filibuster army for occupying East Florida. Farther west, at Natchitoches on the Red River, still other freebooters cast yearning eyes across Wilkinson's neutral ground, toward Texas.

More immediately available than either Florida, Texas, or Ontario was the third beckoning source of land—the last Indian territory east of the Mississippi. The beleaguered red men proved easy prey. Government negotiators, the most adroit of whom was William Henry Harrison, Governor of Indiana Territory, split the tribes into factions, filled rival chiefs with whisky, tempted their followers with promises of annuities, and in the fourteen years between the Treaty of Greenville (1795) and the Treaty of Fort Wayne (1809) finagled forty-eight million acres from the aborigines. Between 1802 and 1806, comparable amounts were taken from the Civilized Nations of the South.

Belated resistance to the land-grabbing brought into prominence two Shawnee brothers: a homely, one-eyed mystic called the Prophet, and austere Tecumseh, invested by history with the dignity of a lost cause nobly handled. Where Tippecanoe Creek runs into the Wabash River in Indiana, the brothers in 1808 founded a sprawling village of bark houses named Prophet's Town. From that headquarters each in his own way worked to knit his disorganized people into an effective whole.

Delegates from hundreds of miles away flocked to the village to hear the Prophet's fiery sermons about rejecting American goods, especially whisky, and regaining strength by a return to the simple ways of their ancestors. Tecumseh, on the other hand, relied on diplomacy. He traveled tirelessly from tribe to tribe, urging unity. To bands west of the Mississippi that he could not reach in person, he sent messengers preaching the same urgent theme. He regularly crossed the Detroit River to Fort Malden,

Canada, and there he conferred with Matthew Elliott, who was British Superintendent of Indian Affairs.

Tecumseh's goal was the worn dream of an independent Indian nation between the Ohio River, the upper lakes, and the upper Mississippi. The idea appealed to the Canadians. Such a buffer state would let them control the Great Lakes waterway to the St. Lawrence, would protect the Ontario Peninsula, and would leave the northern fur trade of the United States tributary to Montreal.

Open support of the plan by the British would involve indefensible meddling with United States Indian affairs. Officially, therefore, the British were circumspect. They merely passed out presents of guns, blankets, and hardware at an annual summer rendezvous at Malden and called it a nonpolitical gesture of good will. Still, the Indians concluded that if trouble arose with the Americans, such generous friends would come to their support.

Tecumseh believed the same thing, evidently on the strength of promises from Matthew Elliott. But he did not wish to strike until he had shored up his proposed Indian confederation as strongly as possible. To that end he told his impatient followers to restrain themselves while he visited the Southern Indians during the fall of 1811 and enlisted their support.

He was being totally anachronistic. By 1811 Indian population in the Old Northwest had dwindled to an estimated forty thousand. Americans numbered more than half a million, most of them strung out near the Ohio River. Between October, 1810, and May, 1811, twelve hundred flatboats, keelboats, and broadhorns floated past Louisville, loaded with emigrants. During the same period, surveys were completed for a graded, all-weather road across the mountains from Cumberland, Maryland, to navigable water on the Ohio at Wheeling, (West) Virginia; in April contracts were let for the first ten miles. Also in 1811, at Pittsburgh, Nicholas Roosevelt, supported by Robert Fulton and Robert Livingston, launched the first successful steamboat of the Western waters, the *New Orleans*.

It was a year long remembered. Vast floods in the spring were followed by unprecedented epidemics. Hordes of squirrels marched insanely from north to south, perishing by tens of thousands as they swam the Ohio. An eclipse and a comet spread wonders through the September sky. As the steamboat neared the mouth of the Ohio, the earth was wrenched by the most terrible quake in the history of the Mississippi Valley. John Latrobe, Nicholas Roosevelt's brother-in-law, wrote that the Ohio was so agitated that many passengers aboard the *New Orleans* "experienced for the moment a nausea resembling seasickness." Many terror-stricken people, linking the steamer's churning paddle wheels to the groaning of the earth, fled as she approached. Chickasaw Indians from the riverbanks near Memphis interpreted the appearance of the snorting monster as a promise of evil to come.

At a great gathering of Southern Indians in Alabama in October, 1811, Tecumseh cried out for a defensive war. No immediate pressure was on the Cherokees and Choctaws, however, and they held back. And the Creeks were fatally divided between "white" towns that favored the Americans and hoped for a peaceful solution, and "red" towns of primitives who hung red war clubs outside their stockades as emblems of hatred and determination.

A leader of the primitives who listened to Tecumseh was William Weatherford. His father was a Scottish trader, his mother the quarter-breed half sister of Alexander McGillivray. That one-eighth Creek heritage was more real to Weatherford than his seven-eighths white strain. He took the name Red Eagle and said that when the time came, he and his followers would join Tecumseh.

Unfortunately for their planning, William Henry Harrison took advantage of Tecumseh's absence in the South to move a thousand militiamen against Prophet's Town at the mouth of Tippecanoe Creek. The Prophet determined to meet the thrust by attacking first. Working himself into one of his mystic frenzies, he promised his spellbound warriors that bullets fired by their enemies would turn as soft as sand. Then, just as the American camp was beginning to stir in the predawn darkness of November 7, 1811, he unleashed his braves.

The militiamen held. In the first glimmer of light, Harrison launched a bayonet countercharge. The Indians fled, pursued by mounted dragoons until marshes checked the horsemen. Harrison burned Prophet's Town, loaded his supply wagons with wounded, and marched, hungry and cold, back to his capital at Vincennes.

Tippecanoe was no clear-cut victory, but the governor's dispatches made what had really been a defensive stand sound like a triumph. Furthermore, his flat declaration that the Indian village had been full of English arms gave Henry Clay and the War Hawks of the new Congress an emotional rallying point. The War Hawks, Southern and Western congressmen united against the appeasement policies of mercantile New England, were convinced that England and her reluctant ally, Spain, were too engrossed by Napoleon to pay effective attention to the New World. Canada would tumble at a push.

By December, 1811, war was inevitable. To create diversionary troubles for Spain, Secretary of State James Monroe resorted to intrigue. George Mathews was encouraged to hurry his preparations for raids on East

Territorial changes in the Southeast, 1810–21, included the purchase of Florida and the admittance of three states.

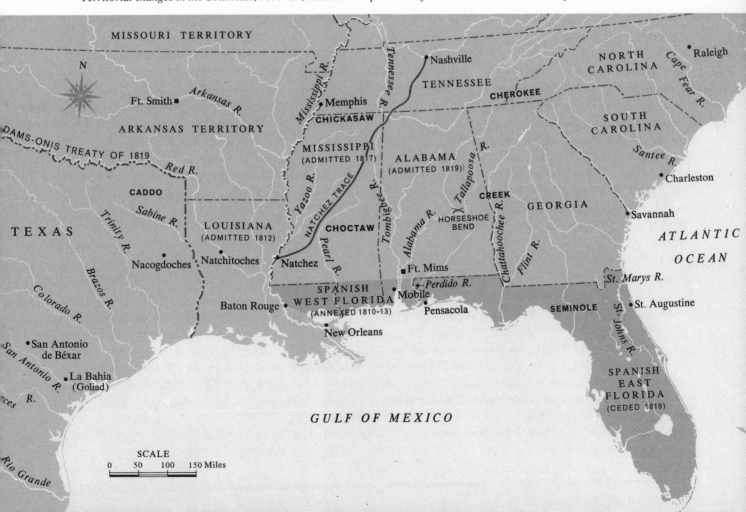

Florida. Of more significance to the West, Monroe also granted audiences to José Bernardo Gutiérrez de Lara, a blacksmith and small merchant from Revilla (today's Ciudad Guerrero), on the lower Rio Grande.

Gutiérrez had survived the crushing of Father Hidalgo's 1810 revolution in northern Mexico. Backed by a handful of other destitute conspirators, he determined to carry on the work until Mexico was independent of Spain. Surely, he reasoned, the United States, home of freedom, would help him. Acting entirely on his own, for no revolutionary junta existed to lend legitimacy to his acts, he journeyed to Washington to present his case.

Monroe made grandiose oral promises—up to fifty thousand troops, as Gutiérrez understood him—but demanded in return that all Texas as far west as the Rio Grande be ceded to the United States. The idealistic blacksmith was horrified. He refused the deal but let Monroe pay his passage by ship back to New Orleans.

From New Orleans, Gutiérrez and other conspirators went by keelboat up the Red River to Natchitoches. The frontier town teemed with plotters—a few men who wanted to fight for freedom, but more who wanted plunder, land grants, and excitement. Gutiérrez picked up a discontented United States Army lieutenant named Augustus Magee and with his help formed an insurgent "army." Late in July, 1812, word reached them that the United States had declared war on Great Britain. Reasoning that Spain would surely be involved and that aid from America would follow, they marched for the Sabine.

Almost unopposed, they swept through Nacogdoches to La Bahia (today's Goliad, Texas). There royalist forces from San Antonio de Béxar besieged them in the town's massive stone fortress. Magee died, either of tuberculosis or, possibly, of self-administered poison. Gutiérrez, who supposedly knew nothing of tactics, engineered a breakthrough and with his eleven hundred ragged followers marched triumphantly on to San Antonio. There the rebel leaders celebrated at a dinner in a mission called the Alamo, which had been turned into a military garrison. Unhappily, Gutiérrez's victory-crazed men got the notion that he meant to pardon the governor and sixteen royalist officers whom they had captured. A hundred self-appointed avengers seized the prisoners, took them outside of town, and butchered them in cold blood.

Texas was free, but Gutiérrez meant to link her to an independent Mexico without rewarding the Americans who had helped him. Furious, the freebooters deposed him and then came to the end of their own road. Spain had not declared war on the United States, and no help arrived from the East. A supporting revolution in southern Mexico flickered out. In August, 1813, a thousand

hard-bitten Spanish regulars smashed the by now completely disorganized rebel forces in vicious retaliation.

Spain's refusal to become involved in the war upset other plans. Even before hostilities opened with Great Britain, George Mathews had to be called back out of East Florida, where he had laid siege to St. Augustine. Later, after war was declared, Madison endeavored to bully the Spanish into fighting by ordering Andrew Jackson of Tennessee to move two thousand militia through bitter cold to New Orleans to support an attack on Pensacola and Mobile. Spain still declined to fight. Confusion in the War Department, lack of support in the North for the conflict, and wirepulling by that perpetual schemer, General James Wilkinson, who wanted no popular rival in New Orleans, led to the cancellation of Jackson's campaign. His militia, waiting at Natchez for marching orders, were instructed instead to disband, five hundred military miles from home.

Declining to obey, Jackson took the men home at his own expense. As he marched on foot beside his soldiers, joking with the footsore and encouraging the sick in their jolting ambulance wagons, someone remarked, "He's tough. Tough as hickory." The label stuck. Old Hickory he became, first to the unwanted column of soldiers and then, in the speeding of the years, to the entire nation.

Northward, the war against Canada limped on the leaden feet of ineptitude. America's obvious strategy was to strike first at Canada's lifeline up the St. Lawrence and through the lakes. With appalling inefficiency, two columns prepared to do just that—one to move along the Hudson River–Lake Champlain route toward Montreal, the other to cross the Niagara River. Long before either force was ready to move—even before war was formally declared—sixty-year-old William Hull, Governor of Michigan Territory, was instructed to plan an invasion of Canada from Detroit. The Government hoped to gain votes and money by snipping off long ravelings of wilderness territory, although the action could hardly inflict lasting damage on the enemy's main military fabric.

Hull recognized the dangers in the plan. Unless the United States first won control of Lake Erie, he would have to be supplied by a long, miry road cut through the Indian-infested forests of western Ohio. Political strategists brushed the objection aside. Yielding, Hull picked up his command at Urbana, Ohio. When war came, he was chopping a route northward in steaming rains.

On July 12 he crossed the Detroit River and occupied Sandwich (modern Windsor, Ontario), but was reluctant to tackle the big guns of Fort Malden guarding the entrance to Lake Erie. As he fiddled indecisively, trying to build his courage by chewing increasingly large cuds of

Sites of events in the strife-torn Northwest, from 1808 through the battles of the War of 1812, are seen above.

tobacco, trouble was brewing for him far to the north.

The British garrison at St. Joseph Island, in the St. Marys River between Lake Huron and Lake Superior, received word of the war long before American messengers reached rival Michilimackinac, some seventy canoe miles to the southwest, around Point Detour. The commander at St. Joseph, Captain Charles Roberts, at once reinforced his inadequate handful of regulars with local products. The North West Company trader on the island, John Askin, Jr., enlisted two hundred and eighty Ottawa and Chippewa Indians. Flamboyant Robert Dickson added one hundred and thirty Sioux, Menominees, and Winnebagos he had brought from Minnesota and northwestern Wisconsin in anticipation of trouble. Canadian fur men added one hundred and fifty French voyageurs.

On July 16, Roberts put his men and two six-pounder cannons aboard a seventy-ton brig requisitioned from the North West Company. Indians and voyageurs traveled by canoe and barge. They landed undetected on the back side of Mackinac at about 3 A.M. on the seventeenth and silently dragged their artillery to a hilltop above the American fort. When Lieutenant Porter Hanks of the garrison realized how completely he had been surprised, he surrendered himself and his sixty-one men.

Two Chippewa Indians carried the word to Hull. He was distraught. With Mackinac fallen, the garrison at

Fort Dearborn, Chicago, could no longer be supplied. Hull sent an Indian messenger west through the Michigan woods with orders for Captain Nathan Heald to withdraw to Fort Wayne. For himself the unhappy general dreamed up nightmares of Indians and voyageurs swarming out of Mackinac onto his rear.

Savages closer at hand caused more realistic trouble: Tecumseh blocked a supply train at the River Raisin, thirty-five miles south of Detroit, and then proceeded to whip the relief column that Hull dispatched to its rescue. Completely unnerved, the general withdrew back across the Detroit River into the town of Detroit.

Discovering quickly that the proposed American invasion of Canada by way of Niagara was far from ready, Major General Isaac Brock shifted his force of British troops against Hull. Tecumseh's Indian auxiliaries closed around Detroit's land approaches, and on August 16 the Canadian artillery began to boom. The combination of events was too much for Hull. The entire front of his jacket befouled with tobacco juice, he surrendered.

One day earlier, acting against the advice of the Chicago traders, Nathan Heald followed Hull's order to abandon Fort Dearborn. Loading women and children into wagons, he marched the garrison out through the sand dunes. His vanguard consisted of thirty or so friendly Miami Indians under William Wells, a relative of Heald's wife and Anthony Wayne's most famous Indian scout during the Ohio campaigns nearly two decades earlier.

Even Wells could be duped. Two miles outside the fort, where hot, deep sand dragged at the feet of horses and men, he walked into an ambush of four hundred Potawatomis. A few of his Miamis escaped. Wells died. So did all but eighteen whites, either in battle or during the hard captivity that followed.

Winter intensified the calamities. Belated American thrusts through Lake Champlain and across the Niagara River fizzled. When Harrison marched north to retake Detroit, he was bogged down in the vicinity of modern Toledo by miserable weather, professional jealousies, and high-level bungling, some of it his own. One of his columns, disobeying orders, reached the River Raisin. There British regulars and Indians surrounded it, killed many men, and captured the rest. Five hundred prisoners were herded to Detroit under appalling conditions. Sixty-four seriously wounded men were left behind in crude huts. Triumphant Indians, crazed with whisky, set fire to the camp, roasted most of the invalids, and tomahawked and scalped those who managed to crawl outside.

The British victories excited the Indians of the entire West. Minnetarees on the upper Missouri drove Manuel Lisa down the river to the vicinity of Council Bluffs. Robert Dickson roamed through northern Illinois, Wisconsin, and southern Minnesota, recruiting red auxiliaries. With a powerful Sauk chief named Black Hawk as his second-in-command, he led them east to join an attack the British intended to launch at the coming of good weather against the defensive forts Harrison was building around the southwestern curve of Lake Erie.

Misinterpreting Dickson's intent, the citizens of St. Louis shivered with dread lest he come to attack them. They had reason to be fearful. The outlying settlements of Missouri were regularly ravaged. Indian pressures mounted so that the commander at Fort Madison, Iowa, burned down his own post and fled. The only answer the frontier militia was able to make was to destroy an inoffensive Indian village at Peoria, Illinois. Fortunately for the isolated towns of the Midwest, traders and Government agents like Thomas Forsythe of Peoria, old Nicholas Boilvin, recently fled from Prairie du Chien, and Manuel Lisa on the Missouri were able to win the support of a few local bands and keep others neutral.

In the South the fury of Weatherford's "Red Stick" Creeks sent some of the peaceful faction, including many half-bloods, hurrying with their families and slaves to shelter with the whites huddled inside half-breed Samuel Mims's stockade north of Mobile. Their guard consisted of seventy Louisiana militiamen, commanded by Major Daniel Beasley, another Creek half-breed. The major's security measures were careless. Weatherford's warriors surprised the stockade on the sultry noon of August 30, 1813, and cut down or burned four hundred or so persons in what was perhaps the most dreadful bloodletting in the long roll of United States Indian massacres.

The private affairs of John Jacob Astor, meanwhile, fared no better. Late in 1810 President Madison had issued a proclamation threatening once again to end commerce between this country and Great Britain. This sent the Montreal owners of the Montreal-Michilimackinac Company (successors to the Michilimackinac Company) back knocking again at Astor's door. Always before, he and other American fur traders had been able to take some goods into the Indian country of the Old Northwest, partly because the United States War Department wanted the tribes supplied. The Canadians assumed that if Astor became their partner in a new company, they would still be able to maintain their trade south of the border. He agreed to their proposal but drove a hard bargain, offering only his U.S. citizenship and connections in return for, roughly, a half interest in a new organization to be known as the South West Company, which would trade south and west of the Great Lakes. Carefully excluded from the agreement were the Missouri and Columbia rivers. In those areas, competition between Astor and the Canadians would remain wide open.

Events did not work out as the Canadians had anticipated. No exceptions were allowed to the Non-Intercourse Act that followed Madison's proclamation. The South West Company was helpless. The only merchandise that reached the Indians during the winter of 1811–12 was brazenly smuggled to them by Robert Dickson and his fellow Britons. Dickson, of course, used the situation as one more proof to the Indians that their true friends were the British, not the Americans. It helped him mightily, after war broke out, in recruiting warriors for the attack on Mackinac and the fighting around Detroit, and in holding United States influence along the border to zero.

The war turned matters in the Pacific Northwest equally bleak for Astor. There the traders of his Pacific Fur Company had scattered far and wide through the interior: along Oregon's Willamette River; at the mouth of the Okanogan in Washington; beside the Thompson River of today's British Columbia. They put up posts cheek by jowl with the North West Company houses at Spokane and on the Clark Fork of western Montana. They prowled the Clearwater River of Idaho and pushed south along the Snake to the mouth of the Boise and beyond.

Because the Indians in the latter two regions proved reluctant to undertake the work of hunting beaver,

Donald McKenzie grew disgusted and went to Spokane to discuss the problem with the Astorian bourgeois there, John Clarke. When he arrived, he found that a Nor'-Wester named John George McTavish had just come across the Canadian Rockies to his own company's nearby Spokane House with triumphant word that war had broken out and that a North West Company ship, the *Isaac Todd*, armed with cannons and carrying letters of marque, was on its way from London to seize Astoria.

McKenzie rushed from Spokane to Astoria, which he reached on January 15, 1813, to sound a warning. Unhappily, Wilson Hunt, who had ultimate authority on the coast, was away in Alaska aboard the ship *Beaver,* trading with Governor Alexander Baranov of the Russian American Company and loading sealskins for transport to Canton. In Hunt's absence, Duncan McDougall was in charge on the Columbia. He and McKenzie, both of them of Canadian birth, decided to evacuate Astoria before it could be captured. McKenzie spent most of February paddling back upstream to alert the other partners, gather his and Clarke's furs, and buy the necessary horses—three hundred or four hundred head.

He was in a hurry, and the Indians' refusal to sell because of certain quarrels exasperated him. Finally, after an almost fruitless spring, he took to pointing at an animal and making an offer; if the owner refused, McKenzie shot the horse, paid the original price, and let his men eat the meat. Clarke, too, asked for trouble by publicly executing a thief who had stolen a silver goblet. Instead of being cowed by these formidable gestures, the Indians grew ugly. Realizing suddenly that they had put themselves into an untenable position, the whites abandoned the few horses they had obtained and fled back down the Columbia to Fort Astoria, arriving on June 14.

John George McTavish and twenty North West voyageurs also paddled to the river mouth, hoping to welcome the *Isaac Todd*. It did not appear. Neither did the American supply ship that was supposed to show up each spring. This left the rivals sitting uneasily side by side, unsupported by their respective Governments, almost helpless, and in mutual suspense about the future.

Thousands of miles away, both Astor and the North West Company's agents were doing their best to get ships around the Horn into the Pacific. Both appealed to their Governments for help. Eventually the Nor'Westers were successful, obtaining not only letters of marque for the *Isaac Todd* but also an armed escort. The ships finally left London early in 1813 with a large, awkward convoy bound for various destinations in the Pacific.

Astor had no such luck. Unable to obtain aid from war-beset Washington, he turned to the Russian consul in New York and with his help (Russia was then an ally of Britain) sprang the three-hundred-ton *Lark* through the British blockade on the grounds that he, Astor, was obligated to send certain necessary supplies to Governor Baranov in Alaska. His idea was to have the *Lark* stop at Astoria along the way. The ship never arrived. A storm drove her aground off the Hawaiian Islands.

To make doubly sure Astoria was supplied, Astor also sent word to his agents in London to spend twelve thousand pounds fitting out a brig there. This ship, the *Forester,* probably sailed with the same convoy that included the North West Company's *Isaac Todd*. Gales broke the group apart. When the *Todd* did not appear at a prearranged rendezvous, the British warship *Raccoon* finally sailed for the Columbia without her. The English

Fort Astoria in 1813 is seen in an illustration from a book by Gabriel Franchère, who served as a clerk at the American post.

crew of the *Forester,* meanwhile, rebelled against taking supplies to enemy Americans. The officers gave in to the crew's demands and diverted the ship to Alaska.

The entire complement of the Pacific Fur Company's inland traders in the meantime had gathered at Astoria at the mouth of the Columbia for their annual summer rendezvous. By that time (late June), the year was too far advanced for them to return to the horse country east of the Cascade Mountains and try again to secure animals for evacuating the post. Besides, several of them wanted to go on trading for another season. This they decided to do. To keep McTavish off their backs, they divided the country with him and sold him supplies. Hunt, who reappeared finally in a brig he had chartered in Hawaii for a short time only, agreed to pull out the next year and sailed back to the islands to purchase a vessel for hauling away furs, equipment, and men when the time came. The inland partners again scattered for their posts.

Shortly thereafter more Nor'Westers appeared from across the Canadian Rockies, convinced that the *Todd* would soon arrive. Giving way afresh to discouragement, McDougall sold Astoria's entire assets to the North West Company—furs, supplies, equipment, inland posts, everything. The purchasers agreed to give work to any Astorian who wished it and to transport the others overland across the Canadian Rockies to the East.

Astor never forgave McDougall and insisted that the prices he accepted were so low as to amount to treachery.

Considering how far from any market the furs and goods were, the accusation seems unreasonable. Astor was lucky, indeed, to receive anything, for the warship *Raccoon* appeared shortly after the bargain had been struck. Disappointed at not having a fort to pound into submission, the captain ran up the Union Jack anyway, declared that the country belonged to King George (Astoria was renamed Fort George), and sailed away. A little later, the long-delayed *Isaac Todd* wallowed over the bar, more Canadian overlanders came from across the mountains, and the Oregon country was firmly in the hands of Great Britain. Anything in American hands then

The Southwest after the War of 1812 was probed by trappers, Santa Fe traders, and the members of Long's expedition.

would have been considered legitimate spoils of war, and the owner would have received nothing. So McDougall really did not do Astor so bad a turn after all.

Farther east, Oliver Perry, in September, 1813, at last gave the frontier something to cheer by outgunning a British fleet on Lake Erie and breaking the British supply lines to Detroit. William Henry Harrison was able to take immediate advantage of the triumph. During the summer his forts near the lake had withstood clumsy British assaults and disheartened Dickson's temperamental Western Indians so much that many went home. Thus when Harrison learned of Perry's triumph, he was able to set out in immediate pursuit of the British and the Indians who remained. At the Thames River in Ontario he defeated them decisively. Tecumseh was slain. His tribesmen said they recovered his body intact, but some frontiersmen did not think so. Years after the battle one wrote boastfully, "I hope [helped] kill Tecumseh and *hope Skin him* and brot Two peices of his yellow hide home with me to my Mother & Sweet Harts."

Although Harrison's victory ended the Indian threat in Ohio and adjacent regions and bolstered morale throughout the West, it did not drive all the invaders off United States soil. Canadian regulars even managed to reinforce Mackinac by way of York and Georgian Bay. They captured the two American schooners that were attempting to blockade the island. Nor'Westers reached Montreal with a canoe brigade carrying a million dollars' worth of fur from the Pacific Northwest and Lake Superior. Voyageurs and Indians crushed an American attempt to establish a fort at Prairie du Chien on the Mississippi, and afterward Sauks led by Black Hawk turned back Zachary Taylor's bumbling attempt to reopen the river.

In the South, Andrew Jackson proved more effective, even though he fought in acute physical discomfort. Five days after the Fort Mims massacre he had brawled in a Nashville tavern with the trigger-tempered Benton brothers, Jesse and Thomas, and Jesse's pistol had shattered his left shoulder. But Jackson remained as indomitable as ever; when a committee of public safety appealed to him three weeks later to lead two thousand five hundred men against William Weatherford's war faction of "Red Stick" Creek Indians, he agreed.

It was a hard, cold, hungry campaign. At last, on March 27, 1814, he threw two thousand men against perhaps half that many "Red Sticks" braced for him on a peninsula in the Horseshoe Bend of the Tallapoosa River in Alabama. The first American to cross the log ramparts and live, though painfully wounded, was Sam Houston, a lean, twenty-one-year-old ensign, six feet two inches tall. Even after hope was gone, the Creeks kept fighting fanat-

ically. An estimated seven hundred and fifty-seven died during the day-long battle. Jackson lost forty-nine killed, one hundred and fifty-seven wounded. As the price of peace, he took half the remaining Creek lands.

Napoleon's abdication and exile to Elba let the English turn full attention to the United States, but, curiously, their success ebbed. A raid on Washington did no strategic harm. Then, in September, 1814, American gunboats on Lake Champlain crushed an English fleet and halted the army with which Sir George Prevost had hoped to cripple New York. Four months later, early in January, 1815, Andrew Jackson succeeded in turning back ten thousand more British soldiers at New Orleans, killing two thousand at a loss of only eight Americans.

Save for the chesty feeling of prowess it brought to the United States, the Battle of New Orleans was fruitless. Peace had been signed two weeks before at Ghent, in the Netherlands, by an England weary from twenty years of war in Europe. By the treaty's terms, territorial boundaries remained as they had been before the war. Boundary commissioners appointed to settle areas of dispute recommended the 49th parallel in 1818 as the dividing line from Lake of the Woods to the crest of the Rockies, putting the headwaters of the Mississippi and Red rivers firmly in United States hands. At about the same time, diplomatic accords ended a potential arms race by ruling that neither country was to maintain a naval force on the Great Lakes. But the negotiators could not agree on the ownership of the Oregon country. Wearily they decided in 1818 to grant citizens of both the United States and Great Britain equal rights of settlement and trade in the Pacific Northwest for ten years, after which time the question of ownership was to be reopened.

Although the United States gained none of the goals with which it began the war, the West counted the peace as a victory. The country around the upper lakes that Great Britain and her red allies had conquered was returned intact, and disputes about fur trade rights in northern Minnesota were ended. Farther south, the Indians were completely cowed; never again in either the eastern part of the Midwest or in the South would they seriously check the spread of settlement.

Only two prewar territorial problems remained unsolved—Spanish East Florida, and Texas. The United States sought to purchase the former, only to have the talks upset when Jackson stormed across the Florida border on a police mission of sorts, occupied foreign territory, executed a couple of British citizens, snapped orders at the Spanish governor, and otherwise caused gasps of consternation in several national capitals. Spain, however, was too beset by troubles at home and revolutions in Latin America to maintain for long her stance of offended dignity. Negotiations resumed. In 1819 she signed the Adams-Onís Treaty, whereby she ceded East Florida, an area she had no hope of holding anyway, and received in return a promise that the American Government would pay the claims of its citizens against Spain up to a limit of five million dollars. The United States further agreed that the southern boundary of the Louisiana Purchase was forever to be a line that jogged from the Sabine north to the Red River, west along the Red to the 100th degree of longitude, north to the Arkansas, westward and north along that river to the 42nd parallel, and so to the Pacific—in effect setting the southern boundary of the Oregon country, which no one yet actually owned, at what eventually became the northern lines of Utah, Nevada, and California.

To frontiersmen, still rumbling about the Rio Grande as the southern boundary of the Louisiana Purchase, the treaty's "surrender" of Texas to a nonbelligerent seemed a far greater defeat than anything suffered in the actual war with England. A filibuster expedition led by a Dr. James Long actually marched across the Sabine to take Texas by force but was handily defeated by Spanish regulars. Henry Clay meanwhile carried Western protests against the Adams-Onís Treaty to Washington, hoping that Spain's crumbling empire might fall completely apart if he waited long enough. For two years Clay's efforts were successful in holding off ratification, but in February, 1821, the treaty finally became law.

The end of fighting brought fresh armies of migrants tramping across the mountains. Between 1810 and 1820, Indiana's population exploded upwards more than six hundred per cent, from 24,000 to 147,178. Missouri's soared two hundred and fifteen per cent; Ohio's doubled.

Transportation projects struggled to keep pace. War-interrupted construction on the National Road was resumed, and in 1818 the graded, stone-paved highway reached Wheeling. (Unfortunately, the Government refused funds for maintenance.) Along this slowly deteriorating trace lurched mountains of freight in colorful Conestoga wagons. The course was not easy. Stagecoaches slithered and bounced through ooze in wet weather, over iron-hard ruts in dry. Lean peddlers trudged along with laden pack mules. Migrating farm families creaked in small wagons amidst flocks of cows and pigs.

At Wheeling (or at other river crossings in Kentucky), some of the travelers ferried their possessions across the Ohio to the network of stump-filled, bone-distressing roads that led throughout the Old Northwest. Some stopped to hew more clearings from the forests. Others continued doggedly on to the Mississippi. During the

boom years of 1817 and 1818, an average of fifty wagons and four hundred to five hundred passengers a day rode the clumsy river ferries to St. Louis and the old French town of St. Charles, a little farther north. Observer Timothy Flint wrote of a typical migrant company that stretched three quarters of a mile along the approach to the St. Charles Ferry—nine wagons, each loaded with two to three tons and pulled by four to six horses; hogs, sheep, loose horses, and a hundred cattle scattered in between; slaves, women, and children strolling beside.

At first those movers who did not travel by land traded their vehicles for leaky flatboats or rafts, bought river guidebooks, and floated to their destinations. Soon, however, steamboats took over the bulk of the traffic. In 1815 the *Enterprise* made the first upstream journey from New Orleans to Louisville. Her time was twenty-five days. Compared with the snail pace of keelboats, the rate was fantastic—but within ten years improved vessels cut the elapsed time to slightly more than a week.

In 1817 the first steamer reached St. Louis—the same year, incidentally, in which New York decided to build the Erie Canal, a move that in time helped break the West away from its long economic and political alliance with the South. In 1818 a steamboat, *Walk-in-the-Water*, appeared on the upper Great Lakes, and another thrashed up the Cumberland to Nashville. By 1819 at least thirty-one boats were competing for the rapidly growing traffic of the Ohio and the Mississippi. Their tapping the National Road at Wheeling proved so powerful a magnet to traffic that Daniel Boone's old Wilderness Trail through Cumberland Gap, once the settlers' great gateway to the West, fell almost into disuse.

These dazzling river craft were creations straight out of fantasy. Streams were so shallow that machinery, paddle wheels, and storage space for barrels, bales, and poorer passengers had to be located on a deck almost at water line. Above this commercial clutter rose another deck, fretted with lacy gingerbread and bright with white paint and gilt, for wealthy planters, merchants, politicians, gamblers, and their ladies. Still higher, almost as high as the ornate tops of the slender smokestacks, rose the Texas deck holding the glassed-in pilothouse.

If this postwar flood of diverse peoples had a common characteristic, it was a renewed mania for speculation in land. Long years of nonimportation decrees and war had stimulated the home processing of agricultural products. Between 1807 and 1815, for instance, the number of cotton spindles in the United States had soared from eight thousand to half a million. Cotton responded by reaching thirty cents a pound in 1816, thirty-four cents in 1818. Other commodities rose at a comparable rate, and the native hunger for good land became insatiable.

The boom psychology was quickened by the Government's policy of selling public domain lands largely on credit. In 1818 and again in 1819, three and a half million freshly surveyed acres were handed over to hopeful citizens. By the latter year, sales on the books totaled forty-four million dollars, but the Treasury actually had received only half that amount. The problem was intensified by the selling of military bounty lands. Immediately after the war the Government repaid its veterans by handing out eight million acres in Illinois and Missouri alone. Warrants for this land changed hands without the need of the grantee even looking at his plot.

Since most hard money went East to pay for freight and manufactured goods, little specie was available in the West for lubricating these freewheeling deals. To provide a medium of exchange, small banks run by amateurs bloomed everywhere, printing paper currency on the flimsiest sort of security. Counterfeiting was easy. A fast-talking sharper simply rode into town, opened an office, and issued crinkly new bank notes as loans in exchange for promissory signatures. The "banker" then sold the paper to a local businessman for cash at a substantial discount and vanished before the borrowers discovered that their "bank notes" were worthless.

Economic trouble was obviously making for the reckless West, but so long as the excitement continued to feed on itself, the merry-go-round spun on. Little energy was left over for resuming the arduous fur trade thrusts that had been gathering momentum before the war. Moreover, the British-oriented Indians of the upper Missouri were of very uncertain temper, and traders were unwilling to risk lives and property among them.

The few new adventures that were launched avoided the Missouri Indians and stayed well to the south. In 1814, even before the war had ended, Joseph Philibert of St. Louis took eighteen French trappers to the base of the Rockies, in the vicinity, roughly, of modern Pueblo, Colorado. He assumed he was on American land, but actually the boundary had not yet been determined. (That was finally done by the Adams-Onís Treaty of 1819.)

Spanish officials in Santa Fe, alerted about the trappers by Indian messenger, indulged in no such presumption. Years of American filibustering in Texas had made them nervous. Out went soldiers to seize the trappers. But then the officials had second thoughts. After keeping the men in the grubby Santa Fe prison throughout the winter, the New Mexicans finally released them in February, 1815, but ordered Philibert to pay the expenses of the captivity.

In spite of the experience, Philibert intended to keep on with his project. He told most of his men to spend the next spring trapping and trading in the mountains and promised to meet them the next fall, with fresh goods, where Huerfano Creek flows into the Arkansas. Accompanied by the remaining hands, he then hurried across the plains to Missouri to make his promise good.

In St. Louis he encountered two substantial merchants, Auguste P. Chouteau and Jules de Mun, who were planning a trading-trapping excursion among the Arapahoes —a big party of forty-five men. Philibert waited until September in order to ride west with them. Evidently their power impressed him. Somewhere along the way he withdrew from competition by selling his goods and the contracts of his men to Chouteau and de Mun.

The party reached the Huerfano on December 8, 1815. No men were there. From Indians they learned that the

Walk-in-the-Water, *the first steamboat on the Great Lakes, was depicted at Detroit by Army surveyor-draftsman George Whistler.*

hungry trappers had waited a while, then had drifted off to Taos, thus launching that sleepy adobe town on its hectic career as the favorite spa of the Southern mountain men. Since de Mun had paid for the defectors' services, he wanted them back. He aimed his horse south and west, past the two vast cones of gray rock that the New Mexicans called *Huajatolla*, Breasts of the World—refined since to Spanish Peaks. He found the men in Taos and rode on to Santa Fe to ask permission to take trapping parties to the headwaters of the Rio Grande.

The governor of New Mexico forwarded the request to his superiors in Chihuahua. While waiting for an answer, de Mun took Philibert's shaggy crew north to join the others on indisputable American ground. During the next season (1816) they developed the idea of meeting at a predesignated point in the field to exchange furs and supplies—an operating pattern much like the more famous rendezvous system that William Ashley invented a few years later in Wyoming. While the bulk of the men stayed in the mountains, a few hurried the fall and spring catch of pelts to the settlements, picked up supplies, and returned to the appointed meeting place.

Hoping to learn what action had been taken on the request to trap in Spanish territory, de Mun early in 1817 again rode to Taos and there discovered that the far-ranging activities of his men had created a fearful hoodoo in the minds of the Spanish. Twenty thousand American troops, they actually thought, were manning a huge fort at the mouth of the Purgatoire, near present-day Las Animas, Colorado. Two hundred Spanish dragoons marched back with de Mun from Santa Fe to investigate, found nothing, and allowed the Americans to proceed—on the condition that they avoid Spanish territory.

Denied access to the Rio Grande, the trappers in the spring of 1817 started north and west across the central Rockies toward the headwaters of the Columbia. Snow in the high country was still too deep to buck through. Disconsolately they turned back toward the Arkansas, scattering out to trap as they traveled. In May they reassembled at the familiar rendezvous where Huerfano Creek runs into the river—the south bank of the stream, unfortunately for them. Troops from Santa Fe swooped down, arrested the entire party—de Mun, Chouteau, and twenty-four men—and took them off to prison.

After forty-four days in jail the Americans were tried by a court-martial whose presiding officer kept pounding the table, denying that Spain had ceded Louisiana, and threatening to shoot the prisoners on the spot. "It is easy," de Mun later wrote William Clark, "to judge of our feelings to see our lives in the hands of such a man."

In the end they were freed, but furs and merchandise worth $30,380.74 were confiscated. After the United States had assumed, under the Adams-Onís Treaty, some five million dollars in claims of American citizens against Spain, Chouteau and de Mun entered bills for the loss. Thirty years later their estates collected principal plus interest—$81,772. The immediate reaction, however, was discouragement. After hearing of the experience, responsible traders in Missouri were no more inclined to risk capital near the Spanish borderlands than among the restive Indians of the upper Missouri.

Astor fared just as poorly in the Pacific Northwest. The treaty-making diplomats of Great Britain and the United States decided that Astoria had been seized as an act of war by the British captain of the *Raccoon* and that the post should therefore be returned to the American. Restitution on paper, however, meant little in the face of

Ramsay Crooks, painted by Jules Emile Saintin

the 1818 convention that allowed citizens of both nations equal rights of trade and settlement in the Oregon country. Deciding that the aggressive Nor'Westers were too deeply entrenched to challenge, Astor made no effort to refurbish his bold dream of a continent-wide monopoly for his American Fur Company.

Elephantine Donald McKenzie had meanwhile returned to the North West Company. Unchallenged by Astor, he set about reforming the Canadian company's Western fur-gathering operations. He abandoned trade in fixed posts and substituted mobile trapping brigades strong enough to resist Indian attack. He based these brigades on a new post, Fort Nez Percés, built on hot, dry sands where the Walla Walla River runs into the Columbia. From there McKenzie ranged southeast to the edges of present Utah, into the valley of the Green River in western Wyoming, and north and east to the erratic line of the Continental Divide in Montana.

The Pacific lost to him, Astor set about closing his pudgy fist tight on the Great Lakes area. Congress aided him by passing a law forbidding foreigners to participate in the Indian trade of the United States. Probably Astor did not instigate the bill, but he was quick to take advantage of it. Using it as a lever, he forced his Montreal partners in the South West Company to sell him their share of the forts, boats, unsold merchandise, and pelts stored in the Indian country. He received this prize for about one hundred thousand dollars.

Having thus frozen out the Montrealers, he then sought permission to void the exclusion order by importing French-Canadian workers for manning his boats and posts. They alone were willing to labor eighteen hours a day moving merchandise on a diet consisting almost exclusively of lyed corn flavored with fat. Since the War Department wanted the Indians supplied and certain foreigners were necessary for doing it, Astor was again able to bend the law to his advantage, as also were his American competitors, notably David Stone of New Hampshire, who also employed French Canadians.

Using the experienced voyageurs as their work horses, Ramsay Crooks, who after the war assumed complete charge of Astor's field operations, and Robert Stuart each year sent scores of barges loaded with merchandise from Mackinac and Detroit to every Indian village between the Wabash of Indiana and the Red River of North Dakota. Ruthlessly they crushed weak opponents but either bought out strong ones, as they did David Stone, or offered them partnerships of a sort. In spite of continued vigilance, however, they were unable to eliminate small peddlers who ingratiated themselves with certain bands by marriage and who then corrupted their customers with smuggled alcohol, an illegal trade weapon that subordinates in the American Fur Company used freely in retaliation rather than lose a single fur.

With private competition largely contained, Crooks and Astor turned on the government trading factories. With Senator Benton of Missouri as the company's Congressional spokesman, they at last (February, 1822) succeeded in having them abolished, largely on the grounds that the public houses were not fulfilling one of their primary functions, civilizing the savages, and hence were an indefensible interference with private enterprise.

During this same period the War Department was busy consolidating its own hold on the wilderness. Shortly after the coming of peace, it hurried troops into the Indian country to erect forts at every center where British influence had been strong. Forts Dearborn and Mackinac were reactivated; new bastions were built at Green Bay, Prairie du Chien, and Rock Island on the Mississippi. These were inner strongholds for controlling the nearby Indians and the Indian trade. Each housed an Indian agent and generally, until the repeal of the factories, a government trading house as well. The frontier's outer line of defense became Fort Smith, on the western boundary of Arkansas Territory; Fort Snelling, near where St. Paul now stands; Fort Brady, at Sault Ste Marie; and, most distantly, a post scheduled for the junction of the Yellowstone and the Missouri.

The Yellowstone Expedition, trying to move upriver in five ill-designed steamboats, broke down long before reaching its goal, which in the meantime had shrunken to the Mandan villages. Troops went into winter quarters (1819–20) at Council Bluffs. Because of inadequate supplies, a hundred of them died of scurvy. The gruesome malady simultaneously afflicted the soldiers working on Fort Snelling, where forty died. The nation was horrified. Appropriations were cut, and the country's westernmost post, Fort Atkinson, was built, not on the upper Missouri, but a few miles north of the site of today's Omaha. The protection was enough, however, so that Manuel Lisa in 1819 took his new wife and her companion up the Missouri to his trading post near the fort. The pair were the first American white women of record to have ventured so far into the wilderness.

Part of the abortive Yellowstone Expedition had been a survey group commanded by Major Stephen H. Long. Unable to reach the original destination, Long went instead, with twenty men—a botanist-geologist, a topographer, a naturalist, a painter, three French Canadians, and several soldiers—to the Colorado Rockies. They traveled light. Each man had a single riding horse. All baggage for the entire summer, including gifts for the Indians and supplementary provisions (pork, corn meal, hardtack, coffee), was carried on eight pack animals.

The group was examining the land but hardly exploring. Ezekiel Williams, de Mun, Chouteau, and others had covered the country thoroughly; Long's guide, Joseph Bissonette, had been one of de Mun's trappers. Without experiencing any particular excitement, the party moved up the Platte and the South Platte to the base of the mountains and turned south toward the Arkansas. In mid-July Dr. Edwin James and two soldiers made the first recorded ascent of Pikes Peak. On reaching the Arkansas, the group separated. Some followed the Arkansas directly to Fort Smith. Long and the others pushed farther south, searching for the Red. They did not find the Red, but they came upon the Canadian and followed it across the Texas Panhandle and today's Oklahoma to its junction with the Arkansas.

The cursory examination left Long as little impressed with the arid, high plains as Pike had been. So bleak a region, he wrote, was not fit for agriculture. The area's best function would be "as a barrier to prevent too great an extention of our population westward." From then on the name Great American Desert went down on the maps to designate the plains from, roughly, the 98th meridian to the Rockies. But though this land was unfit for whites, its enormous herds of wild game made it, Long suggested, a fine home for nomads who lived by hunting. The remark struck Government men who more and more were wondering what to do with the remaining Indians in the East. Might not the best solution be to move Eastern tribes off onto this apparently worthless ground?

The collapse of the Yellowstone Expedition coincided with the crumbling of the West's speculative sand castles. Belatedly trying to halt the frenzy, the Bank of the United States presented Western bank notes for collection. Unable to comply, many local banks failed. Agricultural prices shot down—cotton from thirty-three cents to sixteen and a half cents in six months. A sobered Congress on April 24, 1820, passed a new land law that dropped the mischievous credit provisions while reducing the price per acre to $1.25 in cash.

As trade expired, a few desperate men turned their eyes westward. Among them was Moses Austin, fifty-nine-year-old mine operator, banker, and storekeeper at the lead-mining town of Potosi, southwest of St. Louis. Austin had experienced failure before, in 1796, in Virginia. He had responded by taking his family across the Mississippi and becoming a Spanish citizen in return for land grants in what was then Spanish Missouri. In 1820 he began wondering whether Spanish colonial administrators in Texas might not listen again to proposals for frontier colonies that would act as buffers against aggressive Americans. He was sure he could recruit in impoverished Missouri at least three hundred families who, in exchange for free land, would move to Texas and swear allegiance to Spain and the Catholic Church. But were the Spanish still willing to invite such immigrants? In December he rode to San Antonio to learn.

On the Missouri, Manuel Lisa felt similar stirrings. In 1819, after repeated postwar failures to expand the scope of his Missouri Fur Company, he at last pulled together an energetic group headed by Joshua Pilcher, a St. Louis banker. As a supplier of merchandise he lined up David Stone, who was losing out to Astor's American Fur Company on the Great Lakes and who desperately needed a new outlet for goods.

The intention of this new Missouri Fur Company was to follow the troops of the Yellowstone Expedition to the upper river. As we have seen, Congress ended that hope in the summer of 1820 by refusing further appropriations. In August of the same year, Lisa died. In spite of the double shock, his partners decided to press ahead in 1821 at least as far as the site of Lisa's prewar Fort Raymond, at the junction of the Bighorn and the Yellowstone. From there they would try another gamble in the very mountains that the Blackfeet had made so costly to the original Missouri Fur Company.

Economics fortified their boldness. The depression had reduced the price of the manufactured goods they bought, but the price of furs was holding steady, creating a better margin of profit on barter than had existed

for years. It was so alluring, indeed, that in the summer of 1821 two other companies decided to risk the upper country—Berthold, Chouteau & Pratte, old hands at the trade on the middle river; and William Ashley and Andrew Henry, the latter of whom had learned something of the northern Rockies with Lisa before the war.

Each of these groups was well financed. Less potent companies and individuals had to seek outlets for their goods somewhere away from the Missouri. In June, 1821, William Becknell, of Franklin, in central Missouri, advertised in the local newspaper for seventy men to trade with the Comanches of the Southwestern plains for horses and mules and to catch "Wild Animals of every description." Many men sent in inquiries, but only a few scratched together enough gimcracks to start west with him on September 1. Farther south that same September, Hugh Glenn and fifty-seven-year-old Jacob Fowler, traders in what is now eastern Oklahoma, headed up the Arkansas toward the Rockies with eighteen trappers.

Neither the Becknell nor the Glenn-Fowler party planned to risk Spanish territory. A third group of Missourians did. They were put into motion by John McKnight, whose brother Robert had been one of the leaders of the group that had visited Santa Fe in 1812 and since then had been languishing in a Chihuahua jail. Finally, early in 1821, some of the prisoners had been released. Three of them made their way back to the United States. But Robert McKnight was not one of them, and his brother John was anxious to learn why.

For help he turned to rugged Thomas James. James had been on the upper Missouri in 1809–10 with Lisa's company and since then had kept store in Illinois and St. Louis. The depression ruined him. Creditors were clamoring, and his shelves were loaded with woolens no one could buy. Well, maybe the New Mexicans, or even the Comanches, had silver and furs to barter for his cloth. He and McKnight rounded up seven men (later they hired two more), added more items to James's yardage, loaded the bales into a keelboat, and in May, 1821, started west by a roundabout route—down the Mississippi and up the Arkansas until in eastern Oklahoma the river grew too shallow for their boat. Encountering Glenn and Fowler making preparations at the mouth of the Verdigris tributary of the Arkansas for a similar jaunt toward the southern Rockies, they proposed a union of their parties. They were rebuffed. Undismayed, they bought twenty-three pack horses from the Osage Indians and jogged ahead, trading as they went.

Thus, from the southern border of the United States to the northern, thanks to a disastrous depression, the Far West was stirring again.

Artist Coke Smyth romanticized some of the details of the paintings he made during his travels in the American West, but his works were basically true and honest, as is this picture of a bartering session between a trader and an Indian. Smyth did not forget to include one of the omnipresent Indian dogs.

FUR RIVALRIES

The fur trade was like no other business on earth. Its basic work was carried on in remote wildernesses, it dealt daily with customers who had been known to use arrow and tomahawk in resentment over a bad deal, and some of its most capable men could not have entered another business because they were illiterate. At the same time, it was an occupation where the competition was keen, for the peltries of America were rich beyond measure; it is rather remarkable that the combinations formed to vie for bigger shares of the furs managed to compete with so little bloodshed. However, the historic importance of the fur men lay not in the value of the pelts they marketed but in their role as precursors of civilization. On every frontier, from the Carolinas to the Pacific, they blazed the trails settlers later followed. They prepared the Indians for easy conquest by pitting tribes against each other and by weakening them with alcohol and disease. Their trading posts, from their important locations, often became frontier Army forts and sometimes grew into cities. Such, however, was not the destiny of Michilimackinac (above), painted in 1817 by F. S. Bolton; this once-strategic island in the strait between Lakes Michigan and Huron is today a state park.

113

THE WAR OF 1812

The War of 1812 was a Westerner's war. British harassment of American commerce and impressment of American seamen were the principal causes of the conflict, but the mercantile Northeast, which was most affected by these actions, wanted no part of any war. It was the young, bellicose War Hawks in the Twelfth Congress who forced the conflict. Those from the Northwest demanded the conquest of Canada; those in the Southwest and South called for the seizure of Florida from Spain. But the war, which was to have been won easily and quickly, produced a series of disasters from which the United States was fortunate to emerge without loss of territory. One gain was a strengthening of a spirit of American nationalism; another was the ending of British influence and effective Indian opposition east of the Mississippi.

War Hawk Henry Clay was a peacemaker when sketched at Ghent by P. Van Huffel.

Sick and wounded who were left behind when the British took the rest of a defeated American force prisoner on the River Raisin near Detroit were massacred by Indians. The Americans made propaganda use of the grim episode, as in the print at left by an unknown artist (who almost certainly worked entirely from imagination), and "Remember the Raisin!" became a battle cry.

American troops at Fort Dearborn (right), which guarded the strategic Chicago waterway, were murdered by Indians after surrendering the post in 1812 to the British, who then could not control their native auxiliaries. This military drawing was made in 1808 by Captain John Whistler, builder of the fort, commandant until 1810, and of some interest as grandfather of artist James Abbott McNeill Whistler.

WESTWARD THE COURSE

The Conestoga wagon, pictured above on a Pennsylvania pike in 1814 by Thomas Birch, was the ubiquitous vehicle that carried most of the humans and goods of the westward migration.

The miserable state of early Western roads is indicated in the drawing by George Tattersall, above. Trees have been cut, but stumps remain as perils to horses, vehicles, and passengers. Because vehicles often did get hung up, the expression "to be stumped" became part of the American language.

The steamboat accelerated growth of the West by making the network of rivers into two-way roads for travel and commerce. The Maid of Orleans *was sketched in 1820 by Fleury Generelly.*

Highways and byways
of the South

After the War of 1812 the westward tide increased. The Indians were no longer a barrier, for the Northern tribes had been crushed with the smashing of Tecumseh's confederation, and Andrew Jackson had humbled those in the South. So, unchecked by fear, settlers came by flatboat and steamboat on the rivers and over the grimly rough roads across the land. Traveler Morris Birkbeck wrote in 1817: "Old America seems to be breaking up and moving westward. We are seldom out of sight, as we travel on this grand track towards the Ohio, of family groups, behind and before us." And editor Hezekiah Niles, reviewing in 1819 the advance of settlement since 1812, noted, ". . . St. Louis, now a *port* on the Mississippi, then at about the extreme point of the emigrants voyage in that direction—is turned into a *starting-place*." Population west of the mountains increased more than a million during 1810–20.

A familiar sight on the Wilderness Road was a family by a campfire, as sketched by traveler Joshua Shaw.

The turbulent Missouri proved too much for the pioneer steamboats of the 1819 expedition, with the exception of the Western Engineer, *commanded by Stephen Long; it reached Council Bluffs, where Titian Peale made this sketch.*

Major Stephen H. Long by Charles W. Peale

LONG'S EXPEDITIONS

Major Stephen H. Long did the treeless heartland of America no service with his report on his 1820 exploration over the Great Plains. He categorized the region so thoroughly as arid and useless that it became known as the "Great American Desert," a label that persisted into the 1850's and discouraged any attempts to exploit the region. The previous year, 1819, Long had led the scientific portion of the "Yellowstone Expedition," a project originally planned to establish forts on the upper Missouri but later scaled down to building a fort in present North Dakota. Long's biggest accomplishment was getting his detachment to Council Bluffs by steamboat, for none of the craft had ascended the Missouri before beyond its lower reaches. The force wintered at Council Bluffs; then new orders sent Long up the Platte River, along the Rockies, and, after splitting his forces, back down the Arkansas and Canadian rivers—convinced the plains were worthless. In 1823 he led a party that examined the sources of the St. Peter's (now Minnesota) River, then went on north to fix the point where the national boundary crossed the Red River. Thereafter he led a more prosaic life, principally as a consulting engineer for railroads.

Samuel Seymour, who accompanied Long on his Missouri, southern plains, and Minnesota explorations, was one of the first of the artists who gave the American public glimpses of the trans-Mississippi West. Here, from Seymour's portfolio painted on the plains, are an Indian trio in blankets (above); a war dance being performed in a spacious Kansa lodge (upper right); a plains view of buffalo and the Rockies (a print from the original painting, right); and a busy Western scene of an encampment of Kiowas (below), with the expedition's tent and guard in the foreground.

Great Salt Lake Desert, northwestern Utah

"... we pushed forward, walking as we had been for a long time ... burning with thirst. ... When morning came it saw us in the same unhappy situation pursuing our journey over the desolate waste now gleaming in the sun and more insuportably tormenting than it had been during the night. ... At 10 O Clock Robert Evans laid down ... being able to proceed no further. We could do no good by remaining to die with him and we were not able to help him along. ..."

Jedediah Smith, leading trappers from California to Salt Lake, June 24 and 25, 1827

CHAPTER SIX

SEVEN-LEAGUE BOOTS

1821-1833

In January, 1821, aided by an amiable Hispanicized Dutch adventurer who called himself Baron de Bastrop, Moses Austin at last gained the attention of Governor Antonio Martínez of Texas. American colonists? Martínez hesitated. The idea had backfired before—in Louisiana, around Natchez, in the Floridas. Repeated American filibusters had threatened Texas; largely because of them, the border outpost of Nacogdoches had been all but abandoned. Should the tiger be invited inside the house?

Yet strength had to come from somewhere. Scarcely four thousand impoverished Spanish citizens scratched out a living in Texas, mostly by herding livestock at widely scattered spots along a crescent one hundred and fifty miles deep around the Gulf coast. Facing them were six or seven times that many Indians, unreclaimed by the missionary activities that in California and New Mexico had served Spain so well—cannibalistic tribes like the Karankawas along the coast and the arrogant horse Indians from the interior: Caddoes, Apaches, and, most dreaded of all, the raiding Comanches, who wiped out entire settlements along the Rio Grande and invaded San Antonio (de Béxar) almost at will.

There was no use crying to Mexico City for help. Continued revolutions had sapped the king's forces. Trained soldiers could neither be spared for permanent garrison duty in Texas nor sent in a hurry when trouble occurred. Because Spain rigidly controlled commerce through Veracruz, seaports had never developed in Texas; the undisturbed occupant of Galveston Bay until 1821 was a pirate, Jean Lafitte. The sole link between Mexico proper and Nacogdoches on the eastern frontier of Texas was *El Camino Real*, the King's Highway, bravely titled but actually a wretched trace intermittently blocked by weather, bandits, and Indians.

A succession of officials had proposed remedying the situation by locating strategic colonies strong enough to develop a vigorous trade while holding back the Indians. Neither Mexicans nor Europeans had responded well to invitations, however. That left only North Americans, as the Spanish called citizens of the United States. Dangerous, yes. Still, the temptation was powerful. If applicants were carefully screened for dependability by someone like Moses Austin, whose qualifications were evident, and if the newcomers swore allegiance to king and church, then perhaps the tiger could be tamed. Urged thus by Bastrop, Governor Martínez hesitantly recommended the proposal to his superiors in Monterrey.

Overjoyed, Moses Austin wrote of the results to his twenty-seven-year-old son Stephen, who was studying law in New Orleans, and hurried home to begin his recruiting. Father and son planned to meet in Nacogdoches during the summer, but Moses' thousands of miles of riding, much of it in winter, proved too much for his sixty-year-old constitution. He caught pneumonia and died.

Stephen did not know of the death until messengers overtook his small party between Natchitoches and Nacogdoches. He must have considered giving up the project then and there. His slight frame—he was only five and a half feet tall—did not seem suited to the wilderness. Well educated in Connecticut and at Kentucky's Transylvania College, he liked to read and play the flute for diversion.

He had held office jobs in his father's lead mine and store, had been a banker and a member of the Missouri legislature, and after the family fortunes had collapsed, had turned to the study of law. He was methodical, patient, and meticulously honest. Socially he enjoyed polite dancing, card playing, and moderate wine drinking with his peers. He lacked the gusto of the land breakers he would have to control. Some of his restraint was possibly glandular. He never married.

Above all, he was loyal. When his father's deathbed appeal to keep the project alive reached him, he thrust his reluctance aside and crossed the Sabine River into Texas. Later he wrote, "I came with pure intentions. I bid an everlasting farewell to my native country, and adopted this and in so doing I determined to fulfill rigidly all the duties and obligations of a Mexican citizen."

The hindsight of history recognizes the impossibility of being loyal to Mexico while spreading North Americans throughout Texas. Austin, however, busy with one of the great colonizing exploits of United States expansionism, did not appreciate for years the dichotomy in his goals. And even after understanding of the situation came, he kept trying to be faithful to both sides.

The governor in San Antonio accepted him as his father's heir. Assuming that this gave legitimacy to the plan, young Austin ranged far and wide on horseback, finally selecting as the best area for his colony the contiguous valleys of the Brazos and Colorado rivers. Hurrying to New Orleans, he chartered the ship *Lively* to carry tools, heavy equipment, and workers to the mouth of the Colorado. He himself led more colonists overland through Natchitoches. Others rode down out of Arkansas Territory. The land parties had to tighten their belts when the *Lively* missed the rendezvous, but by March, 1822, signs of progress could be seen: one hundred and fifty men were clearing farms on both the Colorado and Brazos watersheds, and the town of San Felipe de Austin was taking shape beside the latter stream.

The pattern was American South: single-room log cabins amid stumps in well-watered, timbered valleys; or, for larger plantations, two cabins connected by a breezeway. The homes were scattered at random—quite different from the Mexicans' tawny rock-and-adobe shelters clustered in straight lines about a dusty central plaza. Neither nationality admired the other's architecture, food, religion, or customs. The hard impatience of the Americans offended the leisurely Mexicans; the shoulder-shrugging excuses and delays of the Mexicans exasperated the efficiency-minded newcomers.

Just as Austin was seeing hopeful progress, he learned (March, 1822) that the colony might be challenged. Dur-

Davy Crockett's Almanac *regaled readers with its illustrated tall tales of frontier existence.*

ing the summer of 1821, Mexico's ten-year struggle for freedom from Spain had succeeded, and the new Congress in Mexico City was still debating, among a multitude of other problems, a fresh pattern for colonizing procedures. So far Austin's grant had not been confirmed.

Taking alarm, he put Josiah Bell in charge of the colony, stuffed four hundred dollars' worth of doubloons into his pocket, and rode out of the timber into grasslands, then into cactus and sand, across the Rio Grande, and so to Mexico City, twelve hundred miles away. He arrived there on April 9, 1822.

Leading Government figures were too busy with their intrigues to heed the dusty colonizer from the north. A month after Austin arrived, a tumult swept the city, and the leader of the preceding year's republican revolution, Colonel Agustín de Iturbide, had himself crowned Emperor Agustín I. Thereafter, Iturbide devoted far more attention and tax money to the pomp and circumstance of his title than to governing. His doubloons slowly melting away, Austin drew up the usual fulsome memorials, saw them unanswered, studied Spanish, and cultivated influential friends in the capital.

In the spring of 1823, Iturbide was ousted by another upheaval, this one engineered by a crafty young army officer of Veracruz, Antonio López de Santa Anna. Stephen Austin, hoping for a new opportunity, pawned his watch and patiently drew up another set of memorials.

Aside from lack of interest—Texas was infinitely remote from the capital's plotting—his greatest stumbling block was slavery. The Mexican Congress wanted to outlaw it. Austin's own attitude was ambivalent. He decried the institution in principle but felt immigrants would not come to his colony's rich cotton lands unless they were allowed the economic base to which decades of practice had accustomed them. In the end he worked out a compromise: slaves could be imported but not sold after arrival, and their children were to be free at age fourteen. The Government accepted the suggestion, whittled down the amount of land Moses had asked for (from 640 to 177 acres per family for farming, but 4,428 for grazing), and on April 14, 1823, confirmed the grant. Since Negroes were just becoming useful at fourteen, the compromise was not likely to appeal to American Southerners, but at least it kept the door open. Austin went home from his thirteen months of waiting pleased with results.

His grant was a special case. A national colonizing law did not come into effect until a new constitution was promulgated in 1824. Under this constitution, the awarding of colonial land grants was entrusted to the different Mexican states. They dealt, not directly with individuals, but through *empresarios* who promised to bring in a certain number of families (always in multiples of one hundred) and who distributed sites to the settlers.

The responsible state in the northeast was the sprawling giant of Coahuila and Texas, with its capital at Saltillo. Between 1824 and 1829 its administrators awarded fifteen grants calling for fifty-four hundred families. Either alone or in concert with others, Stephen Austin received three of these. During his absence in Mexico City, uncertainty about land titles had kept his colony languishing, but on his return the rush began. His initial three hundred families (approximately eighteen hundred persons, including four hundred and forty-three slaves) were located by 1825. Through additional grants that year and in 1827 and 1828, he raised the total to nine hundred families. Other *empresarios* were not so successful. A few were speculators and never advanced beyond writing high-sounding prospectuses. Others abused their privileges and aroused dangerous resentment among the Mexicans—but more of that later.

The news of Mexico's independence had meanwhile reached Santa Fe in September, 1821. From there the joyful word was spread along the edges of the mountains and out into the plains by soldiers, traders, and buffalo hunters. William Becknell's horse traders and wild animal catchers—who had struck west during the summer—heard the news without immediately understanding the

messengers. The Missourians had drifted westward to the Arkansas River and had moved up it with indifferent luck into present-day Colorado. Following an ancient Indian and Spanish trail that skirted the Purgatoire River's rough, tawny canyon, Becknell's men rode between shaggy mesas into Raton Pass, on what is now the border between Colorado and New Mexico. They evidently lost the main thoroughfare, for they had to spend two days rolling boulders before they could get their pack horses through the rugged gap and see beyond them the stark buttes and hazy yellow distances of a foreign land. With amazing persistence—for they had no reason to suppose aliens would be welcome—they rode southward into the dusty heart of it. No one challenged them until they neared San Miguel, where the road, quite plain now, bent west around a point of timbered mountains. There, on November 13, they encountered dragoons.

For a heart-chilling minute they thought they were going to be arrested. But the swarthy soldiers grinned broadly and with gestures (no one in Becknell's party spoke Spanish) urged them to come to Santa Fe. Apprehensively they visited the whitewashed little city of five thousand exuberant people. A French interpreter introduced them to Governor Malgares. The goods-hungry populace snapped up their merchandise at incredible prices; one of Becknell's companions is said to have realized nine hundred dollars on a sixty-dollar investment. A month or so later, their cloth and hardware gone, Becknell and one or two companions made a hurried, forty-eight-day winter ride to Franklin, Missouri, for fresh supplies. The rest of the adventurers stayed in New Mexico to trap.

Another group also followed the Arkansas westward that autumn of 1821—the eighteen trappers who had left the mouth of the Verdigris in eastern Oklahoma under Hugh Glenn and Jacob Fowler, the self-sufficient pair who had rebuffed McKnight and James. On November 13 they passed the mouth of the Purgatoire, where one of the men was mauled to death by a grizzly. On the seventeenth (the day after Becknell reached Santa Fe), they encountered a huge village of Indians, so rich in horses, Fowler wrote in his journal, "that the Hole Cuntry to a great distance was Coverd." They traded there for a month, in icy weather and a foot of snow.

On Christmas the whites moved with the Indians closer to the mountains. Sixty Mexican traders came by. From them the trappers learned that "the mackeson province Has de Clared Independence of the mother Cuntry and is desirous of a traid With the people of the united States." Glenn and Fowler were short of goods and so could not accept the invitation. But perhaps they could obtain permits to trap on Mexican land. Glenn and four other men rode off with the sixty Mexican traders to find out.

The elderly Fowler settled down with the others near today's Pueblo to trap and await results. The men were convinced that Glenn would simply attract attention to them and they would all be arrested. One morning Fowler had to put down an attempted mutiny. But in time word came back from Glenn that they could go wherever they liked. After a cold trip to Taos—and a rousing warming up at the fandangos there—they pressed far up the Rio Grande toward the stupendous San Juan Mountains of southwestern Colorado, unraveling some of the area's geography in person and learning more from the peak-hatted Spanish peddlers and the Ute Indians whom they encountered along the way.

In Santa Fe, meanwhile, Hugh Glenn had met the third party from the American frontier. This was the Thomas James–John McKnight group that he had refused to join when they had passed his Verdigris post in September. They had had a difficult time. After transferring their goods from keelboats to pack horses, the eleven men had cut cross lots through present Oklahoma, hopping from one sandy, half-dry tributary to another and in between them suffering dreadfully from thirst. Indians had halted them near the New Mexico border, extorted tribute, and might have killed them all had not provincial soldiers out hunting buffalo with friendly natives chanced to rescue them.

From Santa Fe, John McKnight rode south to Chihuahua to look for his brother Robert, whom he found. The workers of the party scattered for the mountains to trap. Merchant James rented a building and displayed the drab woolens he had been unable to sell in depression-ridden St. Louis. Because the New Mexicans wanted bright colors, the fabric did not move well in Santa Fe, either. Besides, Becknell had skimmed off most of the town's loose cash. In the end James had to accept horses and mules in trade, and in June he at last started home with Glenn's trappers, who were also driving mules. The leaders soon quarreled, and the parties separated.

Becknell, heading westward again, left the Arkansas River in present-day southwestern Kansas to avoid the boulders and canyons of Raton Pass. The wheel-clutching sand of the river crossing made his drivers double their teams, and after that the road blazers wandered miserably through a flat, featureless desert, so maddened by thirst that they reputedly killed their dogs and cut off the ears of their mules to drink the blood. Fortunately, they killed a buffalo that had been to water and were able to reach the Cimarron, dig shallow wells in the sandy creek bottom, and revive themselves and their livestock.

This Cimarron Cut-off would always be desperately dry for later caravans and subject to raids by Comanches; but it was passable to wagons, whereas the Raton route was not (until roads were built), and so it became the route of the Santa Fe Trail.

Becknell pioneered again in 1824 when he joined eighty small traders who wanted to band together for the mutual protection of their thirty-five thousand dollars' worth of hardware, cutlery, hats, shirting, linen, hosiery, and other dry goods. For moving the bales, they assembled two wagons, two carts, and twenty dearborns. Named for Henry Dearborn, onetime general and Secretary of War who introduced the vehicle to the Army, a dearborn was a light, four-wheeled vehicle, roofed and equipped with side curtains. It bore scant resemblance to the big, canvas-topped Conestoga wagons used on the plains in a later era. The organization of this column of undersized wagons, however, set the pattern for the future. Following the American instinct for government by compact, the proprietors assembled in a council, divided themselves into messes for more efficiency in housekeeping, elected officers, and drew up a list of rules for behavior on the trail. During the next half century, countless wagon parties bound for Santa Fe, California, and Oregon would follow that basic principle.

A few of the 1824 group's wagons rattled on from Santa Fe to Chihuahua. Profits from the adventure as a whole reached a dazzling six hundred per cent—one hundred and eighty thousand dollars in gold and silver and ten thousand dollars in furs. This extraordinary success, which was never again approached, so bemused later historians of the trail that they tended to concentrate on the storekeeping phases of the caravans and overlooked their importance, during the 1820's, as an adjunct to the swiftly developing fur trade of the Rockies.

The fur merchants of St. Louis were instantly aware of the possibilities opened by the relaxation of Mexico's antiforeign bias. When Hugh Glenn, Jacob Fowler, and John and Robert McKnight arrived in St. Louis on July 17, 1822, Ramsay Crooks of the American Fur Company bought their beaver, worth $4,499.64. More significantly, he seems also to have outfitted one of Glenn's men, Baptiste Roi, for more trapping in New Mexico.

At the same time, Crooks joined another supply firm in equipping James Baird and Samuel Chambers with goods for the Santa Fe mercantile trade. Both Baird and Chambers had spent nine years in the Chihuahua jail for a similar excursion in 1812, but they felt prospects merited another attempt. This time their party was snowbound on an island in the Arkansas for three bitter months before reaching Taos. Baird thereafter became a Mexican citizen, as did his jail companion Robert McKnight, who also changed loyalties and returned to the Southwest.

For various reasons, meanwhile, Baptiste Roi's outfit was switched from the auspices of Crooks and the American Fur Company to those of Berthold, Chouteau & Pratte (or, more popularly, the French Fur Company). The outfit perhaps continued west in the fall of 1822 under the aegis of one of the French company's most fiery partisans, Joseph Robidoux. It is unfortunate that its adventures remain unknown, for this in all probability was the first party organized from its inception solely for trapping in Mexican territory.

A stampede quickly followed. Within a year or two, American trappers were pressing southwest to the headwaters of the Gila along the southern part of today's New Mexico–Arizona border. Even greater numbers worked up the old Escalante Trail into Colorado and then veered west across the Green River into the Great Basin of Utah. Mexican slave traders long since had made the way familiar. Their pattern went like this: first they bartered with the mountain Utes for horses, then rode on into the Great Basin to swap the animals with the wretchedly poor Paiutes of the desert for young children. Children had value as slaves in New Mexico. Beaver were worthless there—until the North Americans came.

Mexican friendliness toward this locust-swarm of aliens was short-lived. In 1824 the Government decreed that only citizens could obtain trapping licenses. Americans promptly evaded the interdict by taking out naturalization papers, by forming partnerships with bona fide

Mexicans, or simply by ignoring the regulations and bribing some poor citizen to let them hide their pelts.

Partly because of the licensing provisions, neither the French Fur Company nor any other big firm took hold for long in the Southwest. Independent trappers moved about in small groups. No company-controlled system was worked out for supplying them. Yet the trappers themselves had no time to go to St. Louis, sell their pelts, buy new outfits, and recruit new helpers. This work of distribution accordingly was undertaken by modest proprietors who annually assembled a few goods and for protection joined the mercantile caravans bound for Santa Fe. Trappers too, including Becknell himself in 1824, went west with the same wagon trains.

Because Taos was close both to the mountains and to the trail, yet relatively free from Government supervision in Santa Fe, it became the base of this boisterous, uncentralized, still vaguely known commerce. Of the scores of scoundrels and empire builders who made their headquarters there—Thomas L. Smith, Céran St. Vrain, Joseph Reddeford Walker, Ewing Young, Kit Carson, and the four Robidoux brothers, most notably Antoine— none was more efficient or has been less honored by history than Etienne Provost.

Provost had first seen the edges of New Mexico with de Mun and Chouteau in 1815–17. In 1824 he and his partner LeClerc worked as far into north-central Utah as a stream that bounds down out of the Wasatch Mountains into Utah Lake—a stream that, with the city on its banks, now bears his name, spelling it Provo. The men

Santa Fe, little changed since the 1820's, was portrayed in this lithograph accompanying an 1848 report by Lieutenant Colonel W. H. Emory. John Mix Stanley, who drew the original sketch, and Emory were with Kearny's Army that took the Mexican city in 1846.

separated to hunt, and Snake Indians attacked the group of trappers under Provost. Only Provost and three or four others escaped to flee back to their main camp, situated beside the Green River.

Rejoining LeClerc's men, they wintered, (1824–25) near the desolate plains where the White River flows into the Green from one side, and the Duchesne from the other. The next spring Provost risked the Wasatches again. There, on the Weber River, which flows into the Great Salt Lake, he encountered a party of Canadians from the Columbia. Astonishment was compounded with the arrival, later that same afternoon, of a gang of Americans from the distant Yellowstone River. Accompanying them were fourteen Canadians whom they had met on the nearby streams, and whom they had attached to their own camp. Puffed with that success and waving a United States flag, the Americans strutted truculently while their leader, Johnson Gardner, told Peter Skene Ogden, the bourgeois of the Canadians, that he had better clear out of American territory—fast.

It was not United States land, however. It was Mexican. Thus two old enemies, Britain and the United States, were squaring off afresh in a lonely valley belonging to yet a third familiar antagonist, Mexico, as the heir of Spain. To understand this inevitable regrouping of forces west of the Rocky Mountains, it is necessary to shift the focus back to the Missouri River.

As noted in the last chapter, three companies were vying for the commerce that could be made to flow along that stream. One was the revitalized Missouri Fur Company, which gained a start on the others by building Fort Benton at the junction of the Bighorn and the Yellowstone in the fall of 1821. The conservative French Fur Company (Berthold, Chouteau & Pratte) moved more slowly, intent on gripping by standard means the trade of the Plains Indians before invading the mountains. The radicals of the river were William Ashley and Andrew Henry, the latter of whom had scoured parts of the northern Rockies before the War of 1812.

Ashley and Henry meant to trap rather than rely solely on trade. To avoid straining their meager capital by hiring men at the usual annual wage of two hundred to four hundred dollars a year, they agreed to transport volunteers to the mountains and outfit them there for a year's hunt in return for one half of the recipient's catch. The other half of the fur would belong to the men; the outfitters hoped to bargain it away from them in exchange for new guns, clothing, alcohol, and "fofarraw" for the Indian girls. There was another merit in the plan. The more energetic the trapper, the higher his income— an economic truth that soon would spur the Taos independents far out along the rugged trails of the Southwest.

Despite losing a keelboat full of goods, Ashley and Henry reached the mouth of the Yellowstone in the fall of 1822, built a stockade called Fort Henry, and sent trappers up the frozen Missouri toward Great Falls. Far ahead of them, Robert Jones and Michael Immell of the Missouri Fur Company set off early in the spring of 1823 for the Three Forks country. Far behind, the French Fur Company built Fort Lookout (also called Kiowa) in present South Dakota and then prepared to move upstream among the Mandans. Complicating the picture was a group of displaced Britons calling themselves the Columbia Fur Company, who unexpectedly moved west to the Missouri from their new post beside Lake Traverse, astraddle today's Minnesota–South Dakota border.

Disasters began almost instantly. During the winter Blackfeet killed four deserters from the Missouri Fur Company and four trappers from Fort Henry. In the spring a band of Bloods trapped Jones and Immell's party along the Jefferson River, killed both leaders and five hands, and made off with horses, traps, and furs.

Two weeks later the Arikaras on the middle Missouri struck. Bound upstream with two keelboats filled with supplies for Fort Henry, Ashley stopped outside their villages in present-day South Dakota to trade for horses. Animals were expensive near the mountains, yet they were necessary for roaming the tributaries of the Yellowstone and—probably the partners already were thinking of this—for crossing the Continental Divide to the watersheds of the Snake and the Green, whose edges Henry had touched a dozen years before. During a day of trading, Ashley obtained nineteen horses and then, pinned to the riverbank by a violent storm, camped within rifle range of the pickets surrounding one of the villages.

Firing began at sunrise. When the brief battle was over, the horses and fifteen whites were dead; nine or ten were wounded; the boat hands were in a jelly of terror. Retreating, Ashley sent pleas for help both upstream to his partner, who promptly joined him, and downstream to the Army at Fort Atkinson, near Council Bluffs. Colonel Henry Leavenworth responded with six companies of infantry supported by a volunteer battalion of fur traders and Sioux horsemen under Joshua Pilcher.

A bombardment of the villages by the Army's little cannons caused only minor harm to the earth-covered huts but did kill an important chief and frightened the Arikaras into begging for a truce. Although Leavenworth granted lenient terms, the attitude of the trappers was so vengeful that the Indians decided to flee. During the night the entire Arikara population disappeared softly from the villages. Unable to locate them, the mortified

Leavenworth ordered his troops back down the river.

This did not suit Angus McDonald of the Missouri Fur Company. His post was nearby, and for a year he had been having trouble with the Arikaras. If the Indians returned belligerent and unpunished to their homes from this last affray, he might be the one to suffer. In order to leave them nothing to come back for, he and a helper moved with torches from hut to hut, setting the interior timbers afire and now and then ducking when unexploded shells embedded in the roofs went off. So far as his own affairs were concerned, the strategy succeeded. The homeless Arikaras settled two hundred miles away, near the Mandans. There they soothed their feelings by butchering some French Fur Company men who had had nothing whatsoever to do with the troubles.

The Missouri was closed. Even if a party succeeded in passing the Arikaras, it would still have to contend with

TO
Enterprising Young Men.

THE subscriber wishes to engage ONE HUN-DRED MEN, to ascend the river Missouri to its source, there to be employed for one, two or three years.—For particulars, enquire of Major Andrew Henry, near the Lead Mines, in the County of Washington, (who will ascend with, and command the party) or to the subscriber at St. Louis.

Wm. H. Ashley.

February 13 ——98 tf

This famous 1822 ad in St. Louis's Missouri Gazette *lured such future mountain-man "greats" as Jedediah Smith and Jim Bridger.*

the Blackfeet, stirred to a murderous pitch by their victory over Jones and Immell. Yet Ashley and Henry could stave off bankruptcy only by pushing trappers into the mountains. They determined to strike directly overland. Though the season was then late, brigades still might reach the eastern base of the Rockies and spend the fall trapping and trading with friendly Crow Indians along Wind River, in today's Wyoming. When spring arrived, the men could continue on across the Continental Divide somewhere south of Blackfoot territory. How the spring furs would be assembled and how fresh supplies could be distributed to the men in the mountains were problems that would have to wait until the partners received specific information from the wanderers themselves.

The decisions reached, Henry and the men he had brought with him started back by land to the fort on the Yellowstone. Along the way a grizzly all but killed old

Hugh Glass. The two men left to watch him die—young Jim Bridger and John Fitzgerald—abandoned him. Recovering, Glass crawled toward Fort Kiowa, living on berries, roots, and wolf-killed buffalo calves. Succored at last, he vowed revenge but gave it up later when he had the defectors in reach.

Ashley meanwhile sent Jedediah Smith, Jim Clyman, Thomas Fitzpatrick, William Sublette, and a handful of others on horseback due west from Fort Kiowa. In the Wind River Valley they met on schedule trappers coming south from Henry's Fort and an unscheduled party from the Missouri Fur Company as well. In February Smith's eleven-man group shook free from the others and tried to cross the Wind River Mountains at Union Pass, which Hunt's westbound Astorians had used in 1811. Snowstorms turned them back. When the weather cleared, they swung south to Sweetwater Creek, searching for an Indian trail around the lower end of the saw-toothed peaks. Late in March, after weeks of hunger and crippling cold, they found the way—the broad sage swales of South Pass, leading easily from Mississippi drainage to the valley of the upper Green.

At the Green they split. A group under Smith trapped downstream toward the magnificent east-west rampart of the Uinta Mountains. (Simultaneously, Provost's men were riding out of Taos toward trails that would take them to the southern side of the same mountains.) Fitzpatrick and the rest of the pioneers turned up the Green. Indians stole their horses. They trapped afoot with dazzling success, chanced across the very savages who had raided them, recovered the horses, and in June met with Smith's party at an appointed rendezvous on Sweetwater Creek, east of the pass.

Melting snow swelled Sweetwater Creek and led Clyman, Fitzpatrick, and two more to suppose they could build skin canoes and float their harvest of furs east to market. While investigating the way, Clyman became separated from the others and hiked alone six hundred starving miles to Fort Atkinson. Fitzpatrick and his two companions had an equally desperate time. Their boats sank. Although they recovered and cached most of the fur, they too had to walk.

Fitzpatrick dashed off a letter about developments to Ashley in St. Louis, obtained pack stock from a Missouri Fur Company trader (to whom he sold the cached pelts), and rode back up the Platte to retrieve the stranded fortune. To Ashley, the news was electrifying. Andrew Henry had just come down the Missouri bearing a fair catch but completely disheartened by the effort and bloodshed involved in getting it. Though many of his men were still roaming the wilderness and needed sup-

BRITISH POSSESSIONS
ASSINIBOIN
TREATY LINE OF 1818

Clark Fork
KALISPEL
Marias R. BLACKFEET
Ft. Piegan
Ft. McKenzie
Missouri R.
Ft. Union
Ft. Henry

Pend Oreille Lake
Coeur d'Alene Lake
Flathead Lake
Flathead Post FLATHEAD

Ft. George ■
Ft. Vancouver ■

MANDAN

CASCADE RANGE
Columbia R.
Ft. ■
Nez Percés NEZ PERCE
Clearwater R.

Salmon R.
Jefferson R.
Three Forks
Yellowstone R.
Ft. Cass
CROW

Arikara Villages
(Ashley's defeat)

Willamette R.

(Smith party massacre 1828)

OREGON COUNTRY

Madison R.
Beaverhead R.
Gallatin R.
Yellowstone Lake

TETON RANGE
WIND RIVER RANGE

Bighorn R.
Tongue R.
Powder R.

SIOUX
Ft. Kiow

UMPQUA

Umpqua R.

SHOSHONI

COAST RANGES

× ✕

TREATY LINE OF 1819

MT. SHASTA +

PAIUTE

Snake R.

UTE

CACHE VALLEY ✕

Bear Lake

UNORGANIZED

N. Platte R.

SMITH 1827-28

SIERRA NEVADA

Humboldt R.

Great Salt Lake

Truckee R.

EBBETTS PASS

SMITH 1827 ➔

Utah Lake

UINTA MTS.
Ft. Uinta ■

Green R.
White R.

ROCKY

S. Platte R.

PAWNEE

Yerba Buena

SMITH 1826 AND 1827

Sevier R.

WASATCH RANGE

PIKES PEAK +

Bent's Ft. ■
CHEYENNE

PAIUTE

SPANISH PEAKS

SAN JOAQUIN VALLEY

OLD SPANISH TRAIL

OLD SPANISH TRAIL

Virgin R.

Purgatoire R.

RATON PASS

TAOS TRAIL

CIMARRON CUT-OFF

KIOW

COAST RANGES

GRAND CANYON

NAVAHO

PUEBLO

Taos

COMANCHE

MOJAVE DESERT

WALAPAI
Mohave Villages
(Smith's defeat 1827)

Colorado R.

Santa Fe

San Miguel

Los Angeles ■
San Gabriel Mission

SAN BERNARDINO MTS.

Albuquerque ●

MEXICAN

POSSESSIONS

San Diego ■

BAJA CALIFORNIA

YUMA

PIMA

PAPAGO

Salt R.

Gila R.

APACHE
Santa Rita
Copper Mines □

MOUNTAINS

PACIFIC

OCEAN

El Paso ●

Rio Grande

Pecos R.

GULF OF CALIFORNIA

CONTINENTAL DIVIDE

COAHUILA

1821-33

Chihuahua ●

Saltil

The Far West, 1821–33, realm of traders and trappers and scene
of Jedediah Smith's historic 1826–28 treks, is shown at left.

plies, he was through with the trade. From that point on,
the company and all its headaches belonged to Ashley.

While Ashley had been preparing to start for the
mountains—by pack train, since water transport up the
Missouri was still highly vulnerable—Fitzpatrick's letter
had arrived, saying that the bulk of the men had crossed
the Rockies to the unknown country beyond. Immediately Ashley adjusted his plans. Guided by Fitzpatrick
and Clyman, he would cross the divide and—the confidence is staggering—somewhere in the immense wastes
beyond would run his hunters to earth.

The trappers were ranging farther than the written
records of the time indicate. Jedediah Smith's tracks are
the only ones even partially clear. Early in July, 1824,
after waving Fitzpatrick's fur carriers Godspeed from
the Sweetwater, he had turned with six men back west
through South Pass. It was not the season for trapping.
Still, they were young—Smith was twenty-five—and a
new world stretched limitlessly before them. Why not
look it over, joyously, with no more care on their minds
than locating streams they might like to revisit in the fall?

There is no record of where they spent the next two
months, but in September they were on the Blackfoot
River in the southeastern part of today's Idaho. There
they encountered a party of Iroquois trappers who had
been detached from a Hudson's Bay Company brigade
working the western Rockies under Alexander Ross. Terrified by Snakes who had robbed them, the Iroquois
offered their cached furs to the Americans in exchange
for protection on the way back to rejoin Ross's brigade.

Having thus located the Canadians, Smith's Americans
learned the brigade's mode of operation and something
of the country in which it operated by blandly following
the exasperated Ross back to headquarters at Flathead
Post on Montana's Clark Fork River, a little upstream
from David Thompson's old Saleesh House. There the
uninvited guests watched a noisy trading fair at which
nearly a thousand Flathead and Nez Perce Indians
swapped beaver, muskrat, and dried meat at abysmal
rates for armament and cloth; and they were very much
on hand when Peter Skene Ogden arrived to put into
effect a new trapping policy designed to keep such Americans as themselves out of the Columbia country.

For years, as Jedediah Smith undoubtedly knew, the
North West and Hudson's Bay companies had been bat-
tering each other into mutual exhaustion. In 1821 they
had at last ended the folly by amalgamating under the
banners of the Hudson's Bay Company. The new broom

was sweeping clean, particularly in the West. In 1824 John McLoughlin, a huge, white-haired, long-experienced trader, six feet four inches tall, took charge of the entire Columbia watershed for the British. Fort George, formerly Astoria, was abandoned in favor of a new headquarters post, Fort Vancouver, to be built a hundred miles upstream on the Columbia, near the mouth of the Willamette, opposite today's Portland. Aware of the advance of American trappers toward the Rockies, the company decided to forestall them by abandoning its normal conservation policies and stripping the country along the Snake bare of beaver. With no fur to tempt the restless mountain men farther west, they might stay away from the Columbia. Because the work was important and Alexander Ross was a bumbler, Peter Ogden was sent to Flathead Post to replace him.

Ogden began poorly. Trailed by Smith's Americans, the ungainly expedition of two hundred and sixty-eight horses and about sixty Indians, half-breeds, and whites, including a few Indian wives, left Flathead Post a little before Christmas, 1824. Heavy snow delayed their approach to the Snake River. As the weather opened, Smith's group went its own way. The departure was small comfort to Ogden, however. By the time he had crossed out of the Snake into Cache Valley, along the lower Bear River of northern Utah, he knew, though he had seen only their traces, that other Americans besides Smith's party had reached the country in force.

Searching for streams that the opposition had not already trapped, he worked south toward the Wasatch Mountains. Great Salt Lake was not far away to his right, but he did not detect it across the flat plains. Americans already knew of it, however—Etienne Provost, perhaps, and certainly Jim Bridger, who had tasted its water either in the fall of 1824 or early in 1825, had spat and reputedly declared in amazement that he had just discovered an arm of the Pacific.

In May Ogden reached the site of the city that today bears his name. From there he turned up a river that later that year would be named the Weber, after one of Andrew Henry's men from the Yellowstone, John Weber; but at the time, the stream seemed untouched. Eagerly the Canadians scattered out. They had many beaver with them when Johnson Gardner, also from the Yellowstone, began running into them here and there. Dazzled by their pelts, Gardner offered more in trade than company policy would let Ogden pay. Fourteen of the men promptly deserted to the Americans.

Before Ogden learned of the defection, Etienne Provost's small party appeared out of Taos. Provost had no idea, either, that some of his countrymen were in the

Aeneas (right), one of many Iroquois trappers with the British traders in the Northwest, lived with Montana Flathead Indians like Chief Adolphe (left). They were drawn by Gustavus Sohon.

area. He and Ogden soon found out. That same afternoon, as noted earlier in the chapter, Gardner and twenty-five Americans arrived in the camp with the deserters. Waving a flag and announcing stentoriously that this was the land of freedom, they offered the remaining *engagés* top prices for their beaver. Several responded; all told, the Americans managed to pick up seven hundred pelts worth more than five thousand dollars in St. Louis. When Ogden showed fight, the United States mountain men cocked their guns, and Gardner snarled that American troops already were marching toward the Columbia to drive Canadians off that river.

(The threat was not pure bluff. Gardner was probably thinking of General Henry Atkinson's Yellowstone Expedition. After the Arikara uprising, the frontier had cried out for a show of force to reopen the Missouri. In 1824, as Gardner may have known, Congress authorized the display, and in 1825 Atkinson started up the river with nearly five hundred men, some of them twisting hand cranks that turned experimental paddle wheels on their eight keelboats. During the summer they reached a hundred miles above the Yellowstone, signing treaties of friendship with all the major tribes except the Blackfeet. But they did not come anywhere near the Columbia.)

Crippled by the defections, Ogden retreated. Gardner's group and the Canadian deserters turned east toward the Green. Provost too rode east with his men, but on the opposite, the south, side of the Uinta Range. Soon he had another unexpected meeting, this time with William Ashley, who was in the middle of an amazing epic.

After conferring with Fitzpatrick at Fort Atkinson, Ashley on November 5, 1824, had started his supply caravan westward along the Platte. The weather was harsh. Wood suitable for fuel was skimpy everywhere on the high plains, but shivering Pawnees told him that there was more along the south fork of the Platte than along the north. The wayfarers bent that way. Blizzards pinned them for nearly a month against the foot of the Colorado Rockies, but by March, 1825, they were moving again, over the Front Range into North Park. From there they slanted across what is now the southern part of Wyoming toward the Green River, losing seventeen horses to thieving Indians and luckily finding at critical moments snow that they could melt for drinking water.

On April 19, 1825, they reached the Green. Ashley deployed most of his men to trap and to look for the wanderers who were somewhere in that transmontane vastness. Rendezvous was set for July at the mouth of Henrys Fork, near the point where the Green begins its wild hairpin surge around the eastern snout of the Uinta Range. With the few men who remained with him, Ashley built two crude boats by stretching fresh buffalo hides over willow sticks. Although he could not swim, he set out in these wobbly craft to explore the river. With him he carried a few goods, in case he encountered some of his own men or Indians with furs to sell.

He did not anticipate the ride he ran into. First he whipped wildly through Flaming Gorge, between reddish precipices half a mile tall. Then the cliffs rounded back into what soon would be known as Browns Hole, thirty miles of romantically beautiful valley that became a favorite wintering spot for trappers and, later on, a hideout for outlaws. Below Browns Hole the canyon narrowed again. The water raged over cataracts and among massive boulders fallen from the cliffs. Today the stretch is part of Dinosaur National Monument; to tourists who have ventured along the snarling chasms, Ashley's feat of navigating them in hide boats waterproofed with tallow seems incredible.

He emerged into barrens. Here and there he found beaver and bottom lands where horses could graze. Two of Provost's men were camped on one flat. Later, after buying horses from Ute Indians and riding westward, the explorers met Provost himself. From the Taos mountaineer they learned of Gardner's clash with Ogden and of the furs the English deserters had brought to the Americans—pelts Ashley hoped to obtain for himself.

Accompanied by Provost's party, he circled the western end of the Uintas and reached the rendezvous site at the appointed time. Every American who had been in the Rockies that year was there, a hundred and twenty men in two camps, whooping, racing horses, swapping gossip —but not loading up on liquor. Ashley had failed to

bring alcohol with him, an oversight that would not be committed again by any other supply caravan.

The men bought the traps, knives, ammunition, and little luxuries they craved—coffee, tobacco, trinkets for their women. Ashley picked up ninety packs of beaver there and another forty-five on his way northeast to the Bighorn. He descended that river, scuffling with Indians along the way, and met General Atkinson's treaty-making expedition at the mouth of the Yellowstone. Luxuriating in the protection of the soldiers, he returned triumphantly to St. Louis, his fortune salvaged.

It was the beginning of the brief, bright days of the Rocky Mountain fur trade. Each summer during the next dozen years, hundreds of trappers and Indians gathered at some centrally located rendezvous—its site varied annually—to sell furs and pick up fresh equipment. Then off they went again. *Engagés* indentured to a company were carefully managed by a "bushway" (bourgeois) and his second-in-command, the "little bushway," or clerk. The squaws of the men set up camp. Hired hands tended

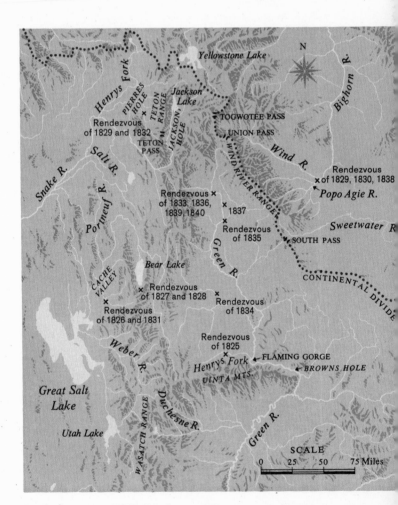

Rendezvous sites, 1825–40, where trappers met supply caravans from the East (sometimes at two places a year) are seen above.

131

the horses, scraped, stretched, and baled the raw furs. At dawn and sunset the hunters waded along the icy streams to destroy their human odor and carefully placed their traps just under the water, baiting them with secretions from the beaver's own glands. Free trappers, a proud title borne by men not contracted to a company, elected their own leaders, established their own rules, and sold their catch at the best prices they could arrange, either at the rendezvous or at Taos.

For those who liked danger, it was an exhilarating life. Sun, blizzards, Indians, and grizzly bears were routine hazards. Thirst-choked men sometimes sought relief by drinking buffalo blood—Thomas James remembered it as tasting like milk—and freezing men sought shelter by wrapping themselves in moist, green buffalo hides that turned hard around them like iron. Starving, they ate

Mohaves like those who attacked Jed Smith were shown rafting the Colorado twenty years later by artist Heinrich Möllhausen.

beaver skin, moccasins, crickets, or tree bark. Ill, they drank buffalo gall mixed with water or hopefully rubbed their rheumatic joints with petroleum that oozed from an oil spring near today's Lander, Wyoming. Some remedies were more heroic. Rattlesnake bites were cauterized by burning gunpowder in them. Assisted by his awed companions, Thomas L. (soon Pegleg) Smith amputated his own shattered limb just below the knee. Jim Bridger carried an iron arrowhead in his back for years until Marcus Whitman finally sliced it loose, without the use of anesthesia, at the rendezvous of 1835.

There were compensations of a sort. The limitless vistas unmarked by trail signs built illusions of freedom. Self-reliance, ingenuity, and physical courage fostered a rough-and-ready individualism that from a distance seems epic. Except for a handful of superior men, how-

ever, the liberty from convention often meant only a lapse into savagery; most trappers were honored to be mistaken for Indians. Though their wants were simple, the men were thralls to the cutthroat transportation system that supplied those wants. The fruits of a year's frightful labor seldom brought them much more than a wild debauch at the rendezvous and equipment enough for another year in the mountains. They destroyed without creating; they were the first of the Far West's many waves of mindless exploiters.

Their frenzied search for beaver swept them into every cranny of the mountains. In the fall of 1826 a brigade under David Jackson and William Sublette discovered the geysers of Yellowstone. Another party, suffering torments of thirst, paddled around Great Salt Lake, searching fruitlessly for the outlet that, in spite of the lake's salinity, they believed must flow out somewhere and lead to the Pacific—a useful highway if they could find it. Farther south, James Ohio Pattie and his father, Sylvester, who mixed trapping with copper mining at Santa Rita, in southwestern New Mexico, followed the Gila to the Colorado, turned up the latter stream, and saw the Grand Canyon, observing in it (one judges from the inconsiderable mention in Pattie's book), not splendor, but only an appalling obstacle.

Far more spectacular were Jedediah Smith's two trips to California. The first came in 1826–27. At the summer rendezvous of 1826, held just south of Bear Lake on the Utah-Idaho border, he and his partners, David Jackson and William Sublette, purchased Ashley's brigades and his goods. Immediately thereafter, Smith led seventeen trappers southwest to learn what opportunities existed in untouched California. Starving, the troop ate their dying horses as they skirted what is now Zion National Park and at last reached haven among the beanfields and melon patches of Mohave Indians on the Colorado River, fifty miles or so below the present site of Hoover Dam. From there native guides took them west across terrible deserts and over the San Bernardino Mountains to the mission of San Gabriel, near Los Angeles.

Lacking proper papers, they ran into trouble with Mexican provincial officials. Fortunately, American sea captains, searching for cheap leather to be used by the new boot factories in New England, had already developed a profitable trade in tallow and cowhides along the California coast. Some of these men persuaded Governor José Echeandia not to jail Smith's party if the trappers agreed to leave California by the same dangerous path they had used in reaching it.

Released, Smith did not comply with the terms but worked due north through the vast, almost totally unknown San Joaquin Valley. Trapping was profitable along the foothills of the Sierra Nevada, but when the time came to take the catch back to the rendezvous of 1827, snow in the mountains stopped the wayfarers.

Since operations for the next year would depend in part on Smith's reports, he felt he had to get back. Leaving furs and most of the men behind, he and two companions, traveling light, started for the high ridges of the Sierra Nevada again on May 20, 1827. This time they broke across the summit of the range at today's Ebbetts Pass. After a nearly fatal traverse of the grisly saline deserts of western Utah, they reached Bear Lake just as the rendezvous was assembling.

Plans made, Smith started again for California to retrieve his men and furs. His group traveled along the trail to the Mohave villages that he had used the year before, moving much faster because he knew the way. At first the Mohaves seemed as friendly as before, but then fell savagely on the party as it was crossing the Colorado River on rafts made of coarse cane grass. Ten men died; nearly all supplies were lost. Smith and eight other survivors fought off pursuit and fled on foot across the desert, suffering hideously under the fiery August sun.

Again the suspicious governor delayed the Americans, and again friendly ship captains helped the party avoid jail. Gathering his men and furs and a herd of horses to sell at the next rendezvous, Jedediah started north through downpours of winter rain. Utter misery went with the party as it forced a snail-slow way through the densely timbered coastal mountains and yawning canyons of northern California and southern Oregon. On July 14, 1828, on Oregon's Umpqua River, Indians struck again, killing fifteen persons and stealing everything the party owned. One hulking trapper named Arthur Black fought free. Smith and two others, out scouting the next day's path, escaped. Eventually all four reached Fort Vancouver, the huge new post the Hudson's Bay Company was building on the Columbia River across from modern Portland.

Almost simultaneously, pudgy George Simpson, the company's governor for all Canada, came down from the Fraser River of British Columbia during the course of one of his whirlwind tours of inspection. He and massive John McLoughlin, chief factor at Fort Vancouver, promptly sent out a police brigade of sorts that recovered most of Smith's furs and horses from the offending Umpqua Indians and then purchased these from the American mountain man at bargain rates.

During the negotiations Simpson questioned Jedediah not only about the fur trade but also about rumbles in United States newspapers regarding settlers searching out, in Simpson's words, the "Wilhamot [Willamette] Country, as a field for Agricultural speculation."

Much of this newspaper talk had emanated from the activities of Congressman John Floyd of Virginia. As we noted earlier, Great Britain and the United States, on October 20, 1818, had signed a convention of joint occupancy that gave citizens of each country equal rights of trade or settlement in Oregon for ten years. Within twenty-six months Floyd had begun introducing into the House a series of bills calling for American penetration of Oregon by military posts and colonial grants.

Nothing came of the proposals. In 1827 the convention of joint occupancy was extended indefinitely, although either power could abrogate the agreement on a year's notice to the other. The frontier protested. More bills to occupy Oregon landed in the Congressional hopper. More colonizing schemes were promulgated, most particularly an 1828 request by Hall Jackson Kelley, a wild-eyed Boston schoolteacher who vowed that if the Government gave him and his associates a hundred miles of land along the lower Columbia (Kelley called it "the grand river Oregon"), he would march west with three thousand settlers. He had no such number of settlers available, and he received no grant—but more of Mr. Kelley in the next chapter.

In the fall of 1828 Governor Simpson may not yet have heard of Kelley's feverish scheme, but he was aware of trends. At Fort Vancouver he pumped his unexpected visitor for more data. Smith reassured him. The deserts he had crossed, Jedediah said, were too barren for travel by untrained families. And the Snake River, so Simpson believed, was likewise too formidable. After his conversations with Smith, he wrote complacently to his superiors in London, "I feel perfectly at ease, unless the all grasping policy of the United States, should induce it, to embark some of its National Wealth, in furtherance of the object [locating settlers in the Pacific Northwest]." Nor were trappers or ship traders likely to become a serious problem. The policy of stripping beaver from the streams ahead of American fur gatherers and of underselling sea peddlers whenever they appeared was removing all attractiveness from the adventures. In short, Simpson thought, Oregon was safe for a long time.

To Jedediah Smith, wandering curiously about Fort Vancouver, the description "all grasping" was best applied to the Hudson's Bay Company. A powerful stockade three hundred and eighteen feet square surrounded warehouses, stores, offices, dormitories, a brick powder magazine, and a deep-porched residence seventy feet long for McLoughlin's family. There were herds of livestock, grainfields, orchards, a dock for ocean-going ships;

farther up the river there would soon be a sawmill. The company's influence over the Indians was "decisive"—the word is Smith's. All told, it looked to him as though the company was turning joint occupancy into a privilege reserved exclusively for Britons.

He carried the sense of injustice with him when he rejoined his partners. For the next year, business engrossed him. Although his own efforts had ended in disasters, Jackson and Sublette had done well. At first there had been little competition. True, Joshua Pilcher had patched up a new firm out of the ruins of the old Missouri Fur Company and had invaded the field in 1827–28, but Indians had stolen so many of his horses, and seepage had spoiled so much of his cached merchandise, that Pilcher had gone bankrupt in a single season. Would-be rivals trying to invade the North from Taos had had no better luck. Save for the constriction of transportation costs and difficulties with Blackfeet Indians in the North and British in the Northwest, the firm of Smith, Jackson, and Sublette had had things its own way.

The situation was too good to last. Increasing numbers of free trappers were roaming streams no longer virgin. A graver threat was Astor's American Fur Company. After General Atkinson had reopened the Missouri in 1825, the firm instituted its famous Western Department by absorbing both the Columbia and French fur companies. Under the ruthless management of Kenneth McKenzie and Pierre Chouteau, Jr., it systematically pushed posts higher and higher up the Missouri. It built massive Fort Union at the mouth of the Yellowstone in 1828–29; Fort Piegan (later Fort McKenzie) at the mouth of the Marias in 1831–32; Fort Cass at the mouth of the Bighorn in 1832. From these posts it planned to dispatch strong brigades throughout the northern Rockies, learning the geography and know-how of the trade by dogging the heels of its better-informed rivals.

The pattern was clear by 1830. That, too, was another year of pioneering for Smith, Jackson, and Sublette, whose summer rendezvous was held just east of the Continental Divide, at the confluence of Wind River and Popo Agie Creek (the site of today's Riverton, Wyoming). Bill Sublette freighted in the firm's supplies in ten big wagons and two dearborns. In the forested East no such trip would have been possible without prepared roads, but beyond the Missouri, as Santa Fe traders long since had demonstrated, the only obstacles were ravines and creek banks—which, to be sure, presented certain dangers: one of Sublette's men out shoveling a way for the wheels was killed by a collapsing bank.

The goods distributed, the partners took a careful look at the future. Something was happening in the Rockies that never before had occurred in America and would not occur in other fields for more years—an end to the land's bounty. When game was exhausted in one section, red hunters and white in times past had always been able to move somewhere else. By 1830, however, the beaver streams had all been found, even in Spanish New Mexico and Arizona. Beyond the mountains lay inhospitable desert or territory dominated by the Hudson's Bay Company. Lacking places to spread, the swarms of free trappers and the brigades of the American Fur Company were going to have to fight the Blackfeet for the forbidden North and rework the streams of Colorado and Wyoming more closely than ever. The time had come, the partners decided, to seek other fields. In August they sold their interests to the Rocky Mountain Fur Company, composed of veteran mountain men Thomas Fitzpatrick, Milton Sublette, Jim Bridger, Henry Fraeb, and Jean Baptiste Gervais. Loading furs and equipment into their ten wagons, they rattled back to St. Louis, arriving in that city in October.

John H. Eaton, Secretary of War in Andrew Jackson's Cabinet, was currently gathering material about the fur trade and the British establishments on the Columbia. His inquiry to the partners gave Smith an opportunity to air his views about Fort Vancouver and the abuses of the Convention of 1818 being wrought by the monopolistic, anti-American policies of the Hudson's Bay Company. The trio mentioned further their feat with the wagons and declared, rather optimistically, that the vehicles could easily have continued to the Great Falls of the Columbia at the eastern foot of the Cascade Mountains, which is not quite what Smith had told Governor Simpson at Fort Vancouver.

Such remarks made fine reading in expansionist newspapers, where they were widely circulated, but the Government made no move—at least nothing official. A curious coincidence might be noted, however. In the spring of 1831, shortly after Eaton had published the testimony he had gathered, a United States Army captain named Benjamin Louis Eulalie Bonneville obtained a two-year furlough to indulge in fur trapping. While engaged in this private commercial flier he would, he wrote his commanding general, Alexander Macomb, also study the British establishments, the Western Indian tribes, and the geography of the area. A year later another Army captain, Richard Bland Lee, obtained from Macomb a one-year furlough to invest in the Santa Fe trading firm of Bent, St. Vrain & Company.

While Bonneville was working around the edges of the Oregon country, Lee examined Santa Fe and Taos. With Kit Carson he took trade goods up the Old Spanish Trail to Antoine Robidoux's Fort Uinta, not far from where Ashley had met Provost in 1825. Like Bonneville, Lee made maps and spoke to the Indians of the United States Government's abiding interest in their welfare. Like Bonneville he overstayed his leave, a dereliction for which neither man was officially punished. Probably the commercial cloaks were honest, and neither captain was a spy in the strict sense. Still, it would be handy for the Army to have their data on hand in case trouble arose with Britain, Mexico, or the Indians of the Far West.

Smith, Jackson, and Sublette, meanwhile, invested their fur trade profits in the booming Santa Fe commerce, adding twenty-three or twenty-four wagons to one of the several caravans that in 1831 creaked west with half a million dollars' worth of assorted goods. It was Jedediah Smith's last adventure. While he was searching for water on the dry *jornada* between the Arkansas and Cimarron rivers, he was killed by Comanche Indians.

Sublette returned to the Northern fur trade. David Jackson joined another pioneering trend by continuing with a few companions to California to buy mules. A small commerce in cloth, mules, and specie was gradually developing with the coast. During the winter of 1827–28 (a few months after Smith's second California incursion), the Patties, father and son, had followed the Gila and Colorado rivers through Arizona to the Gulf of California. From the gulf they had staggered westward across sandy wastes to a mission in Baja California and, promptly, to jail in San Diego, where the elder Pattie died of his sufferings. Two years later (1829–30) a trapping party under Ewing Young completed another successful crossing a little farther north. Indians and terrain made the routes too rugged to endure, however. In 1830–31 William Wolfskill worked out a longer, safer way by following the Old Spanish Trail into central Utah and then bending south in a big horseshoe to join the trail Smith had pioneered across the Mojave Desert.

Mule buyers, trappers, and native traders from New Mexico began regular trips over the roundabout route, meeting on the coast the hide buyers who came around the Horn in sailing ships. A few aliens even located in California. It worried the officials, but they consoled themselves with the thought that if American settlers took out Mexican naturalization papers, all would end well. It was a hope that by that time, 1832 or so, the governor of Coahuila and Texas far to the east would have described as naive indeed.

Not all the Texas *empresarios* were of Stephen Austin's stamp. Particularly obnoxious was Haden Edwards, who in 1825 had been granted a wide sweep of land near Nacogdoches. His arrogant assumptions of power, and his oppressive treatment of Mexicans who lived in the area he claimed, quickly led to a cancellation of his rights and to his expulsion from the country.

Haden Edwards and his brother Benjamin retorted with armed attack. They anticipated help from Austin and from a group of Cherokee Indians who a few years earlier had left unfriendly Georgia and Tennessee for Arkansas and then had moved into northern Texas, yearning for a spot where they could re-establish their lost independence. Some of the chiefs, along with their white advisor, John Dunn Hunter, even supposed they could persuade other tribes to join them in an all-out war of conquest against Texas.

Banking on their support, Benjamin Edwards and a handful of men on December 16, 1826, seized the old

"Shooting Mr. Pattie's Horse" illustrated James Ohio Pattie's narrative of his travels and many adventures in the Southwest.

stone fort at Nacogdoches, raised a flag half-red and half-white to symbolize the two races, and proclaimed the Republic of Fredonia. Nothing happened. An extraordinary adventurer and settler named Ellis Bean, who had first seen Texas with Philip Nolan and who knew the Cherokees well, counseled the majority to restraint. Austin joined his militia to the Government forces. By spring the revolt was over.

In spite of Austin's demonstration of loyalty, the Mexican Government grew increasingly suspicious of Americans. The United States elections of 1828 added to their alarm; the country's new President was Andrew Jackson, plague of Spanish Florida a decade earlier and an avowed expansionist. Nor could the Mexicans avoid the starkness of statistics. By 1830 there were twenty thousand Americans in Texas, and Jackson's ministers in Mexico City were blatantly offering to buy the northern province. The second of the emissaries, unprincipled Anthony Butler, even resorted to bribes to get what Jackson wanted, behaving so crassly that the President eventually had to recall him.

On April 6, 1830, Mexican President Anastasio Bustamante issued a somewhat ambiguous decree closing Texas to further colonizing by Americans, suspending all grants whose terms had been filled, and ordering that further settlement should be made by Mexicans and Europeans. Slavery fell under fresh threats. A seven-year moratorium on importation taxes ended, and payments were complicated by onerous red tape. New troops were sent to strengthen Texas' military garrisons. Meanwhile Mexico herself boiled with revolutionary turmoil, and it became impossible to guess what might happen next.

To the impatient American colonists, the unstable situation was not to be borne. Land speculators busy selling scrip in the United States fulminated against the cancellation of the grants. Cotton growers demanded assurance about slavery. The peremptory way of certain Mexican tax collectors created burning antagonisms. A particular object of fury was John Bradburn, a Hispanicized American in charge of the garrison at the head of Galveston Bay. Bradburn arbitrarily blocked certain land transfers, impressed slave labor without compensation to build forts and then told the Negroes that under Mexican law they really should be free, and substituted military court-martial for civilian procedures in trying rebellious Americans. Eventually he was forced out, but his resignation did not come in time to prevent bloody clashes between Government troops and angry colonists.

Austin, ever loyal, tried to find a solution by supporting the newest revolution of Santa Anna, hoping that if the "liberal" general managed to oust President Bustamante, he would listen to the grievances of the Texas settlers. A mob of two hundred colonists under James Bulloch caught the fever and helped Santa Anna's cause by forcing the surrender of the loyalist garrison at Nacogdoches.

Counting on Santa Anna's gratitude, delegates from the different settlements met on October 1, 1832, at San Felipe de Austin to prepare a list of reforms they wanted. The meeting was premature. Santa Anna had not yet won his fight. Furthermore, the demands did not go as far as some of the colonists wished, particularly in the matter of self-government. Though denying any intent to be disloyal, this radical wing of the settlers believed they could achieve full maturity only if Texas split away from Coahuila and established a semiautonomous legislature of its own. After Santa Anna at last landed firmly in the saddle in Mexico City, a new convention was summoned to meet at San Felipe de Austin in April, 1833, to discuss resolutions looking toward this end.

Riding through the settlements, feeling the pulse of the excited colonists, went a newcomer named Sam Houston. He had arrived in late December, 1832, without a passport, at the end of an extraordinary round of vicissitudes. At the time of Jackson's election he had seemed luck's darling. Aged thirty-five, he was governor of Tennessee and a favorite of Old Hickory's. On January 22, 1829, he had married lovely, eighteen-year-old Eliza Allen, of Gallatin, near Nashville. Three months later, just as Houston was launching his campaign for re-election, the couple separated. No one ever knew why. In the face of Houston's stubborn silence, salacious rumors swept throughout the United States.

Resigning his governorship, he fled to the neighborhood of Fort Gibson, in present eastern Oklahoma, to rejoin Cherokees with whom he had lived for a time during his teen years and who since had migrated west. He seems to have had a wild idea of putting himself at the head of these Indians and conquering Texas. Jackson restrained him, exacting by letter a pledge "that you will never engage in any enterprise injurious to your country that would tarnish your fame."

Thus frustrated, Houston lived dissolutely among the Cherokees for three years, taking one of them, Tiana Rogers, to wife. They changed their name for him from Raven to Big Drunk but let him represent them on missions to Washington. During one trip he beat a congressman on the streets with a cane for imputing fraud to some of his earlier transactions. A sensational trial ended in a public reprimand that jarred him into taking fresh hold of himself. When he returned west, he went soberly, determined to lift himself back into eminence. In December, 1832, he crossed alone into Texas.

On February 13, 1833, he wrote Jackson about the things he had heard during his rides among the settlements—information, as he put it, that "may be calculated to forward your views, if you should entertain any, concerning the acquisition of Texas by the United States." Six weeks later, as a delegate from Nacogdoches, he rode to the new convention at San Felipe to devise some system whereby Texas could live in amity with Mexico.

The delegates overwhelmingly voted for separation from Coahuila. Houston drew up most of the constitution for the proposed new state. Folding a copy of it into his saddlebags, Austin in all optimism rode to Mexico City to lay the plan before Santa Anna.

No one had yet coined the term "Manifest Destiny." But its yeast was bubbling.

Lewis Cass

TO DISTANT CORNERS

The pace with which Americans were moving out to the far limits of their land quickened during the third decade of the 1800's. The frontier east of the Mississippi was almost gone; only Wisconsin, Michigan, and Florida were not states, and as of 1821 there were two states west of the river. Far ahead of the line of settlement, traders opened commerce with Mexican colonies over the new Santa Fe Trail, and fur men explored the mountain country with amazing thoroughness. The source of the Mississippi (above) was, inevitably, one of the far places to give up its secret. In 1820, Governor Lewis Cass of Michigan Territory (left) led an expedition up the river but stopped at Cass Lake, as Zebulon Pike had in 1806, believing that the river began there. But a young scientist with the expedition, Henry Schoolcraft, had some doubts. Not until 1832 did Schoolcraft get a chance to investigate further, but then he established that the river rises from Lake Itasca. The above picture of his expedition meeting with Indians at his Lake Itasca camp is based on one of his own sketches, but it was painted by Seth Eastman, the Army officer-portrayer of the West.

Dr. John McLoughlin

Peter Skene Ogden

Voyageurs, photographed at Fort William on Lake Superior, paddled the wilderness rivers and lakes of half the continent, taking supplies to the Hudson's Bay Company traders and trappers in the West and bringing back the year's load of furs.

Jim Beckwourth   *Jim Bridger*

MEN OF THE BEAVER TRADE

The four men whose portraits appear above, although greatly different in character, were alike in sharing a vocation that demanded something of the quality of giants in its members. All were men of the Western fur trade, members of a fraternity that traced the ridges and valleys and followed virtually every mountain stream to its source in a single-minded pursuit of beaver, exploring as they went an enormous region where white men had never stepped before. The talents of the men pictured were varied. Dr. John McLoughlin, Hudson's Bay Company factor, ran its Columbia District, 1824–46, as a complete autocrat; although a ruthless competitor, he gave aid to rivals (and, eventually, to American settlers) in personal distress. Peter Skene Ogden, leader of fur brigades and McLoughlin's subordinate, explored great areas of Northwest mountains and arid plains from Utah to the Pacific (discovering, among other features, the Humboldt River), but still found time to read and write books. Jim Beckwourth and Jim Bridger were trappers, two of the fabled mountain men who sought beaver, lived lives lonely and wild, and thrived on danger. Beckwourth, a mulatto, became a chief of the Crows and told monumental tales of his exploits, some true, some embellished in mountain man style. Jim Bridger told tall stories, too, but scoffers usually found that they were honest. With Jedediah Smith, Tom Fitzpatrick, Kit Carson, and many others, they found the trails and passes that future generations took West.

DAWN OF "THE WESTERN"

William Ranney's "The Trapper's Last Shot" may well be considered the apotheosis of the mountain man, the point at which he passed from fact into legend. The painting, when reproduced in mid-century as a print (left), brought into unknown thousands of homes the thrill of a new theater of American frontier adventure. The romance of the border of Daniel Boone was eclipsed; farther west was an even vaster arena offering grist for painters and writers of nickel and dime novels. Until today the West has continued to provide a seemingly endless store of dramas, and the movie and television "western," descendant of action-packed paintings like that by Ranney, is still popular fare throughout the world.

A woodcutter's cabin on the Mississippi

The President of the United States, Andrew Jackson

An Indiana camp meeting

"The solemnity of [American] justice"

A TROLLOPE ON WESTERN CULTURE

Mrs. Frances Trollope, mother of Anthony Trollope, spent the years 1827–31 in the United States, and if any aspect of America won her approval in that time, she did not mention it in her book, *Domestic Manners of the Americans*. Most of her stay was in Cincinnati, still a young, raw town, where she and her husband tried and failed to run a fancy-goods shop. The whisky drinking and tobacco chewing, the lack of manners and cultural void, the democratic bumptiousness she criticized did exist, but she refused to recognize that a frontier society needed time to develop social graces. Stung by her caustic wit, defiant Americans reviled her as they did not other critics of their ways. The drawings on these pages are by Auguste Hervieu, who accompanied the English authoress on her travels.

New Orleans steamboat Belvidere

The backwoods settlement of Nashoba, Tennessee, for freed slaves

*Stephen F. Austin in 1833;
miniature by William Howard*

ROOTS OF "THE TEXIANS"

Empty land attracted the westering Americans just as surely as a magnet draws iron filings—and there was a great deal of land in Texas, not only virtually empty (there were only a few thousand Mexicans in the vast province) but much of it very fertile. It would have been attractive to the land-hungry Americans under any conditions; it was especially so after the Panic of 1819 left many of them bankrupt and looking for a place to make a new start. If all Americans had been like Stephen Austin, who completed the arrangements that opened the door to colonists, there might have been no problems, for Austin gave his allegiance to his new country and tried to be a loyal Mexican citizen. But most American colonists brought their independence and dislike of government with them; that, combined with dictatorial Mexican regimes, made trouble inevitable.

An unhappy early attempt at settlement in Texas was made by refugee French Bonapartist soldiers who established a colony, Champ d'Asile (above), on the Trinity River in 1818. But it failed within a year, and the colonists were completely dispersed.

The tremendous extent of Mexican grants to American empresarios is made graphic by this old map of Coahuila and Texas from an 1834 book by a traveler through the region. Stephen Austin, who worked longest and hardest at bringing in and establishing colonists, had by far the largest holdings.

A picturesque and placid aspect of early Texas life (right) is depicted by Theodore Gentilz, himself a settler, though from France. The painting is entitled "The Ox Cart, Returning from San Antonio," and in the background is San Fernando Cathedral, later completely engulfed by San Antonio.

145

The page above is from the field notes of Joseph C. Brown, a civilian who conducted the Government's first instrument survey of the Santa Fe Trail, 1825–27. Brown noted information on landmarks (like the odd hills known as The Rabbit Ears) and when to change course. Such knowledge was important to travelers, since it was easy to lose one's way in the great expanse of plains.

Josiah Gregg was a trader from 1831 to 1840, spending much of that time in Santa Fe and in Mexico and making four round trips over the Santa Fe Trail. Out of his experiences came a book, Commerce of the Prairies, *the best account ever written of this episode in Western history, describing as it does everything from the routine of the trail and encounters with Indians to life in the Mexican towns. The pictures "March of the Caravan" (above) and " 'Dog-Town,' or A Settlement of Prairie Dogs" (left) are from his book, first published in 1844.*

SANTA FE TRADE

The Santa Fe Trail extended some 780 miles, from Westport (now Kansas City) on the Missouri to Santa Fe, where it connected with *El Camino Real*, which led deep into Mexico. Over this road, one of the historic highways of America, moved large caravans of freight wagons, bearing American manufactured goods into the Southwest and returning with a manifest that was largely silver, furs, and mules. It was not a road over most of its course in the sense that there was a narrow beaten track; the wagons followed only a general path over the tough plains grass. While the route was not without its dangers, descriptions of it as colored with blood were grossly exaggerated; Indians virtually never attacked a well-organized caravan, and only eight men died on the trail in its first ten years of use.

The presidio of San Francisco was drawn in 1816 by Louis Choris, artist with a visiting Russian expedition. The humans and horses did not appear in his original but were added when the picture was used in a book of his travels.

THE CALIFORNIOS

When mountain man Jedediah Smith and his party of trappers came out of the hills into the San Bernardino Valley in 1826, the first Americans to enter California overland, they found a culture completely alien to them. The mission system was in full flower; Mission San Gabriel, where they were received, had 30,000 head of cattle and other livestock in proportion, orchards, distillery, looms, and other enterprises, worked by several thousand more or less Christianized Indians under the benevolent but strict direction of a small group of friars. The missions prospered by selling hides and tallow to foreign traders. Richard H. Dana, who shipped in 1835 on a vessel engaged in the hide trade and wrote *Two Years Before the Mast* to tell about it, visited coast villages and found an easygoing land of fandangos, cockfights, casual flirting, horsemanship, and bright clothing. But things changed rapidly. The missions were secularized in 1833, ranches became numerous, and foreigners—sailors, hunters, rovers—drifted in and quietly settled. The California Jedediah Smith had found was soon gone.

Louis Choris depicted two Indians in war dance costumes at San Francisco mission.

This engraving of San Luis Rey mission near San Diego illustrated a travel book by Frenchman Eugène Duflot de Mofras, who saw it in 1841. However, the picture must have been made earlier because all missions were in disrepair by then.

William Coke Smyth entitled the painting from which this lithograph was made "California Mode of Catching Cattle." Smyth was a naval officer and artist with a British Arctic expedition that passed the winter of 1826–27 in California.

A FRONTIER MILITARY ARTIST

Seth Eastman was an Army officer who served for many years on the frontier; he was also a careful observer and an artist of talent. From this combination came one of the finest pictorial records of the Indian ever produced. On graduating from West Point he was sent to Fort Crawford in what would become Wisconsin, then to the upper Mississippi outpost of Fort Snelling. Seven years as an instructor at West Point interrupted his frontier duties, but he returned: to the Seminole War in Florida (1840–41), to Fort Snelling (1841–48), and to Texas (1848–49).

Eastman was no mere casual observer. During his Fort Snelling duty he even learned the Sioux language, and a journalist said he knew the Sioux so well he could "read the private history of a chief or brave by the ornaments which decorate his person." But he did not limit himself to Sioux; he found his subjects wherever he went. In 1850 he was assigned to the Bureau of Indian Affairs to produce the drawings for Schoolcraft's six-volume *Indian Tribes of the United States*. It was a major task, resulting in some 275 pages of drawings on Indian life, implements, and weapons. He returned to frontier duty in 1855, but his prolific output had ended; he did only one known picture until he was retired for disability during the Civil War. His last works, for which he returned to active duty in 1867, were Army and Indian scenes to decorate rooms in the Capitol at Washington. He died in 1875.

2

1

3

(1) "Pawnees Torturing a Female Captive." Actually, this was an annual spring sacrifice, and the torture was only symbolic. The girl captive was given the best of treatment and kept in ignorance of her fate as long as possible. In this sacrifice of a Sioux girl in 1838, she was killed instantly with many arrows at the moment burning brands were pushed at her. Eastman, apparently working from incomplete information, has omitted the arrows and made it a pure torture scene.

(2) "Dakotah Encampment." Eastman includes the elements of Dakota (Sioux) camp life so familiar during his Fort Snelling years: lounging men, gossiping women, bathers, a man on horseback. The woman removing the tepee cover shows the camp is about to move on and raises the question, What will then happen to those canoes?

(3) "Dog Dance of the Dakotahs." A seldom-performed dance whose central feature was the eating of liver of newly-killed dogs, this bizarre activity supposedly made the participants both brave and shrewd.

(4) "Dakotah Village." The Sioux had once all been forest dwellers, and the eastern or Santee Sioux whom Eastman knew had not yet completed the change from forest to prairie. These summer houses are typical woods-Indian dwellings.

(5) "Indian Sugar Camp." Eastman here turns to the Chippewas for a subject. He knew these people of the Northern forests well; they came to Fort Snelling to trade, and he traveled in their country. Here, with his usual attention to detail, he shows women at the various tasks involved in maple sugar-making, an annual activity of the late winter.

(6) "Protecting the Cornfields from Vermin." Naked and trailing her garment, the woman walks around her cornfield in the moonlight to form a magic protective circle against insects and animals. All the pictures on this page were also used as black-and-white engravings in Schoolcraft's Indian Tribes.

151

The Texas Range

"We take up the line of march at bugle-call in the morning, and it may be a long time before I can send a Letter again, as there are no post-offices nor mail carriers in the country where we are now going. . . . I am now to enter upon one of the most interesting parts of the Indian country . . . one of the wildest and most hostile. . . ."

The artist George Catlin, accompanying the U.S. First Regiment of Mounted Dragoons into lands of Comanches and Wichitas, southwestern Oklahoma and Texas, July 14, 1834

CHAPTER SEVEN

THE SOUTHWESTERN BARRIERS

1825-1844

When Great Britain and the Indians proposed several times before the War of 1812 that a nation of red men be established north of the Ohio as a barrier to American expansion, the United States objected indignantly. Yet not long after the war, she created exactly that sort of barrier for herself by establishing a "permanent" Indian Territory immediately beyond the western borders of Missouri and Arkansas. As a consequence, expansion split north and south into twin prongs and, instead of filling the plains, leapfrogged to the alien lands of Texas and the Pacific Coast.

Talk of solving the Indian problem by moving the aborigines to the barren buffalo prairies beyond the 96th meridian had been gaining listeners ever since Zebulon Pike and Stephen Long had returned with their discouraging reports about a Great American Desert. Even a few Eastern Indians seemed to think that moving was a good idea. In 1809 Cherokee hunting parties roaming as far as today's Oklahoma had sounded out their tribesmen about locating there, but when the majority of the nation disapproved, the idea came to nothing.

It revived after the war as the speculative demand for cotton land drew rings of white settlement tighter and tighter around the territories that still remained to the Southern tribes. Wearied by the pressures, a few of the Cherokees of eastern Tennessee and the Choctaws of Mississippi between 1816 and 1820 agreed to swap their Eastern lands for new holdings in what became Arkansas Territory. (After the creation of that territory in 1819, the Indians had to move again. As we shall see, some Chero-

kees settled, to their coming sorrow, in northeastern Texas, on land obtained in 1824 from the Mexican Government.) Northward, in 1818–19, certain Delawares, Shawnees, Miamis, and Kickapoos also agreed to surrender their hunting grounds and move into the eastern part of today's Kansas.

The Government cleared the way by making treaties with the Western Indians, ejecting white squatters illegally located on lands assigned to the newcomers, and assisting the travelers during their migrations. The moves were haphazard. Mass relocations did not become official policy until the closing days of Monroe's administration.

Two popular philosophies justified the upheavals. The "superior race" theory proclaimed that inferior peoples held land in trust only until a race appeared capable of making more productive use of the soil. Humanitarians argued simultaneously that since the Indians had shown themselves particularly susceptible to the vices of the crude frontier, they must be removed to the distant West so that the work of civilizing them could continue free from contaminating influences.

By 1825 a definite boundary between the United States and Indian country had taken shape in governmental minds. It ran from the mouth of Green Bay (northern Lake Michigan) west to the Mississippi, leaving the woods and lakes of upper Wisconsin to the Indians, and after following the Mississippi a ways, swung south through Iowa to the northern border of the state of Missouri. There it bent west to the Missouri River, then dropped south once more along the western edges of Missouri and Arkansas. In general, the area north of the

Platte was to be the home of the tribes already living there. The land south of the Platte to the Red River border of Texas was to furnish a haven for the relocated Eastern tribes. Forever and forever it was to be Indian country. To keep whites back and Western tribes at peace with the arriving Eastern Indians, three forts were established along the eastern edges of the new Indian country —Fort Leavenworth, in today's Kansas; Fort Gibson, in east-central Oklahoma, where the Verdigris and the Neosho join the Arkansas; and Fort Towson, almost on the Texas border.

During the administration of John Quincy Adams, the Government sought to move the Eastern tribes through peaceful persuasion. Except for a brief scare created in 1827 by the Winnebagos of southwestern Wisconsin, the shattered Northern tribes began a resigned, trouble-free drift westward. The Southern tribes, on the other hand, were more stubborn, arguing an unshakable attachment to their ancestral homes.

Additional resentment rose from the fact that each group—Cherokees, Chickasaws, Choctaws, Creeks, and, to an extent, the Seminoles in Florida—had made remarkable strides in agriculture, handicrafts, and self-government. Livestock breeding, cotton spinning, flour milling, and the like improved steadily. A quarter-breed Cherokee, George Guess, or Sequoyah (the giant redwoods of California were later named for him), invented a written alphabet that many Cherokees learned enthusiastically. A newspaper and Bible translations soon appeared; schools sprang up; Christian missionaries were welcomed. Talk about moving the "inferior" Indian races out of the way of "superior" white farmers began, in brief, to sound more and more silly.

Still, the Southern states did have a legal right on their side. When in 1802 Georgia had finally ceded to the United States her Western lands, which stretched to the Mississippi River, she had attached a proviso that the Federal Government should extinguish the Indian titles with all convenient speed. A quarter of a century later, Indians still held millions of acres in Georgia, as well as in Alabama and Mississippi, states that had been created from those ceded lands. Why, Southerners asked, did not the Government keep its promise?

On July 26, 1827, the Cherokees precipitated the issue by declaring themselves, on the strength of early treaties with the United States, a sovereign nation and adopting a constitution modeled after that of the Federal Government. The maneuver in effect declared that Georgia had no authority over the Cherokee nation. The Georgians furiously denied that an independent country could legally exist within their state boundaries and gave force

to their contention by annexing the Cherokee counties.

Andrew Jackson's election to the Presidency in 1828 made the Indians' case hopeless. Under his prodding, Congress in May, 1830, passed an Indian Removal Bill that did not explicitly authorize force in relocating the tribes but was so worded as to make that interpretation possible. Meanwhile, gold was discovered on Cherokee land at Dahlonega, Georgia, and the Indians' rights were trampled remorselessly in the stampede that followed.

Desperately the Cherokees turned to the Supreme Court. Although that body in 1832 declared Georgia's laws null and void in Indian country, the state refused to heed. Nor did Jackson demand compliance with Federal edict, although, cynically enough, he was outraged at the same time because South Carolina had dared defy the Government's rulings concerning the tariff. Encouraged by Jackson's attitude, Alabama and Mississippi also extended the jurisdiction of their laws over the Indian "nations" within their borders.

Armed resistance was hopeless, as Black Hawk was illustrating farther north. Years before (1804), the Sauk and Fox tribes had ceded their Illinois lands to William Henry Harrison but had been allowed to remain on them until the area was needed for settlement. The time came

Choctaw girls of one of the Civilized Tribes, once in the Southeast, were photographed in Oklahoma by W. H. Jackson.

in 1830–31, after a rush of miners to the Galena lead fields brought farmers in their wake. While the bulk of the Sauk tribe was away on winter hunts, white squatters moved into their town of Saukenuk, at the mouth of Rock River, Illinois, destroyed or appropriated homes, made free with cornfields, tore down fences, and beat Indians who remonstrated. Extensive clashes were narrowly averted during the summer, and in the fall of 1831 Black Hawk, who always had denied the validity of the 1804 treaty, promised to return to Iowa forever.

A miserable winter without adequate food or shelter and a mistaken reliance on English and Winnebago support changed the minds of his "British band," so called because of its frequent visits to Malden in Canada. Despite the opposition of Keokuk and a peaceful part of the tribe, Black Hawk in the spring of 1832 crossed back over the Mississippi with four hundred warriors and their families. Although he insisted that his intent was peaceful, alarm shivered through Illinois. Troops marched; militia poured to the colors in overwhelming numbers. Though Black Hawk won an initial skirmish, it served only to bring more men into the field against him. Thereafter, his "war" consisted of an agonizing flight up Rock River and west across Wisconsin, ending in a massacre as his people tried to recross the Mississippi to Iowa.

The crushing of the Sauks added to the discouragement of the peaceful segments of the Southern tribes. Was it not wiser to give up the struggle, sign the best terms possible, and move? The Government tempted those who were undecided by promising migrants rifles, blankets, kettles, and tobacco. It said it would provide caravans for those traveling in groups; families choosing to move on their own would receive subsistence payments varying from fifteen to fifty dollars. As more and more unhappy householders signed up for the trips, it became possible for wily agents to speed the Government's designs by playing off faction against faction.

The United States offered only one alternative to removal. A man could drop membership in his tribe, become a United States citizen subject to state law, and receive a "reservation" of six hundred and forty acres or more, depending on the size of his family. These reservations opened the way to giant frauds. "Ravenous speculators," wrote one registrar of public lands in Mississippi, "are carrying everything before them." By alcohol, trickery, cajolery, and flagrant misrepresentation, white land hogs persuaded Indians to apply for reservations, often illegally, and then sell the rights to their white friends. In Mississippi alone, fraudulent claims ballooned to 3,840,000 acres and invited belated Congressional investigation. Many reservations, how-

From his Saukenuk home, Black Hawk fled up the Rock River, then went back to tragic defeat at Bad Axe on the Mississippi.

ever, stayed in Indian hands. By means of them, as well as by hiding in inaccessible places, a fairly substantial minority of each tribe managed to remain behind when their fellows were transplanted.

The enforced movements were carried out during several years in the 1830's. The long "trails of tears" were in many instances turned into a shambles by incompetent and dishonest contractors of transportation and food, and by the un-co-operative acts of the Indians themselves. Inclement weather, radical changes in diet and climate, whisky, carelessness, steamboat sinkings, cholera, and smallpox killed thousands of the migrants. The stubborn Cherokees, who refused to budge until herded west by troops in 1838, were particular sufferers. Only the Seminoles fought back. Digging into Florida's almost impenetrable swamps, they waged a desperate war that cost the United States Army more than fifteen hundred lives and upwards of twenty million dollars before remnants of the tribe were finally thrust westward among the relocated Creeks in today's Oklahoma.

By the time the job was done, roughly 1842, the United States had acquired, since the Revolution, 442,866,370 acres of Indian land in the East. In 1840 the Government was selling its public domain to settlers for $1.25 an acre. Thus the value of the Indian land can be calculated at $553,583,000. The Government's actual expenditures (apart from the cost of its long series of Indian wars) were $31,331,403 in money and 53,757,400 acres of Western land obtained through the Louisiana Purchase at slightly more than four cents an acre. For good measure, toss in certain continuing annuities and payments made each year to Indian schools and the "general civilization" fund. The total cost of the Indian land in the East then comes to about ten cents an acre, one twelfth of what the Government resold it for. This was not quite as striking a bargain as the Louisiana Purchase. Still, very few of the conscienceless speculators rushing frantically around the frontier during those hectic days managed to do anywhere near as well.

Benefits to the Indians were negligible. They did not escape the contaminations of the frontier, as many humanitarians had hoped they would. Although some of the transplanted Delawares and Shawnees in Kansas adapted themselves to the arid plains and became successful hunters for the fur men and for such explorers as Frémont, they were exceptions. The Southern Indians in particular tried to cling to familiar climates by huddling close to the eastern boundary of Oklahoma. This brought them within easy reach of the Arkansas settlements. In spite of the stringent new laws of 1834 that imposed total prohibition in the Indian country and required passports of all whites crossing the border, whisky peddlers and unscrupulous traders still found ways to cheat the gullible aborigines and subvert the civilizing work of the ill-trained teachers, blacksmiths, and clerks attached to the inadequate agency staffs.

When hunting parties of the relocated tribes did venture west after buffalo, they clashed with the horse tribes of the plains. In 1833, after Delawares had wiped out a Pawnee village in retaliation for an attack on a hunting group, the alarmed Army called a series of peace talks at Fort Leavenworth. It followed these the next year by a march of some four hundred dragoons into the trouble spots of western Oklahoma. The gesture almost ended in disaster. Blazing heat intensified an outbreak of malaria. General Henry Leavenworth sickened and died; at one point, half the column was immobilized. With the other half, General Henry Dodge marched doggedly on almost to New Mexico and extracted a promise of good behavior from Wichitas, Kiowas, and Comanches—"as availing," according to a version written by Philip St. George Cooke, an early Army officer who had literary bents, "as it would be to attempt to establish a truce

between the howling wolf of the prairie and his prey."

At the very time that the United States was setting up this barrier to westward expansion, the demand for land was quickening under the pressures of a new cycle of prosperity and increasing immigration from Ireland, Germany, and England—half a million new arrivals between 1830 and 1840. The Erie Canal, whose tolls in eight years repaid the seven-million-dollar cost of construction, and the busy little steamers of the Great Lakes poured settlers into the hitherto-neglected lowlands of northern Indiana and the "oak openings" of southern Michigan and central Wisconsin. Other pioneers hitched six or more yoke of oxen to giant iron plows and ventured out onto the heavy sod of the Illinois prairies. Still more settlers swarmed across the Mississippi onto the "Black Hawk Purchase" of eastern Iowa, wrested from the Sauk Indians after their stubborn chief's crushing defeat. Eager planters bid frantically for the vacated Indian lands of the South. To sum it up in statistics: Government land sales swelled from a little under four million acres during 1833 to more than twenty million during 1836. Money clinked and clattered into the Federal tills at such a rate that the national debt was extinguished and, fantastic though it sounds today, the Government began debating how best to dispose of the surplus.

Nearly everyone could get money. Jackson's refusal to recharter the Bank of the United States and his placing of Government deposits in certain "pet banks" throughout the country helped inflate credit and bring about higher prices. Inspired by the success of the Erie Canal and hopeful of Federal aid, all the lusty young states east of the Mississippi joyfully waded out into bogs of debt in order to finance a network of canals and roads of their own. These helped bring manufactured goods and immigrants from the East, sped crops to market, and created still more optimism. Eyeing strategic junction points, speculators in townsites became more feverish than ever. Many town schemes were, as usual, pure hokum; but a few, like Chicago, which was visited in 1833 by three hundred ships, though her population at that time was only three hundred and fifty, succeeded mightily.

As the price of wheat, corn, and cotton rose, capital moved toward the frontier, particularly as represented by the "planter aristocracy" of the South. Under pressure of these well-financed competitors, small farmers sold out and moved farther west, looking for untouched lands they could afford to develop. The trend did not bring the West unalloyed delight, however. All public land, good, bad, or indifferent, sold for $1.25 an acre. Inevitably, men raced each other into the wilderness in search of choice plots, while hundreds of thousands of

Fort Butler, an emigration depot for Cherokees being sent west on their "Trail of Tears," was situated on North Carolina's Hiwassee River. The artist of the sketch, drawn during an 1838 survey of Cherokee lands, is unknown.

less desirable acres remained uncultivated close to various hopeful towns in dire need of increased business.

In an effort to induce settlers to consider these overlooked areas, Senator Benton of Missouri led a long battle to graduate prices according to desirability; land that was not purchased within a certain time would even be given away in order to bring it into some sort of cultivation. Though his effort proved fruitless, it did help spread a growing frontier belief that public land should no longer be sold to raise revenue for the Government but should be used instead to furnish homesteads and hence give individual dignity to the nation's growing agricultural population.

Greater success attended the West's demand for preemption—the right of a man to settle on whatever land he wanted and to pay later, in effect a form of credit. Partly because of inadequate appropriations, surveys tended to lag behind settlement. Since Colonial days, impatient "movers" had always jumped paper borders to settle where they wished. Thus, when surveys at last were completed and blocks of land were thrown open to purchase, the best pieces were generally occupied already by squatters who considered themselves not lawbreakers but tamers of the wilderness. Many of these squatters were soon to be disillusioned. When they showed up at the land offices to buy their homes, they often were outbid by well-heeled speculators and so lost the result of their labor, except for what they could pry from the purchasers in exchange for the improvements to the land—buildings, fences, wells, and so on.

In the West's mind, pre-emption would cure this unfairness. The conservative East, which in general opposed cheap land lest it drain away factory workers and raise wages, was horrified. A pre-emption law, in the words of the New York *Courier and Enquirer* (January 27, 1838), would simply give grants-in-aid to "squatters engaged in cheating the government out of the best tracts of public lands." The frontier won, however. Even the sudden, crushing Panic of 1837, the second disastrous depression to visit the speculative Americans in a single generation, did not slow their demands for land reform. The series of limited, temporary pre-emption measures that had begun in 1830 became permanent national policy in 1841. The way was open at last for the home-

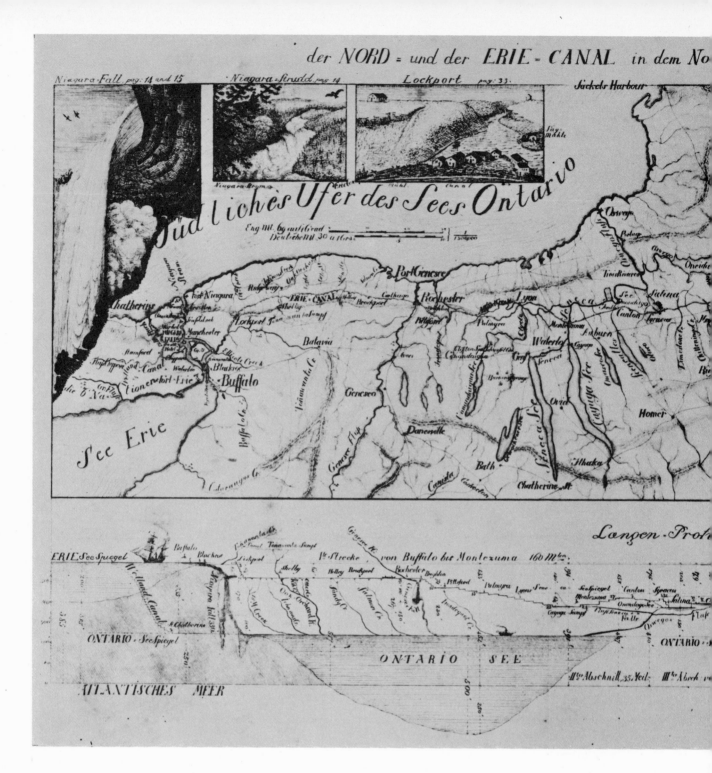

stead acts—the offer of "free land"—of later decades.

This combination of many pressures—swelling population, speculative frenzies, transportation panaceas, the displacement of poorer farmers, and pre-emption—turned more and more eyes westward to land once deemed too remote and too undesirable for agriculture. What they saw was an exasperating barrier, created by the Government itself—the new Indian nation. It was particularly galling beyond Missouri and Arkansas. Northward, the empty lands of Michigan, Wisconsin, and eastern Iowa

temporarily relieved the pressures. In the South, no such outlets existed, yet Southern expansion had always marched geographically ahead of that in the North; Kentucky, for instance, had been sprinkled with towns while Ohio remained a wilderness. Where could new escapes be found, save in the Pacific Northwest, a region that seemed infinitely remote, or in Texas, which was known as an alien land torn by strife?

During 1832 and 1833, it will be recalled, most of the twenty thousand or more Americans in Texas had sup-

158

ERIE = CANALS, 1826.

Interest in New York's Erie Canal, both as an engineering accomplishment and as an aid to emigrants intending to seek new homes in the American West, resulted in the publication even in Europe of detailed maps and views like the illustration at left. Issued in Stuttgart, Germany, in 1835, the map depicted the new water route leading toward the Western states and territories of the United States.

ported the revolution of Antonio López de Santa Anna. As soon as he had seemed on the point of success, a colonial convention had dispatched Stephen Austin to Mexico City to seek a reversal of the harsh tax laws and restrictions against immigration passed in 1830, and to present a new state constitution that would allow Texas to govern herself independently from Coahuila.

Affairs dragged. Santa Anna was out in the provinces, suppressing continued uprisings. Austin was ill much of the time. When he made no progress with minor officials,

he gave way to pique and imprudently wrote to the governing council in Texas suggesting that the settlements form their own state government. Almost immediately thereafter, Santa Anna returned from his military exercises and suavely granted nearly every Texas request except statehood. Feeling his mission at least a limited success and hoping that home rule would follow if the province remained calm, Austin started for home.

The Coahuila legislature also made placatory gestures, passing new laws that improved the Texas judicial system, extended religious toleration, and legalized trade by foreigners—that is, by Americans. None of these apparent changes of heart was likely to endure, however. Coahuila, an arid ranching and mining district without access to the sea, had no true economic rapport with the humid farming areas of east Texas and the Gulf coast, where ports were rapidly being opened to commerce with New Orleans. Mexican absolutism in politics and religion was incapable of any real wedding with the Protestant individualism of most of the Texas colonists. Only the creation of a strong mutual trust could reconcile these antipathies; in its place came Santa Anna, to whom duplicity and cruelty were as innate as breathing.

Austin discovered some of these sad truths on his way home. His imprudent letter had fallen into the hands of Government officials. At Saltillo he was arrested, hauled back to Mexico City, and put into solitary confinement. No official charges reached him. For weeks he could not see a lawyer, apply for bail, or obtain a trial. Then pressures from Texas brought about gradual improvement in his lot, until finally he was permitted to roam Mexico City on his own recognizance.

Persistent uprisings in the meantime so exasperated Santa Anna that he abrogated the constitution of 1824, which had established a federal system of government in Mexico, and replaced it with a strongly centralized national authority. He ordered the strengthening of military garrisons throughout the country and put his brother-in-law, General Martín Perfecto de Cos, in charge of the eastern *Provincias Internas*, which included Texas. Cos suspended all local government in Coahuila and Texas, dispatched advance squads north to tighten customs collections at Anáhuac and Brazoria in Texas, and set a revenue cutter to patrolling the Gulf coast.

During these developments Austin was at last permitted, in the summer of 1835, to leave Mexico. He sailed from Veracruz to New Orleans and thence by American ship to the new Texas port of Velasco, near the mouth of the Brazos River. He went heavyhearted, convinced that autonomy for Texas was impossible so long as Santa Anna remained the dictator of Mexico. What was the answer? More patience? A resort to arms in an effort to wrest concessions from the treacherous general? Or a bloody fight for complete independence?

Gunfire underscored the urgency of the questions. At Anáhuac a trigger-tempered young lawyer named William B. Travis, who once before had used violence to protest against the port authorities, gathered together two or three dozen settlers and on June 30, 1835, chased the new customs garrison out of town. A few weeks later the Mexican revenue cutter outraged American ship cap-

SAN JACINTO MUSEUM OF HISTORY

Santa Anna, the in-again, out-again Mexican ruler, is shown in a daguerreotype made about 1850.

tains plying the coast by taking a United States brig into custody. The vessel bringing Austin home retaliated by opening fire on the cutter and driving it away from the mouth of the Brazos.

Strictly speaking, the naval clashes lay outside the competence of Texas; but they caused great excitement nevertheless, and the echo of the shooting stayed in Austin's ears as he rode back toward his town of San Felipe. An armed struggle against Santa Anna, he decided, was inevitable. But he still hoped to stay loyal to Mexico and so wrote to a "Consultation" of settlers that met at San Felipe in November.

Determined to make an example of Travis, General Cos marched his army toward San Antonio. The commander of the Mexican garrison at that city hoped to welcome the general by presenting him with a six-pounder brass cannon owned by the citizens of Gonzales, seventy-some miles east of San Antonio. The Gonzales settlers upset him by refusing to surrender the gun. Loading it with iron balls and pieces of chain, they frightened the advancing Mexican soldiers, one hundred strong, back to their base. The success was much too easy. The burly-muscled Texans now thought they could handle the entire Mexican army with fly swatters.

Though lacking military experience, Austin put himself at the head of six hundred volunteers and marched to attack Cos, who had just reached San Antonio. As the

Texans neared the town in their turn, Austin belatedly recalled that he lacked adequate artillery. Canceling plans for a pitched battle, he settled his grumbling volunteers to a siege. The main action during the weeks that followed was the routing of a Mexican pack train that had ventured out to cut grass for the livestock that were starving inside the town.

Sam Houston, who since his arrival in Texas late in 1832 had been practicing law and politics between Nacogdoches and Washington, traveled now to New Orleans to appeal for volunteers: "Come with a good rifle and come soon . . . 'Liberty or Death!'" Within days, ten thousand dollars had been contributed, and a company called the New Orleans Grays was hurrying west, afraid they might arrive too late for the fun. The excitement swept throughout the United States. Meetings to raise men and money for Texas became a rage, particularly in the Mississippi Valley. Idealists, farmers hoping for bounties in land, drifters, opportunists, and young men hungry for adventure signed their names to volunteer lists and scurried about looking for equipment. By the end of 1835, the number of Americans in Texas probably exceeded thirty thousand.

Influenced by Austin, the November Consultation in San Felipe voted down a resolution that Texas secede from Mexico. But it simultaneously rejected Austin as provisional governor and elected instead a proponent of independence. Austin was appointed a member of a commission to seek aid from the United States, and accordingly resigned his generalship. The troops thereupon elected in his place an old Indian fighter named Edward Burleson, who proved to be as cautious as his predecessor. The Consultation concurrently named Houston commander in chief of the regular army. Strangely, his authority was not deemed to extend to the volunteers still camped outside San Antonio. All he could do with these independent soldiers, as he set about creating an official force, was make recommendations.

He suggested that the volunteers go into winter quarters. This did not suit the mood of the more impatient members. A leader of the dissidents, Ben Milam, stormed through the camp shouting for an attack.

What followed is almost incredible. Disobeying Burleson, their own elected general, and ignoring Houston, the commander in chief of Texas, three columns began, on the morning of December 5, 1835, to bore their way into the town—literally. A handful of soldiers would force entrance into one house and with battering-rams break through the adobe walls into the next. Sharpshooters at windows and on rooftops gave support by sweeping the streets. House by house, the Mexican soldiers fell back to Cos's headquarters inside the Alamo.

Founded originally as the mission of San Antonio de Valero, the Alamo had long since been abandoned as a center of religious activity. The roof of the church had collapsed. Nevertheless, the establishment made a good fort. Its thick stone and adobe outer walls surrounded an area of about two and a half acres. The cells of the abandoned convent furnished useful living quarters; the stone jail made a fine powder magazine; the plaza around which the buildings were grouped was a convenient gathering place. Cannon could be placed on earthworks above the walls at strategic corners.

With adequate food and water Cos might have held the place indefinitely. But the long siege had left him short of supplies and fuel, and the weather was wet and cold. Perhaps one hundred and fifty of his soldiers had been slain during the house-to-house fighting, but only two Americans had died, one of them Ben Milam. Unnerved, three bedraggled Mexican companies slipped away through the darkness toward the Rio Grande. Panic demoralized the rest, and on December 10, Cos surrendered. He was granted parole on his honor not to oppose the re-establishment of the constitution of 1824; this condition met, he was allowed to march his eleven hundred survivors back into Mexico.

The reaction in Texas was next to suicidal. Francis W. Johnson and Dr. James Grant, the latter a Scottish speculator in lands below the Rio Grande, led a raw gang toward Matamoros, promising plunder. Settlers everywhere cried for the regular army to support the freebooters. Knowing how ill prepared Texas was for a sustained campaign and convinced that Santa Anna would soon launch retaliatory attacks, Sam Houston and Henry Smith, head of the provisional government, opposed the reckless move. The council, however, overruled Houston and Smith, and James W. Fannin was put in charge of a force that reached Goliad (formerly La Bahia) and there bogged down.

Travelers along *El Camino Real* brought word that Santa Anna was massing a formidable army at different points along the Rio Grande, vowing death to every rebel caught bearing arms. The second government convention that assembled in the new village of Washington retorted on March 2, 1836, (Sam Houston's forty-third birthday) with a declaration of independence and Houston's reappointment as commander in chief of the Texas forces. He was greeted to his new term by word of a series of staggering disasters that had befallen his scattered military units even before the convention met.

General José Urrea had killed Johnson and wiped out his Matamoros raiders at San Patricio on February 27.

Grant's turn came a few days later, March 2. By that time, Santa Anna had appeared outside San Antonio, after a far swifter march through wretched weather and across inhospitable terrain than anyone had anticipated.

One hundred and fifty men under William Travis defended the town. They were a stout band. At least two of them have become American legends: David Crockett, the famous bear hunter and backwoods congressman from Tennessee, and barrel-chested James Bowie, inventor of the murderous knife that carries his name. They expected reinforcements daily. The provisional government had ordered Fannin, sitting irresolutely at Goliad, to join them, a move Travis also urged through private messengers of his own. Fannin started but turned back when one of his wagons gave out. Neither man worried much about the failures, however. They were confident that hordes of volunteers from the United States were already on the way to aid them.

Instead, on February 23, 1836, Santa Anna ringed the Alamo, ordered the garrison to surrender or be put to the sword, and began a bombardment with light fieldpieces.

Shown above are the principal sites of Texas' turbulent history from the days of Austin's colony until annexation in 1845.

The shooting killed no one but induced Travis to send his famous appeal "To the People of Texas & all Americans in the world. . . . If this call is neglected, I am determined to sustain myself as long as possible & die like a soldier who never forgets what is due to his own honor & that of his country—VICTORY OR DEATH!"

Thirty-two men and teen-age boys from Gonzales managed to make their way through the Mexican lines, bringing the number of defenders in the Alamo to between 182 and 188—accounts vary. Fewer than twenty of the total were citizens of Texas.

Far greater reinforcements reached Santa Anna, until perhaps three thousand men surrounded the adobe walls. A little before dawn on Sunday, March 6, the Mexicans launched their attack. Massed bands played the fearful *Degüello*—which literally means the throat-cutting, signifying that no prisoners were to be taken.

The carnage was dreadful. The attackers fell dead in heaps but more scrambled on, lodging themselves at last against the walls, where the artillery could not be brought to bear on them. They breached the north barricade and swarmed through the plaza into the church and the convent, clubbing and knifing. All but five defenders died fighting; those five, dragged from hiding, were executed. Texan bodies were piled with brush and wood in front of the mission and burned. Dead Mexicans were buried in the old mission graveyard until it could hold no more; the putrefying remainder were thrown into the river. The man in charge of the disposal complained that he had sixteen hundred Mexican corpses to handle. Santa Anna reported officially that two hundred and twenty-three were wounded and fewer than a hundred killed. The true figure is undoubtedly somewhere in between.

Houston had reached Gonzales on his way to help Travis when he learned of the disaster from the wife of a slain defender, Mrs. A. M. Dickinson, who was carrying a fifteen-month-old baby, and from Travis's Negro slave, Joe, both of whom were spared so that they could warn Houston of what awaited all rebels. Hopelessly outnumbered, Houston began a spirit-withering retreat, holding his resentful army together until he could find time to drill, regroup, and turn a cohesive force around to fight. Along the dismal road east he learned that Fannin had surrendered after a desperate battle near Goliad. The prisoners, together with captives taken at various other small engagements along the coastal plain, were promised clemency by the victor, General Urrea. Santa Anna countermanded the order. Upwards of three hundred men were marched in three columns onto the prairies and murdered. Twenty-seven managed to bolt away during the confusion. The bodies of the others, like the corpses

A survivor of the fall of the Alamo, Susanna Dickinson (above), the widow of one of the defenders, was set free after the siege.

at the Alamo, were tossed into piles and then burned.

A wild panic swept Texas. In what came to be called the Runaway Scrape, distraught families fled toward the border, often supported by nothing more than the possessions they could carry on their backs. In May Comanches and Kiowas took advantage of the confusion to fall on Parker's Fort, forty miles east of present Waco. After massacring most of the men, the Indians carried away the women and children. One girl, Cynthia Ann Parker, later married a Comanche chief. After being "rescued" late in the 1850's, she tried three times to return to the Comanches and, failing, finally starved herself to death.

Saying nothing whatsoever of his intentions to the suspense-torn country, Houston dropped back and back and back, toward the junction, near the present-day city of Houston, of the San Jacinto River and Buffalo Bayou: mingled swampland, prairie, and oak forest, where the only escape was a single ferry across the San Jacinto. Santa Anna followed joyfully. Convinced that all Texas was utterly demoralized, the Mexican let his army rampage along in several semi-isolated columns. He himself

swung toward Harrisburg, hoping to capture the fleeing president of Texas, David Burnet. The man eluded him. In his disgust, Santa Anna burned the town and then drove his weary men on, intending to bring Houston into his grip by reaching the essential ferry ahead of him.

Houston's seven hundred and eighty-three Texans won the race, stopped with their backs to the ferry, and faced around, screened by a line of oaks, evergreens, and magnolias. Beyond a parklike plain rose a low hill crowned with woods. Santa Anna camped there, made a barricade of packsaddles, baggage, and brush, and then let his soldiers rest until nearby reinforcements could reach him. Strangely, Houston did not attack but was content to let his two cannons, a gift from the citizens of Cincinnati, wage a fruitless duel with Santa Anna's single fieldpiece. The Mexican reinforcements arrived. Houston went to bed with orders that he was not to be disturbed. Refreshed by his first full night's sleep in weeks, he woke well after daylight on April 21, 1836— and still did nothing.

Was he canny, lulling Santa Anna into overconfidence? Or was he indecisive, waiting on luck? It is impossible to say. In any event, Santa Anna did grow careless. Convinced that Houston was incapable of attacking, the Mexican general let his army settle down for an afternoon siesta. Houston mounted a white horse and rode along the lines. "Remember the Alamo! Remember the Alamo!" They took the enemy by such total surprise that the Battle of San Jacinto was over in eighteen minutes. During that time, Texans say, six hundred and thirty Mexicans were killed and seven hundred and thirty— more than two hundred of them wounded—were taken prisoner, including Santa Anna. Only nine Texans died. Twenty-six were injured, among them Sam Houston, his right leg bone shattered above the ankle into so many fragments that during the following days he nearly died from loss of blood, exhaustion, and gangrene.

Instead of counterattacking, the other Mexican columns in Texas, between four thousand and five thousand men, fled across the Rio Grande. Although most Texans wanted to hang Santa Anna, Houston and President Burnet kept him safe. Burnet signed treaties with him calling for cessation of hostilities, and Houston released him on Santa Anna's promise to help persuade the Mexican Government to grant full independence to Texas. The Government, which had deposed him for the defeat, of course defied him, and on his return to Mexico, Santa Anna went briefly into ignominious retirement. Yet though the Mexicans insisted Texas was not free, unsettled conditions farther south prevented them for several years from attempting to reassert authority.

163

Unhampered by outside attack, the new nation undertook to remold her destiny. It proved to be rough going.

Most Texans wanted and expected annexation to the United States. To their chagrin, the American Government, tormented by sectionalism and reluctant, in those depression-ridden days, to risk war with Mexico, declined to do more than extend recognition to the new republic. As debates on the matter continued, tempers in the United States leaped out of hand. Quaker Benjamin Lundy wrote two inflammatory pamphlets declaring that Southern slave interests had deliberately fomented the Texas revolution for "the avowed purpose of adding five or six more slaveholding States to this Union." John Quincy Adams included similar charges in an anti-annexation speech he spent three weeks delivering to the Senate. Deciding that annexation would have to await a different political climate, the Texans withdrew their request for admission to the Union. Instead, they set about showing the world that they were completely capable of getting along by themselves.

Guiding the touchy republic along this difficult path became the task of Sam Houston, who was overwhelmingly elected president of Texas in September, 1836. He gained support by inducing his principal opponents, Henry Smith and Stephen Austin, to accept positions in his cabinet. As Secretary of State, Austin worked prodigiously until his untimely death two months later. Financial pressures were eased by suddenly cutting the army to a quarter of its original size, a move Houston dared risk only because of his determined peace policy with the Indians and the inability of revolt-torn Mexico to mount a counteroffensive against him.

Immigration swelled under the stimulus of a land program that gave away two square miles (twelve hundred and eighty acres) to each arriving family, and half that amount to bachelors. The devastating panic that shattered the United States beginning in 1837 made these rainbows of free soil glow still more brightly. In Mississippi the price of a good slave had plunged from fifteen hundred to two hundred dollars. According to James Truslow Adams's *The Epic of America*, nine tenths of the factories in the East closed; fifty thousand Massachusetts shoe workers were idle; more than half the clerks in Philadelphia had no jobs. True, an unemployed factory hand could not easily move his family halfway across the continent. Still, tens of thousands of homemakers and adventurers somehow managed to scrape together outfits and pour across the Sabine or sail on cranky little river boats up the rivers that empty into the Gulf. Even that was not enough. In 1841 the *empresario* system was revived, and colonists were lured from Germany, England,

and France. During the decade immediately following the revolution, the population of Texas was increased by more than one hundred thousand.

Houston's policy of rigid financial responsibility was abandoned by his successor, Mirabeau Buonaparte Lamar, elected president in the fall of 1838. (The constitution outlawed successive terms by the same man.) To gain votes from his restless countrymen, Lamar promised the things Houston had not been able to produce: a place in the international sun for the nation, and the opening of more Indian lands for homes—and for speculation.

He succeeded internationally better than domestically. By pointing out the stability Houston had achieved, his envoys gained recognition from France, England, the Netherlands, and Belgium, but failed to budge Mexico from her adamant refusal to acknowledge Texan independence. The bruised mother country was in no position to back the refusal with force, however. During the winter of 1838–39, a French fleet occupied Veracruz in a quarrel over debts. The fighting gave Santa Anna an excuse to emerge from retirement. On losing one leg below the knee to a bullet, he declared that the defunct member had died gloriously for its country, and he hopped dramatically back into the president's chair. Although the French soon withdrew, revolutions continued. The next winter, 1839–40, Texas filibusterers joined Mexican rebels in an attempt to set up a "Republic of the Rio Grande," stretching grandly, on paper, clear to the Pacific. Betrayed by their own allies and outnumbered one hundred and ten to twelve hundred and twenty-five, the Texan freebooters holed up in a stone hacienda at Saltillo and slew four hundred and eight Mexican soldiers while losing five of their own number, and then withdrew under heavy cavalry attack back across the Rio Grande. There was no effective pursuit. Santa Anna's forces had their hands full trying to patch together the fragments into which the abortive Republic of the Rio Grande had collapsed.

Freed by these Mexican turmoils from outside interference, Lamar turned on the Indians. Attacking under the flimsiest of pretexts, his army crushed the Texas Cherokees in April, 1839, occupied the lands the Indians had gained from Mexico in 1824, and sent the defeated red men fleeing for refuge among their recently relocated tribesmen in present-day Oklahoma.

Next came the Comanches. In March, 1840, a small band was invited to the courthouse in San Antonio to discuss a peace treaty. Shooting erupted over the alleged failure of the Indians to produce certain prisoners. One Texan was wounded. Thirty-six Indians were slain. Twenty-eight women and children were jailed but later exchanged for white captives. Comanches answered by widespread burning and looting until they were defeated at Plum Creek, near today's Lockhart, Texas.

By no means cowed by the setback, the Indians shifted to deadly hit-and-run raids. They were hard to handle out on the naked plains. A single-shot, muzzle-loaded rifle fired from horseback was not very useful against wild-riding Indians, who in one minute could gallop more than three hundred yards while discharging up to twenty arrows. Hunting for equivalent fire power on horseback, the Texas Rangers, an Indian-fighting force stationed in San Antonio under John Coffee Hays, discovered the revolver that had been invented in the mid-1830's by Samuel Colt. It proved to be the answer. Coupling courage to quick firing, small groups of Rangers many times defeated what appeared to be overwhelming numbers of Indians, and the Colt revolver was off on its heady path toward becoming the American folklore symbol of the winning of the West.

No rapid-fire panacea existed to fight off Lamar's financial troubles. Through customs and taxes his government took in one million dollars—but spent five million. Currency depreciated; bonds were next to unsalable. In a frantic effort to recoup, Lamar decided to push west into New Mexico and absorb for Texas the Santa Fe trade, which, in common with many other peo-

ple, he supposed to be more lucrative than it actually was.

Times seemed auspicious. An 1837 revolution had ousted New Mexico's official governor—Pueblo Indians from Taos had cut off the man's head and used it as a football—but a counterrevolution had quickly landed in his place a home-grown tyrant from Albuquerque who was equally oppressive. He was Manuel Armijo, stout, six feet tall, given to gambling and garish red and gold or sky-blue uniforms. Many American traders disliked and distrusted him. Hoping to get rid of him, plotters among them whispered to ambitious Texans that most Mexican nationals and all the Pueblo Indians of the upper Rio Grande would welcome outside help in throwing off Armijo's harsh yoke.

In the spring of 1841, Lamar gave his blessings and half a million dollars in specially printed paper money to a harebrained scheme for capitalizing on the discontent. The idea went like this: A wagon train—eventually it numbered fourteen vehicles, shepherded by fifty merchants and teamsters—was to load up with innocuous trade goods and rattle six hundred desolate miles across the almost unknown Texas Panhandle to Santa Fe. Three official commissioners were assigned to accompany the caravan, equipped with handbills printed in Spanish and English that offered to New Mexicans "a full participation in all our blessings . . . co-aspirants with us for all the

Immigrant families were flooding in, but in 1840 Austin, Texas, seen above, was still essentially a frontier town of cabins. Its inhabitants busily joined expeditions that fought Mexicans and protected the western borders against marauding Plains Indians.

glory of establishing a new and happy and free nation."

Advertisements in the *Austin City Gazette* sought armed volunteers, ostensibly to defend the caravan against Comanche Indians. Two hundred and seventy signed up, bringing with them one small brass cannon. Ten more wagons were needed to haul their equipment. This was a bigger force than necessary for fighting Indians, but it was hardly big enough for conquering a foreign land. But then, the New Mexicans were not supposed to fight back very hard.

A late start (June 18, 1841) ran the adventurers into fiery heat. Grass shriveled; water disappeared. They lost their way, stretching their six-hundred-mile journey to twice that. Prairie fires destroyed some of their wagons; Indians slew five stragglers. Bewildered and starving

THOMAS J. GREEN, *Journal of the Texian Expedition Against Mier*, YALE UNIVERSITY LIBRARY

A view of Texans, bound for Mier, burning Mexican boats on the Rio Grande was drawn by Charles M'Laughlin of the expedition.

in the deep canyons of the Panhandle country, they split into two columns, hoping to speed their rate of travel. As they staggered out of the wastes, Armijo captured every man without firing a shot. Shackling them together, he put them in the charge of Captain Damasio Salazar, who was to take them as far as El Paso on their way to prison in Mexico City. It was a march of unspeakable brutality; during it, Salazar kept tally of those who died by threading their ears onto a bit of rawhide thong. It was a costly triumph, however. When George Kendall's book about the episode was published in the United States in 1844, it aroused widespread indignation against Mexico and helped prepare the popular mind for war.

Meanwhile, in December, 1841, Sam Houston was re-elected president. Again he tried to retrench by disband-

ing most of the army and slashing salaries. The mood of the times worked against him, however. Infuriated by the treatment of the Santa Fe prisoners, the legislature passed an act annexing to Texas six northern Mexican states and Upper and Lower California—at a moment when the republic could not afford firewood for the executive mansion. When Houston returned the paper bombast with a remark that legislative jokes were inappropriate, the lawmakers overrode his veto and adjourned.

Mexican armies reacted in March, 1842, and again in September by raiding San Antonio and several other towns but withdrew without attempting permanent conquest. In retaliation, three hundred hotheads crossed into Mexico and in a cold drizzle on Christmas Day, 1842, seized the town of Mier—only to surrender to the force that immediately surrounded them.

Bound by lariats, these prisoners too were started afoot through bitter weather toward prison in Mexico City. In February, near Saltillo, one hundred and seventy-five of them overpowered their guards and fled. Lost and starving in the nearby mountains, they were soon recaptured. Santa Anna then added another episode to the saga of his cruelty. He ordered that one man in ten be shot as punishment, each man to determine his own fate by drawing blindfolded one bean from a jar containing one hundred and fifty-nine white beans and seventeen black ones. Those who drew the black were lined up and executed by rifle fire on March 25, 1843. The others were tossed into various jails, beside some of the remaining prisoners of the Santa Fe fiasco.

Other Texas forays of revenge were made against New Mexico and Mexican merchants traveling the Santa Fe Trail. Many of the volunteers who signed up under Texas lieutenants in exchange for promises of booty were Missourians or trappers from the southern Rocky Mountains. The members of one small group under Charles Warfield successfully attacked the hamlet of Mora, New Mexico, but lost their horses to a counterthrust by Mexican cavalry and limped away to Bent's Fort, on the Arkansas River, with their saddles on their own backs. Another group under John McDaniel was captured and its leaders executed by the United States Government for the wanton robbing and slaying of a Mexican merchant named Chavez. The largest party of raiders, one hundred and eighty men under Jacob Snively, defeated a detachment of Armijo's ill-disciplined Indian soldiers but soon surrendered to a United States force guarding the Santa Fe caravans of 1843 and was sent, shamefaced and empty-handed, back to Texas.

These foolish maneuvers gave Houston's angry constituents something to chew on while he launched a far more important diplomatic gamble: playing American jingoists off against their favorite bogey, Great Britain. Relations between the countries were strained again. Diplomats quarreled over the boundary of Maine and over the sympathy and material aid that some Americans had extended Canadian insurgents during an abortive revolution in 1837. Alarmists in the United States felt that many Britons were growing altogether too interested in the Far West. During the winter of 1840–41, the Hudson's Bay Company sent traders south from the Columbia to open a post beside San Francisco Bay. In England, a few editorial writers and one or two members of Parliament proposed that Great Britain accept California from Mexico in lieu of certain debts and use the rich coastal valleys thus acquired to haven colonies of poor English and Irish farmers. This plan for British expansion on the American continent received virtually no serious support in England, but in the United States it raised the hackles of professional Anglophobes.

Of even more concern to expansionists was Britain's active interest in Texas. By stabilizing the new republic as a rival to the old South, English industrialists hoped to find a more amenable source of cotton for their mills and a place where they could market their manufactured goods free of American tariff restrictions. Furthermore, Great Britain's humanitarians openly hoped to strike another blow against slavery by having it outlawed in the fledgling Texas republic.

While Houston was weighing these trends, an influential prisoner of the Mier fiasco, James W. Robinson, wrote Santa Anna from his cell, urging that he be allowed to approach the Texas president concerning an armistice between his nation and Mexico. Santa Anna, beset by a revolution in Yucatán, agreed. After listening to Robinson, Houston saw an opportunity to flatter the English by letting Lord Aberdeen step into the picture as peacemaker between the belligerents.

An armistice was arranged, and Santa Anna freed those prisoners captured at Santa Fe and Mier who still remained in jail. An answering gesture was then up to Houston. He made it on July 6, 1843, by withdrawing from the United States Senate his request that Texas be annexed. This pleased the Mexicans, who were afraid of American designs, and also allowed Houston to hint abroad that Britain, peacemaker with Mexico, seemed to be Texas' most useful friend.

As he probably had anticipated, most Southerners and many Northerners reacted with alarm. Great Britain, the ancient enemy, dominating a free Texas! A Texas that might become a permanent check to the United States and a home for runaway slaves! Heaven forbid! In

October, 1843, Abel P. Upshur, Secretary of State in President Tyler's Cabinet, told Houston that instead of canceling talks of annexation, this was the time to resume them. President Tyler had broken with the majority of his party and would listen favorably.

Houston sent ambiguous messages on the subject to both Upshur and the British minister. No doubt he felt that duplicity was justifiable. He did not want to lose the support of either nation, yet he sensed that England's usefulness was wearing thin. Santa Anna had become dangerous again. He had quarreled with the British chargé d'affaires in Mexico City, had freed his armies by ending the revolt in Yucatán, and had induced his Government to pass a decree, which was obviously aimed at Texas, that any foreigner who invaded Mexico would

M'Laughlin, who illustrated Thomas J. Green's account of the Mier foray, showed "Texians drawing the black beans at Salado."

be executed immediately. Under such batterings, the English-arranged armistice was not very likely to endure.

At this point Upshur was accidentally killed during a gunnery exhibition aboard the warship *Princeton.* Tyler appointed John C. Calhoun to take his place as Secretary of State. A Southerner, Calhoun was maneuvered into espousing annexation on the ground that the United States Government was bound to protect slavery against Great Britain's wicked plot to bring an end to the institution throughout the world.

Annexation to protect slavery!—abolitionists raised a fierce cry. Thomas Benton, although a slaveholder himself, supported their opposition, decrying the immorality of extending slavery into lands torn from a foreign country that did not brook human servitude. A proposed treaty of annexation was soundly defeated in the Senate —but not before damage was done: an angry Mexico had reacted to the proposed bill by ending the brief armistice with Texas and making preparations for war.

One can hardly guess what might have resulted if these furies between North and South had been the only issue occupying the nation. Underneath the surface clamor, however, the depression-slowed but perennial western thrust of the "movers" was regaining momentum, bolstered in the early 1840's by a growing conviction that it was the divine right, even the divine duty of their country—not North or South, but their country as a united whole—to spread the blessings of democratic freedom from coast to coast. Anything short of that would leave the United States unfulfilled.

How trace the osmosis of an idea? During the decade that saw the thirteen Colonies win their revolt against England, both John Ledyard, a Connecticut marine aboard a British ship off the Northwest coast, and Jedidiah Morse, a Connecticut minister in his study near the Atlantic, had felt, half-mystically, the indivisibility of their continent. The unity they conceived had not been political, however—distances were deemed too great— but rather a bond springing from similar bloodlines and cultures. Even so ardent an expansionist as Thomas Hart Benton did not at first envision a single continental nation. In a famous 1825 speech in the Senate, support- ing one of Congressman John Floyd's many proposals that the Government aid emigrants from the United States in occupying Oregon, he declared the Rocky Mountains to be a natural western boundary for his country. There "the statue of the fabled god, Terminus, should be raised . . . never to be thrown down." Settlers who ventured beyond the Rockies would erect a sister republic, allied with the Eastern nation by common ideals against encroachment from the Old World.

Yet the very fact that the United States did assert a claim to the Oregon country as against Great Britain made talk of Terminus sound unreasonable to some ears, notably those of Hall Jackson Kelley of Boston. As men- tioned in the preceding chapter, Kelley between 1828 and 1832 had assaulted Congress with a series of requests for help in inducing colonists to settle beside the Columbia. In 1831 he incorporated the "American Society for En- couraging the Settlement of the Oregon Territory" and began enrolling what he hoped would be a total of three thousand emigrants. Although he recognized that his settlement might become the nucleus of a separate na- tion, he earnestly recommended instead, in a "General Circular" advertising his scheme, that the emigrants be regarded as "a Colony, planted, cherished and pro-

tected" by the mother country through an extension of full United States jurisdiction across the disputed area.

He was a dozen years ahead of the times. Both Con- gress and prospective emigrants turned deaf ears. Unde- terred, Kelley in November, 1832, started west on his own by way of New Orleans, Veracruz, and Mexico City. Crossing to Baja California, he rode northward through the peninsula's sterile, dangerous deserts to San Diego. There he met and eventually persuaded Ewing Young, one of the master mountain men of the West, and seven other trappers to go with him to Oregon.

Horse thieves driving fifty-six stolen animals fell in with them. When at length the mixed cavalcade reached Fort Vancouver in the fall of 1834, the Hudson's Bay Company's white-haired chief factor, John McLoughlin, suspected them all of being outlaws. He ordered Young away from the post but allowed Kelley, ill with malaria, to crawl into a hut outside the stockade. Fed by the company, the destitute colonizer spent the winter of 1834–35 recuperating, now and then sending his host angry messages about the respect due "an American on American soil." In the spring he borrowed enough money from McLoughlin to sail home, never to return.

Of itself Kelley's Western plunge was insignificant, but the ripples spread far. Ewing Young and his fellow trappers, filled with an abiding enmity toward all things English, settled on the Tualatin Plains section of the Willamette Valley, a little southwest of the site of modern Portland. More importantly, Kelley's activities in Mas- sachusetts had put into motion a young Boston ice mer- chant named Nathaniel Wyeth. And Wyeth, as the next chapter will show, was still another of history's strange catalysts. By his mere presence he helped initiate the strangely linked coincidences that created in the North- west a known target toward which settlers could aim. This was a factor of some moment, for even the most restless of movers did not simply load tools and seed and kitchenware into his wagon and head west unless he had some sort of goal in mind.

Once located, these settlers would feel scant interest in forming an independent country. Like the majority of Texans far to the southeast of them, they wanted to be part of the continental United States. And if the think- ing in the East changed enough to wish the absorption into the nation of both of these areas, would not the mag- netism of geography drag along everything in between as well—that huge and scarcely known vastness that today makes up western Colorado, Utah, Nevada, New Mex- ico, Arizona, and California?

Such were the thrusts that, during the 1840's, were to overpower even the growing animosities about slavery.

Four Legs, Winnebago

One-Side-of-the-Sky, Chippewa

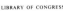

Little Crow, Sioux

Brewett, Miami

EXTINGUISHING THE EXTINGUISHED

There had been a day when the Indian tribes of the Old Northwest could act to defend their own. When William Henry Harrison, a master at bribing, threatening, and hoodwinking Indians into ceding their lands, had pushed them too far, they had united under Tecumseh to save what remained. But now Tecumseh was long dead, the natives' power to fight back was gone, and the tribes were divided again. Hunger came as game grew scarce, thousands succumbed to the white man's diseases, and many, without purpose, turned to alcohol. The treaty makers could not keep ahead of the settlers; almost as soon as a tribe was moved to a new location, the squatters were there, crowding in and demanding more Indian land. In 1830 the Great Removal began, to put all Eastern Indians forever out of the way on the Great American Desert, and by 1842 it was virtually completed, though some tribes managed to cling on beyond the settlements in Wisconsin, Michigan, and Minnesota. A witness to some of these melancholy events was James O. Lewis, hired by the Government to make portraits of Indians at treaty councils that extinguished native land rights in the 1820's. He painted these chiefs at four councils in Wisconsin during 1825–27.

An 1837 scene of the Seminole War shows an Army camp at Tampa Bay. The costly war was ended in 1842, with some Seminoles still hiding in swamps.

Captain Basil Hall, an Englishman, visited the Southeast just as whites were moving in behind the departing Indians. Above is his view of the new log cabin settlement of Columbus, Georgia, in 1828, soon after Creeks had left the area. Below and right are sketches of some of the dispossessors.

Deck passenger on a steamboat

THE DISPOSSESSORS

When it was proposed to the Cherokees in 1817 that they move West, one of them said the President puzzled him. A few years before, he had given them plows and hoes, saying it was not good for them to hunt; now he was telling them there was good hunting on the Arkansas River and offering them rifles if they would go there. Very soon not proposals but demands were being made that all Five Civilized Tribes—Cherokees, Chickasaws, Creeks, Choctaws, and Seminoles—leave the Southeast. With the connivance of President Jackson, the states involved—most notoriously Georgia—abrogated the Indians' treaty rights, seized their property, denied them legal recourse, and contemptuously ignored Federal jurisdiction. "I saw the helpless Cherokees arrested and dragged from their homes, and driven by bayonet into the stockades," wrote a soldier sickened by his part in the removal. Some bands, including fiercely resisting Seminoles, thwarted the dispossessors, but by 1842 they were small islands in their former homelands, now overrun by new owners.

A slave overseer   *Backwoodsman with his rifle*

An 1842 Government patent (right) affirmed Choctaw rights to Western lands given in 1830 when their own land was taken.

170

THE UNITED STATES OF AMERICA,

To all to whom these presents shall come, Greeting:

Whereas by the Second Article of the Treaty began and held at Dancing Rabbit Creek, on the fifteenth day of September, in the year of our Lord one thousand eight hundred and thirty, (as ratified by the Senate of the United States, on the 24th of February, 1831) by the Commissioners on the part of the United States, and the Mingoes, Chiefs, Captains, and Warriors, of the Choctaw Nation, on the part of said Nation, it is provided that The United States under a grant specially to be made by the President of the U.S. shall cause to be conveyed to the Choctaw Nation, a tract of Country west of the Mississippi River, in fee simple, to them and their descendants, to inure to them while they shall exist as a Nation, and live on it Beginning near Fort Smith, where the Arkansas boundary crosses the Arkansas River, running thence to the source of the Canadian Fork, if in the limits of the United States, or to those limits; thence due south to Red River, and down Red River to the west boundary of the Territory of Arkansas: thence north along that line to the beginning. The boundary of the same to be agreeably to the Treaty made and concluded at Washington City, in the year 1825.

NOW KNOW YE, That the United States of America, in consideration of the Premises, and in execution of the agreement and stipulations in the aforesaid Treaty, have given and granted, and by these Presents do give and grant, unto the said Choctaw Nation, the aforesaid Tract of Country West of the Mississippi, to have and to hold the same, with all the rights, privileges, immunities, and appurtenances of whatsoever nature, thereunto belonging, as intended to be conveyed by the aforesaid Article, in fee simple, to them and their descendants, to inure to them, while they shall exist as a Nation, and live on it, liable to no transfer or alienation except to the U. States or with their consent.

IN TESTIMONY WHEREOF, I, JOHN TYLER, President of the United States of America, have caused these Letters to be made Patent, and the Seal of the General Land Office to be hereunto affixed.

Given under my hand at the city of Washington, the twenty third day of March, in the Year of our Lord one thousand eight hundred and forty two, and of the Independence of the United States the sixty sixth.

John Tyler

BY THE PRESIDENT:

Danl Webster
SECRETARY OF STATE

John C Spencer
SECRETARY OF WAR

T. Hartley Crawford
COMMISSIONER OF INDIAN AFFAIRS.

Recorded, Volume 1.   Page 43.

H Williamson
RECORDER OF THE GENERAL LAND OFFICE

Examined in the Bureau of Topographical Engineers.
John J Abert
Col. Corps of Engineers

Entered in the War Department, for the Quarter ended

TEXAS INDEPENDENCE

"Crockett's Last Stand" by Robert J. Onderdonk, reproduced only in part above, is a popular interpretation of the last moments at the Alamo. Its historical accuracy is debatable; the final stand was made inside the mission buildings.

When he posed for J. G. Chapman in 1834, two years before he died, Davy Crockett was 48.

Jim Bowie was in almost every skirmish for Texas independence till he died at the Alamo.

Mathew Brady made this photographic portrait of Sam Houston long after the Texas Revolution.

For many weeks in 1836 the Texas Revolution was a grim tale of defeats and retreats; then in less than half an hour it was overwhelmingly won. It is not the victory at San Jacinto, however, but a defeat, the Alamo at San Antonio, that has been immortalized. There is doubt whether a defense of the Alamo should even have been made. Sam Houston believed not and sent Jim Bowie with men to destroy the old mission—which Bowie then declined to do. Texas Governor Henry Smith thought yes and sent William Travis and other men to defend it. And defend it they all did until overwhelmed by three thousand Mexican troops. One Mexican soldier told how forty comrades fell about him. But the walls were breached. Travis died across the cannon he was serving. Davy Crockett, it is said, killed fifteen of the enemy with his rifle and fell with his knife in the body of a sixteenth. Bowie, too ill and weak to stand, lay on a cot in his room and met the onrushing Mexicans with pistol fire. All 180-odd defenders perished, but they took some 1,500 of the foe with them.

Shown here in color for the first time, the torn, faded guidon of the First Company of New Orleans Volunteers is the only surviving flag of the Alamo defenders. Still a trophy in Mexico City, it had almost disintegrated before it was restored in 1965 for this photograph. In its center was an eagle with the legend, "God and Liberty."

BOTH BELOW: CATLIN, *Letters and Notes on . . . the North American Indians*, VOL. 2, 1841

A Comanche bears a truce flag at the first meeting with the dragoons.

Colonel Henry Dodge

Comanches show why some soon termed them the world's best cavalrymen.

DRAGOONS AND COMANCHES

Few Americans knew much about the Comanches of the southern plains when General Henry Leavenworth and Colonel Henry Dodge led the 1st Dragoon Regiment into their country in 1834. But they had a reputation for ferocity, especially among travelers on the Santa Fe Trail, and the troopers' mission was to demonstrate to them and other tribes the power of the United States and to warn them to live in peace with whites and with the Five Civilized Tribes being removed to Oklahoma from the Southeast. Crossing the Red River into Mexican Texas, the Dragoons found the Comanches hospitable—and luckily so, for a "bilious fever" had incapacitated a large part of the command. Sixty men were left in a Comanche village while the skeletal regiment under Dodge pushed on to the Wichitas. One of the ailing who remained with the Comanches was artist George Catlin, who continued to draw whenever he could hold pad and pencil; these pictures are from his sketches. On the return trip Catlin was carried in a horse litter, but he was lucky, for Leavenworth and a third of the force had died.

A great Comanche village in Texas; according to Catlin it contained six to eight hundred tepees.

Comanche hunters pursuing a buffalo herd break through the column of marching dragoons.

The Teton Mountains

"The Trois Tetons were in full view . . . five in number, but only three of them are so very high as to be seen at a great distance. . . . Here I spent much time in looking over the widely extended and varied scenery, sometimes filled with emotions of the sublime, in beholding the towering mountains. . . . After some hours occupied in this excursion, I descended to the encampment, much gratified with what I had seen of the works of God."

The missionary Reverend Samuel Parker, on his way to convert Indians of the Oregon Country, August 27, 1835

CHAPTER EIGHT

THE GREAT SURGE

1832-1846

Nathaniel Wyeth's Yankee imagination was commercial, not sociological as was Hall Kelley's. After reading the data on the Northwest that Kelley had accumulated in Boston, Wyeth devised a plan similar to the one Astor had envisioned before the War of 1812. He would establish, in conjunction with Kelley's proposed agricultural colony, a headquarters post on the Columbia and use it as a base for supplying trapper brigades in the mountains. To this he added a subsidiary idea—pickling Columbia River salmon for sale in the East.

While Wyeth's plans were maturing, Congress rejected another of Kelley's pleas for aid. Impatiently Wyeth and two dozen followers cut loose on their own. They chartered a brig largely on credit and sent it around the Horn with trapper supplies and barrels for their fish. The men themselves went overland. At Independence, Missouri, they attached themselves to a long supply train of pack mules William Sublette was leading to the annual trappers' rendezvous, held that year (1832) in Pierres Hole, at the western base of the Teton Mountains.

At Pierres Hole half of Wyeth's men deserted, discouraged by the hardships of the trail and alarmed by the sight of the experienced power they would have to buck if they entered the fur trade. The rest roistered through the gathering, helped the mountain men fight a bloody battle with Gros Ventre Indians, and drifted on to Fort Vancouver, arriving late in October, 1832. There they learned that their brig had been wrecked.

Most of the men quit then, taking jobs with the Hudson's Bay Company. Not Wyeth. In the spring he and two men from his original party journeyed east with a Hudson's Bay Company brigade into Montana and then swung with a great conclave of Indians south to the rendezvous of 1833, gathered beside Green River near present-day Daniel, Wyoming. During the frolicking, he undercut William Sublette and won a contract to supply the Rocky Mountain Fur Company in 1834. Back to Boston he went to place his orders and obtain fresh financing for his own fur trade plans. With him he took two Indians, a twenty-year-old Nez Perce employed as a roustabout, and an alert thirteen-year-old mixture of French and Flathead named Baptiste, whom Wyeth planned to train to serve as an interpreter.

By coincidence, Methodist churchmen were at that moment preparing to send missionaries to the Columbia. In 1831 three Nez Perce Indians and one Flathead had traveled to St. Louis with a party of fur trappers, and a notion spread about that they had made the journey to appeal for religious instruction for their tribes. A Protestant merchant named William Walker, himself part Indian, picked up a garbled report of the episode during a visit to St. Louis and fired off an excited letter that eventually was published in the Methodist *Christian Advocate*. The upshot was that black-bearded Jason Lee, a powerful ex-farm-hand more than six feet tall, and his nephew Daniel Lee, only three years younger, volunteered to plant a Methodist mission in the Northwest.

The Lees hurried to Boston to interview Wyeth. Though a nonbeliever, Wyeth let them borrow his Indian boys to raise funds at church meetings, said they could ship their equipment around the Horn in his new vessel,

177

and invited them to travel west from St. Louis with his supply caravan in the summer of 1834. Thus buoyed, they prevailed on a schoolteacher, Cyrus Shepard, of Lynn, Massachusetts, to join them, and on the Missouri frontier they rounded out their entourage by hiring two hands to help with the daily packing and unpacking and with the herding of their three milk cows.

Although the fur men and missionaries in Wyeth's cavalcade did not realize it at the time, the economic pattern of the West they were invading was undergoing a minor revolution. On June 1, as their horses splashed through crystal Laramie Creek just above its junction with the North Platte, the travelers saw several men hewing timbers for a stockaded post like the big trading forts on the upper Missouri. A similar post, except that it was built of adobe brick, was taking shape on the Arkansas River, two hundred and eighty air-line miles to the south. This was the massive Bent's Fort, the creation of a trio of traders from Santa Fe, Charles and William Bent and Céran St. Vrain.

They were the children of changing styles. In the early 1830's, manufacturers began to use substitutes for beaver in making hats—cheap nutria from South America and, more ominously, silk, which was soon to become more fashionable than beaver itself. Overproduction of beaver combined with these substitutes to bring about a collapse in prices: from $6.00 a pound in St. Louis in the fall of 1832 to $3.50 in October, 1833. The best streams meanwhile had been exhausted by frenzied overtrapping. There were still beaver to be had, of course, but not enough after the mid-1830's to attract the big brigades of the powerful companies. The cleanup, so to speak, could best be handled by small, independent groups willing to take their chances with the Indians.

All this while, the price of buffalo hides was slowly rising. So many were shipped in 1834—most of them from the upper Missouri posts of Pratte, Chouteau & Co., which had just purchased the Western Department of the American Fur Co.—that their total value for the first time exceeded that of mountain beaver. Skinning the ungainly animals, then laboriously scraping and tanning the hides, was a work white men gladly left to Indian women, particularly when it became obvious that the Federal Government intended, as part of its program for the new Indian country, to be much more severe about whites' hunting on Indian lands. Pelt gathering, in short, was swinging back into the hands of the natives. This brought about a reawakening, out on the dry plains of the West, of the old-style trading posts that once had dominated the fur trade. It proved to be only a last flicker, however. The colorful era of the bewhiskered,

rambunctious Rocky Mountain trapper was all but over.

Wyeth's concerns were too urgent for him to pause at the unbuilt fort on Laramie Creek to study its prospects. William Sublette was ahead of him, intent on being first at the Ham's Fork rendezvous (southwestern Wyoming) with his pack train of goods and four hundred and fifty gallons of raw alcohol. Fearing a double cross, the Bostonian tried hard to overtake Sublette, but failed. Sublette reaped the trade, and Wyeth's merchandise was refused. To dispose of his goods, Wyeth rode on to the vicinity of present-day Pocatello, Idaho. There, near the south bank of the Snake, he built a post he named Fort Hall—not in imitation of the posts east of the Rockies, for very few buffalo remained in the area, but as a means by which he could attract trade away from the rendezvous system that had betrayed him.

The move alarmed the Hudson's Bay Company. To keep Northwestern Indians from drifting into Fort Hall with their beaver, brigade leader Tom McKay constructed the precursor of Fort Boise, two hundred and twenty miles farther down the Snake, near the mouth of Boise River. And thus, in the same year, 1834, the yet unnamed Oregon Trail received three of its principal caravansaries—Forts Laramie, Hall, and Boise. The effort, however, brought Wyeth no benefit. Indians, illness, bad luck, and genteel throat-cutting by the Hudson's Bay Company bankrupted him. In 1837 he sold Fort Hall to the English concern and returned to his ice business in Massachusetts.

Dr. John McLoughlin, out of natural kindness (and perhaps to keep the missionaries from unsettling the fur-producing Indians of the interior), helped Lee's party establish itself in the Willamette Valley, near the site of modern Salem. Superannuated French voyageurs, retired with their Indian wives from the Hudson's Bay Company, had already broken out crude farms not far away. Some miles to the south, Ewing Young's ranch formed the nucleus of a little settlement of ex-mountaineers. A few of Wyeth's disenchanted followers located near each of these centers. Except for a spectacular view of Mount Hood's shining white cone, the rolling, tree-dotted land looked so much like the farm country the Americans had known in the East that inevitably they began to envision it as part of the same country.

Early in 1836, a fifty-seven-year-old Presbyterian minister named Samuel Parker came riding up to the Lees' mission—house, barn, school for Indian children, and thirty acres of plowed land, created in little more than a year. The newcomer said that he too had been interested in the Northwestern mission field by William Walker's letter in the *Christian Advocate*. To explore

William Bent

potentials, he and a lay companion, Dr. Marcus Whitman, in 1835 had traveled with a fur caravan—a dreadfully godless experience, Parker clucked—to the rendezvous beside Green River. The field for religious effort was enormous, they had discovered, and time was short. To hurry things along, Whitman had returned East to fetch helpers, equipment, and his betrothed, blond Narcissa Prentiss. Parker had continued exploring for a site, crossing the Idaho mountains with an escort of Nez Perce Indians. But instead of waiting for the Whitmans, he said farewell to the Lees, caught a Hudson's Bay Company sailing ship, and returned home.

Wives!—Jason Lee, worn down from doing household chores along with farming and missionary work, listened enviously. On March 15, 1836, he said in a letter to the Methodist board, "A greater favour could not be bestowed upon this country, than to send to it pious, industrious, inteligent females."

By that time Marcus Whitman, a new recruit, Henry Spalding, and their wives were already on their way west. The first to cross the American continent, the white women created a sensation among the Indians and trappers at the Green River rendezvous. Helped, as the Lees had been, by the Hudson's Bay Company, the Whitmans built their station east of the Cascade Mountains at Waiilatpu on the Walla Walla River, twenty miles above its junction with the Columbia. In time Waiilatpu too would be a haven for immigrants. The Spaldings, who

did not get along with the Whitmans, located farther away from the main route of travel, in the heart of the Nez Perces' country, where Lapwai Creek flows sparkling into the Clearwater Fork of the Snake.

That same winter (1836-37) a ship bearing reinforcements to Lee reached the Columbia. Five of the party were women, three of them single—a state Jason Lee and Cyrus Shepard quickly altered for two of them in a ceremony in a grove of fir trees. Other civilizing changes were wrought during the summer by Ewing Young. With two French Canadians, three Indians, and eight Americans he sailed to California and drove back overland—with incredible toil and running fights against marauding savages—six hundred and thirty cattle.

As stability increased, the fifty-one settlers of the Willamette Valley began to discuss the future. They had good farms and livestock. All around them was a plethora of soil awaiting development. But without political organization to guarantee land titles, they lacked security. Gathered at Lee's mission in March, 1838, a group of them petitioned Congress for United States jurisdiction, writing confidently, "We flatter ourselves that we are the germ of a great state." Three dozen men signed the declaration, nine of them French Canadians. Jason Lee put the document into a tin box to carry horseback across the continent.

His main reason for the arduous journey was to obtain more help for his station. As aids in enlisting sympathy he took with him two teen-age Chinook Indian boys. Rescuing the heathen was, of course, his mission's primary purpose. Still, if immigration should start, would not a strong Christian establishment be equally serviceable to the arriving Americans?

The Hudson's Bay Company was worrying about the same possibility. James Douglas, a factor at Fort Vancouver, wrote London, "We have all along foreseen . . . that the formation of a Colony of United States Citizens on the banks of the Columbia was the main or fundamental part of their [the missionaries'] plan." Then who would become the owner of Oregon?

The shrunken rendezvous of 1838 was held east of Wyoming's Wind River Mountains, beside Popo Agie Creek. There Lee, eastbound, met three more missionary couples journeying west with the fur caravans to strengthen Whitman and Spalding. Traveling with them was an odd civilian who spoke with a heavy foreign accent, sported military whiskers, and had wide round eyes in a big round head. His polished, somewhat ingratiating manners shone out against the dark vulgarity of the trappers. His name was Johann August Sutter, and since in time he would be the one who would draw more settlers to the Pacific coast than any other man or missionary establishment, he merits a bit of digression.

Debt-strangled in Switzerland, John Sutter had told his wife and children good-by in 1834 (years later they followed him) and fled to Missouri. Twice thereafter he tried his luck rather fruitlessly in the Santa Fe trade. That brought him in touch with one more of the unlikely heralds of expansionism, fugitive John Marsh, searching westward like Sutter for a new life.

Marsh, two hundred pounds big, had graduated from Harvard in 1823 and immediately had traveled to Fort Snelling, the new Army outpost (first called Fort St. Anthony) at the junction of the Minnesota and Mississippi rivers, as tutor to the officers' children. He had studied some medicine at Harvard, and at Fort Snelling he resumed the work under the post surgeon. He married the half-breed daughter of a French trapper and a Sioux mother and because of her stayed in the wilderness as an Indian agent. When she died, Marsh was grief-stricken. At about the same time, he was indicted by the Government for illegal dealings with the Indians. Slipping away to Independence, he kept store for a time (this is probably where he met Sutter) and in 1835 moved on to Santa Fe. In Santa Fe he heard enough intriguing rumor about California's pastoral paradise so that he made the long jump across the desolate Gila River route of southern Arizona to the sleepy adobe hamlet of Los Angeles. By showing his Harvard diploma, he won from the authorities a license to practice medicine.

Sutter too soon heard the siren song of California and in 1838 started West, planning to skirt the awesome Sierra Nevada Mountains to the north rather than to the south, as Marsh had done. After bidding eastbound Jason Lee farewell at the rendezvous, he rode on with the three missionary couples to Waiilatpu and then continued with a handful of companions to Fort Vancouver, arriving late in October, 1838. Deterred by traders from trying to press south to California in the teeth of winter, he caught a ship to the Sandwich (Hawaiian) Islands. From there he sailed on a trading venture to Sitka, Alaska, and then, in the summer of 1839, to Monterey, capital of the Mexican province. Brushing off a French military uniform he had bought in exchange for a beaver skin, he paid a call on the governor.

Years of practice had made Sutter a master dissembler. Wherever he went, he pretended that he had noble antecedents and often managed to gull important people into writing him letters of introduction. He had an impressive sheaf of these letters in hand when he asked the governor for a grant of land somewhere above San Francisco Bay. There he promised that he would establish a colony that,

in event of trouble, would be a bulwark of defense.

Tentative permission granted, he chartered two tiny schooners and a rowboat, loaded them with supplies, and pushed northwest out of the bay to the junction of the American and Sacramento rivers. Disembarking with Kanaka laborers whom he had hired in Hawaii, he began building a huge adobe fort on what became the heart of California's present-day capital, Sacramento. To the original dwellings, kitchens, and trading store, he soon added a distillery and a tanning factory. He sent trapping parties into the mountains. Indian workers dug irrigation ditches and planted wheat and fruit trees. When the Russians abandoned their agricultural colony at Fort Ross, near Bodega Bay, a hundred miles to the west, he acquired their movable property on credit.

He soon learned that his old acquaintance, John Marsh, had relocated some seventy miles to the southwest, at the foot of Mount Diablo, just across the hills from today's Berkeley. Less than a year in indolent, poverty-stricken Los Angeles had persuaded Marsh to move north. Purchasing a broad rancho for a song, he built a crude, unfloored home—he was turning into a miser—and added to his herds by charging his distant neighbors exorbitant fees in cattle for medical advice.

Between them, John Marsh and John Sutter changed the California pattern. When they founded their ranches, perhaps seven thousand persons, not counting Indians, lived in clusters around a chain of twenty-one missions that stretched near the seacoast from San Diego north to Sonoma, above San Francisco Bay. This scattered population raised enormous numbers of cattle and swapped the hides and tallow (the latter used to make candles for the silver mines of Peru) for articles of luxurious personal adornment brought them by ship. The English and American agents of these hide buyers, together with a few stray sailors and trappers, lived in the somnolent towns that were scattered along the coast.

Until Marsh and Sutter appeared, no one had heeded the province's central valley. Hot, dry, and enormously fertile, this huge depression, four hundred miles long, was entirely walled by mountains except where its rivers (the Sacramento from the north, the San Joaquin from the south) joined in a confused delta and broke through the hills into San Francisco Bay. By settling on the lower reaches of these rivers, Sutter and Marsh shifted California's center of gravity inland and north, away from the earlier centers of population. More importantly, their settlements, like the ones rising around Lee's mission in the Willamette Valley of Oregon, gave emigrants from the United States a target at which to aim. Marsh in particular wrote ecstatic letters about California to friends on the Missouri frontier, in hopes of attracting enough people to the vicinity of Mount Diablo so that the value of his land would rise.

Other men were reaching wider audiences. America's most famous author, Washington Irving, published *Astoria*, a history of the Astorians on the Columbia, in 1836, and in 1837, a book about Bonneville's wanderings. Samuel Parker (1838) and ornithologist John Townsend (1839) wrote accounts of their experiences in the West. All four of those books and a handful of others decried British influence in the Northwest. In 1840 Richard Henry Dana added California to the lore with his popular *Two Years Before The Mast*.

Members of the various missions sent back letters to the religious press. During his 1838–39 quest for reinforcements, Jason Lee delivered at least eighty-eight lectures. Though his request to present the petition of the Oregon settlers to Congress in person was denied, Representative Caleb Cushing of Massachusetts distributed, free of charge, ten thousand copies of a Congressional document containing long statements by William Slacum, Kelley, Wyeth, and others. The excitement reached a high enough pitch so that Lee's church gave him forty thousand dollars to charter a ship and take fifty new

helpers, men and women both, to the Willamette Valley.

Here and there along the frontier the words struck wistful ears. The back country of Iowa, Missouri, and Arkansas had not proved the shining paradise that many pioneers had hoped for. The doldrums that followed the depression of 1837 still shriveled the value of their land and the price of their crops. They cursed the frozen or muddy roads they had to use on the way to market, and they dreaded the malaria that ravaged the bottom lands that once had promised so much.

Then rumor began whispering. Neither snow nor ague existed in California's golden valleys; the black soil of Oregon was bottomless; vast rivers afforded easy transportation; the Hudson's Bay Company at first, and later the hordes of hungry Asia, would absorb as much grain as they could grow. No forests barred the way to emigrating wagons. South Pass opened an easy gate through the Rockies, and perhaps they could float the last long miles down either the Columbia or a stream called San Buenaventura, which, according to widely circulated maps, drained from Great Salt Lake to the Pacific.

Conceivably, the very ignorance of the first migrants let them advance where more exact knowledge would have rooted them with apprehension. But although they

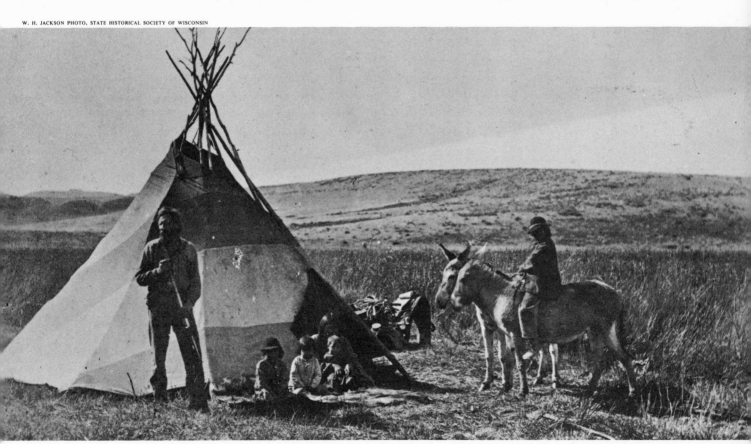

Familiar Western "drifters" after the collapse of the fur trade: a former mountain man, his Indian wife and half-breed children.

underestimated the land, there was much they did understand. Most of them were farm folk and had pioneered before. They were adept with wagons, livestock, rifles, and axes. The women were used to walking beside the men as wilderness equals. Above all, they were restless. Once a farm had been tamed, the narrow horizons of the backwoods communities closed around them. Bored, they were ready to try again.

The first considerable group of them set out for California from Sapling Grove, in what is now eastern Kansas, in the spring of 1841. There were fifty-four men, five women, and ten or so children—as nearly as one can resolve the conflicting records. Three of the women were married. Of the two unattached women, one was a widow. Both got husbands before the trip was finished.

Times were still hard. Among them the entire group could not muster one hundred dollars in cash. But most

Fort Hall, fur post and stopping point on the Overland Trail, was drawn by California-bound J. Goldsborough Bruff in 1849.

of them were young and healthy. John Bidwell, one of the leading spirits of the venture, was twenty-one. Nancy Kelsey, married to Benjamin Kelsey and carrying a year-old baby, was eighteen. They had fourteen good wagons and a sizable herd of horses, mules, and draft oxen. They were hard-twisted, a trait that not all of their contemporaries found admirable. Joseph Williams, a wild, lone, sixty-four-year-old preacher who overtook the party a few days later on the plains, cried out against the general tone of the train, its irreligion and "dreadful oaths . . . O, the wickedness of the wicked."

Not one of them knew which way to go, except west. Fortunately, mountain man Thomas Fitzpatrick came along, guiding Father Pierre Jean De Smet. After an exploratory trip across the plains the previous year, the Jesuit had returned to St. Louis and there had enlisted two priests to help him establish a mission station for

the Flathead Indians in Montana's lovely Bitterroot Valley. They carried their supplies in four squealing, two-wheeled Red River carts and a wagon and were assisted by six or seven stout roustabouts.

The parties joined forces. This let the migrants benefit from Fitzpatrick's knowledge of the country and of Western travel as far as Fort Hall, where the mountain man would strike north with the Catholics. After trudging on to the ford over the Kansas River (modern Topeka engulfs the site today), the laymen elected John Bartleson to serve as their captain and drew up a set of rules that would govern their travel.

In calling this meeting, as in many other matters, the caravan of 1841 was an unconscious prototype for scores of followers. Most of the subsequent caravans would be larger. Save in 1842 and again in 1843, there would be not one but several groups on the trail each year. There would always be a certain number of men who tried to cut their travel time by using pack stock instead of wagons—and did not often succeed because of the greater hardship on the animals. For the sake of this account, it may be useful to describe here conditions in general and not just the affairs of the 1841 group.

Traveling often by steamboats whose holds and decks were jammed with their cows, chicken coops, washtubs, plows, and furniture, the migrants gathered each year at the little Missouri towns of Independence, Westport (modern Kansas City), or St. Joseph. When a group had reached what its members deemed to be the appropriate size, they hired a guide, generally some mountain man like Fitzpatrick. Then they had to decide the time of their departure. They dared not move onto the prairie before grass was high enough to feed stock, yet they dreaded following big trains whose hunters would drive away the buffalo and strip the campgrounds of forage.

They used ordinary farm wagons with boxes ten feet long and four wide—not the big, slope-sided freighters of the Santa Fe Trail. The canvas that arched them was sometimes lined with pockets for holding small items; additional storage space might be created by building a false bottom. A prosperous family generally took two or more wagons. They tried to leave enough room for sleeping and privacy, but after flour sacks and farm equipment had been piled on, not much space remained.

The first miles were a monstrous hubbub. Ill-broken oxen and mules either bolted or sulked in harness, tangled themselves in picket ropes, or escaped entirely and sped back to the starting point. When not busy rounding them up, the exuberant males of the party felt obligated to prove themselves to their neighbors and continued the turmoil by quarreling over firewood and water holes and racing for preferred positions in line.

During this initial shakedown period the men eyed each other as potential candidates for captaincy of the train or for one of the lesser offices. Elections were spirited, filled with scheming, bargaining, and backbiting. The best men did not always win, and those chosen were seldom obeyed. Very rarely did a train make the crossing without either deposing its captain somewhere en route or watching part of its membership pull away in a huff. Sometimes the group as a whole would rally to help an unfortunate member in trouble; but more often, if their first gestures were unsuccessful, they abandoned those who were causing the delay to such individual friends as were willing to stand by. After all, they had a long way to go. Indeed, the great difference between the overland migrations of the 1840's and 1850's and the earlier ones across the Alleghenies was the enormous distance, two thousand miles, that had to be covered in a single season.

At daylight the men rounded up and harnessed the stock in a swirl of dust, shouts, brays, and bellows. The guide and his scouts started ahead in order to stake out the best stream crossings and, eventually, the next night's campground. The train plodded slowly behind them, pausing to rest at noon in spite of the miles stretching ahead. Too much hurrying wore down the stock. The main thing was steadiness, twelve, fifteen, or sometimes, on easy land, twenty miles a day.

A train of fifty wagons might stretch out as much as a mile. Occasionally, where the terrain allowed, travel was in parallel columns to facilitate corralling at night or in case of an Indian attack—the latter a thing that never occurred during the 1840's, though the Kansas and Pawnees that hung around the camps to beg would sometimes rob and, on occasion, even kill unfortunate stragglers.

Eastern Kansas was exhilarating—rolling hills spangled with wild flowers but often shaken by spectacular thunderstorms that "rolled the whole circle of the firmament with a peculiar and awful vibration." One dazed diarist reported a gale that covered the ground a foot deep with water, drove rain through the wagon covers "like as though they had been paper," and scattered "the cattel . . . to the far ends of the earth."

As they toiled up the broad, shallow Platte River, the country grew sandier and more arid. Pungent sagebrush appeared, its narrow gray leaves glinting with silver when the wind turned up the undersides. Gradually the bordering ridges took on fantastic shapes—the slender spire of Chimney Rock, domed and crenelated Scotts Bluff. There was no wood, save for a fuzz of cottonwoods on the river islands. Cooking was done over dry buffalo dung glowing in shallow trenches. The buffalo herds were still enormous, though beyond South Pass the great herds of previous years had disappeared for some reason that has never been satisfactorily explained.

Alkali dust stung the travelers' eyelids and rasped their throats. Alkali water griped their bowels. "A fatal, febrile complaint" known as camp fever was attributed by one traveler to using the milk of hot and feverish cows. Gunshot accidents accounted for far more casualties than assaults by Indians ever did. Bored children fell from the wagons more often than one would suppose, and sometimes they were run over.

A brief rest came at Fort Laramie. Women turned eagerly to washing clothes. (Narcissa Whitman had been able to do laundry only three times on her transcontinental journey.) Supplies were replenished. Iron tires were refitted onto wheels that had been shrunken by the dry air. Sore-footed oxen were thrown onto their backs in

Fort Bridger is seen in a sketch believed to have been done in 1849 by W. H. Tappan, who rode with mounted riflemen to Oregon.

trenches and shod while their hooves waved helplessly.

On the travelers crawled, past poisonous springs that mocked their thirst. As oxen grew gaunt, "ancient claw-footed tables, well waxed and rubbed, or massive bureaus of carved oak" were jettisoned, "stern privations of the journey." On and on, up Sweetwater Creek past Independence Rock; higher and higher to the backbone of the continent, South Pass. They crossed with cheers and gunfire. The Pacific lay ahead!

And then they recoiled. Westward past the Sandy toward Green River there stretched, one dismayed traveler wrote, "an unmeasurable and sterile surface. . . . The resolution almost faints when contemplating the . . . ground that is yet to be traveled over."

After 1842 some of the emigrants swung southwest to trade at Jim Bridger's new, ramshackle fort on Blacks Fork of the Green River, in southwestern Wyoming. Impatient souls plunged directly ahead, fifty hard, water-less miles across Sublette's Cut-off. In the blessed green vales of Bear River, Idaho, the routes rejoined and coiled northward toward Fort Hall.

But to return to the particulars in 1841. The original goal of that year's single caravan had been California. Guide Fitzpatrick, however, could tell them nothing about the intervening land to the Mexican province save that it had discouraged beaver trappers during the preceding decade. Certainly they would find no San Buenaventura River to float down in comfort. Dismayed, half the train, including four of the five women, lost heart and decided on Oregon. But teen-age Nancy Kelsey stayed

with her husband when he and thirty other men clung stubbornly to their original goal, California's valleys.

The parties separated where the north-flowing Bear makes its hairpin curve and drops south toward Great Salt Lake. Those seeking California pushed their nine wagons to the grisly edges of the inland sea, then bent west. Knotted sagebrush shook the vehicles mercilessly. The skimpy grass they found was so crusted with salt that often the animals could scarcely eat it. On a few nights they had to make dry camps, but the next day they always managed to find a spring.

By the time they had passed gaunt Pilot Peak, just west of today's border between Utah and Nevada (north of

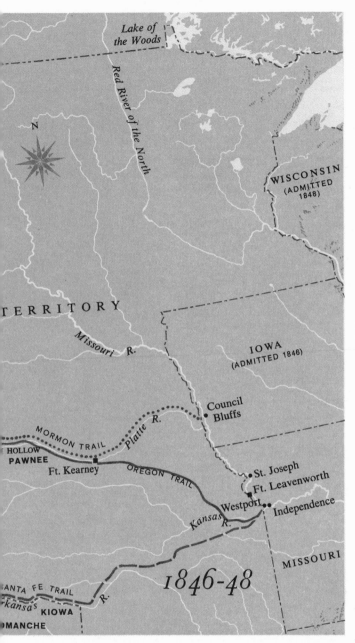

Lake of
the Woods

N

Red River of the North

WISCONSIN
(ADMITTED
1848)

TERRITORY

Missouri R.

IOWA
(ADMITTED 1846)

Platte R.

Council
Bluffs

MORMON TRAIL

HOLLOW
PAWNEE

Ft. Kearney

OREGON TRAIL

St. Joseph

Ft. Leavenworth

Westport

Independence

Kansas R.

MISSOURI

1846-48

ANTA FE TRAIL

Arkansas R.

KIOWA

OMANCHE

*Roads of empire, the Oregon Trail and its principal cut-offs,
followed by thousands of Western emigrants, are seen above.
Later, many travelers took the Mormon and California routes.*

dismal Wendover, on modern U.S. Highway 40), the
Kelsey brothers' livestock could no longer pull their two
wagons. The brothers abandoned the vehicles and transferred their goods to packsaddles made on the spot. Soon
the rest of the party gave up their wagons, too.

In time the thirty-one males and the lone girl, carrying
her baby, reached Marys River, named years earlier by
Peter Skene Ogden of the Hudson's Bay Company but
redesignated Humboldt in 1844 by Frémont. So far as
western migration was concerned, the Humboldt was a

geographic miracle—three hundred and sixty-five miles
of water and grass through an otherwise all but impassable desert. Later emigrants reached it by traveling from
Fort Hall west down the Snake for forty miles to Raft
River and slanting southwest up that stream through the
stark spires called City of Rocks. A long, dull pull down
Goose Creek then brought them to the head of the
Humboldt, well above the point at which the party of
1841 reached the river—a longer way, but one that
avoided the Great Salt Lake Desert.

The Humboldt's sparse, tepid water finally disappeared
in a broad tangle of swamp and salt puddles called
Humboldt Sink. The migrants of 1844 learned from Indians to cut southwest from the sink to Truckee River
and follow the Truckee up into the Sierra foothills, bang-
ing miserably back and forth across the canyon-pinched,
boulder-littered stream bed until they reached what came
to be called Donner Pass. The pioneers of 1841, however,
missed the Truckee, reaching instead the Walker River
farther south, so bright and cold as it danced out of the
Sierra that they named it the Balm. They turned their
pack animals up it. It was already October and dangerously late. Pushing and pulling at their gaunt livestock
and made fearful by the ice that formed each night, they
crossed Sonora Pass, so hungry that they ate the scrawny
mules they butchered "half roasted, dripping with
blood." Then, toward the end of October, they killed
twenty-six deer and feasted. Revived, they found their
way to Marsh's ranch at Mount Diablo.

No one followed them to California in 1842, and
relatively few in 1843. The latter was overwhelmingly
Oregon's year. Bills in Congress promised to *give* every
male settler over eighteen in the Northwest six hundred
and forty acres, another one hundred and sixty to his
wife, and one hundred and sixty to each child—this at a
time when the head of a family in the United States
proper *paid* the government $1.25 an acre for a maximum
of one hundred and sixty acres. Since sovereignty of the
Oregon country was in dispute with Great Britain, the
bills did not pass, but the frontier was convinced that
one soon would. In the spring of 1843 a thousand restless
emigrants owning five thousand head of cattle started
west on the tracks of the scant hundred who had gone to
Oregon the year before.

Traders at Fort Hall told the sprawling party of 1843,
as they had told their predecessors the year before, that
wagons could go no farther; but Marcus Whitman, traveling with the train on his return from mission business
in the East, persuaded the group to try. Stretched loosely
out for miles behind their road builders, they swung
along the rims of the black lava canyons of the Snake

River, their wagon beds tortured by the knotted sage.

Twice they risked the deep crossings of the Snake—fatal for some—then dragged up Burnt Canyon into present-day Oregon. Next they skirted the treacherous swamps of the lovely Grande Ronde Valley, and then they were climbing slowly among the cold evergreens of the Blue Mountains. Far ahead, glinting in the sunlight, they saw at last the curving sweep of the Columbia, breaking a gateway through the tawny mesas that guard the approach to the Cascade Range.

Unable to drive wagons through the Columbia's steep-walled, heavily timbered gorge, they switched to Indian canoes and Hudson's Bay Company bateaux or else made precarious rafts, wheeled the hard-used vehicles aboard, and took their chances with the turbulent water. Lice-infested, thievish Indians charged them exorbitant rates for portaging goods around the rapids. The first rains of winter dripped soddenly from the trees. Exhausted and numbed, the travelers stumbled into Fort Vancouver. There McLoughlin gave them generous succor, although he knew many had left home intent on helping drive his company out of the Northwest.

This dangerous river trip at the end of the long journey was an ordeal for everyone. The Oregon-bound parties of 1844 lost half their animals while swimming them across the broad stream to a better trail on the north bank. Part of the train of 1845 tried to avoid the stretch by striking due west across the deserts east of the Cascades. Lost in the rocky canyons, the emigrants fell into a panicked shambles; during their wanderings twenty or more died. But one offshoot of that year's fragmenting caravans did find a usable way across the high, forested hogbacks south of Mount Hood. Samuel Barlow shortly thereafter built a toll road along their route and so spared thousands of travelers the terrors of the Columbia gorge.

Actually, no more than ten thousand people moved to the entire Pacific coast during the critical years from 1841 to 1846. Out of a total United States population of nearly twenty million, it was hardly a significant figure; during that same period, more than fifty times that many immigrants, principally Irish and German, arrived in this country from overseas. Yet, like foam from a shaken bottle, the western outpouring was suggestive of a heady ferment taking place inside.

Many yeasts were at work. One that excited some politicians was a new twist to the old belief that splendor and wealth attended those nations that dominated the trade of Asia. In 1844 Asa Whitney, onetime China merchant, began an agitation for rails to speed goods across the continent from Eastern factories and farms to Western harbors and thence to the Orient. "Awake," he cried

"to the real importance of the Oregon question." Stephen Douglas of Illinois echoed him, urging that Indians be cleared out of the Platte Valley, territorial governments established in Nebraska and Oregon, and a transcontinental railroad surveyed at once, so that this nation would be in a position to "drive Great Britain and her ships and commerce from China."

Another venerable concept, the desire to assure land to future generations, also operated powerfully. In 1844 a New Jersey Democrat cried to eager cheers in his state's political convention, "Make way, I say, for the young American Buffalo—he has not land enough. . . . I tell you, we will give him Oregon for his summer shade and the region of Texas as his winter pasture. . . . The mighty Pacific and the turbulent Atlantic shall be his."

Idealists lent a philosophic tinge to the mood. Boundaries and crowds, they said, were a frustration; the free spirit of man needed actual physical space in which to grow. Even the utopians of New England caught the feeling: it was the God-given duty of Americans to carry their democratic customs across the continent, even, if necessary, "robbing Mexico of another large mass of her territory," to quote Brook Farm's high-minded paper, *The Harbinger*. For in this dark and inscrutable way, *The Harbinger* continued, "Providence is operating on a grand scale to accomplish its designs"—a feeling summed up by the phrase Manifest Destiny.

The Democrats had read trends more accurately than had the Whigs. In searching for a candidate to recapture the Presidency, they cast aside their party leaders, settled on James K. Polk, a dark horse against whom nothing very damning could be said, and elected him, just barely, on a platform that demanded, in a wry semantic perversion of history, "the re-annexation of Texas" and "the re-occupation of Oregon," the latter of which was deemed to reach north to 54° 40' (or fight)—that is, almost to the southern tip of Alaska. Although the platform said nothing of California—openly clutching for it as well as for the other regions would have seemed too blatant—Polk feared England meant to absorb the coastal province, and he was determined to get there first.

The outgoing Whig President, John Tyler, stole some of Polk's thunder just before the inauguration by signing, on March 1, 1845, a joint resolution of Congress that called for the annexation of Texas if that republic expressed, through a plebiscite, a desire to join the Union. Mexico retorted by breaking off all diplomatic relations with Polk's administration.

England meanwhile was growling about Oregon. Faced with the prospect of war on two fronts, Polk for several months after his inauguration talked less belligerently and sent feelers toward both nations suggesting compromises. Meanwhile, the Cabinet took a casual glance at the country's military potential. What they discovered was not reassuring.

The Regular Army consisted of seventy-two hundred soldiers, geared mainly toward keeping the Indians quiet. The men were underpaid (a private earned seven dollars a month), poorly trained, ill disciplined. Equipment and morale in the dusty, isolated frontier garrisons were, in most cases, wretched. War as England or Mexico might be expected to wage it was remote from the Army's experience. No adequate supply system existed to move any sizable number of forces quickly into the field. The officers would hardly know even where to go. Maps of the Texas frontier were full of white spots, and those of California and Oregon almost useless.

Singularly little was done to remedy the defects. As tension with Mexico mounted, General Zachary Taylor was ordered to move as large a force as he could muster to Corpus Christi, near the mouth of the Nueces River, ready to defend Texas in case Mexico attacked. Simultaneously, three little reconnaissance groups moved up the Platte and Arkansas rivers to study the terrain and awe the Indians into staying neutral. That was the extent of the country's preparation.

The stoutest of the exploring forces consisted of two hundred and eighty mounted dragoons from Fort Leavenworth under Colonel Stephen Watts Kearny. On June 16, 1845, Kearny assembled twelve hundred Sioux on a meadow near Fort Laramie. It was a gray, drizzly morning, but he managed a good show nevertheless. He fired his two howitzers, shot off some gaudy rockets, and warned the astounded Indians to be good. That point made, he moved on to South Pass, took a quick look toward what one of his officers, Philip St. George Cooke, described as "the mountain edge of Oregon . . . land of promise and fable," and then turned back, swinging along the eastern base of the Rockies to Bent's Fort on the Arkansas. On August 19 he was once more at Fort Leavenworth. He had marched twenty-two hundred miles in ninety-nine days. For his dragoons it was a useful trip. If trouble came, they would be an experienced core around which to build a fast-striking, mobile force—but not a very big one.

Two reconnaissance groups of topographical engineers a little later moved in concert up the Arkansas to Bent's Fort, arriving August 2. One, commanded by Lieutenant James W. Abert, had been ordered to swing south of the fort, study the formidable Comanches and Kiowas, and map their country in what is now the Texas Panhandle and western Oklahoma. The other group—forty-eight

cartographers, scientists, soldiers, and famous trappers (Kit Carson, Joe Walker, Dick Owens, Lucien Maxwell), and twelve Delaware Indians—was commanded by John Charles Frémont, thirty-two years old. It seems impossible to determine exactly what his mission was.

Brilliant in mathematics, adept at wilderness living, and ambitious, Frémont had been soundly grounded in his work during two years spent on the Dakota prairies with Joseph Nicollet of the War Department's recently expanded Corps of Topographical Engineers. On October 19, 1841, he married Jessie Benton, the seventeen-year-old daughter of Senator Thomas Hart Benton of Missouri. This made him the protégé of the most powerful expansionist voice in the United States Senate. It also brought him, as an unexpected bonus, his literary wife's

Mount Shasta, one of many Western wonders reported by Frémont, was depicted somewhat grotesquely in his Memoirs of My Life.

remarkable skill at translating into readable prose her husband's boundless enthusiasm for the more picturesque aspects of the Western scene.

In 1842 and again in 1843 Frémont had examined the Oregon Trail. During his second trip he had disobeyed orders about returning directly east. Counting perhaps on Benton's protection and hoping to learn conclusively whether there really was a river outlet to the sea from the Great Basin (his name for the landlocked depresssion that embraces most of Nevada and Utah and bits of California, Oregon, Wyoming, and Idaho), he had swung south along the eastern toes of the Cascade and Sierra Nevada Mountains. No river existed. And still he had not gone home. Instead, in February, 1844, he had made a foolhardy, desperately harrowing, incredibly lucky crossing of the snow-heaped Sierra at Carson Pass. After recuperating at Sutter's Fort, he rode south to the Old Spanish Trail and followed it into Colorado on his belated way back to the settlements.

The report of this and of his earlier trip to South Pass —unfurling a special flag after a breathless climb of Fremont Peak in the Wyoming Rockies; risking the Great Salt Lake in a rubber raft; battling snowdrifts; wandering about Sutter's exotic barony; skirmishing with Indians in the Mojave Desert—all this had fired the excitement of the nation. The accounts had been practical as well, for they had given westbound emigrants dependable information about distances, campgrounds, stream fords, grazing conditions, and mountain gateways.

Now, in 1845, Frémont was traveling West again. Instructions from the Bureau of Engineers told him simply to examine the southern Rockies and return with his data before Congress adjourned, "in order that if [military] operations be required in that country the information may be at command." Yet the frontier believed that he was on a broader mission to search out "a new and straight road both to Oregon and California" (*Western Expositor*, Independence, Missouri, June 26, 1845). There may have been secret orders as well—or perhaps just a hint from Benton, confident of his power to smooth out repercussions, that American rifles in California might be handy in case trouble with Mexico came to a head.

Whatever the truth, Frémont left Bent's Fort in mid-August, 1845. He moved slowly, not reaching the south shore of Great Salt Lake until October 10. Elsewhere, history was marching rapidly. On October 13 the voters of Texas declared in favor of annexation. Fearful of England and hoping still to placate Mexico, Polk sent envoy John Slidell to Mexico City to pay off the damage claims American citizens held against Mexico if Mexico would agree to the Rio Grande rather than the Nueces River as the border of Texas. If that gesture succeeded, Slidell was then to offer up to forty million dollars for everything west of the Rio Grande to the Pacific. Bald cash, however, might not succeed with the proud Mexicans. To copper bets, Secretary of State James Buchanan on October 17 wrote the American consul in Monterey, Thomas Larkin, that it might be a good idea for Californians to separate from Mexico on their own initiative and then ask "to unite their destiny with ours . . . as brethren"—annexation, Texas style. It was ever so pure: if the Californians themselves made the necessary overtures, how could anyone, even Mexico, accuse the United States of acts of aggression?

One copy of this letter was sent by ship. Another was given to a Marine lieutenant, Archibald Gillespie, who was also entrusted by Senator Benton with a packet of

Sam Brannan

private letters for delivery to Frémont. Disguising himself as a traveler in search of health, Gillespie sailed early in November to the east coast of Mexico and started across the country by foot and horseback. In Mexico City crowds were howling through the streets for war on the North Americans. After memorizing the contents of Buchanan's letter, Gillespie prudently destroyed it. He kept the packet for Frémont intact, however, as he continued to Mazatlán and took ship for Monterey.

From Great Salt Lake, meanwhile, Frémont pushed west to Pilot Peak. Eighty miles of the way lay across a waterless waste, crushed white with salt. From Pilot Peak he slanted southwest to Walker Lake, crossed the Sierra in December untroubled by snow, and reached Sutter's Fort on the ninth. During the trip, detachments from his party made side explorations. The first one, led by Frémont himself, found a direct route from the vicinity of Pilot Peak to the emigrant trail down the Humboldt. A later one, guided by Joseph Walker, swung far south to cross the Sierra at Walker Pass, intending to meet Frémont in the upper San Joaquin Valley. They missed connections, and on January 15, 1846, Frémont returned from that valley to Sutter's. There he met Lansford W.

Hastings, an adventurer whose schemes, from this distance, look every bit as enigmatic as do Frémont's.

Hastings had gone to Oregon with the party of 1842. The Willamette Valley fell short of his expectations. Away he went with several other malcontents to California in 1843. There his imagination began to soar. The sight of Sutter's feudal empire; the inability of Mexico to suppress the revolutions, waged mostly by manifesto, that rippled the province almost annually; the endless reaches of land on which to base speculations like those he had seen in the Ohio Valley—it is impossible to say what put him to scheming or what he schemed about.

In pursuit of the necessary people, he boarded a sailing ship early in 1844 and went east by way of Mexico. At his home in Ohio he picked up his pen. Grandiloquent phrases tumbled out—sixty bushels of corn and up to a hundred and twenty bushels of wheat per California acre, oats eight feet tall, strawberries and grapes beyond belief. No "noxious miasmatic effluvia" existed, nothing to cause catarrh or "consumptive affections." Snow on the mountains, but in the valleys, perpetual summer.

Reaching paradise was no problem, he said, although he had not seen the deserts and mountains that had to be crossed on the last half of the journey. One simply left the Oregon Trail at a point vaguely east of Fort Hall and drove "west southwest about fifteen days, to the northern pass, in the California mountains, thence three days, to the Sacramento," over a road that was easier than the section of the trail around Fort Hall—a cavalier distortion of geography that could prove disastrous if many people succumbed to it.

Giving his propaganda the dignity of book publication cost money. To raise funds, Hastings took to lecturing. Early in 1845 he reached New York City and there touched the edges of another scheme, this one involving the possible shifting of thousands of Mormons from the East to new homes in California. And that necessitates another digression.

Founded in 1830 by Joseph Smith, a young farm hand of upper New York State, the Church of Jesus Christ of Latter-day Saints had been driven from its home at Kirkland, Ohio, to Jackson County in western Missouri, near Independence. There the newcomers quickly absorbed the bulk of the available land and gained control of the local courts. Abolitionists in a slaveholding region, tightly knit in an area of freewheeling frontier individualism, and haughtily convinced of their superiority as a chosen people, they again roused violent antipathies among their neighbors. In 1838, riots exploded. Both sides indulged in barn burnings, night floggings, even murder. In October Governor Lillburn Boggs sent six thousand members of the state militia into the area: "The Mormons . . . must be exterminated or driven from the State if necessary for the public peace."

They fled to the east bank of the Mississippi in Illinois and founded Nauvoo. By taking advantage of an even political division between Democrats and Whigs, Joseph Smith won a charter from the state that enabled him to set up an almost autonomous principality, defended by its own militia. A carefully organized missionary system carried Mormon gospel throughout the East and England. "They speak," wrote John Greenleaf Whittier, "a language of hope and promise to weak hearts, tossed and troubled." The stream of converts swelled until Nauvoo and its environs boasted two thousand neat brick homes housing perhaps fifteen thousand people.

Callously bartering the votes he controlled, Smith grew so arrogant that he said no Illinois law could be recognized in the city without his consent. The climax of resentment came with his espousal of polygamy. This doctrine split his own church. Mormons opposed to plural wives established a newspaper, the *Nauvoo Expositor*, to fight him. The Prophet ordered the press destroyed. Meanwhile, non-Mormons were gathering in ugly bands throughout the surrounding countryside.

Smith, his brother Hyrum, and two others surrendered to the authorities, perhaps hoping to check violence. Promised state protection, they were thrust into jail in the nearby town of Carthage. The promise meant nothing. At five in the afternoon, June 27, 1844, a mob broke into the building and shot the brothers down.

The church threatened to crumble under the crisis. Brigham Young, forty-three years old, square-set, blunt, and inspiring, stepped into Joseph's shoes and held it together. But he knew, from the experiences of the past, that the Mormon movement could not endure unless relocated in a wilderness so isolated that its development would not be interrupted again by mob assaults.

What wilderness? And how were the people to get there? By the spring of 1845, when Lansford Hastings reached New York City, Mormons everywhere were discussing the problem of their future, although in Nauvoo itself Brigham Young was still saying nothing—he had not yet reached a decision.

One of New York's leading Mormons was twenty-six-year-old Samuel Brannan, an Irishman out of Maine who ran a newspaper for the Saints in the East. After Joseph Smith's death, Brannan had briefly supported a candidate opposed to Brigham Young, then had seen the error of his ways and had gone to Nauvoo to seek forgiveness. On his return, bursting with new faith, he encountered Hastings—who had finally managed to get his book pub-

189

lished—heard him lecture, mentioned the book in his re-invigorated paper, and evidently talked to Hastings about resettling the Mormons in the West. He was particularly impressed by what Hastings said of California, "a portion of the new world," Brannan wrote in his columns, "which God made choice above all others."

Hastings also talked in New York to A. G. Benson and Amos Kendall, the latter of whom had been a member of Jackson's Kitchen Cabinet and later had served as Postmaster General of the United States under Martin Van Buren. These men led the promoter to believe that their firm, A. G. Benson & Company, intended to establish branches in California and the next year (1846) send ships around the Horn laden with merchandise and emigrants. When Hastings left New York on July 6, 1845, he

Frémont's May, 1846, fight with Klamath Indians near Oregon's Klamath Lake was portrayed by this illustration in his memoirs.

was convinced that an enormous migration—up to twenty thousand persons—would roll westward in '46. Presumably he expected many of the participants in this surge to be displaced Mormons.

He and nine companions made their own transcontinental crossing with horses and pack mules dangerously late in 1845, not leaving Independence until August 17. At Fort Laramie they ran into Jim Bridger. To avoid hostile Indians, Bridger led them through the Wind River Mountains on a trail one of them called the worst on the American continent—precipitous mountains, wild chasms, canyons where sunlight never penetrated. In December they climbed along the Truckee River and crossed Donner Pass. They were hungry at times but otherwise as lucky as Frémont had been three weeks

earlier. No snow fell during their four-month journey. They reached Sutter's Fort on Christmas Day, 1845.

When Frémont reappeared at Sutter's in January, he told Hastings about the fine new short cut that he had discovered running south of Great Salt Lake past Pilot Peak to the Humboldt River. He probably used language like that he employed in a letter he wrote to his wife on January 29. "The mountains were covered with grasses of the best quality, wooded with several varieties of trees, and containing more deer and mountain sheep than we have seen in any other part of our voyage. . . . I can ride in thirty-five days from the *Fontaine qui Bouit* River [about modern Pueblo, Colorado, on the east side of the Rockies] to Captain Sutter's; and for wagons, the road is decidedly better."

These were extraordinary statements. Isolated summits may have been clothed with grass, but not the salt-crusted desert or the seared valleys beyond it, although by implication Frémont seemed to include them all. And it had taken him three times thirty-five days to make the crossing, an excess not entirely explained by his exploring.

Hastings spent a couple of weeks laying out a townsite below Sutter's Fort. Then, as time dragged, he began to think of riding east to the Oregon Trail, intercepting the flood of wagon trains somewhere around Bridger's Fort in southwestern Wyoming, and deflecting the travelers toward their golden opportunity—and his. In due time he made connections with a small eastbound party that included Jim Clyman in its numbers and in April started back over the Sierra.

By then the Mormons were moving. In September, 1845, anti-Mormons had begun burning farms and harrying the people who lived on the outskirts of Nauvoo. Meeting with Illinois officials, Brigham Young and the Council of Twelve accepted the inevitable, and in return for a promise of protection, agreed to evacuate Nauvoo during the spring of 1846. As a destination Young suggested to the council, rather vaguely, Upper California, in those days a loose designation for the great sprawl of land between the Wasatch Mountains (present-day Utah) and the Pacific. The coastal valleys did not really interest him, however. Migrants were drifting that way in numbers, and a Mormon community might find itself beset with the same old problems. An environment too harsh to attract enemies would be better.

More and more often his thoughts dwelt on the arid plains between the Wasatch Range and Great Salt Lake —seemingly sterile, yet capable of being irrigated by mountain streams. He did not want to start discussions and raise objections, however, by a premature announcement of what he was planning. Until he had obtained

190

more information, he would keep his counsel to himself.

In Nauvoo, wagon shops manufactured hundreds of vehicles. Agents scoured Illinois buying firearms, draft oxen, and supplies. Women made clothes, tents, and blankets; they dried vegetables and meat. On the Iowa side of the Mississippi, men began building cabins beside Sugar Creek for a temporary refuge called Camp of Israel.

Sam Brannan was delegated to charter a ship for those Mormons in the East who wished to sail around the Horn. During his search he fell into the hands of A. G. Benson & Company and was completely duped. They told him that Mexico would protest the influx of so many armed religionists opposed to Catholicism, and that the United States would then halt and disarm the Mormons . . . unless friends intervened. Amos Kendall, the former Postmaster General and confidant of Polk (he said), offered himself as such a friend. He would secure passports for the Mormons if church officials promised to deed to his company one half of all land, including town lots, that they acquired in California!

Brannan signed the infamous agreement. He possibly received in return financing for the ship he rebuilt for two hundred and thirty-eight passengers (one hundred of them children) and loaded with seed, tools, farm equipment, and animals. The exiles sailed February 4, 1846, bound for San Francisco Bay. A little later, Brigham Young received a copy of the contract and tore it into pieces. It was never honored.

Persecutions continued in Nauvoo in spite of the governor's promise of protection. Finally Young decided the Saints would have to start moving immediately, even though only thirty or so cabins had been completed at Camp of Israel. On February 4 the exodus began. Floating ice filled the Mississippi. A north wind whined. Ferryboats loaded with weeping people, with cows, pigs, and furniture, dumped their cargoes and returned for more. Later the river froze and people could walk over the ice to shelter in half-built cabins, canvas-covered wagons, and cold-stiffened tents—exalted, a reader of their accounts cannot help feeling, by their sense of martyrdom. Those who stayed behind, unable to obtain wagons and equipment for fleeing, were harried meanwhile not by the weather but by the mobs of Gentiles who sporadically howled and rioted throughout Nauvoo during the rest of the spring and summer.

On February 17 Young mounted a wagon box at Sugar Creek and berated Camp of Israel for its internal quarreling and its wickedness. The next day he divided the group into companies, each with a captain over it, and then, as discipline asserted itself, announced plans for the migration. This was to be no blind flight. Within days, small,

highly organized advance parties would start west to prepare rest camps and plant crops for the horde who followed on the way to . . . Brigham was not yet prepared to say exactly where they were bound. But wherever their destination, "the angels of God will go with you, even as they went with the children of Israel when Moses led them from the land of Egypt."

During this time, relations between the United States and Mexico steadily deteriorated. In December, 1845, Texas formally became a state of the Union. The Mexican Government refused to receive envoy Slidell. On February 3, 1846, General Taylor received orders to cross the Nueces and advance to the Rio Grande.

Although he had been at Corpus Christi for months, Taylor had neglected to learn very much about the coun-

An early panorama of Mormon history by C. C. A. Christensen included this scene of the crossing of the Mississippi in 1846.

try beyond the Nueces or to prepare adequate supply facilities. Fortunately, rain turned the plains into such a quagmire that he could not have moved anyway. He used the time to scramble an organization together and on March 9 got underway, his four thousand soldiers relieved of boredom and feeling very chesty in the clear spring air, among the sudden profusion of wild flowers.

In California Joseph Walker's contingent at last joined Frémont. Sixty hard-twisted, well-armed mountaineers was a more formidable force than had won many a California revolution in the past. Highly suspicious when Frémont marched into Salinas Valley within striking distance of Monterey, Mexican officials ordered him out of the province. Bristling at the insult, Frémont fortified himself on Gavilan (Hawk's) Peak and told the Californians to try to make him go. They prepared. After three uneasy days, Frémont thought better of creating an international incident and, slipping away under darkness, headed toward Oregon.

A month later Lieutenant Gillespie landed at Monterey. He gave Consul Larkin Buchanan's instructions to establish, if possible, an independent California republic that would favor annexation to the United States, and then he set out with a small party to overtake Frémont. On May 8 he reached the camp, situated in the heavy forests close to the southern shore of Klamath Lake. Historians have been speculating ever since about what sort of message he might have delivered to Frémont late that evening around the smoky fire.

One way or another, it probably suggested the imminence of trouble. Frémont decided to march back into California and improvise on whatever situation developed. He was so excited that he went to bed without posting sentries. Indians crept into camp and began tomahawking the sleepers. A furious melee erupted under the dark evergreens. Three of Frémont's men and one attacker died. During subsequent days, the grimly revengeful Americans hunted out the Indians' village, set it afire, and slaughtered many of the fleeing inhabitants. Then they rode for California.

On May 9, word reached President Polk that Mexican soldiers had crossed the Rio Grande—onto American territory, the United States claimed, although Mexico would not admit it—and had clashed with sixty-three of Taylor's dragoons, killing or wounding sixteen and making captives of the rest.

To timorous observers, the timing of the incident was appalling, for the quarrel with England over Oregon seemed also rushing to a climax. Late in April, at about the time Taylor's dragoons were tangling with the Mexicans, Congress had passed a resolution recommending that the President end the agreement of joint occupation of the Northwest. The next step would be either a declaration of war or the signing of a treaty settling the longstanding boundary dispute. Many feared—and a few hoped—that war would be England's response.

Actually, the causes for conflict were fading. The geographic area under contention had shrunk. Although England once had demanded the 42nd parallel (the northern boundary of California) as her limit, she long since had grown reconciled to pulling back at least as far as the Columbia. And in spite of eagle-screaming American talk of 54° 40′, Polk had quietly renewed offers made by his predecessors to settle for the 49th parallel, already established as the boundary east of the Rockies. Disputes, in short, had narrowed to the western

two thirds of what is the modern state of Washington.

Was that relatively small area worth fighting about? The powerful Hudson's Bay Company thought not. Fur returns from the Columbia country had dwindled. Moreover, many of the newly arrived Americans had struck Factor John McLoughlin as dangerous. Some of them already had threatened to burn Fort Vancouver, holding supplies worth one hundred thousand pounds. If international clashes developed, the newcomers were numerous enough to turn talk into action. In 1845, accordingly, the company, though maintaining Fort Vancouver, shifted headquarters operations north to Fort Victoria, on the southern tip of Vancouver Island, closer to trading posts recently opened in what is now British Columbia. No "special interests" remained in the Northwest to exert pressure on the English Government.

Other considerations were at work. England needed peace to settle problems throughout the world. She wanted to keep her commerce with the United States flowing; her manufacturers bought most of their cotton and disposed of at least fifteen per cent of their cloth and machinery in this country, and as a result Polk's moderate tariff stand won good will in England. One more consideration: Great Britain did not need a Pacific harbor but realized expansionist America was determined to have one, either San Francisco Bay or Puget Sound. Why fight to hold them from the sound, especially after investigators sent to evaluate the area described it as a "pine swamp"?

The British Government began an adroit propaganda campaign in the newspapers to prepare the English public for a settlement at the 49th parallel. In January, 1846, the powerful London *Times* swung into line, and it was evident that any sort of accommodation by the United States would result in a peaceful compromise.

Official offers of a settlement had not reached Polk when he read Taylor's reports of the clash on the Rio Grande. Still, he sensed the trend and so was willing to take a chance that a clash with Mexico would not be complicated by another one with Great Britain. He spent much of the night of May 9 and Sunday, May 10, drafting an angry message to Congress:

"War . . . exists by the act of Mexico herself."

At the moment the message was read, Frémont was hurrying into California, ripe for anything; Hastings was riding east to lure immigrants into the same area; an advance party of Mormons was moving from Camp of Israel on Sugar Creek across Iowa toward the Missouri River; Sam Brannan's ship was on the high seas; and Taylor had collided again with the Mexicans on the Rio Grande. It promised to be a busy year.

Western lands needed more people; this 1836 poster promoted a new townsite in Illinois.

EXPANDING FRONTIERS

As the nineteenth century neared its mid-point, the frontier was well beyond the Mississippi, and a small forerunner of settlement had even leap-frogged the Great Plains to the Oregon country. East of the Mississippi the frontier was at last gone except in the pine forests of upper Michigan, Wisconsin, and Minnesota; the emphasis now was on laying down roads and railroads, building better houses, and acquiring such amenities of civilization as debating societies, village brass bands, and sewing circles. The development of lands around the Great Lakes had been helped tremendously by the completion of the Erie Canal in 1825, which had brought an influx of settlers and cheap water-borne commerce. As a result, there was an obsession with canal building, although no other route had the advantages of location and terrain that made the Erie such a money-maker. Pennsylvania, in order to get its canal boats over the Alleghenies, put them on its Portage Railroad (above, as painted by George Storm), where they were pulled up the steeper slopes by cable. Though all but the Erie lost money, the canals helped develop backwoods regions.

193

MECHANICS' MAGAZINE,

AND

REGISTER OF INVENTIONS AND IMPROVEMENTS.

VOLUME IV.]   FOR THE WEEK ENDING OCTOBER 11, 1834.   [NUMBER 4.

"It is a strange thing to behold what gross errors and extreme absurdities men do commit for want of a friend to tell them of them. The help of good counsel is that which setteth business straight."—BACON.

CYRUS H. M'CORMICK'S IMPROVED REAPING MACHINE.

To the Editor of the Mechanics' Magazine:

DEAR SIR,—I send you a drawing and description of my Reaping Machine, agreeably to your request.

References—A, the platform; B, tongue; C, cross-bar; D, hinder end of the tongue; e e, projections in front; F, broad piece on each side; G, circular brace; H, diagonal brace; I, upright post; J, upright reel post; K, braces to upright; L, projection to regulate the width of swarth; M, main wheel roughened; N, band and cog wheel of 30 teeth; O, band; p, small bevel wheel of 9 teeth; Q, do. of 27 teeth; r, do. of 9 teeth; s, double crank; T, cutter; V, vibrating bar of wood, with bent teeth; U, reel pulley; W, reel; X, wheel of 15 inches diameter; Y, reel post.

The platform A is of plank, made fast to a frame of wood, for receiving the grain when cut, and holding it until enough has been collected for a sheaf, or more. The projections in front, e e, are two pieces of the platform frame, extending about 1½ feet in front, and one or more feet apart. On each outside of these pieces is to be secured a broad piece of wood, as at F, by screw bolts, as at 1 1, passing through them and the pro-

VOL. IV.   14

Cyrus McCormick's reaper, patented in 1834, was the first of the great labor-saving inventions that kept improving farm production.

B

EXPLANATION

194

DEVELOPING THE PRAIRIES

*ohn Dixon's ferry over the Rock
River at Dixon, Illinois (left)
was painted by Henry F. Ainslie
n 1842. Abraham Lincoln was sta-
ioned here with his militia com-
any during the Black Hawk War.*

*To help Ohio and Indiana finance
heir canal systems, the Government gave them public lands in a
heckerboard pattern of sections
below) along the canal routes.
The same help was later granted
o railroad builders in the West.*

American pioneering technology had been so completely based on the forest and an
abundant supply of wood that settlers avoided the first open prairies as long as possible.
In Illinois they cleared the wooded river valleys and passed up the grasslands, and in
Missouri they settled the forested rocky areas before the rich prairies. It was not only
that they depended on trees for everything from houses and fuel to furniture and fencing; they believed that grassland was too sterile to grow trees and, hence, to grow crops.
Latecomers were forced to farm prairieland; when they found how wonderfully fertile
it was, the treeless country of Iowa was settled rapidly. The invention of a steel plow by
John Deere greatly promoted the opening of the prairie, for the cast-iron plows of the
period were unsuited to the tough sod and sticky soil. Deere made his first plow from
a saw blade in 1837; eventually he was producing them from cast steel in a factory.

VALLEY
OF THE
MAUMEE RIVER
OHIO

RING-TAILED ROARERS

The log cabin above was set up in Buffalo during the 1840 campaign by Whigs who portrayed their candidate as a simple, cabin-dwelling, cider-drinking man. Actually, he came from a wealthy family. The political candidate (left) and riverman (below), both by George Caleb Bingham, were Western types.

Exaggeration was part of the natural idiom of the West. No boast was too big, no tall tale too outrageous. Men declaimed ridiculous brags that ran on to considerable length: they were ring-tailed roarers, half-horse, half-alligator; they were sired by a hurricane and rode the lightning, and on and on. Boasting came naturally in a big, new land where everything was in superlatives, even self-descriptions. The ring-tailed roarers believed in doers rather than thinkers; it was natural that when they elected a fellow Westerner, Andrew Jackson, President in 1828, they did so mainly because he had been a noted Indian fighter and general. The roarers, unhappily, brought a new demagoguery into politics. Westerner William Henry Harrison was easily elected President in 1840, although he had no platform other than being the hero of the indecisive victory over the Indians at Tippecanoe.

Behind Andrew Jackson, in a heroic lithograph, men fight the Battle of New Orleans, which made him a national figure.

An 1835 map of the Fort Snelling area, though completely wrong in its scale and directions, does show buildings and Indian villages of the time. The fort is the square object above and to the right of the confluence of the rivers.

THE NORTHWEST BORDER

Although the frontier continued to advance rapidly in the south and center, it came almost to a standstill in the north, halted by the great forests of northern Michigan, Wisconsin, and Minnesota. Fort Snelling, from its establishment in 1819 until a small outpost was built about a hundred miles farther up the Mississippi in 1849, remained the most remote Northwestern bastion of American strength. Nor was there any other to the west on the upper Missouri; no Army fort would be built there till 1855. Over this vast region the military at Fort Snelling tried to keep out Canadian fur men, control the Indians, and enforce laws.

But civilization was on its way. Copper and iron had been discovered in upper Michigan in the 1840's, and the Soo Canal that would open Lake Superior to ore-carrying ships would come in 1855. Lumbermen were working their way up rivers into Wisconsin as early as the 1830's. And that surest herald of an advancing frontier, the settler with his plow, was moving up the Mississippi. By mid-century, emigrants were coming as far as Fort Snelling by steamboat and going out into nearby land.

Fort Snelling (above), built of stone, was as solid as it looks in this 1844 painting by J. C. Wild. However, in its long career it was never under attack. Michigan's Fort Michilimackinac (below), painted in 1842 by Henry F. Ainslie, who shows Chippewas camped to receive their annuities, gradually lost its strategic importance after the War of 1812.

Kenneth McKenzie

MISSOURI KNIGHTS
AND A KING

George Catlin, an awed observer of the Mandan O-kee-pa ceremony, drew the above sketch of one of the dancers, the black-painted Evil Spirit.

In 1834, three years before they were almost wiped out, Karl Bodmer painted the scene (right) of Mandans crossing the frozen Missouri.

Kenneth McKenzie of the American Fur Company did what no other American fur man had ever managed; he was able to trade with the Blackfeet, the lordly warriors of the upper Missouri, who until then had been in the habit of murdering every American they met. But then, McKenzie was an unusual man. He hired only bold, hardy, experienced men, and he directed them with a firm hand from Fort Union, where the Yellowstone joins the Missouri. They called him "The King of the Missouri," and he lived the part with ruffled shirts, old brandy, and fine furniture, brought upriver by company steamboats. He built posts in the 1830's on the Marias and Bighorn rivers, sent his men among the proud warrior tribes of the high plains, and developed the buffalo hide trade. But he could not control all forces. Smallpox swept his domain in 1837, killing thousands of Indians. All the tribes suffered, but none so terribly as the Mandans; of 1,600 people, it is said that only 31 survived.

In his "*Attacking the Grizzly Bears*" George Catlin captured the primitive violence of a strug

...ween the fiercest of American beasts and Plains Indians wielding lances and knife-tomahawks.

203

Alfred Jacob Miller painted "Trappers" (above), as well as the scenes opposite, during a trip to the West in 1837.

Fort Laramie was a major fur trading post from 1834 until the Army bought it in 1849 to protect the Oregon Trail.

SUNSET OF AN ERA

For a time, when the West was untracked and wild, it had belonged to the mountain men alone. Then the world's demand for beaver pelts had been insatiable, and there had been unlimited beaver in myriads of streams in mountain ranges without end. But, incredibly, the beaver began to grow scarce just as a change in men's fashions from beaver hats to silk toppers cut the demand for pelts. The 1838 trappers' rendezvous was the last big one; the next year it was so much smaller that the dispirited mountain men did little drinking or roistering.

Some mountain men continued to trap. Some of the best, among them Kit Carson, Thomas Fitzpatrick, and Jim Bridger, put their incomparable knowledge of the West to other uses and became scouts and guides. And when they began leading emigrant parties through mountain passes they had discovered, then the day of the mountain man was indeed past.

"Escape from Blackfeet"; a trapper's worst fear was Blackfeet Indians.

205

The turkey vulture of America was among the creatures examined by expedition scientists.

WILKES'S
WONDERS

The huge Pacific Northwest trees were a source of amazement, and expedition artist Joseph Drayton used a camera lucida to record an especially big one (above) in a pine forest near Astoria.

The crater of Kilauea (left) on Hawaii was painted by Titian R. Peale, artist-naturalist with the expedition. All three pictures shown here appeared in Wilkes's long narrative of the voyage.

206

In 1838 the United States Exploring Expedition, a squadron of six criminally inadequate Navy ships commanded by an opinionated, duty-driven martinet, Lieutenant Charles Wilkes, set sail from Hampton Roads. However, without Wilkes to drive it on, it is doubtful the miserable squadron could have carried out its mission, which included not only a survey of Pacific islands and coasts but also deep explorations into dangerous Antarctic seas. When the expedition returned in 1842, it had mapped 280 Pacific islands, charted 800 miles of the coast of Northwest America, and sailed along 1,600 miles of Antarctica to prove it a continent. In addition, a small corps of scientists had collected a wealth of specimens and facts. Wilkes was never commended by an Administration too mean-spirited to praise a project sent out under another political party, but his surveys of the Oregon country shortly became important to the Northwest by adding strength to the hand of the United States when the future of Oregon was being argued with Great Britain.

Father Pierre Jean De Smet built a mission for the Flatheads of Montana.

THE MACEDONIAN CRY

With the exception of priests, active in the Southwest since the days of New Spain, missionaries were a long time getting to Indians west of the Mississippi River. In the 1820's, the Hudson's Bay Company sent several boys of Northwest tribes to an Anglican school at Red River in Canada. Influenced by them and by Catholic Iroquois in Montana, Nez Perces and Flatheads became interested in Christianity—more as a "medicine" that would give them new power than as a religion that would supplant their own beliefs. In 1831 four Nez Perces, traveling with fur traders, arrived in St. Louis, and the distorted fiction that they had come seeking the white man's book of God went eastward. "It was a Macedonian cry of 'Come over and help us,'" the excited writer for one church paper put it. By 1834 the first missionaries had started to Oregon.

Spokan Garry, son of a Spokan chief, spread interest in Christianity among neighboring tribes after his return from Red River. The missionaries' feuding later embarrassed him.

Five Crows, a Cayuse headman, was converted by Spalding, who named him Hezekiah. After the Whitman massacre, he forced a white captive to live with him briefly as his wife.

James, a Nez Perce shaman, bedeviled Spalding, who squatted on his land and tried to turn the Indians against him. These three heads were drawn by Gustavus Sohon in 1855.

208

JESUS CHRIST.

In the Oregon country the missionaries rapidly set to fighting among themselves. To win converts from their rivals, Catholics distributed pictures of "Catholic Ladders," showing Protestants as withered ends of the branches of the true Church. Henry H. Spalding (below), who set up a mission for the Nez Perces, retaliated by devising a "Protestant Ladder" (left, with a section omitted for space), mapping the paths to heaven and hell and portraying the Catholic Church as hell-bent. The feuding disillusioned the natives and contributed to the massacre of Spalding's associates, the Whitmans, and the eventual failure of almost all of the missionaries.

THE OREGON COUNTRY

Fort Vancouver (above), the great Hudson's Bay Company post on the Columbia, was painted by Captain Henry J. Warre, who made a military reconnaissance of Oregon for the British Government in 1845–46. Below are two views of the American settlement of Oregon City in 1846, also by Warre; the one at left shows the falls of the Willamette River.

American expansionists had called for occupation of the Oregon country, and the Administration itself had insisted, "Fifty-four forty or fight!" But that was all quietly forgotten as American and British negotiators split the huge region along the 49th parallel. The treaty, in June of 1846, extended the United States to the Pacific and added the territory that is now Washington, Oregon, Idaho, and part of Montana and Wyoming. It was not a populous region: a few missionaries, a scattering of trappers, and several thousand settlers, almost all in the Willamette Valley. But the wagon trains rolled across the plains, new cabins went up daily, and this was the best yet of promised lands.

Fort Nez Percés (later Fort Walla Walla), here seen in an old lithograph, was built in 1818 as a base for British fur brigades trapping Idaho's Snake Basin.

Kettle Falls on the Columbia was painted in 1847 by Paul Kane, Canadian portrayer of Indians of his country and the northern United States. Here the Colville Indians caught enough salmon in two months to feed them all year.

In legend, according to artist Paul Kane, Chimney Rocks on the Columbia near Walla Walla were t

ayuse Indian women turned to stone. Actually, they are the uneroded cores of ancient volcanoes.

213

A YANKEE IN CALIFORNIA

Presidio of S. Diego   California

William H. Meyers was a gunner in the American Navy from 1841 to 1848, but his hobby was painting, and his vivid though unpolished watercolors now form a valuable record of his times. Those shown here were made while he was on the U.S.S. *Cyane*, 1842–45, in California waters. As the pictures indicate, duty there left a sailor time for such diversions ashore as horseback riding and hunting grizzly bears. The hide houses sketched by Meyers (near right, center) were used by traders to store the cattle hides that were almost the sole export of the province.

Hide houses at S. Diego   California

The martial scene on the opposite page commemorates the blunder by Commodore Thomas Ap Catesby Jones, who hastened from Peru to seize Monterey in 1842 on hearing a false report that Mexico and the United States were at war. After learning of his error, Jones made such deep apologies that he left few hard feelings. But there was no sword waving such as Meyers depicts; a landing party raised the American flag unopposed after the Governor capitulated. Meyers plainly had tongue in cheek when he dramatized the scene and wrote in the turgid exhortation that ends, ". . . storm the works, there is only one soldier in the fort."

Meyers was in California again in 1846–48 and made a picture record of the Mexican War as it was fought in that region. Two of those works appear on page 245.

Hunting the Grizzly Bear.

Monterey California

Taking of Monterey Oct 20th 1842 by the frigate United States & Sloop of War Cyane — Lat 36° 38' N in West California

San Francisco (left) and Los Angeles (right) were sketched in 1847 by William R. Hutton, who went to California with American troops. Gold-rush growth completely changed the appearance of San Francisco within the next few years.

In his "Fandango," artist Charles Nahl captured the carefree spirit of early California life, at least among the more prosperous. Nahl, who went west as a gold seeker in 1850, must have seen this society in its waning days.

216

As the American flag indicates, Sutter's Fort had already transferred its allegiance to the United States when the above picture was painted in 1847. The famous private fort was manned chiefly by Sutter's own Indian workers.

ELYSIUM

California was a province of Mexico, but the bonds between the two were weak. Several times Mexican governors had been chased home in bloodless revolutions, and there had been talk of independence; but the *Californios* could not overcome their sectional and personal differences and work together. American visitors described the people as indolent and pleasure-seeking, with no higher ambition than to dress in fancy clothes and dance the fandango. If true—and it was, to an extent—it was a way of life that drew foreigners. A considerable number of them, mostly Americans, came after 1840, and many received generous land grants.

The largest grant of all, some 49,000 acres, went to John Sutter, a Swiss. From his fort, Sutter ruled a virtually independent principality with its herds, flocks, grainfields, orchards, gristmill, tannery, workshops, and all else necessary to a self-contained existence. Sutter was generous and hospitable to a fault; his door was always open, and he had a partiality for Americans that made his place their unofficial headquarters. But in 1846 the end was near for both his lordly living and the carefree life of the *Californios*.

John Augustus Sutter

217

The Pathfinder and his pathfinder: Frémont (seated) and his guide, Kit Carson

CHARTING THE PATHS WEST

Fremontia vermicularis, *a plant of Oregon and northern California discovered by a Frémont expedition, was named for the explorer.*

Mountains and deserts lay on the path to the Pacific, and though there was no easy way through or around them, the major routes to the West were traced in less than two decades. In the winter of 1830–31, William Wolfskill and George Yount led a party that first traced the entire line of the Old Spanish Trail from Santa Fe to Los Angeles. In 1832, Captain Benjamin Bonneville took a two-year leave from the Army to make a fortune in furs. He did not get rich, and he was dismissed for overstaying his leave, but part of his party explored from Utah to California the route that would soon be the California Trail. Fur men pieced out what became the Oregon Trail with the passage of the first wagons in 1841. And most active of the pathfinders was John C. Frémont, who made five exploring trips into the West. Few areas escaped his attention; he did engage in dubious enterprises, and one of his expeditions ended in disaster, but he pioneered new trails and surveyed new territories.

Captain Benjamin L. E. de Bonneville

The map of the Great Salt Lake (left) and the drawing of the American Falls of the Snake River (below) were both by Charles Preuss, German cartographer with three of Frémont's expeditions. Although Preuss hated every minute of his service, he turned out the first maps of any regions west of the Mississippi River that were based on modern cartographic principles.

LEFT AND ABOVE: FREMONT'S REPORT, 1845

THE OREGON TRAIL

Albert Bierstadt's "Nooning on the Platte" depicts one of the midday rests so essential to conserve the strength of the animals. Farther west, nooning was not always so idyllic since water and grass might be entirely lacking.

"Fording the Platte" was sketched by William Tappan, who went to Oregon in 1849 with a rifle company. Quicksand made crossing the shallow Platte an adventure.

The Indians used to watch the endless lines of covered wagons on the Oregon Trail in awe-struck wonder at the unlimited number of white men. The red men were witness to one of the longest treks in history; an 1846 guidebook of the trail that gave accurate distances between landmarks tallied exactly 2,000 miles from Independence, Missouri, to Fort Vancouver—and then there were still a few miles to go to settle in the Willamette Valley.

The route of the trail was soon marked clearly and grimly. Beginning in western Nebraska, as the land became hillier, drier, more barren, the road began to be littered with furniture, tools, even food thrown out to lighten loads. Dead animals rotted by the way. Sanitation was elementary, and the romantic Oregon Trail was, in fact, often a menace to health. It is not surprising that it was scourged with epidemics and became dotted with graves.

William Tappan probably also made this 1849 sketch of Fort Laramie, the same year in which the Government purchased this most important post on the Oregon Trail.

221

PIONEERS! O PIONEERS!

223

South Pass and the Wind River Mountains, Wyoming

"Yesterday at noon we arrived at the 'culminating point,' or dividing ridge between the Atlantic and Pacific.... Thus the great day-dream of my youth and of my riper years is accomplished. I have seen the Rocky mountains—have crossed the Rubicon, and am now on the waters that flow to the Pacific! It seems as if I had left the old world behind, and that a new one is dawning upon me."

Letter to his brother from Charles T. Stanton, emigrant to California with the ill-fated Donner Party, "South Pass," July 19, 1846. Snow-blinded and alone, Stanton died soon afterward in the Sierra Nevada Mountains.

CHAPTER NINE

NEW EMPIRES

1846-1848

General Zachary Taylor opened the war with a spectacular flourish. He was a short-legged, thickset man with sharp eyes in a dark, seamed face. Indifferent to military polish, he was given to appearing before his troops in a sloppy straw hat and an unkempt uniform, astride his old horse Whitey or even on a yellow mule. Taylor's soldiers referred to him as Old Rough and Ready and were prepared to follow him anywhere.

In March, 1846, he had occupied a tongue of land protruding toward the Mexican city of Matamoros, a few miles above the mouth of the Rio Grande. There his engineers threw up massive earth walls enclosing an area six-pointed like an asterisk and named the place Fort Texas. Because of sand bars at the entrance to the Rio Grande, supplies for Fort Texas were landed at Point Isabel, nine miles north of the estuary.

The obvious Mexican strategy was to cut the road between Fort Texas and Point Isabel and defeat the North Americans when they sallied forth to reopen the vital line. To this end, a succession of Mexican generals massed numerically superior forces at Matamoros. On May 1, they moved across the Rio Grande.

Taylor marched forth to push them back, strengthen Point Isabel, and bring more ammunition to Fort Texas. Blinded by poor scouting, the opponents missed each other completely, and Taylor reached Point Isabel without incident. Behind him, the Mexicans in Matamoros began a desultory bombardment of Fort Texas. An exploding shell fatally wounded Major Jacob Brown, who had been left in charge (the stronghold was renamed

Fort Brown in his honor; eventually it grew into today's Brownsville), but otherwise the cannonade did little harm. Taylor meanwhile loaded two hundred and fifty wagons and started his force back toward the river in a single long, tight column.

The Mexicans slid in across his road. There was a crunching collision, the dry grass caught fire, and under cover of the smoke Taylor's West Point artillerymen slashed devastatingly with their light guns, killing three hundred and twenty Mexicans and wounding more than four hundred. Taylor's casualties were fifty-three.

The next day, May 9, the Mexicans regrouped stubbornly at Resaca de la Palma, an old river bed bordered by four-foot banks and rattling palm trees, its uneven bottom dotted with lagoons and choked with chaparral. The position was formidable and the afternoon blistering hot. The Mexicans did not anticipate Taylor's sudden attack. After a short period of stout resistance in the heavy undergrowth, they broke and stampeded across the river, many drowning in the rout. Casualties soared above two thousand. The Americans lost thirty-three dead, eighty-nine wounded. That same night, completely unaware of the clash, Polk began the preparation of his war message to Congress.

The legislators responded by appropriating ten million dollars and authorizing an army of fifty thousand men. The bulk of the requisitions for men fell on the West and the South—wisely, for this was a war the frontier wanted and the East did not. In the end the West furnished forty thousand men, many on short-term enlistments; the South, twenty-one thousand; and the far more populous

Northeast, only eight thousand. In Tennessee so many answered the call that they had to be selected by lot.

Polk and the War Department evolved their strategy by looking at outline maps that showed next to nothing of actual topography. The basic plan was to pinch off Mexico's northern provinces by means of three widely separated but roughly parallel columns. Taylor, currently bogged down at Matamoros by inadequate supplies, was to drive for Monterrey and Saltillo. From San Antonio, General John Ellis Wool would advance directly west on Chihuahua—actually impossible because of the rough Sierra Madre Oriental and, beyond it, the vast, high desert of Bolsón de Mapimí, which even today few roads touch. Much farther north, Stephen Watts

Some 10,000 people clustered, 1846–47, in the Mormons' Winter Quarters at present Omaha, here painted by C. C. A. Christensen.

Kearny was to leave Fort Leavenworth for Santa Fe and then, if the situation warranted, move on across Arizona to California. The Atlantic squadron was to lend support by blockading the east coast of Mexico and occupying Tampico, the principal port north of Veracruz. The Pacific squadron was already under orders, issued originally with one eye on England, to occupy the California coastal towns in case of trouble with either nation.

A good deal of fuzzy hope was mixed with this fuzzy geography. As usual, dissension shook the Mexican Government; American strategists fondly believed the discontent would bring about revolts in favor of the invaders, especially in the north. Their scheming even embraced Santa Anna, again in exile. The United States helped him return to Mexico in the fatuous hope that he

would declare for peace and let the northern provinces slip, for cash, into American hands. As soon as the opportunistic general was back in Mexico, however, he made a ringing declaration in favor of the constitution of 1824 (which he himself had once suppressed) and leaped to the head of an army of liberation. Of that stage in Santa Anna's career, more later.

Three nonmilitary columns were also on the move when war was declared—more truly conquerors than the Army, for they were embodiments of the relentless surge that was dragging the military in its wake. One was the biggest mercantile caravan yet seen on the Santa Fe Trail, upwards of four hundred wagons carrying merchandise estimated at $1,700,000. A little farther north, twenty-seven hundred emigrants, undeterred by winter-long rumors of trouble, were toiling toward the Platte on their way to the West Coast. Most of them learned of war's declaration in eastern Kansas. It was too late then to turn back without severe loss. On they plodded, fifteen hundred toward California, twelve hundred toward Oregon, where England's intentions in the conflict were very much in doubt.

Still farther north, fifteen thousand Mormons were stringing out across Iowa on their agonizing flight toward a goal still unannounced. The advance parties had started from Sugar Creek on March 1, 1846, before grass existed for their stock. Cold rains liquefied the dormant earth, sent streams out of their banks, and spread chills and rheumatism into every joint. In spite of heroic feats of organization, shortages of food, medicine, clothing, and money were chronic. The Saints quarreled and grumbled; apostates tugged at the disaffected and lured a few. But most held fast, inspirited by the endless prayers, threats, fervors, and psychological tricks of Brigham Young and the Twelve Apostles. Brass bands played regularly. Every night, fiddle music stirred dances beside the blazing logs of the big campfires. Lifted out of selfishness by a faith in the utter rightness of what they were doing, the first groups erected a string of shelters for those who followed, split rails and built fences, planted crops, dug wells, and established blacksmith and wagon shops to service the caravans.

Accommodations for the winter of 1846–47 were built on the west bank of the Missouri River, a few miles above modern downtown Omaha—a cluster of more than six hundred 12- by 18-foot cabins, some of logs and some of sod bricks. The emigrants called the settlement Winter Quarters. They had no business whatsoever being there, for Winter Quarters was on Indian land, which by law was closed to settlement of any sort. But an Army officer eager to recruit Mormons for service in the Mexi-

General Stephen Watts Kearny

can War granted them permission in hopes of gaining Brigham's good will. The Indian Bureau was outraged. Finally, in 1848, it ordered the Saints to evacuate—in Mormon eyes, another proof of their persecution by the Government of the United States.

Anticipating war, meanwhile, the traders bound for New Mexico had hit the trail as fast as they could load their vehicles, hoping to cash in on the high prices that were bound to attend the approach of armies to Santa Fe and Chihuahua. Kearny sent dragoons to stop them. Although a few traders in the van slipped by, the majority, swearing furiously, obeyed orders to await the Army at Bent's Fort on the Arkansas, jumping-off place for Kearny's military invasion.

Behind them, Kearny pulled his plains-hardened dragoons together and began rounding up transportation and food. Simultaneously, he braced himself to absorb the volunteers who inundated him early in June and who elected as their colonel a popular, able, huge-framed Missouri lawyer named Alexander Doniphan. A lark, the volunteers thought: they knew all they needed to know about horses and rifles. They were profoundly mortified when Kearny drilled them so hard during the next twenty days that they had little edge left for the camp followers who swarmed after them.

The first detachments left Leavenworth June 16. The main group departed ten days later. All told, Kearny had sixteen hundred and sixty men: his tough regulars, the half-disciplined volunteer cavalry, some footsore infantry, and a handful of topographical engineers delegated to prepare maps that would have been very useful

right then. The horde was moved by an incredible confusion of transport and supply—fifteen hundred wagons and close to twenty thousand draft horses, oxen, and pack mules, plus cattle for eating.

Griping and straggling, the heterogeneous mob plodded through searing heat and dusty winds. They cooked their meals on hundreds of little fires of buffalo dung, shot at rattlesnakes and antelope, broke ranks to chase buffalo, disregarded every military rule in the books—and averaged twenty miles a day. At the end of July they gathered at Bent's Fort with the disconsolate traders, and there they prepared to make the final lunge across the Raton Mountains.

From the trading post, Captain Philip St. George Cooke and trader James Magoffin went ahead under a flag of truce to Santa Fe. They convinced slippery Governor Armijo that resistance was hopeless. Magoffin, a secret agent of Polk's, probably added persuasion by making use of the Mexican tradition of the bribe, the exact amount of which remains uncertain.

Armijo played his part well. He issued sonorous proclamations calling for resistance unto death, erected defense works at the Apache Canyon approach to Santa Fe, and suddenly turned tail. His dumfounded, ill-equipped militia scattered instantly, and on August 18, Kearny entered Santa Fe without having fired a shot.

He reassured the frightened inhabitants by attending mass and giving a great ball in the Palace of the Governors. More practically, he organized a territorial government and appointed Charles Bent as its head. In mid-September he dispatched contingents of Doniphan's volunteers throughout northern and northwestern New Mexico to chide the Utes and the Navahos for stealing thousands of sheep from the outlying ranchos. And he kept thinking of California.

Why not go? Except for the Indians, New Mexico was prostrate. Strong bodies of American reinforcements were approaching along the Cimarron Cut-off. Among them was a Mormon Battalion of five hundred men who had enlisted in Iowa so that the church hierarchy, desperate for money to speed the migration, could draw their pay. While waiting for these troops to arrive, Doniphan could complete the Indian campaign with a big council near present-day Gallup. That done and the management of the conquered territory handed over to the newcomers, Doniphan could then march south to Chihuahua. Kearny himself would continue across the bleak southern parts of today's New Mexico and Arizona to California with three hundred regular dragoons, followed in due time by the Mormon Battalion—an expedition of epic proportions for both groups, since they

The fearful desert that confronted overland travelers west of Great Salt Lake was depicted by artist Stanislas Schimonsky. The Donner Party, following the Hastings Cut-off, had to race across this waterless area to survive.

would be entirely removed from their sources of supply.

Kearny began his eight-hundred-mile leap on September 25, marching southward down the Rio Grande past Albuquerque. Trader James Magoffin started with him. A resident of Chihuahua, Magoffin planned to continue south to that city after separating from Kearny. There, if all went well, the trader would subvert the military commander, as he had Armijo, so that Doniphan could enter the city without bloodshed. The mere prospect delighted the American merchants who annually traded in Chihuahua or beyond but this year had been confined to Santa Fe. Harnessing their teams, they straggled along behind Kearny's army down the Rio Grande with three hundred and fifteen wagons.

They traveled scarcely one hundred and forty miles. Rumors rolled up from the south that a huge Mexican army was massing in Chihuahua for the reconquest of New Mexico. Although Magoffin continued south into the teeth of the scare, Kearny ordered the civilians to wait until adequate security could be guaranteed them. Disgruntled yet fearful, they went into camp near the ruins of a long-abandoned settlement named Valverde. Fortunately, game abounded—ducks and geese on the river, deer, rabbits, and quail in the thickets and gullies that stretched off toward the mountains to the east. The traders put their wagons into a strong defensive square under the cottonwoods, set up their tents and their brush shanties, and whiled away the time at such activities as

hunting, playing cards, and shooting at bull's-eyes that they made by coloring white bark with wet powder.

Kearny meanwhile continued toward California. Shortly after leaving Valverde, he encountered Kit Carson and fifteen men, six of them Delaware Indians, hurrying dispatches from Frémont to Senator Benton and President Polk. From these messengers the general learned what had been going on in California—and that leads into a long digression.

After hurrying back from Klamath Lake with Gillespie in May, Frémont's explorers had gone into camp on the Sacramento River several miles above Sutter's Fort. Rumors of war were flying, and the region seethed with excitement. Frémont's strong band, commanded by an officer of the United States Army, became a natural magnet for adventurers and malcontents. As they hurried to consult with him, they automatically ended Consul Larkin's hope of prevailing on the native Californians to establish an independent republic of their own, as suggested in Buchanan's instructions. This gathering was an act of aggression, and the *Californios* prepared with clumsy anger to meet it.

How much prompting Frémont gave the American filibusters cannot be said; probably it was considerable. Anyway, one gang opened the brief affray by seizing horses being gathered by Mexican officials. Another group, thirty-three strong, invaded the sleepy hamlet of Sonoma, north of San Francisco Bay, made a prisoner of the garrison's commanding officer, raised a crude flag decorated with a fat, shapeless animal said to be a bear, and proclaimed the California Republic. Frémont appropriated Sutter's Fort in the name of the United States, put it in charge of his topographer, Edward Kern, with directions to "if necessary shoot any person who shall endanger the safety of the place," and against Sutter's violent objections, confined the Sonoma prisoners inside its walls. He then galloped on to Sonoma itself and took over the Bear Flag Republic.

When his men caught three "spies" crossing by rowboat from Yerba Buena, Frémont ordered Carson to slay them, partly in revenge for two Americans killed in an earlier tiff. In July he learned that United States naval vessels had occupied San Francisco and Monterey harbors. Repairing to the latter place, he and one hundred and sixty Bear Flag revolutionists were enlisted by the fleet's Commodore, Robert Stockton, as the California Battalion. They went south by ship and seized San Diego while Stockton invested Santa Barbara and Los Angeles by land. By the end of August California had been conquered, and Carson was sent East carrying dispatches that announced the feat.

Well before this, in June, 1846, England and the United States had agreed to draw the Oregon boundary at the 49th parallel. The emigrants on the plains knew nothing of the decision. Sun-beaten and wind-scoured, they toiled painfully ahead, speculating now and then on what might be happening in their new homelands but engrossed for the most part by each day's pressing need to reach the evening's campground.

Sirens sang to them of short cuts. After following Frémont's tracks back across the salt desert, Lansford Hastings had swung northeast through the rugged canyons of the Wasatch Mountains and had picked up the normal trail near the squalid collection of log huts called Fort Bridger. From there to the head of Sweetwater Creek he spread his propaganda. Both his own trail companion, Jim Clyman, and Joe Walker, who had crossed the salt desert with Frémont, sounded warnings, but the prospect of shrinking travel time was more temptation than some of the wayfarers could resist. Hastings gathered forty wagonloads of emigrants at Bridger's Fort and on July 20 led them southwestward.

The Weber River seemed to offer an easier passage through the Wasatch Mountains than did the brushy, up-and-down trail by which he had come. A Hobson's choice. In places, the emigrants had to shovel out breathless passages high on the ragged sides of the canyons; at one point a wagon and its oxen slipped seventy-five feet to destruction. In other places, the travelers moved all the way down to the cliff-pinched river bed itself, half floating their wagons on the rowdy water.

Twenty-six more vehicles overtook this Hastings party just south of the Great Salt Lake. An additional twenty-three captained by elderly George Donner did not. In a sense Hastings betrayed the Donner group. During the struggle with the Weber's grim canyons, Hastings had left a note in a cleft stick advising future travelers to avoid the river and follow his original pack trail. But where was that? By heroic riding, three scouts from the Donner group overhauled Hastings to ask. He returned several miles with one of them, James Frazier Reed, and with his finger pointed out such landmarks as he could recognize. Returning then to his own train, he led the sixty-five wagons across the sun-blasted white hell of the salt desert. Eighty waterless miles—though Hastings had said forty. The strongest outfits barely reached the cool springs at the foot of Pilot Peak. Gathering grass and water, they returned to help the companions whose oxen had collapsed along the way.

Behind Hastings, the Donner party spent twenty-one aching days in the Wasatch Mountains, rolling boulders, shoveling, chopping through mats of willows and alders. On some stretches their progress amounted to only a mile a day. They were completely exhausted when they reached the edge of the salt plains.

How could they possibly cross? Yet where else could they turn?

One man died. That left twenty-five adult males, three of them elderly. There were fourteen women and forty-four children under eighteen—a total of eighty-six persons. Seventeen of the children had not yet turned six.

They cut grass, filled every vessel they had with water, and goaded the weary oxen ahead. The train straggled out for miles. Some of the loose, thirst-crazed stock stampeded and were lost. After forty-eight hours of pulling day and night without pause, the yoked animals began to lie down at widely scattered spots. The desperate men unyoked them, left wagons, wives, and children behind in isolated groups under the remorseless sun, and drove the faltering beasts to grass and water at Pilot Peak, where they rested for a few hours and then returned to the stranded vehicles.

On they crept. Skulking Indians shot or stole more of their oxen. Tempers snapped. James Reed stabbed a man to death in a quarrel and was banished by the others, who promised to look after his family as he rode on ahead. Another man was callously left behind to perish when he could not keep up; a third was secretly murdered; a fourth died from an accidental gunshot. Charles Stanton, sent ahead with one other man to Sutter's Fort for food, managed to return with two Indian helpers and seven loaded mules. But the season was late—mid-October—and the crippled train was straggling badly as it turned up Truckee Canyon toward the Sierra.

Both in time and in twisting miles, the Hastings Cutoff had proved far longer than the normal route. The train Hastings led reached the summit well behind the emigrants who had swung around by Fort Hall. But at least Hastings got his group over the mountains that autumn. The Donners, as we shall see, did not. First, however, a glance at the Oregon emigrants of 1846 who were simultaneously testing a new short cut that wound through the Black Rock Desert of Nevada, slanted across the northeastern tip of California, and entered Oregon's Willamette Valley from the south.

This rough trail had been worked out with difficulty and suffering, early in the summer of 1846, by fifteen Oregonians under Levi Scott and Jesse Applegate. After reaching the Humboldt River, the explorers sent five of their number on east to Fort Hall. There the quintet bought supplies, left word that they had opened a better road to the Willamette, and hurried back with a few tools to smooth it a little. By then many Oregon immigrants had already gone on past Fort Hall, but those still moving along the interminable trail felt their spirits quicken. Anything shorter was certain to be preferable—or at least so they thought.

The long drag down the Humboldt and west across the Black Rock Desert sapped the fiber of men and beasts. Indians shot at the oxen in order to have the carcasses when the train passed on. This necessitated night penning of the livestock, shorter grazing hours, and a further weakening of strength.

Disaster struck in October, in the heavily timbered mountains beyond Klamath Lake and in the deep, raging canyon of the Umpqua River. Down from the Gulf of Alaska swept the first of the storms that every winter batter the entire Pacific coast of North America. That year (1846–47) the deluges came earlier and more frequently than usual—the worst winter, according to one Oregon resident, that anyone could remember. Shrouded in icy fog, the dense trees dripped continually. Creeks flooded. Despairing people, unable to dry their clothes for days at a time, jettisoned household possessions they had lugged halfway across the continent. As more cattle died each day, many travelers had to abandon their wagons as well. Indians killed two persons; a few others died of exhaustion. The strongest slogged ahead through the mud to the Willamette Valley for help; others gave up, built shanties, and waited numbly for relief. The last of the marooned did not escape until February. And yet

the Applegate Trail really was shorter than the desolate road along the Snake River, over the Blue Mountains, and down the Columbia gorge. In later years, as experience accumulated and various improvements were made, it became heavily traveled.

The same storms that winter caught the Donner party just short of what soon would be called Donner Summit, atop the Sierra Nevada Mountains of California. The advance group occupied an abandoned cabin and built some squat, windowless huts beside Donner Lake. The laggards, including the Donner family, halted five miles farther down the trail in hutches covered with wagon canvas and buffalo robes. The great, soft snowflakes fell inexorably. "Difficult to get wood," Patrick Breen noted in his diary on Christmas Day. The last oxen and horses strayed away and were covered with drifts.

Five women, two boys, and ten men, including Sutter's two Indians, contrived snowshoes out of oxbows and hides. Gasping and falling, they struggled up the summit ridge. Two turned back. The others froze their feet, wept the scalding tears of snow blindness. Once, their nighttime fire burned through a platform of green logs that held it above the snow and dropped them into a well of ice water. They crawled out and crouched under blankets while the blizzard raged. One man went mad at that camp, and four, including Charles Stanton, died; the others, famished from five days without a morsel, butchered the dead. Later another man grew crazed and killed Sutter's two Indians for food. All told, seven men and a boy perished—but no women—and were consumed, some of them while their relatives watched. After thirty-three nightmare days, the survivors stumbled into an Indian camp and were saved.

At intervals rescue parties set out for the threescore people still stranded in the mountains. The first could not get through. Later groups succeeded. At the lake and at the camp five miles below it, they found a melancholy repetition of the cannibalism on the trail. Since the initial rescuers could not provide for everyone, they packed out the weakest children on their backs. On the mountain the grim death and grimmer survival dragged on. By the time the ordeal was over, nearly half the party had perished.

Such were the conquerors. But the widely scattered armies engaged in war against Mexico were the visible carriers of the flag. Slow carriers at times. Zachary Taylor sat at Matamoros most of the summer of 1846, waiting for supplies, neglecting reconnaissance, and giving interviews to correspondents who already were booming him as a candidate to bring the Presidency back to the Whigs. Ten thousand or more soldiers and an infestation of camp followers poured in on him. Bored stiff

This lithograph of General Zachary Taylor (third from left) at his headquarters near Monterrey was part of the publicity of his war exploits (often exaggerated) that helped build him into a hero and send him to the White House.

in the steamy heat, they got out of hand. They drank, yowled, pillaged, raped—and died. Taylor, knowing nothing of sanitary measures, did not ask for even elementary neatness. Epidemics raged. The death march of fifes and muffled drums through the filthy tent cities was so incessant that mockingbirds, it was recorded, took to trilling snatches of the tune.

Using shallow-draft steamboats and often marching at night to avoid the heat, the debilitated army at last moved, late in the summer, one hundred and thirty miles up the Rio Grande and then a bit inland to the dusty stone-and-adobe village of Camargo. There it paused again while nineteen hundred mules were gathered—not nearly enough, but a vast problem nevertheless for those who had to pack them every morning and line them out along the trail toward Monterrey.

On September 20, Taylor attacked the mountain-girt city from opposite sides, driving by bloody street fighting from house to house. On September 24, the Mexican

general offered to evacuate the city in exchange for an eight-week armistice. Needing time to bring up supplies and hoping that a gesture of leniency would woo the northern provinces into his arms, Taylor agreed.

In the United States the press whooped up the affair as a great victory. Polk was furious. Victory indeed! By granting the armistice, Taylor had let the Mexicans escape to fight another day. Admitting at last that the war could not be won by nipping away at the outlying provinces, and eager besides to clip the wings of Taylor's Presidential aspirations, Polk gave the green light to General Winfield Scott's plan of capturing Mexico City itself after a landing at Veracruz. This involved drawing away many of Taylor's regiments and settling him down to defensive operations.

Bitterly resentful, Taylor determined to press ahead anyway. He established a base camp at Saltillo, fifty-four miles beyond Monterrey, and sent advance detachments eighteen miles farther to Agua Nueva. Then he realized he was in trouble. Santa Anna had gathered twenty thousand men at San Luis Potosí, three hundred miles to the south, and was preparing to strike.

Luck brought Taylor reinforcements. General John E. Wool, ordered to take Chihuahua, had marched a small army west from San Antonio to the Rio Grande during late September and early October. Belatedly learning that he could not take his men across the inhospitable terrain ahead of him, he veered south, planning to reach his goal by a long circle through Saltillo and Parras. Delayed several weeks by the ill-judged armistice, he had just reached the latter town when Taylor summoned him back to Saltillo with word that Santa Anna was coming.

They braced to meet the Mexicans at an *estancia*, or ranch, called Buena Vista. Santa Anna, his men fagged out by forced marches, approached the American lines along a rough, narrow valley between soaring mountains. Although two thousand Mexicans had dropped out during their cruel march, the rest still outnumbered the 4,759 Americans three or four to one.

When Santa Anna saw Taylor's advance detachments fleeing back up the valley toward Buena Vista, he thought the whole army was retreating and decided to strike at once. On the afternoon of February 22, he

feinted toward the American right, which was anchored on a road that wound along the western side of the valley. The bulk of his force, both footmen and cavalry, he sent along the gully-sliced lower slopes of the mountains to the east. Little more than skirmishes had developed when darkness halted the action.

The next morning, Santa Anna launched his bid against the American left. Taylor's lines bent back and back and back . . . but never quite broke as the farm-boys-turned-soldier made up for the wretchedness they had caused in camp. At one critical moment, Jefferson Davis led a Mississippi infantry regiment, dressed in red shirts and white duck trousers and using eighteen-inch Bowie knives, on a counterattack that perhaps turned the tide of the battle—and, moreover, helped pave the way for a presidency for Davis, too.

The day ended with the lines about as they had started. Conceivably Santa Anna could have won if he had charged once more the next morning. But there was no fight left in his hard-used troops. During the night they slipped quietly away. Whig newspapers ballooned what had been a remarkable defensive stand into another earth-shaking triumph for Taylor, and his election as the twelfth President of the United States was assured.

Quite unwittingly, meanwhile, Alexander Doniphan, colonel of the Missouri volunteers who had occupied Santa Fe with Kearny, undertook to do Wool's neglected job of capturing Chihuahua. Kearny, it will be recalled, had started for the coast and soon afterward had learned from Kit Carson that the war in California was apparently over and that his dragoons were not needed there. He decided to continue nevertheless, for his orders read, "Should you conquer and take possession of New Mexico and Upper California . . . you will establish civil governments therein." He interpreted this to mean that although no conquering remained to be done, he was still responsible for establishing the sort of government he had just set up for New Mexico.

To facilitate this march, he detached two hundred of his dragoons with orders that they guard the traders' camp at Valverde, then go with Doniphan to Chihuahua. Kearny also left his wagons behind, for Carson said they could not be driven over the Gila River route to California. But since a wagon road to the coast was desirable, he ordered Philip St. George Cooke to take command of the Mormon Battalion coming along behind him and find a way for vehicles. He then impressed Kit Carson into service as guide and moved on toward California with his remaining hundred horsemen.

By December Doniphan had completed his Indian pacification assignments (the treaties and the marching

The theatre of the war with Mexico, 1846–48, is seen above, together with principal routes followed by the American forces.

Colonel Alexander W. Doniphan

brought no lasting relief, however) and had turned over New Mexico to reinforcements that had recently arrived in Santa Fe under Sterling Price. By the twelfth he had started south for Chihuahua, unsupported by artillery, which he left behind for Price because of rumors of a projected revolt in Santa Fe. Doniphan's was a motley column, the traders' wagons mixed indiscriminately with the Army transport, and most of the eight hundred and fifty-six soldiers slouching along as they pleased. But when a Mexican army, superior in numbers, tried to halt the column at the campground of El Brazito, thirty miles above El Paso, the Missourians managed to brush it aside in a battle that lasted only half an hour.

Learning in El Paso that Magoffin's efforts to subvert Chihuahua had failed, and realizing that the city could be taken only by fighting, Doniphan sent back to Santa Fe for artillery. Price, still fearful of an uprising, would release only six cannon. He soon found use for the guns he retained. A revolt erupted at Taos on January 19, 1847. Pueblo Indians brutally killed Governor Charles Bent and the handful of American sympathizers in the ungarrisoned town. Several more died in nearby hamlets. Raiders swept away beef cattle, mules, and draft oxen from two transport camps on the Santa Fe Trail, and with a shiver of alarm the Army realized just how fragile its supply lines were—especially since Comanches had

begun staging raids along the trail farther to the east.

Doniphan heard of the Taos uprising just after he had started south from El Paso. A revolt behind, an army of unknown strength ahead—well, it was too late then to panic. On the column slogged, through the dry sand, up the long, long hills, hoping that while they attended to the front, Price would handle matters behind.

He did. Quickly gathering upwards of four hundred soldiers and sixty-five mountain men recruited by Bent's partner, Céran St. Vrain, Price marched up the Rio Grande, smashed through fifteen hundred disorganized rebels at La Cañada (present Santa Cruz), and wallowed on through deep snow to Taos. On February 4, 1847, he cornered the remnants of the Indians inside the massive old mission church at their pueblo. Sappers forced a breach in the thick adobe walls and lobbed shells inside the crowded building. By evening the carnage was over— at least one hundred and fifty dead Pueblos, at a loss to the attackers of seven killed and forty-five wounded.

Doniphan's victory on February 28, four days after the battle of Buena Vista, was even more spectacular than Price's at Taos. Three thousand Mexican troops and a thousand ragged militia, who otherwise might have been helping Santa Anna's drive against Taylor, had built heavy fortifications at Sacramento Creek, fifteen miles north of Chihuahua. They knew they outnumbered the invaders nearly five to one, and many local residents had ambled out to watch their warriors blast the hated gringos apart. The troops had even brought along a thousand lariat ropes for tying up the prisoners.

Doniphan mixed infantry, cavalry, artillery, his own wagons, and the traders' vehicles in four columns, used the remarkable skill of the teamsters to cross the creek where the enemy did not expect him, and wheeled his moving fort against the Mexican flank. The six cannon Price had reluctantly sent him blew gaping holes in the charging enemy lines. The Mexicans broke into a shambling rout. The pursuing Missourians killed more than three hundred, wounded at least that many more, captured forty, and took quantities of booty. One American trader and one sergeant died; seven soldiers were wounded. After that there was nothing left but to slog on through Monterrey to transports waiting near the mouth of the Rio Grande to take the men home. In a year's time they had marched thirty-five hundred miles and had won two crackling fights. Not bad for farmers, they thought.

Kearny meanwhile was marching his own shrunken force of regulars toward California. The men outlasted the horses. By the time they reached the point where the Gila River flows into the Colorado (today's Yuma, Arizona), most of the dragoons were afoot; Kearny was on a mule. They mounted themselves again, after a fashion, by capturing a herd of Mexican horses and requisitioning some of the wild, scrawny, half-broken animals.

From the herders they learned that uprisings in Los Angeles and Santa Barbara had chased out the scanty American garrisons there. Except for San Diego, which was protected by three warships, all southern California was again in the hands of the Mexicans.

Unable to turn back across the long deserts, Kearny decided to continue his laborious path just north of today's international border and somehow break through the enemy lines into the friendly port of San Diego. He sent messengers ahead to Commodore Stockton and, after crossing the coastal mountains in a freezing downpour, was met by forty marines under command of Frémont's friend, Archibald Gillespie.

Thirty miles north of San Diego, at the Indian village of San Pasqual, the combined force was challenged by hard-riding *vaqueros*, well mounted but armed with little more than lances. Kearny elected to charge them over unfamiliar terrain in a predawn fog. Powder wet by the night's rain sputtered in the guns. The *Californios* jerked men from their mounts with lassos, captured a howitzer, stabbed twenty or so of the invaders to death with their lances, and wounded seventeen more before withdrawing.

Dragging their wounded on travois hastily built of willow poles, the Americans started again toward San Diego but forted up on a rocky hill, foodless and exhausted, when the enemy reappeared ahead of them. Unless help came soon, they were finished. Under cover of darkness Kit Carson, Lieutenant Edward Beale, and a friendly Indian took off their shoes for the sake of quiet, wriggled over stones and through cactus until they were in the clear, and by different routes made an agonizing dash to San Diego. Two hundred marines and sailors responded, and the *Californios* melted away.

Wrangling over who had supreme authority—both had received orders to set up a civil government in California—Commodore Stockton of the Navy and General Kearny of the Army led six hundred ill-equipped men north against Los Angeles. Twice the enemy feinted ineffectually at them and then fled across the hills into the San Fernando Valley. There, on January 13, they surrendered to Frémont, who had been moving slowly down from the north, through dismal rains, with a ragtag collection of four hundred regulars, retired mountain men, glory-hungry settlers, and newly arrived immigrants.

Hostilities in the West were thereafter confined to a struggle for power between the American commanders. In time, Kearny's authority was confirmed. Frémont, who continued to defy him after a more judicious man would have read the handwriting, was eventually tried by court-martial in Washington, D.C., for mutiny and insubordination. The affair brought Senator Benton roaring bull-voiced into the lists in support of his son-in-law and filled the nation with an unsavory scandal. Although the court found Frémont guilty, President Polk, sorely embarrassed, mitigated the sentence and urged him to return to the service. The touchy-tempered lieutenant colonel (he had been promoted) hotly refused and soon sought fresh fields of glory where he could wipe away the tarnish from his fame.

During the Kearny-Stockton controversy, the Mormon Battalion had limped into southern California at the end of its own arduous crossing from Santa Fe. Only five of its twenty wagons had survived the trip, but they had fulfilled their instructions: they had found a road that could be made usable through Tucson to the coast. (Today the Southern Pacific Railroad follows most of the route.) While waiting for their enlistments to expire in July, they did garrison duty at various points between San Diego and Los Angeles. After that, eighty-one re-enlisted for another six months. Most of them, however, wanted to rejoin the families they had left in Iowa in the early summer of 1846. But where exactly, they began to wonder, were the Mormons?

Others were wondering. On July 31, 1846, bumptious young Sam Brannan and his two hundred and thirty-eight Saints had landed at Yerba Buena, at one stroke more than doubling the population of the sleepy hamlet soon to be known as San Francisco. They paid the captain of their ship for their passage by crossing to the north side of the Golden Gate and cutting a cargo of redwood lumber. Brannan, a onetime printer, set up a press and a store. Others built gristmills. A party under William Stout went by cutter with tools, seed, and livestock to the junction of the Stanislaus and San Joaquin rivers and there founded New Hope, nucleus, so Brannan intended, of the new Mormon empire in the West.

None of it was done in harmony. The immigrants felt timid and insecure. They had expected to land in a foreign province. Instead they found themselves surrounded by an American occupation force. They were by no means sure the church really meant to come to California. Before leaving home they had heard rumors of Texas, the Rocky Mountains, the Great Basin, Vancouver Island. As months passed without a line from Brigham Young, doubts increased. Brannan, only twenty-eight, was not the man to hold them together. When his followers accused him of mismanaging the common property and of gross self-seeking, he retorted by excommunicating his most vocal critics (they picked up dis-

The hard-marching Mormon Battalion was commanded jointly by military and church leaders. This idealized view of the unit in the Mexican War was the work of George M. Ottinger, a pioneer painter and photographer in the West.

contented followers, of course) and haranguing the rest about their duties as revealed through him, a chosen elder.

Matters grew so bad that in the spring of '47, Brannan determined to ride east until he met Young, get his advice and blessings, and, if necessary, add words of persuasion about the golden coast. It was an extraordinary trip. In April, floundering afoot, he and two companions drove their horses across snowdrifts that still humped a hundred feet deep in places on Donner Summit. They passed the cabins housing the unburied skeletons of the Donner party, rode unmolested by Indians across Nevada and southern Idaho, and on June 30, reached the banks of Green River in southwestern Wyoming. An advance party of Mormons was there. Shrouded with mosquitoes, some were hammering together rafts for crossing the swollen current; others lay in their wagons, mournfully ill with "mountain fever," an ailment that it is now no longer possible to diagnose.

The group had started its march west from Winter Quarters in April—seventy-two wagons for one hundred and forty-three men, three wives (including polygamous Brigham Young's nineteen-year-old Clarissa), and two young boys. In his own mind Young had pretty well settled on the eastern part of the Great Basin as their destination. It was Mexican territory and so grimly unattractive that the church could gather strength before large numbers of American immigrants washed in with

fresh persecutions. But the exact point in the Great Basin had not been selected, and the matter was urgent, for the pioneer group had to plant crops to help feed the fifteen hundred people who would follow close behind.

As they marched west under Young's exacting discipline, the pioneers picked up a few more men and women. They also dropped off a party to build a ferry over the North Platte near today's Casper, Wyoming. Boats would speed the main group—and also raise funds by exacting tolls from non-Mormon travelers.

Just beyond South Pass they encountered mountain man Black Harris and a small party out of Oregon and, a little later, Jim Bridger. Young pumped both of them. What he heard about several locations helped narrow his focus toward the valleys lying southeast of the Great Salt Lake, a dry, difficult land but creased by creeks that sparkled out of the mountains.

He was in no mood to heed Brannan's excited talk about California. To get rid of the young man's importunities, Brigham finally sent him east to meet the so-called Sick Detachment, members of the Mormon Battalion, including several wives, who had been discharged in New Mexico and who had wintered near a grubby little trading post that eventually grew into today's Pueblo, Colorado.

Minus Brannan, the advance party—by then it numbered one hundred and forty-seven men, nine women,

235

and the same two children—went southwest from Bridger's Fort along the trail the Donners had blazed. It was rough, slow going, and many of the group, Young among them, were wobbly still with the mountain fever that had spread among the party. Finally Brigham had to drop behind with a few wagons while the rest of the group toiled ahead in a snail's race against time.

Two anxious scouts caught the first glimpse of Great Salt Lake, glittering in the harsh sunlight. "We could not refrain from a shout of joy." Dropping out of the mountains, they discovered "the soil of a most excellent quality . . . yet the grass nearly dried for lack of moisture." Uneasily they noted "large crickets, about the size of a man's thumb." But crops might grow. They turned

A climactic moment in Mormon history, the descent into Great Salt Lake Valley in July, 1847, was painted by Christensen.

back, marking out a route by which vehicles could travel.

Two days later the first wagons reached the valley. After prayers of thanksgiving, plowing began. The baked earth was stubborn. In desperation the pioneers dammed a nearby creek (today's City Creek) and used the water to soften the ground.

A shower fell just after Brigham Young arrived on July 24. Work quickened, as it had to, and by the next day the people were planting potatoes, beans, peas, and corn. When Brannan arrived with some of the Sick Detachment and plumped again for California, he was ignored. This was to be the new homeland—but not on Mexican territory, as Young had hoped.

Far to the south, during the preceding March, 1847, General Winfield Scott had bombarded Veracruz into

submission and had started west toward Mexico City. He smashed through the chasms of Cerro Gordo, seized Puebla, and paused to bring up supplies and replace the volunteers whose enlistments had expired. On August 8 he started ahead again, crossed a pass between the colossal snow peaks that guard Mexico's central valley, and after a fruitless attempt to negotiate with Santa Anna, fought slowly ahead toward the capital city through lakes and swamps and lava fields. The climax of the bloody business came with the successful storming of the stone fortress of El Molino del Rey and the terraced hill of Chapultepec. On September 13, 1847, the invaders burst into Mexico City. The next dawn the defenders surrendered, and the war was over.

Sam Brannan was returning meanwhile to San Francisco, practically in disgrace. Brigham Young desperately needed the pay that had fallen due the Mormon Battalion settlers on the expiration of their enlistments in July, but he did not want the men themselves to come to the uncultivated valley, where they would have to be fed and housed. Accordingly he sent James Brown to California to collect the money and instruct the discharged troops to find jobs on the coast for the winter. Brannan, who considered himself leader of the California Mormons, was reduced to being guide for Brown's small party.

In the Sierra foothills, Brannan quarreled with the others. In a huff he and Charles Smith, who had ridden east with him to meet Young, pushed ahead up the Truckee River. On September 6, not far from the Donners' cabins, they met a large contingent of the Mormon Battalion riding east.

After their discharge in southern California, several score of the Battalion soldiers had trudged north to San Francisco, hoping to find news of their people from the Mormons there. Learning that Brannan had gone east earlier in the summer to intercept Young, many of the wanderers had started after him. Now suddenly Brannan and Smith were in front of them, bearing disquieting information. Through some wild folly of Young's, Brannan said, the Mormons were settling in Great Salt Lake Valley. One winter would convince them of the impossibility of subsisting there, and then the church would move on west. The thing for the Battalion to do, he advised, was to turn back and wait. He and Smith then rode on toward the Sacramento.

The next day James Brown arrived at the Battalion camp with orders that the soldiers do as Brannan had suggested, though for different reasons. After perplexed debate, half of them declined to obey: they had been too long away from their families. But the other half followed Brannan's tracks down to Sutter's Fort. Charlie Smith was there. He and Brannan had decided to open a store in a single-room adobe hut in the small settlement taking shape outside the fort's walls. Brannan himself had gone on to San Francisco to buy merchandise. He remained sure the church would follow in time, but the members of his quarrelsome colony at New Hope, would-be center of Mormonism, broke up at the news that Young had stayed at Great Salt Lake, and abandoned their farms. Brannan soon found himself liquidating all the communal church property on the coast. Somehow much of it stuck to his own fingers during the process.

Sutter meanwhile was delighted to see the Battalion members. Frémont's recruiting of volunteers to suppress the previous winter's revolt in southern California had brought work at the fort to a standstill. The stagnation hurt. Sutter was heavily in debt, principally to the Russians for his purchases at Fort Ross, and needed to expand rapidly to recoup. He wanted to add several buildings to his complex, and to do this he had to have lumber. None grew in the vicinity, but his head carpenter, James Marshall, had come up with a bold idea. Why not build a sawmill in the foothills, prepare what they needed, and float the planks down the American River?

Sutter agreed. After careful exploration, Marshall found a good site forty miles east of the fort, in the Coloma Valley. As soon as he could manage to recruit the necessary labor . . . and at that moment, in came the members of the Mormon Battalion.

Some went to work at various projects around the fort. Marshall hired from nine to thirteen others (accounts vary), a few non-Mormons, one wife to be cook, and some Indians. After outfitting the group at Brannan's and Smith's new store, he went with his draft oxen into the hills. The workers spent the autumn and early winter felling trees, building a crude dam, and erecting the mill. The building was completed by mid-January, 1848, but adjustments needed to be made in the race. The men cut and dug, and turned water through the channel to wash out the debris. On the morning of January 24, 1848, Marshall shut off the flow and walked along the bank to study results. A tiny yellow object caught his eye. Stooping, he picked it up, examined it, and with growing excitement showed it to the boys. Afterward Henry Bigler, one of the Mormons, described the momentous event in his journal: "This day some kind of mettle was found in the tail race that looks like goald, first discovered by James Martial, the Boss of the Mill."

Nine days later, on February 2, 1848, at little Guadalupe Hidalgo near Mexico City, representatives of the United States and Mexico signed a peace treaty that formally ended hostilities. By its terms, the victors acquired, for fifteen million dollars and the assumption of certain claims against the Mexican Government, all of present-day California, Nevada, and Utah, most of New Mexico and Arizona, and much of Colorado. In December, 1853, Mexico sold for ten million dollars the Gadsden Purchase—enough more land south of the Gila River to give the United States control of the railway route that the Mormon Battalion had unraveled on its long march west.

It was a good bargain—for the United States. By the end of December, 1853, California's gold production alone would amount to more than ten times the total purchase price; one estimate sets the figure at $276,516,186.

Throughout the war years, the settlers in the Willamette Valley of Oregon found little reason to congratulate themselves on *their* luck. Prewar slogans like "Fifty-Four Forty or Fight" had led them to suppose that Congress fully intended to absorb them as soon as possible. But once the Government settled its boundary quarrel with Great Britain, it seemed to lose interest in the area. No territorial governor arrived; no instructions came about establishing proper legislative machinery. Something was awry, but the ten thousand or so Oregonians south of the Columbia (only a handful had ventured north to Puget Sound) had no idea what it was.

The matter was of acute concern. Although the settlers had formed a provisional government for themselves in 1843, they wanted more permanent assurance than it could offer about land titles, military protection, mail, navigational aids, and a dozen other benefits—things that would automatically accrue, they thought, if the Congress of the United States granted them territorial status, with its guarantee of eventual statehood.

Economics were equally deplorable. So little cash money existed in Oregon that most business was transacted by barter or by warehouse receipts for wheat and flour. But wheat was losing its magic. Once, the Hudson's Bay Company, which had contracts to supply Russian Alaska, had absorbed the settlers' entire harvest. By 1847, however, so many immigrants were farming the rich soil that the company could no longer buy all their output. The skimpy market in Hawaii for wheat, dried salmon, and lumber scarcely dented the growing stock piles. Prices sagged. Newcomers felt poorer than they had back home. Unable to remedy the problems, the provisional government fell into factional quarrels between the so-called Methodist party, sprung from Jason Lee's mission, and newcomers who resented what seemed to them the Methodists' entrenched selfishness.

The doldrums were ended late in 1847 by the searing shock of the Whitman massacre. For some time, the Northwest Indians east of the Cascade Mountains had watched the steady march of the immigrants with increasing antagonism. Angry little clashes broke out over trampled grass and slain game on the one hand, and over stolen horses and pilfered camps on the other. A firebrand Delaware Indian named Tom Hill told the Nez Perces and Cayuses how his tribe had been despoiled of its lands in the East; grimly he warned that unless steps were taken, the same would happen in the Northwest.

Anger came to a head when the immigrants of 1847 brought with them an epidemic of measles that killed half the Cayuses under unspeakable conditions. The missionary doctor, Marcus Whitman, although engrossed in establishing a branch mission at The Dalles and in building a sawmill and gristmill near Waiilatpu, did what he

The Methodist-built Dalles mission, painted by W. H. Tappan, was a base for fighting the Cayuses after the Whitman massacre.

could to alleviate the suffering. The deaths continued. Hotheads whispered that the doctor was deliberately poisoning the Indians to get their land. Nearly seventy whites, many of them sick and destitute after the summer's long trip, had gathered at his mission to recuperate. *They* weren't dying, though Indians were. And was it not tribal custom to slay a medicine man who failed?

On the dark, foggy morning of November 29, 1847, the Cayuses killed Whitman, his wife, and twelve white workers. Two small girls, sick with measles, died for want of attention. One man fleeing for help drowned in the Columbia River. Five more men, eight women, and thirty-four children were held captive by the Indians until they were ransomed by Peter Skene Ogden of the Hudson's Bay Company for shirts, blankets, ammuni-

tion, and tobacco that were worth five hundred dollars.

Promptly Oregon's provisional government raised a small army, supplied it through contributions and promises, and sent it up the Columbia to fortify The Dalles and arrest the ringleaders of the attack. But what if Indians throughout the Northwest fought back? Oregon was incapable of carrying on a large conflict.

Hurriedly a legislative committee drafted still another petition to Congress: "Our forefathers complained that they were oppressed by the mother country. . . . We do not complain of oppression, but of neglect." This document was entrusted for delivery to a former mountain man, Joe Meek, whose half-breed daughter had been one of the two girls to die of neglect after the massacre—and who by chance was a cousin of the wife of President Polk.

With nine companions, Meek made a dangerous winter crossing of the continent, arriving in Washington in the spring of 1848 dressed in trail-dirty buckskins and announcing himself, to the delight of the newspapers, as "Envoy Extraordinary and Minister Plenipotentiary from the Republic of Oregon to the Court of the United States." Simultaneously another delegate, Samuel Thurston, representing a rival political faction, traveled to the capital by sea. While Meek made headlines about Oregon's predicament, Thurston worked with Congress, trying desperately to achieve the territorial status that had been delayed for such a long time.

The stumbling block was slavery. Was the institution to be permitted everywhere in the vast area just acquired from Mexico? In some of it? Or in none of it? Was slavery a matter to be decided by the states themselves or by the Federal Government? Could it be rightfully extended to New Mexico and California, regions from which it had been excluded by Mexican law? And what were the boundaries of New Mexico? Texas claimed to reach as far west as the Rio Grande. If the contention was accepted, she would gain Santa Fe and most of the other populous areas of the province; and the Texans would extend slavery there if possible. Was it to be allowed?

Actually, as discerning Southerners realized, the arid lands of the West were not suited to cotton culture and a slave economy. But perhaps Southern political control could be extended, even if cotton could not; then the North's grip could be broken and leadership of the nation returned to the South. Surely justice was on their side, or so they argued. The North had no right to dictate the laws of the West when the region had been won by the whole nation's expenditure of blood and treasure.

The sectional strife grew so bitter that nothing official could be done for the Far West. Military governments continued to function in Monterey and Santa Fe, the provisional government in Oregon. A gesture was made toward keeping the trails open by building Fort Kearney on the Platte River in today's Nebraska and grubby little Fort Mann on the Arkansas River in Kansas. William Gilpin led a slashing campaign against raiding Comanches and Kiowas. And in April, 1848, a mail contract was awarded to William Aspinwall, a trader to Panama who believed that the quickest way to California was by ship connections across the Isthmus. Very little else was done for the new territories.

At the time Aspinwall won the mail contract, no one in the East had the least inkling of what was going on in California. In that territory, however, rumors of the discovery at Coloma were beginning to leak, even though Sutter and Marshall swore their workers to secrecy and actually prevailed on them to stick to their jobs until the mills were finished. At first little attention was paid to the talk, though some of the workers at Coloma were scratching gold out of cracks in the rocks with butcher knives and spoons made from the horns of cattle. Finally Brannan decided to ride to Coloma to investigate. When he

Former trapper Joe Meek is shown as he appeared in Washington after hurrying across country with Oregon's appeal for help.

arrived, he took fire at what he saw. Obviously, a stampede would be the making of his and Smith's store.

Filling a small bottle with gold dust, he returned to San Francisco on May 12. Legend has it that he strode through the streets bellowing, "Gold! Gold! Gold from the American River!" Possibly he passed the bottle more quietly from hand to hand. In any event, the rush to the hills began. Within weeks San Francisco was deserted, and the ripples were spreading swiftly—to Oregon, to Hawaii, and to places where men knew mining: Sonora in northern Mexico, Peru, and Chile. Still ignorant of the excitement, William Aspinwall ordered for his new Pacific Mail Steamship Company three wooden side-wheelers, each of one thousand tons burden, two hundred feet long, moved by steam and by twenty thousand square feet of supplemental canvas. Each had room for two hundred and ten passengers. Each would pick up mail, freight, and ticket holders from the East on the Pacific side of Panama and carry them at scheduled intervals to San Diego, San Francisco, and the Columbia. He promised that his first ship, the *California*, would start around the Horn for Panama in October. Immediate prospects were not bright. Uncertainty about the fate of the new territories had slowed emigration to a trickle. But Aspinwall was an optimist. He felt that as soon as Congress got over its bickering and established workable governments, the tide would pick up again.

The only area in the West that received more people in '48 than during the years immediately preceding was Utah. That summer, Brigham Young came back over the trail from Winter Quarters with perhaps three thousand Mormons. The newcomers very nearly moved into desolation. As Sam Brannan had predicted, frost killed most of the vegetables planted in the spring. Then a crawling mass of black crickets attacked the wheat. But in the nick of time, gulls swarmed up from the Great Salt Lake, probably as they swarmed every year, ate crickets until they threw up, and began again. "It seems," one observer wrote Young, "the hand of the Lord is in our favor."

Affairs relating to the West were so unstable, indeed, that private capitalists—aside from Aspinwall, who was working on government money—backed only one major project that year, Frémont's ill-considered survey for a Pacific railway. There had been plenty of talk about such a road. Since 1844, Asa Whitney had been showering the country with propaganda advocating that Congress aid the job by granting to some construction company a strip of land sixty miles wide across Indian country to Puget Sound, jumping-off place for Asia.

This was too far north to suit the sectional ill will of the times, and nothing was done. Senator Benton then sought to compromise the objections by recommending a central route that would draw equal amounts of traffic from both north and south to St. Louis and strike due west from there to the newly acquired harbor of San Francisco. As in Whitney's proposal, access to the Orient was the prime objective.

The great problem facing the central route was the finding of a suitable pass through the Colorado Rockies. When Congress refused to appropriate funds for a survey, Benton produced part of the money from his own pockets, raised more funds in St. Louis, and offered the leadership of the expedition to his ambitious son-in-law, John Charles Frémont, who was smarting still from the setback caused by his court-martial.

Frémont jumped at the chance to redeem himself. With a burst of optimism he proposed to do the work in the dead of winter, just to prove that trains could run in winter also. Furthermore, he would leave the East for good and settle on a ranch Thomas Larkin had supposedly bought for him near Santa Cruz, California. (Actually Larkin had bought instead, without authorization, the remote Mariposas grant, northeast of present-day Merced. Frémont would be furious—until he learned that gold had been discovered in the area.) While he was exploring the continent by land, his wife would sail to Panama, cross the Isthmus, and catch one of Aspinwall's new ships to San Francisco.

Frémont began his preparations at Benton's Washington home in August, 1848, as an overheated Congress argued its way toward adjournment. During the closing session, Northerners, supported by popular outrage over the Whitman massacre, managed to break a bill establishing Oregon Territory, without slavery, away from the debates about the Mexican cession. It passed. Joe Meek was appointed United States Marshal and ordered to escort the new territorial governor, Joseph Lane of Indiana, to his office.

Nothing was done about California. Benton thereupon whipped off a proclamation to the neglected residents advising them to set up an independent government of their own, Oregon-style, until the United States got around to acting. He handed the document to Frémont for delivery, with the implication that his son-in-law was just the man to be governor of the self-constituted republic. Polk was infuriated by the arrogation of authority; but Polk had declined to run again for the Presidency, and Benton was indifferent to his fuming. Insult his son-in-law? They'd see.

Meek and Governor Lane did not get away from St. Louis until September. To avoid running into snow on the way to Oregon, the old mountain man led the entourage by way of Santa Fe and the Gila River to Los Angeles, where they would be able to transfer to a ship. Frémont should have been equally circumspect. The winter proved to be a howler, every bit as bad as the one that had crushed the Donners.

It smothered the Mormons at Salt Lake City—where, in December, they drew up a petition twenty-two feet long, bearing 2,270 signatures, asking that they be given some kind of government. In March, shivering in endless blizzards and all but starved, they took the matter into their own hands, formed a legislature, and elected Brigham Young governor. Someone had to do something. Congress would not.

In December Frémont was bulling his way across the snow-heaped Sangre de Cristo Mountains and the broad San Luis Valley of Colorado, guided by an eccentric trapper, Old Bill Williams. The one hundred and thirty bushels of shelled corn carried by the party's hundred mules disappeared, and the skeletal beasts, their backs running with sores from frostbite, grew so ravenous that they took to eating one another's tails. Blinded by continual blizzards and in desperate need of grass and shelter, the thirty-three men turned up a canyon they thought might lead to a haven. It did not. At the ridgetop, 12,287 feet above sea level, they were blasted by so terrible a hurricane that they broke into fragments and scrambled back down into the canyon. A third of them died, some raving mad. After recuperating at Taos, Frémont went on to Los Angeles by the route Meek had used. Behind him, Old Bill Williams and another of the expedition's survivors, Dr. Benjamin Kern, returned to the mountains to retrieve the abandoned baggage. Presumably Indians killed them. They were never seen again.

By then the East had grown aware that something astounding enough to change the course of American history really was happening in California. On December 5—Frémont was then plowing through the Sangre de Cristos in sub-zero cold—Polk told Congress in his final message: "The accounts of the abundance of gold in that territory are of such an extraordinary character as would scarcely command belief were they not corroborated by the authentic reports of officers in the public service."

Two days later a special messenger from California's military governor, Colonel Richard Mason, arrived with two hundred and thirty ounces of pure gold, which was put on display in the War Office.

That did it. In the single year of 1849, one hundred thousand or more people poured West. When they arrived, they would go ahead without authorization from Washington and do whatever they considered to be necessary for the management of their own affairs.

YALE UNIVERSITY LIBRARY

CHICAGO HISTORICAL SOCIETY

Thomas Hart Benton

MANIFEST DESTINY

The American eagle never soared quite so confidently nor screamed so challengingly as it did in the decade 1840 to 1850. Those were the years when a nation of twenty million people came to consider half a continent as not a bit more than their birthright. They were the years of the annexation of Texas, of "Fifty-four forty or fight!" and the acquisition of Oregon, of the Mexican War and the conquest of the Southwest and California. In 1845 New York editor John O'Sullivan gave a name and a justification to rampant nationalism when he declared that it was "our manifest destiny to overspread the continent allotted by Providence for the free development of our yearly multiplying millions." Many agreed with his heady vision of a United States extending from the Atlantic to the Pacific and from the Arctic Ocean to the limits of Central America. A few beat even more stirring drums; Congressman John Wentworth of Illinois told his fellow members he hoped they would one day hear the Speaker recognize "the gentleman from Nova Scotia, the gentleman from Canada, the gentleman from Cuba, the gentleman from Mexico, aye, even the gentleman from Patagonia." Some counseled restraint: Thomas Hart Benton, himself no violent enemy of expansion, rose in the Senate to speak against annexing Texas under conditions that would anger Mexico, and to ridicule the vainglory of "Fifty-four forty or fight!" But there was no halting the tide; the armies marched, the settlers' wagons rolled, and overhead floated the banner of the spreading eagle. John W. Audubon, son of the naturalist, caught on canvas (above) a vignette of the advance west.

An early lithograph shows General Zachary Taylor's camp, improbably neat and trim, at Corpus Christi, Texas, in October, 1845, just before the war.

THE MEXICAN WAR

Samuel E. Chamberlåin painted Gen. John Wool's division crossing San Antonio's Grand Military Plaza at the outset of its 900-mile march into Mexico.

The Mexican War was not a completely popular conflict. It was denounced in Congress as "flagrant," "unconstitutional," and "a war of robbery," and a good part of the public was just as unhappy about it. There was a strong suspicion that President Polk had not tried to settle the differences between the two nations peaceably but had deliberately provoked war in order to obtain California and the Southwest. That suspicion grew when expansionists began to talk even of annexing all of Mexico. More temperate views prevailed, but even so, Mexico lost about one third of her territory.

It was the smallest of all American wars in numbers involved, but it was also the deadliest: one sixth of the Army perished. But disease, not enemy bullets, was the dreaded killer, taking seven times as many men as died on the field of battle. A small bright note was the appearance of the anesthetic ether at dressing stations, for the first time taking the worst of the ancient horror from battlefield surgery.

Another of Samuel Chamberlain's rude but vivid pictures is this battle scene, which he labeled "U.S. Troops Storming the Bishop's Palace, Monterrey, Mexico." Chamberlain, a private, deserted in California in 1849 to hunt gold.

The Battle of Buena Vista has a curious bloodless, toy-soldier quality in this lithograph. Otherwise, it should be an accurate portrayal of that action, for it was made from an on-the-spot sketch by General Taylor's aide-de-camp.

CALIFORNIA IMBROGLIO

Serving as a captain's clerk, 16-year-old John Elliott Montgomery, son of the commander of the U.S.S. Portsmouth in San Francisco Bay, sent a letter to his mother in Massachusetts on July 25, 1846, drawing on it the banner (above) under which Americans in northern California had proclaimed their short-lived Bear Flag Republic in June. The town of Sonoma (below), where the revolutionists made their somewhat comic-opera seizure of power, is seen as it looked in 1847 to an unknown artist.

Commodore Robert Stockton

The conquest of California might well have been a bloodless one. The Californians had no close ties with Mexico and offered no resistance when Commodore John Sloat took possession of port cities in early July, 1846, and promised the people American citizenship. But Sloat was soon replaced by grim-faced Commodore Robert Stockton, who at once made bellicose statements. With John Frémont he marched an army all through the province. At Los Angeles, meanwhile, Captain Archibald Gillespie enforced a stern curfew and forbade certain popular recreations. The easy-going Californians rebelled, and by late September the occupation had become a fighting war that lasted almost four months. When it was over, Stockton and Frémont fought with Stephen W. Kearny over who should govern the conquered province, an unseemly quarrel that the Government settled in Kearny's favor.

The last engagement in California was the Battle of the Plains of Mesa near Los Angeles on January 9, 1847. William H. Meyers (see page 214) painted a sanguinary view of the fight, but his imagination may have gotten the better of him, for history records it as an almost bloodless clash. Below, Meyers pictured one of the Californians whose skillful horsemanship and unorthodox use of lances and lassos in battle caused the Americans much trouble.

From 1846 to 1848, artist Henry Lewis painted a huge panorama of the Mississippi River. This section shows Nauvoo, still the Mormon capital and the largest city in Illinois when Lewis saw it. The Mormon Temple on the hill overlooks the city.

The murder of the Mormon brothers Joseph and Hyrum Smith after a mob took them from the jail at Carthage, Illinois, was depicted by G. W. Fasel. The artist shows a Mormon calling on a slayer to desist, a note of very dubious accuracy.

BY THE
GREAT SALT LAKE

Brigham Young organized and led the settlement of the Utah country. This engraving is from a Frederick Piercy sketch.

Men went west for furs, for gold, and for land, but before the Mormons, none save a few missionaries had seen in the setting sun a vision of a land of Zion on earth. The Mormons, although not faultless themselves, had borne the agony of persecution, mainly for the sin of being different. Hounded from Missouri, they had started anew in Illinois, only to be driven from there too. Homeless, some 600 of them died in Nebraska's bleak Winter Quarters in 1846–47. Then, still unbowed, they left their dead in the spring of 1847 and commenced the trek across the plains that ended in a desolate Utah valley. Strong in faith and toughened by the trials they had endured, they ploughed harsh land, planted crops, dug irrigation ditches, built homes, and raised towns; then, in the security of their isolation—where few would have given them a chance to survive—they could sing at last, "All is well, all is well."

Salt Lake Valley as the Mormons saw it was drawn by Piercy, an Englishman who traveled to the Mormon capital in 1853. Despite its desolate look, the country east of the lake had fertile soil and ample water for irrigation.

A Western mountain stream

"... Marshall pulled out of his trousers pocket a white cotton rag which contained something rolled up in it.... Opening the cloth, he held it before me in his hand.... 'I believe this is gold,' said Marshall, 'but the people at the mill laughed at me and called me crazy.' I carefully examined it and said to him: 'Well, it looks like gold. Let us test it.'"

John Augustus Sutter's reminiscence of January 28, 1848, Sutter's Fort, California

CHAPTER TEN

THE MISERIES OF RICHNESS

1848-1854

One prime wonder of the California gold rush is that so many people survived it. They poured out of Atlantic seaboard cities, Ohio villages, and Southern plantations in abysmal ignorance of the geographic and social obstacles that loomed ahead. Had the deluge dropped onto an unprepared California, the results would have been disastrous. Thanks to the continent's width, however, men who were familiar with the West had a year's grace during which they could attack the knottier problems connected with geology, mining technology, transportation, and political order that were raised by the frenzy.

Even among experienced Westerners, the madness was acute. "The whole country," wrote one San Francisco newspaper editor, ". . . resounds with the sordid cry of 'gold! GOLD! *GOLD*!' while the field is left half planted, the house half built, and everything neglected but the manufacture of shovels and pick axes." The alcalde of Monterey described the situation there: "All were off for the mines, some on horses, some on carts, and some on crutches, and one went in a litter."

Breathless talk like that suggests, inaccurately, that torrents of people washed immediately through the mountains. Actually, the rush developed slowly. In mid-1848, California's non-Indian population, women and children included, amounted to no more than fourteen thousand. Perhaps seventy-five hundred of these were native *Californios*, many of them living on isolated ranchos in the south and less susceptible to the fever than the Americans and Englishmen in the towns farther north. Probably there were no more than a thousand

people who were directly involved with the initial rush.

New surges soon followed, however, as fast as ships spread the news along the Pacific shores. The first groups appeared during the summer from Hawaii—nineteen vessels in three weeks. Their clamor for supplies sent prices skyrocketing. Flour that sold for twenty dollars a barrel at Stockton early in the summer soared in the mountains, during moments of pinch, to eight hundred dollars. Eggs at times brought three dollars each.

Hoping to capitalize on the shortages, the captain of the ship *Honolulu* sailed to the Columbia River and purchased every pick, shovel, crowbar, butcher knife, and staple food item on which he could lay hands. When he told the cash-starved Oregonians why he was so interested in their merchandise, they too rushed south, traveling with pack trains or else paying outrageous prices for sleeping space between piles of lumber on the decks of sailing ships hurrying to the new markets. The first wagon caravan from Oregon set out in September, hewing its own road through the dense forests and forbidding canyons beyond Mount Shasta. At the head of the train was Peter Burnett, who was destined to become the first elected governor of California.

In northern Mexico eager workers arranged grubstakes with local *patrones* and tossed a minimum of supplies onto muleback or into crude *carretas*. Accompanied by their wives and children, even babies in arms, they streamed in gabbling confusion across the dread deserts of southwestern Arizona. At the beginning of each winter's rainy season most of them returned to their homes in Sonora, paid their *patrones*, made new arrangements,

An engraving of a ship, groping inland through one of the narrow waterways of the delta of the Sacramento River, adorned a navigational chart published by the Government to aid gold seekers trying to reach Sacramento by water. The chart was one of a series prepared by Commander Cadwalader Ringgold, who headed a survey of San Francisco Bay and adjoining coastal waters, 1849–50.

and hurried back to California with their families in the spring. One of their favorite foothill camps in the California gold fields eventually became a town whose name, Sonora, still commemorates them.

Only the Mormons resisted, though they might well have cashed in. Several members of the Mormon Battalion, it will be recalled, had been working at Sutter's sawmill when James Marshall made his discovery. During the wet, cold spring, they had scratched nuggets out of cracks between the rocks, moved on to new localities, and found gold there too. All the advantages that accrue to firstcomers might have been theirs. Instead, forty-eight of them, accompanied by one wife, determined that as soon as the high passes were clear of snow in the spring of 1848, they would go east to rejoin their people.

Their caravan consisted of three hundred head of livestock and seventeen wagons. Because of those wagons they were reluctant to tackle Donner Pass, whose eastern approach along the Truckee River was interrupted by twenty-seven wheel-bruising fords. Surely they could find some easier way.

Indians killed the first three scouts they sent out. Undeterred, other explorers located a usable route up the long ridges to Carson Pass, named for the Carson River, which Kit and Frémont had followed during their own foolhardy crossing four years earlier. The descent of the Carson on the Nevada side required only three crossings, compared to twenty-seven along the Truckee. Because of this (and despite the grim Forty-mile Desert between the lower Carson River and the Humboldt Sink), their route became one of the principal highways of the Forty-Niners.

This same eastbound Mormon party unraveled another usable wagon road north of Great Salt Lake and so guaranteed that Salt Lake City would become a supply point for thousands of stampeders. They themselves reached the city on September 20, 1848. The year's migration of Mormons from Winter Quarters, on the Missouri, was just crawling into Salt Lake Valley. As a matter of routine interest, the Battalion members displayed some of the nuggets they had brought with them. Everywhere else in the world, tales of such things bred epidemics of excitement, but not in Utah. Gold, Brigham Young said, was for paving streets. The Saints would find a surer reward by attending to their business of establishing God's new kingdom on earth. His people heeded. When the crushing winter of 1848–49 ended and trails were open in the spring, only a handful of intransigents left for the rainbow land.

To the Mormons already in California, Young sent emissary Amasa Lyman with warnings against the corruptions of the yellow metal. Still, the work in Utah did need money. Accordingly, Lyman was also entrusted with a letter to Sam Brannan, who had not yet remitted to the church his own tithings or anything from the tithes he was supposedly collecting from the California Saints. Yet Sam was prospering. In nine summer weeks, his and Charlie Smith's little adobe store in the tent-and-plank city of Sacramento, which was springing vigorously alive beside Sutter's Fort, grossed thirty-six thousand dollars. At year's end Sam bought out his partner for fifty thousand dollars and began to spread new enterprises from San Francisco to the mountains.

Brigham Young felt that Brannan should share the prosperity. By letter he asked bluntly for forty thousand dollars, warning with underscoring, ". . . should you withhold when the Lord says give, your hopes and pleasing prospects *will be blasted in an hour you think not of— and no arm can save.*"

In an angry scene with Amasa Lyman, who brought the letter, Brannan refused. Later he was read out of the church. He always felt guilty, and in the end he did die destitute, ruined by injudicious promotions—or, if you like, by God's visitation. Being what he was, however, he could hardly have helped himself. He had glimpsed a different kind of empire from Brigham's, sinewed by different men. Brigham was clinging, with religious colorations, to the familiar sturdy-yeoman concept of the first American frontier. Until 1848, farmers had been the mainstays of the western thrust. No longer. The impact of mining—its changed demands and its eventual concentrations of capital—would forever modify Western history. Corrupt or not, Brannan's lot was with the new.

The thousand Californians who hurried toward the mountains during that first spring of 1848 lived in pure romance. They climbed from hot valleys into rolling hills dotted with live oaks and vivid with orange poppies. The canyons deepened, singing with water. No rain came until late fall; they camped in comfort under the flimsiest shelters of brush, or under nothing at all. The great drawback was a dearth of food. Hunting took time, and as a result, the length of a man's stay in the diggings was determined by what he could carry with him.

Even the climate co-operated. The annual summer drought shrank the streams, exposing deposits of gold-bearing gravel called bars. These had formed during high water wherever the current was slack: opposite bends in the river channel, behind boulders, and in potholes in the stream bed. Gold had settled with the gravel. Heavier than the sand, it worked its way into cracks and cavities in or near bedrock. Receding water opened these spots to the crude tools of the early miners. Other deposits were found in ancient channels that had been left dry following changes in the stream's course.

Rewards were sometimes extraordinary. One lump of gold unearthed at Sonora weighed twenty-eight pounds; eight other nuggets from the same district exceeded twenty pounds. A small group of friends from Monterey, aided by hired Indians, took two hundred and seventy-three pounds from the Feather River in seven weeks. The first five prospectors to reach the Yuba River gleaned seventy-five thousand dollars in three months. In ten days one soldier off on a furlough picked up fifteen hundred dollars. These strikes and similar ones in '49 and even '50 were exceptions; yet even those unoriginal souls who clung near the familiar bars at Coloma, the site of Marshall's discovery, are said to have averaged twenty-five to thirty dollars a day, at a period when skilled labor elsewhere in California commanded about three dollars daily. Under such conditions a man did not mind standing in icy water all day while a hot sun beat on his head, his shoes turned to pulp, and his stomach, assaulted with insufficient amounts of monotonous food, sent forth calls of distress.

The geology that accounted for the gold was, in general terms, simple enough. During the upheaval of the Sierra, magma had welled up from the earth's interior, then had cooled and cracked, forming in the foothills a relatively narrow north-south band seamed with ribbon-like veins, or lodes. Gold-bearing ore had filled sections of these veins. Streams born in the mountains had sliced across them, gradually worn the gold free of its gangue, and tumbled it downward until it came to rest in the bars.

This geologic information was unknown to the discoverers. Still, many of them were shrewd observers, familiar with California. John Bidwell, for example. He had reached the coast with the pioneer overland party of 1841 and thereafter had worked for Sutter until he was able to acquire a ranch of his own. He examined the Coloma region in March, 1848, remembered similar formations along the Feather River seventy miles or so to the north, and made sensational strikes up there.

By year's end, perhaps five thousand men had reached the diggings. Guided only by common sense, they fanned slowly out across nearly two hundred miles of the mineral belt—as far as their numbers allowed, for they were working as well as prospecting. (Eventually the mineral region was found to extend almost seven hundred miles, from southwestern Oregon past Mount Shasta and then south along the eastern side of the central valleys as far as the Kern River.) They evolved sound practical theories from their experience, and when the greenhorns from the East swarmed in during the next years, a body of knowledge existed to tell them where to go. Otherwise, the waste in energy would have been incalculable.

The pioneers of '48 were less successful in learning how to separate gold from sand and gravel. At first they simply picked out the coarse grains with their fingers or the points of their knives. Then a Georgian, Isaac Humphrey, who had learned mining on the Cherokee lands near Dahlonega, visited Coloma in March—the month Bidwell was poking about the region—and taught the local prospectors the mysteries of gold pan and rocker. These primitive mechanisms, fabulous to the neophytes, had been known to Agricola in sixteenth-century Europe and probably to the Roman miners in Spain long before that.

Both devices let the miner imitate and concentrate the action of the streams that had deposited the gold in the first place. A pan might be either wooden (the batea of the Mexicans) or metal. A frying pan would do, but a larger receptacle with flaring sides was more efficient. A worker dumped a shovelful of pay dirt into his pan, removed the pebbles, and added water. Holding the pan at a slant, he swirled it about so that the water carried away the light earth, leaving a thread of "color" in the lowest edge of the dish. Tales are told of men earning

251

a thousand dollars a day without using other equipment.

A rocker increased the scope of the operation. It was an oblong box set at a slant on rockers like those of a cradle. One or two men shoveled dirt into buckets or a wheelbarrow; another transported the material to the rocker. A perforated metal sheet screened out the biggest pieces of waste rock. The rest fell through onto the slanting bottom. A fourth man bailed in water and shook the cradle to separate the mass. As the earth washed through the box, the gold settled behind a series of transverse slats, or riffles, and was spooned up at the day's end.

Both pan and rocker permitted fine "dust" to escape. Both trapped sand with the metal. To get rid of the dross,

The region of the gold rush, together with sites of the principal diggings and routes into the mining country, is seen above.

the miner lightened it by drying his pile over his camp-fire and gingerly blowing away the unwanted material with his breath. Mexicans who were accustomed to dry diggings could make separations without using water. They tossed pebble-free earth into the air, let the wind, bellows, or their lungs winnow away the lightest material, and caught the enriched remnants on a blanket. Although they were surprisingly adept—Americans seldom caught the knack—that method was too wasteful.

In those days a miner could afford to be wasteful. Prospectors scrambled for rich new bars rather than try to improve on the pan and rocker, though Europeans and Latin Americans had for centuries been familiar with various refinements. Essentially these more sophisticated devices simply elongated the box containing the riffles, added mercury to catch the dust in an amalgam, and by their size enabled many men to pool their labor. Called long toms or sluices in America, according to their pattern, they seem not to have been reinvented in California until well into 1849. But at least the basic principles of separation by water had been worked out by the time the newcomers came panting in from the East.

Sutter at first tried to collect royalties from the trespassers on his land. The miners ignored him—rightly, for Mexican land grants were agricultural and did not convey the mineral rights. Presumably, therefore, the United States Government owned those rights along with the millions of empty acres it had recently taken from Mexico. The gold rush had been underway for months, however, before Congress heard about it, and accordingly the lawmakers had developed no policy for transferring ownership to private hands.

The stampeders turned to themselves for a solution. As soon as any considerable number of them had reached a new strike, they gathered at a central point amidst their tents and shanties, elected officers, and selected a committee to draw up laws governing their "district." Undoubtedly some of them knew that in the lead regions of Illinois and the new copper country around Lake Superior, a man could acquire forty acres of mineral land from the Government for five dollars an acre. But forty acres was an unrealistic unit in California.

From the beginning, one feature was common: everyone was to have equal opportunity to dig and not be thrust aside by hogs. Early in the rush various persons, Sutter included, tried to use Indian labor in order to cover more ground. Indignant individualists soon stopped them. A man had to work his way to this kind of wealth with his own hands.

Save for a discoverer, who sometimes was awarded two claims, no individual could hold more than a single

A typical Forty-Niner with pickaxe, Joseph Sharp, sat for this portrait.

plot, though contiguous claim holders might operate their ground in common. Boundaries were carefully defined in a book kept by the camp recorder. An owner held title only so long as he actively worked the ground; whenever he failed to meet requirements concerning the amount of labor to be expended during a given period, the claim reverted to the public domain and could be reappropriated. Because the first camps were often very rich, the area allotted was small, sometimes as little as ten feet square per claim. In later days, after the best ground had been picked over, claim sizes increased but remained smaller in California than in other mineral sections of the West.

The insistence on one claim per man regardless of wealth or influence is often cited as an example of the democracy of the gold camps. Well, yes—if you happened to be of the right nationality or color. Indians, South Americans, and Frenchmen were subject to various restrictions, including mob action. Chinese had to pay special taxes and often were not allowed into a district until after the whites had abandoned it. Persecution of Mexicans was so virulent that by 1854 they had ceased their annual treks north from Sonora. Many of the Mexicans already in California turned to crime, notably Joaquín Murieta, a swarthy Robin Hood probably compounded in the folk imagination from several bandits.

In spite of this dislike of Mexicans, the mining camps drew heavily on Spanish custom in administering their laws. The chief official was generally an alcalde. His role was broad. He could act as arbiter and advisor in matters involving trespass, claim abandonment, priority of recording, and so on. Arbitration failing, he could hear trials, reach decisions, impose sentences. In criminal cases he sometimes appointed juries, but more often the populace elected juries to serve under him or, in serious cases, appointed themselves as juries-of-the-whole.

Because jails did not exist, justice inclined to be summary. Trials were held as promptly as a general meeting could be called and a jury arranged. Punishment consisted of flogging, banishment, the cutting off of ears, or immediate hanging. Memoirs of '48 insisted that there was little crime in the first camps, although fortunes in gold, lacking vaults for safekeeping, might lie unattended in flimsy tents or under logs. Still, no Eden lasts forever. In January, 1849, the camp of Dry Diggings had to perform certain executions that brought it the name of Hangtown, later changed to Placerville.

Since no camp conceived of itself as any more permanent than its gold deposits, society was atomistic. Early laws ignored such civic matters as cleaning up the appalling streets and such private affairs as debt, slander, contract violations, and the like. Jurisdiction never extended beyond the immediate boundaries of the camp concerned, and there was no provision for co-operation with other districts. Consider Sutter's case, for instance. While gold was sitting undisturbed in ragged mountain tents, his barony in the valley was plundered without check. His workers deserted, leaving his mills silent, his hides rotting in the tannery, his crops unharvested, his herds untended. Dead beats hit him for loans and grubstakes they refused to repay, and no court came to his help. Believing that gold had made him rich, "creditors" heaped him with fraudulent charges he had no means of countering. Droves of squatters clustered on his land and paid no rent. Emigrants stole from his store, helped themselves to his tools and horses, raided his fields, and butchered his cattle. Eventually Sutter died in poverty, virtually unrecompensed.

Still, if the mining districts of '48 had not partially filled the legal wastes, the invasion of '49 might have come even closer to anarchy than it did. It was a tremendous, chaotic inpouring. Just how many people were involved seems impossible to determine. Estimates for 1849 range between sixty thousand and one hundred thousand. Many went home disappointed. But more kept coming. By the end of 1852, a special census set the state's population at 223,856.

Perhaps a fifth of the total arrived by ship from Asia, Australia, South America, and western Europe. The rest hailed from practically every American county east of the Indian frontier. Considering the nation's population as a whole (close to twenty-five million), the figure is not extraordinary. But the count was sufficient to give much of the East an acute personal interest in the West. Almost every family had either a member or a friend off on the mysterious coast—which inevitably lost its mystery as "Intelligence from the West" became a regular feature of many village newspapers. Overnight, almost, the young land's thinking became more solidly continental than it ever had been at any time in the past.

Adventure inspired many of the prospectors. They wanted to break away from their humdrum routines long enough to see the huge snow peaks and colorful Indians of whom they had read in Frémont's and Parkman's books. Veterans of the war with Mexico and men who had left home to freight Army supplies or to work in the overnight factories wanted one last fling.

A few hoped to find farms or business careers or political offices in the West, but most intended to come home after having made their fortunes. For that reason, family units going to California were rare. One conservative estimate suggests that of 30,000 persons crossing South Pass in 1849, 25,500 were men, a mere 3,000 were women, and only 1,500 were children.

Perhaps thirty thousand more travelers sought California by sea, either circling South America or taking a short cut across the Isthmus of Panama. Historian John E. Pomfret says in *California Gold Rush Voyages* that during 1849, seven hundred and seventy-five vessels sailed from Eastern ports for the new Golconda. One impulse was comfort, for many city greenhorns feared the privations and dangers involved in crossing the continent by covered wagon. In the early days, speed was another consideration. Land travel could not begin until spring. Fearful that the nuggets would all be picked up before latecomers arrived, the most eager stampeders began clamoring at shipping offices even before President Polk on December 5, 1848, officially confirmed the discoveries. By February 8, 1849, one hundred and thirty-six vessels had taken to the wintry seas from Atlantic ports.

Both speed and comfort proved illusory. The average sea trip dragged out to one hundred and ninety-nine days, more than half a year. Accommodations were abominable. To meet the unexpected demand for ships, owners pressed coastal freighters, fishing smacks, even top-heavy river steamers into service, hastily fitted them with tiny staterooms, hired inexperienced crews, and then, in the face of one of the world's toughest ocean trips, loaded their facilities far beyond capacity. Passengers grew gaunt on unpalatable food, lived in dread of

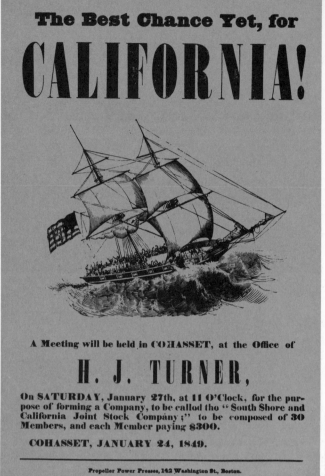

An advertising card, reflecting the excitement of the day, attracted customers for the sea trip to the distant El Dorado.

tropical doldrums and of Cape Horn's violent tempests (there were amazingly few sinkings, however), and finally slumped into a paralysis of boredom.

A crossing of the Isthmus of Panama beckoned as a way to shorten the ordeal. The first of William Aspinwall's three Pacific Mail Company steamers, the *California*, left the East in October, 1848, to sail around the Horn. Many persons, hearing of the gold discoveries after the ship's departure, bought tickets in New York for the trip from Panama to San Francisco in anticipation of intercepting the *California* on the far side of the Isthmus. Others went without tickets. They raced by the hundreds to the port of Chagres on Panama's eastern coast and transferred first to dirty little river steamers for the Isthmus crossing and then to uncomfortable *bungas* poled by natives. At the head of navigation they switched at exorbitant rates to muleback, generally discarding some of their baggage, and rode the exotic but steaming jungle trails through strange odors, drenching rains, and swarms of insects.

The *California* was late in arriving on the west coast of Panama. Her machinery broke down, and strong head winds battered her. In Callao, Peru, her fortune apparently changed. Seventy-seven Peruvians, babbling something about gold in California, wanted to buy tickets. The purser happily filled his empty berths—a coup! But when the steamer put in at Panama City, far out in the shallow bay, she was greeted by fifteen hundred men camped on the beach in a miserable, disease-ridden, unsanitary scramble of tents and hutches.

Riots threatened until finally the captain stuffed four hundred men aboard a vessel built for only two hundred. Passengers slept on the deck; the water was rationed; provisions ran so low that the steward took on a stock of monkeys, which left one nauseated diner feeling he had been served "the charred remnants of a small child." When the vessel reached San Francisco, the crew deserted. Weeks later the captain of a sister ship, the *Oregon*, picked up more hundreds from the distressing beaches at Panama and in San Francisco kept his crew by anchoring under the guns of an obliging warship. Eventually the third Pacific Mail paddle wheeler, the *Panama*, appeared. The *California* rounded up new hands. Shuttling busily, the three steamers brought Aspinwall revenue he had in no wise anticipated when applying for the mail contracts in 1848. Between 1851 and 1855 he helped build a railroad across the Isthmus, and at about the same time, competitors appeared along the shipping lanes. Until then, Panama remained a dismal irritant in the minds of thousands of gold seekers.

Land travelers had a choice of routes, including several trails across Mexico. Others went to Santa Fe, then either looped into southern California by the Old Spanish Trail through Utah or dropped southwest to the Gila River. In spite of the hundreds of horsemen who traveled those trails and the thousands who went by sea, the popular image of the gold rush remains a covered wagon. That in turn suggests South Pass, the gateway through which all but a handful of the vehicles creaked.

A few arrived at the pass by following the Santa Fe Trail up the Arkansas to the Rockies and then bending north. Far more jumped off from Independence, Westport, St. Joseph, or from Council Bluffs, in those days called Kanesville by the Mormons who had founded the town. The different strands knit together in the Platte Valley near Fort Kearney, built in 1848 by the Army. It was a glum, dusty spot; but to the plodding emigrants, it furnished the psychological boost of protecting troops, a blacksmith shop, a post office for sending mail home, traders with fresh horses and oxen to sell, and a Mormon family from whom one could occasionally obtain fresh milk and eggs. In both 1849 and 1850, the villain along this stretch of the trail was not hardship, but a cholera

epidemic that was then ravaging the Mississippi Valley. Travelers carried the disease along the Platte with them and died by the hundreds, far from their families, with many of their graves left unmarked.

The disease burned itself out in the high plains, and the terror it caused was beginning to evaporate when the travelers staggered into the trail's most famous caravansary, Fort Laramie in eastern Wyoming. (Seventy-five miles northeast of today's city of Laramie, Fort Laramie had been purchased from its fur-trading owners by the Army just that spring, 1849.) "A place of general renovating," one diarist called it, for by then, hard usage and dry air were splitting wood, loosening tires, and in general creating unexpected problems for the overloaded wagons. And the most difficult part of the long and demanding trail still wound ahead.

Oddments of help appeared almost as if by spontaneous generation. Mormons ran ferries at the crossings of the North Platte and Green rivers. Mountain men from as far away as New Mexico set up shop here and there to sell essential livestock, buckskin clothing, jerky, and a violent whisky called Taos Lightning.

Beyond South Pass, hard choices faced the travelers. Should they save time by striking due west toward Fort Hall across the bone-dry Sublette's Cut-off? Or circle by way of Fort Bridger's repair shops? Or go through Salt Lake City, where the Mormons would sell or swap, at merciless prices, fresh produce and husky livestock to replace the emigrants' dwindling stores? Refreshed, a man could then swing north around the lake to rejoin the Fort Hall trail in the monotonous valley of the Humboldt, or else drop south to the Old Spanish Trail through Las Vegas. The latter was a long detour to the gold fields, but reassuring to travelers who came late and feared the snows of the Sierra.

Ignorant people persisted in striking off on short cuts to nowhere. William Lewis Manly and five or six companions furnished the most famous example. They tried to float down Wyoming's Green River, supposing it emptied into the Pacific. After wrecking themselves in Lodore Canyon in Colorado, where William Ashley had all but foundered, they crawled out into the Uinta Basin and from Indians learned how to reach Salt Lake City. Arriving too late to risk the Sierra, Manly joined a caravan bound for southern California over the Old Spanish Trail. Again sirens sang of short cuts. In southwestern Utah the travelers quarreled and split. Segments of the train eventually landed in a grisly desert depression lower than sea level. Before they were able to work out an escape, thirteen died, bringing a lasting name to the locale and giving to Western history one of its classic

The buildings of Peter Lassen's 18,000-acre Rancho Bosquejo in northern California, near present-day Red Bluff, were drawn by Forty-Niner J. Goldsborough Bruff. A nearby peak was named for Lassen, whose ranch was an aiming point for many travelers.

published tales of endurance, Manly's *Death Valley in '49*.

The so-called Lassen route into northern California was almost as dreadful. It had been "discovered" the year before by an incompetent Dane named Peter Lassen, who owned a ranch in the upper Sacramento Valley. Early in '48, quite unaware of Marshall's discovery, Lassen rode east to the Humboldt River to lure farmers close to his property so that its value would increase. Ten wagons heeded him. He led the party along the Applegate Trail until they were far north of where they should have gone. Totally lost, Lassen then floundered toward the Pit River, a tributary of the Sacramento. Hung up on high ridges between sheer canyons, the panicking travelers probably would have starved had not Peter Burnett's gold-eager wagon train from Oregon chanced by and helped them through.

In 1849, reports of the difficult passes farther south prompted other travelers to turn along the tracks of the Lassen party. Before the year was over, thousands of them followed each other into trouble like sheep. The Black Rock Desert of western Nevada exacted immediate toll. Forty-Niner J. Goldsborough Bruff, who left many sketches of the country as well as a diary, reported that in one fifty-mile stretch he counted five hundred and eleven dead oxen, ten mules, nine horses. Eighty-two of the bloated carcasses were scattered so densely around Rabbit-hole Spring that Bruff's party could scarcely work its wagons through. Crazed beasts had fallen into the shallow wells, hindquarters still out, plugging them. The stench . . . but there was no other place to camp.

Because the Forty-mile Desert on the familiar trail between Humboldt Sink and Carson River in Nevada was more heavily traveled, it produced even more shocking statistics. "I should think," wrote one man, "I passed the carcasses of 1,200 head of cattle and horses and a great

many wagons—Harness, cooking utensils—tools water casks &c &c that cost in the United States $50,000." On this stretch and on all the trails, skulking Indians further shattered morale by killing many animals from ambush, although they killed few people.

As winter neared, a reputed ten thousand persons were still toiling in the wilderness. Taking alarm, General Persifor Smith, commander of the American troops in California, appropriated one hundred thousand dollars for relief operations, accepted private donations, and told Major D. H. Rucker to start organizing parties. Without the Army's timely work, the Lassen route in particular would have turned into a charnel house for people as well as for animals. As it was, and in spite of the incompetence of many of the wayfarers, relatively few lives were lost to the desert and the mountains.

Before the aching rear guard of the 1849 migration reached shelter, rambunctious California learned by ship news that antipathies between Northern and Southern congressmen were freezing action on the establishment of territorial governments for the lands wrested from Mexico. President Zachary Taylor grew impatient. The West Coast might break the deadlock, he suggested, by hurdling the territorial stage and applying for direct admission into the union as a full-fledged state. The notion had already occurred to many Californians, and early in 1849, mass meetings gathered in several villages to discuss calling a state convention.

The situation in San Francisco gave urgency to the talks. A jungle town was growing there, disordered, unkempt, unpoliced. Hundreds of abandoned ships clotted the harbor. In time some were dragged close to the shore and scuttled, to be used as dwellings, stores, and brothels; one was transformed into San Francisco's first prison. Throughout this wooden spider web, ashore and afloat,

256

buzzed riffraff drawn from every land facing the Pacific.

A man named Sam Roberts organized several discharged American soldiers and a few Sydney Ducks from Australia's penal colony into a group that called themselves the Regulators but were more generally known as the Hounds. They masked their lawlessness under a grinning mask of patriotism: foreigners had to be controlled. Their principal target was San Francisco's ragged tent settlement of Chileans and Peruvians.

After an arrogant parade on July 15, 1849, the bullyboys swarmed into the district, robbing and smashing. One woman was clubbed to death for trying to defend her daughter against rape. Protests boiled, but the alcalde only wrung his hands, saying he was helpless. Sam Brannan then climbed onto the roof of the alcalde's own office and harangued the crowd until it formed vigilante committees. They broke the Hounds, banished the leaders, and gathered donations to help the victims recover.

It was dramatic. Perhaps it was necessary. But it certainly was not government.

Four weeks later, on August 1, Californians elected forty-eight delegates to a state constitutional convention that met in Monterey the following September. By October 13, the group had prepared a constitution that, among other things, prohibited slavery and established the state's boundaries as they now exist. The document was ratified by the voters in November. At the same time, they chose a legislature and elected Peter Burnett to serve as governor of a region that called itself a state but that in actuality had no legal sanction whatsoever.

In December, 1849, this first governing body selected California's initial senators: big, six-foot William Gwin, and explorer John Charles Frémont. The latter had just whirled through another storybook change in fortune. In January, 1849, it will be recalled, blizzards had shattered his fourth expedition high in the Colorado Rockies. After resting in Taos, he and twenty-five men continued to California by the Gila River. Near the Gila they met a caravan of Mexican miners and learned of the gold discoveries near Sutter's sawmill. Legend insists that Frémont immediately decided, on the basis of no evidence whatsoever, that surely there was also gold on the Mariposas grant that Thomas Larkin had purchased for him, against Frémont's desires, for three thousand dollars.

Promptly he entered into an arrangement with twenty-eight of the traveling Sonorans to mine his land on a share basis. That fall, according to his wife's memoirs, the Mexicans brought gold to his home in Monterey in bulging buckskin sacks. No longer walking the edges of destitution, Frémont declined an appointment to head the commission being formed to survey the new boundary with Mexico and entered politics. After his election as senator, he and Gwin drew lots to see who would serve the long term, the short one having only months to run. Frémont lost—but in 1856, a senatorship tucked among his other trophies, he became the first nominee of the

This graphic view of vultures circling above the carcasses of abandoned animals at Rabbit-hole Spring, where the California Trail crossed Nevada's desert, was one of many sketches with which Bruff illustrated his diaries of his gold rush adventures.

Republican party for the Presidency of the United States.

Immediately after their election, the senators hurried to Washington to present their credentials and urge Congress to accept what California had created—a full-fledged state in which slavery was prohibited. Other Western "officials" joined them, hoping to force the Government's hand. Almon W. Babbitt of Salt Lake City urged recognition of the Mormons' self-declared state of Deseret—all of present-day Utah and Nevada, most of Arizona, parts of Wyoming and Colorado, and enough of southern California to provide an outlet to the sea. The handful of Americans in New Mexico, aided by a few of the onetime citizens of Mexico, also formed a state (like Utah, they claimed jurisdiction over present Arizona) and sent "Representative" W. S. Messervy and

Southwest Wisconsin lead mines, active since early in the century, were served by this open-hearth furnace in Platteville.

"Senator" Richard H. Weightman to Washington, just as though they had been legally elected to the offices.

While these Westerners watched, Congress hammered out the Compromise of 1850. California entered the Union as a free state. The other two sections became territories. Deseret's name was changed to Utah; it was stripped of Arizona (which went to New Mexico) and of southern California but still reached from the crest of the Rockies to the eastern foothills of the Sierra. As for slavery, each territory could make up its own mind through its own constitution when the time arrived for statehood. The vociferous demands of slaveholding Texas for that part of New Mexico lying east of the Rio Grande were gagged, to Texas' indignation, by the Federal Government's assuming debts incurred by Texas

during its career as an independent republic. A more stringent fugitive slave law and an act abolishing the slave trade in the District of Columbia completed the horse trading, and the West rejoiced in the assumption that government would now cure all its ills.

Optimism filled the rest of the country as well. Once more the ugly issue of slavery had been swept under the rug. The stagnation that follows most wars ended, and prosperity shone. Floods of emigrants (nearly 2,700,000 between 1847 and 1854) crossed an Atlantic Ocean no longer so difficult or expensive to negotiate. As pools of surplus labor built up in the East, industrialists lost their fear that the opening of attractive new lands in the West would siphon away workers and raise wages. The headlong development of shipping on the Great Lakes, the growth of canals, and the spread of railways through the North began to divert Mississippi Valley freight away from the port of New Orleans and gradually broke the historic alliance that had existed between South and West. As Horace Greeley summed up the situation in his influential *New York Tribune*, "Every smoke that rises in the Great West marks a new customer to the counting rooms and warehouses of New York."

The 1846 repeal of England's corn laws opened new markets to American agriculture. Wheat farmers moved out of New England to the prairies of Illinois and Iowa, to the oak openings of Michigan and Wisconsin. Improved plows, reapers, and other machinery enabled farmers to break more sod and harvest more acres than ever before. A revolution in attitude followed. Once, men had sought forest land, believing that nut-bearing trees signified good soil. Then, in the 1850's, Wisconsin lumbermen began to float white pine timber for houses, fence rails, and posts down the Mississippi to railroads that hauled it out onto the prairies. Farmers using this cheap wood began to say that trees were a nuisance on farmland. With increasing covetousness they looked across the boundary of the Permanent Indian Country at the rolling hills of eastern Kansas and Nebraska.

Lead production boomed in Missouri, Wisconsin, Illinois, and Iowa. Copper and iron rushes developed around the edges of Lake Superior. The output of these mines and of the northern lumber camps built mountains of freight for the bustling lake steamers and the railroads feeding dozens of overnight cities.

With increasing insistence, Westerners demanded Government help in solving their transportation problems. Finally, in 1850, Stephen Douglas, who had a personal interest in the outcome, pushed through Congress a bill awarding the Illinois Central Railroad 2,572,800 acres in alternate sections along either side of the road's right of way. In 1852, Missouri obtained 1,764,711 acres to help finance two lines in that state. Although President Franklin Pierce tried to halt the enormous giveaway, he was only partly successful. During 1856–57, the Western and Southern states received twenty million acres for aiding forty-five different railroads, many of them little more than flagrant speculations. Before the policy was ended two decades later, approximately one hundred and thirty million acres, an area twice that of New York, New Jersey, and Pennsylvania combined, had passed without charge into the hands of the corporations. Some of it they still hold.

As real estate values rose throughout the nation, partly in response to the inflationary effects of California's flood of gold, the Midwest resumed its demands for a more liberal treatment of settlers. By law, an acre of the public domain, regardless of its quality, still cost private purchasers $1.25. Yet if public land could be given to corporations, why not also to individuals, in quarter-section (one-hundred-and-sixty-acre) plots called homesteads? The cry was taken up by labor leader George Henry Evans, who saw free land as a safety valve that would draw off excess labor from the East, thus bringing about higher wages and better working conditions. Galusha Grow of Pennsylvania became the homestead measure's chief proponent in Congress; Horace Greeley, its most vocal and persistent supporter in the press. "Shame on the laws," Greeley thundered in the *New York Tribune*, "which send an able, willing man to the almshouse . . . when the soil which he would gladly work and produce is . . . accorded by this government of freedmen to those alone who have money to pay for it."

"Vote Yourself a Farm" became a popular political slogan among radical groups. Much was made of the sturdy-yeoman concept—the truehearted, independent farmer gaining his land by virtue of his labor, the only morally valid title, Evans argued, that land could have.

In earlier days the South had supported the West's demands for a liberal land policy, but during the 1850's, her tune changed. Save perhaps for bits of California, the newly acquired Western territory was not suited to cotton. Throwing the domain open in one-hundred-and-sixty-acre plots would fill the West with small farmers opposed to slavery. Bitterly, therefore, the South mocked the romantic vision of the ennobled yeoman. Agricultural labor, her writers said, brutalized the worker rather than sanctified him. The true enlightenment necessary to a democracy came from a leisured class supported by slave labor. Giving land to the poor would simply sap the fiber of the recipient. Good Heavens! If the trend continued, the radicals soon would be proposing that actual money be disbursed to the indigent in the form of doles.

In spite of Southern opposition, some liberalization did result. In 1854, Thomas Hart Benton's principle of "graduation" was finally allowed—that is, a scaled reduction of prices to as low as twelve and a half cents an acre for federal lands that had been on the market for thirty years. Extraordinary bonuses were extended to veterans; by 1856, any man who had served as much as fourteen days in any war since the Revolution, and in many cases his heirs, could claim one hundred and sixty acres in certain localities free of charge.

To encourage the settlement of Oregon Territory (and later of Washington Territory, formed in 1853), half-section grants were made to citizens of the United States who had tilled, or promised they would till, the soil for four years. If a man married by December 1, 1851, his wife also received free land. By the time this Oregon Donation Law expired in 1855, 8,455 settlers had claimed nearly three million acres throughout the new Northwest. The mania was such that in 1851, more wagons went to Oregon than to the gold fields of California. Because of the premium that the law put on wives in a frontier land that was starved for females, girls twelve and thirteen years old were swept into matrimony by men who were often old enough to be their grandfathers.

The rights of the Indians were, as usual, ignored. Farmers hungry for Donation Law lands swept relentlessly across newly formed reservations. Gold seekers appeared at about the same time in the Rogue River and Umpqua canyons of southern Oregon. Isolated little wars erupted in the remote canyons and forest, spread to include Indian attacks on immigrant trains following the Applegate Trail, and then leaped north into Washington. In 1856, Seattle itself was briefly under siege. Yakima warriors for a time closed the Columbia gorge to traffic, and in 1858, in a quarrel brought on by gold seekers at Fort Colville, the Spokan, Coeur d'Alene, and Palouse Indians came within an ace of wiping out a column of troops led by Colonel E. J. Steptoe.

Untroubled by these incidental mischiefs, the House of Representatives in far-off Washington, D.C., was willing to extend its generosity with the public domain to the entire nation. Three times, in 1852, 1854, and 1859, it passed homestead laws. On each occasion, the Senate defeated the measure. Each time, sectional lines were more sharply drawn. If the South could find means to prevent it, free land would not help to draw free-soil yeomen into the rest of the West.

California meanwhile settled down to grappling with her own peculiar problems. Gold production for the year 1852 soared to eighty-one million dollars. By that time, most of the easy-to-handle placer gold had been skimmed away, and new sources had to be found. Companies were formed to dam rivers in order to work the exposed channels, or to construct long flumes for transporting water to erstwhile dry diggings. High-pressure nozzles washed mountains of gravel into batteries of sluice boxes and by sheer volume wrung a profit from the light dusting of gold the material contained. Other men followed gold-bearing veins of quartz deep into the earth and then had to learn, by trial and error, how to mill the ore they mined. Although by 1858 the annual output of metal had dropped to a relatively meager forty-six million dollars, an estimated hundred thousand men still found employment in trades directly connected with the mines. More importantly, they were developing skills they soon would spread throughout the West.

Capital concentrated in banks to finance these more sophisticated mining procedures, then branched out to foster other activities. Fabricating plants of many sorts took root. Thanks to the demands of the gold fields for supplies, truck farming became profitable in the Willamette Valley of Oregon, lumbering beside Puget Sound in Washington. In New Mexico, Kit Carson, Uncle Dick Wootton, and other retired mountain men threw together herds of small, coarse-wooled sheep and drove them across desert and mountains to the insatiable market—one hundred and thirty-five thousand head made the weary trip to California in 1853. Texas cowboys and Mormon farmers added trail herds of rangy steers. An estimated one hundred and fifty men dug oysters at Budd Inlet in Puget Sound for San Francisco's new nabobs. High prices for ice—seventy-five dollars a ton in 1852—led to the building of oceanside freezing ponds near Sitka, Alaska. Only in wheat did early California achieve self-sufficiency. During the decade of the 1850's, output jumped from seventeen thousand bushels a year to five million nine hundred thousand, and grain ships from Europe, hunting food for soldiers fighting the Crimean War, began anchoring at inland ports alongside the two rivers that empty into San Francisco Bay.

Violence accompanied these whiplash releases of energy. During the eighteen months between December 24, 1849, and July 22, 1851, six major fires swept San Francisco. Some of the blazes were set by incendiaries. After the fifth one, Sam Brannan helped form another vigilante committee that eventually hanged four men, flogged one, deported twenty-eight, turned fifteen over to the authorities—and released forty-one. Many other criminals escaped retribution by fleeing. But human nature inclines to relax, and in 1856 the job had to be done over again. Similar extralegal upheavals shook the min-

ing camps, reaching a zenith of sorts at Downieville in 1851 when a pregnant Mexican girl was hanged for stabbing an American during a quarrel. In the same year, Los Angeles experienced forty-four killings without a conviction. Throughout the state, cattle rustling and stage robberies were commonplace. Even politics was brutal. In 1859, David Terry of the state supreme court killed David Broderick, boss of San Francisco, in a duel arising out of a struggle to control the Democratic party.

Legalized robberies were equally flagrant. By treaty the United States was bound to honor land grants made by the Mexican Government. California courts placed the burden of proving ownership onto the grantees, made them travel long distances to present their cases, and by sheer harassment forced many an erstwhile Mexican to forfeit his holdings. "Our inheritance is turned to strangers," mourned Don Juan Bandini. ". . . Our necks are under persecution—we labor and have no rest."

The fragmented bands of Indians in the central valleys were harried like those in southern Oregon. When they resisted, they were cut down in what historian Hubert Howe Bancroft described as "butcherings." There was even an unexpected side gain for the whites. Militia hunting Yosemite Indians in 1851 followed their quarry into the valley that bears the tribe's name, returned awed by the towering cliffs and waterfalls, and with their tales launched that spectacular mountain area on its career as one of America's favorite scenic attractions.

The picture was equally grim in New Mexico and Arizona. Between 1846 and 1850, according to statistics kept by United States marshals, Indians stole 7,050 horses, 12,887 mules, 31,581 horned cattle, and 453,293 sheep. In spite of severe losses at the hands of punitive expeditions under William Gilpin, Kiowas and Comanches continued to raid the Santa Fe Trail. The growing aggressiveness of the Indians, added to personal dissatisfactions, led William Bent to abandon and partially destroy the once-great fur trading post that he had built on the Arkansas River.

In the face of the depredations, the Southwest's dry mesas, wind-scoured deserts, and colored canyons were insufficient lures to attract any considerable number of settlers. The area thus became primarily a military frontier. Immediately following the war with Mexico, the Bureau of Topographical Engineers sent survey parties throughout the new domain, from Texas to California, to locate forts and roads for supplying those forts and to map the location of Indian trails and villages. Long-range questions also intruded. Could river navigation be developed? Did the section offer snow-free passes for a transcontinental railroad that would reduce the expenses

Fort Union, built in 1851 north of today's Watrous, New Mexico, held in check Apache and Ute Indians. This view of the post was done by German-born lithographer Joseph Heger, who served with the Army in the Southwest, 1855–60.

of maintaining the distant military establishments? As incidents to these investigations, what could be learned about mineral resources and the amounts of arable land that would be available for farming?

In pursuit of answers, small parties thrust into northern California. Captain Howard Stansbury circled Great Salt Lake and returned home well south of the traditional Sweetwater trail, marking out the Bridger Pass crossing that would soon become the route of the overland stages and the Union Pacific Railroad. By far the greatest effort of the engineers, however, was expended in the region making up today's New Mexico and Arizona. This area became the scene of slow, patient probes of the Indian country carried out by such dedicated Army career officers as Captain Randolph Marcy, Captain Lorenzo Sitgreaves, and Lieutenant James Simpson.

New Mexico's military installations were turned over to Colonel Edwin Vose Sumner, called Bull-Head by his men after a musket ball bounced off his skull without doing appreciable damage. He went out in 1851, found his troops garrisoned in the little towns along the river valleys, and was horrified by their morale. "My first step," he reported to his commanding officer, "was to break up the post at Santa Fe, that sink of vice and extravagance, and to remove the troops and public property to Fort Union"—a post he erected beside the

Santa Fe Trail in northeastern New Mexico and turned into the key bastion of the Southwest. Other troops were dumped into isolated posts—some built of raw planks, some of adobe bricks—scattered far and wide between the Rio Grande border of Texas and Fort Yuma in the inferno deserts beside the lower Colorado.

A march against the Navahos reached into spectacular Canyon de Chelly in northeastern Arizona but accomplished nothing. Nor did New Mexico's longed-for civil government seem to Sumner to be doing any better in its field. All branches had failed, he declared: "the executive, for want of power; the judiciary, from the total incapacity and want of principle in the juries; and the legislative, from want of knowledge." There was, he added, "no possibility of any change for the better . . . [no] inducement for any class of our people to come here whose example would improve this people [the native New Mexicans]."

In Colonel Sumner's opinion, the Army should relieve itself of its heavy expenses on this discouraging frontier by furnishing weapons to the native populace and letting them take care of themselves, as they had done under Mexico's rule. The Government declined to abrogate its responsibilities, however. Troops stayed in the lonesome posts, now and then escorting high brass out to sign impotent treaties with blank-faced Indian chiefs. These failing, punitive patrols would ride into the wilderness,

A group of Mormon missionaries sent out from Salt Lake City posed for their picture in Echo Canyon, on the road between the Mormon capital and Fort Bridger. Many like them went to Europe as well as various parts of the West.

sometimes winning a skirmish and sometimes dying in ambush, until eventually even danger grew to be as monotonous as the sun-washed rocks.

Utah's settlement was far more orderly. Under the church's iron authority, a Mormon who had proved himself as a farmer or a craftsman might be "called" to uproot his family, join a caravan of similarly designated persons, and move along the valleys to found another settlement. To select just one example: the California city of San Bernardino was established that way in 1851 by Mormons traversing the desert from Salt Lake City in a self-sufficient train of one hundred and fifty wagons.

To help needy Mormons from outside Utah reach their promised land, Brigham Young in 1849 instituted the Perpetual Emigrating Fund, financed by donations of cash and livestock. Recipients of these funds promised to repay their loans after establishing themselves in Utah so that others might also benefit from the perpetually renewed pool. By 1852, nearly every Mormon inside the United States who wished to join his coreligionists in Utah had made the journey. Attention centered thereafter on bringing converts from abroad. At first, most of the newcomers were pallid refugees from England's rising factory towns. Later, vigorous Scandinavians began

to appear on the scene, lured, as the English had been, by thoughts of land as well as by promises of heaven.

The new arrivals spread quickly among the embryo villages, helping dig irrigation ditches, break fields, herd the communal flocks. Soon they came into contact with Ute Indians. Relations were generally friendly. Mormon religion taught that though the Indians, whom they called Lamanites, were cursed with dark skins for early errors, they were capable of redemption and reunion with the white race. Furthermore, as Brigham Young kept pointing out, it was cheaper to feed the Indians than to start wars that might bring the United States Army marching into Utah, an intrusion that the Saints strongly wished to avoid at all costs.

Thanks to this policy of conciliation, no major clashes developed until the territorial government infuriated the Utes by forbidding them to sell captive Indian children to slave traders from New Mexico. To make their point, Ute war parties began attacking towns and travelers in the central valleys. Even then, Young would not let his people take the offensive, as most American frontiersmen would have done. "I have not made war on Indians," he said in the Salt Lake tabernacle on July 31, 1853, "nor am I calculating to do it. My policy is to give them presents and be kind to them." During the height of the conflict, while Utes were waving fresh Mormon scalps, stealing stock, and burning outlying mills, Young sent Wakara, principal chief of the Utes, "tobacco for you to smoke in the mountains when you get lonesome. You are a fool for fighting your best friends. . . ." Unconvinced at first, the Utes kept on; but gradually the strange policy prevailed, and by November, 1853, the war had sputtered out for lack of fuel.

Greater troubles came to the Mormons from men of their own nation. Although Utah, unlike most territories, had been allowed to select its own governor, the other executive and judicial officers were, in the main, political hacks appointed in Washington as a reward for party faithfulness. Arrived in Utah, they swelled arrogantly. They clashed with the stiff-necked legislature, which was little more than an arm of the church; they offended ordinary Mormons by publicly denouncing church-sanctified polygamy as a gross immorality; they quarreled regularly with Brigham Young—whom they suspected of any number of evils, including treason—and then went home to charge that he used hired assassins, the Danites, for maintaining his power and that he was accumulating an immense personal fortune at the expense of his duped followers. Mormon apostates added to the clamor. The 1856 platform of the Republican party attacked Negro slavery and Mormon polygamy as twin relics of barbarism and promised to extirpate both offenses if their candidates were elected. As tensions mounted, the Mormons began to wonder whether their mountain isolation would provide sufficient protection after all.

To other parts of the West, isolation was a maddening frustration, and it was continually attacked. Builders of New England sailing ships, responding to the challenge of steam, designed graceful clipper ships that by 1854–55 were carrying freight around the Horn in eighty days. Mail and passengers could travel from New York to California by way of Aspinwall's Panama railroad, completed in January, 1855, in twenty-six to thirty days. Costs were high, however—up to eighty cents an ounce for mail—and of course a route through Panama was no solace to points within the interior of the United States.

Mail was brought to Santa Fe from Independence, Missouri, once a month in a six-mule coach protected against Indians by eight guards so heavily armed that they could fire one hundred and thirty-six shots without pausing to reload. The only cross-country mail line to the Pacific consisted of two sections. The first part, from Independence to Salt Lake City, was opened in 1850 by Samuel Woodson under a Government subsidy of nineteen thousand five hundred dollars a year. The other,

from Salt Lake City to Sacramento, was pioneered in 1851 by Absalom Woodward and George Chorpenning for fourteen thousand dollars a year. Both contracts called for a trip once a month from either terminus, Independence or Sacramento, to Salt Lake City. Return trips supposedly operated on the same schedule. Actually, the time requirements were seldom met, especially in winter, when the California end of the line had to swing around the Sierra by way of Los Angeles.

There were no relays of horses. Either the same teams made the entire round trip, or the driver was forced to heroic substitutes. Feramorz Little, a Mormon subcontractor on the South Pass crossing, once replaced a failing team by buying four wild mules at Fort Laramie, thrusting them blindfolded into harness, and breaking them by letting them run themselves to exhaustion. Although workers with mauls sometimes tried to pack snowdrifts hard enough to hold the winter sleds, the vehicles often stalled completely; the drivers then cached the mail sacks in whatever shelter they could find and beat their way on foot to the nearest succor. Sharper troubles came on occasion from Indians. In 1851 they killed Absalom Woodward, one of the partners of the newly opened California end of the line.

All this while, visionaries were crying to the nation that a transcontinental railroad would solve the prob-

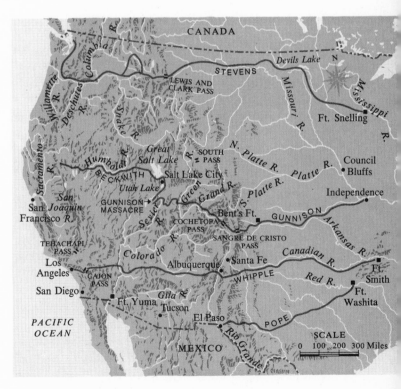

Moving west in roughly parallel lines, topographical engineer groups sought the best route for a transcontinental railroad.

lems. At first, a southern route seemed the most logical. Northward, from Texas on to Canada, the Permanent Indian Country loomed as a barrier. Due west of the Indians towered the Rockies and the Sierra Nevada. By striking from New Orleans or Vicksburg through Texas and New Mexico, however, a railway could avoid both the Indian country, inviolable by solemn treaty, and the mountains—or so southern enthusiasts argued.

Cities farther north that wished to grab the Western trade for themselves—Chicago, St. Paul, St. Louis, Memphis, and the satellites of each—bridled at the plan. Slavery muddied these economic issues still more. Settlers carrying their doctrines with them would follow whatever line was built. The new states they created would eventually control the balance of power in the nation, and both North and South were determined to hold this advantage for their own sections.

Hoping to break the bitter deadlock, Senators William Gwin of California (a Southern sympathizer) and Richard Brodhead of Pennsylvania suggested that survey parties examine all potential routes and then let the cool objectivity of science determine which one was best from an engineering standpoint. Secretary of War Jefferson Davis agreed, possibly because, as a Southerner, he felt that the snow-free southern route through Texas would prove to be the inevitable winner.

The bill that Congress passed in March, 1853, instructed the Bureau of Topographical Engineers to map wide east-west strips across the entire West and have the reports ready for Congress on January 1, 1854, only ten months away. This was manifestly impossible. To avoid waste of time and money on unnecessary duplication, Davis sent no survey parties along the two best-known routes, the central one up the Platte Valley and through southern Wyoming, and the one farthest south, through lower New Mexico and along the Gila River. Earlier reports prepared by Frémont, Stansbury, and the engineers traveling with Kearny's army during the war were deemed to have made the topography of these crossings familiar enough. Effort was concentrated instead on surveying three lesser-known areas.

Isaac I. Stevens headed the largest party, which struck out from Fort Snelling, Minnesota, through today's Montana to Puget Sound. Since Stevens had just been appointed governor of newly created Washington Territory, he could be expected to see this most northerly of the routes in a favorable light—and he did. The exploration of a central route through the Cochetopa Pass area of the Colorado Rockies was entrusted to Captain John Gunnison. A third party under Lieutenant Amiel Whipple went from Fort Smith, Arkansas, through Albuquerque to Los Angeles. Two limited surveys fleshed out these studies. Captain John Pope examined the Staked Plains of western Texas, while another party, even more curiously constrained, examined the Sierra passes in central California only. Finally and belatedly, still another small group was hurried out to fill in, from an engineering standpoint, some of the more glaring deficiencies of the wartime Gila River examination.

Private interests, suspicious of Jefferson Davis's intent, sent out three additional parties to supplement the Government's work. Iowa financiers, annoyed by the neglect of the Platte Valley, dispatched young Grenville Dodge into western Nebraska to make careful cost studies to reinforce their arguments in favor of that route. St. Louis interests, led by Thomas Hart Benton, sent out two survey parties to counteract any negative reports Captain John Gunnison might turn in concerning the central Colorado crossing that they favored. The first of these St. Louis groups, traveling rapidly in summer weather, was headed by Edward Beale and was equipped with its own press agent, an Eastern newspaper reporter named Gwinn Heap. The second was led by ubiquitous John Charles Frémont. Once again Frémont traveled in winter, hoping to prove that snow was not the threat to construction that it had seemed during his debacle of 1849. This time he reached Cochetopa Pass, Benton's famous Buffalo Trail—supposedly a "natural" highway, since migrating herds used it—and after severe suffering got through with the loss of only one man. The experience was too rugged, however, to serve as an effective counter to Gunnison's pessimistic findings.

Gunnison, slain by Indians with seven of his men in central Utah on October 26, 1853, was the only one of the surveyors not to reach his destination. The next year his job was completed, though not very thoroughly, by Lieutenant E. G. Beckwith. The reports of the various reconnaissance parties eventually filled thirteen handsome volumes. They added enormously to America's knowledge of Western fauna and flora, Indian life, soil, and mineral resources. But although each party made a stab at cost estimates, the reports turned out to be skimpy on just the sort of detailed engineering data that a railroad builder would need.

To no one's surprise, Jefferson Davis evaluated the material in favor of the southern route along the Gila. Dispassionate rebuttal of his arguments was no longer possible, however. For by that time, Senator Stephen Douglas of Illinois had come up with his infamous Kansas-Nebraska Bill of 1854. It split the country asunder. In the fierce heat of that fission, the cool voice of science was completely overwhelmed.

James W. Marshall

MARSHALL'S DISCOVERY

James Marshall was a tragic figure of the California gold rush. Though he made the discovery at Sutter's Mill on January 24, 1848, gold thereafter eluded him. He could not even prospect in peace, for other miners, convinced he was lucky, dogged his steps and began to dig near him whenever he stopped to test for pay dirt. Finally, under the delusion that he was the rightful owner of all the gold in California, he became so cantankerous that he was driven from most mining camps.

News of Marshall's find was a long time reaching the East. In the first months of 1848, reports of the magnitude of the deposits were so confused by the time they reached Monterey that the military governor, Colonel Richard Mason, went in June and July to the gold area with his adjutant, Lieutenant William Tecumseh Sherman, to assess the situation. Sherman drew maps of the site of discovery at Sutter's Mill (above) and of a second find at Mormon Diggings. These maps, with a letter from Colonel Mason and a sample of gold, were sent by courier to Washington via Panama and were the basis for President Polk's glowing report of the richness of the California gold fields in his annual message on December 5. This, the first official confirmation of California newspaper reports that had begun reaching the East in August (one of them was carried across country by Kit Carson), set off the gold rush that in 1849 alone sent some 100,000 people hurrying off to California.

San Francisco Harbor in the early 1850's held hundreds of abandoned ships whose crews had deserted to hunt gold.

WHAT WAS YOUR NAME IN THE STATES?

"A Good Freight" was one of many sketches of miners painted in 1849 by Augusto Ferran and fellow Cuban José Baturone and published in Havana.

There was a favorite ditty of the California diggings: "Oh, what was your name in the States?/ Was it Thompson or Johnson or Bates?/ Did you murder your wife and fly for your life?/ Say, what was your name in the States?" But not many of the Forty-Niners were there to escape a posse or the gallows at home. The average miner was an amiable young man planning to return East with enough to pay off a mortgage or start his own business. But the rich strikes were only for a lucky few; most miners had a hard time making ends meet, and many stayed on as settlers because they did not have enough money to return home. After the first year or two, the throngs of newcomers included more criminals and other undesirables. Most of them went to cities, especially San Francisco. Few became miners; they preferred to get gold by taking from those who did the hard work.

San Francisco Vigilantes, the main force for order in a lawless city, made a show of strength in an 1856 parade.

Hangtown (later Placerville), here pictured by W. R. Hutton, was so named after three men died by miners' justice.

267

268 THIS IS THE WAY IT WAS

Miners (and guest) use a "long tom" to wash gold from pay dirt in Auburn Ravine on the American River in 1852.

EXPLORING
THE NEW TERRITORIES

Randolph B. Marcy

The Mexican War added a third of a billion acres to the nation, but much of the newly acquired land was unknown, and exploration was a first order of business. A commission surveying the new Mexican boundary found a good railroad route, and the Gadsden Purchase was made to put the right of way within the United States. Captain R. B. Marcy pioneered a road from Fort Smith, Arkansas, to Santa Fe in 1849. Lieutenant J. H. Simpson, who went with him, continued west and discovered ancient pueblos. Captain Howard Stansbury, in 1849–50, surveyed and studied the arid reaches about the Great Salt Lake. In 1851 Captain Lorenzo Sitgreaves crossed an unknown part of Arizona, past hostile Indians, to reach San Diego. By these and a number of other expeditions, more limited in scope, many previously empty spaces on maps of the Southwest were rapidly filled in.

JOHN RUSSELL BARTLETT, *Personal Narrative*, VO

LEFT AND RIGHT: HOWARD STANSBURY, *Exploration and Survey of the Valley of the Great Salt Lake of Utah*, 1852

Surveyors with Stansbury's Great Salt Lake expedition are shown setting up a base line station in the Utah desert.

Fort Yuma (opposite shore), overlooking the Colorado, was drawn by Mexican boundary commissioner John R. Bartlett.

Stansbury's report, published in 1852, included this scene of bird life on Gunnison's Island in Great Salt Lake.

Arizona sandstone formations resemble man-made fortifications and buildings in one of Richard H. Kern's water colors.

A warrior was painted in Navaho country by Richard Kern.

Hosta, a Pueblo Indian, guided the expedition.

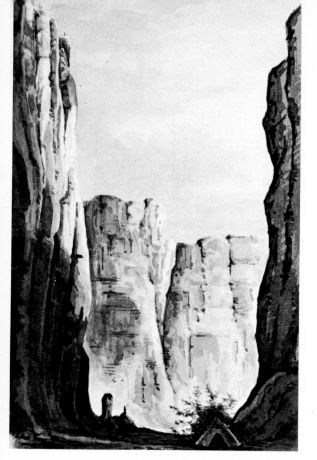

Richard drew this view of the Navahos' Canyon de Chelly.

THROUGH THE EYES
OF THE KERNS

An indefatigable trio of brothers from Philadelphia, Benjamin, Richard, and Edward M. Kern, artists and explorers, saw much of the Southwest when it was new and fresh and, though stalked by tragedy, left a rich visual record of what they had seen. Edward was a topographer for Frémont's 1845–46 expedition; all three brothers were with Frémont's disastrous fourth expedition, on which Benjamin was killed by Indians. Edward and Richard were topographers with James H. Simpson in 1849, and in 1851 Richard was with Sitgreaves in Arizona. In 1853 Richard was slain with Gunnison during a railroad survey in Utah. Only Edward survived his Western adventures. These paintings by Edward and Richard, reproduced for the first time, are typical of the Kerns' work, which as lithographs adorned many Government reports. They are from the Simpson journey in Arizona in 1849.

At Jemez, near Santa Fe, Simpson's men watched Pueblo Indians perform the Green Corn Dance, here painted by Edward.

The Indians got little of what was promised them at the Traverse des Sioux council, here sketched by Francis Mayer.

Mendota's first signer: Sioux Chief Little Crow by Mayer

THE MINNESOTA FRONTIER

In the northern Midwest in 1849, Minnesota became a territory with a huge area extending west to the Missouri. Of this, all save the small portion east of the Mississippi was Indian country, closed to settlers. But the Government was skilled in handling such problems, and at Traverse des Sioux in July, 1851, and Mendota in August, the eastern Sioux signed away their domain—the southern half of present Minnesota and more besides—retaining only a narrow reservation along the Minnesota River.

While the settlers pushed the farm frontier forward, a trade frontier was also vigorously developed, and a traffic in pelts grew up with the Red River settlements in central Canada. An annual caravan of oxcarts—some 600 in the peak year, 1858—ground southward to St. Paul from the area between Pembina and Fort Garry (Winnipeg); and St. Paul, a Mississippi port, became a great fur market.

Kittson's trading post (above) was a fur station at Pembina on the Red River. Pierre Bottineau (right), a Red River métis, or half-breed, became a prominent scout, guiding many Western hunting and exploring expeditions. The French-Indian métis were the trappers and hunters of the Red River country and adjoining plains. In 1870 and 1885, they attempted, in the Louis Riel rebellion, to set up an independent nation. It was Canada's only Indian warfare, though it was almost incidental that the métis had Indian blood.

The 1858 caravan of Red River carts was camped near St. Paul when this picture of resting métis drivers was taken.

SEARCH FOR A PACIFIC RAILROAD ROUTE

Everyone agreed there should be a transcontinental railroad to tie the Pacific coast to the rest of the country; the trouble was that no one could agree on the route. The North wanted it across the north, the South across the south, and the central Mississippi Valley was convinced it should cut across the West's mid-section. As Western population increased, the matter became more pressing, but every railroad bill brought up in Congress could muster only the votes of the men from the section where it would start; all others voted against it. Thus, it eventually seemed a wise compromise to have the Army Topographical Corps make a number of roughly parallel surveys across the West, from which the Secretary of War, on the basis of the evidence, could decide which was the best route. The plan's weakness was that the Secretary, Jefferson Davis, was a Southerner and was therefore convinced that the southernmost route was the best. But in 1853 four major Topographical Corps expeditions, together with several smaller and even private ones, started west.

The topographers with the railroad survey parties were not just map makers but also artists skilled at depicting terrain. Often their pictures were panoramic views to supplement the maps, but they also drew details of Indian life, natural history, and the workaday existence of the expeditions. These views are among dozens that they made of the West, as a part of their official records.

A pack train of the party led by Lieutenant R. S. Williamson is shown on the opposite page heading out across a California desert. This was the southernmost survey near the Mexican border, the one favored by Jefferson Davis. At upper right are the Spanish Peaks of southern Colorado, from an original sketch by Richard Kern but finished for a lithographer by John Mix Stanley. Kern, topographer with the expedition under Lieutenant John W. Gunnison surveying between the 38th and 39th parallels, was killed with Gunnison and six other members of the party by Indians in Utah in October, 1853.

Lieutenant Amiel Whipple led another party that went from Fort Smith, Arkansas, through Albuquerque to Los Angeles. The painting (right, center) by H. B. Möllhausen, Whipple's artist, shows expedition members crossing the Colorado near a Mohave Indian village. And the lithograph of buffalo dotting the northern plains (lower right) was made from a drawing by John Mix Stanley, already a noted artist of the West, who accompanied Isaac I. Stevens's party that conducted the northernmost of the surveys, traveling from Minnesota to Puget Sound between the 48th and 49th parallels.

BLACK RANGE   GREAT BOILING SPRING POINT

Jefferson Davis

THE CENTRAL ROUTE

The results of the railroad surveys surprised Jefferson Davis and the Topographical Corps by indicating that other routes might be better than the southernmost one. But Davis's bias prevented an impartial judgment, and he decided in favor of the southern route. It made no real difference, for the Kansas-Nebraska Act engendered so much bitterness that Congress failed to agree on the route until Southerners withdrew from Washington during the Civil War. The line then chosen was a central one, paralleling for part of the way the route surveyed by the group led at first by Lieutenant John W. Gunnison, then later, after Gunnison's death, by Lieutenant E. G. Beckwith, who completed the survey. The panoramic view and map are both of Nevada's Humboldt Valley and were drawn by Beckwith's topographer, F. W. von Egloffstein. The panorama shows what the surveyors saw when looking toward the top of the map from within the encircled point at bottom; features like the Black Range, Mud Lake, and Lassen's Meadows on both depictions help orient the viewer. The Central Pacific in time closely followed the proposed map route.

NORTHERN MUD LAKE   COLD SPRING RANGE   LASSEN'S MEADOWS

BOTH: U.S. PACIFIC RAILROAD SURVEY, 1855, VOL. XI

The San Juan Mountains, Colorado

"If any young man is about to commence in the world, with little in his circumstances to prepossess him in favor of one section above another, we say to him publicly and privately, Go to the West; there your capacities are sure to be appreciated and your industry and energy rewarded."

Advice circulated by Horace Greeley, Editor of the *New York Tribune*, 1850's

CHAPTER ELEVEN

THE GREAT PRIZE

1852-1861

During the 1840's, expansionists began arguing that it was absurd for the geographic continuity of the United States to be broken by "foreign nations" of wild and half-wild Indians. Some sort of restraint, it was said, should be put on the tribes. At the very least the transportation routes between the Midwest and the Pacific coast ought to be cleared—a contention that appealed particularly to railroad promoters.

As a step in that direction, white negotiators in September, 1851, assembled ten thousand Indians in a barbarically resplendent council near Fort Laramie. There the tribes that once had roamed at will across the northern and central plains were persuaded to accept limited reservations—the Sioux north of the North Platte River, the Crows in the Powder River Basin of what today is southern Montana, the Cheyennes and Arapahoes on a broad tract that reached from western Kansas to the toes of the Colorado Rockies. Also, the Indians granted unrestricted transit rights along the main trails to white emigrants and freighters. They furthermore allowed the United States, a potential enemy, to locate military forts in the heart of their territory. In return, the signers of the Fort Laramie treaty were promised fifty thousand dollars' worth of goods each year for fifty years—a time span later reduced by Congress without the Indians' consent to fifteen years. In 1853 treaties with similar provisions were signed with the Comanches and Kiowas living south of the Arkansas River.

Though few of the Plains Indians could have realized it at the time, they had helped to guarantee their own eventual defeat. For when settlers demanded additional land in the future, negotiators could whittle it away first from one tribe and then from another without arousing concerted resistance.

Some of the relocated Eastern tribes, however—the Wyandots, Potawatomis, Delawares, Shawnees, Kickapoos, Miamis, and others who inhabited a narrow north-south tier just outside the western borders of Iowa and Missouri—were more aware of what these increasing white pressures might portend. They had been kicked out of the way of settlement once before. Apparently it would happen again unless they devised an effective counter.

By 1852 most of the Eastern tribes had learned to worship in Christian churches, practice farming, and govern themselves by written codes of law. Led by the Wyandots, they next decided to embrace white neighbors as well, hoping that an influx of land-hungry settlers would raise the values of the Indian holdings. This meant turning their section of the Indian country into a territory so that the Federal Government would open it to settlement. Once a territory had been formed, those Indians who so desired could become citizens of the United States (as some Creeks and Cherokees in the South already had), take over private ownership of their shares of the communal lands, and, by assuming responsible roles under the new white man's government, avoid being sent into exile once again.

These Indian maneuvers to establish a territory won the support of the seven or eight hundred whites who already lived among them. A few of those whites were squatters, but most were employees of the United States

281

Indian Department or of the trading posts and missions —Indian agents, teachers, freighters, storekeepers, blacksmiths, and the like. Unhappily, however, the efforts also attracted the attention of whites who lived outside the Indian country but who had their own reasons for wanting to see the territory take shape.

The first outsiders to interfere were Missourians interested in promoting Thomas Hart Benton's proposed central railroad to the Pacific, a line that would run up the Kansas River and through today's Colorado. On July 26, 1853, they called a meeting in the Council House of the Wyandot tribe at Wyandotte City, near the junction of the Kansas and Missouri rivers, the site of today's Kansas City, Kansas. To be governor of what they called Nebraska Territory, a huge region stretching west toward the Rockies and north toward Canada, the gathering selected the Indian leader of the territorial movement, fifty-three-year-old William Walker, son of a white trader and a half-French, half-Wyandot mother. As nominee for delegate to Congress, to be voted on in October, the territory makers named Abelard Guthrie, a Scotch-Irish native of Ohio who on marrying his Indian sweetheart, Quindaro Nancy Brown, in 1843 had been adopted into the Big Turtle clan of the Wyandots, which was also William Walker's clan. Next, the convention whooped through a resolution putting "Nebraska" on record as favoring a central railway (this was the Missourians' real reason for muscling in on the Indians' affairs in the first place) and adjourned. None of the actions had legal sanction, of course, for only Congress could authorize the formation of a territorial government.

The gathering made no pronouncement about slavery, assuming that the Missouri Compromise would hold in the new territory and that slavery would be prohibited north of 36° 30', the line of Missouri's southern boundary. This did not suit slaveholders in western Missouri. They believed, probably erroneously, that the areas just beyond the border would be as suited to the slave cultivation of hemp and tobacco as were their own counties. They feared, moreover, that additional free territory directly to the west would intensify the severe economic drain already being occasioned by runaway slaves. But mostly they hated the Missouri Compromise as a matter of principle. The Western lands, they argued, belonged to the nation as a whole, and Congress had no right to exclude slavery from any part of them. The instant they heard of the new "territory," they determined to use it as a device for ending the Compromise.

Leader of this newest movement was one of Missouri's United States Senators, David R. Atchison, a florid, barrel-bodied stump screamer from Platte County, just

A Delaware mountain man, Black Beaver, settled on his tribe's Kansas reservation after years as a trapper and Western guide.

across the river from Wyandotte City. Immediately after the adjournment of the first "territorial" convention, Atchison summoned a rival convention. This one met at a Shawnee mission house south of Wyandotte City. As its nominee for delegate to Congress, Atchison's group named Thomas Johnson, a portly missionary among the Shawnees. A Virginian by birth and breeding, Johnson sincerely believed that slavery carried divine sanction. (Slavery, it should be noted, was not uncommon at the Kansas trading posts and missions, and it was even practiced among the Indians themselves.)

Thomas Johnson was, of course, endorsed by the missionaries. He was also supported by George Manypenny, a proponent of slavery who, as Commissioner of Indian Affairs, controlled trading licenses and agency jobs. The effect of these pressures was startling. For example, the precinct of the Miami Indians returned no votes for Abelard Guthrie, fifty for Thomas Johnson.

The missionary's election seemed assured until unexpected returns arrived from the northern precinct, Peter Sarpy's trading post at Bellevue, near the mouth of the Platte. At that single polling place a candidate unknown to the other groups, Hadley Johnson (no kin to Atchison's candidate), garnered three hundred and fifty-eight votes. Thomas Johnson's total from the entire "state" was only three hundred and thirty-seven.

What had happened was this: A small-town Missouri newspaper carrying a brief mention of the forthcoming election had fallen by chance into the hands of certain Iowans interested in promoting a transcontinental railroad from Chicago across their state and up the Platte Valley. They took fright. If Missourians captured the new territory, they would locate its capital somewhere along the lower Kansas River. Settlers would follow and so would the transcontinental railroad.

Hoping to counter the threat, nearly four hundred Iowans crossed the Missouri on the morning of election day, swarmed into Sarpy's, and voted for Hadley Johnson. These results they defiantly sent to "Governor" William Walker in Wyandotte City for certification.

Walker was no particular friend of Thomas Johnson, but he did want the railroad to come through Wyandotte City. Throwing out all ballots marked for Hadley Johnson on the ground that the voters were not bona fide residents of the "territory," he declared Thomas Johnson to be Nebraska's delegate.

Arrived in Washington, Johnson was refused recognition. He stayed around anyway, for Senator A. C. Dodge of Iowa and Representative J. G. Miller of Missouri had just introduced bills to create the very territory Johnson's constituents desired. If the measure passed, it might be that he would be seated.

The Senate version of this newest Nebraska bill was referred in December, 1853, to the Committee on Territories, of which Stephen A. Douglas of Illinois was chairman. During the subsequent months, it underwent radical transformations, one of which was suggested to Douglas by Hadley Johnson, the rejected delegate from Sarpy's.

Hadley had also gone to Washington, not to contest the election of his namesake, but to prevent the Kansas Valley from becoming the sole railroad magnet for whatever territory was formed. To Douglas he suggested two territories: Kansas, occupying the lands west of Missouri, and Nebraska, occupying the plains west of Iowa and north to Canada. This division would allow both Missouri and Iowa railroad promoters an equal chance to develop the routes they favored.

Douglas listened sympathetically. (The idea of two territories, incidentally, had been suggested before as a way to please both North and South and was not as novel as Hadley Johnson liked to think.) The Illinois Senator owned real estate both in Chicago and at the western tip of Lake Superior, and a bill that allowed a railroad to cross any part of the northern Indian country would enhance property values in both regions. The touchy South, however, was not likely to allow the formation of a territory from which slavery was excluded. Nor were Northerners likely to allow an indiscriminate spread of slavery throughout the remaining

wilderness. But if *two* territories were formed, every section could find a route for a railroad; and if the settlers of each of the new territories were allowed to decide for themselves whether or not to permit slavery—free-soilers in Nebraska, slaveholders in Kansas . . . ah, there was a reasonable compromise!

Douglas—the little steam engine in britches, his friends called him—was not being baldly expedient. As a practical politician he believed in give-and-take. As a Westerner he insisted on the right of free individuals to determine their own destinies. If the future inhabitants of Kansas wished slavery and those of Nebraska did not, who had a better right than they to say so?

On January 19, 1854, Douglas proposed to the Senate's Pacific Railroad Committee the building of three transcontinental lines financed by government land grants—one in the North, one across the central plains, a third through Texas and southern New Mexico. Meanwhile he was hard at work in his own Committee on Territories. On January 23, it produced his brain child—the Kansas-Nebraska Bill, which repealed the Missouri Compromise and submitted popular sovereignty in its place.

Backed by President Pierce as an Administration measure, the bill was pushed through to passage on May 25. Squatters immediately began pouring across the border. Some of these newcomers were the usual adventurers, hoping to cash in by being first on the scene. Many more were ordinary movers, looking for fresh farms on which to settle their large families. The majority came from north of the Ohio River. Very few owned slaves and as a matter of stark economics did not wish to compete with slave labor. The bias did not make them tolerant. Like their peers in Oregon who in 1857 wrote into the Oregon state constitution a clause excluding every Negro, free or slave, from the state, they wanted white neighbors only. If outside pressures had not interfered, the first-comers to Kansas probably would have created anti-slavery communities with no more than the normal amount of frontier turbulence.

Unfortunately, "popular sovereignty" guaranteed meddling. In 1854, abolitionists led by Eli Thayer and industrialist Amos A. Lawrence formed what became the New England Aid Company. Its avowed aim was to send enough free-soil squatters to Kansas to seize control of the government. A five-million-dollar capitalization and twenty thousand settlers were the figures aired by the society's exuberant propagandists.

There was utterly no chance that the group could raise that much money or recruit that many idealistic New Englanders to send west. Most of the settlers of Kansas came without its help. The first Emigrant Aid party, founders of the antislavery town of Lawrence, forty miles west of the Indian settlement of Wyandotte City, consisted of twenty-nine persons. During the rest of 1854 approximately seven hundred more Emigrant Aid settlers followed. Perhaps nine hundred reached Kansas the next year. This was hardly a population surge, but rumor roared swiftly off ahead of reality. Twenty thousand free-soilers supported by five million dollars! David Atchison and his proslavery adherents reacted with furies of resentment. One Fourth of July orator screeched in 1854, "I am ready to go, the first hour that it shall be announced that the emigrants have come, and with my own hands, will help hang every one of them on the first tree." And he was not alone in such sentiments.

The election to choose Kansas' delegate to Congress came in that fall, 1854. Seventeen hundred Missourians, one group led in person by David Atchison, galloped across the border. Some of them made a cynical gesture toward establishing residence by cutting blazes on trees or driving claim stakes as evidence of their intent to pre-empt farms. They then voted, changed their minds about staying, and went home. Others did not even bother to pretend. Of the 2,871 ballots counted, at least half were fraudulent. Nevertheless, the newly appointed territorial governor, fat Andrew Reeder, a Democratic party wheel horse from Pennsylvania, certified the election of the proslavery candidate, John W. Whitfield.

Elated by the success, five thousand Missourians—"enough," Atchison boasted, "to kill every God-damned abolitionist in the Territory"—crossed the line in March, 1855, with flags, bands, and even artillery, to rig the election for legislators. The body they chose promptly passed laws limiting office holding in Kansas to proslavery men, decreed the death penalty for helping a slave escape, and authorized two years' imprisonment for anyone who questioned the legality of slavery in the territory.

This was too much even for Governor Reeder. He challenged the returns from some of the more flagrant precincts. He vetoed the legislative acts (they were re-passed over his veto) and went to Washington to protest personally to the President. Instead he landed in hot water: Indian Commissioner George Manypenny had discovered that Reeder was mixed up in a shady scheme to purchase land from certain half-breeds for speculative purposes. The governor was removed. As his successor, President Pierce named Wilson Shannon, a proslavery hack from Cincinnati. Since the judiciary was also controlled by proslavery sympathizers, the hold of the South on the territory seemed unbreakable.

Angry free-soilers decided to outflank the enemy by forming a "state"—illegally, since only Congress could pass the necessary enabling act. They set their election for December 15, 1855. Uproar was instantaneous. Twelve hundred bullyboys marched from Missouri to seize the town of Lawrence, stronghold of the state makers. Free-soilers flocked to defend the hamlet. At the last moment Governor Shannon had second thoughts about unleashing civil war and arranged a truce. Unopposed, the free-soilers formed their state—hardly a representative entity, since slavery advocates abstained from voting on the proposed constitution.

Pierce refused to recognize Kansas State. This left the fraudulently elected proslavery territorial legislature the only government. A seething indignation filled the North. They would send in enough money, men, and arms really to guarantee the next election. Preacher Henry Ward Beecher donated twenty-five Bibles and added twenty-five Sharps rifles, which thereafter were known in Kansas as "Beecher's Bibles." Farther south, Colonel Jefferson Buford marched out of Alabama with his own Bibles, Sharps rifles, and four hundred fighting men. In western Missouri a newspaper screamed, "Blood for Blood! . . . all [imported free-soilers] who do not leave immediately for the East, *will leave for eternity!*"

The spark came in the spring of 1856 when Sheriff Samuel Jones of Douglas County, a slavery man, visited Lawrence to make a routine arrest. Someone shot him. Friends spirited Jones away and pretended he was dead. Investigators dispatched by the territorial government to subpoena witnesses reported that they were obstructed by disorderly persons. Chief Justice Samuel Lecompte, a hard-drinking proslavery lawyer from Maryland, thereupon ordered the grand jury to indict Lawrence's leading free-soilers for treason. The jury not only obliged but added indictments for sedition against Lawrence's two newspapers, and also against the hotel on the ground that it was a gathering place of undesirables.

The serving of these papers was entrusted to the United States Marshal, J. B. Donaldson. Anticipating resistance, Donaldson marched into the town on May 21, 1856, with a posse of eight hundred proslavery men. Atchison was among them. Colonel Buford and one hundred of his Alabamans appeared. Less noticeable but also present was the "deceased," Sheriff Jones.

The townspeople of Lawrence agreed among themselves to surrender without resistance to the authority of the United States. Marshal Donaldson thereupon ordered the posse to disband and went off to dinner with Atchison, Buford, and other leaders of both sides. Instead of dispersing, the posse—an illegitimate mob now—surged up in front of the hotel and newspaper offices. Jones showed himself. A roaring cheer went up. Despite

A contemporary of John Brown in "Bleeding Kansas" was Dr. John Doy (seated), who was kidnapped for stealing slaves and setting them free. Lawrence friends posed with him in this picture after rescuing him from a Missouri jail.

their earlier ranting, Atchison and Buford rushed out and pleaded for calm. It was no use. Jones had control. A red flag emblazoned "Southern Rights" waved, and the mob went to work. It destroyed both newspaper plants, ransacked the hotel, then gutted it with fire, and burned down the home of the antislavery "state" governor.

On May 20, the day before the raid, Charles Sumner of Massachusetts finished in the United States Senate a two-day speech as intemperate in its way as the action at Lawrence. During the diatribe he sprinkled aspersions on Senator Andrew Butler of South Carolina, who was absent from the chamber. On May 22, the day after the attack on Lawrence, Senator Butler's six-foot nephew, Congressman Preston Brooks, also of South Carolina, approached Sumner as he sat at his Senate desk and beat him insensible with a cane. During the next weeks, jubilant Southerners showered Congressman Brooks with testimonial canes of many sorts.

Word of the attack on Sumner flashed swiftly to Kansas over the new electromagnetic telegraph. On May 24 it reached a wild-eyed patriarch named John Brown, who even then was leading a stealthy group of eight men, four of them his own sons, toward Pottawatomie Creek. Each of them was armed with a heavy, short saber. When they heard the news of the attack, one

of them recalled later, "The men went crazy—*crazy.*"

During the warm spring night, they reached proslavery territory. They knocked at the door of lonely cabins, dragged the men who answered outside, and methodically hacked or shot them to death—five, all told. Now the North had its hero to approve, one whose obsessions would not end until he was martyred, as some interpreted it, at Harpers Ferry three years later.

During the rest of the summer the territory earned the name that history still uses: "Bleeding Kansas." Border ruffians from both sides murdered an estimated two hundred people, destroyed crops, burned and pillaged. The disintegration, which in Kansas was manifested by violence, showed itself in a variety of other ways throughout the rest of the nation.

The Whig party crumbled. As the Presidential election of 1856 drew near, dissatisfied Northerners flocked to the new Republican party and its nominee, explorer John Charles Frémont. Southerners retorted by swinging to the Democratic party and pushed James Buchanan into the White House in a close election. When the Supreme Court the following year declared in its sinuously reasoned Dred Scott decision that Congress could not bar slavery from the territories, Northern wrath swelled higher. Lincoln crystallized the resentment during his debates with Douglas, then gathered more Western support when Buchanan in 1860 vetoed a homestead (free land) bill that finally had squeaked through both Houses of Congress after a decade of defeats. The Democrats meanwhile had fallen into a bitter split. Thanks to that, the Republicans won the 1860 election, and for the first time in American history a man from the frontier Northwest, as Illinois at that time was designated, became the President of the United States.

The Wyandot Indians, who had played their small part in launching the cataclysm, got what they thought they wanted. In 1855 they became citizens and divided their communal lands into individual holdings. Then a conservative minority of about three hundred reconsidered. Using funds obtained by the sale of their Kansas homes, they bought from Seneca Indians an area near the Neosho River in the northeastern part of the last remaining Indian country (today's Oklahoma), moved there, and reinstated their old forms of tribal government. Other bands retreated before the whites to other parts of Indian Territory, and by 1868 very few natives were still making their homes in Kansas.

Sectionalism also shattered Douglas's railroad plans. The Senate committee that during early 1854 discussed his proposal for three lines to the coast was appalled by the cost and on March 2 recommended a single road instead. The Republican platform of 1856 proposed building this single line up "the most central and practical route." By that time, however, North and South—Chicago, St. Louis, Memphis, Vicksburg, and New Orleans—were clutching so fiercely for control of the line and were so suspicious of each other that nothing concrete could possibly be achieved by a direct approach.

California decided on an indirect attack. On May 28, 1856, Senator John B. Weller of that state presented to Congress two enormous leather-bound, gilt-stamped books containing a petition signed by seventy-five thousand Californians calling for the construction of a transcontinental wagon road via the familiar Platte Valley–South Pass–Humboldt River route. Since hundreds upon hundreds of wagons had been traversing the stretch for years without government help, this massive appeal seemed to smack of redundancy. To be sure, improvements were possible. Grades could be gentled, streams bridged. Accurate surveys could determine which of the variants along the way really were the shortest. But the purpose behind Weller's proposal, as most congressmen realized, was to prepare the public mind for a railroad by first building a humbler wagon way. As a bonus the road might also demonstrate, by staying open all winter, that a central crossing of the country, the route that was

favored by most Californians, in fact would prove more practical than Southern scoffers were willing to admit.

As proposed by Weller, this central road was to start at Fort Kearney, Nebraska. It would end either at Honey Lake near California's northeast boundary, where easy passes across the Sierra existed, or at the little Mormon settlement of Genoa, just south of today's Carson City, Nevada. These limitations, halting the road at the California border, were the result of an opinion, prevalent in the 1850's, that Federal aid to improvements within state borders was unconstitutional. Weller and his allies concentrated therefore on the territories, over which Congress had full control.

In order to win broad geographic support for the measure, Weller added other routes. Southerners, who already had Army-road connections through San Antonio, Texas, with El Paso, and through Fort Smith, Arkansas, with Fort Defiance, west of Albuquerque, were promised extensions of those roads to the Colorado River boundary of southern California. The El Paso extension would end at Fort Yuma, and the other, near the Mohave villages, some fifteen miles north of present-day Needles.

Northerners were promised a branch line that would run from Fort Ridgely, Minnesota Territory, to the vicinity of South Pass and there join the central route. Minnesota, incidentally, was a more logical starting place for a road to California than may appear today. The territory was experiencing a phenomenal growth. In 1853 the United States had ratified a treaty, signed in 1851 by the Sioux, that confined those Indians to a narrow reservation embracing both banks of the upper St. Peter's (now Minnesota) River and opened the rest of their rich prairie lands in the territory to settlement. In 1854–55, Chippewa cessions yielded up the lumber country in the north. Non-Indian population jumped from 6,077 in 1850 to an estimated 150,000 in 1857.

Tingling with this inpouring of energy, Minnesotans changed the name of their metropolis from Pig's Eye to St. Paul and began dreaming of their state as the new heartland of the West. Not Chicago, not St. Louis, but one of their own strident cities, so they proclaimed, was the logical terminus of a railway to the gold fields and ocean ports of the Pacific coast. Senator Weller of California was willing to nod agreement, at least insofar as a branch wagon road from Fort Ridgely to South Pass might help him garner votes for his central route.

The War Department was the logical supervisor of any road work in the wilderness. Its topographical engineers were experienced in Western exploration. It understood procurement and supply, for during the early 1850's it had built scores of miles of military roads in Minnesota,

Oregon, Washington, Utah, and New Mexico. But the Secretary of War was Jefferson Davis, a Southerner, and Weller questioned Davis's impartiality toward a central road that might be precursor to a railway. The Californian therefore asked the Senate to transfer control of territorial road building to the relatively new (1849) Department of the Interior.

A digression of sorts is necessary. During the debates on the road measure, the perils of Western travel were gruesomely underscored by tragedies befalling two companies of impoverished Mormon emigrants traveling across the plains under the auspices of the church's Perpetual Emigrating Fund. The fund was shrunken that year. In the fall of 1855 grasshoppers had plagued crops in Utah, and during the subsequent winter, blizzards had played havoc with livestock; in Cache Valley alone, twenty-three hundred cattle from a single herd of twenty-six hundred had frozen to death. As a result of the widespread losses, there was a falling off in contributions to the Emigrating Fund, designed to help European converts reach their faith's promised land. In order that these dependents might still be moved in 1856, in spite of lack of money for buying wagons and draft animals to transport them, Brigham Young suggested handcarts.

Mounted on a single axle and covered with hooped canvas, the handcart was a shallow wooden box capable of carrying on its two wheels three to five hundred pounds of luggage. Shafts protruding from the front of the box were connected at their outer ends by a transverse wooden bar. Emigrants stood between the shafts and moved the carts by pushing on the bars—human draft animals trudging fourteen hundred miles from eastern Iowa to northern Utah. At a rough average, one handcart served five persons. Wagons, approximately one to each seventy-five persons, hauled communal provisions. There were never enough tents—as few, in instances, as one for twenty people. Anyone who fell too sick to walk (and cholera ravaged the trail again in 1856) had to be added to the load in his family's cart.

During the spring, while carpenters in Iowa City built carts and seamstresses stitched covers, eight chartered ships crossed the Atlantic with 4,395 Welsh and English converts, far more than the workers in the United States expected. Half of the newcomers were able to pay for passage in well-organized wagon trains, but 2,012 of them, scourings of the factory towns, had to depend on the Perpetual Emigrating Fund. The average age of the adults was higher than in most pioneer bands. Women outnumbered men. There were widows with families, and even blind men and cripples. Most of the children were scrawny and pale; many of them died in Iowa's sul-

try heat before the columns even started out for Utah.

Three companies totaling about nine hundred people got off during June. Brigham had said that an efficient group ought to be able to cross the plains through rain, sandstorms, and sun glare in seventy days. The relentless leaders assigned to the companies set out to prove him right, even passing wagon trains in their zeal—save for three dozen or so (there seems no exact tally) who literally walked themselves to death in testimony to their faith.

Late in June the final fifteen hundred immigrants poured into Iowa City. The unprepared workers there had to scurry about finding wagons for four hundred travelers who had paid their passage in advance. Far more dismaying, the organizers also had to hammer together out of green lumber two hundred and fifty hand-

A Mormon handcart company, financed by the Perpetual Emigrating Fund, fights on west through a blizzard on the plains.

carts for the destitute. They managed with amazing dispatch. Five hundred people under Captain James Willie departed from Iowa City on July 15. Another five hundred and seventy-six under Captain Edward Martin followed them eleven days later.

Sand wore out the wooden axles. Green lumber shrank in the dry air. Carts fell apart; delays mounted. At Fort Laramie the toilers discovered that earlier trains had stripped the shelves and they could not replenish their food stocks. Half-starved, they crawled along the North Platte and turned up Sweetwater Creek.

In October the blizzards struck. After dragging the carts all day, the exhausted men and women, their wet clothing freezing on them, had to stagger out to find fuel in an almost woodless land. Often it was not enough, and there were cases of men who went to sleep in the arms of their wives for mutual warmth and died without waking.

Rescuers pushed out from Salt Lake City. Heroism was a commonplace, but for a fifth of the immigrants it came too late. More than two hundred people died. Dozens of others were crippled for life from the loss of their frostbitten limbs. Yet in spite of the catastrophe—and possibly because Brigham Young wished to justify the experiment—upwards of a thousand people crossed the plains with handcart companies during the three following summers. It was cheap. One group made the fourteen-hundred-mile trip at an expenditure of $22.30 per person. Public roads, if they had existed, might have brought the expenditures of energy within reason as well.

During the closing days of Pierce's administration, while stragglers of the Willie and Martin debacle were still being helped into Salt Lake City, Congress passed the last of two bills appropriating six hundred thousand dollars for surveying and building the Western wagon roads that Senator Weller had proposed. The largest amount, three hundred thousand dollars, was assigned to the central route, and an additional fifty thousand dollars was added for the branch from Fort Ridgely, Minnesota, to South Pass. The southern route from El Paso to Fort Yuma was awarded two hundred thousand dollars. The remaining fifty thousand dollars was allocated to the distant stretch that lay between Fort Defiance and the Mohave villages.

A related problem for Weller and his colleague from California, Senator William Gwin, was mail service. Until 1856, letters to the coast had traveled either by the circuitous, twice-a-month Panama route or by the once-a-month connection through Salt Lake City. In August of that year, Western pressures made a small gain by winning from the Post Office Department another twice-a-month service, this one to run between San Antonio and remote San Diego. This route by no means satisfied California's populous northern areas, however, and Weller kept hammering away at Congress. In March, 1857, almost simultaneously with the road bill, he won a subsidy of six hundred thousand dollars for linking the Mississippi Valley with San Francisco. The Post Office bill authorizing the sum called for an elapsed time on the run of no more than twenty-five days. To avoid a sectional fight during debate, it specified that the successful contractor was to choose the route he preferred to follow.

Nine groups entered bids. Prominent among them was a syndicate headed by a personal friend of President Buchanan, John Butterfield, a highly able New York expressman. Butterfield's associates in the syndicate included board members of the nation's four major express companies, notably William Fargo of Wells, Fargo &

Company. Their long-range intent was a monopoly that eventually could wrest not only California mail but passenger and freight service as well from the Pacific Mail Steamship Company. With so large a stake at issue, the Butterfield group was willing to play along with whatever the Administration suggested.

All nine of the bidders naturally considered the mileage involved in reaching San Francisco, and not one of them named a route any farther south than Albuquerque. This did not suit President Buchanan's new Postmaster General, Aaron Brown of Tennessee. In direct violation of the appropriation bill, he specified that the eastern branches of the line must begin at St. Louis and Memphis, unite at Little Rock (later the junction point was changed to Fort Smith), and swing through Texas to the vicinity of El Paso. From that point, he said, it should follow "the new road being opened and constructed under the direction of the Secretary of the Interior, to Fort Yuma, California; thence, through the best passes and along the best valleys . . . to San Francisco."

This "ox-bow route," as one indignant newspaper termed it, added six hundred miles to the longest line suggested by the bidders. Brown, of course, defended himself. His southern route, he said, would stimulate commercial relations with Mexico, would give impetus to the mines being opened in what is now southern Arizona, and would enjoy better weather and easier mountain grades than lines farther north. Protest nevertheless was instantaneous. A "foul wrong," cried the Sacramento *Union*. "One of the greatest swindles ever perpetrated upon the country by the slave holders," was the way the Chicago *Tribune* described the plan.

Because of the help that the new El Paso–Fort Yuma road would give them, all nine contractors agreed to let their original bids stand for the southern route also. On September 15, 1857, the contract was awarded to the Butterfield Overland Stage Company. Twice-a-week mail service by way of Fort Smith, El Paso, and Fort Yuma was to begin one year later, September 15, 1858. The South was triumphant.

During the summer of 1857, while Butterfield was edging in as the favorite of the Post Office Department, the road builders took to the field. Through a clerical error in printing the bills, the fifty-thousand-dollar project from Fort Defiance to the Mohave villages remained under the supervision of the War Department. The man in charge of the work was a onetime naval lieutenant turned civilian, Edward Beale. Beale, who by this time had become a veteran frontiersman, added an exotic touch to his road work: his party used twenty-five camels as pack animals. The camels performed their functions well. So, indeed, did all of Beale's expedition.

It was the only one that did. Although the Secretary of the Interior picked competent engineers for the other three groups, the superintendents turned out to be another breed entirely. James Leach, of the El Paso–Fort Yuma road, was accused first of "frisking, gambling, and frolicking" and later indicted for fraud. The Fort Ridgely road, which incurred the wrath of the Indians by starting a rush of speculators for townsites along the right of way, reached no closer to its proposed destination than the Missouri River in what is today South Dakota. Meanwhile the central route, for which three hundred thousand dollars had been appropriated, fell into the hands of a rascal named William M. F. Magraw.

Magraw knew the country well. From 1854 until the middle of 1856 he had held a contract for carrying mail once a month from Independence, Missouri, to Salt Lake City. Because of the high claims Magraw entered in compensation for loss to Indians, the Postmaster General canceled the contract and turned it over to a Mormon who was backed by Brigham Young. Furious, Magraw joined the chorus of anti-Mormon protests filling Congress. And that leads into another digression connected with the turbulent history of Utah.

Clashes between the Mormon Church and a series of Federal judges sent from the East had raged steadily from 1851 to 1856. In 1856 three Mormon lawyers raided the office of their newest bête noire, Justice George P. Stiles, heaped his lawbooks and personal papers in a privy, and burned them—but did not touch official court records, as Stiles later charged. Stiles's colleague, Justice W. W. Drummond (who took a mistress to Utah and passed her off as his wife while denouncing the lewdness of church-sanctioned polygamy), declared Utah law to be in error and refused to recognize the decisions of the Mormon probate courts. Retreating to Washington from the bitter antagonism he aroused, Drummond wrote the Attorney General of the United States an open letter in which he accused the Mormons of inciting Indians to kill surveyor John Gunnison in 1853, of poisoning a Federal official named Leonidas Shaver, and of sending private assassins called Danites out to the plain to murder Territorial Secretary Almon W. Babbitt, who himself was a Mormon. Disgruntled freighters, Indian agents, surveyors, travelers—and William Magraw—added more charges of murder, corruption, and lawlessness. The Mormons' arrogant defiance of all outside "interference" did nothing to soften the exaggerated charges. By May, 1857, the uproar had reached such a pitch that President Buchanan declared Utah to be in open rebellion, appointed Alfred Cumming governor in Brigham Young's place, and ordered Colonel Albert Sidney Johnston to march west with an army of twenty-six hundred men.

Moving the Army's four and a half million pounds of supplies was the responsibility of the giant freighting firm of Russell, Majors & Waddell, which held a monopoly on all Army transport west of the Missouri River. For handling the job, they assembled forty-one wagon

Soon after road-builder Edward F. Beale began trying to use Arabian dromedaries in the arid Southwest, miners imported Mongolian camels to Nevada (above). The Westerners did not take to the animals, however, and the use of camels was eventually abandoned.

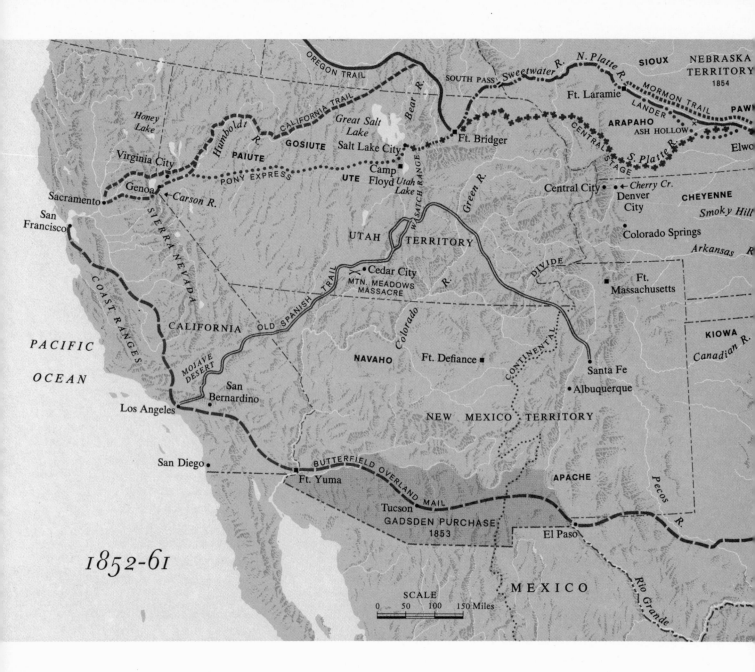

trains. The long strings of ponderous vehicles could well have used help from road builder William Magraw and his hundred roustabouts. Magraw, however, was drinking excessively, muddling his reports, and planning with mountain man Tim Goodale to haul, quite illegally, three tons of liquor to Fort Laramie, to soothe the huge thirst Johnston's soldiers would develop while marching up the Platte Valley. Save for a little grade smoothing by Magraw's crews near Ash Hollow in western Nebraska, the advance wagon trains had to prepare their own wheelways as they lumbered off toward Utah.

Word of the coming invasion reached the Saints on July 24, 1857, the tenth anniversary of the Mormons' arrival in Salt Lake Valley. Intense excitement shook the territory. More persecution—as the Mormons saw it. Young alerted the militia and made plans for fighting back. Colonists in San Bernardino, California, and also at Genoa in the Carson Valley were instructed to dispose of their property, buy as much ammunition as possible, and hurry to Utah to join their beleaguered brethren. Food was to be stock-piled. Emissaries were sent among the Indians, urging unity against the common enemy.

Into this tension came the Fancher Company of one hundred and forty emigrants bound from Arkansas to California. It was traveling late and did not reach Salt Lake City until August 3 or 4. Fearful of meeting snow in the Sierra if they continued due west, the emigrants swung south on the trail to Los Angeles. When the

The principal emigrant and express trails to the West, and the sites of important events while the frontier continued to move forward during the decade from 1852 to 1861, are located above.

been used to shoot the guts out of Prophet Joseph Smith. All of them snarled that soon the United States Army would teach these lecherous polygamists a lesson that would make the destruction of Nauvoo look like a picnic.

Certain church officials in Cedar City in southern Utah decided, on their own authority, that as a justifiable first step in the coming war, they would prevail on a band of Utes to exterminate the party. The attack came at daybreak on either September 7 or 8, 1857, at a grassy swale called Mountain Meadows. Driven off after having killed seven men and wounding perhaps thirteen more, the Indians settled to a siege. Three of the migrants tried to ride for help. Indians killed two; a Mormon killed the third. Fearing implication if the train escaped, the Mormons decided to finish the job themselves.

Entering the camp under a white flag on September 11, John D. Lee prevailed on the emigrants, by then desperately short of ammunition, to accept an extraordinary plan in exchange for a promise of safe escort to Cedar City, thirty-five miles away. The eighteen youngest children were loaded into a wagon and sent off ahead. The most seriously wounded followed in another wagon. Behind the second wagon straggled the women and older children. At the rear walked the men, unarmed and in single file, each individual under the watchful eye of an armed Mormon guard.

After the wagon of children had pulled out of sight around the hill, someone gave a signal. Indians rose from ambush with knives and hatchets to dispatch the wounded, the women, and the older children. The escort turned on the men. About one hundred and twenty people died; the exact toll remains unknown. The littlest children, who did not see the slaughter, were spared on the ground that they would never remember enough to bear witness. Eventually seventeen of them were surrendered and returned to relatives. One, a girl, evidently grew up as a Mormon and married among them.

The Mountain Meadows Massacre occurred September 11. On September 15, Brigham Young, who knew nothing of the horror until after it had happened, declared martial law. "CITIZENS OF UTAH—We are invaded by a hostile force. . . ." Guerrillas moved toward what today is the southwestern corner of Wyoming, where the advance units of Johnston's army and the first supply trains were beginning to rendezvous. On the night of October 4, raiders under Lot Smith burned three trains and made off with seven hundred cattle. Army groups, swinging toward Bear River in an effort to outflank the Mormon forts in the deep canyons of the Wasatch Mountains, found the fall-dry grass burned ahead of them. Oxen grew gaunt with starvation; trains began to

travelers tried to buy supplies, the Mormons, who were stockpiling, refused them with a toplofty contempt that was born in part of a religious revival then sweeping the territory. Annoyed, the emigrants snapped the heads off chickens with their whips, turned their cattle into Mormon fields, and began shouting that the Mormon women were whores. Missourians who were among the travelers boasted of having been at Haun's Mill, where in 1838 a mob had killed seventeen Mormons and had wounded fifteen, including several children. One emigrant bragged that he carried with him the gun that had creak to a halt. Then the snows came. Realizing he could not reach Salt Lake City that season, Johnston ordered the Army into winter quarters at what remained of the famous Fort Bridger.

The stockaded trading post had been taken from Bridger by the church in 1853 during the Wakara War on the ground that the old mountain man was selling guns and ammunition to the Utes; together with Fort Supply, nearby, the place had then been developed into a haven for incoming immigrants. At Johnston's approach the Mormon defenders burned both spots and the surrounding forage, and fled. So many Army horses starved or froze that enlisted men had to harness themselves to sleds and drag firewood from the mountains on foot. Growing desperate, Johnston late in November ordered one of the West's great frontiersmen, Captain Randolph Marcy, to ride with sixty soldiers and mountain men south for reinforcements to Fort Massachusetts in the San Luis Valley of present Colorado, a dangerous trip through the heart of the snow-laden central Rockies.

By this time, William Magraw had abandoned road building altogether in favor of fighting his old enemies, the Mormons. He turned his wagons and stock over to Johnston, who was short of both, volunteered his own services, and persuaded most of his workers to follow him. In the end it turned out that there was no need either of Magraw's gesture or of the wagon train of food, the five companies of soldiers, and the fifteen hundred head of livestock that Captain Marcy brought back after a nearly fatal trip across the Continental Divide.

Brigham Young had had second thoughts. Realizing that when spring came he could no longer keep the Army out of Utah, the Mormon leader had threatened to burn the northern settlements and march his people south, away from the invaders, in still another desperate flight to . . . the destination remained indefinite.

Whether he meant business or was executing a masterly propaganda stroke (it stirred powerful sympathy in the East, where the truth of Mountain Meadows was still unknown) cannot be said. In any event, the evacuation had begun when Thomas Kane, a non-Mormon friendly to Young and his followers, appeared in Salt Lake City after a difficult trip by way of Panama and Los Angeles. From Salt Lake City, Kane rode to Fort Bridger, picked up Governor-designate Alfred Cumming, and brought him back to Utah for talks with Young. The upshot was a compromise. The Mormons were pardoned by Buchanan for their "rebellion." (They considered the affair another persecution.) Young yielded his governorship to Cumming, but as head of the church continued to be the most powerful man in the territory. The Army agreed not to settle in Salt Lake City but instead to establish its headquarters, Camp Floyd, in the barren country that stretched west of Utah Lake.

Well before this time, Magraw had been replaced as superintendent of the central road project by his own chief engineer, Frederick Lander, a veteran of Isaac I. Stevens's northern railroad survey of 1853. The Lander Cut-off, which the new superintendent built west from South Pass, was of scant help to the residents of Utah. Although it provided good pasturage for the wagon trains and large herds of livestock that were being moved west each summer, the Lander road stayed well to the north of the Mormon settlements.

To the new mail contractors who had to serve Salt Lake City—John M. Hockaday in the east and George Chorpenning in the west—time was more important than grass. Ignoring the Lander Cut-off and relying in part on the trail blazing of Army surveyors hunting a short way to Camp Floyd, the pair opened a direct run through Fort Bridger to Salt Lake City and on across the grisly deserts that had betrayed the Donner party in 1846. Such hay as Chorpenning needed at his stations on the desolate western leg of the route he imported from Mormon ranches in Utah and the Carson Valley.

Between them the two men had a subsidy of three hundred and twenty thousand dollars for carrying the mail once a week over their nineteen-hundred-mile line in an elapsed time of thirty-eight days. Since their route was much shorter than John Butterfield's southern ox-bow loop, they were sure they could outspeed him if granted equal money—six hundred thousand dollars.

It would not be easy. Butterfield had spent a million dollars distributing eighteen hundred horses and mules at one hundred and sixty-five wooden and adobe stations strung across the wilderness. Mail and passengers were whisked over the desolate central portions of the route in "celerity wagons," light vehicles covered with a flat top and equipped with side curtains to keep out some of the dust and rain. At either end, ornate Concord coaches took over, their egg-shaped bodies cradled in leather thorough braces designed to protect the horses, not the passengers, from excessive jolting. Service was launched with calculated fanfare on September 15, 1858. (The eastern terminus had been shifted to the railhead at Tipton, in central Missouri.) Both the east and west runs were completed in roughly twenty-four days, which meant that the coaches maintained an astounding average of nearly one hundred and twenty miles a day. This rate was maintained by traveling by night as well as day, a testimonial to the skill of the drivers—and to the stamina of passengers—for long stretches of the route proved to be noth-

A Butterfield Stage Line "celerity wagon" crossing the desert near Tucson was sketched by William H. Hilton in 1859. The springless seats of this vehicle had one advantage: the backs could be let down to make a bed of sorts.

ing more than jolting, rock-strewn tracks across the land.

In October, 1858, service began on still another California route, this one out of New Orleans by steamer and across the narrowest part of Mexico to Tehuantepec Bay. Hockaday and Chorpenning thought they could beat it too—in winter, to quiet Southern talk about snow —and spent eight thousand dollars scattering temporary camps eighteen miles apart along their central route.

Batons in this three-way race were to be advance copies of Buchanan's December message to Congress, which Government agents were supposed to deliver simultaneously to each contender. None reached Hockaday's starter, however. He had to wait eight days for a newspaper version. The other lines received their copies on schedule, and Butterfield pulled triumphantly into San Francisco early on December 26, after an elapsed time of twenty-two days. The ocean-borne copy arrived December 28. Chorpenning's weary man appeared on January 1, 1859—but his elapsed time was only seventeen days, twelve hours. The central route, said the San Francisco

Bulletin in grim summation of what had occurred, had been the victim of "jugglery" when it should have won.

No record says, incidentally, how Chorpenning's newspaper copy crossed the Sierra. If snow was deep, it probably was carried by Snowshoe Thompson, a vast bear of a man, who several times during the winter of 1858–59 loaded a hundred-pound mail sack on his back and toiled over the drifted summit on "Norwegian snowshoes"—today we would call them skis. More dependable even than Thompson was a telegraph line that Frederick Bee had completed that fall (1858) from Sacramento to Genoa, stringing much of the wire from tree to tree. But of course a telegraph line could not transport written documents or personal letters.

Two sudden mining rushes, the first into what became Colorado and the other soon thereafter into present-day Nevada, added still more pressure to Western demands for better mail and stage service along the central route. Indians were the initiators of the Colorado excitement. In 1850 a party of Cherokees and white relatives from

293

the gold fields at Dahlonega, Georgia, had crossed the area en route to California. Pausing along the way to prospect, they had detected glints of gold in the streams that shimmer out of the eastern foothills of the Rockies into the South Platte River. It had not been enough to detain them then. Later, after they had returned home and the panic of 1857 had closed over the East, they remembered. Early in 1858 William Green Russell—he boasted a Cherokee wife and wore his beard in two neat braids—led a party of whites and Indians from Dahlonega westward up the Arkansas River. Along the way they joined forces by prearrangement with a party of Cherokees from Indian Territory under the leadership of a red Baptist preacher named John Beck.

While Russell had been making his plans in Georgia, two Delaware Indians of eastern Kansas, Fall Leaf and Little Beaver, had guided an Army detachment against Northern Cheyennes who had been raiding emigrant trains near Fort Kearney, and then had ridden off toward the Rockies to hunt. Somewhere near the foothills, according to one story, the pair met Missourians who had paused to prospect while riding home from the Utah hullabaloo. From those whites the Delawares obtained a few grains of gold they carried with them in a goose quill to Lawrence, Kansas. Depression-ruined townspeople, led by the butcher, John Easter, began saying, "Remember California? Why can't it happen again?" And so, when spring made travel possible once more, eleven covered wagons from Lawrence started west a few days behind the Russell party. Here and there others fell in with both groups. When finally the parties joined near the confluence of Cherry Creek and the South Platte River (the Denver railroad yards are there now), they numbered more than a hundred men.

They unearthed very little gold. Discouraged, the Indians and most of the whites went home. Russell too went east, but he was sanguine enough over the traces of metal he had seen so that he intended to return in the spring with supplies and fresh recruits. In eastern Kansas he found that rumor had built up a thundering head of excitement. On September 4, 1858, the *Weekly Press* of Elwood, Kansas, carried this frantic headline:

GOLD! GOLD!! GOLD!!! GOLD!!!!

Russell tried to cool the heat. The gold fields had not been proved, he said, and he even mentioned the discouraged returnees of his own party. If a mass of unprepared, undersupplied greenhorns rushed recklessly west and found nothing, the hardships would be terrible. No one heeded him. Although the season was late, a few small parties started immediately for the diggings. Thousands more, the exact number indeterminate now, waited

for the first thin showing of spring and then swarmed across the plains. A few walked, pushing a dab of supplies in wheelbarrows or carrying them in knapsacks. Some ingenious hopefuls rigged huge sails onto their wagons— and generally ended upside down in ravines. Companies that traveled in more normal fashion with pack trains and wagons discovered too late, as their animals faltered and died, that the new grass had not yet sprouted. Seeking short cuts, hundreds thronged directly up the Republican and Smoky Hill forks of the Kansas River and found themselves on the dry, barren plains of what is now eastern Colorado. Late blizzards roared; the trail was littered with discarded goods.

Many people died. When the survivors reached Cherry Creek, they experienced total anticlimax.

Only two men were actually at work in the mountains, twenty miles farther west. One was George Jackson of Missouri, a cousin of Kit Carson's. The other was an unkempt, red-bearded Georgian named John Gregory. Traveling separately, the two men had heard at Fort Laramie that some crazy gold seekers were at work off to the south, and they had come down to have a look. Bored a little later by the inactivity that winter laid on the Cherry Creek camp, they had moved, still separately, onto different forks of Clear Creek, a nearby foothill stream. Jackson, who was using his hunting knife as a shovel, settled near the site of today's Idaho Springs. Gregory located a few miles north of him, across a high ridge. Neither knew of the other's whereabouts.

The Cherry Creekers meanwhile were gambling incessantly, drinking the Taos Lightning that the old trader, Uncle Dick Wootton, had brought north to swap with Arapaho Indians, and laying out, on paper, rival, speculative townsites—Montana City, Auraria, St. Charles, and, in honor of James W. Denver, who served at the

A view of the times shows a "wind ship wagon," one method attempted in the race across the plains to the Colorado mines.

time as the territorial governor of Kansas, Denver City.

Paper towns were no solace to the storm-buffeted thousands who began staggering into the camp during April. This—a gold field! There wasn't work enough to earn food. Hundreds upon hundreds turned home, some numb with despair, others furious at what they believed a hoax perpetrated by speculators with town property to sell. As they met fresh thousands hurrying along their tracks they advised earnestly, "Go Back!" For years afterward, "Goback" was a term of scorn in Colorado.

A terrible confusion swept the plains. Scores did wheel around. But inertia kept thousands more plodding on.

Late in the spring, the news flashed out that both Jackson and Gregory had made rich strikes. Catching wildly at the straw, two or three thousand frantic, desperate men raced for Clear Creek.

Out on the plains uncertainty rippled once more: go back, go ahead, what should a man do? At that point, in came three newspaper men. Two were young—Henry Villard, twenty-four, of the *Cincinnati Daily Commercial*, and A. D. Richardson, twenty-six, of the *Boston Morning Journal*. The third, aged forty-nine, was Horace Greeley himself, august editor of the *New York Tribune* and long-time supporter of frontier hopes in Congress. After looking over the mines, the trio prepared a joint report to the nation, dated June 9, 1859. They listed production statistics, dazzling to unemployed workers in the Middle West, and closed with a warning about the disappointment and suffering that must occur if a rush developed "as ill advised as that of last Spring."

People already on the trail ignored the caution. An estimated thirty thousand prospectors flowed up Clear Creek into Gregory Gulch that summer, found the ground staked, and washed with new optimism into nearly every cranny on the eastern slope of the central Rockies. Here and there some of them made modest strikes—except that mining camps never admit a strike is modest. Local historians of Central City, the metropolis of Gregory Gulch, still enjoy calling its environs "the Richest Square Mile on Earth." It never was, of course. During 1862, the peak year of Colorado's early rush, the entire territory produced $3,400,000 in gold; the total for the first decade, 1858–67, approximated $25,000,000—as compared with California's peak year, 1852, of $81,295,-000 and first-decade total of $502,576,000, or (to cast briefly ahead) the $300,000,000 eventually taken from a square mile of Nevada's Comstock Lode.

Kansas farm boys were not the only people bemused by Colorado's premature rainbow. John S. Jones and William Hepburn Russell, the latter a partner in the freighting firm of Russell, Majors & Waddell (he had no blood connection with miner William Green Russell), grew so excited that they proposed a stage line from Leavenworth, Kansas, to Denver. Russell's partners, Alexander Majors and William Waddell, refused to go along with him. The Army had exceeded appropriations during the Utah war, bills for transport could not be collected, and years might pass before the company was reimbursed for wagons and oxen lost to Mormon guerrillas. Government belt-tightening, brought about by the lingering depression of 1857, had squeezed some of the fat out of their normal freight contracts to Santa Fe and Camp Floyd. This was not the year to expand.

Undeterred, Russell and Jones in April, 1859, inaugurated the Leavenworth & Pike's Peak Express Company. Forage, wages for one hundred and seventy-five men, and amortization charges against equipment came to one thousand dollars a day. On top of that, Russell agreed to pay one hundred and forty-four thousand dollars for the Independence to Salt Lake City line, controlled by J. M. Hockaday, who had been brought to the edge of ruin by Government economy measures concerning his mail subsidy. This purchase was promptly consolidated with the Pike's Peak line.

The brave new runs added up to more ambition than Colorado's gold fields could support. To keep Russell from collapsing into a bankruptcy that might swallow it too, the firm of Russell, Majors & Waddell in October, 1859, absorbed the Pike's Peak line and set up the Central Overland California & Pike's Peak Express Company. They dickered with George Chorpenning, who was also being troubled by the Government's economy measures (in May, 1860, they took his line over), and began casting thoughtful eyes toward Butterfield's subsidy. If their central route could supplant the southern line as the Government's principal carrier of mails to the West Coast, the new firm would be riding high.

To press the case, Russell went to Washington late in 1859. There he encountered Frederick Bee, who had strung the telegraph line across the Sierra and who was agitating for a Government-supported transcontinental wire along the central route. From Bee, Russell almost certainly heard of the West's second new mining fever, centered on the southern slopes of Mount Davidson in the western part of what soon became Nevada Territory.

Since 1849, thousands upon thousands of emigrants had trudged past the mouths of two small Nevada ravines that sliced down the side of the stark mountain and debouched into Carson Valley. Some travelers halted to prospect. They found gold—not much, but enough to keep a few eccentrics scratching away. As the yield dwindled, they moved higher up the slopes. Early in

1859 a small group in Gold Canyon, and another a short distance away across a ridge in Six-mile Canyon, almost simultaneously made strikes at either end of what became known as the Comstock Lode.

At first neither group realized what it had. They and a handful of hopefuls who hurried up the canyons after them were washing for gold and were annoyed by a heavy blue sand that kept clotting up in their sluice boxes. Then one of them sent a sackful of the stuff across the mountains to California for assay. Silver as well as gold—as much as $3,876 a ton! The word leaked, and a fantastic stampede developed. Almost overnight a roaring, miserable collection of tents and shanties called Virginia City sprang up on the inhospitable sides of the barren peak. As Bee undoubtedly pointed out to Russell, those people too would want mail, and they were only a few miles removed from the regular central-route stage line through Carson Valley.

Northern congressmen meanwhile were beginning to worry about the vulnerability of the southern mail route, should the slave states actually secede, as they were threatening to do. Bills proposing to shift contracts to more northern lines were introduced in both houses. At that point, someone—Russell, Bee, Senator Gwin of California, or perhaps all three of them working together—dreamed up a dazzling publicity stunt to attract attention to the central line. This was the famed pony express, designed to carry letters across half the continent in ten days by means of dashing relays of horses. Bee was interested because the speeding messengers would bridge the gap between Western and Eastern telegraph lines and he could accept telegrams in San Francisco for delivery in New York: charge $2.45 for ten words, as compared to $5.00 for a half-ounce letter. California newspapers, sick of reporting world events three weeks or more after they had happened, would be Bee's principal subscribers.

Again Russell's timing was inopportune. The freighting firm had just lost to a howling blizzard (January, 1860) thirty-three hundred of thirty-five hundred oxen being driven from Camp Floyd to California for sale. The loss was estimated at one hundred and fifty thousand dollars. Other company enterprises were in trouble. Under the circumstances, buying more horses, building stations, and hiring scores of riders as a mere stunt seemed risky indeed. But the stakes were huge. On January 27, 1860, Russell announced that the company would begin the express.

By prodigies of effort and by using stations already in operation, the firm had riders ready to go in April. The messengers ran into instant trouble—heavy snow in the Sierra and an uprising of the Great Basin's Gosiute

and Paiute tribes, made sullen by the mining stampede across their land. Though the Indians swept off scores of horses and burned a few stations, most of the riders were able to get through, sometimes by heroic feats. Buffalo Bill Cody later claimed that at the age of fifteen he rode a distance of three hundred and eighty-four miles without relief and with very little rest.

How much influence the stunt actually had on Congress is impossible to determine. In any event, a bill authorizing an eight-hundred-thousand-dollar subsidy for mail service on the central route passed the Senate but died in the House. Grandly the company announced that it would continue the pony service without a subsidy for one more year.

Finding the necessary funds was something else, however. Desperate, Russell began embezzling government bonds through a Treasury clerk who soon lost his nerve and confessed. Both men were jailed, then released on bail. The clerk vanished; Russell was freed more prosaically through the clever work of his lawyers.

As sanguine as ever, he hoped for the mail contract in 1861. Lincoln had been elected, and the South was seceding. Butterfield's line (Butterfield himself had retired as its president) was doomed. Why shouldn't the contract go to the Central Overland?

The bond scandal was too unsavory for Congress to overlook. The contract for daily mail service was offered instead to the Butterfield company, provided it shifted operations to the central route. The firm agreed, and the original Central Overland found itself reduced to working for its rival as a subcontractor along parts of the line. The pony express meantime continued shuttling back and forth between the closing ends of the telegraph line until, on October 24, 1861, the wires joined in Salt Lake City.

With Southern opposition removed from Congress, other aids desired by the West seemed attainable—a homestead law for disposing of the rest of the public domain, and a railroad up the Platte Valley and past roaring Virginia City to San Francisco. Both measures had been promised by the Republican platform, and the Republicans were in control in Washington.

The Republicans also had a war to fight. As the first terrible victories went to the South, the West began to realize that years might pass before promises could be turned into actuality. Well, the frontier was used to that. Impatient, shocked to repeated excitement by one new gold strike after another, and too far removed from the conflict to feel the East's deep agony, Westerners set about carrying on their business in as nearly a normal fashion as Confederate raiders, restless Indians, and their own lawless fellows would allow.

Stephen A. Douglas

THUNDER IN KANSAS

Historians are still debating the motives of Stephen A. Douglas in contriving the Kansas-Nebraska Act of 1854; was it to get Southern backing for a Presidential bid, or to influence the route of the proposed Western railroad—or something else again? Whatever he was after, he paid too high a price, for to get Southern support for his bill he had to back repeal of the Missouri Compromise, a statute that for some thirty years had maintained a truce between North and South. It was not surprising that the first violence resulting from the end of that truce should come in Douglas's own creation, Kansas. Open warfare raged between proslavery border ruffians from Missouri and Free State Jayhawkers; Free Staters finally won control in 1858. As the 1856 daguerreotype of a Free State artillery battery (above) shows, the fighting was more than an occasional shot from ambush.

The act bore bitter fruit for Indians, too. The two territories included almost all the Great American Desert, once promised them forever. George Manypenny, Indian Commissioner and a man of scruples, had the unpleasant duty of telling the erstwhile Eastern tribes that the Government had erred a bit when it had told them they would never have to move again. Sam Houston pleaded the case of the Indians in the Senate—but Old Sam was an eccentric who actually believed promises to Indians should be kept. By 1854, only the nomadic plains tribes and those of the far Northwest and Southwest remained free—and their turn was coming.

Making a grass bridge acost a swamp.

Edwin Whitefield was an artist who took up real estate on coming to Minnesota in 1856 and joined a company to promote new towns. The project failed—only one town survives—but Whitefield left pictures of its activities. Above, the group, including John Stevens, first Minneapolis settler, lays a grass bridge across a swamp. The first hut built in Karns City (below) was a hopeful start, but today the site is a farmer's field.

Never far behind the frontier and the first settlers came the townsite speculators who, with cords stretched between stakes driven into the prairie, tried to evoke visions of gleaming cities. In Minnesota, having her first spurt of growth in the 1850's, it was estimated that some 700 towns were platted in 1854–57. Many never got one house. The promoters ranged from enthusiasts, wanting to play a part in building up a new land, down to out-and-out swindlers. A typical example of fraud was Rollingstone on the Mississippi River in Minnesota, a site that Eastern swindlers promoted, with the aid of faked maps, as a utopian community. Some 400 settlers arrived by steamboat in 1852 and found absolutely nothing there. Some stayed on in caves and shacks; but, unequipped for pioneering, many sickened and died with cold weather. The colony was soon deserted.

THE REALTORS
MOVE WEST

The first Minneapolis real estate office (right) was set up in 1855 when the town was platted. Minneapolis later was united with the older village of St. Anthony across the river. Furniture on the St. Paul levee (below), about 1865, is an indication of the continuing emigration to Minnesota country.

NATURAL WONDERS FARTHER WEST

Washington's Palouse Falls was painted by James Alden of the Canadian boundary survey.

By the 1850's the West was no longer quite the land of the unknown that it had been. Too many mountain men, too many settlers' parties, too many government surveys had crossed the region to leave it a land of mystery. And yet, the West was so vast that there was always something new to be found. Oregon's Crater Lake did not reveal its unbelievably blue waters to the eyes of a white man until 1853. Surveyors of the Canadian-American boundary in 1859–60 traversed long, unexplored stretches along the 49th parallel between the Rockies and the sea. Captain James H. Simpson, seeking a better route across the Utah and Nevada deserts in 1859, discovered much of interest along the way. The year before, Lieutenant Joseph Ives led the first party into the bottom of the Grand Canyon; they looked up in awe when their measurements told them that they were a mile below the rim. The fascinating reports of such expeditions were a part of the magnet that continued to draw men West.

Lake Tahoe (then Lake Bigler) on Captain Simpson's route was painted by J. J. Young from an expedition sketch.

Colorado Exploring Expedition, General Report, 1857–58

F. W. von Egloffstein, with Ives's expedition, pictured the terrain near Grand Canyon. Note the tiny human figures.

THE SERENITY OF THE VIRGIN LAND

Unspoiled, the West inspired visiting artists, including Albert Bierstadt, who did this "Western Sunset."

SWEEP IT AWAY

A lumber raft is assembled on a Wisconsin stream for delivery to downriver towns.

For decades, logs and lumber were floated downriver from the pine forests of Minnesota and Wisconsin to provide housing for the growing population of the Mississippi Valley. Ard Godfrey (left), a Maine Yankee, built the first sawmill on the Falls of St. Anthony in 1849. Above are the falls, partly jammed with logs from upstream cutting.

YOUNG MAN IN A HURRY

Isaac I. Stevens

From 1855 to 1858 the Northwest was rocked by Indian wars stemming from the efforts of a young man who tried to achieve a lot in a hurry. Isaac I. Stevens was only 35 when he became first governor of Washington Territory in 1853. A West Pointer who had led the northernmost of the Pacific Railroad surveys, he envisioned a railroad from Minnesota to Puget Sound, carrying settlers to build up his territory. To clear the railroad's right of way and to gain more land for settlers, he held a whirlwind series of councils and pressured many powerful tribes into ceding their lands. When whites almost at once violated these treaties, the tribes, smarting from Stevens's pressure, fought back. Costly warfare, raging from Puget Sound to Idaho, finally ended with the Indians defeated and on reservations, and their lands in white hands.

In the Walla Walla Valley, May–June, 1855, where Stevens counciled with 5,000 Indians of the interior, an artist, Gustavus Sohon, drew this scene (below) of Nez Perces entertaining the Americans with a scalp dance.

M. & M. KAROLIK COLLECTION, MUSEUM OF FINE ARTS, BOSTON

Fort Steilacoom, west of the Cascades, was almost captured by Indians in 1855. The painting is by W. B. McMurtrie.

SMITHSONIAN INSTITUTION

CENTER AND RIGHT: WASHINGTON STATE HISTORICAL SOCIETY

Owhi, proud Yakima headman of eastern Washington, opposed selling his tribe's lands but gave in to Stevens at Walla Walla. When his people revolted, Owhi became enmeshed in the war. He surrendered to troops in 1858 and was brutally shot by his guards.

Kamiakin, drawn by Sohon at the Walla Walla council, resisted Stevens and finally led Yakimas and their allies into war after miners and settlers ignored the treaty. Later, he fled to Canada.

Peopeo Moxmox, Wallawalla headman and friend of whites, was falsely accused of hostility. Oregon volunteers, who seized him, outraged Federal troops by murdering him and mutilating his body.

307

NEW STAMPEDES

Hopeful prospectors kept on poking away in the California hills, but the chances of a loner finding much were slim after the middle 1850's; by then almost all the easy placer gold had been taken out, and deep-rock and hydraulic mining, either one requiring a great capital investment, were necessary to recover any gold. Then, in 1859, the gold hunters deserted the California streams to hurry across the mountains to Nevada's rich Comstock Lode (named for a drunken but aggressive miner who pressured the discoverers into giving him a share). It was a gold rush until they learned that the ore was much richer in silver, and strike after strike was made during the following years, reaching a climax in the Big Bonanza of 1873. More than $145,000,000 in gold and silver came from the lode in a dozen years. Colorado's gold rush also came in 1859, although some gold had been found and had set off an abortive rush the summer before. The Pikes Peak rush was pretty well over by the end of 1859, for most of the gold was embedded in quartz and would need costly mining machinery—no place for a shoestring prospector. But farmers and ranchers had come to supply the miners, Denver and other towns were started, and Colorado was on its way.

"Mining on the Comstock" (above) was made at Gold Hill, Nevada, in 1876 and shows some of the operations involved in the mining, which by then had tunneled the earth like an anthill. The picture by Tim O'Sullivan of a miner (below, left) was one of the first American flash photographs and was made in the same Comstock mine as the other photo.

A wagon train fords the Smoky Hill River near Ellsworth, Kansas, in 1867. The Smoky Hill Trail remained the main Kansas City–Denver road after the gold rush and then became the approximate route of the Kansas Pacific Railroad.

In the Plains Indian, one of the world's most superb horsemen, the Army was soon to find a stubborn and worthy foe.

WHITETOPS AND RED EARTH

The Colorado gold rush brought no joy to the hearts of Indians on the central plains. The long lines of wagons that rolled along the Smoky Hill River through Kansas to the Denver region raised such a mighty cloud of dust and so much commotion that the buffalo shied away from this clamorous avenue across the plains, as they had from the Oregon Trail. This —today's western Kansas and eastern Colorado —was Cheyenne and Arapaho country. The two tribes had been generally friendly, but friendship had cooled as traffic over the Smoky Hill Trail continued and adventurers not only slaughtered buffalo for the fun of it but now and then shot an Indian going about his own business. Not surprisingly, young braves retaliated in kind; however, older and cooler heads kept the tribes in check. It was not yet time for war.

Plains Indians mutilated their slain enemies for religious reasons; foemen with crippled bodies would not be threats in the spirit world.

Union & Central Pacific Railroad Line.

Thos. L. Kimball

Gen'l Ticket Agent, U. P. R. R.

8554

ONE CONTINUOUS
EMIGRANT PASSAGE
—FROM—
OMAHA
TO STATION CANCELED,

Good for TEN DAYS only from and including date punched or indicated in the margin, after which time it will be "Void," and full fare will be charged for the whole or remainder of the trip, as the case may be.

Kelton.	Marysville.
Elko.	Terminus Oregon Division
Palisade.	Sacramento.
Battle Mountain	Stockton.
Winnemucca.	Lathrop.
Reno.	Terminus So. Pacific R. R.
Truckee.	San Jose.
Colfax.	San Franci

NOT TRANSFERABLE.

No Stop-over privileges given on this Ticket.

Baggage Checked only to Destination.

Whole | 1876 | Half | 1877

Cost of one-way fare, straight coach, Omaha to San Francisco, 1869: $111. Time: 4 days, 4 hours, 40 minutes, buffalo and Indians permitting. Cost of same today: $53.45. Time: 1 day, 12 hours, 5 minutes.

CHAPTER TWELVE

CLEARING THE WAY

1854-1870

In spite of the protests of Sam Houston, Texas in February, 1861, voted 46,129 to 14,697 to secede. On the instant, fiery Ben McCulloch, Indian fighter and Texas Ranger, galloped with three hundred state militia into San Antonio's Main Plaza. There he accepted the surrender of General D. E. Twiggs, a Georgian, the twenty-seven hundred Federal troops Twiggs commanded, and every bit of United States property in Texas, worth an estimated $1,500,000. Chesty with triumph, the trans-Mississippi South then began stitching its ambitions into the grand design of Confederate strategy. So far as the West was concerned, this involved laying clamps on the wavering border state of Missouri and, more ambitiously, reaching out for the gold fields of Colorado, Arizona, Nevada, and California.

After failing to rig a Missouri convention that would declare in favor of secession, the state's governor, Claiborne Jackson, assembled seven hundred militiamen at a camp on the edge of St. Louis. The authority of his office gave him full right to do this. But for what ends did he intend the troops? The Union commander in St. Louis, Nathaniel Lyon, swathed his red beard in a veil, toured the camp as a farm woman selling eggs, and decided Jackson meant to seize the St. Louis arsenal. Moving first, Lyon and Francis Blair, Jr., whose brother sat in Lincoln's Cabinet, surrounded the militia with Union troops and irregular German guards and forced their surrender. During these military maneuvers, civilian riots erupted that left twenty-eight dead in the streets.

Jackson fled with a strong core of Confederate sympathizers into the southwestern part of the state. With Sterling Price, an ex-governor of Missouri and conqueror of the Pueblo Indians of Taos during the Mexican War, he began raising an army in order to recapture what had been lost. To support their effort, Jackson and Price called on Texan Ben McCulloch, who had recently been installed at Fort Smith as the commander of the Confederacy's Department of Arkansas.

At that point McCulloch and Albert Pike, a transplanted New Englander, were busily wooing the Five Civilized Tribes of Indian Territory, hoping to gain the Indians' beef herds as a source of provisions and the warriors as auxiliary fighters. The Missouri call left the Indian intrigue entirely in Pike's hands. A learned lawyer, poet (one version of "Dixie" was his), and pen-wielding booster of a southern railway line to the Pacific, he moved and spoke with Olympian loftiness. He was more than six feet tall and bearded like Zeus; his curly locks cascaded to his shoulders.

In meeting after meeting, Pike reminded the Indians of the rapacity with which the United States had gobbled up their lands in the East. Sweepingly he promised, among other things, that a victorious Confederacy would reverse the trend and accept an Indian state, with full equality, into the new nation. Choctaws, Chickasaws, and part of the Creeks were impressed. Not so John Ross, seven-eighths white and head chief of the Cherokees, who pointed out that Southerners, not Northerners, had led the original drive to evict the Indians from their homes. Moreover, Ross argued, neutrality might preserve what the displaced red men had created in this new land. The wealthier Cherokees, many Creeks, and some Seminoles supported him, and a long dialectic, inconclusive for a while, developed among the Indians themselves.

The fortunes of war tipped the balance. Price and McCulloch pulled together an army of thirteen thousand men in southwestern Missouri and there made contact with Nathaniel Lyon, the Union commander. Lyon had only five thousand effectives, and his transport to the railhead at Rolla, one hundred and twenty miles away, was in a snarl. Rather than flee, he decided on a bold, infinitely hazardous attack.

The battle began at dawn on August 10 (less than three weeks after Bull Run), near a sluggish stream called Wilson's Creek. For a staggering hour it seemed Lyon's gamble might win. Then the Confederates rallied and massed their fire along a line less than a thousand yards wide. "Within its limits," wrote historian Allan Nevins in his biography of Frémont, "it was one of the fiercest encounters of the Civil War." Twice wounded and leading a last despairing charge, Lyon was shot through the heart. After that, the rout began.

Triumphant Confederate guerrillas roared unrestrained through central Missouri, burning bridges, wrecking trains, spreading terror. Pressing his advantage, Sterling Price thrust one hundred and sixty miles north to Lexington, Missouri, and on September 20, captured twenty-eight hundred Federal troops and wagonloads of booty. Overextended, he fell back as John Charles Frémont, commander of the Department of Missouri, organized a pursuit force of thirty thousand men. For Frémont the effort came too late. The odor of defeat throughout his department, his own mismanagement, politics, and internecine rivalries led to his replacement by Samuel Curtis, a West Point graduate and a railroad engineer in Iowa. Fighting gave way for a time to reorganization.

The North's apparent weakness led the half-blooded Cherokees, many of them slaveholders, to put heavy pressure on Ross to join the Confederates. In November he capitulated and signed a treaty with Pike. Many individuals among the Civilized Tribes, Cherokees included, refused to accept it. Loading what possessions they could into their wagons, several thousand fled toward Kansas. Twice they fought off pursuing Texans and Indian auxiliaries, but on December 27, 1861, they were shattered just short of the border and turned back. Only a few hundred reached Union haven, destitute and starving; scores had limbs so badly frozen they had to be amputated.

Union fortunes farther west seemed equally precarious. Immediately after Texas' secession, Colonel John R. Baylor, a flamboyant adventurer who had been raised in Indian Territory, marched a ragged force of volunteers through the blazing heat of July from San Antonio to the

Confederate General Sterling Price

Rio Grande and without opposition laid hold of Fort Bliss, near El Paso. Forty miles farther up the river, at Fort Fillmore, Major Isaac Lynde was dug in with seven hundred Union regulars. Baylor probed at them with no more than two hundred and fifty men. During the desultory shooting, Lynde lost three or four killed, six wounded.

An inexplicable panic shook him. During the night he ordered Fort Fillmore abandoned. Supplies—including whisky—that could not be loaded into available wagons were to be destroyed. The enlisted men demolished the liquor by consuming it and using it to fill their canteens for the march. The next day, July 27, 1861, a crushing sun caught soldiers, mules, and carriages carrying wives and children strung out for miles along a sandy, waterless road leading toward Fort Stanton, one hundred and fifty miles to the northeast. When Baylor's two hundred and fifty men galloped up, the hung-over, thirst-crazed Federal troops surrendered without a shot.

Twenty hours later, a little cavalcade of buggies, horsemen, and pack animals reached the Rio Grande over the old Butterfield mail road from the west. The leader of the group was Albert Sidney Johnston. A Texan, Johnston had relinquished command of the United States Army's Department of the Pacific, whose headquarters were in San Francisco. Traveling by way of Los Angeles, he rode east to offer his services to the Confederacy.

On their swift trip through what is now Arizona, Johnston and his party passed the charred ruins of forts abandoned by loyal garrisons as they withdrew toward Fort Union in northeastern New Mexico, where they were to regroup under Colonel Edward Canby. Except for raiding Apache bands, Johnston told Baylor, the

314

way to California was wide open to Confederate forces.

Baylor lacked men enough to take advantage of the situation. But more were being readied in Texas by General Henry Hopkins Sibley, long familiar with the Southwest and, by coincidence, a brother-in-law of the Union commander in New Mexico, Colonel Canby. To prepare the way for Sibley, Baylor on August 1 proclaimed the Confederate Territory of Arizona, a long east-west strip embracing, roughly, the lower third of today's New Mexico and Arizona. He named himself military governor and sent a hundred cavalrymen west to seize the tough little mining supply center of Tucson.

Sibley reached New Mexico toward the end of the year, his original brigade of thirty-five hundred Texans sorely shrunk by an epidemic of measles and the hardships of the six-hundred-mile march from San Antonio. Canby meanwhile had moved part of his forces down the Rio Grande, past Albuquerque, to an adobe cantonment called Fort Craig, across the river from the frowning bluffs of Valverde. Eager though the Confederates were for the gold of California, Sibley dared not move on west while his brother-in-law sat so close to his flanks. In February, 1862, accordingly, he swung north, marching along the river bank opposite the Union stronghold.

On the twenty-first, Canby's men swarmed across the fords to challenge him. The leaden shock of the meeting sent the Union troops reeling back. Many died in the turbid water before the terrified survivors fled inside Fort Craig. Sibley thereupon by-passed the stronghold and easily occupied both Albuquerque, March 2, and Santa Fe, March 23. Dazzling new possibilities beckoned to him. Why not crush undermanned Fort Union and seize the Pikes Peak gold regions? After that, if luck continued and adequate forces could be mustered, the Confederates could perhaps cut the Overland Trail and sweep on toward Nevada and northern California in a pincer movement co-ordinated with drives through Arizona.

Sibley's victories marked the high point of Confederate success in the West. Then, from Missouri to New Mexico, the crumbling began. About the time that Sibley was by-passing Fort Craig, Samuel Curtis moved his reorganized Union army of ten thousand five hundred infantry and cavalry through southwestern Missouri toward sixteen thousand Confederates and Indians commanded by Generals Earl Van Dorn, Ben McCulloch, and Albert Pike. The forces collided on March 7, 1862, at Pea Ridge, just inside the border of Arkansas.

Sharpshooters killed McCulloch early in the battle. Pike's poorly armed, ludicrously uniformed Indian auxiliaries achieved a moment's success, then broke under heavy artillery fire and fled from the field. The Confederate whites retreated the next day. The way cleared, Federal troops occupied Fort Gibson in eastern Indian Territory and in July, 1863, at Honey Springs, on Creek land, soundly whipped six thousand Confederates who tried to dislodge them.

Henry Sibley's forces in New Mexico fared no better. Their earlier victories had made them overconfident. On March 26, 1862, as they advanced toward Fort Union, scouts reported Federal patrols moving toward them through the boulders of Apache Canyon. "Out we marched," wrote Texan George Brown to his wife, ". . . expecting an easy victory, but what a mistake. Instead of Mexicans and regulars, they were regular demons, that iron and lead had no effect upon, in the shape of Pike's Peakers from Denver City Gold mines."

More Pike's Peakers were a little way behind. They had volunteered earlier in Colorado for the relief of Fort Union and had covered the last one hundred and seventy-two wintry miles of their march in five days. Ill-drilled and worse disciplined, they had terrorized the little settlements along the way with their ruffianly behavior. But they were spoiling for a fight. They got it March 28, in La Glorietta Pass, east of Santa Fe.

Until evening, the battle was a draw. Unknown to the Confederates, however, several hundred Coloradans had spent the day climbing the almost impassable mountains to the south of the battlefield. The commander of the detachment was a former Methodist preacher, Major John M. Chivington, six and a half feet tall, round-headed, crop-bearded. As a roaring abolitionist in the proslavery frontier counties of Missouri, Chivington had delivered his sermons, it is said, with a cocked revolver lying beside his Bible. In 1860, he had been sent to Colorado to establish the Rocky Mountain Conference for his church. Shortly after the outbreak of the war, he left his pulpit for the Army. He was a dynamic leader with almost hypnotic powers over his men.

Letting themselves silently down the mountainside with ropes or by swinging from tree to tree, Chivington's men caught the Confederate supply column by total surprise. They burned at least eighty-five wagons loaded with food, blankets, and tents, and ruthlessly bayoneted to death five or six hundred mules and horses. Hungry and shelterless, the dismayed Southerners had no choice but to fall back to their advance base at Santa Fe.

More trouble was making for them in California. Twin motives prompted the Pacific activity. First, word came that Baylor's Confederates had captured Fort Fillmore and Tucson. Almost simultaneously, heavy snow closed the central mail route, which had recently replaced the southern crossing. Sneering at the northern service as

The following text appears on the map:

Lake of the Woods

Red River of the North

LAKE SUPERIOR

MICHIGAN

MINNESOTA
(ADMITTED 1858)

WISCONSIN

LAKE MICHIGAN

Mississippi R.

Minnesota R.

Ft. Ridgely

Missouri R.

SPIRIT LAKE

IOWA

Chicago

WNEE

Platte R.

Kearney

St. Joseph

Lexington

St. Louis

ILLINOIS

Ft. Leavenworth

Kansas City

Hays

Smoky Hill R.

Lawrence

Rolla

. Larned

KANSAS
(ADMITTED 1861)

MISSOURI

WILSON'S CREEK

CHEROKEE

Arkansas R.

PEA RIDGE

CREEK

SHITA SEMINOLE

Ft. Gibson

INDIAN TERRITORY

CHOCTAW

ARKANSAS

Mississippi R.

CHICKASAW

MISSISSIPPI

Red R.

Fort Worth

Sabine R.

Trinity R.

Colorado R.

Brazos R.

LOUISIANA

Austin

PLUM CREEK

New Orleans

San Antonio

GULF OF MEXICO

Rio Grande

SCALE
0 50 100 150 Miles

"a gigantic humbug and swindle," the Los Angeles *Star* demanded a reopening of the southern route. To placate the so-called cow counties, the Pacific commanders ordered vainglorious General James H. Carleton to march east from Los Angeles with two thousand men, drive the Confederates back into Texas, and establish communications through New Mexico with the East.

Hampered by unprecedented rains, Carleton did not start until late in March, 1862. During April he sent his men across the California desert in small detachments so as not to overstrain the watering places. "Blinding white sand," wrote one correspondent, ". . . reflects the rays of the sun with terrible lustre and withering effect. Men, mules and horses sink under its power. . . ." Mismanagement added to the inertia. The column spent ten months investing Tucson, which had been abandoned by the Confederate cavalry, and then dragging on to Santa Fe, a total distance of eight hundred and fifty-nine miles —an average of less than three miles a day, as the New Mexico papers sarcastically pointed out. Still, Carleton's advance accomplished its purpose. Sibley retreated into Texas, and after that the Confederates made no further gestures toward the Far West.

Eastward, in Missouri and Kansas, war degenerated into barbaric raids and counterraids. The latter state suffered particularly. On January 21, 1863, William Clarke Quantrill, operating under a captain's commission in the Confederate army, seized the old Free-Soil stronghold of Lawrence, burned nearly two hundred buildings, shot down or cremated a hundred and fifty men—but, he insisted, molested no women. Disguising themselves afterward in Federal uniforms, the raiders fled through Indian country toward Texas. Before they were well started, they surprised a detachment of Union soldiers, hailed them as friends, and slew a hundred of them. Finding the device rewarding, they continued it against lonesome garrisons and runaway Negroes. All told, Quantrill's bloody guerrillas are reputed to have killed a thousand persons during 1863.

Meanwhile, the far longer conflict against the American Indians was at last coming to a head. In general, the natives' motive remained what it had been for two and a half centuries: the defense of their homelands against an influx of whites whose own yearnings toward the New World the tribes could not possibly grasp. Within this broad area of mutual resentment there were, of course, numerous specific grievances. To comprehend them, it is

The Great West of the initial mail and stage routes, the Civil War period, the mining rushes, the Pacific Railroad, and the intensifying resistance of the Indians is shown at left.

necessary to backtrack several years to the early 1850's.

The whites who surged in growing numbers along the Oregon and Santa Fe trails during those years brought with them terrifying epidemics of cholera, which the Indians did not understand and which seemed in some obscure way a deliberate malice on the part of the invaders. At the same time, white fire builders from regions where wood was cheap casually chopped down the thin ribbons of irreplaceable trees along the streams of the barren plains. Hunters killed or frightened away the buffalo, around which the entire economy of the Indian tribes was built. Thousands of livestock moving back and forth along the trails each year stripped grass away from favorite village campgrounds.

The Indians on their part annoyed the wagon trains by incessant begging and pilfering and by the occasional killing of a straggler. The inevitable major incident boiled up near Fort Laramie on August 17, 1854. A camp of Miniconjou Sioux butchered a cow belonging to a Mormon emigrant. Acting on an appeal from the cow's owner, young Lieutenant John Grattan marched forth from Laramie with twenty-nine troopers, an interpreter, and two small cannons. One story has it that the interpreter was drunk and that his clumsy translations caused tempers to flare. Be that as it may, fighting erupted, and every white man died.

The next summer, General W. S. Harney was sent west with twelve hundred men to awe the Indians. One Sioux village near Ash Hollow on the Oregon Trail failed to learn of his order for friendly bands to cross to the south bank of the North Platte River. Impatiently, Harney sent his cavalry around to the rear of the camp. He himself approached its front under a flag of truce, parleyed until he felt the cavalry were in place, and then told the Indians to fight. It was quick and vicious: five slain soldiers to eighty-six dead Indians, some of them women.

Still rattling his saber, Harney swung from Fort Laramie northeast back across the plains to Fort Pierre, a fur trading post on the Missouri River recently purchased by the Army. (Pierre, capital of South Dakota, now stands across the river from the site.) The next March, 1856, he assembled many of the Sioux at the new post and won from them a promise never again to molest travel along the Platte Valley or on a new White River military road between Forts Pierre and Laramie. Enforcement of this promise Harney would have left to the Indians themselves, working through a police force of seven hundred warriors fed and uniformed by the United States. Such a unit might have brought to the tribe's restless young men a sense of pride and responsibility and a desire to cooperate with the white authorities. Unhappily, the costs that would be involved so horrified the bureaucrats in Washington that they rejected the idea out of hand.

During the talks with Harney, the Sioux gathered that henceforth no whites (except licensed traders) would be allowed to cross their lands anywhere except along the Platte Valley and White River roads. They were incensed, accordingly, when two unwarranted groups immediately violated the promise.

One party was a hunting excursion led by Sir George Gore of Ireland. After a warm-up venture into present-day Colorado, Gore had moved north to winter (1855–56) in Yellowstone Valley. To care for and transport his seventy-five sporting rifles, his fifteen shotguns, dozens of pistols, bundles of fishing rods, his special tents, collapsible brass bedstead, and folding tables, he had one hundred and twelve horses, forty men, six wagons, and twenty-one two-wheeled carts, plus Jim Bridger as guide. When he passed through Fort Union at the mouth of the Yellowstone on his way home, he boasted to the Indian agent, Alfred Vaughan, that he had killed that spring "105 Bears and some 2,000 Buffalo Elk and Deer 1600." Angrily Vaughan added, "The Inds have been loud in their complaints." Bitterly he asked, "what can I do against so large a number of men coming into a country like this so very remote from civilization. . . ." And in dejection he answered his own question: "Nothing. . . ."

Just as Gore left the Yellowstone country, Lieutenant G. K. Warren entered it at the head of a surveying party that included in its numbers one of the West's most brilliant young geologists, Ferdinand V. Hayden. Just what, the Indians wondered, were these men looking for? After watching the party for a time, they came to an angry conclusion: more roads and sites for more military posts. What, then, did Harney's promises amount to?

The next year, Warren expanded his activities. After exploring southern Nebraska, he moved north into the Black Hills of present South Dakota. There a large force of Sioux halted him. The Indians were carefully holding a herd of buffalo within a certain area until, so Warren reported, "the hair would answer for robes," which they would sell to their traders. The hunters feared that the whites would frighten the animals away. "Their feelings . . . were not unlike what we would feel toward a person who should insist upon setting fire to our barns." Pointedly the Sioux spokesmen added, according to Warren's report, that "having already given up all the country they could spare to the whites, these Black Hills must be wholly left to themselves."

Warren judiciously withdrew. To the Indians, this was a triumph. Immediately they had a bloodier one to think about. Far east at Spirit Lake, on the northern border of Iowa, renegades led by an outlaw named Inkpaduta massacred about forty settlers and carried off a few women. Partly because most of the troops at the nearest post, Fort Ridgely, Minnesota, had been withdrawn to participate in the Mormon War, no retribution followed the attack. This, like Warren's retreat, seemed to some of the Indians a proof of weakness.

Additional portents of the times continued to appear. In order to speed troop movements into the Northwest, the War Department in 1859 directed Lieutenant John Mullan, a veteran of Isaac Stevens's 1853 railroad survey across the northern Rockies, to spend one hundred thousand dollars building a road between Fort Walla Walla in eastern Washington and Fort Benton, a fur trading post some forty miles below the Great Falls of the Missouri. Mullan began work in July with ninety workers guarded by one hundred and forty soldiers. From Fort Walla Walla he moved north across the rolling hills of eastern Washington, bridging streams as he went. Near the site of today's Spokane he bent east through heavy timber along the shore of Coeur d'Alene Lake. Winter caught him in the rugged Bitterroot Mountains on the present-day border between Idaho and Montana. Temperatures dropped to forty below. Most of the horses died; one man lost both legs to frostbite; twenty-five others came down with scurvy.

Moving again in the spring, Mullan finally reached Fort Benton in August. Two specially built shallow-draft steamboats were already there, loaded with three hundred troops and their equipment. To prove the usefulness of his road, Mullan loaded the soldiers' gear into his wagons and in fifty-seven days marched the men back to Walla Walla, six hundred and twenty-four miles away. The teamsters were shaken up considerably by rough spots here and there; after all, the one-hundred-thousand-dollar appropriation had enabled Mullan to spend, on the average, only a hundred and sixty dollars a mile.

The Army also decided to link the Oregon Trail with Mullan's new thoroughfare. Locating the best routes became the responsibility of Captain William F. Raynolds. Using Forts Pierre and Union on the Missouri as his bases and guided in part by Jim Bridger, Raynolds spent parts of two years, 1859 and 1860, prowling an aggregate of five thousand miles through contiguous parts of the Dakotas, Wyoming, and Montana. The Indians watched uneasily. They thought they had driven Warren away. But obviously these implacable whites were not going to stay away.

Legend has it that during his travels with the Raynolds expedition, guide Jim Bridger picked up gold ore in the Black Hills but discarded the specimens at the behest of his employer, who feared the excitement might break up the survey. Mullan too worried lest gold discoveries "lead to a stampede of my men . . . and thus destroy the possible consummation of my work." Such alarms were still another sign of the times. The gold fever, never really cured since '49, had been heated again by major strikes in 1858 along the Fraser River of British Columbia and, shortly thereafter, by the discoveries in Colorado and Nevada. Once more, prospectors began dreaming of truly lucrative "poor-man's diggings" like those in California —sand and gravel placers whose exploitation demanded nothing more than simple tools and honest muscle.

Indian talk led Elias Pierce, onetime California miner and later a trader among the Nez Perce tribe, to believe there might be such diggings on the forbidden lands of

John Owen's post in Montana's Bitterroot Valley, painted by Peter Tofft, a guest in 1865–66, was often host to John Mullan.

the Nez Perce reservation, where bright creeks flowed out of the Bitterroot Mountains into the Clearwater Fork of the Snake. During the fall of 1860, he managed to sneak in with a small party. He made his discovery on what he called Orofino Creek. Softened perhaps by bribery, certain Nez Perce chiefs agreed to allow mining within a rigidly limited area.

The stampede of whites who followed never heeded those boundaries. Steamboats snorted up the Columbia River into the Snake and docked at the overnight tent city of Lewiston, Idaho, sprawled across a favorite Nez Perce campground at the mouth of the Clearwater. From there, swarms of prospectors moved south to Florence and other diggings in the Salmon River district, joined other throngs working out of Oregon and California, and by the end of 1862 had raveled wildly off through the fabulously rich hills to the north of today's city of Boise.

Convinced afresh that the world was at their fingertips, other miners pushed from Idaho into what is now the southwestern corner of Montana. Bannack City became 1862's wonder town. The next year, the rush pressed on east to a barren, creek-seamed gulch whose ribbon of trees looked, in the words of the discoverer, "so nice and green" that he named the trickle Alder Creek. This indeed was California over again—the supreme accolade. Within a year, according to one set of statistics, fourteen thousand men had plastered a thousand claims along both sides of the gulch from mouth to source and with their pans and rockers had stripped ten million dollars in gold from the sandy earth. The gulch's sprawling heart was first called Varina for the wife of Jefferson Davis. An outraged Federal judge changed the name to Virginia City—commendable patriotism perhaps but an unimaginative choice, for it meant that two of America's most spectacular mining camps thereafter bore the same title.

Nor was that the end. In the fall of 1864, ninety air-line miles north of Montana's Virginia City, a group of disgruntled prospectors paused on their way out of the country to make a final effort in what they called Last Chance Gulch, just off Little Prickly Pear Creek. The eventual result: twenty million dollars in placer gold and the development of a boisterous frontier town, Helena, which grew to be the capital of the territory. Southern influence was strong there, too. Off to the southeast was Confederate Gulch; in 1866, two shipments of gold

were weighed out of the district quite literally by the ton.

By their very nature, the quickly exploitable placer camps of the West attracted an unstable population, men whose chief motto was "Cash in and get out." The characteristic was intensified in Idaho and Montana by large numbers of political self-exiles: draft dodgers from the North and embittered Southern sympathizers fleeing from the war-torn farmlands of Kansas, Missouri (where Price's Confederates were raiding again in 1864), and northern Arkansas. The severe winters increased their restive opportunism. Since placer mining under snow in frozen gravel was almost impossible, there was a heavy exodus of workers each fall, an inpouring each spring. Anonymity became easy—and this in a country whose sole wealth was highly concentrated and simple to handle. Under the circumstances, lawlessness was inevitable.

Most notable of the many organized gangs was one led by handsome, soft-voiced, philandering Henry Plummer. Since Plummer doubled at the same time as sheriff of both Bannack and Virginia City, no help came from the law. Impatient citizens finally formed California-style vigilante committees and on January 10, 1864, hanged handsome Harry on a scaffold he himself had erected for the execution of a horse thief. Twenty-three more hoodlums followed. The rest oozed away in fright, and order of a sort returned to the mountains.

Another plague to the mining towns of Montana and northern Idaho was inadequate transportation. The nearest sources of food were the farms of Utah, an advantage quickly exploited by Mormon suppliers and freighters. Fabricated material had to come from either St. Louis or San Francisco. The existing land routes were roundabout—either east or west along the Overland Trail to Fort Hall, and then north through eastern Idaho. Short cuts such as those Warren and Raynolds had been looking for were desirable, but the Civil War had stopped Army road building. In the spring of 1863, accordingly, two civilians decided to fill the gap. One was John Jacobs, a big, red-bearded trapper; the other, John Bozeman, a Georgian turned miner. With Jacob's little half-breed daughter in tow, they left the Overland Trail near where Douglas, Wyoming, now stands beside the North Platte River. After slanting north past the east side of the Bighorn Mountains to the Yellowstone River, they bent west across Bozeman Pass into the gold country. Convinced that wagons could follow their route, they returned to the main trail and offered themselves as guides. A small wagon train gathered, but Sioux and Cheyenne Indians terrified it into turning back.

Disgusted, Bozeman and ten men leading pack horses managed to slip through by riding mostly at night. In

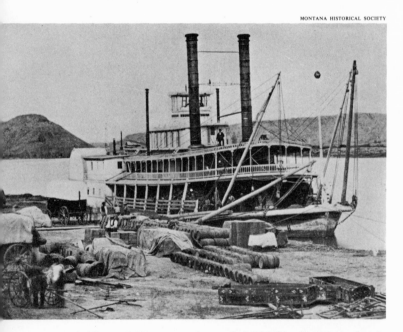

A Missouri River steamboat of the 1860's discharges freight at Fort Benton, head of navigation, 2,300 miles up the river.

320

1864, he determined to try again with wagons. Warning that Bozeman was asking for trouble with the Indians, mountain man Jim Bridger worked out an alternate route on the west side of the Bighorns, farther from hostile territory. The road he found was shorter as well as safer than Bozeman's, but rough and scanty in grass. Hundreds of wagons accordingly chose the Bozeman trace. And this too intensified the grievance of the Indians.

The sinuous rivers carried still more freight toward the gold fields. Each spring, St. Louis merchants sent steamers thrashing twenty-three hundred miles up the snag-filled Missouri to the clanging docks of Fort Benton. Wholesalers in San Francisco countered by shipping their material to Portland. There it was taken in charge by a lusty young monopoly called the Oregon Steam Navigation Company. In order to defeat the howling rapids of the Columbia River gorge through the Cascade Mountains, the company constructed, as a portage device, the Northwest's first steam railway.

Mullan's road should have been a godsend to the inland freighters who took over at the head of navigation on the Columbia. Unfortunately, no appropriations were forthcoming from Congress to remove fallen timber or repair flood-ruined bridges. As a result, most goods moved into early-day Montana from the west by pack train. One skinner estimated that during the height of the rush, a braying maelstrom of six thousand mules and a herd of pack camels imported from Manchuria shuttled goods and gold back and forth along the different trails.

Farther south, black-bearded Ben Holladay in 1862 absorbed the bankrupt remnants of the once-great freighting empire of Russell, Majors & Waddell. Insatiable for empire, Holladay thrust new lines deep into Colorado, Utah, Nevada, Oregon, Idaho, and Montana. Soon his plunging stagecoaches and ponderous freight wagons were coursing thirty-three hundred miles of mountains and desert road, garnering, among other rewards, government mail subsidies of one million dollars a year.

Meanwhile, a transcontinental railroad to absorb some of this freight burden was at last becoming a reality. One prime figure in the final attack was Crazy Judah—Theodore Dehone Judah—a civil engineer who had gained his first experience working on various railroads in New York and New England. In 1854, aged twenty-seven, Judah had traveled to California to help build a twenty-one-mile line from the river docks at Sacramento eastward to Folsom, jumping-off place for the deepening mines of the Mother Lode country. The road's iron rails and diminutive locomotive were brought by ship around the Horn, which struck Judah as ridiculous. Backed by California promoters, he journeyed to Washington in

1856 and again in 1859, to mill around the capitol with other railroad lobbyists. Frustrated by Congress's sectional animosities, he decided early in 1860 to better his time by finding the most usable pass across the Sierra for his nonexistent road. After long tramps through the alpine meadows and spruce forests of the high country, he settled on Donner Summit, near the scene of the cannibalistic disaster of 1846.

An untamed pass raised no money. When Judah kept using the same breath to talk about Donner Summit and the Mississippi Valley, hundreds of millions of dollars away, San Francisco capitalists just shook their heads. Without Government help, the thing was impossible, and who could say what the strife-torn Government might do?

Growing practical, Judah narrowed his sights to the booming Comstock mines of Nevada (then part of Utah Territory), just beyond the California border. By then the wild silver rush was drawing a fantastic amount of wagon traffic across the mountains. Using that bait as honey, Judah caught the attention of four Sacramento merchants: Collis Huntington and Mark Hopkins, who owned a thriving hardware company; Charles Crocker, a red-faced, two-hundred-and-forty-pound dry-goods entrepreneur; and Leland Stanford, prosperous wholesale grocer and Republican nominee for the governorship of California. Scenting new markets, the quartet financed studies to determine the cost of building a railroad over Donner Pass to the California-Nevada line. The price came to a staggering $12,500,000. Drawing a deep breath, the four told Crazy Judah to try Washington again. Lincoln had just been elected on a platform calling, among other things, for a Pacific railroad, and Government help just might be forthcoming at last.

Iowans hoping to lure traffic across their state from Chicago were also hard at work in the capital. How effective their efforts and Judah's actually were cannot be measured. Times were ripe for a railroad. Southern obstruction was gone. The North needed California's gold. It also needed, many worriers believed, tight bonds with the coast in order to forestall Confederate propaganda. Yet no railroad could pay for its construction to the Pacific out of current income; not enough traffic existed in the intervening wilderness. Therefore, so the argument ran, the nation, which would benefit as a whole from the line, should be willing to help finance its building. The fact that Leland Stanford of the Central Pacific Railroad's board of directors had just been elected the first Republican governor of California in no wise detracted from this line of reasoning.

In the early summer of 1862, Congress passed and Lincoln signed a bill authorizing the railroad. In this initial bill (it was later modified several times), the lion's share of the Government's subsidies went not to Judah's firm but to an Eastern amalgamation called Union Pacific, which was authorized to build as far west as the California-Nevada border or until it met the eastward-thrusting Central Pacific. For every mile of track it built, each road would be awarded ten alternate sections of land (a total of sixty-four hundred acres) checkerboarded throughout a twenty-mile-wide strip embracing the rights of way. Later the grants were doubled, so that eventually the roads received roughly nineteen million acres of free land, which, as the country grew, they could sell to settlers as a recompense for their efforts. Also, each company was promised generous loans for each mile of track laid—sixteen thousand dollars a mile in level country, thirty-two thousand dollars a mile in the rough country between the Rockies and the Sierra, and forty-eight thousand dollars a mile in the mountains themselves. The loans eventually totaled ninety-six million dollars. The state and various counties of California pumped more funds into the Central Pacific. And finally, both roads were permitted to float generous public stock issues.

Although the potentials were dazzling, realization lay in the distant future. The incorporators of both roads wanted more immediate profits. To gain them, the directors of each line set up construction firms, from which ordinary stockholders were excluded, and awarded themselves fat contracts for laying track: the Charles Crocker Construction Company (later the Contract and Finance Company) for the Central Pacific and, in 1864, the infamous and far more sophisticated Crédit Mobilier for the Union Pacific. When Judah objected to the way his partners were milking the Central Pacific, they squeezed him out. Hurrying eastward across Panama to find means for fighting them, he caught yellow fever and died just as he reached New York City.

In spite of the juggling and heavy personal investments by the incorporators, initial progress on both lines was snail-slow. The war had tightened labor markets and had ballooned expenses; rails, for example, had jumped from $55 a ton in 1861 to $115 in 1863. Speculators in California were more interested in the soaring stock of the Comstock mines than in the Central Pacific. Eastern investors were concentrating on the North's war-exhilarated industrial complex. Although the original Pacific Railway Act was liberalized by generous amendments in 1864, money still came in so slowly that at the end of 1865, neither railroad could boast of more than fifty miles of track.

In other fields, the nation's energy was phenomenal. On May 20, 1862, six weeks before signing the Pacific railroad bill, President Lincoln fulfilled another part of the Republican platform by affixing his signature to the Homestead Act. Under terms of this law, all heads of families and all males over twenty-one who had not borne arms against the Government were given the right to acquire full title to one hundred and sixty acres of public domain land by simply residing on it for five years and completing certain improvements in the way of building and cultivation. Or, after six months' residence and trivial improvements, an entrant could acquire title by paying the Government $1.25 an acre. By the close of the war, more than fifteen thousand persons had laid claim to nearly two and a half million acres.

Throughout the Civil War, migration to the West continued almost unabated. In spite of continuing draft troubles, the Government each year appropriated from twenty-five to fifty thousand dollars to protect travelers on the Overland Trail. Farther north, Captain James Fisk, acting under Army authority, in 1862, 1863, and 1864 guarded wagon trains traveling through Sioux country from Minnesota to Montana. Denied further appropriations in 1865, Fisk resigned from the Army and, in a private venture, hired a company of riflemen to protect a train of one hundred and sixty wagons.

These escorts were stopgap measures. At the outset of the Civil War, the troops garrisoning the West's scattered posts were pulled east, and the Indians were quick to take advantage of the fact. Apaches brought mining in Arizona to a standstill. In New Mexico, during the single month of August, 1861, they killed forty-six settlers and carried several women and children into captivity. During that same thirty days, Navahos stole forty-five thousand sheep. Bannocks burned stage stations in Utah and Idaho. In 1862, Cheyennes, Sioux, and Arapahoes struck so hard at the North Platte and Sweetwater road across Wyoming that Ben Holladay shifted his newly acquired Overland Mail farther south, following roughly the line now used by the Union Pacific. In order to keep the way open, the Government hurriedly established a new post, Fort Halleck, in the Medicine Bow Mountains. The defense of the western end of the trail was assigned to redheaded, hot-tempered Colonel Patrick Edward Connor of California. Instead of seeking a wilderness base, Connor offended the Mormons, their memories of the Utah war still fresh, by building Camp Douglas just north of Salt Lake City, as though he meant to keep the Utah Saints as well as the Indians under surveillance.

The first major uprising occurred not in the Far West, however, but in heavily settled farming regions near the Minnesota River. The different bands of Santee Sioux who once had roamed the area had been crowded, 1851-53, onto a narrow strip of land along the upper half of the stream. They appeared peaceful. The thirty-two hundred Indians centered around the Lower Agency, at Redwood Creek, fifteen miles or so above Fort Ridgely, farmed thirteen hundred acres. Between the Upper Agency at Yellow Medicine River and the main river's head at Big Stone Lake, another forty-five hundred Indians farmed fifteen hundred more acres. Missionaries conducted schools. The Government ran gristmills and sawmills and blacksmith shops and once a year passed out annuities, most of them in the form of goods.

These annuities were late arriving in 1862, to the annoyance of five thousand would-be recipients who were already angry over excessive charges of their traders and encroachments of whites on their land. As hunger grew, the Indians listened with increasing approval to the promptings of a militant secret society of young warriors. The North was not to be feared, after all. Had it not suffered heavy reverses at the hands of the South? Was it not further betraying its weakness by sending out recruiting officers to enlist even half-breeds? And finally, as every Indian knew, at least five thousand volunteers had left Minnesota for the battlefronts; very few troops remained in the Northern forts.

The spark came in August when a small party of Sioux hunters proposed a shooting match with some whites gathered at a farm house near Acton. As soon as the guns of the whites were empty, the Sioux attacked, killing three men and two women. They then galloped to the camp of Chief Little Crow near the Lower Agency and told him what they had done.

Fearful of retribution against the entire tribe and hopeful of restoring his waning prestige, Little Crow called in his warriors. At dawn on August 18, they wiped out the Lower Agency and swept on through the valley. Refugees scrambled into undermanned Fort Ridgely, no stockaded post, but a sprawl of unfortified wooden buildings. Eight hundred Indians charged the post but were beaten back. They turned then against the town of New Ulm, burned one hundred and ninety structures, and forced the evacuation of the settlement—but did not crack the orderly defense and retreat. Other brutal attacks bloodied the countryside west to Dakota Territory, south into Iowa. There is no way of knowing how many people died; one careful estimate suggests seven hundred civilians and one hundred soldiers. Hundreds more were taken prisoner and hideously abused by the Indians until a slow-moving relief column under Henry Hastings Sibley (no kin to Texan Henry H. Sibley, the Confederate invader of New Mexico) brought Little Crow to bay near Wood Lake on September 23. After defeating the Sioux, Sibley seized fifteen hundred prisoners—though Little

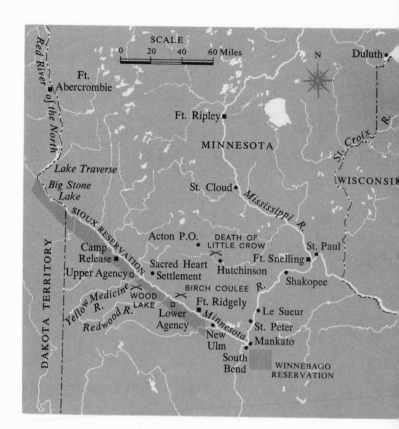

Above is the area of conflict of the sudden and desperate Minnesota war of 1862-63 with Little Crow and eastern Sioux.

Crow himself escaped—and freed the white captives.

A perfunctory trial sentenced three hundred and six Indians to death for arson, rape, and murder. Lincoln stayed execution and ordered details sent to Washington. Minnesotans were incensed. On December 6, a mob surged around the prisoners' camp at Mankato, but it was turned back by soldiers. Shortly thereafter, Lincoln authorized the hanging of thirty-eight of the condemned. On December 26, they were executed simultaneously on a single huge scaffold. The bands involved in the massacre were eventually shunted out of Minnesota to a reservation in Nebraska.

The punishment was not enough to suit the frontier. In 1863, Sibley marched nineteen hundred infantry and cavalry west through central North Dakota to about the site of today's Bismarck. Another punitive force under General Alfred Sully moved up the east bank of the Missouri River. The intent was to crush the eastern Sioux between the columns, but low water delayed Sully's supply steamers, and Sibley reached the meeting place a month ahead of his colleague. Although he surprised a large village of buffalo hunters under the wily renegade Inkpaduta, leader of the 1856 Spirit Lake massacre in Iowa, and fought three sharp skirmishes with them, the

Indians managed to escape across the river. The whites turned home. Promptly the Sioux recrossed the Missouri River to resume their hunt.

Along came Sully, his columns badly scattered. Inkpaduta's warriors trapped a battalion but paused for a dance of triumph before moving in for the kill. This gave Sully's cavalry time to race to the rescue. They saved their trapped fellows and killed three hundred Sioux at a loss of twenty-two whites dead, fifty wounded. The next year, 1864, Sully resumed the chase. After leaving part of his troopers a few miles below today's Bismarck to build Fort Rice, he pressed on with the rest toward the head of Knife River, in the badlands of what is now the western part of North Dakota.

Because of interruptions by the military the year before, the Sioux had taken few buffalo robes to trade with the English north of the border and consequently were short of ammunition. Trying to avoid a fight, they sought refuge in a spot so remote the whites would not follow. But Sully persisted. On the rough sides of Kildeer Mountain, sixteen hundred Indian braves turned on him but broke under cannon fire and scattered, contenting themselves thereafter with dogging the whites' flank as the foot-sore detachment moved north to the Yellowstone River to meet its supply boats.

While Sully was bearing down on the Sioux in the north, General James Carleton was crushing the Apaches and Navahos in the Southwest. His motives were mixed. The harried settlers of the region appealed to him for relief against a foe that never yet had been subdued. The prospect appealed both to Carleton and to his California volunteers, who had arrived too late to fight the retreating Confederates and were grumbling under such anticlimactic tasks as repairing roads and guarding mail wagons in the large and lonely country.

In addition, Carleton was convinced that New Mexico and Arizona were full of precious minerals—"one of the richest gold countries in the world . . . millions on millions of wealth," to use his own words—and that a rush comparable to California's would develop as soon as the Indians were removed. He ordered that all Apache and Navaho males "are to be slain whenever and wherever they can be found." Women and children were to be taken prisoner. Or—and this part of the notorious extermination order is not so generally repeated by offended historians of a later date—the tribes were to let themselves be confined to a reservation at Bosque Redondo, a long strip of timbered bottom land along the Pecos River in central New Mexico.

Troops under General Joseph R. West used promises of a peaceful conference to capture massive, six-foot-six-inch Mangas Coloradas, the seventy-year-old chief of the Mimbreños band of Gila Apaches, then prodded him into trying to escape. One story has it that soldiers burned the chief with a hot bayonet while he was asleep, shot him down when he leaped to his feet, and cut off his head. Terrified by his death, the Mimbreños went into hiding in their rough country and for the next few years caused no serious trouble. The Mescalero Apaches and the Navahos, better armed, fought harder. During 1863, the troopers lost seventeen dead and twenty-five wounded while killing or injuring three hundred and eight Indians. They also made prisoners of seven hundred and three, mostly Mescaleros, who were promptly penned up under guard at Bosque Redondo.

In January, 1864, Kit Carson, now a colonel in the U.S. Army, marched three hundred and seventy-five men through deep snow to Canyon de Chelly in northeastern Arizona and surprised the bulk of the Navahos in that vast, red-walled stronghold. He destroyed their crops, including three thousand peach trees, defeated a contingent of them in a brief battle, and persuaded twenty-four hundred men, women, and children to surrender. On March 5, the glum column of prisoners started east to Bosque Redondo on the "Long Walk" still remembered in Navaho tradition. They drove three thousand sheep with them—little more than one animal per person—and 473 horses. Thirty army wagons were enough for their possessions. After they had reached the Bosque, guards from nearby Fort Sumner watched them while they built mud huts as shelters in this new and meager land. In time, some six thousand of them were confined to the Bosque. Bad weather and cutworms destroyed their feeble attempts at farming. They lived in miserable degradation, subsisting on Government handouts, but were numerous enough, nevertheless, so that their reluctant neighbors and ancient enemies, the Mescalero Apaches, risked Army wrath one November night, 1865, to get away from the Navahos and flee from Bosque Redondo back to the hills.

Northward, on a sub-zero day in January, 1863, Patrick Connor's Californians attacked a village of Bannocks and Shoshonis huddled around some hot springs near the Utah-Idaho border. The whites killed two hundred and twenty-four people, took many prisoners, and cowed the survivors into peace. Farther east, the Cheyennes and Arapahoes of the high plains proved harder to pin down. Throughout 1863, they slashed sporadically against stations on the main roads up the Platte, Smoky Hill, and Arkansas rivers. Sioux to the north and Kiowas and Comanches to the south sometimes joined them. In between raids, they collected guns and ammunition from their agents and traders, ostensibly for use in hunting.

As their armament increased, so did their opposition to the growing number of whites in their countries. In the summer of 1864, bitter fighting swept western Kansas and eastern Colorado. Scores of settlers were scalped and mutilated; women were kidnaped and violated; ranches and hayfields were destroyed by fire. Troops retaliated by ruthlessly obliterating such villages as they managed to catch before the Indians could dismantle them. This bred fresh furies among the tribes. Freight reached Denver erratically. Mail to the Rocky Mountains was routed by way of San Francisco, and Ben Holladay claimed that Indian depredations drove his stage companies to the edge of bankruptcy.

Trying to segregate potentially peaceful bands from the hostiles, Governor John Evans of Colorado urged friendly Kiowas and Comanches to report to Fort Larned, on the Arkansas River in Kansas, and Southern Cheyennes and Arapahoes to Fort Lyon, two hundred and fifty miles farther up the same stream, in southeastern Colorado. The strategy collapsed. At Fort Larned, Chief Satanta of the Kiowas fell into a shooting scrape with a trigger-happy sentry, whereupon his followers stampeded the post's horseherd and fled with the animals into the Texas Panhandle. Many Comanches and Arapahoes joined them there.

Angrily, General James G. Blunt moved a column from Fort Larned against the defiant tribes. To support Blunt, Kit Carson marched east from New Mexico with three hundred and twenty-five men. On November 25, a thousand Indians hit Carson near Adobe Walls, the remnants of an old fur trading post beside the Canadian River. The startled troopers rallied and shot the attackers to pieces with two little howitzers they were transporting on pack mules. They then burned the abandoned Indian village and withdrew. This victory and Blunt's quieter maneuvering farther east slowed but did not halt Kiowa-Comanche raids on the Santa Fe Trail.

Affairs in Colorado were less clear-cut. After peace talks in Denver, a few Cheyenne and Arapaho chiefs led several hundred of their people at intervals into Fort Lyon. They may have been prompted more by a desire for free handouts during the coming winter than by a yearning for peace. Certainly far larger numbers of the tribes stayed belligerently away from the forts, holding war councils along the Smoky Hill River farther north.

Whatever the Indians' motives, the commanding officer at Fort Lyon received the bands that appealed to him, fed them for a time, and sent them off to hunt. About seven hundred of them, mostly Southern Cheyennes under Black Kettle, set up a hunting camp at Sand Creek,

forty miles north of the fort. Women considerably outnumbered men in the village, which suggests that the younger braves were away listening to the war drums at Smoky Hill. Still, having been sent to Sand Creek by the Army, the Indians there had no reason to anticipate attack.

One came nevertheless, delivered November 29, four days after Carson's fight at Adobe Walls. Most of the nine hundred and fifty whites involved were Colorado volunteers who had enlisted during the summer alarms and who wanted a fight before disbanding. Their leader was Colonel John Chivington, hero of the victory over the Confederates in New Mexico in 1862. Inasmuch as Chivington passed through Fort Lyon, where he picked up reinforcements and two cannon, he almost surely knew that the Indian village on Sand Creek was under military sanction. But perhaps he felt, on evidence appearing adequate to him, that Black Kettle's supposedly peaceful Cheyennes were actually leagued with the hostile camp on the Smoky Hill. Anyway, he attacked without warning and killed somewhere between one hundred and fifty—as estimated by a half-breed on the scene—and five hundred Indians, as Chivington himself estimated. Many women and children were among the slain. The whites committed certain atrocities. Today, a century after the battle, controversy still rages over its motives and details.

Whatever the truth, the attack inflamed rather than quieted the Indians. The Sioux made common cause with the Cheyennes. Employing their bewildering mobility with devastating effect, they again briefly isolated Denver but left off fighting in the spring of 1865 to follow the buffalo herds into northeastern Wyoming.

As the Civil War drew to a close, humanitarians in the East, shocked by the Sand Creek massacre, urged the Government to approach the Indian problem with something other than force. The upshot was one Congressional commission to investigate the condition of the tribes, and other committees to enter into fresh treaties looking toward peace. Unhappily, the Government's left hand seldom kept track of the right. In October, 1865, the treaty makers prevailed on the Kiowas, Comanches, Southern Cheyennes, and Arapahoes to consent to reservations south of the Arkansas River in western Kansas and Oklahoma. But when the documents relating to the Cheyennes and Arapahoes reached the Senate, that body added an amendment forbidding the establishment of reservations in Kansas. This contradiction left the two tribes no legal home to which to repair.

Similar inconsistencies brought about graver troubles farther north. Yielding to pressure from the Montana miners, Congress in March, 1865, authorized improvements to, and protection for, the road through central

Wyoming located by John Bozeman. The Sioux repeatedly had insisted that such a road violated earlier treaties and vowed never to permit it. The Army nevertheless ordered Colonel Henry B. Carrington into the area to build three forts. Almost simultaneously, in the fall of 1865 and again in the spring of 1866, treaty commissioners holding out olive branches summoned the chiefs to Fort Laramie for peace talks.

Carrington's march abruptly gave the lie to the blandishments. Grimly and yet with strange indecision when it came to attacking, the Sioux under Red Cloud watched Forts Reno and Phil Kearny rise in north-central Wyoming, Fort C. F. Smith beside the Bighorn River in southern Montana. While this was going on, there ar-

Fort Laramie was sketched by C. Moellman, a bugler with the 11th Ohio Cavalry that patrolled the Overland Trail in 1863.

rived in Wyoming the precursors of a more dangerous threat to Indian economy than the Sioux could have realized at the time—six hundred or so Texas longhorn cattle driven by Nelson Story and twenty-six cowboys.

Story was a Montana placer miner who in 1866 had sewn ten thousand dollars into the lining of his clothes and had ridden south with two friends to buy beef for the hungry mining camps around Virginia City. He bought his herd near Fort Worth, worked a way through the Indian country of eastern Oklahoma, cut north to the Oregon Trail, and then moved slowly west to Fort Laramie. By that point, he had covered some twelve hundred saddlesore miles and was unimpressed when Army officers told him the Indians along the Bozeman Trail

were feeling ugly. Purchasing new repeater rifles for his men, he pointed his longhorns northwest and kept going.

Indians attacked as predicted, wounded two men, and swept off the herd. The cowboys tracked the raiders down, annihilated them, and kept the recovered steers pointed toward Montana. They disdained Carrington's orders to wait for reinforcements and had no more trouble with the Sioux. In the opinion of one of the drovers, the Indians had no desire for a second taste of the new rifles. Or perhaps the Indians were busy preparing to challenge the troops, who were armed with old-style, muzzle-loading, single-shot Springfields.

As the fall buffalo hunts ended, skirmishes quickened. The climax came on December 21, 1866, when Captain William J. Fetterman recklessly marched eighty-one men out of Fort Phil Kearny on Powder River to relieve a besieged train of woodcutters. Red Cloud's Sioux killed every soldier. For a time after that, cold weather slowed hostilities, but with the arrival of spring, the persistent harassment of the forts' patrols, horseherds, woodcutters, and hay gatherers began again. Meanwhile, the Indians of the entire Platte watershed were becoming aware of still another invasion of their lands, this one by railroad builders, laying track westward.

Both the Union Pacific and a subsidiary, the Kansas Pacific, were on the move. In 1865, the brawny Casement brothers, Jack and Dan, the former a brigadier general in the Union army, had taken charge of the UP's construction work. Hiring thousands of Irish immigrants and discharged soldiers, they set them a goal of a mile of track per working day. The next year, hard-driving General Grenville M. Dodge, who had made railroad surveys in the Platte Valley as early as 1853, was released by the Army to take charge of the Union Pacific's location work. The new vigor was needed, for in 1866 the Central Pacific, pushing eastward across California, had suddenly loomed as a formidable rival for hundreds of thousands of acres of grant land.

In 1864, while amending the earlier Pacific railroad bill, Congress had decreed that the Central Pacific should build no farther than one hundred and fifty miles east of the California-Nevada border. So long as the booming Comstock mines of Virginia City held a paramount place in the thinking of Crocker, Hopkins, Huntington, and Stanford, the restriction did not chafe unduly. But the once-fabulous diggings were running into borasca, as barren ground was called. Ore returns dwindled by half between 1865 and 1869, a trend painfully evident as 1866 got underway. In the shadow of this collapse, the possibility of a lucrative commerce with the growing Mormon communities of northern Utah and connections with freight outfits supplying Montana began to look bright indeed to the Central Pacific's owners, especially since building that far would bring additional land grants and construction contracts.

Journeying to Washington in 1866, Collis Huntington prevailed on Congress to let the Central Pacific move on east until it met the Union Pacific. This political triumph buttoned safely in his pocket, he ordered sixty-six thousand tons of rail under the noses of the UP purchasing agents and acquired twenty-three ships for hauling it around the Horn. Meanwhile, Charles Crocker met the challenge of the Sierra Nevada with prodigies of effort, cutting trackway along the canyon wall of the American River by swinging Chinese and Irish blasters down the cliff faces in bosun's chairs. During the winter of 1866-67, while powder monkeys gouged out tunnels under the snowy ridges, he hauled rails, cars, and dismantled locomotives over Donner Summit on sleds so that his tracklayers could race up Nevada's relatively flat Humboldt Valley without waiting on the slow work in the mountains.

Although favored with easier terrain, the Union Pacific faced gigantic supply problems of its own. Railroads from the East did not establish connections at Omaha until 1867. Until then, all materials—forty carloads of ties, spikes, rail, food, and the like for each mile of track—had to come up the Missouri by steamboat. While Dan Casement managed logistics, his brother Jack pushed his tracklayers relentlessly on the heels of the wagon-supplied graders and set a record that at the time seemed phenomenal—266 miles of track in the single year of 1866. The next year, they progressed even faster. By the end of 1867, the UP's notorious "hell-on-wheels" construction camps had passed Cheyenne, and the clanging tracklayers were toiling toward the summit of the Laramie Hills.

This route, entering Wyoming at its southeastern corner, brought deep pain to Denver. Merchants in that young city had assumed their traffic would lure the railroad to their gates, just as it had lured the earlier stagecoaches; but by 1866, the mines of Colorado were languishing because of complex low-grade ores that no one could yet smelt economically. More importantly, bustling Grenville Dodge, the road's locator, saw no reason to waste time and miles on a long southern dip into Colorado—or, for that matter, on a northern bulge along the traditional trail up the North Platte and the Sweetwater. Instead, he drove as straight ahead as terrain allowed: over the Laramie Hills, around the point of the Medicine Bow Mountains, and west across Wyoming's sagebrush plains and Red Desert.

Denver's hurt was somewhat assuaged by the eastern branch of the Union Pacific, in those days more gener-

ally known as the Kansas Pacific. Projected originally as a branch road to connect Kansas City with the transcontinental line at the 100th meridian in the Platte Valley, the KP freed itself of the limitation in 1866. Promised generous land grants of its own (eventually they totaled six million acres), the new line in 1867 moved swiftly across central Kansas toward Colorado, meantime sending surveyors far ahead in an abortive attempt to find usable ways through the central Rockies to the coast.

This was the year the United States purchased Alaska from Russia for $7,200,000, a gesture as expansionistic as the Louisiana Purchase had been two thirds of a century earlier. But in 1867, the Yukon River seemed as remote from practical considerations as the Columbia

An 1868 view shows the American flag flying over Sitka shortly after Alaska was transferred from Russia to the United States.

had been in 1803. Of more immediate concern to the frontier was the Indians' continued resistance to white advances. In April, General W. S. Hancock tried to subdue the Southern Cheyennes and Arapahoes in Kansas by wantonly destroying one of their abandoned villages on the Pawnee Fork of the Arkansas River. George Armstrong Custer, whose dashing cavalry exploits in the Union Army during the Civil War had won wide praise, capped the "campaign" by zigzagging his famous Seventh Cavalry a fruitless thousand miles through the arid hills in the western part of the state. His main accomplishment was trouble for himself; on hearing that his young wife was ill of cholera at Fort Hays, he went AWOL to visit her and was suspended for a year without pay. Meantime, the Southern Cheyennes continued harassing the KP's surveyors and construction crews, and on August 6, at Plum Creek, Nebraska, two hundred and thirty miles west of Omaha, they wrecked a Union Pacific freight train and massacred its crew.

On their part, the Sioux killed several Union Pacific surveyors in Wyoming and attacked grading crews so methodically that shovelers had to work within reach of their stacked rifles. The Bozeman Trail to Montana stayed all but closed, its three forts under intermittent siege. Red Cloud's warriors twice more fought pitched battles with white soldiers patrolling the area, but the Army's powerful new breech-loading rifles prevented a repetition of the Fetterman debacle.

In March, 1867, the Congressional committee investigating the condition of the Indian tribes issued a report sharply critical of the Government's past Indian policies. Bolstered by this, advocates of a vigorous peace program again took charge of developments and initiated still another series of treaties. In the fall of the year, an incomplete roster of Cheyennes, Arapahoes, Kiowas, and Comanches assembled at Medicine Lodge Creek near Fort Larned, Kansas, and were cajoled into accepting barren lands in western Oklahoma as a new reservation —lands, incidentally, that had been stripped from the Five Civilized Tribes, loyal and Confederate alike, as a blanket punishment for their participation in the Civil War. The young warriors of the plains tribes hated the new lands and denied having agreed to the treaties. To teach them an object lesson, Custer in November, 1868, launched a winter campaign against their villages on the Washita River. Resorting to a surprise dawn attack, he smashed a Cheyenne town even more thoroughly than Chivington had smashed the camp at Sand Creek. After that, peace of a sort came to the Kansas area.

Elsewhere in 1868, the push to confine the Indians to reservations moved ahead with less bloodshed. The Utes settled peacefully in the western third of Colorado; the Bannocks agreed to a reservation near Fort Hall, Idaho. The Navahos promised never again to take up arms (a pledge they have faithfully kept) and were allowed to leave Bosque Redondo for a new reservation embracing part of their old homelands in the contiguous corners of northern New Mexico and Arizona. One of the chiefs, Manuelito, later told about the home-coming: "When we saw the top of the mountain from Albuquerque we wondered if it was our mountain and we felt like talking to the ground, we loved it so, and some of the old men and women cried with joy."

The Sioux also capitulated in 1868, after the Government had agreed to abandon the Bozeman Trail and its three forts. Joyfully the Indians burned down the hated posts. Afterward, in November, they signed a treaty that gave them the western half of South Dakota as a reservation and established the Powder River country of eastern Wyoming as a hunting ground for themselves and the Crows, who were confined to the south side of the Yellowstone River in central Montana.

By the time the Sioux treaty had been completed, the Union Pacific was thrusting toward the Central Pacific at a steadily accelerating pace. As the lines neared each other, the competition leaped out of hand. No junction point had been specified, and so, hoping to grab as much land as possible, the rival roads hurried up their Chinese and Irish laborers and kept on grading side by side in parallel lines, letting the exuberant workers now and then pummel each other instead of the earth with their pick handles. After more refined jockeying in Washington, Congress specified drab Promontory, in the alkaline desert north of Great Salt Lake, as the meeting point. On May 10, 1869, special engines touched nose to nose, dignitaries whose plug hats gleamed incongruously against the wastelands made speeches, and Leland Stanford, after missing with his first wallop, hit the golden spike a symbolic blow with his sledge hammer. The halves of the frontier were joined at last.

Tremendous energies chafed to fill the empty places still remaining. New railroads inched west. The Atchison, Topeka and Santa Fe broke ground in 1868. In 1869, Jay Cooke took over the financing of the stalled Northern Pacific, chartered in 1864 to build between Lake Superior and Puget Sound and promised the most generous land grant in American history: the total eventually reached thirty-nine million acres. In 1870, Denver and Salt Lake City linked themselves to the Union Pacific with branch lines to Cheyenne and Ogden, respectively.

The swiftly spreading transportation network promised Western farmers, miners, and cattlemen access to Eastern markets. Technology, which continued to improve agricultural machinery, quickened mining with the introduction of powerful steam drills. In 1868, Nathaniel Hill devised smelting procedures that released Colorado miners from the frustrations of their refractory ores. Lumbermen, whose ships were reaching Australia and South America, began looking for new ways to tap the seemingly inexhaustible forests of northern Minnesota, of Washington and Oregon.

Richness beckoned everywhere, and for the first time in America's wildly speculative course, neither isolation nor Indians loomed as serious threats to the harvesting— or so it seemed as a new decade opened on the most turbulent era of exploitation the frontier had yet experienced.

William C. Quantrill

BLUE AND GRAY IN THE WEST

The Civil War in the West was seldom a very orthodox kind of conflict. The opposing forces were composed largely of untrained local boys who often ran at the first shot, and who sometimes fought like heroes. It was waged over a huge area—one skirmish was as far away as Arizona—and while its battles are little remembered today, they kept Missouri in the Union and denied the mineral wealth of the Southwest to the Confederacy. Like all warfare, it fell heavily on civilians. On the Kansas-Missouri border the guerrilla fighting of the 1850's, much intensified, was repeated; it reached a hideous climax in the attack on Lawrence, Kansas, by William Quantrill and his band (above, as sketched a few hours later by a soldier, Sherman Enderton, after talking to survivors). The atrocity was an indefensible episode of the war, and in retaliation, Kansas Unionist guerrillas ravaged northern Missouri so thoroughly that it became known as the Burnt District. The Five Civilized Tribes in Indian Territory were also tragic victims of the Western wars. Wanting no part in the conflict, they were forced to choose sides and then suffered rapine, hunger, house burnings, and exile. After the war, the Government took half of the land of those who had joined the South, but it also took as much from those who had been loyal. The tribes won one distinction: Cherokee leader Stand Watie became the first Indian general and was the last Confederate general to surrender.

ACTION IN THE SOUTHWEST

Left: A guard at Fort Sumner on Bosque Redondo keeps watch over Navahos during a counting of the captive Indians at the beginning of their confinement.

Right: Fort Canby was established in the heart of Navaho country to serve as the principal military base during the 1863-64 campaign to suppress the tribe.

Below: Canyon de Chelly—most of it less accessible than the portion in this photograph of the 1870's—was the inner bastion of the Navahos; once it was penetrated, they were forced to surrender.

The United States inherited an ancient Indian problem when it annexed the Southwest. The conquering Spanish had made mortal enemies of the Navahos, and things had not bettered in two hundred years. Navahos were still raiding Mexican villages for horses, sheep, and young Mexicans to adopt; Mexicans in return enslaved hundreds of Navahos. American attempts to make treaties with the Indians and bring peace between the old enemies were only fitfully successful; by 1858 the Navahos were warring with the Army itself. Attacks increased, as Army garrisons were reduced during the Civil War, until Colonel Kit Carson was sent to teach the Navahos a lesson. He harried them during the winter of 1863–64, invading their Canyon de Chelly stronghold to destroy homes, orchards, and sheep flocks. When the starving Indians surrendered, they were marched some 300 miles to the Bosque Redondo, a wind-swept reservation on the Pecos. Many died on the bitter trip, which is still known as the "Long Walk." There was a happy ending; farming failed on the Bosque Redondo, and in 1868 the captives were sent back to their own land to settle down as herdsmen, never going to war again.

Before the Bosque Redondo captivity, a Navaho man was both warrior and sheepkeeper; afterward, he gave up all his warmaking activity.

WHILE THE TROOPS WERE AWAY

Refugees from the Minnesota Sioux uprising of 1862 pause to rest on the prairie during their flight.

333

AFTERMATH

Henry Benjamin Whipple, Episcopal Bishop of Minnesota

The Indians gave Bishop Henry Whipple a high compliment for a white man; they called him Straight Tongue. He had long warned that white treatment of the Indians would end in violence, but after the 1862 Minnesota Sioux uprising, all he could do was pick up a few of the pieces. It was his intercession that led Lincoln to commute the death sentences of all but 38 of the 306 Sioux condemned for war crimes—and for this, the wrath of the revenge-hungry frontier fell on the Bishop. But there was little more he could do for his Indian friends, for Minnesota now took advantage of the situation to rid itself of all its Sioux. Nearly 2,000 of them, almost all neutral or actively friendly during the war, had been rounded up. They were kept over the winter on the river flats below Fort Snelling, then were sent to a barren reservation in Nebraska. The 268 prisoners whose death sentences had been set aside had been sent from Mankato to a prison camp a little earlier. Most had become Christians during the winter; as their steamboat passed the camp below Fort Snelling, where many had relatives and friends, they sang the hymn, "Have Mercy Upon Us, O Jehovah."

Under Fort Snelling's guns, almost the very last of Minnesota's Sioux wait in a dreary camp (above) for spring and deportation. Chief Shakopee, a ruthless killer during the uprising, was photographed (right) while awaiting his execution, which came in 1865.

334

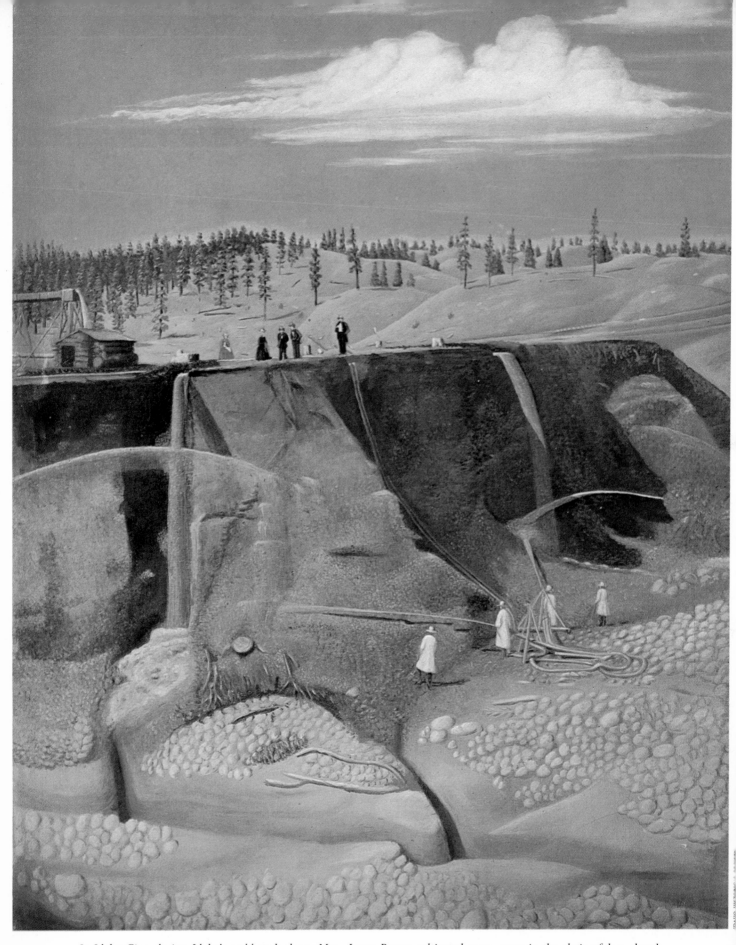

In Idaho City, during Idaho's gold rush days, Mrs. Jonas Brown cultivated roses, sang in the choir of her church, and painted pictures like the one above of hydraulic miners. But Idaho City was not all roses: of 200 men who died in a period of eighteen months, only ten perished of natural causes. The rest either "stretched rope" or were shot.

ROAD AGENTS
AND
VIGILANTES

One night in December, 1863, nine men gathered in a store in Virginia City, Montana. Standing in a circle with hands raised, they dedicated themselves to "the laudable purpose of arresting thieves and murderers and recovering stolen property." Thus, to cope with outlaws infesting the West's new gold regions, were born Montana's vigilantes. The first big strike in the northern country, at Pierce, Idaho, in 1860, had been followed by other finds in Idaho and Montana. Soon the hills from Boise Basin to Helena were full of prospectors—and rogues. Among the latter, the most celebrated was Henry Plummer, sheriff at Bannack and Virginia City who also led a gang of road agents. Men of his kind in almost every camp were ultimately hanged by vigilantes.

As tough head of the Montana vigilantes and, later, deputy marshall, John X. Beidler (left) brought scores of desperadoes to gallows and hanging trees like the one at Helena (above). At top is Helena (first called Last Chance Gulch) during gold rush days, 1865.

CONNECTING THE CENTERS

An 1860 view shows a pony express rider hurrying past an emigrant train on the plains.

In an Indian attack, like the one below painted by George Simons, the heavy iron and wood body of a stagecoach was like an armored car.

The growth of populated centers, many of them far from each other and all of them remote from the East, increased the need for reliable communication and transportation facilities across the West. Stagecoaches and mail carriers first linked settlements in California and Oregon, but by the late 1850's, Butterfield Overland stages, subsidized by Congress, were carrying passengers and mail between the Mississippi Valley and San Francisco. Swifter mail service was provided in 1860 by the pony express, but its dramatic history ended abruptly the next year with the opening of the transcontinental telegraph. Freight service meanwhile became big business. Steamers carried cargo 2,300 miles up the Missouri to Fort Benton, while caravans of oxen-drawn freight wagons, many from the firm of Russell, Majors & Waddell, plied a network of routes to the new mines and towns in the West.

Until comparatively recent times, bull trains like the one winding over Ute Pass, Colorado (right), could be seen delivering freight to isolated Western settlers.

Laying rails on the Union Pacific

A work train on the central plains

Pushing the Central Pacific eastward

THE RAILROAD AT LAST

Union Pacific engines on completed track

uilding a tunnel for the transcontinental road

Making a cut in California's Sierra

nstructing a bridge abutment in Wyoming

341

The Battle of Beecher Island in 1868 (top left) occurred when a company of fifty scouts was surprised in eastern Colorado by a band of Sioux and Cheyennes they were hunting. After a siege of several days, the Indians withdrew, leaving five whites dead. Controversy continued for years over Custer's dawn attack on the village of the Cheyenne chief Black Kettle (left center), on the Washita River in present Oklahoma. Many denounced it as the masscre of a friendly sleeping camp. The captives taken by Custer were herded back through the snow (lower left) and on arrival were forced to pass in a triumphal review before General Sheridan.

ALL THIS PAGE: *Harper's Weekly,* 1868

STRUGGLE ON THE PLAINS

Comanches, Kiowas, and Southern Cheyennes and Arapahoes agreed at Medicine Lodge Creek in Kansas in 1867 to go on reservations. Private Hermann Stieffel, who was there, painted the council (above) as the great Kiowa Chief, Satanta, was speaking. A magazine artist called his idealized drawing of President Grant and Indians (below) "Let Us Have Peace." Usually such meetings cost the Indians their land.

The 1862 Sioux uprising in Minnesota shattered the uneasy peace that had prevailed on the plains; for many years after, the Army would always be fighting Indians somewhere. Sioux, Cheyenne, Arapaho, Comanche, and Kiowa warriors had all been drawn into fighting even before the Civil War had ended; after the war the tribes took new alarm as railroad builders pushed westward across the plains.

General William T. Sherman took command of the Army in the West and began to talk of "extermination" as a solution to Indian problems. Among his lieutenants was General Philip Sheridan, an expert at ruthless destruction during the war. Sheridan's favorite officer was George A. Custer, a man who wept with his wife at sentimental drama but who could ride whooping with his troopers over an Indian village full of women and children. It was not a happy time for Indians.

Harper's Weekly, 1870

Custer Battlefield, overlooking the Valley of the Little Bighorn, Montana

"The soldiers stopped and got off their horses. . . . In a few minutes the warriors were all around these soldiers. Then Lame White Man called out: 'Come. We can kill all of them. . . .'"
Wooden Leg, Northern Cheyenne, in *Wooden Leg, A Warrior Who Fought Custer*, interpreted by Thomas B. Marquis, 1931

CHAPTER THIRTEEN

HIGH, WIDE, AND UGLY

1870-1890

In 1881, the cattlemen of southeastern Colorado presented to the Government, through Silas Bent, what seemed an incredible suggestion. Let three hundred and sixty thousand square miles of the "Buffalo Plains" east of the Rockies be classified as pastoral land and leased under twenty-year terms to stock raisers, in blocks ranging between twenty thousand and three hundred thousand acres each. Since some ranches already were spreading across greater areas, the proposal seemed modest to its makers. But to most American sociologists and congressmen, habituated as they were to a different yardstick for evaluating the public domain, the notion was monstrous.

East of the Mississippi, a democratic land unity had been defined in effect as the amount of ground an individual family could clear and cultivate on its way to self-sufficiency. Eventually, as we have seen, this definition crystallized into a figure of one hundred and sixty acres, handed out free to whoever spent five years preparing his homestead for cultivation. That the land might be wholly grazed and not cultivated at least in part never entered into the calculations.

Even the awarding of enormous acreages to the railroads was no real contradiction of these equalitarian philosophies. Congress still intended that individual holdings should remain small. To prevent consolidation for speculative purposes, the long strips of grant land were broken into checkerboards, each square a mile to the side. Squares belonging to the railroad alternated with squares of public domain land that were subject to the normal homestead entry of one hundred and sixty

acres—or eighty acres close to the tracks. Yet the stockmen of southeastern Colorado were blandly proposing to distribute almost an eighth of the nation's area—enough land, on paper, to provide 1,440,000 family units—among five thousand or so cattlemen. Of course to many others in the country it seemed like an outrage.

Actually, the dry climate of the plains was such that 1,440,000 farmers could not possibly have wrung a living from one-hundred-and-sixty-acre plots. The Colorado stockmen may have been selfish in the substitute they proposed, but at least they understood the realities of the situation. Congress did not. It clung instead to time-hallowed theories evolved from a different environment and by so doing invited the very sort of vested monopolies that an equal distribution of free mineral and agricultural lands to those who wanted them was supposed to avoid. The resultant scramble to hog everything in sight was often dramatic, but it also furnishes some of the sorriest reading in the history of the frontier.

Corruption was easy under the Homestead Act. In spite of repeated appeals, the General Land Office never received funds enough to provide an adequate number of investigators for its widely scattered offices. Those who did serve were overworked and underpaid, and hence susceptible to bribery. Results were predictable. For a first instance, let us return to the checkerboarded areas embraced in railroad land grants. A company interested in land speculation first purchased several of the railroad's more desirable squares. It then obtained the intervening pieces by manipulating military land warrants or by sending out fraudulent entrymen to lay claim to homesteads. Since none of these entrymen intended to occupy the land, they had no interest in obeying specifications about improvements. They rented cabins that had been put on wheels and moved them from claim to claim as needed, or they built Alice-in-Wonderland structures, twelve by fourteen—inches, not feet—then went to the nearest land office and swore that a dwelling stood upon their land. Very seldom did an investigation follow.

After six months' residence on the claim, actual or pretended, those entrymen secured full title by "commuting" the homestead to a pre-emption claim and paying the government $1.25 an acre for it. They then transferred the plot to the speculator. He combined several such fragments with his railroad squares and sat back to wait for increased population to raise the price of the whole.

Temporary shacks like this one, often moved from site to site on the plains, were set up to establish ownership of claims.

Often the plungers were content merely to double their money, but special circumstances might result in spectacular profits—the South Dakota wheat boom of the early 1880's, for instance, shot prices up to thirty-five dollars an acre. Lured by similar prospects in Oregon, Ben Holladay, the erstwhile stagecoach king, in 1871 spread the taint of bribery as far as justices of the United States Supreme Court during his titanic financial battle to control the Oregon Central Railroad and its promised four million acres of grant land.

Too many of the speculative land companies were, like Holladay's, closely related to the railroads. Aroused by this, by shoddy track construction born of a hurry to complete the mileage on which grants depended, and by rate juggling in favor of large shippers, Congress in 1871 refused to make any further gifts of land to railroads.

The harm had been done, however. Landless men who really hoped to farm were pushed back outside the land-grant boundaries, where schools and churches and market places would be slow to reach them. No wonder the railroads and speculators smugly advertised their lands as "Better Than A Homestead."

Other handy devices existed for shoving aside the men for whom the homestead law had been designed. One sprang from the Morrill Act of 1862, which handed out to every state and territory in the nation generous amounts of Western land—the total reached one hundred and forty million acres—that could be sold to raise funds for establishing agricultural colleges. Locators employed by the recipient states naturally picked out the most valuable Western lands they could find. The states then sold these lands in big blocks at low rates to speculators. This too tended to thrust homesteaders into less desirable regions—if they went at all.

Eager to lure purchasers to their holdings, railroads and the speculators filled the eastern United States and western Europe with outrageous propaganda. Salesmen for the Northern Pacific, which in the early 1870's was building across Minnesota into eastern North Dakota, sang such paeans of praise that the northern prairies became known sardonically as Jay Cooke's banana belt, after the New York financier who was underwriting the construction of the railroad. Whole colonies succumbed to the advertising. Santa Fe agents made contact with Mennonites emigrating from the Crimea to escape military conscription and during the winter of 1873–74 settled two thousand of these hard-working Russian farmers (who brought with them $2,500,000 for equipping their farms) in south-central Kansas.

The first strips of prairie that the advancing farmers encountered were not unduly demanding. The transcontinental railroads and the shorter "Granger" lines that by 1870 had reached across Iowa to Council Bluffs and Sioux City imported enough lumber for essential building. When the cost of wooden fences leaped out of hand, the settlers found workable substitutes. Kansans, some Iowans, and Texans used thick hedges of prickly osage orange, boosted by their advocates as "pig tight, horse high, and bull strong." Demand for osage-orange seed became a madness; in the early 1870's, its price soared from eight dollars a bushel to fifty dollars or more. In Nebraska, where the hedges were winterkilled, homesteaders built walls of sod bricks, cut from the root-matted earth and heaped up three or four feet high.

Log cabins vanished from the pioneering scene. Houses were sometimes dug back into hillsides and roofed so nearly to the line of the earth that they were really caves. If suitable hills were not available, house walls were built, like fence walls, of sod bricks and roofed with poles covered by dirt and grass—permanent images now in the American historical consciousness.

Household water was another plains problem that had seldom occurred in the humid East. The nearest creek might be half a dozen miles away; ground water, from thirty to three hundred feet below the surface. A man often had to spend a year or more hauling water in barrels before he found time between his other chores to dig a deep well through the hard, compacted earth. However, springtime invariably brought a soft green loveliness to the land and to the hearts of those who loved it; and during the rest of the year, there was rain enough, in those first belts of prairie country, to support the kind of agriculture most of the settlers had learned in the East. Encouraged by this and by good prices for wheat and corn, they edged still farther west. They developed stoves that gulped down twists of hay instead of wood. They learned to outface the thunder of prairie fires, the blinding sweep of winter blizzards, the knife-edge of cold so intense that they took their seed potatoes to bed with them to keep them from freezing. They even mastered, although it was harder for women than for men, the deadly spiritual oppression of so much inescapable sky.

About the 98th meridian there is a climatic line, visible where prairie grass gives way to short, curly buffalo grass, west of which average rainfall will not support ordinary farming. Average—but during the late 1860's, precipitation was above average. The Great Salt Lake, for example, increased ten feet in depth, six hundred square miles in area. Betrayed by this, the advance guard of farmers crossed the danger line in Kansas, Nebraska, and eastern Dakota Territory before the cycle changed.

As rain dwindled, settlement slowed. The General Land Office thereupon showed its misapprehension of the entire plains problem by suggesting that the character of the country be improved. Let there be trees! Congress responded in March, 1873, by passing the Timber Culture Act. If a would-be landowner planted and nurtured forty acres of trees for ten years (reduced in 1878 to ten acres and eight years), he would acquire title to a full quarter-section (one hundred and sixty acres, again!) surrounding his wood lot. Trees can indeed be grown in certain sections of the plains, and in time handsome groves did shade many a prairie farm. But in 1873, tree culture was beyond the resources of most homesteaders, and the act became merely another device whereby dishonest entrymen could hog still more land.

Congress notwithstanding, the drought intensified, crops shriveled, dust storms raged. As if to make nature's threat completely clear, grasshopper swarms floated down out of the hot skies. Nightmares of clicking teeth stripped vegetation to stubble, shred laundry, chewed into hoe handles for the taste of impregnated human sweat. The grease of hordes of insects' crushed bodies on train tracks halted locomotives.

The ecology should have been clear: this was not farming country. But patterns of thinking are the hardest of all habits to break. Besides, when a man has bet his existence on a hundred and sixty acres of free land, it is not easy just to let go and find something else. After viewing the distress caused by the grasshopper plague of 1874, a frontier preacher named Thomas Henry Tibbles decided that something had to be done. By nature, Tibbles was a reformer; later he would become a vice-presidential candidate on the Populist ticket. But in 1874, it did not occur to him to reform attitudes about land. Instead, he thumbed his way east and persuaded railroads—which had an interest in keeping people on the plains—humanitarians, and agencies of the Federal Government to send relief funds to the destitute of Kansas and Nebraska so that they could hang on in the same old way.

Other agricultural reformers were no wiser. Stirred to outrage by the Panic of 1873, they flocked by the thousands to join the Patrons of Husbandry, more popularly called the Grange, and through it attacked monopolistic manufacturers, grain elevator operators, and railroad barons. The abuses they battled needed correction. But in the excitement, the need for acquiring new knowledge about the plains was overlooked.

Ironically, four Federal land surveys were hard at work throughout these years to provide information about the mountains and deserts farther to the west. The leaders of three of these groups were civilians: Ferdinand V. Hayden, who gravitated toward the Rockies of Wyoming and Colorado; John Wesley Powell, who, despite an arm lost during the Battle of Shiloh, prowled tirelessly through the eroded plateau and canyon country of Utah and northern Arizona; and Clarence King, a Rhode Island Brahmin of dazzling personal charm who at the age of twenty-four persuaded Congress that it was possible to learn the general nature of all the West by examining a cross section of it along the 40th parallel. The fourth party was led by Lieutenant George M. Wheeler. A pompous young martinet, Wheeler, West Point '66, felt exploratory work to be the rightful prerogative of the Army. It was his particular dream to produce a topographic map, useful for marching troops, of the entire nation west of the 100th meridian.

The public at large was impressed most by the natural spectacles the surveys made familiar. Powell's two boat

N

CANADA

WASHINGTON
(ADMITTED 1889)

Seattle

NORTHERN PACIFIC R.R.

Coeur d'Alene
Lake

NEZ PERCE

Portland

Columbia R.

CASCADE RANGE

COAST RANGES

Ft. Benton

GREAT NORTHERN R.R.

Missouri R.

NORTH DAKO
(ADMITTED 1889)

MONTANA

Ft. Keogh

NORTHERN PACIFIC R.R.

Bismarck

Ft. Rice

Helena

Butte

Salmon R.

Ft. Ellis

Virginia
City

Bozeman

Yellowstone R.

LITTLE
BIGHORN

ROSEBUD

CROW

Rosebud C.

Tongue R.

Powder R.

SLIM BUTTES

SOUTH DAKOT
(ADMITTED 1889)

OREGON

IDAHO
(ADMITTED 1890)

Snake R.

YELLOWSTONE
NAT'L PARK

WOLF
MTN.

NORTHERN
CHEYENNE

SIOUX

Lead

Deadwood

Rapid City

BLACK HILLS

Custer

WOUNDED
KNEE

White

WYOMING
(ADMITTED 1890)

BIGHORN MTS.

BOZEMAN TRAIL

SOUTHERN PACIFIC R.R.

Goose C.

Promontory
Pt.

Humboldt R.

SOUTH PASS

Ft. Fetterman

WARBONNET
CREEK

CENTRAL PACIFIC

R.R.

Great Salt
Lake

Ogden

UNION PACIFIC

R.R.

Ft. Laramie

N. Platte R.

NEBRASKA

CENTRAL OVERLAND ROAD

Salt Lake
City

UTE

Cheyenne

ARAPAHO

Sacramento

Virginia City

NEVADA

UTAH
TERRITORY

Green R.

S. Platte R.

JULESBURG

San
Francisco

SIERRA NEVADA

COLORADO
(ADMITTED 1876)

Denver

MEEKER
MASSACRE

Aspen

Leadville

PIKES PEAK +

Colorado
Springs

KANSAS PACIFIC

R.R.

COAST RANGES

UTE

Ouray

Telluride

Silverton

ROYAL
GORGE

Pueblo

APISHAPA
CANYON

SOUTHERN
CHEYENNE

CALIFORNIA

GRAND
CANYON

Trinidad

ATCHISON TOPEKA & SANTA FE R.R.

Dodge C

OKLAHOMA TER

Los Angeles

ARIZONA
TERRITORY

Colorado R.

SALT RIVER
CANYON

Salt R.

Taos

Santa Fe

Albuquerque

ADOBE WALLS

KIOW

PALO DURO
CANYON

San Diego

Ft. Yuma

Gila R.

APACHE

BOSQUE
REDONDO

NEW MEXICO
TERRITORY

Rio Grande

COMAN

Tucson

Tombstone

El Paso

GOODNIGHT-LOVING CATTLE TRAIL

TEXA

Ft. Con

PACIFIC

OCEAN

Pecos R.

Con

SOUTHERN PACIFIC R.R.

1870-93

GULF OF CALIFORNIA

Chihuahua

MEXICO

The West of 1870–93 was the busy scene of the final subjuga-
tion of the nation's Indians, the expansion of mining frontiers,
fevered railroad building, and great cattle drives from Texas.

trips through the chasms of the Colorado River system
(1869, 1871) established the Grand Canyon as a symbol
of national grandeur. Hayden's fiery arguments, backed
by the wet-plate photographs of William Henry Jackson,
led Congress in 1872 to establish Yellowstone National
Park, first proposed two years earlier by a group of Montana citizens. (Yosemite, dating from 1866, precedes
Yellowstone as the country's initial gesture at conservation, but Yosemite began as a California, not a Federal,
project.) Painter Thomas Moran so awed legislators with
his glowing canvases of the grand canyons of both the
Colorado and Yellowstone rivers that the nation purchased the paintings for ten thousand dollars each, to
hang in the Capitol at Washington, D.C. Jackson's spectacular photograph of the Mount of the Holy Cross made
that remote Colorado summit almost as familiar as Pikes
Peak to armchair travelers in the East.

Not spectacle, however, but knowledge was each survey's reason for being—practical knowledge as well as
scientific. When Clarence King received his first appropriation, he was told to broaden his survey of the 40th
parallel enough to embrace the line of the Union Pacific
and Central Pacific railroads, so that farmers, miners,
and lumbermen might know what to expect. (It proved
to be not much.) One of the first reports issued by the
scientists who accompanied him was, accordingly, James
Hague's epochal *Mining Industry*, published in 1870,
whereas Othneil Marsh's *Extinct Toothed Birds of North
America* waited until 1880.

Far more dramatic than publications was King's ex-
posure of two extraordinary bunko artists, Philip Arnold
and John Slack. The South African diamond fields were
just then booming into prominence, and the pair realized
that American investors would spring at similar escalators
to easy fortune. They sprinkled several thousand dollars'
worth of second-rate, uncut gems about a remote section
of northwestern Colorado and then sold their "discovery"
for upwards of half a million dollars to a syndicate of
reputable California financiers. The purchasers thereupon eagerly readied a ten-million-dollar public stock
issue, meanwhile keeping the exact location of the spectacular "diamond field" a careful secret.

All this nonplused King and his chief assistants. They
had just traversed the general area of the find and had
detected no geologic conditions favorable for precious
stones. Either they had made a major slip, in which case
their survey would be discredited, or something was

amiss. Through brilliant detection they pinpointed the site, visited it in the bitter cold days of late October, 1872, and proved that the "mines" had been salted.

Science triumphant! That single revelation, one Colorado newspaper editorialized, saved the investing public enough money to justify the entire cost of King's survey of the 40th parallel. But no survey undertook to unmask the land frauds that, among other things, were bleeding away the nation's timber by dishonestly claiming it as agricultural land. Not until 1874–75, when King's field work was already finished, were Hayden, Powell, and Wheeler instructed to classify the land they surveyed as agricultural, timber, pastoral, or barren. By that time, it was almost too late. In 1876, Commissioner S. B. Burdett of the General Land Office told Congress, "A national calamity is being rapidly and surely brought upon this country by the useless destruction of the forests. Much of this destruction arises from the abuse of the beneficent laws for giving land to the landless."

Of the four surveyors, Ferdinand Hayden was the one most inclined to turn his research to economic ends. Attracted by this trait, Colorado promoters arranged in 1872 for him to help them harvest certain commercial riches that they felt were rightfully theirs.

The matter sprang out of a race between railroads. The arrival of the Kansas Pacific in Denver and the linking of that city with the Union Pacific at Cheyenne, both in 1870, had touched off almost as much excitement as the original gold rush. An eager short line, the Colorado and Central, reached toward the mines of Gilpin County, and Denver began to dream of herself as a railroad hub. Then, to the dismay of the promoters, an outside line, the Atchison, Topeka and Santa Fe, pushed toward the southeastern part of the territory, invigorated by a promise of land grants from Kansas if the tracks reached the Colorado border by 1873. This meant that traffic from southern Colorado would escape to Kansas City—unless Denver devised an effective counterstroke.

The man who selected himself as savior was General William Palmer, leader of the Fifteenth Pennsylvania Cavalry during the Civil War and afterward construction boss and Manager of Surveys for the Kansas Pacific. His inspiration was dazzling. So far, all Western railroads had been designed to run from east to west. Why not, Palmer asked, vary the pattern by building a narrow-gauge line from Denver south along the base of the Rockies to Mexico City? He chose narrow gauge (three feet between rails, instead of the standard four feet eight and a half inches) because the tighter roadbeds, smaller rails, and lighter rolling stock were economical, a prime consideration in view of the Government's growing nig-

gardliness with free land. Besides, narrow gauge was more adaptable to the mountains, and Palmer envisioned many mountain branches pointing the way to vast resources of stone, timber, minerals, and even farmland in the peak-cupped interior valleys. Furthermore, the building of these lines would forestall the Santa Fe and keep Kansas hands off Colorado treasure.

His Denver and Rio Grande Railroad, financed principally by Eastern and English capital, was incorporated on October 27, 1870. The next year, the city of Colorado Springs was launched as a railroad promotion, pure and simple. The year after that, the Federal Government directed Hayden to provide the sort of topographical information that would help locate not just trackways but also promising sites for the mines, ranches, sawmills, and farms that Palmer had dreamed of. The Panic of 1873 halted the railroad race for a time, but not Hayden's survey. During four years, 1872–76, his far-ranging men compiled detailed observations for the magnificent atlas, useful as well as scientific, that for decades caused Coloradans to speak his name in reverent tones.

Balancing the other side of the scale is Hayden's share in advancing the frontier's most pernicious myth: the notion that the benign influences of civilization can somehow or other stimulate rainfall. The cyclical nature of weather was not understood in those days, and when precipitation did increase throughout the West in the late 1860's, a folk theory ascribed the change to an increase of plowing and planting. Hayden picked up the notion while head of the Geological Survey of Nebraska in 1867 and noted in his annual report his belief, as a respected scientist, that tree propagation would be helpful in "affecting the climate. . . increasing the moisture and adding greatly to the fertility of the soil." Later, as a Federal surveyor, he let Cyrus Thomas and other members of his exploring parties include similar speculations in the annual reports he submitted to Congress. This was official talk. Drought-stricken farmers took courage from it, and when a new wet cycle occurred during the late years of the 1870's, it encouraged them, as we will see, to break hundreds of thousands of prairie acres that should never have been maimed by a plow.

All this while, a suspect race of horsemen driving herd after herd of longhorn cattle north from the Texas range was heaping up visual evidence of what the short-grass country really was suited for. Habit-stultified agrarians refused to heed what was happening. Cattle, generally herded afoot back East, were adjuncts to other farm activities. The idea of making livestock a person's principal goal seemed preposterous. For one thing, how could a farmer, who was not a horseman by instinct, control his animals out on the boundless plains, where extensive fences, in the early 1870's, simply could not be built?

The animals the cowboys drove were equally suspect. They were the gaunt offspring of low-quality cattle that during the 1700's had escaped from Spanish missions in southern Texas and had found congenial breeding grounds in the thorn-spiked thickets and brassy, hot valleys that transect the lowest tip of the state, from San Antonio down past the Nueces River to the present border with Mexico. In time, animals that belonged to American settlers had mingled with these wild, scrubby herds. The eventual product varied slightly from region to region, but the general type—variegated, pinch-nosed, lean-flanked, and hardy—became known, from its most prominent characteristic, as the longhorn.

When men who had learned phenomenal horsemanship in order to fight Indians and Mexicans decided to move farther out onto the Texas frontier, they hazed as many of these ferocious animals out of the brush as they could handle and took them along. By the time of the Civil War, the creatures were ranging as far north as the upper Brazos River, northwest of Fort Worth.

Markets were a long way off—New Orleans first, then west over mountains and desert to the gold fields of California, or northeast along the so-called Shawnee Trail through Indian Territory to St. Louis. Some of the herds were even ferried across the Mississippi for fattening in Illinois and Ohio.

After viewing one of these herds in 1854, a reporter for the St. Louis *Intelligencer* sniffed, "We have seen some buffaloes that were more civilized." Farmers along the route in southeastern Kansas and Missouri found a deadlier cause for resentment in a fever spread among their domestic cattle by ticks that the longhorns carried. They tried to turn the animals back, and trouble was on the verge of breaking loose when the Civil War interrupted the drives. It took no prophet to guess that if the drivers and their trail herds reappeared afterward, war hatreds would inflame differences still more.

According to one estimate, nearly five million head of untended cattle were ranging the frontier counties of Texas when Confederate soldiers drifted back to the prostrate state in 1865. Meanwhile, the North and, as is less generally recognized, the Rocky Mountain West were clamoring for beef. Promptly the impoverished cowmen of Texas set about obliging their erstwhile enemies.

In 1866, several dozen herds totaling more than a quarter of a million animals moved along the familiar Shawnee Trail toward the nearest railhead at Sedalia, Missouri. Before following them, however, it will be useful to note two thousand history-making steers, bulls, cows, and calves pointed toward a different outlet by crop-bearded Charles Goodnight, thirty years old, and hard-twisted Oliver Loving, aged fifty-four.

Goodnight had spent the war years as a Texas Ranger. On his return to his ranch near the upper Brazos, he began dodging Indians to salvage what cattle he could. It was desperate work, and he was reluctant to risk the meager results among the angry farmers of southeastern Kansas and Missouri. Instead, he decided to try his luck around the Colorado mining camps. As he was making preparations, he fell in with Oliver Loving. Loving had reached Denver with cattle in 1860 by going north through Indian Territory and then west along the Arkansas River. In 1866, however, Kiowas and Comanches were infesting that route, and accordingly the pair decided to approach

Setting for movie and television westerns, the real Dodge City looked like this at the height of its wild gaminess in 1879.

Colorado by a roundabout way through New Mexico.

They hired eighteen cowboys and on June 6 started their herd southwest along the dimming ruts of Butterfield's old Overland Mail road. Beyond the head of the Middle Concho River lay eighty waterless miles. At the end of the third fiery day, the thirsty animals were uncontrollable. On reaching the Pecos River, they poured headlong over six-foot banks. Several were trampled to death in the turbid red water; hundreds more bogged down in the quicksand.

After a three-day rest, the men moved the survivors up the twisting, sterile Pecos Valley into New Mexico. An unexpected market greeted them at Bosque Redondo. The Navahos confined there were starving, and their agent bought every steer the partners had. He would not take the cows and calves, however. Loving and most of the cowboys drove these on into Colorado as planned. Goodnight and three others loaded twelve thousand dollars in gold onto a pack mule and rode seven hundred miles back to Texas to gather another herd for the Indians. Save for a brush with stampeding buffalo, they had no particular trouble. The partners rejoined at the Bosque and spent the winter in a cave dug into a bank.

They repeated the thirsty drive in 1867. Along the way, Loving stumbled into an ambush of Comanches and received wounds from which he died. Working alone after that, Goodnight became an entrepreneur, receiving Texas cattle in New Mexico or Colorado and passing them on to contractors supplying Army camps and Indian agencies.

One Texas trail boss who delivered tens of thousands of longhorns to him was John Chisum. After the Navahos left Bosque Redondo, Chisum moved in, took squatter and homestead rights along the Pecos, and soon was running a hundred thousand head of animals on a range that reached from Fort Sumner (the abandoned post at the Bosque) two hundred miles south to the Texas border. Rustlers hired by Major L. G. Murphy, a store- and saloonkeeper at dusty Lincoln, off to the west, began raiding his herd, or so Chisum believed. Their vendetta, heated by political and economic rivalries, ballooned in 1878 into the infamous Lincoln County War and made a folk hero out of a nineteen-year-old, unprepossessing little assassin called Billy the Kid.

Goodnight kept his hands cleaner. Seeking a grassy place for holding the cattle he received from Texas, he moved into rimrocked Apishapa Canyon, northeast of Trinidad, Colorado. There, in the spring of 1868, he was visited by John Iliff, who during the war had begun running a few head of domestic cattle in the South Platte Valley for sale to Denver butcher shops. In 1867 the Union Pacific, then building into Wyoming, had given Iliff a contract for supplying beef to its construction crews and their Army escorts. Unable to supply the demand from his own herds, he rode south to the Apishapa and ordered forty-five thousand dollars' worth of steers from Goodnight. Goodnight went to Texas for them.

It was the beginning of large-scale ranching on the plains. Although the construction workers soon moved on, the mining towns and Army posts furnished a steady market. The Union Pacific offered an outlet to the East. More importantly, men who were able to tap outside capital, particularly in England and Scotland, began to appreciate the nutrient qualities of the endless, tawny carpet of buffalo grass. By the end of 1883, so reported the *Colorado Livestock Record* with somewhat implausible accuracy, 4,707,976 head of Texas longhorns had

moved into eastern Colorado or on through to Wyoming and Montana. The most famous of these ranches of the central plains was the Prairie Cattle Company, a Scotch corporation, which was founded in 1881, ran 139,000 cattle on five and a half million acres in Texas, New Mexico, and Colorado, and in the second year of its operations showed a net profit of $250,000 on its original investment of $4,416,484.

Ranching took hold a bit more slowly farther east. The original efforts there were toward reaching railheads, and in 1866, the troubles involved were every bit as bad as Charles Goodnight had feared they might be. Aroused farmers in the Baxter Springs area of southeastern Kansas were only part of it. Outlaws took advantage of the unrest to levy tribute on the cattlemen for passage—flogging those who resisted—and sometimes made off with entire herds. Trail bosses who circled the danger areas ran into wooded hills where feed was so sparse that the animals grew lean as paper. On top of that, both Kansas and Missouri added obstacles in the form of county quarantine laws against the fever-bearing Texas imports.

The scant number of animals that reached market disturbed the McCoy brothers, livestock merchants in central Illinois. One of them, Joseph McCoy, in 1867 set about remedying matters by building shipping pens at the drab little hamlet of Abilene, beside the advancing Kansas Pacific Railroad, well west of interference from either farmers or quarantines. Late that summer, riders who knew the land went south to intercept the Missouri-bound herds and turn them north. Most of the thirty-five thousand head that responded followed wagon tracks left during preceding years by a half-breed Scotch-Cherokee Indian trader, Jesse Chisholm (no connection with John Chisum of New Mexico), as he moved goods and furs into and out of Indian Territory.

Four years later, 1871, seven hundred thousand longhorns moved over the Chisholm Trail to Abilene's hectic stockyards. All told, in the five years 1867–71, approximately forty thousand freight cars carried a million and a half beef animals east to the new meat-processing plants in Chicago and in Kansas City. When the Santa Fe Railroad sliced across southern Kansas on its way to New Mexico, it seized most of the shipping business. In lurid succession, Wichita, Ellsworth, and Dodge City helped send another two and a half million animals to the meat-hungry factory workers of the newly industrial East.

Few boomtime mining camps ever equaled these cattle-shipping points in all-round hell raising. The cowboys were spoiling for fun. In late years, most herds were moved by professional drovers on contract with the ranchers, but in the beginning, the ranch's own hands

Dime novel hero Wild Bill Hickok

did the job. After a dreary winter on the range, they rode off on the spring roundup, gathered cattle out of immense areas, separated them into herds according to ownership, then branded and castrated the calves in an uproar of flashing ropes, bellows, dust, manure, spurting blood, heat of sun and branding fires. They selected the animals to drive north (the average herd numbered twenty-five hundred), and after shaking the bunch into trail shape by pushing it hard along the initial stretches, they settled to a creep of twelve miles or so a day. They sat cross-legged on the ground while wolfing down their miserable food and whiled away time by inventing some of America's very limited, truly indigenous folk music. Although they were slaves to a particularly stupid and unattractive animal, they became symbols of the West's vaunted freedom. Violence was their normal escape from monotony: sucking quicksand, occasional quarrels with other trail herds over grazing grounds, or nighttime stampedes, when the animals took fright and ran in blind frenzy over whatever happened to lie in the way.

After that, even the wares of the cowtown gambling saloons and bawdy houses looked good. Ablaze with energy, the celebrants fought each other in exuberance —or the townspeople, whom they suspected of cheating them, with more earnestness. To keep peace, the towns imported professional gunmen, some of whom became legends—Tom Smith, the marshal who first imposed order on Abilene but was shot to death while trying to arrest two murderers; his successor, Wild Bill Hickok, who afterward was mortally wounded during a card game in a Black Hills saloon; lanky Wyatt Earp, who kept order in Wichita and Dodge City, then drifted on to Tombstone, Arizona, and as a deputy town marshal shot his way to wild West immortality during a ferocious,

sixty-second-long gun duel at the OK Corral; Bat Masterson; Uncle Billy Tilghman—but the reader no doubt can draw his own list. The names are more familiar than those of the towns' leading bankers and cattle brokers, to say nothing of the first ministers and schoolteachers.

It soon occurred to various cattle owners and buyers that growing the animals in Kansas and Nebraska would be more efficient than trailing them north from Texas every year. The trend was quickened by the Panic of 1873. Unable to obtain satisfactory prices in Eastern markets, ranchers decided to hold the herds back for a time. In their search for temporary grass, they found permanent homes. Thereafter they spread rapidly. But neither in Kansas and Nebraska nor on the plains farther west and north would the expansion have been possible without two coincidental strokes of luck: the fantastic slaughter of the buffalo and, a little later, the removal of the Indians to reservations.

Since the days of Lewis and Clark, the tribes had been whittling briskly away at the herds in order to obtain robes, which they traded to the whites for ammunition, kitchenware, woolen clothing, beads, and whisky. By the mid-1840's, the Indians of the central plains were selling one hundred thousand buffalo hides a year to the American Fur Company, and comparable amounts were being turned in at Bent's Fort and its satellite posts in eastern Colorado. In addition, the Indians used large numbers of robes to wear and to stitch into conical tepee covers. These skins, which the patient Indian women stripped from the slain animals, pegged flat to the ground, and laboriously scraped clean of hair and fat, were relatively light and pliant cowhides. (A dry bullhide weighed up to fifty pounds and was correspondingly stiff.) This concentration on females, of course, served to reduce the natural increase of the herds.

About 1871, leather factories discovered methods of handling bullhides also and offered up to three dollars for one. The advance of the railroads made the shipment of the ponderous skins possible. Swarms of hunters armed themselves with .55 caliber Sharps rifles that could kill at fifteen hundred yards, loaded their wagons with a ton or so of lead for bullets, and rolled away from the railroad towns in search of fortune.

The totals stagger imagination. Beginning in 1872 and continuing for a decade, more than a million buffalo were slain each year. After the skinning, the hides were sorted, tied, and placed in piles as big as haystacks, ready for the wagon trains that creaked out from the railroad towns to pick them up for shipment. For a time, malodorous Dodge City was as important as a center for hides as for cattle. And after the hideless carcasses had rotted away

353

out on the prairies, the bones, worth five dollars a ton when gathered for delivery to fertilizer factories, became a source of pin money for farmers inching west along the railroad lines. It takes a lot of dry bones to make a ton, yet in 1874, the Santa Fe alone hauled thirty-five hundred tons of bones out of western Kansas and eastern Colorado.

After exterminating the herds near the Santa Fe, the hunters moved south into the Texas Panhandle. There they clashed with Kiowas and Comanches, many of whom had never accepted the reservations assigned them by the Medicine Lodge Treaty of 1867. One fiery leader of the Comanches was Quanah Parker, half-breed son of Cynthia Ann Parker, who had been carried off by raiders during the attack on her father's post east of Waco in 1836. Leaders of the Kiowas were Satanta and Big Tree. That pair had been imprisoned in 1871 for the slaying of seven men in a Texas wagon train, and during their incarceration, the tribe, considering them to be hostages, stayed quiet. In 1873, humanitarians in the East secured the release of the two chiefs. Immediately the Kiowa leaders gathered their warriors, joined Quanah Parker's Comanches, and declared war on the hide hunters.

The climax came in the summer of 1874, after the allies had unsuccessfully attacked twenty-eight men and one woman huddled in a palisaded sod-and-log post near Adobe Walls (not the Adobe Walls where Kit Carson had fought Kiowas and Comanches ten years earlier). Roused by this eruption, the Army set out to defeat the hostiles by destroying their horses, tepees, and stores of arms and food. In September, Colonel Ranald Mackenzie surprised a Kiowa village in Palo Duro Canyon, slaughtered fourteen hundred horses, and sent Satanta back to prison. There, four years later, the chief committed suicide by jumping from a window.

Although bitter flare-ups continued for three more years, the Palo Duro fight ended effective Kiowa-Comanche resistance. Quanah Parker helped the transition to peace by serving as a judge on one of the Courts of Indian Offenses established in 1878 to settle certain disputes within the reservations.

The Indians gone, the broad expanse of the Panhandle was open to stockmen. One of the first to take advantage of it was Charles Goodnight. The open ranges of southern Colorado that he had pioneered had grown crowded. In 1875, he moved back south, pausing first near Adobe Walls and then continuing to Palo Duro Canyon. He chased out the buffalo that remained, obtained financing from an Irish friend, John George Adair, and created the million-acre JA ranch. It was not exactly puny—but the neighboring XIT was even larger: 3,050,000 acres, all deeded land awarded at the close of the decade by the

state of Texas to a group of Chicago capitalists in return for their erecting a new state capitol building at Austin.

The Sioux farther north were whisked aside during the same period. Their young warriors, like those of the Comanches and Kiowas, refused to heed reservation boundaries. They roamed the valley of the North Platte as though it were still theirs, and in 1871 Red Cloud infuriated the whites by prevailing on the Government to open a special agency for his Oglala band thirty miles downstream from Fort Laramie. After two years of mounting friction, the agency was shifted to the White River, in southwestern South Dakota, within reservation boundaries. This enraged the Indians in their turn, a resentment deepened by the poor-quality, short-measure annuities passed out to them by their corrupt agents.

The Indians were equally careless about the boundaries of the unceded hunting grounds east of the Bighorn Mountains, which the treaty of 1868 allowed them to roam. Whether or not this unceded region stretched on north to the Yellowstone and included the superlative game regions of Powder and Tongue rivers was a moot point. Many whites thought not. The Indians, however, insisted on the whole area. In their defiance, they often crossed to clearly forbidden ground north of the Yellowstone and at times rode west into the Crow reservation to make war on those ancient enemies.

In 1872, the Northern Pacific Railroad began surveying in the Yellowstone Valley for its transcontinental line. Although the locators stayed north of the river, the Indians were incensed. During the summer of 1873, they hit so hard at a troop-escorted party that came downstream from Bozeman that the civilian leader lost heart, quarreled with the military commander, saved face by pretending to examine the Musselshell country farther north, and then abandoned the work. Another survey party that meanwhile moved upstream from Fort Rice was more formidable—373 civilians, 1,500 troopers of the Seventh Cavalry under George Armstrong Custer, and a supply train of 275 wagons. The Sioux followed them undaunted and struck twice when they caught detachments of Custer's troops away from the main body. On each occasion, the Indians were beaten off.

The attacks gave the Army an excuse to order a reconnaissance of undisputed Sioux territory, the Black Hills in the western part of today's South Dakota. Supposedly it was a military foray, but actually the Government was interested in more than Indian war trails.

For years, rumor had whispered of gold in the *Paha Sapa*, the sacred hills. In 1872, Charles Collins, a promoter who lived in Sioux City, Iowa, and T. H. Russell, a onetime Colorado placer miner, tried to promote a prospecting expedition into the area but cooled off when the Army threatened to arrest them. Talk persisted, however, particularly in frontier communities hard hit by the depression of 1873. Finally the Government decided to investigate, perhaps as a preliminary to making the Indians an offer for the area. When Custer conducted his reconnaissance in the summer of 1874, he took with him, in addition to the usual complement of scientists, newspaper correspondents, and photographers, a few miners.

Near the site of the town now called Custer, these miners found gold both in creek gravel and in shallow deposits scarcely deeper than the grass roots. Anyone could duplicate the feat, Custer reported on August 15. "Men without former experience in mining have discovered it at the expense of but little time and labor."

Poor man's diggings! Although Collins was again forced by Army orders to stay out of the area, he put into motion, in September, a train of six wagons, twenty-six men, one boy, and Mrs. Annie Tallent, aged forty-seven. On December 23, after a rugged trip, they found gold on French Creek, exactly where Custer had said it was, built a stockade, and set to work. In April the Army escorted them out. Throughout the first part of 1875, soldiers kept on turning back prospectors, most of whom were outfitting in Cheyenne. In September Government negotiators offered the Sioux six million dollars for the sacred hills. The Indians refused, and after that the Army gave up trying to halt the rush.

Rapid City, Deadwood, and Lead sprang boisterously alive in the northern part of the Hills. Near Lead, brothers Fred and Moses Manuel discovered three claims, one named the Homestake, which they sold for one hundred and fifty thousand dollars to a San Francisco syndicate headed by George Hearst, whose original fortune had come from the Comstock. The purchasers added more claims, acquired water, built a costly mill, and turned the Homestake into one of the great gold producers of the Western Hemisphere—a gross output to the present day of more than a third of a billion dollars.

Hostile bands among the Sioux struck back with unco-ordinated raids, not so much against stations in the Black Hills as at ranches in the Platte Valley and eastern Montana. In November, 1875, the exasperated Indian Office ordered all Sioux outside the reservation to report to their agents by the following January 31.

Few appeared. A three-pronged winter invasion was promptly launched against the Powder River country. The first icy maneuvers produced no useful results, but with the coming of spring, the pincers tightened. Colonel John Gibbon's Montana column moved slowly down the Yellowstone Valley. Brigadier General Alfred Terry's Dakota column, twelve hundred strong, including most of Custer's Seventh Cavalry, marched west from Fort Abraham Lincoln, near Bismarck, North Dakota. General Crook repeated his previous winter's thrust northward from Fort Fetterman on the Platte, this time with a thousand men. No one expected that the Sioux could possibly hold out against so much power.

George Crook, six feet tall and imposing behind a forked Jovian beard, was renowned as an Indian fighter.

Shotgun-armed Wells Fargo guards take $250,000 in gold out of Deadwood in this photograph by John C. H. Grabill.

CRAZY HORSE ATTACK
Col. CUSTER
CO. C,
T. W. CUSTER
CO. F, YATES
CO. I, KEOGH
CO. L, CALHOUN
CO. E, SMITH
N
Cheyenne Camp
Little Bighorn R.
GALL ATTACK
CUSTER ADVANCE
Crossing attempt repulsed?
Sioux Camp
WEIR PT. +
BENTEEN
RENO'S 1st POSITION
RENO'S 2nd POSITION
RENO-BENTEEN DEFENSE
RENO RETREAT
BENTEEN
RENO ADVANCE
MONTANA TERRITORY
Reno Creek
SCALE
0   1/2   1 Mile

The movements of Custer's men, as well as they are known, are seen in this map of the Little Bighorn fight, June 25, 1876.

Cavalry under his command had whipped the Apaches of Arizona at Salt River Canyon and Turret Butte in 1871–72. Thereafter, tempering firmness with fair play, he had kept the Southwestern Indians on their reservations until his transfer north in 1875. (In 1882, after chiefs Victorio and Geronimo had broken loose again, he would have to return to Arizona for a grimmer campaign, completed finally by General Nelson A. Miles.) But in all his experience, Crook had never met an Indian charge like the one that hit him beside rocky Rosebud Creek, southern Montana, on the morning of June 17, 1876. Completely jarred by a thousand of Crazy Horse's Oglala warriors, the whites fell back to a base camp on Goose Creek, inside the Wyoming border, and sat tight.

Meanwhile, on July 7, Gibbon's and Terry's columns had met at the mouth of the Powder. Scouts discovered signs of the village whose warriors had halted Crook but learned nothing of the battle itself. On July 22, the combined force launched its drive to run the hostiles down. Gibbon and Terry led the bulk of the troops up the Bighorn. Custer and six hundred of his cavalry rode up the Rosebud and then swung west to the Little Bighorn to

meet Gibbon's men. Learning of a village ahead of him and eager for victory, Custer divided his force into three sections for the attack: Captain Fred Benteen to the south with one hundred and twenty-five men "to pitch into anything he might find"; Major Marcus Reno across the Little Bighorn with one hundred and fifteen men; Custer along the river's northeast bank with the bulk of the forces. Everything went wrong. Reno was driven back; Benteen never reached his commander; Custer and two hundred and twenty-four men were annihilated.

The nation, its forty million people proudly reviewing a century of accomplishment since the signing of the Declaration of Independence, was stunned—and in a sense remains stunned; partisans still paw the irreconcilable records, hunting for whatever meaning there may be in the defeat. For the Sioux, however, the meaning was immediate—disaster. Reinforcements ran down the fragmenting bands, seized the Black Hills and Bighorn Basin, and in 1877 forced the Sioux and Northern Cheyennes (except for a few who, with Sitting Bull, escaped briefly into Canada) onto a number of cramped reservations situated beside the Missouri River.

Before this human roundup had been completed, the Nez Perces sent a fresh shiver of alarm across the Northern frontier. Ever since the discovery of gold in Idaho in 1860, whites had been slicing into the tribe's lovely homeland in the plateau and mountains where Idaho, Washington, and Oregon join. When new orders told some of the Nez Perce bands early in 1877 that they must move again, a group of resentful young warriors broke out of hand and killed eighteen settlers. Out came the troops. The Indians thrashed the first overconfident contingents. Then, fearing retribution, more than seven hundred men, women, and children decided to flee east across the Rockies and join the Crows.

Chief Joseph is generally considered the Indians' inspiring force, but several able leaders shared the masterful strategy of that fantastic, seventeen-hundred-mile, zigzag flight: Joseph's brother, Ollokot; a wise elder named Toohoolhoolzote; a proved fighter, Looking Glass. Three white columns pursued them. The Indians dodged when they could, fought when cornered. The enmity of the Americans was such that the fugitives realized they could find no refuge anywhere within the United States. Abandoning the plan to reach the Crows, they turned desperately toward Canada. Cold and hunger and General Nelson Miles trapped them thirty miles short of the border. On October 5, under snowy skies, his brother and the other leaders dead, Joseph surrendered.

There were other Indian spasms, most seriously the Meeker massacre of northwestern Colorado. Utes there killed their agency workers, including Nathan Meeker, founder of the agricultural colony of Greeley, Colorado, and came within an ace of destroying Major T. T. Thornburgh's relief force of a hundred and fifty cavalrymen. In punishment, the tribe, except for a small band in the southwestern corner of the state, was swept off to a desert reservation in eastern Utah.

Hide hunters first, then cattlemen and farmers, poured onto the vacated plains. The panic was easing, grasshoppers dwindled, wheat prices bounced back toward the dollar mark. Bonanza wheat farmers discovered the marvelous adaptability of steam tractors and threshing machines to the sweep of the Dakotas, to the rolling, lava-ash soil of eastern Oregon and Washington, to the inland valleys of California. Farms in North Dakota's Red River Valley sprawled across as much as one hundred thousand acres. A California joke said that in the rich, interior Sacramento Valley a man plowed only one furrow a day—twenty miles long.

Land consolidation quickened again, often dishonestly through the tried-and-true method of fraudulent homestead entries. Cattlemen, who could not possibly survive on one-hundred-and-sixty-acre farm plots, added their own trade wrinkle. By purchase, or by ordering their employees to file homestead claims, they gained control of desirable stream banks. By controlling the water, they became masters of huge pastures of "free grass" bordering the streams. Thus, by owning fifteen thousand acres along the South Platte, John Iliff of Colorado was able to graze thirty-five thousand cattle across six hundred and fifty thousand acres of the public domain—enough, if the homestead theory had worked on the plains, to have supported four thousand sturdy yeomen and their families.

Obviously the homestead law was not working. But what policy should be substituted in its place? In 1877, President Rutherford B. Hayes recommended that the short-grass grazing lands west of the 100th meridian be sold to ranchers, thus putting an end to the one-hundred-and-sixty-acre absurdity and "legalizing"—the words are Hayes's—"the business of cattle raising which at present is carried upon [the plains]."

A compromise suggestion came the next year from surveyor John Wesley Powell. His hope was to adapt the democratic policy of giving land to those who improved it to the realities of the Far West's subhumid climate. In his famous *Report on the Lands of the Arid Regions of the United States*, he proposed a unit of 2,560 acres, sixteen times the former size. He suggested abandoning the rectilinear boundaries that had prevailed since 1785 and allowing adaptation to natural features so that a maximum number of homesteads in any given district could

have access to water. Title to enough water for irrigating twenty acres should accompany each unit—a flat contradiction to the riparian water laws then prevailing—and supervision should rest not with federal or state governments but with local boards elected within each watershed.

No change resulted. The unit was too small to suit cattlemen (Silas Bent, as noted earlier in the chapter, proposed a minimum leasehold of twenty thousand acres instead) and yet was so large that it offended Easterners. Unrestrained except by land-hungry rivals in the same business, stockmen went right on absorbing all the grass they could get away with. Cattlemen fought sheep remorselessly, especially along the fringes of the Rockies in Colorado and Wyoming, clubbing the helpless animals to death on their stinking bed grounds or driving them by thousands over high cliffs. When other cattlemen elbowed them too closely, they bought barbed wire, invented in 1873 for farms by an Illinois farmer, Joseph Glidden, and with it turned huge chunks of the public domain into private baronies.

When the number of longhorns coming from Texas failed to meet the demands for stock, ranchers journeyed to Oregon and bought better-quality animals whose ancestors had been driven west along the Oregon Trail decades earlier. Out on the plains, giant herds changed hands by "book count" alone—a figure expressing the size of the original herd plus its assumed natural increase, as computed, often enough, on the back of an envelope.

Farmers too felt the world was theirs. Joseph Glidden's barbed wire had solved their fencing problem. Machines took over the drilling of deep wells; windmills began lifting enough water for a home, kitchen garden, and domestic animals from depths far beyond the capacity of hand pumps. Those deterrents to plains living removed, the endless landscape no longer looked so bleak.

Moreover, precipitation was increasing again. Hayden and the other theorists, the farmers said, had been right after all. Rhapsodically Charles Dana Wilbur, an Omaha promoter, wrote in 1881 in a book extolling *The Great Valleys and Prairies of Nebraska and the Northwest*, ". . . in the sweat of his face, toiling with his hands, man can persuade the heavens to yield their treasures of dew and rain upon the land he has chosen for his dwelling place." Or, more tersely, "Rain follows the plow." And with that as their faith and buckler, a new wave of agrarians again flowed across the danger line of the subhumid West.

This was grist for the railroad's mill. Settlers meant land sales for the line that owned grants, traffic for those that did not. The Northern Pacific in 1884 wooed purchasers at home with advertisements in six hundred American and Canadian newspapers, those abroad with eight hundred and thirty-one agents in the United Kingdom and one hundred and twenty-four on the continent. Special targets were Scandinavian ministers, who sometimes prevailed on their entire congregations to migrate with them to the country of infinite promises. Lacking land grants, the Chicago and Northwestern boomed homesteads by captioning maps of South Dakota with such sentiments as "You Need a Farm! Here is one you can get simply by occupying it! 30 Millions of Acres of the Most Productive Grain Lands in the World."

Railroads that crossed Indian Territory fretted that those lands were closed to settlement—and hence to freight. Then they discovered that after the Civil War, the Creeks and Seminoles had been punished for their adherence to the Confederates by being stripped of 1,920,-000 acres, which had not yet been assigned to any other tribe. This unoccupied area surely should be made available to homesteaders. While lobbyists began to agitate for a legal destruction of the Indians' last stronghold, heavily armed Kansas boomers illegally crossed the border and posted claims, only to be regularly driven back, year after year, by Federal troops.

In March, 1889, the Government capitulated. It paid the Creeks and Seminoles $1.25 an acre for such rights as they still claimed in the unassigned territory in the central part of today's Oklahoma and ordered the tract surveyed into one-hundred-and-sixty-acre parcels. Entry could be made beginning at high noon on April 22, 1889.

Farmers in the neighboring states went wild. At least fifty thousand wagon drivers, horsemen, bicycle riders, and even men pushing their possessions in wheelbarrows lined up at different entry points on three sides of the area and waited for the pistol shot that sent them charging across the flower-bright prairies. Within twenty-four frantic hours, every farm and town lot in the newly opened region had been staked.

Ten more "openings" occurred during the next few years. Much of the land involved fell to whites through a cynical inversion of the Dawes Severalty Act, passed in 1887 as a benefit to the Indians. This act decreed that the Government should dissolve the old tribal entities and treat the Indians as individuals—as white individuals, to boot. The communally held reservations were to be divided. Every individual was to receive the white man's highest reward, a farm plot (generally in one-hundred-and-sixty-acre pieces, though there were variations), regardless of whether or not the recipient wanted to be a white-style agriculturist, or even whether he could be one on some of the impoverished pieces that were handed about. After division of the reservation, quantities of land were left over. Absurd to suppose the Indians re-

ceived it. Rather, the Government paid each tribe a pittance for its rights and tossed the chunks of acquired property, sometimes catch-as-catch-can and sometimes by lottery, to impatient white boomers.

After the Santa Fe and Southern Pacific railroads had linked southern California to the Midwest, the land madness spread there. Fighting to attract dewy-eyed investors, the railroads cut the cost of a passenger ticket to the coast from Kansas City to as low, briefly, as one dollar. California real estate prices zoomed so high that dismayed purchasers banded into colonies to increase their bargaining power. Obviously, speculators benefited most from the scramble. Some of them even hung oranges to desert-twisted Joshua trees and solemnly sold the sandy acres as citrus groves.

Miners too hopped aboard the mad era's quickening merry-go-round. Silver was the new darling. After years of indifferent results, the deepening Comstock mines of Virginia City, Nevada, again encountered bonanza ore, first in the Crown Point and then, even more spectacularly, in the Hale and Norcross and the Consolidated Virginia. Consolidated Virginia stock that in July, 1870, sold for one dollar a share hit seven hundred dollars in 1875. But these were rich man's diggings. Forests of Sierra Nevada lumber had to be floated along mountain sides and over canyons in spider-legged flumes, to be used in massive cribworks for supporting the cavernous stopes. Huge blowers were necessary for ventilating the sweltering depths, huge pumps and hoists for removing water and lifting ore. The four roughneck Irish saloonkeepers and mine superintendents who wrested control of the Consolidated Virginia from the Bank of California—James Fair, James Flood, William O'Brien, and John Mackay—poured $31,000,000 into the property . . . but took out $105,000,000 before Virginia City's new and final decline set in about 1880.

As Virginia City faded, Leadville soared into prominence. Located ten thousand feet above sea level in the Colorado Rockies, the district had attracted several thousand stampeders to its gold placers in the 1860's, but the cream had soon been skimmed, and the restless population had vanished like smoke. In the early 1870's, two hydraulic operators, Alvinus Wood and William Stevens, took another look, hoping that improved efficiency might enable them to wash a little profit out of the old gravels. Instead of gold they found lead-silver ore. This involved consulting St. Louis smelting interests. They grew excited, secrets leaked, and suddenly, in 1877–78, another rush was under way in the mountains.

Hopeful prospectors struggled in the dead of winter over the heaped snow of the Mosquito Range. Speculators warred over town lots, and vigilantes hanged the worst of them. Railroads raced each other for bonanzas of freight. In a clash over the strategic right of way through the half-mile-deep Royal Gorge of the Arkansas River, construction crews of the Santa Fe and the Denver and Rio Grande faced each other with loaded rifles. In a last-minute settlement worked out in court, William Palmer gave up his ambitions farther south in exchange for a tight hold on the Colorado mountains; the Santa Fe, abandoning the silver temptation of the mines, resumed its drive through New Mexico toward California.

Leadville's mayor, elected January 14, 1878, when the town had a population of three hundred, was Horace A. W. Tabor, a garrulous storekeeper with sweeping handle-bar mustaches who had been drifting fruitlessly around the mountains with his wife Augusta for nearly twenty years. In April, Mayor Tabor grubstaked two poor Germans who chanced to start digging at almost the only spot where a fabulous vein later called the Little Pittsburg came close enough to the surface to be readily reached with a pick and shovel. Seeing that Tabor was in an expansive mood over this, a prospector known as Chicken Bill stole some rich ore from the Little Pittsburg, dumped it into his own barren shaft, and sold the salted claim to the gullible mayor for one thousand dollars. Tabor shrugged and told his miners to blast a few feet farther on, just to see. He sold a half interest in the Chrysolite vein that they uncovered for five hundred thousand dollars. A little later, he paid one hundred and seventeen thousand dollars for another property, the Matchless mine, and for a period netted one hundred thousand dollars a month from it.

How could you beat luck like that? Although Tabor had been mayor of Leadville for hardly a year (its population meanwhile had reached fifteen thousand), awed Coloradans elected him lieutenant governor of the state. He acquired a dazzling blonde mistress known as Baby Doe, divorced his wife, and by pouring money into the coffers of the Republican party won a thirty-day interim appointment as United States Senator. He had already wed Baby Doe in secret, but now he decided to do it all over again at a glittering Washington ceremony attended by President Arthur. Smelling like a rose, as the boys back in Colorado would have said.

Other Colorado silver mines, fed by corkscrewing narrow-gauge railroads, built ambitious towns in the most remote sections of the state—Aspen, Silverton, Ouray, Telluride. In 1883, attention swung to the Coeur d'Alene section of Idaho and to Butte, Montana, which for a time was considered as still another fair-to-middling silver camp. To exploit Butte's ores, William Clark, a Deer

Lodge banker, financed several claims, foreclosed, and then persuaded a smelting group from Colorado to build a plant near his properties. Simultaneously, a mining scout named Marcus Daly, supported by the same Hearst syndicate that was developing the Homestake in South Dakota, bought the Anaconda mine in Butte as a silver speculation. While deepening the Anaconda shafts, Daly discovered he had acquired a gigantic copper mine. Closing its tunnels, he prepared to develop it on a truly colossal scale. His icy little enemy, William Clark, who hated Daly bitterly because of quarrels over smelter sites, followed suit with his property. When operations resumed, Butte almost overnight became a roaring, fume-choked industrial complex, challenging the Hecla and Calumet mines of the Lake Superior district for dominance of the American copper market.

Small outlaws, unable to match the sophisticated legalisms of their richer brothers, resorted to more direct action. Rustlers preyed on the carelessly handled herds of the cattlemen, infuriating them to the point of violent vigilante action. Grimmest of the drives was the 1884

Posed in a studio (presumably between raids) are (front row, from left) Frank and Jesse James, (rear) Cole and Bob Younger.

359

sweep through eastern Montana led by Granville Stuart, onetime California gold rusher and Montana pioneer, ranching friend of Theodore Roosevelt's, and later United States minister to Uruguay and Paraguay. With ropes and guns, Stuart's fourteen possemen brought peremptory justice to somewhere between nineteen and seventy-five victims. The situation was not one that lent itself to accurate statistics.

Other outlaws preyed on banks and trains. A surprising number were kinfolk: Frank and Jesse James, the Younger brothers, the five Daltons. The public tended to glorify them and even a handful of women of similar stripe—a tobacco-chewing bawd called Calamity Jane; Belle Starr, a swaggerer with a six gun on either ample hip; Cattle Annie McDougal and Little Britches (Jennie) Metcalf, who started their careers bootlegging whisky to the Indians and switched to rustling. Part of the reason for their apotheosis is literary and beyond our concern here. But another cause rose out of the mockeries of the Western spoils system. Opportunity for all had too often turned into exploitation by a few. The outlaw became a symbol of defiance: Robin Hood on a cow pony, striking against entrenched privilege.

Resentment gradually forced attention from Washington. William Andrew Jackson Sparks, appointed Land Commissioner by Grover Cleveland in 1885, pointed bluntly to "widespread, persistent public land robbery under guise of the various forms of public land entry" and suspended further claims in all or parts of eight Western states until investigations could be completed. Cleveland ordered two hundred thousand cattle out of Indian Territory, where they were being grazed under illegal leases, and instructed the Army to remove unauthorized fences from the public domain. Cleveland's one-shot orders met with some success, but the more sweeping reforms proposed by Sparks caused such a din of protest from men who hated to give up either their special interests or their traditional ways of thinking that in November, 1887, he was forced to resign.

Nature stepped in with a drought that shriveled ranges already thin from overgrazing. This was followed, throughout the winter of 1886–87, by unprecedented blizzards. Cattle drifted with the wind until they were trapped against fences—many of them illegal—or in ravines and died there in heaps. After the spring roundups were over, some owners calculated that they had lost two thirds of their animals. Careless "book counts" probably magnified the figures, but actuality was bad enough. According to Granville Stuart, the ranchers of eastern Montana alone lost twenty million dollars during those few desperate winter months. Inefficient stockmen never recovered. Those who did pull themselves back by their bootstraps had to adopt new economies—better-quality animals closely managed on smaller land units.

Continuing drought and sinking prices, 1887–93, all but depopulated many overextended farming communities in the western parts of Kansas, Nebraska, and the Dakotas. Some of the displaced families joined the land rush into Oklahoma; some returned sullenly to the humid lands they had recently left. In 1891, eighteen thousand covered wagons fled from Nebraska back into Iowa. Often the men who lost their farms to mortgage holders entered into tenancy arrangements with larger operators. By 1890, a quarter of the farmers in Kansas were working not for themselves but for absentee landlords.

These economic woes coincided with a shocked realization that the nation had filled up more rapidly than anyone had dared predict a few decades earlier. With the passing of Indian Territory, every foot of land between the Atlantic and the Pacific was finally organized into the Federal system. Of the forty-nine entities (Hawaii had not yet been annexed), only Oklahoma, New Mexico, Arizona, Alaska, and Utah remained territories—and Congress would grant Utah statehood as soon as she officially renounced polygamy.

Viewing the widespread population that had brought about these political developments, the Superintendent of the Census reported in 1890 that his department could no longer draw a line marking the frontier. Except in Alaska, unbroken areas of unsettled—and hence unexploited—wilderness had ceased to exist.

The psychological impact was profound. Some observers, connecting the agonizing slowdown of the Western merry-go-round to the passing of the frontier, concluded that at least part of the American dream was over. No longer could the poor of the world find new lives simply by moving to the frontier and taming a piece of it with their own hands. Other Westerners, hurt that corruption and exploitation by monopolies had kept the dream from working anyhow, called for reappraisal. If the West had changed, then attitudes also had to change —quickly, while there was time to save what still remained.

A thousand reformers cried their solutions to all the land's many economic woes. None crystallized the ferment into words better than a golden-voiced Kansas housewife, Mary Elizabeth Lease, who carried her protests to lecture platforms throughout the state: "The people are at bay. Let the bloodhounds of money who have dogged us thus far beware. What you farmers need is to raise *less corn and more hell.*"

And that is exactly what a great many of them, not just farmers, set about doing.

THE GREAT SURVEYS

For almost five years, American energy was divided between the westward thrust and the Civil War. With the fighting over, the nation renewed its passion for fresh land and its interest in unsettled areas. Although general knowledge had been accumulated by the Topographical Engineers and other surveyors and explorers, little of solid, scientific substance was yet known of most of the West, particularly of the mountains and the Great Basin between the 100th meridian and the Sierra Nevada. From 1867 to 1879, four Government scientific groups, later known as the Great Surveys, ranged over huge expanses of territory, making maps, compiling data on geology, geography, and natural history, and providing a foundation of knowledge for settlement and for the efficient use of resources. With the parties, also, went artists and photographers whose works, like Thomas Moran's painting of the Colorado Rockies (above) and T. H. O'Sullivan's view of Mohave Indians watching the start of a Wheeler survey up the Colorado River in 1871 (left), provided a new, exciting visual record of the West.

361

The Green River's Labyrinth Canyon was photographed by E. O. Beaman in 1871 during Powell's Utah explorations. The river flows from left, curves behind the viewer, and continues downstream at right, a water distance of six miles.

WEST OF THE 100TH MERIDIAN

A William H. Jackson photograph shows Dr. Ferdinand V. Hayden (right) and members of his party at dinner in the field.

There was no lack of wondrous scenery to inspire the artists and photographers on the Great Surveys. Moran's paintings and William H. Jackson's photographs of the geysers, great canyon, and waterfalls of the upper Yellowstone River, made in 1871 on one of Ferdinand V. Hayden's many expeditions, helped persuade Congress to set aside the area as the country's first national park. Pictures taken on other Hayden surveys revealed to the nation Colorado's Mount of the Holy Cross and the cliff dwellings of Mesa Verde. Timothy O'Sullivan, with Clarence King's survey along the 40th parallel, captured the dramatic features of Pyramid Lake and the Great Basin. O'Sullivan, a Mathew Brady protégé, also accompanied Lieutenant George M. Wheeler on surveys in the Southwest but lost many of his negatives of Colorado River views. He was not, however, the only recorder of the beauty of that river and the surrounding canyon country. John Hillers and E. O. Beaman, photographers, and artist Moran were also active on John Wesley Powell's trips down the Colorado (1869) and mappings of the Utah plateau (1871–72).

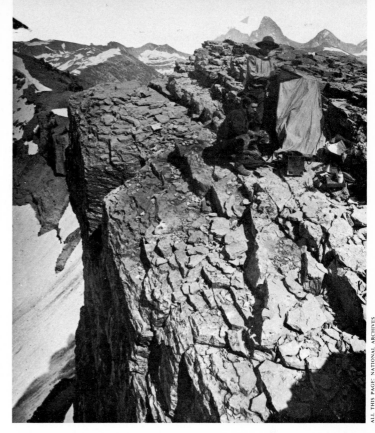

This 1871 Jackson view of Thomas Moran at Mammoth Hot Springs was among the first from what is now Yellowstone Park.

Perched on a pinnacle beside a tent that served as his darkroom, Jackson (sitting) prepared to photograph Wyoming's majestic Teton Range.

Described earlier by mountain men and explorers, the Snake River's Shoshone Falls in southern Idaho were at last photographed by O'Sullivan during the King survey. Today, irrigation dams have diminished the falls' spectacle.

SHOCK ON THE LITTLE BIGHORN, JUNE 25, 1876

Custer's Last Stand: white man's version

A disconsolate Sitting Bull poses with his ninth squaw and three of his children at Standing Rock reservation in 1882, the year after he returned from exile in Canada. The identities of the white woman and child are not known.

THE END
OF
FREEDOM

There was only empty present and bleak future for the Indian as the 1800's drew to a close. He could no longer gain prestige either as a warrior or as a hunter, and the reservation onto which he was forced was usually too sterile to farm. Indians went ·hungry because food issues were erratic and insufficient; they were hard hit by disease. In this unhappy state they turned to religion for help.

When a Nevada Paiute named Wovoka revealed that a certain dance would bring back friends long dead and wipe out the white man, the revelation was accepted eagerly. On the South Dakota Sioux reservations, the so-called Ghost Dance was performed with such fervor that the Army was called in. Sitting Bull died resisting arrest for his part in the Ghost Dance. In a tragic episode, cavalrymen guarding a Sioux camp at Wounded Knee Creek lost their heads and killed almost 300 Indians, mostly women and children. The date was December 29, 1890; it was the final fight between Army and Indians.

The Arapahoes (top right) were only one of the many tribes dancing the Ghost Dance in 1890 to bring back old times. Cavalrymen (right center) look over the scene of the massacre at Wounded Knee the next day. Of the millions of buffalo, nothing remained by 1884 but piles of bones (lower right), gathered by settlers to earn extra money.

WHERE THE BUFFALO ROAMED

Cowboys above are branding calves in a busy scene at a roundup on the Salt Fork, Kansas, 1890's.

The chuck wagon picture below was taken during a roundup in Dakota's Belle Fourche country in 1887.

Pointing out of Texas after the Civil War came the great herds of longhorns, first along the Goodnight-Loving Trail to New Mexico and Colorado, then on the Chisholm and Western trails to Kansas railheads. Living in the open under the stars and big sky, moving the stock by day across rivers and great distances, keeping them quiet at night, the cowboy in big hat, chaps, and spurs became a new romantic symbol of the American West. At the railheads, most of the animals were shipped East to markets, but many were driven on north to fatten on the sea of grass on the central and northern plains. The end of Indian hostilities and the slaughter of the buffalo herds opened the floodgates. Thousands of head of cattle poured across the fenceless ranges of Wyoming, eastern Montana, and Dakota Territory, and ranches were built up where only a year or two before, Indian tribes had hunted. By the late 1870's the cowboy called half the West his home.

371

BAD MEN

Ne'er-do-wells, casual killers, and just ordinary bad types had inevitably followed every frontier, and from the beginning, the West had had its share of them. After the Civil War, the homeless and foot-loose drifted West in greater numbers than ever before, and crime bloomed spectacularly, first in the "end of the track" towns of the Union Pacific Railroad, and then in the cattle railheads in Kansas. Cowboys, reaching the ends of trails, were ready for a toot, and for a decade, towns such as Abilene, Ellsworth, Hays, and Dodge City reached heights of notoriety. In desperation, law-abiding citizens fought fire with fire by hiring men adept with guns (often with shady records themselves) to keep the peace. Some of them forgot which side they were on and were fired as fast as they were hired. Billy Brooks (right), a policeman in Newton and Ellsworth in 1872, was reputedly hanged two years later for stealing mules. During all of the mayhem, men died with their boots on, and peace officers such as Wyatt Earp, Wild Bill Hickok, the Mastersons, and "Doc" Holliday became a part of American lore.

372

End of a brawl in Hays, Kansas: Two dead soldiers, the object of a small boy's curiosity, lie sprawled in front of a saloon, awaiting cartage back to nearby Fort Hays cemetery.

This job by vigilantes was photographed by A. C. Hull at Laramie on the UP line, 1868.

John Henry "Doc" Holliday

The real Wyatt Earp

William B. "Bat" Masterson

BREAKING THE PLAINS

A settler turns the first sod on his homestead in Montana.

The McCormick Harvesting Machine Company used a scene from the 65,000-acre Grandin farm in North Dakota (right) in its 1884 catalogue; it gives an idea of the scale of bonanza farming. Eighteen mules were required to pull an early combine thresher (above) through Oregon grainfields. The horse-powered threshing machine in Idaho (below) was soon replaced, for bonanza farms made use of the most modern power machinery.

BONANZA FARMS

Nothing had a bigger, wider Western-style sweep than the bonanza farms that flourished in the last quarter of the 1800's. The Northern Pacific Railroad, with almost worthless bonds after the Panic of 1873, used its North Dakota land to pay off some stockholders, two of whom formed a 12,000-acre farm near Fargo in 1875. This was the first of the bonanza farms; there were soon 300 in the Red River Valley of Minnesota and North Dakota, two of them of 65,000 acres. Everything was done on a huge scale with modern machinery; squadrons of plows and reapers moved in echelon over fields a mile across. The bonanza system was ideal for the flat Red River Valley and was used farther west where there was sweeping land and rich soil: in Idaho, Washington, Oregon, California. But it was strictly a one-crop system, and when crops other than wheat were introduced, the Red River Valley bonanzas were gradually broken up. Almost all were gone by 1915.

Small farmers had problems, too. Cattlemen often fenced public lands and water; then homesteaders, like these Nebraskans of 1885, masked against recognition, retaliated with wire cutters.

TAMING THE SOUTHWEST

As frontiers elsewhere disappeared, the one in the Southwest lingered on. Troops at lonely posts guarded scattered settlements and mines and policed the arteries of travel against Apaches, Yumas, Mohaves, and other Indians. But it was not until Geronimo finally surrendered in 1886 that wagon trains and stagecoaches like the one below could cross the vast, dusty expanses of Arizona without fear of attack. Meanwhile, wild and woolly towns, based generally on the mines, grew up in the desert. Although the majority of the people were law-abiding, saloons and gambling halls proliferated, and gunfights were frequent. Even Phoenix in one week in 1879 had two shootings, two stabbings, and two hangings.

Faro holds the attention of these gamblers in a saloon in wide-open Morenci, Arizon

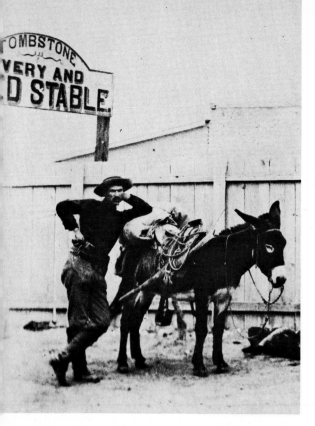

TOP THREE: ARIZONA PIONEERS' HISTORICAL SOCIETY

A desert prospector was photographed by Camillus Fly.

Bettors of both sexes urge on their favorite in an 1885 Tombstone cockfight.

Though traveling in style, wealthy Eastern excursionists felt like old plainsmen at the end of a hunt. Note the wag in feather and blanket.

WESTERNERS ALL

A young trooper poses while policing Cheyenne country.

Chinese at the Deadwood mines in Dakota form a colorfully garbed hose team.

Industrious Mormons were photographed by W. H. Jackson cutting granite for the Salt Lake City temple.

A Wisconsin lumberman puts on an impromptu dance for the others aboard a raft bringing timber downriver.

A sod house on a Nebraska claim was home for these daughters of a rancher.

Members of a communal French colony who introduced silk culture to Kansas display rabbits they shot for a Christmas feast.

GUTHRIE, OKLAHOMA TERRITORY, 1889

Two participants of the land rush guard their claim in this photograph by H. T. Swearingen.

Columbia Basin irrigation project, eastern Washington

"It may be anticipated that all the lands redeemed by irrigation in the Arid Region will be highly cultivated and abundantly productive, and agriculture will be but slightly subject to the vicissitudes of scant and excessive rainfall."

John Wesley Powell, *Report on The Lands of The Arid Region of the United States*, Washington, D.C., 1878

CHAPTER FOURTEEN

NEW VALUES

1890-1914

The fierce confrontation that arose in the 1890's between entrenched capital and solidifying numbers of poor men was of course a national, not just a Western, problem. But in the West, where the traditions of individualism were strong, the pangs had a sharper focus. In spite of railroads and telegraph lines, wide areas remained relatively isolated and devoted to one or two dominant economic pursuits. Conflicts took on an elemental directness, as witness the cattlemen's invasion of Johnson County, northern Wyoming.

After the Sioux had been driven out of the area, farmers had hurried in to build dirt-roofed log cabins and take up homesteads along the upper tributaries of Powder River. At the same time, cattlemen had pushed north from the broad North Platte Valley, intending to lay claim to sweeping reaches of the new range. Antipathies between the groups were instantaneous.

Power seemed to be on the side of the cattlemen, tightly organized in the Wyoming Stock Growers Association. This association dictated, as a matter of state law, the schedule and method of every cattle roundup in Wyoming. It hired detectives to ferret out thieves. It stationed brand inspectors at all railroad shipping points to challenge the ownership of suspect animals. In some minds, the association used these broad powers not only to regulate the industry, but also to harass small operators whom they did not want muscling in on what the cattlemen ironically called the "open" range.

One source of trouble was mavericking—a maverick being an unbranded bull or heifer that had left its mother before her brand, and hence her ownership, could be determined. A custom of the range said that the finders of mavericks were the keepers. Ranch operators paid their cowboys small bonuses for each maverick branded with the ranch mark. Some cowboys, however, preferred to build up herds of their own by claiming the mavericks for themselves. Since the unmarked animals probably had come from one of the main herds in the locality, the cattlemen ordered the practice stopped. The directive accomplished nothing. Accordingly, the stockmen in 1888 prevailed on the legislature to pass a bill decreeing that all mavericks found during a roundup were to be marked with the brand of the Stock Growers Association and sold at auction for the benefit of the association treasury. To help enforce the law, the association adopted the practice of blacklisting cowboys who persisted in following the old range custom about mavericks.

Unable to find employment because of the blacklisting and outraged by what seemed an arrogant interference with an established freedom of the range, many cowboys became out-and-out thieves, stealing unbranded calves whose mothers were known and sometimes reworking brands into different patterns for their own benefit.

In Johnson County, cattle stealing, or rustling, became socially acceptable. Farmers, resentful of crowding by cattlemen, saw nothing wrong in occasionally killing someone else's steer to eat—rustling as a sideline, so to speak. Professional thieves meanwhile farmed as a sideline, raising hay for their horses and potatoes and beans for themselves. The outlines between the groups became increasingly hazy, and soon juries were declining to find guilty any local people who were charged with cattle theft.

In final exasperation the cattlemen decided to resort to vigilante action, not just in Johnson County, but wherever normal law activity in the state seemed to be unable to check the depredations. Although the Stock Growers Association was not involved officially, there is little doubt of its unofficial connivance.

The opening move of the campaign took place south of Johnson County, near Independence Rock on the old Oregon Trail. There a homesteader named Jim Averill ran a store that was considered a rustlers' hangout. On an adjoining homestead, Cattle Kate (Ella) Watson dispensed her personal favors in exchange for animals, most of them stolen. In July, 1889, ten cattlemen cleaned out this sinkhole, as they regarded it, by lynching both Jim

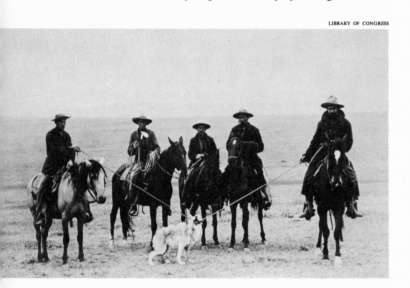

Wyoming cowboys, in this photograph from the 1880's by J. C. H. Grabill, have roped a gray wolf, an enemy of the range herds.

and Cattle Kate. "A horrible piece of business," admitted association president John Clay, who was not involved. Then he asked rhetorically, for all Wyoming cattlemen, ". . . what are you to do? Are you to sit still and see your property ruined with no redress in sight?"

A year later, a man suspected of being a rustler killed association detective George Henderson near Three Crossings on Sweetwater Creek, also on the old Oregon Trail. "He would rather hunt a thief than eat," John Clay said of Henderson in tribute. The year after that, another association detective, Frank Canton, was suspected of assassinating two Johnson County residents from ambush. Tried for one of the killings, Canton was acquitted.

Meanwhile, the homesteaders of Johnson County had elected as their sheriff Red Angus, a man known to be friendly with suspected rustlers. They formed their own roundup in their own way. To the Wyoming Stock Growers Association, this was equivalent to letting known jewel thieves conduct the inventory at Tiffany's.

Association detectives drew up a list of seventy rustlers in Johnson County. Since there seemed no possibility of bringing these men to justice through legal trial, twenty-five association members (but not the Stock Growers Association as an official entity) determined to do it without any trial at all. Calling themselves the Regulators, they raised a war chest of one hundred thousand dollars, imported twenty-five professional gunmen from Texas, and early in April, 1892, rode north along muddy roads, through flurries of snow, toward Buffalo, Johnson's county seat. Detective Frank Canton was one co-leader. His partner was Frank Wolcott, whose brother was a United States Senator from Colorado. Two newspaper correspondents went along. There seemed no doubt in the invaders' minds that their action was laudable. Had not Granville Stuart's fourteen Stranglers been praised for a similar cleanup in eastern Montana eight years before?

The Regulators found two of their quarry, Nick Ray and Nate Champion, in a cabin at the KC Ranch, fifty miles south of Buffalo. They mortally wounded Ray without warning when he stepped outside the door. Alone, Champion held off fifty men. Another Johnson County resident, chancing by, survived a burst of gunfire and raced to Buffalo with word of what was happening. The Regulators meanwhile stepped up their attack and ran a flaming wagon against the cabin walls. Champion broke for a ravine. They shot him down, pinned a note, "Cattle Thieves Beware," on his shirt, and rode on.

Sheriff Red Angus and a hundred or more angry men whom he had sworn in as deputies met the invaders twelve miles outside of town. This time it was the cattlemen who were pinned down without trial in a ranch house. When night came, one of the reporters who had accompanied the stockmen managed to reach Fort McKinney, near Buffalo. He telegraphed the governor, who in turn wired Wyoming's two senators in Washington. They routed President Benjamin Harrison from bed with tales of insurrection in the West. Telegraph wires hummed again. Three troops of cavalry rode out of Fort McKinney and took the cattlemen into protective custody.

Pretty bad, admitted association president John Clay, who had wintered in Europe, ". . . and yet if you had lived in such times the critic of today would probably have been the performer of a far away yesterday. In this world of complex conditions it is hard to define where law ends and individuality begins."

Embittered Johnson County ran up bills of twenty-eight thousand dollars (less than half of which were paid) trying to build a case against those fifty individuals. Witnesses melted away, and in the end the county gave up. For years afterward, popular sympathy stayed on the side of the rustlers. The Hole-in-the-Wall section in the southern part of the county became notorious as a haven for outlaws. No stockman dared enter the region—it was barricaded on the east by a thirty-five-mile reef of red sandstone, broken only by the "hole" of the middle Powder River canyon—until 1897, when Bob Devine of the CY tried to shoot a way in. He did not make it, but the next year a roundup, supported by the sheriffs of the neighboring counties, brought out five hundred and fifty head of stolen stock. After that, order slowly returned—legal order, not triumphant individuality on either side.

In 1892, the year of the cattlemen's invasion of Johnson County, comparable struggles were wracking the Coeur d'Alene silver-mining section of the Idaho Panhandle. Gold placers had lured the first stampeders there in 1882–83. Silver-lead discoveries followed in 1884, and still more prospectors poured wild-eyed across the passes. Among them was Noah Kellogg, an unemployed carpenter sixty years old. In the early spring of 1884, Kellogg found the mines that joined to become the Bunker Hill and Sullivan, one of North America's fattest producers of lead and silver. Noah sold his share of it for three hundred thousand dollars. In the years since then, the Bunker Hill and Sullivan has paid out something like seventy-five million dollars in dividends.

Other mines, some of them almost as rich, were quickly discovered throughout a mountainous, heavily timbered area about thirty miles in length and less than that in width. Several raucous towns—Wallace was the largest—crowded into the narrow canyons. One gulch was so cramped that the branch-line railroad that served it had to be built underneath the hotel and mills. Although the district's swiftly growing volume of traffic led both the Northern Pacific and the Union Pacific to build railroad lines, rates remained high. Grimly the mine owners set about forcing a readjustment.

They based their arguments on the sagging price of silver. In 1873 the United States Government had ceased coining silver dollars and had gone onto the gold standard, as had a number of countries in western Europe. Immediately thereafter, floods of silver from the Comstock, Leadville, and other silver-mining areas had dropped the price of the metal, in terms of gold, from an average of $1.32 an ounce in 1872 to $1.15 in 1878.

Prices of other Western commodities declined proportionately. Thus a farmer burdened by a loan that he could have repaid in 1873 with a thousand bushels of wheat found that in 1877 he had to offer eleven hundred.

In the opinion of the debtor West, prices could be returned to former levels by increasing the amount of money in circulation—that is, by inflation. When Greenback movements in support of paper money made no headway, inflationists turned to silver as a compromise. The Government yielded an inch in 1878 by passing the Bland-Allison Act, which required the Treasury to purchase between two million and four million dollars' worth of silver each month for coinage into dollars.

Each Administration after 1878 had held purchases to the legal minimum, and the effect on prices, even of silver, had been negligible. After a spell of prosperity in the middle 1880's, the long decline continued. By the end of the decade, wheat had touched sixty-five cents a bushel, silver eighty-four cents an ounce.

Owners of silver mines, who of course were capitalists, made an unnatural alliance with the criers for agrarian reform and in 1890 helped prevail on Congress to pass the Sherman Silver Purchase Act. This bill approximately doubled the amount of white metal bought each month by the Treasury. Again the effect on silver prices was negligible. After a brief jump to $1.05 an ounce, the metal slid back to eighty-seven cents.

Seeking economies, the Coeur d'Alene mines closed operations and suspended shipments from January 1 to April 1, 1892. This blackjack forced a freight reduction of two dollars a ton from the railroads. The triumphant mine owners then announced that when work resumed after April 1, it would be at a reduced wage scale.

The workers were incensed. Even before the closures, friction had sparked between their local union and the Mine Owners Protective Association, which the operators had formed as a counter to the union. Led by the Bunker Hill and Sullivan, the Protective Association had hired Pinkerton detectives to spy on union leaders, had favored hiring nonunion men, and had been recalcitrant about deducting hospital fees from the wages of the men themselves. To then turn the men, during the most rigorous months of the northern winter, into shivering pawns in the owners' contest with the railroads was bad enough. To top the arrogance with an announcement that the workers must accept a wage cut, though the mines could now save money on freight, was unendurable. By an overwhelming majority they voted to strike.

The employers imported strikebreakers and guards. On July 10, violent clashes erupted in narrow Burke Canyon. During the shooting, five men were killed, sixteen wounded. The surface workings of the Frisco mine were shattered with dynamite. Other strikers slipped more dynamite inside the huge concentrating mill at the Bunker Hill and Sullivan and by threatening to touch off the explosives forced the management to discharge its strikebreakers. While the unarmed scabs were waiting at Cataldo for a steamer to take them out across Coeur d'Alene Lake, union men fell on them, killed two, and savagely beat as many more as they could catch.

State militia arrived and herded the unionists into stockades called bull pens. Five hundred or more of them were indicted for various crimes; a handful were sentenced for short terms but freed by court order. The workers gained nothing else, however. Protected by the militia, which stayed in the district until November (approximately the date when other Federal troops were imposing peace on union strikers at the Homestead, Pennsylvania, plant of the Carnegie Steel Company), the mines resumed hiring nonunion men. Leaders of the crippled Coeur d'Alene union, seeking a wider basis of strength, thereupon met with other organizers in Butte, Montana, and in May, 1893, formed the Western Federation of Miners, ancestor of both the radical Industrial Workers of the World and of the more law-abiding International Union of Mine, Mill, and Smelter Workers.

Throughout those uneasy days, depression-pinched farmers were desperately seeking remedies to their own woes. One classic answer to falling prices had always been to raise more crops by seeking fresh land. Increasing mechanization and swifter transportation strengthened the temptation, only to have the "movers" come hard up against the sobering fact that the eight hundred and fifty million acres of public domain remaining in the United States were arid and not adaptable to farming—unless the land could be irrigated.

Irrigation was no new panacea, even in America. A thousand years ago, the Indians of the Southwestern deserts had brought water to their fields through long canals. Later, Spanish colonists built crude little communal *acequias* to tap the Rio Grande in New Mexico and the undependable streams of coastal California. The Mormons of Utah, also acting communally, had learned not only to dig ditches but also to build reservoirs for storing spring runoff from melting snow. In 1870, a utopian colony backed by Horace Greeley and led by Nathan Meeker had founded the town of Greeley, Colorado, and by the end of 1871 had completed two big canals that helped the settlers transform several thousand acres of the parched brown plains into an emerald oasis. Denver had its "Platte Ditch," twenty-four miles long, and Spanish Americans in the southern part of the state had built other successful canals.

Bemused by these accomplishments with water diversion, Colorado's governor, S. H. Elbert, invited delegates from Kansas, Nebraska, Wyoming, Utah, and New Mexico to an irrigation congress in Denver on October 15, 1873. This convention forwarded to the Government a memorial advocating land grants as an aid to building irrigation canals and reservoirs—the nation's first reclamation proposal. President Grant thought highly enough of the idea so that he recommended Federal aid in creating a green belt across the plains by means of a huge ditch from the foot of the Rockies to the Missouri River. The notion was impractical—later engineering studies showed that not enough water was available to keep streams and canal both flowing—but that was not what killed the plan. In 1873 land grants had gone out of fashion. Besides, cynics said the scheme was merely another device whereby speculators could hog still more land, which just possibly might have proved to be the case.

Instead, Congress tried by means of the Desert Land Act of 1877 to stimulate irrigation through individual enterprise. This incongruous bill allowed a man to *buy* six hundred and forty acres of arid land for $1.25 an acre (the Homestead Act was meanwhile granting settlers, for a small registration fee, one hundred and sixty acres of more valuable agricultural land) if the claimant irrigated the acreage within three years. In most areas the expenses involved prohibited success. But since six hundred and forty desert acres could be secured for several years by an initial down payment of twenty-five cents an acre, cattlemen gladly supplied fraudulent entrymen with the necessary fee, had them swear that water had been brought to the land (generally in a bucket), grazed it to death, and let the claims lapse.

Irrigation projects fell more and more into the hands of companies that could command capital. The initial purchase price of "water rights," to which an annual water "rent" was often added, soared toward the stratosphere on the wings of the sellers' own ecstatic propaganda. In the excitement to cash in, many companies overreached. The Grand Valley Ditch Company of western Colorado, for instance, borrowed two hundred thousand dollars from an insurance company in 1884, foundered almost immediately, and in 1888 sold its assets at foreclosure for forty thousand dollars, to the distress of several hundred families who needed water. Success stories were equally common, however. One firm in southeastern Colorado completed a canal one hundred and thirteen miles long, forty-five feet wide, six and a half feet deep. Southwest Idaho boasted a corporation-built ditch fifty miles long that watered twenty-five thousand acres. Another private ditch in the San Joaquin Valley of California was fifty-two feet wide and forty miles long. In Wyoming, as the 1890's opened, a five-thousand-mile mélange of individual and company ditches (many in Johnson County) watered almost two million acres.

Chaos threatened. Western water law, springing from diversions miners had first made for operating placer claims, was based on priority of appropriation. In most states and territories, an early filer could claim more than he needed himself and sell the rest. Late filers could shoot for the moon and hope some water might be left over after prior rights had been satisfied. The pyramiding became fantastic. As early as 1886, the bed of the Gallatin River in Montana would have been dust dry if every claimant had possessed ditches enough to assert his rights. Oregon's Umatilla River actually was sucked empty in three different places during the drought year of 1909. The height of absurdity was reached along Idaho's Boise River. In September, 1898, the stream flowed 8,750 second-feet. Against that trickle stood claims for 1,590,450 second-feet!

Under the circumstances, farmers often sat up all night watching their head gates with loaded shotguns. More importantly, what of interstate rights? Could growers of sugar beets in Colorado drain the Arkansas River to the detriment of wheat farmers in Kansas?

Before order could be imposed, the potential yield of each watershed had to be determined by accurate surveys, and the flow stabilized by reservoirs. Private companies, however, were not interested in co-operating on the studies and not able to finance adequate dams. Demands accordingly grew for intervention by the Federal Government, and in October, 1888, Western congressmen achieved passage of a bill authorizing the United States Geological Survey, under John Wesley Powell, to conduct the nation's first irrigation study.

Powell, too, ran afoul of "individuality." Speculators stalked his survey crews and took up homestead or desert claims, often fraudulently, wherever they anticipated a reservoir site. The practice drew such loud complaints from Idaho that in 1890 the Administration in effect closed the public domain throughout the United States to settlement and canceled all land entries made after October, 1888. The intent was to reopen the land, district by district, to normal homestead entry as fast as the water studies were completed.

The social implications were enormous, for by regulating the land openings, the Government could, for the first time, directly control the process of settlement. This of course ran counter to a century of tradition. Western congressmen, eager for untrammeled population movements into their districts, were so incensed by what had happened to their own idea that they immediately emasculated the survey by cutting off its appropriations. As a result of their action, Federal supervision of recla-

mation efforts would have to wait for another decade.

Some reform was achieved, however. In 1891, Congress passed a General Revision Act that repealed the old Pre-emption and Timber Culture laws, reduced Desert Land entries to three hundred and twenty acres while lightening irrigation requirements, and extended from six to fourteen months the time needed to commute a homestead claim into a pre-emption right under which title could be bought for $1.25 an acre—an extension of residence stipulations that chilled temptations to fraud. More importantly, the General Revision Act empowered the President to protect watersheds by closing forestlands, at his discretion, to all forms of use. Heeding the eloquent appeals of John Muir in California and of the Colorado Forestry Association, President Harrison during his two years in office set aside fifteen widely scattered reserves totaling thirteen million acres.

Unfortunately, the General Revision Act had left untouched the Timber and Stone Act of 1878, passed originally to let settlers in the Pacific Coast states and Nevada buy one hundred and sixty acres of forest in order to obtain necessary wood for their farms and mines. The price was $2.50 an acre, an appalling trivia when applied to the towering redwoods of California and the Douglas fir of Washington. Undismayed by Harrison's relatively small reserves, Northwest lumbermen went right on using fraudulent entrymen to engross the best of the easily reached timber. Like reclamation, forest conservation would also have to await the new century.

Waiting did not suit the mood of the farmers on the Great Plains and in the South. They wanted quick relief for their miseries, and the newly formed Populist party offered a promising program: an ending of political corruption through the initiative and referendum and the direct election of senators; a checking of price drops through the free coinage of silver; restraints on capital through a graduated income tax and Government ownership of telegraph lines and railroads.

Slogans were as direct as a knife blade. This, cried "Sockless" Jerry Simpson, a Populist leader of Kansas, "is a struggle between the robbers and the robbed." Aided by the silver barons, the Populists in 1892 won the electoral votes of Kansas, Colorado, Idaho, and Nevada and elected governors in Kansas, Colorado, and North Dakota. Outside of the West, however, success was slim. The Populist Presidential candidate, James B. Weaver, polled only 9 per cent of the national vote.

Price declines continued. A run to convert silver certificates into gold developed, and the country's gold reserve slipped below the mystic safety mark of one hundred million dollars. At the same time, mints in India ceased coining silver and drove the price of the metal still lower. Suddenly, in the summer of 1893, the nation found itself gripped by a terrifying economic crisis.

President Cleveland prevailed on a special session of Congress to repeal the Sherman Silver Purchase Act. The West was outraged. The new Populist governor of Colorado, Davis Waite, roared to a mass meeting in Denver, ". . . it is better, infinitely better, that blood should flow to the horses' bridles rather than our national liberties should be destroyed!" Scoffers promptly nicknamed him "Bloody Bridles Waite," but such sentiments, plus Davis's threats to coin state money and even lead a Western secessionist movement if necessary, were no laughing matter to most conservatives. Neither was Jacob Coxey's "army" of unemployed, which was to gather from all parts of the United States at Massillon, Ohio, in the spring of 1894, and march from there with their protests to Washington. The depression-tormented West furnished the largest proportion of "troops." The "armies" recruited in the Rocky Mountains and the Pacific Northwest were, says Donald McMurray, a historian of the movement, "the most intractable and troublesome" of the groups. One band in Montana stole a train but was stopped by cavalry. Another commandeered a train in Utah and rode undisturbed to Omaha, only to learn Coxey had gone ahead without them. Mounted police drove those marchers who did reach Washington off the Capitol grounds, and nothing was accomplished.

As the elections of 1896 approached, the Democrats absorbed the Populists and challenged the gold-standard Republicans with young William Jennings Bryan of Nebraska and the cry of free silver. Bryan lost, and much of the West was in despair—yet even then, the economic cycle was swinging upward once more.

Unexpected gold discoveries throughout the world loosened currency strictures and helped raise prices without the need of fiat money. Two of the extraordinary finds were on American territory: one near meandering Cripple Creek, on the southwestern slopes of Pikes Peak, eighteen air-lines miles from populous Colorado Springs; the other, in remote Alaska.

Cripple Creek came first. After twelve years of desultory search across a region already well covered, a bibulous cowboy named Bob Womack in October, 1890, discovered what became, local boosters say, the greatest single gold-producing area in the world—a total of about six hundred and twenty-five *tons* of the metal. Womack benefited little himself, but others reaped astonishingly. Winfield Stratton located the Independence mine on July 4, 1891, netted $2,500,000 from it, then sold it in 1899 for a net to himself of $10,000,000. By 1900, fifty

thousand people had crowded into the district, and by 1901, three railroads were competing for their traffic.

In 1896, rich placers were discovered near the junction of the Klondike and Yukon rivers, inside Canada. Sourdoughs who for years had been combing the wastes along the upper Yukon rushed in to found the storybook town of Dawson. During the winter they heaped up mounds of frozen earth that they washed for its treasure the following spring. For some of them returns were fabulous— one hundred thousand dollars or more each—and they were in a hurry to get outside and spend it. The stories they told when they docked in San Francisco and Seattle started a frantic rush northward. Thousands of persons sailed to Skagway and reached the headwaters of the Yukon by struggling through the mud and boulders of White Pass or by climbing with their packs on their backs up a dreadful, single-file staircase chipped out of the solid ice of Chilkoot Pass. Backwashes of the rush swept west from Canada to Nome beside the Bering Sea, to Fairbanks in the middle Yukon Basin, to a dozen other Alaska camps. Under the stimulus of the Alaska traffic, Seattle became the Northwest's most populous city.

The United States was ready for expansion. Some historians believe that the closing of the frontier sent investors farther afield and resulted in war with Spain over Cuba, the seizure of Puerto Rico and the Philippine Islands, and, as a corollary to that imperialistic adventure, the annexation of Hawaii in 1898. Perhaps the theory is sound, but other exploiters found that the West still afforded ample opportunities.

James J. Hill, who without the help of land grants had completed his Great Northern Railroad from St. Paul to Seattle in 1893, stimulated freight revenue by fostering trade with the Orient, lumbering in the Northwest, and agriculture on the high plains. He popped the eyes of Minnesotans by using twenty horses to drag a single log of Washington Douglas fir through the streets of St. Paul and used various forms of trickery to obtain enormous timber holdings. Thus when rising agricultural prices led prospering farmers on the Midwestern plains to increase their demands for Pacific Coast lumber, Hill was ready to oblige them by loading an endless supply of logs into his freight trains. After a series of laws, 1904–16, had increased the number of acres a homesteader might acquire, he lured thousands of settlers to Montana by sending around exhibits of hardy crops and by promoting dry farming. It was again an injudicious disdaining of the weather cycle. The deep plowing and constant soil pulverizing required by dry farming worked as long as rain averages held; but in due time drought came again, fierce dust storms blew seeds right out of the ground, and

New settlers for "rich, free" Western farm lands: Dunker families, lured from their homes in Indiana by agents of James J. Hill's Great Northern Railroad, pass through St. Paul in 1894 en route to North Dakota's Red River Valley.

another retreat took place to the more humid East.

Industrial technology opened other fields. In 1890, L. L. Nunn, of Telluride, Colorado, ran a copper wire from a generator beside the San Miguel River 2.6 miles along a rugged mountain slope to a motor at the Gold King mine, twelve thousand feet above sea level. It was the world's first long-distance transmission of alternating current for industrial purposes, and it dropped the costs of running the machinery at the Gold King from twenty-five hundred dollars a month to five hundred dollars. Even before this, a few cities here and there had started using direct-current electricity for lighting. An extraordinary technological revolution followed, with tremendous economic implications for the metal-producing West. In 1893, the United States generated one and a quarter billion kilowatt-hours of electric power and used two hundred million pounds of copper. In ten years, amounts more than doubled: three billion kilowatt-hours and four hundred and fifty million pounds of copper, most of which was destined to be mined in Montana, Utah, Arizona, and New Mexico.

Steam shovels, which came into general use during the same decade, helped the development. Engineer Daniel C. Jackling and a group of Colorado Springs entrepreneurs, needing new fields for investing their Cripple Creek profits, applied the monsters to vast low-grade copper deposits in Bingham Canyon, south of Great Salt Lake, and in thirty years added six *billion* pounds of copper to the nation's supply. The techniques developed in Utah spread to Arizona and gave that remote territory (a state in 1912) her first really considerable industry.

Oil exploitation was equally spectacular. Once, the liquid had been used mostly for producing kerosene (electric lighting doomed that), for lubricating machines, and, in California, for fueling a few locomotives. But various inventors had learned that another distillation from it, gasoline, could be employed to propel motors. By 1900, eight thousand strange-looking horseless carriages were chugging along dusty roads in the nation, so that when the great Spindletop gusher blew in at Beaumont, Texas, January 10, 1901, two new industries were ready to join hands and change the habits of the world. Texas, Oklahoma, southern California, and Wyoming no longer depended almost solely on agriculture as a primary economic resource. And within a few more years, scoffers who had denigrated the spreading national parks as mere playgrounds for the rich grew aware that everyone in the newly mobile population would have a concern in conserving the beauties of the land.

The vaunted individualism that Americans had carried West with them yielded stubbornly to changing social conditions. As the new century opened, both capital and labor continued, at times, to seek self-aggrandizement by defying the public weal. In October, 1903, Amalgamated Copper, a highly watered trust formed when Standard Oil bought control of the Anaconda Mining Company, blackmailed the Montana legislature into passing certain laws it wished by closing its mines, smelters, lumber camps, and mills, and threatening to leave twenty thousand men out of work during the winter. In

391

their own way, labor agitators could be equally ruthless. In June, 1904, during a strike in the Cripple Creek mining district of Colorado, Albert Horsley, alias Harry Orchard, who claimed to be acting at the behest of Big Bill Haywood of the Western Federation of Miners, killed thirteen scabs and dreadfully injured fourteen more by blowing up the Independence depot where they were waiting for a train. Eighteen months later, in Caldwell, Idaho, Orchard wired a bomb to the residential fence gate of Frank Steunenberg, ex-governor of the state, and obliterated him in revenge for Steunenberg's having used troops to quell an 1899 strike in the Coeur d'Alene mines.

In time Federal intervention helped curb such industrial willfulness. Simultaneously, other needs for Federal help became apparent. Individual states had failed to solve the irrigation problem, even with the aid of generous land grants made available under the Carey Desert Land Act of 1894. Only the Federal Government could marshal enough money to meet the high costs of large irrigation projects. Spurred by Theodore Roosevelt, Congress in 1902 accordingly passed the Reclamation Act. The bill's intent was not merely to provide water but also to frustrate speculation while aiding a maximum number of small farmers. Homesteads as tiny as forty acres were authorized. One of the land-grabber's favorite devices, commutation of a homestead claim to a pre-emption claim so that title could be purchased after a few months' residence, was forbidden. The act further decreed that owners of large tracts within a reclamation area could receive only as much water as was needed to irrigate one hundred and sixty acres.

Almost instantly it became evident that other factors than irrigation were going to complicate the allocation of available Western water. Shortly after the passage of the act, Los Angeles, her growth strangled for want of water, persuaded the Reclamation Service to drop a proposed project in the Owens Valley east of the Sierra Nevada Mountains. The city then moved in, against the sometimes violent opposition of five thousand farmers, and by means of a giant, 250-mile-long conduit, completed in 1913, whisked off enough water to supply a population of two million—which proved to be just a beginning. During the same period, San Francisco outraged nature lovers by building a storage reservoir in spectacular Hetch-Hetchy Canyon of Yosemite National Park. In 1911, Denver's civic leaders began plans for a tunnel under the Continental Divide that would divert water to their city from the upper Colorado River.

Private power interests also laid claims to dam sites throughout the mountainous West. Since power sales provided means for financing irrigation projects, Federal planning extended into the field also, and still more reservoirs were projected. As water studies proliferated, engineers soon learned that save in the Pacific Northwest, there simply were not rivers enough to satisfy all the demands. As one solution, the planners built bigger and still bigger dams. Mere size, however, has not proved to be a panacea. Controversies over the control of water still spark between private power interests and the Government, between state and state, between reclamation groups and citizens determined to preserve the remaining canyons from encroachments by artificial lakes.

Early attempts to conserve the land's remaining timber also stirred antagonisms. When President Cleveland established thirteen new forest reserves almost without warning in 1897, Congressman John L. Wilson of Washington spoke for the individualistic part of the West by crying out against this check on independence. People in the East, Wilson shouted, had developed their domain without government planning. Were those in the West any less competent? When an Easterner, A. A. Anderson, was appointed superintendent of the new Yellowstone Reserve in Wyoming, the Meeteetse (Wyoming) *News* all but swooned: "Mr. Anderson can by a single stroke of his diamond-bedecked hand, put out of existence that noble animal [the sheep] that clothes his unclean body."

Compromise softened the intransigence. At first, the forest reserves—by the end of Theodore Roosevelt's administration there were one hundred and fifty-nine of them, embracing more than one hundred and fifty million acres—had been closed to every form of exploitation, even to settlers needing fence posts. Under Western pressures they were reluctantly opened to controlled grazing, lumbering, and mining. But few people recommended a return to unbridled utilization. The educational programs of such organizations as the American Forestry Association and the sharper warning of a series of ferocious, death-dealing forest fires throughout the Northwest, 1902–10, had brought home to the entire nation the need for adequate control of what trees were still left.

In 1907, the forest reserves became national forests. Perhaps the change in name, suggestive of benefits for everyone, was symptomatic. Throughout the century and a half following the end of the French and Indian War in 1763, the West had been absorbed in learning how to master a vast, varied, sometimes stern but generally fruitful land. By 1914, when the nation could at last transfer some of its enormous energies to America's newer responsibilities as a world power, the frontier had also learned, in part, how to master itself. And that, as even the individualists beyond the Missouri began to realize, was the nation's truest freedom.

THE WEST LIVES ON

As the nineteenth century waned, astute showmen and writers realized that the history of the West was a mother lode of entertainment riches, that American schoolboys (and their fathers) liked nothing better than a seemingly authentic tale or display of Old West derring-do. William F. Cody, called Buffalo Bill because of his prowess as a hunter of buffalo meat for railroad workers, was among the first to capitalize on this love for the romanticized West. A former scout and pony express rider, Cody took his Wild West Show of Indians and "rough riders" across the nation and throughout Europe (above is a climactic moment of the show, photographed in London in 1903), bringing fame not only to himself but also to sharpshooting Frank Butler and Annie Oakley. Boys became readers of the dime novels (left) that deified outlaws as well as intrepid marshals. And in nickelodeons, *The Great Train Robbery,* made in 1903, featured horseback chases, fights atop moving trains, and plenty of gunplay—all to be standard ingredients in countless later films glorifying a West that became only a memory.

Dragging their supplies on a makeshift cart, prospectors (above) ford an Alaskan stream on their way to the gold fields in 1897. Below, a bevy of actresses, headed for Dawson in the Klondike, pose in hiking garb at a camp en route.

THE KLONDIKE

George Washington Carmack, an American with prospecting in his blood (his father had been a Forty-Niner in California), was the first to strike gold in Canada's far northern Klondike. It took almost a year for news of his and of subsequent discoveries to reach the United States; but when it did, a new gold rush fever swept the country. In 1897–98, some one hundred thousand hopefuls quit their jobs and headed north for Alaska and the Yukon. Some who went were experienced prospectors, but most had never seen a placer before. Nor had they any idea of the rigors that lay ahead of them: freezing cold weather, illness, and countless days of struggling over steep, icy trails. Of those who started out, less than forty thousand made it to Dawson, the boomtown that sprang up in the Klondike. And of those, only a few hundred struck it rich. The big rush finally ended when the Spanish-American War began, but it had familiarized the country with still another of its frontiers.

Prospectors, pulling their supplies, trek grimly along a rugged, snow-covered trail.

WEALTH
INEXHAUSTIBLE

Uncapped gushers like "Heywood No. 2" (above), brought in at Beaumont, Texas, during the Spindletop boom in 1901, wasted thousands of barrels of oil a day.

Timber for a growing nation poured out of forests from the Great Lakes to the Northwest. Above, lumber from the Wisconsin woods is hauled by sledge in 1901.

In Minnesota's Mesabi Range, the Mahoning iron mine (right), a few years old when this 1899 picture was taken, became the world's largest open-pit mine.

396

There was no end to the bounty of the West—or so it seemed. Besides the gold and silver, there was copper and lead and a host of other minerals; some of the world's richest iron ore deposits were discovered in Minnesota in the 1880's, and during the next decade the first commercial tappings were made of the vast pools of oil under Texas, Wyoming, Oklahoma, and California. Forests of prime timber trees covered much of the West Coast and the Rockies, and grazing land was still plentiful. But there were disturbing danger signs. By 1900, only 200 million of the country's original 800 million acres of forest remained, and inestimable amounts of coal, oil, and other minerals were being lost by careless extraction. Rivers ran low because of the denuding of forest lands, overgrazing, and bad irrigation practices, while arid land begged for water. Waste was the order of the day.

ERA OF TURMOIL

For many pioneers the promise of the West was never fulfilled. Homesteaders found their fields producing only debt; once-hopeful prospectors were forced to hire out for wages to big mining operators. The farmers turned to both political action and panaceas to solve their difficulties. They used the Granger movement to fight unfair railroad freight rates and sharp grain-grading practices by elevators. They sought—and partially gained—political power in the Populist party. They demanded the cure-all of easy money and almost saw their dreams come true when the Democrats nominated Bryan in 1896 on a Free Silver platform. As for the miners, their hope for getting better wages lay in organizing, but the mineowners met them head-on with lockouts and strikebreakers. The strikers always lost; it was a day when unions were suspect, so if there was violence, the militia was called and the strike was broken. It was decades before turmoil at last gave way to orderly progress.

Three times Democratic party Presidential nominee—and three times loser—William Jennings Bryan (right) based his 1896 campaign on the Western demand for free silver coinage.

Troops march into Wallace, Idaho (below), in July, 1892, after fighting had broken out in the Coeur d'Alene gulches between miners protesting a wage cut and guards hired by owners.

Embittered striking Idaho miners, enjoined by the courts from picketing or any other action against the operators, used dynamite to destroy the Frisco Mill (left) at Gem in July, 1892.

The militant Industrial Workers of the World roused stern opposition. Below, armed citizens evict 1,200 IWW members from Bisbee, Arizona, during a strike in the copper mines in 1917.

CONSERVATION

The nation was still only slowly awakening to the need for conservation. A beginning had been made with the Forest Reserve Act in 1891, which empowered the President to set aside public timberland. But the first big impetus came in 1908 when Theodore Roosevelt called a White House Conference to inquire into the state of the nation's resources. It was a milestone in conservation; the meeting showed that the country knew little about its resources, and it excited public interest and action. Even though there were no sweeping immediate results, Roosevelt set aside more forest reserves, established five national parks, created bird and game preserves, promoted irrigation, and gave to Americans their first real consciousness of the need for conservation.

Despite opposition by strong lumber and mining interests and by many utility companies, Theodore Roosevelt doggedly pushed forward a program for Western land reclamation. It involved the securing for the Federal Government of watersheds and water-power sites by withdrawing them from entry, and the construction of dams and irrigation projects with the proceeds from the sale of public land. The first major undertaking was the building of a series of dams and irrigation ditches in the Salt River Basin of Arizona. By 1906, canals were bringing water to desert lands in central Arizona (above), and by 1910, Roosevelt Dam (right) and its power facilities were nearing completion. Meanwhile, President Roosevelt, shown at left in Las Vegas, Nevada, during the 1904 Presidential campaign, gradually won support from many Western leaders for conservation. Eventually, even lumber barons like C. A. Weyerhaeuser would recognize the advantage to themselves and would come to the support of Roosevelt's goals.

THEY DID NOT VANISH

The start of the long road of adjustment: Arapahoes greet President Chester A. Arthur in Wyoming in 1883.

AND SO AT LAST...

Owen Wister

Three ladies and their escort pose atop the peak Pike saw but could not climb in 1806.

Tourists motor through Mount Rainier National Park, cleared of Indians in the 1850's.

With Indians no longer a danger, and with paintings, photographs, and writings whetting interest in America's scenic wonders, increasing numbers of Easterners ventured West to spend vacations. Prim teachers from Boston gazed at the geysers that Jim Bridger had once described to incredulous listeners, and city families hiked along trails that had been blazed by men like Jedediah Smith. One of the most enthusiastic dudes was Owen Wister, Pennsylvania-born and Harvard-educated, who spent several summers in Wyoming in hopes that the rigorous life would improve his health. Wister came to love the West, and the stories he wrote in the 1890's gave a true picture of a cowboy's life. His most famous novel, *The Virginian* (published in 1902 and dedicated to his friend Theodore Roosevelt), caused many a reader to forsake his armchair and travel West. The book also gave American folklore the prototype of one of its most beloved heroes: the brave cowboy who was soft-spoken with the schoolmarm but brooked absolutely no nonsense from the outlaw; it was to the latter (Trampas) that he spoke his famous line: "When you call me that, *smile.*"

Above: Coach-borne vacationers in 1905 hurry along through Yellowstone Park, viewing wonders that Moran painted.
Below: Progress and the timeless: in a 1902 car, a visitor contemplates the Grand Canyon, the West as it always was.

"Caught in the Circle"
by Frederic Remington

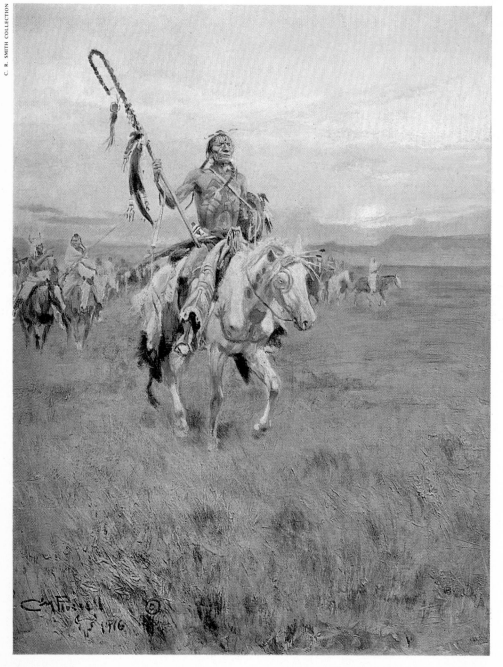

"Stoic of the Plains" by Charles M. Russell

LONG LIVE THE WEST

In 1905, the Western artist Frederic Remington lamented the passing of an era: "I knew the wild riders and the vacant land were about to vanish forever.... I saw the living, breathing end of three American centuries of smoke and dust and sweat, and I now see quite another thing where it all took place, but it does not appeal to me." Fortunately, Remington saved the image of what had passed. Like Charles M. Russell and other artists, he captured on canvas the courage of troopers, the dignity of free Indians, the stamina of cowboys on the unfenced range. In these paintings the spirit of a West now vanished is preserved for future generations.

"Wyoming Blizzard" by W. H. D. Koerner

Hear the wind
Blow through the buffalo-grass,
Blow over wild-grape and brier.
This was frontier, and this,
And this, your house, was frontier.
There were footprints upon the hill
And men lie buried under,
Tamers of earth and rivers.
They died at the end of labor,
Forgotten is the name.

Stephen Vincent Benét, Western Star

*North Dakota durum wheat along the Missouri,
near the site of the former Mandan villages
and of Lewis and Clark's 1804–5 winter fort.*

ACKNOWLEDGMENTS AND INDEX

The Editors appreciate the generous assistance provided by many individuals and institutions during the preparation of this book. They especially wish to thank the following:

Academy of Natural Sciences of Philadelphia: Mrs. Venia T. Phillips
Alamo Library, San Antonio, Texas: Carmen Perry
Alaska Historical Library and Museum, Juneau
American Antiquarian Society, Worcester, Massachusetts
American Museum of Natural History, New York
American Philosophical Society, Philadelphia: Gertrude D. Hess
N. J. Anthony, Washington, D. C.
Archivo General de Indias, Seville
Archivo Historico Nacional, Madrid
Arizona Pioneers' Historical Society, Tucson: Andrew Wallace
Mr. and Mrs. J. B. Arthur, San Antonio
Mrs. Caroline Backlund, New York
Bancroft Library, University of California, Berkeley: Dale L. Morgan
Miss Miriam Bennett, Wisconsin Dells
Bibliothèque Nationale, Paris: Département des Cartes & Plans
Ray Allen Billington
Boot Hill Museum, Dodge City, Kansas: George Henrichs
Bostonian Society, Old State House, Boston
British Museum, London: John McKenzie
California Historical Society, San Francisco: James de T. Abajian, Kent Seavey
California State Library, Sacramento
Carnegie Library of Pittsburgh
Chicago Historical Society: Mrs. Paul M. Rhymer
Church of Jesus Christ of Latter-day Saints, Salt Lake City, Utah
Cincinnati Art Museum: Pinkney Near
City Art Museum of St. Louis: Agnes Grey
William L. Clements Library, University of Michigan, Ann Arbor: Nathaniel N. Shipton
Corcoran Gallery of Art, Washington
E. B. Crocker Art Gallery, Sacramento
Custer Battlefield National Monument: Andrew M. Loveless
Daughters of the Republic of Texas Museum, Austin
Daughters of Utah Pioneers, Salt Lake City: Kate B. Carter
Peter Decker, New York
Denver Public Library: Western Collection
Detroit Public Library: Burton Historical Collection
Mrs. Byron Dexter, South Woodstock, Vermont
Duke University Library, Durham, North Carolina: William R. Erwin, Jr.
George Eastman House, Rochester, New York
Filson Club, Louisville, Kentucky: Mrs. Dorothy Thomas Cullen
Fordham University, New York
Glenbow Foundation, Calgary, Alberta
Mrs. Isabel Haynes, Bozeman, Montana
J. Hefter, Mexico City
James Jerome Hill Reference Library, St. Paul, Minnesota: Russell F. Barnes
Thomas A. Hogan, Pomona, California
Historical Society of Pennsylvania, Philadelphia
Houghton Library, Harvard University, Cambridge, Massachusetts
Warren Howell, San Francisco
Henry E. Huntington Library and Art Gallery, San Marino, California: Robert O. Dougan, Carey S. Bliss, Herbert Schulz, Lyle H. Wright
Idaho Department of Commerce and Development, Boise: Louise Shadduck
Idaho Historical Society, Boise: H. J. Swinney, Merle W. Wells
Independence National Historical Park, Philadelphia
Mrs. Lucie A. Jenkins, Orleans, Indiana
Joslyn Art Museum, Northern Natural Gas Company Collection, Omaha, Nebraska: Mildred Goosman
Kansas State Historical Society, Topeka: Nyle H. Miller, Robert W. Richmond
Kit Carson Memorial Foundation, Inc., Taos, New Mexico: Jack K. Boyer
Library of Congress, Washington: Edgar Breitenbach, Virginia Daiker, Milton Kaplan, Mrs. Renata Shaw, Walter W. Ristow
Lilly Library, Indiana University, Bloomington: Doris M. Reed, Elfrieda Lang
Maryland Historical Society, Baltimore: John D. Kilbourne, Thomas S. Eader
Massachusetts Historical Society, Boston: Malcolm Freiberg
Mrs. Nina Hull Miller, Lexington, Nebraska
Minnesota Historical Society, St. Paul: Eugene D. Becker, Mrs. Helene Thomson
Missouri Historical Society, St. Louis: Mrs. Ruth K. Field
Montana Historical Society, Helena: Michael Kennedy, Mary K. Dempsey
Museo Naval, Madrid
Museo de Historia, Chapultepec, Mexico: Mrs. de la Luz Peredo, Carmen Velasco
Museum of Fine Arts, Boston: Elizabeth P. Riegel, Caroline P. Wistar
Museum of the City of Solothurn, Switzerland
Museum of Science and Industry, Chicago

National Archives, Washington: Herman R. Friis, Josephine Motylewski, A. P. Muntz
National Gallery of Canada, Ottawa
National Maritime Museum, Greenwich, England
Nebraska State Historical Society, Lincoln
New-York Historical Society: James J. Heslin
New York Public Library: Mrs. Maud Cole, Wilson G. Duprey
North Carolina Department of Archives and History, Raleigh: H. G. Jones, Mrs. Joye E. Jordan, Mrs. Peggy Hopson
Oakland Art Museum, Oakland, California
Ohio Historical Society, Columbus: Mrs. Elizabeth R. Martin
Mrs. Ruth Koerner Oliver, Santa Barbara, California
Oklahoma Historical Society, Oklahoma City
Oregon Historical Society, Portland: Thomas Vaughan, Allan Gibbons, Mrs. Barbara Elkins
Pack Memorial Public Library, Asheville, North Carolina: Margaret H. Ligon
Peabody Museum of Archaeology and Ethnology, Harvard University: Mrs. Katherine B. Edsall
Pennsylvania Historical and Museum Commission, Harrisburg
Public Archives of Canada, Ottawa
Franklin D. Roosevelt Library, Hyde Park, New York
Royal Ontario Museum, Toronto
Royal United Service Institution, London: David Erskine
St. John's Cathedral Archives, Winnipeg: Harry Shave
St. Louis Mercantile Library: Mrs. Elizabeth Kirchner
San Jacinto Museum of History Association, Texas
Shelburne Museum, Shelburne, Vermont: Bradley Smith
C. R. Smith, New York
Waddell F. Smith, Pony Express History and Art Gallery, San Rafael, California
Smithsonian Institution, Washington: Robert Elder
State Historical Society of Colorado, Denver: Mrs. Laura Allyn Ekstrom
State Historical Society of Iowa, Iowa City: William J. Petersen
State Historical Society of North Dakota, Bismarck
State Historical Society of Wisconsin, Madison: Paul Vanderbilt, Josephine L. Harper, Alice E. Smith, Mrs. Deloris Willard
Tennessee Historical Society, Nashville
Texas Memorial Museum, University of Texas, Austin
Texas Technological College, Lubbock: Southwest Collection, Roy Sylvan Dunn
Bronson Trevor, New York
Howard-Tilton Memorial Library, Tulane University, New Orleans
Union Pacific Railroad, Omaha, Nebraska
United States Bureau of Reclamation, Washington: Mrs. M. Farrell
United States Forest Service, Washington: Leland J. Prater
University of California Library, Santa Barbara: Wyles Collection
University of Oklahoma Library, Norman: J. D. Haley
University of Wyoming Library, Laramie
Utah State Historical Society, Salt Lake City: Mrs. Margaret D. Shepherd
Valentine Museum, Richmond, Virginia
Walters Art Gallery, Baltimore
Mrs. Al Warner, San Antonio
Washington State Historical Society, Tacoma: Bruce Le Roy
Washington University, St. Louis
West Point Museum, United States Military Academy
Western Reserve Historical Society, Cleveland: Mrs. Alene Lowe White
Whitney Gallery of Western Art, Cody, Wyoming: Harold McCracken
Roscoe G. Willson, Phoenix, Arizona
Witte Memorial Museum, San Antonio
Yale University Library, Western Americana Collection: Archibald Hanna
Brigham Young University, Provo, Utah

Grateful acknowledgment is also made for permission to use material from the following works:

The Field Notes of Captain William Clark (1803–1805), edited by Ernest Staples Osgood. Copyright © 1964 by the Yale University Press

George Caleb Bingham: River Portraitist by John Francis McDermott. Copyright © 1959 by the University of Oklahoma Press

Shutters West by Nina Hull Miller. Copyright © 1962 by Nina Hull Miller. The photograph on page 373 reprinted by permission of the publisher Alan Swallow (Sage Books)

The West of Alfred Jacob Miller, with an account of the artist by Marvin C. Ross. Copyright 1951 by the University of Oklahoma Press

Western Star by Stephen Vincent Benet. Copyright 1943 by Farrar & Rinehart, Inc. The quotation on page 409 reprinted by permission of Brandt & Brandt

Wooden Leg, interpreted by Thomas B. Marquis. Copyright © 1957 by the University of Nebraska Press

410

ABERT, JAMES W., 187
ABILENE, KANS., 352–53, 372
ACTON, MINN., 323
ADAIR, JAMES., 25–26
ADAMS, CASSILLY, 365
ADAMS-ONIS TREATY, 108, 110
ADOBE WALLS, 325, 354
ADOLPHE, CHIEF, 130
AENEAS (INDIAN), 130
AGRICULTURE, 32, 99, 194–95, 258–60, 345–47, 357, 376–77, 387–89, 392
AGUA NUEVA, MEX., 231
AINSLIE, HENRY F., 195
AIRD, JAMES, 84, 85
ALABAMA, 33, 34, 43, 101, 107, 154
ALAMANCE, BATTLE OF THE, 21
ALAMO, THE, 102, 161–62, 163, 172–73
ALASKA, 45, 58, 73–74, 93, 105, 186, 237, 327, 360, 390, 394–95
ALBUQUERQUE, N. MEX., 165, 228, 264, 277, 286, 288, 315, 328
ALDEN, JAMES, 300
ALDER CREEK, 320
ALLEGHENY MOUNTAINS, 15, 18, 51, 57, 78, 99, 183
AMERICAN FORESTRY ASSOCIATION, 392
AMERICAN FUR CO., 93, 110–12, 124–25, 134, 178, 201, 353
AMERICAN RIVER, 180, 237, 239, 269, 327
AMOS BAD HEART BULL (INDIAN), 367
ANACONDA MINING CO., 359, 391
ANAHUAC, TEX., 160
ANDERSON, A. A., 392
ANGUS, RED, 386
APACHE CANYON, 227, 315
APISHAPA CANYON, 352
APPALACHIAN MOUNTAINS, 16, 49, 57
APPLEGATE, JESSE, 230
APPLEGATE TRAIL, 230, 256, 259
ARIZONA, 125, 134–35, 168, 180, 226–27, 237, 249, 258, 260–61, 270, 273, 288, 313, 314, 315, 322, 324, 328, 329, 347, 356, 360, 378, 391, 400
ARKANSAS, 122, 135, 153, 156, 158, 181, 291, 315, 320
ARKANSAS RIVER AND VALLEY, 70–72, 96–97, 108–12, 118, 123–24, 135, 166, 170, 178, 187, 227, 239, 255, 260, 281, 294, 324–25, 327, 351, 359, 389
ARMIJO, MANUEL, 165–66, 227–28
ARNOLD, PHILIP, 349
ARROYO HONDO, 71
ARTHUR, CHESTER A., 359
ASH HOLLOW, 291, 318
ASHLEY, WILLIAM, 110, 112, 126–32, 135, 255
ASKIN, JOHN, JR., 103
ASPEN, COLO., 359
ASPINWALL, WILLIAM, 239–40, 254–55, 263
ASTOR, JOHN JACOB, 71, 93–97, 104–7, 110–12, 177
ATCHISON, DAVID R., 282, 284–85
ATCHISON, TOPEKA AND SANTA FE RAILROAD, 328, 350, 352–53, 358–59
ATHABASKA PASS, 94
ATHABASKA REGION, 48
ATKINSON, HENRY, 130–31, 134
AUBURN RAVINE, 269
AUDUBON, JOHN W., 241
AURARIA, COLO., 294
AUSTIN, MOSES, 112, 121, 123
AUSTIN, STEPHEN, 121–23,

135–36, 144–45, 159–62, 164
AUSTIN, TEX., 165, 354
AVERILL, JIM, 386

BABBITT, ALMON W., 258, 289
BABY DOE, 359
BAD AXE, 155
BAIRD, JAMES, 97, 124–25
BAKER, JIM, 7
BANCROFT, HUBERT HOWE, 260
BANK OF THE UNITED STATES, 112, 156
BANNACK CITY, MONT., 320, 337
BAPTISTE (INDIAN), 177
BARANOV, ALEXANDER, 105
BARLOW, JOEL, 40, 57
BARLOW, SAMUEL, 186
BARTLESON, JOHN, 182
BASTROP, BARON DE, 121
BATON ROUGE, LA., 100
BATURONE, JOSE, 266
BAXTER SPRINGS, KANS., 352
BAYLOR, JOHN R., 314–15
BEALE, EDWARD, 234, 264, 288–89
BEAMAN, E. O., 362
BEAN, ELLIS, 135
BEAN, ROBERT, 21
BEAR RIVER (UTAH), 130, 292
BEASLEY, DANIEL, 104
BEAUDOIN, LOUISON, 85, 87
BEAUMONT, TEX., 391, 396
BEAVERHEAD RIVER, 66, 69
BECK, JOHN, 294
BECKNELL, WILLIAM, 112, 123–25
BECKWITH, E. G., 264, 278
BECKWOURTH, JIM, 139
BEE, FREDERICK, 293, 295–96
BEECHER ISLAND, BATTLE OF, 342
BEIDLER, JOHN X., 337
BELL, JOSIAH, 122
BENSON, A. G. (& CO.), 190–91
BENT, CHARLES, 178, 227, 233
BENT, ST. VRAIN & CO., 134
BENT, SILAS, 345, 357
BENT, WILLIAM, 178–79, 260
BENTEEN, FRED, 356
BENTON, THOMAS HART, 23, 107, 111, 157, 167–68, 187–88, 228, 234, 239–40, 241, 259, 264, 282
BERTHOLD, CHOUTEAU & PRATTE, 112, 125–26
BIDDLE, NICHOLAS, 95
BIDWELL, JOHN, 182, 251
BIERSTADT, ALBERT, 220, 303
BIG TREE, CHIEF, 354
BIGHORN MOUNTAINS, 320–21, 354
BIGHORN RIVER, 61, 88, 89, 112, 131, 201, 326, 356
BIGLER, HENRY, 237
BILLY THE KID (WILLIAM H. BONNEY), 352
BINGHAM, GEORGE CALEB, 25, 196
BINGHAM CANYON, 391
BIRKBECK, MORRIS, 117
BISBEE, ARIZ., 399
BISMARCK, N. DAK., 323–24, 355
BISSONETTE, JOSEPH, 111
BITTERROOT RIVER AND VALLEY, 66, 69, 86, 182, 319
BLACK, ARTHUR, 133
BLACK HAWK, CHIEF, 104, 154–55, 195
BLACK HILLS, 318, 353, 354–56
BLACK KETTLE, CHIEF, 325, 342

BLACK ROCK DESERT, 230, 256
BLACKFOOT RIVER, 129
BLACKS FORK, 183
BLAEBERRY RIVER, 86
BLAIR, FRANCIS, JR., 313
BLANCO, MANUEL, 96
BLAND-ALLISON ACT, 387
BLENNERHASSETT, HARMAN, 68, 71
BLOUNT, WILLIAM, 40, 47
BLUE MOUNTAINS, 186, 230
BLUNT, JAMES G., 325
BODMER, KARL, 200
BOGGS, LILLBURN, 189
BOILVIN, NICHOLAS, 104
BOISE RIVER, 178, 389
BOLTON, F. S., 113
BONNEVILLE, BENJAMIN L. E., 134–35, 218–19
BOONE, DANIEL, 16, 19–22, 23, 25, 28, 32, 36, 59, 78, 141
BOONESBOROUGH, 23–24, 28, 29, 32, 46
BOSQUE REDONDO, 324, 328, 330–31, 351–52
BOTTINEAU, PIERRE, 275
BOWIE, JAMES, 162, 173
BOWMAN, JOHN, 29, 32
BOZEMAN, JOHN, 320–21, 326
BOZEMAN PASS, 69, 89, 90, 320
BOZEMAN TRAIL, 326, 328
BRADBURN, JOHN, 136
BRADDOCK, EDWARD, 19
BRADY, MATHEW, 173, 362
"BRAITHWAITE, GENERAL," 86–87
BRANNAN, SAMUEL, 188, 189–91, 234–37, 239, 250–51, 257, 260
BRANT, JOSEPH, 37–38
BRANTZ, LEWIS, 53
BRAZORIA, TEX., 160
BRAZOS RIVER, 122, 160, 351
BREEN, PATRICK, 230
BREWETT (INDIAN), 169
BRIDGER, JAMES, 7, 127, 130, 139, 190, 205, 235, 292, 319, 321, 404
BRIDGER PASS, 261
BRITISH COLUMBIA, 58, 86, 104, 133, 192, 319
BROCK, ISAAC, 103
BRODERICK, DAVID, 260
BRODHEAD, RICHARD, 264
BROOKS, PRESTON, 285
BROWN, AARON, 288
BROWN, JACOB, 225
BROWN, JOHN, 285
BROWN, MRS. JONAS, 336
BROWN, JOSEPH C., 146
BROWNS HOLE, 131
BRUFF, J. GOLDSBOROUGH, 182, 256, 257
BRYAN, WILLIAM JENNINGS, 390, 398
BRYANT'S STATION, KY., 34
BUCHANAN, JAMES, 188, 192, 228, 285–86, 288–89, 293
BUENA VISTA, MEX., 232–33, 243
BUFFALO, 50, 178, 311, 353–54, 369
BUFFALO, WYO., 386
BUFFALO BAYOU, 163
BUFFALO BILL (WILLIAM F. CODY), 296, 393
BUFORD, JEFFERSON, 284–85
BULLOCH, JAMES, 136
BUNKER HILL AND SULLIVAN MINE, 387
BURDETT, S. B., 350
BURKE CANYON, 387
BURLESON, EDWARD, 161
BURNET, DAVID, 163
BURNETT, PETER, 249, 256–57
BURNT CANYON, 186
BURR, AARON, 66–69, 71–72, 84

BUSTAMANTE, ANASTASIO, 136
BUTLER, ANTHONY, 136
BUTLER, FRANK, 393
BUTTE, MONT., 359, 388
BUTTERFIELD, JOHN, 288, 292–93, 295–96
BUTTERFIELD OVERLAND STAGE CO., 288, 314, 338, 351

CACHE VALLEY, 130, 287
CAHOKIA, ILL., 28
CALAMITY JANE (MARTHA JANE BURKE), 360
CALDWELL, IDAHO, 392
CALHOUN, JOHN C., 167
CALIFORNIA, 45, 62, 74, 108, 121, 124, 132–33, 135, 149, 166, 167, 168, 179–81, 184–85, 186, 187–92, 214, 216–18, 226, 228–30, 232–40, 241, 242, 243, 244–45, 249–63, 265–66, 277, 286–88, 290, 293, 295–96, 308, 313, 315, 317, 319, 321–22, 326, 349, 351, 357–59, 377, 388–89, 397
CALIFORNIA TRAIL, 218, 257
CAMARGO, MEX., 231
CAMELS, 288–89, 321
CAMERON, ALEXANDER, 27
CAMP CHARLOTTE TREATY, 23
CAMP DOUGLAS, UTAH, 322
CAMP FLOYD, 292–93, 295–96
CANADA, 34, 38, 47–48, 57, 61–62, 73–74, 82–84, 93–94, 100, 102–4, 114, 155, 274–75, 300, 356, 390, 395
CANADIAN RIVER, 111, 118
CANALS. See Water supply; Water travel
CANBY, EDWARD, 314–15
CANTON, FRANK, 386
CANYON DE CHELLY, 261, 273, 324, 330–31
CARDERO, JOSE, 45, 74
CAREY DESERT LAND ACT, 389, 392
CARLETON, JAMES H., 317, 324
CARMACK, GEORGE WASHINGTON, 395
CARMEL, CALIF., 74
CARONDELET, HECTOR, 48–49
CARRINGTON, HENRY B., 326
CARSON, CHRISTOPHER (KIT), 7, 125, 134–35, 139, 187, 205, 218, 228–29, 232, 234, 250, 260, 265, 294, 324–25, 331, 354
CARSON PASS, 187, 250
CARSON RIVER AND VALLEY, 250, 256, 290, 292, 295–96
CARTHAGE, ILL., 189, 246
CARVER, JONATHAN, 51
CASCADE RANGE, 64, 66, 105, 134, 179, 186, 187, 237–38, 307, 321
CASEMENT BROTHERS (JACK AND DAN), 326–27
CASS, LEWIS, 137
CATALDO, IDAHO, 388
CATLIN, GEORGE, 152, 174–75, 200, 202
CATTLE INDUSTRY, 148, 260, 326, 328, 345, 349–53, 357, 359–60, 371, 385–87
CEDAR CITY, UTAH, 291
CENTRAL CITY, COLO., 295
CENTRAL OVERLAND CALIFORNIA & PIKE'S PEAK EXPRESS CO., 295–96
CENTRAL PACIFIC RAILROAD, 278, 321–22, 326–28, 340–41, 349
CERRO GORDO, MEX., 236
CHAMBERLAIN, SAMUEL E., 242–43
CHAMBERS, SAMUEL, 97, 124

411

CHAMPION, NATE, 386
CHAMPLAIN, JEAN BAPTISTE, 91, 96–97
CHAPULTEPEC, MEX., 236
CHARBONNEAU, TOUSSAINT, 65–66
CHARLESTON (CHARLES TOWN), S. C., 22, 25, 26, 57, 59
CHERRY CREEK, 294
CHEYENNE, WYO., 327, 350, 355
CHEYENNE MOUNTAIN, 72
CHICAGO, ILL., 81, 103, 156, 283, 286, 321, 352
CHICKASAW BLUFFS (MEMPHIS), 60
CHIHUAHUA, MEX., 69, 72, 85, 97, 109, 124, 226–28, 232–33
CHILKOOT PASS, 390
CHILLICOTHE, OHIO, 29, 34, 59
CHIMNEY ROCK, NEBR., 183
CHIMNEY ROCKS, WASH., 212–13
CHISHOLM, JESSE, 12, 352
CHISHOLM TRAIL, 352, 370–71
CHISUM, JOHN, 352
CHIVINGTON, JOHN M., 315, 325, 328
CHORIS, LOUIS, 148
CHORPENNING, GEORGE, 263, 292–93, 295
CHOUTEAU, AUGUSTE PIERRE, 88, 109–11, 125
CHOUTEAU, PIERRE, JR., 134
CHOUTEAU, PIERRE, SR., 81, 83, 90
CHRISTENSEN, C. C. A., 191, 226, 236
CIMARRON CUT-OFF, 227
CIMARRON RIVER, 124, 135
CINCINNATI, OHIO, 39, 48, 79, 99, 143, 163
CIVIL WAR, 296, 313–17, 322, 329
CLAMORGAN, JACQUES, 85, 87
CLARK, GEORGE ROGERS, 24, 28–29, 32, 34, 43, 47, 58–59, 63
CLARK, WILLIAM, 63–69, 71–72, 76–77, 84–90, 93, 95, 110
CLARK FORK, 86, 94, 104
CLARKE, JOHN, 105
CLAY, HENRY, 101, 108, 114
CLAY, JOHN, 386
CLEAR CREEK, 294–95
CLEARWATER RIVER, 66, 69, 86–87, 104, 179, 319
CLEAVELAND, MOSES, 59
CLEVELAND, GROVER, 360, 390, 392
CLEVELAND, OHIO, 34, 78, 99
CLINCH RIVER AND VALLEY, 20, 21, 25
CLYMAN, JAMES, 127, 129, 190, 229
COAHUILA AND TEXAS, MEX., 123, 135–36, 145, 159–60
COCKE, WILLIAM, 42
COEUR D'ALENE, IDAHO, 359, 387–88, 392, 398
COLLINS, CHARLES, 354–56
COLLOT, VICTOR, 32, 54–55, 75
COLOMA VALLEY, 237, 239, 251
COLORADO, 123, 125, 134, 168, 188, 237, 258, 277, 282, 292–95, 308, 311, 313, 315, 321, 325, 327, 328, 342, 345, 347, 349–54, 356–59, 371, 388–90, 392
COLORADO AND CENTRAL RAILROAD, 350
COLORADO RIVER, 122, 132–33, 135, 233, 261, 286, 349, 361–62, 392

COLTER, JOHN, 85, 88–91, 95, 96
COLTER'S HELL, 89
COLUMBIA, 47
COLUMBIA FUR CO., 126, 134
COLUMBIA RIVER, 47, 58, 61–64, 66, 71, 73, 76, 84, 86, 90–97, 104, 105, 110, 126, 129–30, 133–34, 167, 177, 179, 181, 186, 192, 210, 211, 212, 230, 237–39, 249, 259, 319, 321, 327
COLUMBUS, GA., 170
COMPROMISE OF 1850, 258
COMSTOCK LODE, 296, 308–9, 321–22, 326, 355, 358, 387
CONEJOS RIVER, 72
CONFEDERATE GULCH, 320
CONGRESS, CONTINENTAL. *See* Colonies
CONGRESS, UNITED STATES. *See* United States
CONNECTICUT, 15, 34
CONNOLLY, JOHN, 22, 47
CONNOR, PATRICK EDWARD, 322, 324
CONTINENTAL DIVIDE, 58, 64, 66, 69, 86, 87, 89, 91, 95, 110, 126–27, 129, 134, 292, 392
COOK, JAMES, 45, 58, 73
COOKE, JAY, 328, 346
COOKE, PHILIP ST. GEORGE, 156, 187, 227, 232
COPPER MINING, 359, 391
CORPUS CHRISTI, TEX., 187, 191, 242
COS, MARTIN PERFECTO DE, 160–61
COUNCIL BLUFFS, 65, 104, 111, 118, 126
COURTER (COURTIN, CORTA), CHARLES, 85–88, 90–91
COXEY'S ARMY, 390
CRAWFORD, WILLIAM, 34
CRAZY HORSE, CHIEF, 356
CREVECOEUR, ST. JOHN DE, 60
CRIPPLE CREEK, 390–92
CROCKER, CHARLES, 321–22, 326–27
CROCKETT, DAVID, 122, 162, 172–73
CROOK, GEORGE, 355–56
CROOKS, RAMSAY, 80, 84, 85–86, 88, 95–97, 110, 111, 124–25
CUMBERLAND GAP, 20, 21, 23–25, 28, 31–32, 108
CUMBERLAND RIVER, 20, 29, 31–33, 71, 108
CUMMING, ALFRED, 289, 292
CURTIS, SAMUEL, 314, 315
CUSTER, GEORGE A., 48, 327–28, 342–43, 344, 354–56, 365–66
CUTLER, MANASSEH, 38–39

DAHLONEGA, GA., 154, 251, 293–94
DALTON GANG, 360
DALY, MARCUS, 359
DANA, RICHARD HENRY, 148, 181
DAVIS, JEFFERSON, 232, 264, 276–78, 287, 320
DAWES SEVERALTY ACT, 358
DAWSON, CANADA, 390, 394–95
DEADWOOD, S. DAK., 355, 380
DEARBORN, HENRY, 84, 124
DEERE, JOHN, 195
DENVER, JAMES W., 294–95
DENVER, COLO., 96, 294–95, 308, 310, 312, 315, 325, 327–28, 350, 352, 388, 390, 392
DENVER AND RIO GRANDE RAILROAD, 350, 359
DESERET, STATE OF, 258

DE SMET, FATHER PIERRE JEAN, 182, 208
DETROIT, MICH., 28, 38, 48, 60, 82, 102–4, 107, 109, 111
DETROIT RIVER, 100, 102–4
DIAMOND MINING, 349–50
DICKINSON, SUSANNA, 162, 163
DICKSON, JOSEPH, 85, 88
DICKSON, ROBERT, 82, 103–4, 107
DISCOVERY, H.M.S., 45
DIXON, JOHN, 195
DIXON, ILL., 195
DODGE, AUGUSTUS C., 283
DODGE, GRENVILLE M., 264, 326–27
DODGE, HENRY, 156, 174
DODGE CITY, KANS., 351, 352–53, 372
DONALDSON, J. B., 284
DONELSON, JOHN, 18, 29, 32–33, 40, 42
DONIPHAN, ALEXANDER, 227–28, 232–33
DONNER PARTY, 224, 228, 229–30, 235–36, 240
DONNER PASS, 185, 190, 250, 321
DONNER SUMMIT, 230, 235, 321, 327
DOUGLAS, STEPHEN A., 186, 258–59, 264, 283, 286, 297
DOY, DR. JOHN, 285
DRAGGING CANOE, CHIEF, 23, 27, 29, 31
DROUILLARD, GEORGE, 63, 87–90, 95
DRUMMOND, W. W., 289
DUBUQUE, JULIEN, 67
DUER, WILLIAM, 39–40
DUNMORE, LORD, 21, 23–24
DU PONT DE NEMOURS, PIERRE S., 61

EARP, WYATT, 353, 372–73
EASTER, JOHN, 294
EASTMAN, SETH, 137, 150–51
EATON, JOHN H., 134
EATON'S STATION, 27
ECHEANDIA, JOSE, 132–33
EDWARDS, BENJAMIN, 135
EDWARDS, HADEN, 135
EL BRAZITO, MEX., 233
EL PASO, 286, 288–89
ELBERT, S. H., 388
ELLIOTT, MATTHEW, 100
ELLSWORTH, KANS., 310, 352, 372
EMIGRATION AND IMMIGRATION, 13, 16, 59, 61, 78, 100, 108, 121–25, 135–37, 156–59, 164–65, 168, 180–86, 189–93, 199, 218, 221, 226, 229–30, 234–40, 247, 249–51, 253–60, 262, 274, 283–84, 286–92, 294–95, 298–99, 310–11, 318–20, 346, 357–58, 360, 374–75, 378–83, 390–91
ERIE CANAL, 108, 156, 159, 193
ESCALANTE TRAIL, 125
EVANS, GEORGE HENRY, 259
EVANS, JOHN, 325

FALL LEAF (INDIAN), 294
FALLEN TIMBERS BATTLE, 48, 53
FALLS OF ST. ANTHONY, 51, 305
FALLS OF THE OHIO, 24, 54–55
FANNIN, JAMES W., 161–62
FARGO, WILLIAM, 288
FASEL, G. W., 246
FEATHER RIVER, 251
FERRAN, AUGUSTO, 266
FETTERMAN, WILLIAM J., 326

FINLAY, JACQUES, 86, 94
FINLEY, JOHN, 19–20
FISK, JAMES, 322
FITZGERALD, JOHN, 127
FITZPATRICK, THOMAS, 127–30, 134, 139, 182, 184, 205
FIVE CROWS (INDIAN), 208
FLATHEAD POST, 129–30
FLINT, TIMOTHY, 78, 108
FLORENCE, IDAHO, 319
FLORIDA, 47, 57, 59, 61, 100–102, 107–8, 114, 137, 154, 155
FLOYD, CHARLES, 63
FLOYD, JOHN, 133, 168
FORESTER, 105
FORESTS. *See* Lumber industry
FORT McINTOSH TREATY, 37
FORT STANWIX TREATY, 37
FORT WAYNE TREATY, 100
FORT WORTH, TEX., 351
FORTS: Astoria, 94, 97, 104–6, 110, 130; Atkinson, 111, 126, 127; Benton, 126, 319, 321, 338; Bent's, 166, 178, 187, 188, 227, 353; Bliss, 314; Boise, 179; Brady, 111; Bridger, 183, 229, 236, 255, 262, 292; Brown, 225; Butler, 157; Canby, 330; Cass, 134; C. F. Smith, 326; Colville, 259; Craig, 315; Dearborn, 103, 111, 115; Defiance, 286, 288; Fetterman, 355; Fillmore, 314, 315; Franklin, 49; Gibson, 154, 315; Hall, 178, 182, 184, 185, 230; Halleck, 322; Harmar, 37, 38–39; Henry, 126; Kearney, 239, 255, 286, 294; Kiowa (Lookout), 126, 127; Laramie, 178, 183, 205, 221, 255, 263, 287, 290, 318, 326; Larned, 325; Leavenworth, 154, 187, 226–27; Lyon, 325; Mackinac, 103, 111; Madison, 104; Malden, 100, 102; Mandan, 90, 91, 96, 97; Mann, 239; Manuel, 97; Massac, 54, 67; Massachusetts, 292; Mims, 107; Natchez, 55; Nez Percés, 110, 211; Osage, 90; Phil Kearny, 326; Piegan (McKenzie), 134; Pierre, 318–19; Pitt, 18, 22, 28; Raymond, 88–90; Reno, 326; Ridgely, 286, 288, 323; Robertdeau, 43; Ross (Russia), 94, 180; Smith, 111, 264, 270, 277, 286, 313; Snelling, 111, 150, 180, 198–99, 264, 323, 334; Stanton, 314; Steilacoom, 307; Sumner, 330; Supply, 292; Sutter's, 188, 190, 217, 229, 236–37, 250; Texas, 225; Towson, 154; Uinta, 135; Union, N. Dak., 318, 319, 201; Union, N. Mex., 134, 261, 314–15; Vancouver, 130, 133–34, 168, 177, 180, 186, 192, 210; Victoria, 192; Vincennes, 29; Walla Walla, 211–12, 307, 319; Washington, 48; Watauga, 27; Wayne, 103; William, 82, 94, 138; Yuma, 261, 271, 286, 288–89
FORTY-MILE DESERT, 250, 256
FOUR LEGS (INDIAN), 169
FOWLER, JACOB, 112, 123–24
FOX RIVER, 81–82
FRAEB, HENRY, 134
FRANCE, 15, 25, 29, 34, 40, 57, 60, 62–63, 74, 94, 143
FRANKLIN (FRANKLAND), 41–42, 44, 46
FRASER, SIMON, 86
FRASER RIVER, 58, 133, 319
FREDONIA, REPUBLIC OF, 135
FREEMAN, THOMAS, 68
FREMONT, JOHN CHARLES, 72, 156, 185, 187–92, 218, 228–29, 234, 237, 239–40, 245, 250, 254, 257–58, 264, 273, 285, 314
FREMONT PEAK, 188

FRENCH AND INDIAN WAR, 16, 18
FRENCH BROAD RIVER, 25, 41–42
FRENCH CREEK, 355
FUR TRADE, 26–27, 34, 38, 45, 47–48, 57–58, 62–63, 68–69, 71, 73–74, 81–97, 104–13, 120, 123–34, 137–41, 148, 177–79, 182, 192, 199, 201, 204, 205, 210–11, 260, 274–75

GADSDEN PURCHASE, 237, 270
GALLATIN, ALBERT, 63, 65
GALLATIN RIVER, 89–90, 389
GALLIPOLIS, 40, 57
GALVESTON BAY, 121, 136
GARDNER, JOHNSON, 126, 130–31
GARDOQUI, DIEGO, 42–44
GENET, EDMOND CHARLES, 59
GENOA, NEV., 286, 290, 293
GEORGIA, 15, 27, 34, 40–44, 47, 60, 135, 154, 170
GEORGIAN BAY, 82, 107
GERONIMO, CHIEF, 356, 378
GERVAIS, JEAN BAPTISTE, 134
GIBBON, JOHN, 355–56
GILA RIVER, 125, 132, 135, 180, 232–33, 237, 240, 255, 257, 264
GILLESPIE, ARCHIBALD, 188, 192, 228, 234, 245
GILPIN, WILLIAM, 239, 260
GLASS, HUGH, 127
GLENN, HUGH, 112, 123–24
GNADENHUTTEN, 34
GOLD MINING, 237, 239–40, 249–55, 257, 259, 265–66, 269–70, 293–96, 308, 319–20, 336, 390, 394, 395
GOLIAD, TEX., 102, 161–62
GONZALES, TEX., 160, 162
GOODNIGHT, CHARLES, 351–52, 354, 371
GORE, SIR GEORGE, 318
GRAND CANYON, 132, 300–301, 349, 405
GRANGER MOVEMENT, 347, 398
GRANT, DR. JAMES, 161–62
GRANT, ULYSSES S., 343, 388
GRATTAN, JOHN L., 318
GRAY, ROBERT, 47, 58, 62, 73
GREAT BASIN OF UTAH, 125, 126, 234–35, 361–62
GREAT BRITAIN, 15–18, 21–25, 27–29, 34, 38, 45, 47, 48, 49, 57–59, 61–63, 67–68, 72, 73, 74, 81–87, 90–94, 97, 99–111, 114–15, 126, 130–31, 133–35, 153, 155–56, 164, 167–68, 179–81, 185–87, 192, 207, 210–11, 226, 229, 237, 258, 287, 358
GREAT FALLS OF THE MISSOURI, 66, 126, 319
GREAT KANAWHA RIVER, 23, 40
GREAT LAKES, 28, 34, 38, 74, 82, 93–94, 100, 104, 107–10, 112, 156, 193, 258
GREAT NORTHERN RAILROAD, 390–91
GREAT SALT LAKE DESERT, 120, 185
GREAT SALT LAKE VALLEY, 236, 247, 290
GREELEY, HORACE, 258–59, 280, 295, 388
GREELEY, COLO., 357, 388
GREEN BAY, WIS., 81, 82, 111, 153
GREEN RIVER, 91, 96, 110, 125–27, 130–31, 177, 179, 183, 235, 255, 362
GREENVILLE TREATY, 48, 53, 100
GREGG, JOSIAH, 146

GREGORY, JOHN, 294–95
GROW, GALUSHA, 259
GUADALUPE HIDALGO TREATY, 237
GUITERREZ DE LARA, JOSE BERNARDO, 102
GUNNISON, JOHN, 264, 273, 277–79, 289
GWIN, WILLIAM, 257, 264, 288, 296

HAGUE, JAMES, 349
HAMILTON, ALEXANDER, 58–59, 66
HAMILTON, HENRY, 28–29
HAM'S FORK, 178
HANCOCK, W. S., 327
HANDCOCK, FOREST, 85, 88
HANKS, PORTER, 103
HARD LABOR TREATY, 18
HARMAR, JOSIAH, 37, 48
HARNEY, W. S., 318
HARRISON, BENJAMIN, 28, 33, 386, 389
HARRISON, WILLIAM HENRY, 61, 100–101, 104, 107, 154, 169, 196
HARROD, JAMES, 22
HARRODSBURG, KY., 22–24, 46
HART, NATHANIEL, 23
HASTINGS, LANSFORD W., 188–90, 229–30
HASTINGS CUT-OFF, 228, 230
HAUN'S MILL, MO., 291
HAWAIIAN (SANDWICH) ISLANDS, 105, 180, 206, 237, 239, 249, 360, 390
HAYDEN, FERDINAND V., 318, 347, 349–50, 362
HAYES, RUTHERFORD B., 357
HAYS, JOHN COFFEE, 165
HAYWOOD, WILLIAM D. (BIG BILL), 392
HEALD, NATHAN, 103
HEAP, GWINN, 264
HEARST, GEORGE, 355, 359
HELENA, MONT., 320, 337
HELLS CANYON, 80
HENDERSON, RICHARD, 15–16, 18–24, 29, 31–33
HENRY, ANDREW, 90–91, 95–97, 112, 126–27, 130
HENRY, PATRICK, 15, 28
HENRYS FORK, 91, 96–97, 131
HERVIEU, AUGUSTE, 143
HETCH-HETCHY CANYON, 392
HICKOK, JAMES B. (WILD BILL), 353, 372
HIDALGO, MIGUEL, 96, 102
HILL, JAMES J., 390–91
HILL, NATHANIEL, 328
HOCKADAY, JOHN M., 292–93, 295
HOGG, JAMES, 24
HOLLADAY, BEN, 321–22, 325, 346
HOLLIDAY, JOHN HENRY (DOC), 372–73
HOLSTON (RIVER AND SETTLEMENT), 20, 22, 25, 27, 31–33, 41, 59
HOMESTAKE MINE, 355, 359
HOMESTEAD ACT, 322, 345–46, 388. See also United States, land policies
HONEY SPRINGS, 315
HOPEWELL TREATY, 42
HOPKINS, MARK, 321, 326
HORSLEY, ALBERT (HARRY ORCHARD), 392
HOUSTON, SAM, 107, 136, 161–64, 166–67, 173, 297, 313
HOWSE PASS, 86, 90
HUDSON'S BAY CO., 64, 73, 82, 86, 95, 129, 133–34, 138, 139, 167, 168, 177–79, 181, 185–86, 192, 208, 210, 237–38
HUERFANO CREEK, 109–10

HUFFEL, P. VAN, 114
HULL, A. C., 373
HULL, WILLIAM, 102–3
HUMBOLDT, ALEXANDER VON, 68
HUMBOLDT RIVER AND VALLEY, 139, 185, 188, 190, 230, 250, 255–56, 278–79, 286, 327
HUMPHREY, ISAAC, 251
HUNT, WILSON PRICE, 80, 94–97, 105, 127
HUNTER, JOHN DUNN, 135
HUNTINGTON, COLLIS, 321, 326–27
HUTCHINS, THOMAS, 37–38
HUTTON, WILLIAM R., 216, 267

IDAHO, 63, 69, 80, 87, 89–91, 97, 104, 129, 132, 179, 187, 211, 235, 319–20, 321, 324, 337, 359, 363, 376–77, 387–89, 398
ILIFF, JOHN, 352, 357
ILLINOIS, 28, 59, 63, 104, 109, 154–56, 190–91, 247, 252, 258, 286, 351–52
ILLINOIS CENTRAL RAILROAD, 258–59
ILLINOIS RIVER, 81, 86
IMMELL, MICHAEL, 126–27
IMMIGRATION. See Emigration and immigration
INDEPENDENCE, MO., 177, 180, 182, 190, 255, 263, 289, 295
INDEPENDENCE ROCK, 183, 386
INDIANS: agreements with, 16–18, 23, 25, 27, 37, 48, 53, 59, 153–55, 274, 281, 286, 306, 325, 326, 328; Apache, 121, 261, 314, 322, 324, 356, 378; Arapaho, 96–97, 109, 281, 322, 324–25, 327–28, 343, 369; Arikara, 88, 90, 96, 126–27, 130; Bannock, 322, 324, 328; Bella Coola, 58; Blackfeet, 69, 86, 88, 89, 90–91, 93, 96–97, 112, 126, 130, 134, 201, 205; Caddo, 121; Cayuse, 208, 238; Cherokee, 18, 20–27, 29, 41–42, 44, 60, 101, 135, 153–54, 155, 157, 164, 170, 281, 293–94, 313–14; Cheyenne, 281, 294, 320, 322, 324–25, 327–28, 342–43, 344, 356; Chickamauga, 27, 29, 31; Chickasaw, 23, 26–27, 34, 40–41, 101, 154, 170, 313; Chippewa, 85, 103, 286; Choctaw, 26–27, 41, 101, 153–54, 170–71; Coeur d'Alene, 259; Colville, 211; Comanche, 84, 112, 121, 124, 135, 152, 156, 163, 164–65, 166, 174–75, 187, 233, 239, 260, 281, 324–25, 328, 343, 351–52, 354; Creek, 26–27, 40–41, 44, 47, 60, 101, 104, 107, 154, 155, 170, 281, 313, 315, 358; Crow, 61, 88, 89, 91, 97, 127, 281, 328, 356; Delaware, 28, 34, 90, 153, 156, 187, 281, 294; Five Civilized Tribes, 170, 174, 313–14, 328, 329; Flathead, 69, 76, 87, 91, 129, 130, 208; Fox, 154; Ghost Dance, 369; Gosiute, 296; Government policy toward, 59–60, 62, 153–56, 157, 169, 170, 174, 297, 324–25, 328, 334, 354, 357; Gros Ventre, 177; Hidatsa, 65; Iroquois, 18–20, 29, 51, 129, 208; Kansa, 119, 183; Karankawa, 121; Kickapoo, 153, 281; Kiowa, 119, 156, 163, 239, 260, 281, 324–25, 328, 343, 351, 354; Klamath, 90; Kutenai, 86; Maha, 85, 87–88; Mandan, 10, 64, 65, 71, 85, 88, 127, 200–201; Menominee, 103; Miami, 20, 103–4, 153, 169, 281–82;

Minnetaree, 65, 90, 97, 104; Mohave, 132–33, 286, 361, 378; Navaho, 227, 261, 272–73, 322, 324, 328, 330–31, 351–52; Nez Perce, 66, 87, 129, 208–9, 238, 319, 356; Nootka, 74; Osage, 69, 71, 84, 112; Oto, 84; Ottawa, 103; Paiute, 125, 296; Palouse, 87, 259; Pawnee, 71, 82, 84, 151, 156, 183; Piegan, 86, 87, 94; Potawatomi, 104, 281; Pueblo, 165, 233, 272–73; Sauk, 107, 154–55; Seminole, 154, 155, 170, 313, 358; Seneca, 29, 49, 286; Shawnee, 18–21, 23, 28–29, 34, 90, 153, 156, 281–82; Shoshoni, 65–66, 324; Sioux, 65, 67–68, 88, 90, 96, 97, 103, 150–51, 169, 187, 274, 281, 286, 318–19, 320, 322–24, 328, 334, 342, 343, 354–56, 369, 385; Six Nations, 18; Snake, 96, 129; Spokan, 259; Umpqua, 133; Ute, 124, 125, 131, 227, 262–63, 291–92, 323, 362–63, 369; Wallawalla, 87, 307; wars and conflicts with, 22–23, 27–29, 33–34, 38, 48, 52–53, 89, 101, 103–4, 107, 126–27, 133, 155, 163–65, 192, 233, 237–38, 259, 260–63, 275, 291–92, 311, 318–19, 322–28, 330–31, 334, 342–43, 354–57; Watauga, 29; Wichita, 152, 156, 174; Winnebago, 103, 154, 155, 169; Wyandot, 20, 281–82, 286; Yakima, 259, 307; Yosemite, 260; Yuma, 378
INDIAN TERRITORY, 153, 286, 294, 313, 315, 351, 352, 358, 360
INDIANA, 48, 52, 82, 100, 108, 142, 156, 195, 391
INKPADUTA (INDIAN), 319, 323–24
INTERIOR DEPARTMENT, 287, 289
IOWA, 153, 155–56, 158, 181, 191, 192, 195, 226–27, 234, 258, 264, 281, 283, 287, 319, 321, 323, 346, 360
IOWA CITY, IOWA, 287
IRON MINING, 199, 396
IRRIGATION. See Water supply
ISAAC TODD, 105–6
ITURBIDE, AGUSTIN DE, 122
IVES, JOSEPH C., 300–301

JACKLING, DANIEL C., 391
JACKSON, ANDREW, 33, 102, 107, 135–36, 142, 154, 156, 170, 190, 195, 197
JACKSON, CLAIBORNE, 313
JACKSON, DAVID, 132, 135
JACKSON, GEORGE, 294–95
JACKSON, WILLIAM HENRY, 154, 349, 362–63, 381
JACKSON COUNTY, 189
JACKSON HOLE, 89
JAMES BROTHERS (FRANK AND JESSE), 359, 360
JAMES, EDWIN, 111
JAMES, THOMAS, 89, 112, 123–24, 132
JASPER'S HOUSE, 95
JAY, JOHN, 43, 48
JAY'S TREATY, 82–84
JEFFERSON, THOMAS, 28, 36, 39, 56, 58, 60–68, 71, 72, 77, 83, 88, 95
JEFFERSON RIVER, 66, 89–90, 126
JESSAUME, RENE, 65–66
JOHNSON, FRANCIS W., 161
JOHNSON, HADLEY, 282–83
JOHNSON, THOMAS, 282–83
JOHNSON COUNTY WAR, 385–87
JOHNSTON, ALBERT SIDNEY, 289–90, 291–92, 314–15
JONES, JOHN GABRIEL, 24

JONES, JOHN S., 295
JONES, ROBERT, 126–27
JONES, SAMUEL, 284–85
JONESBOROUGH, 41–42
JOSEPH, CHIEF, 356
JUDAH, THEODORE DE-HONE, 321–22

KANE, PAUL, 211–12
KANESVILLE (COUNCIL BLUFFS), IOWA, 255
KANSAS, 124, 156, 183, 239, 258, 281–86, 294–95, 297, 311, 314, 317, 320, 325, 327–28, 329, 346–47, 350–54, 358, 371–72, 388, 389
KANSAS CITY, MO., 310, 327, 350, 352, 358
KANSAS-NEBRASKA ACT, 264, 278, 283, 297
KANSAS PACIFIC RAILROAD, 310, 326–28, 350, 352
KANSAS RIVER AND VALLEY, 182, 282–83, 294
KASKASKIA, ILL., 28, 59
KEARNY, STEPHEN WATTS, 125, 187, 226–28, 232–34, 245, 264
KELLEY, HALL JACKSON, 133, 168, 177, 181
KELLOGG, NOAH, 387
KELSEY FAMILY, 182, 184–85
KENDALL, AMOS, 190–91
KENDRICK, JOHN, 47
KENTUCKY, 18–25, 28–29, 31, 34, 38, 41–43, 46, 47, 59, 67, 108, 158
KENTUCKY RIVER, 18, 22–23
KEOKUK, CHIEF, 155
KERN, BENJAMIN, 240, 273
KERN, EDWARD M., 229, 273
KERN, RICHARD H., 272, 273, 277
KETTLE FALLS, 211
KILDEER MOUNTAIN, 324
KING, CLARENCE, 347–50, 362–63
KING, RUFUS, 60
KINZIE, JOHN, 85
KLONDIKE RIVER, 390, 394–95
KNIFE RIVER, 324
KOERNER, W. H. D., 407
KULLYSPELL HOUSE, 90

LA GLORIETTA PASS, 315
LAHONTAN, BARON DE, 50
LAKES: Athabaska, 57–58; Bear, 132–33; Cass, 68, 137; Champlain, 38, 102, 104, 107; Coeur d'Alene, 319, 388; Crater, 300; Erie, 20, 48, 51, 59, 78, 82, 102, 104, 107; Great Salt, 126, 130, 132, 181, 184, 188, 190, 219, 235–37, 239, 250, 261, 270–71, 328, 347, 391; Huron, 81, 82, 103, 113; Itasca, 67, 137; Klamath, 190, 192, 228, 230; Lake of the Woods, 34, 107; Leech, 67; Michigan, 81, 85, 113, 153; Nipissing, 82; Ontario, 82; Pend Oreille, 90; Pyramid, 362; Rainy, 94; Simcoe, 82; Superior, 34, 81–82, 85, 103, 107, 138, 199, 252, 258, 283, 359; Tahoe, 301; Utah, 125, 292; Windermere, 86
LA LANDE, BAPTISTE, 69, 72
LAMAR, MIRABEAU BUONAPARTE, 164–65
LANDER CUT-OFF, 292–93
LANE, JOSEPH, 240
LAPWAI CREEK, 179
LARAMIE, WYO., 373
LARAMIE CREEK, 178
LARAMIE HILLS, 327
LARKIN, THOMAS, 188, 192, 228, 240, 257
LAROCQUE, FRANÇOIS, 88
LASSEN, PETER, 256

LAST CHANCE GULCH, 320
LAS VEGAS, NEV., 255, 400–401
LATROBE, JOHN, 100
LAWRENCE, THOMAS, 73
LAWRENCE, KANS., 284–85, 294, 317, 329
LEACH, JAMES, 289
LEADVILLE, COLO., 358–59, 387
LEAL, ANTONIO, 47
LEAVENWORTH, HENRY, 126–27, 156, 174
LEAVENWORTH, KANS., 295
LEAVENWORTH & PIKE'S PEAK EXPRESS CO., 295
LECOMPTE, SAMUEL, 284
LEDYARD, JOHN, 58, 168
LEE, DANIEL, 177–78
LEE, JASON, 177–81, 237
LEE, JOHN D., 291
LE RAYE, CHARLES, 61
LEWIS, HENRY, 246
LEWIS, MERIWETHER, 62–69, 71–72, 77, 83, 90, 93, 95
LEWIS, REUBEN, 90
LEWIS AND CLARK PASS, 69
LEWIS'S RIVER, 87
LEWISTON, IDAHO, 319
LEXINGTON, MO., 314
LICKING RIVER, 79
LIMESTONE (MAYSVILLE), KY., 32
LINCOLN, ABRAHAM, 195, 285–86, 294, 313, 321–23, 334
LISA, MANUEL, 84–85, 87–93, 95–97, 104, 111–12
LITTLE BEAVER (INDIAN), 294
LITTLE BIGHORN RIVER, 48, 89, 344, 356, 364
LITTLE CROW, CHIEF, 169, 274, 323
LITTLE PRICKLY PEAR CREEK, 320
LITTLE TALLASSEE, 26, 40
LIVELY, 122
LIVINGSTON, ROBERT, 60–61, 100
LOCHABER TREATY, 18
LODORE CANYON, 255
LOGAN, BENJAMIN, 23
LOLO TRAIL, 66, 69
LONG, JAMES, 108
LONG, STEPHEN H., 98, 106, 111, 118, 153
LOOKING GLASS (INDIAN), 356
LOS ANGELES, CALIF., 180, 216, 218, 229, 234, 240, 245, 260, 263, 264, 277, 290, 314, 317, 392
LOUISIANA, 34, 43–45, 47, 56, 59–63, 68–69, 71, 81–83, 87, 104, 110, 121
LOUISIANA PURCHASE, 56, 60–63, 66–68, 72, 74, 99–100, 108, 156
LOUISVILLE, KY., 34, 54–55, 100, 108
LOVING, OLIVER, 351–52
LUMBER INDUSTRY, 199, 304–5, 328, 389–90, 392, 396–97, 400–401
LUNDY, BENJAMIN, 164
LYMAN, AMASA, 250
LYNDE, ISAAC, 314
LYON, NATHANIEL, 313–14

McCLALLEN, JOHN, 84–85
McCLELLAN, ROBERT, 86, 88, 96–97
McCORMICK, CYRUS, 194
McCOY BROTHERS, 352
McCULLOCH, BEN, 313–15
McDANIEL, JOHN, 166
McDONALD, ANGUS, 127
McDONALD, FINAN, 86, 90–91, 94

McDOUGALL, DUNCAN, 105–7
McGILLIS, HUGH, 68
McGILLIVRAY, ALEXANDER, 26–27, 40, 42, 47, 48, 101
McGILLIVRAY, DUNCAN, 86
McGILLIVRAY, LACHLAN, 25–27, 40
McKAY, ALEXANDER, 58
MACKAY, JAMES, 64
MACKAY, JOHN, 358
McKAY, TOM, 178
MACKENZIE, ALEXANDER, 57–58, 61–62, 64, 73
McKENZIE, DONALD, 94, 105, 110
McKENZIE, KENNETH, 134, 200–201
MACKENZIE, RANALD, 354
MACKINAC (MICHILIMACKINAC) ISLAND, 38, 58, 81–82, 84, 93–95, 103–4, 107, 113
McKNIGHT, JOHN, 112, 124
McKNIGHT, ROBERT, 97, 112, 124–25
M'LAUGHLIN, CHARLES, 166, 167
McLOUGHLIN, JOHN, 130, 133, 138–39, 168, 178, 186, 192
McMURRAY, DONALD, 390
McMURTRIE, W. B., 307
MACOMB, ALEXANDER, 134
McTAVISH, JOHN GEORGE, 105
MADISON, JAMES, 100, 104
MADISON RIVER, 90–91
MAGEE, AUGUSTUS, 102
MAGOFFIN, JAMES, 227–28, 233
MAGRAW, WILLIAM M. F., 289–90, 292
MAHONING MINE, 396
MAID OF ORLEANS, 116
MAJORS, ALEXANDER, 295
MALGARES, FACUNDO, 69, 71–72, 123
MANGAS COLORADAS, CHIEF, 324
MANIFEST DESTINY, 186, 241
MANKATO, MINN., 334
MANLY, WILLIAM LEWIS, 255–56
MANUEL BROTHERS, 355
MANUELITO, CHIEF, 328
MANYPENNY, GEORGE, 282, 284, 297
MARCHAND, SEHOY, 26
MARCY, RANDOLPH B., 261, 270, 292
MARIAS RIVER, 69, 134, 201
MARIETTA, OHIO, 37, 39, 42, 48, 54, 71
MARSH, JOHN, 180, 185
MARSH, OTHNEIL, 349
MARSHALL, HUMPHREY, 21
MARSHALL, JAMES, 237, 239, 248, 250–51, 256, 265
MARTIN, EDWARD, 287–88
MARTIN, JOSIAH, 23
MARTINEZ, ANTONIO, 121–22
MARTINEZ, ESTEBAN JOSE, 47
MASON, GEORGE, 33
MASON, RICHARD, 240, 265
MASSACHUSETTS, 15, 34, 42
MASSIE, NATHANIEL, 59
MASTERSON, WILLIAM B. (BAT), 353, 373
MATAMOROS, MEX., 161, 225–26, 230
MATHEWS, GEORGE, 100–102
MATTAWA RIVER, 82
MAUMEE RIVER, 48
MAXWELL, LUCIEN, 187
MAYER, FRANCIS, 274
MAYSVILLE (LIMESTONE), KY., 32, 59
MAZATLAN, MEX., 188
MEARES, JOHN, 47
MEDICINE BOW MOUNTAINS, 322, 327

MEDICINE LODGE TREATY, 328, 343, 354
MEEK, JOE, 238, 239, 240
MEEKER, NATHAN, 388
MEEKER MASSACRE, 356–57
MEIGS, JOSIAH, 37
MEMPHIS, TENN., 264, 286, 288
MENARD, PIERRE, 87, 90–91
MERO DISTRICT, 44
MERRILL, MRS. JOHN, 32
MESA PLAINS (BATTLE), 245
MESABI RANGE, 396
MESSERVY, W. S., 258
METIS, 275
MEXICAN WAR, 187–89, 191–92, 225–37, 241–43, 245, 260, 270
MEXICANA, 45
MEXICO, 40, 45, 47, 57, 60, 67–68, 96, 102, 121–26, 132, 135–36, 144, 147, 153, 159, 160–68, 184, 186, 188–89, 191–92, 214–15, 217, 225–26, 237–39, 241, 249, 251–52, 255, 257–58, 260, 270, 288, 292, 331, 351
MEXICO CITY, 121–22, 136, 159–60, 166–68, 173, 188, 231, 236–37, 350
MEYERS, WILLIAM H., 214–15, 245
MICHAUX, ANDRE (FATHER AND SON), 57–59
MICHIGAN, 81–82, 102–3, 137, 156, 158, 169, 193, 199, 258
MICHILIMACKINAC. See Mackinac
MIDDLE CONCHO RIVER, 351
MIER, MEXICO, 166–67
MILAM, BEN, 161
MILES, NELSON A., 356
MILLER, ALFRED JACOB, 204
MILLER, J. G., 283
MILLER, JOSEPH, 95, 97
MIMS, SAMUEL, 104
MINING, 132, 199, 237, 239, 250–53, 257–60, 268–69, 295–96, 308–9, 317, 319–22, 326–28, 348–49, 354–55, 358–59, 379–81, 387–88, 391, 394–401
MINNEAPOLIS, MINN., 298–99
MINNESOTA, 71, 82, 103, 104, 126, 169, 193, 199, 274, 277, 286, 298–99, 306, 322–23, 328, 332–34, 343, 346, 377, 390, 396–97
MINNESOTA RIVER, 68, 82, 118, 180, 274, 286, 322–23
MIRANDA, FRANCISCO, 57
MIRO, ESTABAN, 40, 43–45, 47–48
MISSISSIPPI, 34, 36, 43, 44, 153–55, 164
MISSISSIPPI RIVER AND VALLEY, 15, 28, 33–34, 40, 42–45, 47–48, 49, 51, 54–55, 60–63, 67–68, 72, 74, 79, 81–84, 97, 100, 107, 108, 112, 114, 117, 127, 137, 150, 153–56, 161, 180, 191, 193, 199, 246, 255, 258, 274, 288, 304–5, 321, 338, 351
MISSOURI, 36, 59, 66, 69, 78, 96, 104, 108–10, 112, 153, 158, 166, 178, 181, 195, 199, 201, 247, 258, 259, 281–84, 291, 294, 297, 313–15, 317, 320, 329, 351–52
MISSOURI COMPROMISE, 282–83, 297
MISSOURI FUR CO., 90, 95, 112, 126–27, 134
MISSOURI RIVER, 54, 58, 62–66, 69, 75, 81–90, 95–97, 104, 109, 111, 112, 118, 126–27, 130, 134, 147, 153, 178, 192, 200–201, 226, 250, 274, 289, 320, 321, 323–24, 327, 338, 356, 388
MOBILE, ALA., 29, 102
MOBILE BAY, 60

MOJAVE DESERT, 135, 188
MOLINO DEL REY, MEX., 236
MÖLLHAUSEN, HEINRICH B., 132, 277
MONONGAHELA RIVER, 32
MONROE, JAMES, 33, 61–62, 101–2, 153
MONTANA, 64, 85, 88, 94, 104, 110, 129, 177, 182, 208, 211, 264, 281, 319, 320, 321, 322, 325–26, 337, 344, 349, 352, 355–56, 359, 360, 371, 374–75, 386, 389, 390, 391
MONTANA CITY, COLO., 294
MONTEREY, CALIF., 180, 188, 191–92, 214–15, 229, 238, 249, 251, 257, 265
MONTERREY, MEX., 121, 226, 231, 233, 243
MONTGOMERY, JOHN ELLIOTT, 244
MORAN, THOMAS, 349, 361–63, 404–5
MORGANTOWN, N. C., 44
MORMONS, 8, 26, 189–91, 226–28, 232, 234–36, 239, 240, 246–47, 250–51, 255, 258, 260, 262–63, 287–93, 295, 322, 326, 381, 388
MORRILL LAND GRANT ACT, 346
MORRISON, WILLIAM, 87, 90
MORSE, JEDIDIAH, 60–61, 168
MOUNT DAVIDSON, 295
MOUNT DIABLO, 180, 181, 185
MOUNT HOOD, 64, 178, 186
MOUNT OF THE HOLY CROSS, 349, 362
MOUNT SHASTA, 187, 249, 251
MOUNTAIN MEADOWS MASSACRE, 291–92
MUIR, JOHN, 389
MULLAN, JOHN, 319, 321
MUN, JULES DE, 109–10, 125
MURPHY, L. G., 352
MUSCLE SHOALS, 31, 33, 40, 44
MUSKINGUM RIVER AND VALLEY, 37, 38–39, 59

NACOGDOCHES, TEX., 47, 71, 102, 121, 135, 136
NASH BROTHERS, 29
NASHOBA, TENN., 143
NASHVILLE (NASHBOROUGH), 16, 29, 31–34, 42, 44, 107, 108
NATCHEZ, MISS., 25, 29, 31, 33, 40, 43, 59, 69, 102, 121
NATCHEZ TRACE, 47, 71, 77, 99
NATCHITOCHES, LA., 69, 71, 72, 100, 102, 121, 122
NATIONAL PARKS SYSTEM, 349, 362, 391
NATIONAL ROAD, 108
NAUVOO, ILL., 189–91, 246, 291
NEBRASKA, 9, 82, 85, 186, 221, 239, 247, 258, 264, 282–83, 290, 318, 323, 334, 346–47, 350, 353, 360, 381, 388
NEOSHO RIVER, 286
NEVADA, 108, 168, 184, 187, 230, 235, 237, 250, 256, 278–79, 289, 293, 295, 300, 308, 313, 315, 319, 321, 327, 389
NEW HOPE, CALIF., 234, 237
NEW MEXICO, 69, 72, 84, 87, 109, 112, 121, 123–25, 134–35, 156, 165–66, 168, 227–28, 232–33, 235, 237–38, 255, 258, 260–64, 283, 287, 315, 317, 322, 324–25, 328, 351–52, 359–60, 370–71, 388, 391
NEW ORLEANS, LA., 25, 42–47, 54, 57, 61, 66–68, 99–100, 102, 107, 122, 143, 160–61, 168, 197, 258, 264, 286, 293, 351

NEW ORLEANS, 100–101, 108
NEW ULM, MINN., 323
NEW YORK, 14, 18, 33, 37, 107–8
NEWTON, KANS., 372
NIAGARA, 38, 48, 82, 103
NIAGARA RIVER, 102, 104
NICHOLSON, FRANCIS, 22
NICOLLET, JOSEPH, 187
NILES, HEZEKIAH, 117
NOLAN, PHILIP, 44, 47–48, 68, 72, 135
NOLICHUCKY RIVER, 25, 42
NOME, ALASKA, 390
NOOTKA SOUND, 45, 47, 58, 74, 93–94
NORTH CAROLINA, 15–16, 18, 20–21, 23–25, 27–29, 31, 33–34, 40–42, 44, 157
NORTH DAKOTA, 64–65, 82, 85, 96, 118, 319, 323–24, 346–47, 355, 357, 360, 370–71, 377, 389, 391, 408–9
NORTH PLATTE RIVER AND VALLEY, 178, 235, 255, 281, 287, 319–20, 322, 327, 354, 385
NORTH WEST COMPANY, 48, 57, 64, 82–84, 86, 88, 90, 93–94, 97, 103–7, 110, 129
NORTHERN PACIFIC RAILROAD, 328, 346, 354, 357–58, 377, 387
NORTHWEST ORDINANCE OF 1787, 36, 39, 52
NORTHWEST PASSAGE, 45, 73
NORTHWEST TERRITORY, 29, 39, 48, 54, 79, 100, 103–4, 108
NUECES RIVER, 187–88, 191, 351
NUNN, L. L., 391

OAKLEY, ANNIE, 393
O'BRIEN, WILLIAM, 358
O'FALLON, JAMES, 44–45, 47
OGDEN, PETER SKENE, 126, 129–31, 138–39, 185, 238
OHIO, 29, 37, 39–40, 48, 52–53, 59, 71, 102, 107–8, 158, 195, 351
OHIO COMPANY, 38–40, 42
OHIO RIVER AND VALLEY, 15, 18–21, 23–25, 28, 31–34, 37–38, 40, 43, 45, 48, 52–54, 59, 61–63, 78–79, 100, 108, 117, 153, 283
OKANOGAN RIVER, 95, 104
OKLAHOMA, 68, 111–12, 123–24, 152–56, 174, 187, 286, 325–26, 328, 342, 358, 360, 391, 397
OLD SPANISH TRAIL, 134–35, 188, 218, 255
OLLOKOT (INDIAN), 356
OMAHA, NEBR., 226, 312, 327, 357, 390
ONDERDONK, ROBERT J., 172
ONE-SIDE-OF-THE-SKY (INDIAN), 169
ONTARIO, 99–100, 107
ORDINANCE OF 1784, 36, 38
OREGON, 63, 80, 104, 106–8, 110, 124, 133–34, 168, 176, 179–81, 183–90, 192–93, 207–11, 218, 221, 226, 229–30, 235, 237–41, 249, 251, 256, 259–60, 283, 287, 300, 307, 321, 328, 338, 356–57, 376–77, 389
OREGON CITY, OREG., 210
OREGON STEAM NAVIGATION CO., 321
OREGON TRAIL, 178, 185, 187, 189–90, 205, 221, 311, 319, 326, 357, 386
OROFINO CREEK, 319
OSAGE RIVER, 69, 71
O'SULLIVAN, JOHN, 241
O'SULLIVAN, TIMOTHY H., 309, 361, 363
OTTAWA RIVER, 82

OTTINGER, GEORGE M., 235
OURAY, COLO., 359
OVERLAND MAIL, 322
OVERLAND TRAIL, 182, 315, 320, 322, 326
OWEN, JOHN, 319
OWENS, DICK, 187
OWENS VALLEY, 392
OWHI, CHIEF, 307
OXFORD, N. C., 24

PACIFIC FUR CO., 94, 96–97, 104–5
PACIFIC MAIL STEAMSHIP CO., 239, 254–55, 288
PADUCAH, KY., 67
PALMER, WILLIAM J., 350, 359
PALO DURO CANYON, 354
PALOUSE FALLS, 300
PANTON, LESLIE & CO., 40, 60
PARIS, TREATY OF, 34, 57
PARKER, CYNTHIA ANN, 163, 354
PARKER, QUANAH, 354
PARKER, SAMUEL, 176, 178–79, 181
PARKMAN, FRANCIS, 254
PARRAS, MEX., 232
PATTIE, JAMES OHIO, 132, 135
PATTIE, SYLVESTER, 132, 135
PAWNEE RIVER, 327
PEACE RIVER, 58, 86
PEA RIDGE (BATTLE), 315
PEALE, CHARLES WILLSON, 41, 77, 118
PEALE, TITIAN R., 118, 206
PECOS RIVER, 324, 331, 351–52
PEGUIS, CHIEF, 85
PEMBINA, N. DAK., 274–75
PENNSYLVANIA, 16, 18–19, 21, 37, 38, 42, 43, 48, 49, 116, 193
PENSACOLA, FLA., 29, 102
PEOPEO MOXMOX, CHIEF, 307
"PERCH, ZACHARY," 86–87
PERDIDO RIVER, 100
PERRY, OLIVER HAZARD, 107
PEYTON, EPHRAIM, 33
PHILIBERT, JOSEPH, 109
PHOENIX, ARIZ., 378
PIERCE, ELIAS, 319
PIERCE, IDAHO, 337
PIERCY, FREDERICK, 247
PIERRES HOLE, 177
PIG'S EYE, MINN., 286
PIKE, ALBERT, 313–15
PIKE, ZEBULON M., 66, 67–72, 82, 84, 137, 153
PIKES PEAK, 70, 72, 111, 308, 315, 349, 390, 404
PILCHER, JOSHUA, 112, 126, 134
PILOT PEAK, 184, 188, 190, 229
"PINCH, JEREMY," 86–87
PITTSBURGH, PA., 22, 37, 53, 100
PLACERVILLE, CALIF., 253, 267
PLATTE RIVER AND VALLEY, 82, 84, 88, 90, 97, 111, 118, 127, 131, 154, 183, 187, 220–21, 226, 239, 255, 264, 283, 286, 290, 296, 318, 324, 326, 335, 355
PLAYFAIR, WILLIAM, 40
PLUM CREEK, NEBR., 328
PLUM CREEK, TEX., 165
PLUMMER, HENRY, 320, 337
POE, DAVID, 9
POINT DETOUR, 103
POINT ISABEL, 225
POINT PLEASANT, 23
POLK, JAMES K., 186, 188, 192, 225–26, 231, 234, 238, 240, 242, 254, 265

POMFRET, JOHN E., 254
POND, PETER, 48
PONTIAC, CHIEF, 18
PONY EXPRESS, 296, 338
POPE, JOHN, 264
POPO AGIE CREEK, 134, 179
PORTLAND, OREG., 321
POTTS, JOHN, 87, 89
POWDER RIVER, 281, 326, 328, 354, 356, 385, 387
POWELL, JOHN WESLEY, 347, 350, 357, 362, 384, 389
POWELL RIVER, 25
POWELL'S VALLEY, 20, 33
PRAIRIE DU CHIEN, WIS., 67, 82, 104, 107, 111
PRATTE, CHOUTEAU & CO., 178
PRESQUE ISLE, 51
PREVOST, GEORGE, 107
PRICE, STERLING, 233, 313–14, 320
PROCLAMATION OF 1763, 16, 23–24
PROMONTORY, UTAH, 328
PROPHET'S TOWN, 100–101
PROVOST, ETIENNE, 125–27, 130–31, 135
PRYOR, NATHANIEL, 88
PUEBLA, MEX., 236
PUGET SOUND, 192, 237, 239, 260, 264, 277, 306, 328
PURGATOIRE RIVER, 110, 123
PUTNAM, RUFUS, 38, 42

QUANTRILL, WILLIAM CLARKE, 317, 329

RABBIT-HOLE SPRING, 256, 257
RACCOON, H.M.S., 105–6, 110
RAFT RIVER, 185
RAILROADS, 186, 195, 234, 237, 239–40, 255, 258–59, 263–64, 270, 273, 276–79, 282, 283, 286–87, 296, 306, 312, 321–22, 326–27, 340–41, 345–46, 349, 350, 354, 357–59, 387, 390, 398
RAISIN RIVER, 103–4, 115
RANCHO BOSQUEJO, 256
RANNEY, WILLIAM, 140–41
RATON PASS, 123, 124
RAY, NICK, 386
RAYNOLDS, WILLIAM F., 319
RAYNOLDS PASS, 91
RECLAMATION ACT, 392
RED CLOUD, CHIEF, 326, 328, 354
RED RIVER, 68, 72, 100, 102, 108, 154, 174
RED RIVER OF THE NORTH, 82, 111, 118, 274–75, 357, 377, 391
REDWOOD CREEK, 323
REED, JAMES, 85
REED, JAMES FRAZIER, 229
REEDER, ANDREW, 284
REGULATORS (N.C.), 20–21
REGULATORS (SAN FRAN-CISCO), 257
REGULATORS (WYO.), 386
REMINGTON, FREDERIC, 406–7
RENO, MARCUS, 356
REPUBLICAN RIVER, 71, 294
RESACA DE LA PALMA (BATTLE), 225
RESOLUTION, H.M.S., 45
RICHARDSON, A. D., 295
RINGGOLD, CADWALADER, 250
RIO GRANDE, 68, 72, 91, 102, 121, 124, 161, 163–66, 188, 191, 192, 225, 228, 231–33, 238, 258, 261, 314–15, 388
RIO GRANDE REPUBLIC, 164
ROADS, 59, 108, 116, 147, 156, 221, 270, 319, 320–21, 338

ROBERTS, CHARLES, 103
ROBERTS, SAM, 257
ROBERTSON, JAMES, 16, 21, 22, 27, 29–32, 44, 47
ROBIDOUX, ANTOINE, 125, 135
ROBIDOUX, JOSEPH, 125
ROBINSON, JAMES W., 167
ROBINSON, JOHN, 69, 71–72
ROCK ISLAND, ILL., 111
ROCK RIVER, 155, 195
ROCKY MOUNTAIN FUR CO., 134, 177
ROCKY MOUNTAIN HOUSE, 86
ROCKY MOUNTAINS, 64–65, 67, 72, 76, 84, 86, 88, 91, 93, 95, 109–12, 124, 126–31, 134, 166, 168, 181, 190, 192, 224, 234, 240, 255, 264, 292, 294, 295, 300, 322, 325, 327, 345, 347, 356, 357, 358, 361, 388, 390, 397
ROGERS, ROBERT, 51, 58
ROGUE RIVER, 259
ROI, BAPTISTE, 124
ROLLA, MO., 314
ROLLINGSTONE, MINN., 298
ROOSEVELT, NICHOLAS, 100
ROOSEVELT, THEODORE, 360, 392, 400, 404
ROOSEVELT DAM, 400–401
ROSE, EDWARD, 88
ROSEBUD CREEK, 356
"ROSEMAN, JAMES," 86
ROSS, ALEXANDER, 129, 130
ROSS, JOHN, CHIEF, 313–14
ROYAL GORGE, 70, 359
RUCKER, DANIEL H., 256
RUSSELL, CHARLES M., 406–7
RUSSELL, MAJORS & WAD-DELL, 289–90, 295, 321, 338
RUSSELL, T. H., 354–56
RUSSELL, WILLIAM GREEN, 294
RUSSELL, WILLIAM HEP-BURN, 295–96
RUSSIAN AMERICAN FUR CO., 93, 105

SABINE RIVER, 71, 100, 102, 108, 122, 164
SACAJAWEA, 65–66
SACRAMENTO, CALIF., 180, 250, 263, 288, 293, 321
SACRAMENTO RIVER AND VALLEY, 180, 189, 228, 236, 250, 256, 357
ST. ANTHONY, MINN., 299
ST. ASAPH'S, 23, 28
ST. CHARLES, COLO., 294
ST. CHARLES, MO., 108
ST. CLAIR, ARTHUR, 39, 48
ST. JOSEPH, MO., 182, 255
ST. JOSEPH ISLAND, 103
ST. JOSEPH RIVER, 81
ST. LOUIS, MO., 54–56, 59, 68, 71, 75, 82–83, 90, 93, 104, 108, 109, 112, 117, 124–25, 130, 131, 134, 177–78, 182, 208, 240, 264, 286, 288, 313, 321, 351, 358
ST. MARYS RIVER, 81, 103
ST. PAUL, MINN., 68, 264, 274, 286, 299, 390, 391
ST. PETER'S (MINNESOTA) RIVER, 68, 82, 118, 180, 280
ST. VRAIN, CERAN, 125, 178, 233
SALAZAR, DAMASIO, 166
SALEESH HOUSE, 90, 94, 129
SALINAS VALLEY, 191
SALMON RIVER, 86, 87, 319
SALT FORK, KANS., 371
SALT LAKE CITY, UTAH, 240, 250, 255, 258, 262, 288, 290, 293, 322, 328, 381
SALT RIVER, 356, 400
SALTILLO, MEX., 123, 160, 164, 166, 226, 231–32

SAN ANTONIO, TEX., 47, 102, 112, 121, 122, 145, 160–62, 165, 166, 173, 226, 232, 242, 286, 288, 313, 314–15, 351
SAN BERNARDINO, CALIF., 262, 290
SAN BERNARDINO MOUN-TAINS, 132
SAN BUENAVENTURA RIVER, 181, 184
SAN DIEGO, CALIF., 135, 149, 168, 180, 229, 234, 239, 270, 288
SAN FELIPE (DE AUSTIN), TEX., 122, 136, 160, 161
SAN FERNANDO VALLEY, 234
SAN FRANCISCO, CALIF., 45, 74, 94, 148, 216, 229, 234, 236, 237, 239, 240, 249, 254–57, 260, 266–67, 288, 293, 296, 312, 314, 325, 338, 355, 390, 392
SAN FRANCISCO BAY, 167, 180, 191–92, 228, 240, 244, 250, 260, 266
SAN GABRIEL, CALIF., 132, 148
SAN ILDEFONSO TREATY, 60
SAN JACINTO RIVER, 163, 173
SAN JOAQUIN RIVER AND VALLEY, 133, 180, 188, 234, 388
SAN JUAN MOUNTAINS, 124, 280
SAN LORENZO TREATY, 48
SAN LUIS POTOSI, MEX., 232
SAN LUIS VALLEY, 72, 240, 292
SAN MIGUEL, TEX., 123
SAN MIGUEL RIVER, 391
SAN PASQUAL, CALIF., 234
SAN PATRICIO, TEX. (BAT-TLE), 161
SAND CREEK, 325, 328
SANGRE DE CRISTO MOUN-TAINS, 240
SANGUINET, CHARLES, 97
SANTA ANNA, ANTONIO LOPEZ DE, 122, 136, 159–64, 166–67, 226, 232–33, 236
SANTA BARBARA, CALIF., 234
SANTA CRUZ, CALIF., 233, 240
SANTA FE, N. MEX., 68–69, 72, 84–85, 91, 93, 96–97, 106, 109–10, 112, 123–25, 134–35, 165, 167, 178, 180, 227, 232–34, 238, 240, 255, 261, 263, 270, 273, 295, 315, 317, 346, 354
SANTA FE TRAIL, 124, 137, 146–47, 166, 174, 182, 226, 233, 255, 260–61, 319, 325
SAPLING GROVE, KANS., 182
SARPY, PETER, 282–83
SASKATCHEWAN RIVER, 62, 69, 91, 95
SATANTA, CHIEF, 325, 343, 354
SAVANNAH, GA., 25
SCHIMONSKY, STANISLAS, 228
SCHOOLCRAFT, HENRY, 137, 150–51
SCIOTO CO., 39–40
SCIOTO RIVER, 34
SCOTT, LEVI, 230
SCOTT, WINFIELD, 231, 236
SCOTTS BLUFF, 183
SEATTLE, WASH., 259, 390
SEDALIA, MO., 351
SEVIER, JOHN, 16, 27, 40, 41, 42, 44, 47
SEYMOUR, SAMUEL, 119
SHAKOPEE, CHIEF, 334
SHANNON, WILSON, 284
SHARP, JOSEPH, 253
SHAVER, LEONIDAS, 289
SHAW, JOSHUA, 117
SHAWNEE TRAIL, 351
SHE-HE-KE, CHIEF, 71, 88, 90, 95
SHELBY, EVAN, 29

SHEPARD, CYRUS, 178–79
SHERIDAN, PHILIP H., 343
SHERMAN, WILLIAM T., 265, 343
SHERMAN SILVER PUR-CHASE ACT, 387, 390
SHOSHONE FALLS, 363
SHOSHONE RIVER, 89
SIBLEY, HENRY HASTINGS, 323
SIBLEY, HENRY HOPKINS, 315
SIERRA NEVADA, 133, 180, 185, 187, 190, 224, 230, 236, 251, 255, 258, 263–64, 286, 291, 293, 296, 321–22, 327, 341, 358, 392
SIMONS, GEORGE, 338
SIMPSON, GEORGE, 133
SIMPSON, JAMES H., 261, 270, 273, 300
SIMPSON, SOCKLESS JERRY, 389
SIOUX CITY, IOWA, 63, 346, 354
SITGREAVES, LORENZO, 261, 270, 273
SITKA, ALASKA, 74, 180, 260, 327
SITTING BULL, CHIEF, 356, 368–69
SIX-MILE CANYON, 296
SKAGWAY, ALASKA, 390
SLACK, JOHN, 349
SLACUM, WILLIAM, 181
SLAVERY, 123, 125, 136, 143, 164, 167–68, 170, 238–40, 257–59, 262–64, 282–85, 297
SLIDELL, JOHN, 188, 191
SLOAT, JOHN, 245
SMITH, CHARLES, 236–37, 239, 250
SMITH, DANIEL, 44
SMITH, HENRY, 161, 164, 173
SMITH, HYRUM, 189, 246
SMITH, JEDEDIAH, 120, 127–30, 132–35, 139, 148, 404–5
SMITH, JOSEPH, 189, 246, 291
SMITH, LOT, 292
SMITH, LUCY, 8
SMITH, PERSIFOR F., 256
SMITH, THOMAS L., 125, 132
SMITH, TOM, 353
SMOKY HILL RIVER, 294, 310–11, 324–25
SMOKY HILL TRAIL, 310–11
SMYTH, WILLIAM COKE, 113, 149
SNAKE RIVER, 66, 80, 86–87, 91, 94–97, 104, 126, 130, 133, 178–79, 185–86, 211, 219, 230, 319, 363
SNIVELY, JACOB, 166
SOHON, GUSTAVUS, 130, 208, 306–7
SONOMA, CALIF., 180, 228–29, 244
SONORA, CALIF., 250–51, 253, 257
SONORA, MEX., 239, 249–50
SONORA PASS, 185
SOO CANAL, 199
SOUARD, ANTOINE, 75
SOUTH CAROLINA, 15, 16, 25, 27, 34, 154
SOUTH DAKOTA, 65, 82, 86, 88, 126, 289, 318–19, 323, 328, 346–47, 354, 357–60, 370–71
SOUTH PASS, 88, 97, 127–29, 181, 183, 187–88, 224, 235, 253, 255, 263, 286, 288, 292
SOUTH PLATTE RIVER AND VALLEY, 72, 96, 111, 294, 352, 357
SOUTH WEST CO., 104
SOUTH YAZOO CO., 44, 47
SOUTHERN PACIFIC RAIL-ROAD, 234, 358
SOUTHWEST TERRITORY, 44, 47, 106, 126
SPAIN, 15, 29, 34, 40–49, 51, 54, 57, 60–63, 68–72, 74–75, 82,

84–85, 87, 96–97, 99–102, 107–10, 112, 114, 121–22, 126, 208, 251, 331, 388, 390
SPALDING, HENRY H., 179, 208–9
SPANISH-AMERICAN WAR, 390, 395
SPANISH PEAKS, 109, 277
SPANISH RIVER, 91
SPARKS, WILLIAM A. J., 360
SPINDLETOP WELL, 391, 396
SPIRIT LAKE, 318, 323
SPOKAN GARRY, CHIEF, 208
SPOKANE, WASH., 94, 104–5, 319
SPOKANE HOUSE, 105
STAGE TRAVEL. *See* Wagon travel
STAKED PLAINS, 264
STANFORD, LELAND, 321, 326, 328
STANISLAUS RIVER, 234
STANLEY, JOHN MIX, 125, 277
STANSBURY, HOWARD, 261, 264, 270–71
STANTON, CHARLES T., 224, 229–30
STARR, BELLE, 13, 360
STEPTOE, E. J., 259
STEUNENBERG, FRANK, 392
STEVENS, ISAAC I., 264, 277, 292, 306–7, 319
STEVENS, JOHN, 298
STEVENS, WILLIAM, 358
STILES, GEORGE P., 289
STOCKTON, ROBERT, 229, 234, 244, 245
STOCKTON, CALIF., 249
STONE, DAVID, 111–12
STONER, MICHAEL, 22
STORM, GEORGE, 193
STORY, NELSON, 326
STOUT, WILLIAM, 234
STRATTON, WINFIELD, 390
STUART, DAVID, 94–95
STUART, GRANVILLE, 360, 386
STUART, HENRY, 27
STUART, JOHN, 18, 20–21, 27
STUART, ROBERT, 96–97, 111
SUBLETTE, MILTON, 134
SUBLETTE, WILLIAM, 127, 132–33, 135, 177–78
SUBLETTE'S CUT-OFF, 184, 255
SUGAR CREEK, 191–92, 226
SULLIVAN, JOHN, 29
SULLY, ALFRED, 323–24
SUMNER, CHARLES, 285
SUMNER, EDWIN VOSE, 261
SUTIL, 45
SUTTER, JOHN AUGUSTUS, 179–80, 189, 217, 237, 239, 248, 250–53, 257, 265
SWEETWATER CREEK, 127–29, 183, 229, 287, 322, 327, 386
SWEETWATER TRAIL, 261
SYCAMORE SHOALS, 23, 25, 27
SYMMES, JOHN CLEVES, 39

TABOR, HORACE A. W., 359
TALLAPOOSA RIVER, 107
TALLENT, ANNIE, 355
TAMPA BAY, 170
TAMPICO, MEX., 226
TAOS, N. MEX., 109–10, 124–27, 130, 132, 134, 165, 233, 240, 257, 313
TAPPAN, WILLIAM H., 183, 221, 238
TARGHEE PASS, 91
TATTERSALL, GEORGE, 116
TAYLOR, ZACHARY, 107, 187, 191–92, 225–26, 230–33, 242–43, 256
TECUMSEH, CHIEF, 100–103, 107, 117, 169
TEHUANTEPEC BAY, 293

TELEGRAPH SERVICE, 293, 295, 338
TENNESSEE, 18, 21, 23, 31, 34, 40–44, 59–60, 135, 153, 226
TENNESSEE RIVER, 20, 23, 31, 33, 48
TERRY, ALFRED, 355–56
TERRY, DAVID, 260
TETON MOUNTAINS, 176–77, 363
TETON PASS, 89, 96–97
TEXAS, 40, 47, 67–69, 71–72, 96, 100, 102, 107–9, 111–12, 121–23, 135–36, 144–45, 150, 153–54, 158–68, 173–75, 186–88, 191, 234, 238, 241, 258, 260–61, 264, 283, 285, 313–15, 317, 325, 346, 350–54, 357, 370–71, 386, 391, 397
TEXAS RANGERS, 165
THAYER, ELI, 283
THOMAS, CYRUS, 350
THOMAS, ISAAC, 27
THOMPSON, DAVID, 85–87, 90–91, 93–95, 129
THOMPSON, SNOWSHOE, 293
THOMPSON RIVER, 104
THORN, JONATHAN, 94
THORNBURGH, THOMAS T., 357
THREE CROSSINGS, WYO., 386
THREE FORKS, 66–67, 90–91, 126
THURSTON, SAMUEL, 238
TIBBLES, THOMAS HENRY, 347
TILGHMAN, WILLIAM M., 353
TIMBER AND STONE ACT, 389
TIMBER CULTURE ACT, 347
TIPPECANOE CREEK, 100–101, 196
TIPTON, JOHN, 16, 42
TOFFT, PETER, 319
TOLEDO, OHIO, 48, 104
TOMBSTONE, ARIZ., 353, 379
TONGUE RIVER, 354
TONQUIN, 94–95, 97
TOOHOOLHOOLZOTE, 355
TOWNSEND, JOHN, 181
TRANSYLVANIA CO., 23–25, 29, 32–33
TRAVERSE DES SIOUX COUNCIL, 274
TRAVIS, WILLIAM B., 160, 162, 173
TREATIES: Adams-Onís, 108–10; Convention of 1818, 133–34; Fort Laramie, 281; Fort McIntosh, 37; Fort Stanwix, 37; Fort Wayne, 100; Ghent, 107; Greenville, 48, 100; Guadalupe Hidalgo, 237; Hard Labor, 18; Hopewell, 42; Indian, see Indians, agreements with; Jay's 82–84; Lochaber, 18; Medicine Lodge, 328, 343, 354; Paris, 34, 57; San Ildefonso, 60; San Lorenzo, 48
TRINIDAD, COLO., 352
TRINITY RIVER, 145
TROLLOPE, FRANCES, 143
TRUCKEE CANYON, 230
TRUCKEE RIVER, 185, 190, 236, 250
TRYON, WILLIAM, 20
TUALATIN PLAINS, 168
TUCSON, ARIZ., 234, 293, 315, 317
TUPPER, BENJAMIN, 38
TURRET BUTTE, 356
TWIGGS, DAVID E., 313
TYLER, JOHN, 167, 186

UINTA BASIN, 255
UINTA MOUNTAINS, 127, 130–31
UMATILLA RIVER, 389
UMPQUA RIVER, 133, 230, 259

UNION PACIFIC RAILROAD, 261, 312, 321, 326–28, 340–41, 349–50, 352, 372–73, 387
UNION PASS, 96, 127
UNIONS, LABOR, 387–88, 392, 398–99
UNITED STATES: land acquisition, 16–32, 39, 41, 46, 48, 57–72, 83–87, 99–101, 107, 137, 153–56, 188, 191, 211, 237, 241, 258, 270; land claims, 19, 29, 34, 47–48, 68–71, 73–74, 126, 133–34, 168, 211; land grants, 195, 258–59, 322, 327–28, 345–47, 350, 358, 388; land policies, 35–39, 41–42, 47, 49, 52, 59–62, 109, 112, 153–58, 178, 185, 252, 259–60, 286, 296, 322, 345–46, 357–58, 389, 392
UNITED STATES ARMY: exploration and surveys, 63–72, 77, 98, 130, 134–35, 150, 187–90, 218–19, 260–64, 270–71, 273, 276–79, 286–87, 292–93, 300, 306, 318–19; peace-keeping activities, 37, 52, 111, 126–27, 155–56, 187, 199, 261–62, 289–90, 292, 319, 322–28, 342–43, 354–57, 369, 378, 386
UPSHUR, ABEL P., 167
URREA, JOSE, 161–62
UTAH, 8, 108, 110, 125, 132–33, 135, 139, 168, 184, 187, 190, 218, 237, 239–40, 247, 250, 255, 258, 262–63, 273, 277–78, 287, 289–90, 293–95, 300, 320–22, 324, 326, 347, 357, 360, 362, 388, 390–91
UTE PASS, 339

VALVERDE, N. MEX., 228, 232, 315
VAN BUREN, MARTIN, 190
VANCOUVER, GEORGE, 64, 86
VANCOUVER ISLAND, 45, 74, 192, 234
VANDALIA COLONY, 18–19
VAN DORN, EARL, 315
VARINA, MONT., 320
VAUGHAN, ALFRED, 318
VELASCO, TEX., 160
VERACRUZ, MEX., 121, 160, 164, 168, 226, 231, 236
VERDIGRIS RIVER, 112, 123–24
VICKSBURG, MISS., 264, 286
VICTORIO, CHIEF, 356
VIGILANTES, 257, 260, 267, 320, 337, 359–60, 373
VILLARD, HENRY, 295
VINCENNES, IND., 28–29, 48, 101
VIRGINIA, 15, 18, 21–25, 27–31, 33–34, 41, 47
VIRGINIA CITY, MONT., 320, 326, 337
VIRGINIA CITY, NEV., 296, 326, 358

WABASH RIVER, 28, 43, 48, 59, 81, 100, 111
WACO, TEX., 163, 354
WADDELL, WILLIAM, 295
WAGON TRAVEL, 116–17, 124, 147, 182–86, 220–21, 226, 229–30, 235–37, 241, 250, 255–57, 259, 262, 275, 287–94, 310, 316–17, 320–22, 325, 338–39
WAIILATPU, 179–80, 238
WAITE, DAVIS, 390
WAKARA, CHIEF, 263, 292
WALKER, JOSEPH REDDEFORD, 125, 187–88, 191, 229
WALKER, WILLIAM, 177–78, 282–83
WALKER PASS, 188
WALKER RIVER, 185
WALK-IN-THE-WATER, 108, 109

WALLA WALLA RIVER AND VALLEY, 110, 179, 306
WALLACE, IDAHO, 387, 398
WALNUT HILLS (VICKSBURG), MISS., 44–45, 47, 62
WALTON ROAD, 59
WAR OF 1812, 101–8, 114–15
WARD, NANCY, 27
WARFIELD, CHARLES, 166
WARIN, JOSEPH, 54
WARRE, HENRY J., 210
WARREN, GOUVERNEUR K., 318–20
WARRIOR'S TRACE, 20
WASATCH MOUNTAINS, 125–26, 130, 190, 229, 292
WASHINGTON, GEORGE, 15, 18, 30, 33, 36, 39, 42–44, 47–48, 59–60
WASHINGTON (STATE), 91, 104, 192, 211, 259–60, 264, 287, 301, 306–7, 319, 328, 356–57, 377, 389, 392
WASHINGTON, TEX., 161
WASHITA RIVER, 328, 342
WATAUGA ASSOCIATION, 21–22, 25
WATAUGA RIVER, 20, 23, 27, 41–42
WATER SUPPLY, 347, 357, 388–89, 392, 397, 400–401
WATER TRAVEL, 32–33, 42, 45, 57–59, 73, 78–79, 81–83, 99–100, 108, 116–18, 132, 138, 156, 159, 170, 186, 193, 195, 199, 239–40, 250, 253–55, 293, 304–5, 320–21, 338
WATIE, STAND, 329
WATROUS, N. MEX., 261
WAYNE, ANTHONY, 48, 52–53, 59
WEATHERFORD, WILLIAM, 101, 104, 107
WEAVER, JAMES B., 389
WEBBER, JOHN, 74
WEBER, JOHN, 130
WEBER RIVER, 126, 130, 229
WEIGHTMAN, RICHARD, 258
WELLER, JOHN B., 286–88
WELLS, FARGO & CO., 288, 355
WELLS, WILLIAM, 103–4
WENDOVER, UTAH, 185
WENTWORTH, JOHN, 241
WEST, JOSEPH R., 324
WEST VIRGINIA, 15, 18–19
WESTERN ENGINEER, 118
WESTERN FEDERATION OF MINERS, 388, 392
WESTERN RESERVE, 34
WESTPORT, MO., 147, 182, 255
WHEELER, GEORGE M., 347, 350, 361–62
WHEELING, WEST VA., 59, 100, 108
WHIPPLE, AMIEL W., 264, 277
WHIPPLE, HENRY BENJAMIN, 334
WHISTLER, JOHN, 115
WHITE, JAMES, 42, 44
WHITE PASS, 390
WHITE RIVER, ARK., 126, 318
WHITE RIVER, S. DAK., 354
WHITEFIELD, EDWIN, 298
WHITEFIELD, JOHN W., 284
WHITMAN, MARCUS, 132, 179, 185, 208–9, 237–38, 240
WHITMAN, NARCISSA PRENTISS, 179, 183
WHITNEY, ASA, 186, 239
WICHITA, KANS., 352–53
WILBUR, CHARLES DANA, 357
WILDERNESS TRAIL, 23, 32, 46, 59, 108, 117
WILKES, CHARLES, 206–7
WILKINSON, JAMES, 43–45, 56, 66–67, 69, 72, 83–85, 87, 100, 102
WILKINSON, JAMES BIDDLE, 71
WILLAMETTE RIVER AND

VALLEY, 104, 130, 133, 168, 178–81, 189, 210–11, 221, 230, 237
WILLIAMS, BILL, 240
WILLIAMS, EZEKIEL, 97, 111
WILLIAMS, JOSEPH, 182
WILLIAMSBURG, VA., 24, 28
WILLIAMSON, ROBERT S., 277
WILLIE, JAMES, 287–88
WILSON, JOHN L., 392
WILSON'S CREEK, 314
WIND RIVER MOUNTAINS, 89, 97, 127, 179, 190, 224
WIND RIVER AND VALLEY, 96, 127, 134
WISCONSIN, 81–82, 103–4, 137, 150, 153–56, 158, 169, 193, 199, 258, 304–5, 381, 396
WISCONSIN RIVER, 67, 81–82
WISER, PETER, 87, 91
WOLCOTT, FRANK, 386
WOLFSKILL, WILLIAM, 135, 218
WOMACK, BOB, 390
WOOD, ALVINUS, 358
WOOD RIVER, 94
WOODEN LEG, CHIEF, 344
WOODSON, SAMUEL, 263
WOODWARD, ABSALOM, 263
WOOL, JOHN ELLIS, 226, 232, 242
WOOTTON, DICK, 260, 294
WOUNDED KNEE CREEK, 368–69
WOVOKA (INDIAN), 369
WYANDOTTE CITY, KANS., 282–84
WYETH, NATHANIEL, 168, 177–78, 181
WYOMING, 89, 97, 110, 127, 131, 134, 178–79, 183, 187–88, 190, 211, 255, 258, 264, 292, 319, 322, 325–28, 340–41, 347, 352, 356–57, 363, 370–71, 385–86, 388, 391, 397, 402–5
WYOMING STOCK GROWERS ASSOCIATION, 385–86

XY COMPANY, 82–83, 86

YADKIN REGION, 16, 19–20
YAZOO RIVER, 44–45
YELLOW MEDICINE RIVER, 323
YELLOWSTONE EXPEDITION, 111–12, 118, 130–31, 362–63
YELLOWSTONE GEYSERS, 132, 404–5
YELLOWSTONE PARK, 89, 91, 349, 363
YELLOWSTONE RESERVE, 392
YELLOWSTONE RIVER AND VALLEY, 56, 69–72, 84, 89–90, 111–12, 126–27, 130–31, 134, 201, 319–20, 324, 328, 349, 354–55, 362
YERBA BUENA ISLAND, 229, 234
YOSEMITE NATIONAL PARK, 349, 392, 404–5
YOUNG, BRIGHAM, 189–91, 226–27, 234–37, 239–40, 247, 250–51, 262–63, 287–92
YOUNG, EWING, 125, 135, 168, 178–79
YOUNG, J. J., 301
YOUNGER BROTHERS (COLE AND BOB), 359–60
YOUNT, GEORGE, 218
YUBA RIVER, 251
YUKON RIVER, 327, 390, 395
YUMA, ARIZ., 233

ZANE, EBENEZER, 59
ZANESVILLE, OHIO, 59
ZION NATIONAL PARK, 132

416